Praise for Anne C. Heller's

AYN RAND AND THE WORLD SHE MADE

A *Bloomberg* Best Book of the Year
A *Library Journal* Best Book of the Year

"Heller has taken the forbidding author of the novels *The Fountainhead* and *Atlas Shrugged* and made her real, a person of greater complexity than Rand herself would admit. . . . She crafts a narrative that gains force from its engagement with Rand's writing. Yet this is very much the story of Rand's life, underscoring the contradictions between her strident philosophy and her very human, very messy existence. . . . [A] fine work." —*San Francisco Chronicle*

"Dramatic and very timely." —*The New York Times Book Review*

"Offer[s] ammunition for fans and skeptics alike." —*The Washington Post*

"A thoroughly researched, immensely readable portrait of a sui generis thinker who was fiercely committed to her ideals yet whose life contained fascinating contradictions." —*The Wall Street Journal*'s Speakeasy

"The champion of individuality who insisted on obedience and conformity from her followers (including Alan Greenspan), Rand emerges from Heller's superbly vivid, enlightening, and affecting biography in all her paradoxical power." —*Booklist* (starred review)

"Engrossing and unsparing, an excellent introductory course on Rand written with a shrewd eye." —*New York Post*

"The picture of Rand that emerges from Ms. Heller's book is all the more damning because the biographer is obviously fair-minded and, indeed, something of an admirer of her subject." —*The New Criterion*

"Worthwhile and engrossing." —*City-Journal*

"[An] excellent biography. . . . A vivid yet objective portrait of this gifted, brilliant, ultimately monstrous author. . . . Brings to life not only Rand but her circle and their milieu, making the book readable if only for its glimpse into a not-so-distant past where serious literature was widely influential, the television new, the railroad a common mode of travel. It's strangely quaint to read about a world without computers or cell phones, a world where typists were a must and people wore hats as a matter of course. Even more extraordinary is [Heller's] rendition of this wildly divided woman, who could create some of our most unique literature yet remain unable to make that most fundamental of connections: unconditional love for another." —PopMatters.com

Anne C. Heller

AYN RAND AND THE WORLD SHE MADE

Anne C. Heller is a magazine editor and journalist. She has been the managing editor of *The Antioch Review,* a fiction editor of *Esquire* and *Redbook,* the features editor of *Lear's,* and the executive editor of the magazine-development group at Condé Nast Publications, with a special emphasis on money and finance. It was Ayn Rand's writing about money that first aroused her interest in the author, who is one of the most passionate defenders of capitalism of all time. Heller has written for a number of national magazines.

www.annecheller.com

AYN RAND AND THE WORLD SHE MADE

AYN RAND

AND THE WORLD SHE MADE

Anne C. Heller

ANCHOR BOOKS

A Division of Random House, Inc.
New York

FIRST ANCHOR BOOKS EDITION, NOVEMBER 2010

The Library of Congress has cataloged the Nan A.
Talese/Doubleday edition as follows:
Heller, Anne C.
Ayn Rand and the world she made /
Anne Conover Heller.—1st ed.
p. cm.
Includes bibliographical references and index.
(alk. paper)
1. Rand, Ayn.   2. Novelists, American—20th century—
Biography.   3. Philosophers—United States—Biography.
4. Objectivism (Philosophy).   I. Title.
PS3535.A547Z68 2008
813'.52—dc22   [B] 2008027638

Anchor ISBN: 978-1-4000-7893-6

*Author photograph © Brennan Cavanaugh
Book design by Jennifer Ann Daddio /
Bookmark Design & Media Inc.
Title page photograph by Phyllis Cerf*

www.anchorbooks.com

Printed in the United States of America
10   9   8   7   6   5   4   3   2   1

For David Harter de Weese

Alas, that you would understand my word: "Do whatever you will, but first be such as are able to will."

—*Thus Spake Zarathustra*, 1885

CONTENTS

Preface   xi

ONE   Before the Revolution
          1905–1917   1

TWO   Looters
          1917–1925   22

THREE   Freedom to Think
          1926–1934   52

FOUR   We Are Not Like Our Brothers
          1934–1938   81

FIVE   *The Fountainhead*
          1936–1941   107

SIX   The Soul of an Individualist
          1939–1942   123

SEVEN   Money
          1943   149

EIGHT   Fame
          1943–1946   161

NINE   The Top and the Bottom
            1946–1949   185

TEN   The Means and the End
            1950–1953   218

ELEVEN   The Immovable Mover
            1953–1957   245

TWELVE   *Atlas Shrugged*
            1957   270

THIRTEEN   The Public Philosopher
            1958–1963   291

FOURTEEN   Account Overdrawn
            1962–1967   317

FIFTEEN   Either/Or (The Break)
            1967–1968   352

SIXTEEN   In the Name of the
            Best Within Us
            1969–1982   383

Afterword   411

Acknowledgments   415

Abbreviation Key   417

Notes   419

Selected Bibliography   529

Permissions Acknowledgments   541

Index   543

PREFACE

Ayn Rand died in her Murray Hill apartment in New York City in 1982, at the age of seventy-seven. Although she had spent her last thirty years as a familiar presence in the city where I lived, offering lectures and readings, I never met her. With no particular evidence, I assumed that her best-selling novels, *The Fountainhead* and *Atlas Shrugged* (the only ones I knew about), were potboilers or propaganda. They certainly had an eerie effect on some of my acquaintances who read them and who began to talk about "the earned and the unearned," "free markets and free minds," and an individualist hero named John Galt. Besides, in the 1970s, when I moved to New York, I was busy reading E. L. Doctorow, J. M. Keynes, and Little Magazines.

Hence, unlike most of Rand's readers, I came across her books not as a young person but in my forties, while working as an editor on a financial magazine. A contributor, Suze Orman, showed me the two-thousand-word text of Francisco d'Anconia's famous "money speech" from *Atlas Shrugged*. "So you think that money is the root of all evil?" the capitalist hero Francisco asks a group of New Deal–style lobbyists and bureaucrats. "Have you ever asked what is the root of money?" Rand's answer, in part, is that money is the "tool and symbol" of a society built on mutual, voluntary trade rather than forced labor, duty to the state, or war. It is an engine of economic progress. "But money is only a tool," she writes. "It will take you wherever you wish, but it will not replace you as the driver. It will give you the means for the satisfaction of your desires, but it will not provide you with desires." Orman appended a note: This was exactly what *she* was trying to say in the essay I was editing.

The passage surprised me by defending limitless wealth in a way that was logical, original, complex, and, though somewhat overbearing, beautifully written. I learned that Rand had often presented this long passage as a test of intelligence and literary acumen to potential new disciples, including her most famous follower, Alan Greenspan. I went on to devour her novels and, later, to read her speeches, essays, letters, journals, screenplays, and theatrical plays. (A complete list of her published works appears on page 529.) I became a strong admirer, albeit one with many questions and reservations.

Although Rand is rarely taught in universities, new readers, most in their teens and twenties, have always found their way to her books. Together *The Fountainhead* (1943) and *Atlas Shrugged* (1957) have typically sold more than 300,000 copies a year, easily making them the equivalent of best-sellers. Recently, in the midst of a financial crisis greater than any since the Great Depression—the proximate setting of *Atlas Shrugged*—sales of her last and most ambitious book have nearly tripled. More than thirteen million copies of the two books are in print in the United States.

Because most readers encounter her in their formative years, she has had a potent influence on three generations of Americans. Her controversial themes and racy romantic scenes made her famous in the 1940s and 1950s. She attracted a youthful right-wing following in the 1950s and 1960s and became the guiding spirit of libertarianism and of White House economic policy in the 1970s and 1980s. In a 1991 survey jointly sponsored by the Library of Congress and the Book-of-the-Month Club, Americans named *Atlas Shrugged* the book that had most influenced their lives (second only to the Bible). When the Modern Library asked readers in 1998 to name the twentieth century's one hundred greatest books, *Atlas Shrugged* and *The Fountainhead* were numbers one and two on the list; *Anthem* and *We the Living* were numbers seven and eight, trumping *The Great Gatsby, The Grapes of Wrath,* and *Ulysses.* Her defense of radical individualism and of selfishness as a capitalist virtue has won her scores of contemporary public champions, including former SEC chairman Christopher Cox, congressman and 2008 presidential contender Ron Paul, Libertarian Party founder John Hospers, *Wall Street Journal* editorial writer Stephen Moore, Alan Greenspan, and even Chris Matthews, MSNBC news commentator and former chief aide to liberal congressman Tip O'Neill. *Forbes* and *Fortune* regularly mention her as a heroine of young Silicon Valley entrepreneurs, game theorists, and chess masters. Yet she has stood outside the pale of respected American literary practitioners and social critics, and a quarter century after her death most readers of her novels know little about her.

Rand was Russian by both birth and temperament. Born into a bourgeois Jewish family during the reign of Czar Nicholas II, she was twelve years old when the Bolshevik Revolution overturned her native city, St. Petersburg, and caused her family to flee south, newly impoverished and hungry. Although her characters and themes have always impressed readers as being distinctly American, it was her hatred of Russian tyranny that underlies her best and most famous work. Her followers have often proclaimed that she was born an American in spirit and was merely trapped during her formative years in a dark and alien Slavic land. I have tried to document how Russian and Jewish culture and history color some of the most interesting features of her character and work.

Rand immigrated to America from Soviet Russia in 1926, without much English, to pursue a career in writing. Her early years in America were hard, but not as hard as she later claimed they were. "No one helped me, nor did I think it was anyone's duty to help me," she wrote in an afterword to *Atlas Shrugged*. In fact, many people helped her. I have tracked her relationships with a variety of helpmates and with the influential thinkers and writers of her time.

Rand wanted to be the architect of an American utopia that looked backward to the gilded age of American industrial titans. But like many of her Russian predecessors, she was a far shrewder social critic than she was a visionary. As a deconstructionist of liberal American economic and political assumptions, considered against a background of twentieth-century Russian history, she displayed breathtaking insight and remarkable courage. Whatever one thinks about her positive program of rational selfishness, egoism, and unregulated capitalism, her ability to spot and skewer cowardice, injustice, and hypocrisy is at least as keen and passionate as that of her ideological opposite Charles Dickens.

Like Dickens, Rand's art is the art of melodrama. At heart, she was a nineteenth-century novelist illuminating twentieth-century social conflicts. Her novels and the best of her essays are well worth reading now, when issues of wealth and poverty, state power and autonomy, and security and freedom still disturb us.

Because I am not an advocate for Rand's ideas, I was denied access to the Ayn Rand Papers at the Ayn Rand Institute in Irvine, California, where copies of her unpublished letters and diaries, calendars, photographs, and other documents reside. Nevertheless, I have been able to add much that is new to the record of her life. An exhaustive search of Russian government archives by a Russian research team yielded fascinating new information about her parents' and forebears' limited freedom as Jews in the anti-Semitic Russian empire, about her formal education in St. Petersburg and the Crimea, and about her experiences during the Russian Revolution. I listened to half a dozen unpublished tape recordings of speeches, interviews, and lectures presented over the years by archivists at the Ayn Rand Institute and enjoyed unprecedented access to forty hours of taped biographical interviews with Rand conducted by Barbara Branden in the early 1960s, all of which filled in many details of the writer's childhood and troubled young adulthood. Freedom of Information Act documents cast light on her first years in America and, among other things, helped to explain the timing of her 1929 marriage to her husband, Frank O'Connor. Journalist Jeff Walker and collector Marc Schwalb let me listen to privately recorded interviews with Rand's friends from the 1920s through the 1970s, many of them now dead, whose comments suggested aspects of Rand's character that were new to me. I conducted more than fifty interviews with Rand's still-living, often elderly American relatives, intimates, employees, and adversaries, including three long interviews with her former protégé and lover, Nathaniel Branden. Further insights came from viewing original letters to and about Rand and her followers housed in libraries and archival collections in Hollywood; San Francisco; New York; Washington, D.C.; Auburn, Alabama; Scottsdale, Arizona; Provo, Utah; Bloomington, Indiana; and West Branch, Iowa, and from drafts and galley proofs of Rand's four novels on file at the Library of Congress.

Gallant, driven, brilliant, brash, cruel, as accomplished as her heroes, and ultimately self-destructive, she has to be understood to be believed.

ANNE C. HELLER
FEBRUARY 2009

AYN RAND AND THE WORLD SHE MADE

ONE

BEFORE THE REVOLUTION

1905–1917

*If a life can have a theme song, and I believe every worthwhile one has,
mine is a religion, an obsession, or a mania or all of these expressed in
one word: individualism. I was born with that obsession and have
never seen and do not know now a cause more worthy, more misunderstood, more seemingly hopeless and more tragically needed. Call it fate
or irony, but I was born, of all countries on earth, in the one least suitable for a fanatic of individualism, Russia.*

—Autobiographical Sketch, 1936

When the fierce and extraordinary Ayn Rand was fifty-two years old,
about to become world famous, and more than thirty years removed from her birthplace in Russia, she summed up the meaning
of her elaborate, invented, cerebral world this way: "My philosophy,
in essence, is the concept of man as a heroic being, with his own
happiness as the moral purpose of his life, with productive achievement
as his noblest activity, and reason as his only absolute." It was a world in
which no dictator, no deity, and no well-meaning sense of duty would
ever take away the moral right of the gifted individual—Ayn Rand—to
live according to her own high-wattage lights.

This was not the world she was born into. Ayn Rand was born Alissa
Zinovievna Rosenbaum, a Russian Jew, on February, 2, 1905, in St. Peters-

burg, then the capital city of the most anti-Semitic and politically divided nation on the European continent. Later, she would say that she
loathed everything Russian, and while this was not entirely true—she
retained her appetite for Russian classical music and Russian sweets
until the end of her life—she hated the passivity, brutality, and primitive
religiosity of the Russia of her youth.

She had good reason for this. Her birth came barely three weeks after
the brief but bloody uprising known as the 1905 Revolution, where, on
a bright January Sunday morning, twelve thousand of Czar Nicholas II's
cavalrymen opened fire on thirty thousand factory workers, their wives
and children, labor organizers, and students who had walked to the
Winter Palace to petition for better working conditions and a role in the
czar's all-powerful government. The protest was led by a Russian Orthodox priest named Father Gapon, and many marchers were said to be
praying as they died. The slaughter gave rise to days of rioting throughout the city and set the stage for the Bolshevik Revolution of October
1917, which would end not in the quick and brutal suppression of the
rebellion's leaders, as this one did, but in a revolutionary coup that would
shake the world and mold Ayn Rand's worldview.

Rand's parents, who in January 1905 were thirty-four and twenty-
five and had been married for just nine months, could hear the gunfire
from the windows of their new apartment above a pharmacy on Zabalkanskii Prospekt—the street on which, later that evening, the popular writer Maxim Gorky would hold a meeting of the city's liberal
intellectuals and announce, "The Russian Revolution has begun."
Rand's father, born Zelman Wolf Zakharovich Rosenbaum but known
outside the family by the non-Jewish variant of his name, Zinovy, was a
pharmaceutical chemist and the manager of the shop downstairs. Her
mother, a homely but self-consciously stylish woman named Khana
Berkovna Kaplan, known as Anna, had been trained as a dentist but had
stopped practicing after her marriage and pregnancy.

By the time Ayn Rand was born, Zabalkanskii Prospekt and the
streets around it were calm again. It was an illusory calm: all over Russia and the vast Russian territories to the south and east, massive labor
strikes, anti-czarist peasant insurrections, and anti-Jewish violence were
erupting. This would continue, in waves, until 1914, when World War I
briefly united the nation against the Germans, and would grow yet more
explosive from 1915 to 1919, when the country was war torn and starv-

ing. Meanwhile, Marxist political organizations, their leaders in and out of exile in Siberia and Europe, gained a following.

In these years, it was dangerous to be a Jew. As the economy deteriorated and the czar grew more repressive, the brunt of popular anger often fell upon Russia's five million Jews. At Czar Nicholas II's court, as elsewhere in Europe, Jews had long been identified with the supposedly pagan notions of a money economy, urbanization, industrialization, and capitalism. Given traditional Russian fear of modernity and fierce anti-Semitism, Jews were ready-made scapegoats onto whom the czar, the landowners, and the police could easily shift workers' and peasants' resentment for their poverty and powerlessness.

For Jews outside the capital city, this period brought the worst anti-Semitic violence since the Middle Ages. In the fall of 1905 alone, when Rand was not quite a year old, there were 690 anti-Jewish pogroms and three thousand Jewish murders. In one pogrom in Odessa, in the Crimea, where Rand and her family would relocate in 1918, eight hundred Jews were killed and one hundred thousand were made homeless. The czar's police were said to have supplied the largely illiterate Russian Orthodox rioters with arms and vodka.

St. Petersburg was relatively safe from pogroms, which was one reason the Rosenbaums had migrated there. But it had its own complicated forms of official anti-Semitism. By 1914, the statutes circumscribing Jewish activities ran to nearly one thousand pages, and anything that wasn't explicitly permitted was a crime. For decades, Jews who didn't possess a trade or profession useful to the czar were barred from St. Petersburg; in most cases, unqualified Jews couldn't even visit for a night. By law, Jews made up no more than 2 percent of the city's population, and residency papers had to be renewed each year. Jews often changed their names to avoid detection. They and their homes were subject to police searches at all times. Rand's father, who was born in the poor and pogrom-ridden Russian Pale of Settlement—a vast checkerboard of Jewish ghettos encompassing much of Lithuania, Latvia, and Poland—went variously by the names Zelman, Zalman, and Zinovy. He seems to have become a pharmacist, at least in part, because this was one of the professions that permitted Jews to enter the city relatively freely. But the laws were fickle and crafted to give the czar maximum flexibility, and arrest and/or exile were a constant danger.

It was in this volatile and often frightening atmosphere that Rand grew up. She was the eldest of three daughters of this upwardly mobile pharmacist and his religiously observant, socially ambitious wife; Anna would later appear in her daughter's novels as a series of superficial or spiteful characters. When Rand was two and a half, her sister Natasha was born; when she was five, her youngest and favorite sister, Eleanora, called Nora, entered the family.

By the time Nora was born, in 1910, Zinovy had advanced to become the manager of a larger, more centrally located pharmacy. The Zabalkanskii drugstore, along with one a few streets away, in which the young chemist had worked before his marriage, were owned by Anna Rosenbaum's sister Dobrulia Kaplan and her husband, Iezekiil Konheim; the new store, called Aleksandrovskaia, belonged to an affluent and professionally distinguished German Lutheran merchant named Aleksandr Klinge. Klinge's shop faced Znamenskaya Square on the Nevsky Prospekt, the city's resplendent main thoroughfare, built extra wide by Peter the Great to accommodate his cavalry and cannons against the insurrections of the eighteenth century. Zinovy, now newly established among the Jewish bourgeoisie, moved his wife and daughters into a large, comfortable apartment on the second floor, adjoining the pharmacy. Another one of Anna's sisters and her husband, a prosperous medical doctor named Isaac Guzarchik, settled with their two daughters on the floor above. There the family lived until they fled the starving city for the Crimea in the wake of the October 1917 Revolution.

Intelligent, self-directed, and solitary from an early age, Rand must have been a difficult child to raise in the first decade of the twentieth century. In spite of the era's violence and turmoil, the ambience was Victorian: the fashions were for frills, family loyalty, and the feminine arts, all of which went utterly against her grain. Some of her earliest memories were of being unreasonably treated in such matters by her mother, who was the dominating personality in the household and even at times "a tyrant." In one memory, during the family's move to the Nevsky Prospekt apartment, Rand and her younger sisters were sent to stay with a neighboring aunt and uncle, perhaps the Konheims. When they returned to Rand's new home, she asked her mother for a midi blouse like the ones she'd seen her cousins wearing. Anna Rosenbaum refused. She didn't approve of midi blouses or other fashionable garments for children, Rand recalled fifty years later. Anna was serving tea at the time, and—perhaps as an experiment—Rand asked for a cup of tea. Again her mother refused; children didn't drink tea. Rand refrained from arguing, although even then the budding logician might have won the argument on points. Instead, she asked herself, Why won't they let me have what I want? and made a resolution: Someday I will have it. She was four and a half or five years old, although all her life she thought that she had been three. The elaborate and controversial philosophical system she went on to create in her forties and fifties was, at its heart, an answer to this question and a memorialization of this project. Its most famous expression was a phrase that became the title of her second nonfiction book, *The Virtue of Selfishness,* in 1962.

Rand's first memory is worth describing here. The future author of *Atlas Shrugged,* a novel whose pulse is set by the rhythms of a great American railroad, recalled sitting at a window by her father's side, aged two and a half, gazing at Russia's first electric streetcars lighting the boulevard below. Her father was explaining the way the streetcars worked, she told a friend in 1960, and she was pleased that she could understand his explanation. Although she did not know it then, the American company Westinghouse had built the streetcar line, in a gesture to the city's workers from the embattled czar. Such seeming coincidences—this one suggesting that even as a young child she showed an affinity for the bright beacon of American capitalism—abound in Rand's life, and later became the threads from which she and her followers would spin her legend.

While the czar's regime grew more unpopular, and the Marxist Mensheviks and Bolsheviks competed for the allegiance of the nation's workers, the Rosenbaums prospered. In 1912, Rand's father became the co-owner of Klinge's pharmacy, a thriving business that employed not only Klinge and Zinovy, but also six assistant pharmacists, three apprentices, and a number of clerks. In 1914, at the outbreak of World War I, Klinge transferred full ownership of the drugstore to Zinovy, presumably because, as the Russian troops advanced against the German army to the west, anyone bearing a German name was even more at risk than a Jew in the streets and government offices of St. Petersburg. As Zinovy's income grew, he bought the deed to the building that housed both the store and the family apartment. Anna hired a cook, a maid, a nurse for her daughters, and even a Belgian governess to help the three girls improve their French before they entered school, French being the language of the Russian educated classes. The girls also took music and drawing lessons.

Rand respected her father and strongly disliked her mother, whom, oddly, she called by the Russian variant of her patronymic, Borisovna. From the beginning, she and Anna Rosenbaum did not get along. The daughter viewed her mother as capricious, nagging, and a social climber, and she was painfully convinced that Anna disapproved of her. Anna considered her eldest daughter to be "difficult," Rand recalled. It's easy to imagine that she was. Although formal photographs from the time show a beautifully dressed, long-haired little girl with an arresting composure and huge, dark, intelligent eyes, her face is square and her features are slightly pudgy; when animated, they assume the stubborn, hawkish look of her adulthood. She had few friends and little inclination to make new ones, and she was physically inert in an era of passionate belief in physical exercise. Her mother nagged at her to be nicer to her cousins and more outgoing and athletic ("Make motions, Alice, make motions!" Anna would cry)* and was exasperated by her penchant for becoming violently enthusiastic about the things she liked—certain European children's stories and songs, for example—and immovably indifferent, even hostile, to the things she didn't. But Anna also articulated many of the values that Rand would later become famous for expressing. In a letter from the 1930s, for example, Anna wrote to Rand, "Every man is an architect of his own fortune" and "Every person is the maker of his own happiness." Anna liked the idea of America and wanted to visit; she even named the family cats after American states and cities.

Anna came from a more privileged background than Zinovy did. She seems to have been born and raised in St. Petersburg, which was a marked advantage in the late nineteenth and early twentieth centuries, and this gave her an air of sophistication and social polish that her husband lacked. Anna's father, Rand's maternal grandfather, was a prosperous St. Petersburg tailor named Berko (or Boris) Itskovitch Kaplan who owned a factory that made military uniforms for the czar's guards, an occupation that would have afforded the family some protection in times of trouble. Anna's mother, Rand's grandmother, named Rozalia Pavlovna

---

*After coming to the United States, Rand referred to herself as Alice, the English equivalent of her name Alissa.

Kaplan, was a pharmacist, just as Zinovy and Anna's sister Dobrulia's husband were. All lived within a few streets of one another, including the Konheims, the Guzarchiks, and two of Anna's brothers, Josel and Moisha, called Mikhail. Since many members of Anna's extended family also lived nearby, and at least a few of Zinovy's eight brothers and sisters eventually joined him in St. Petersburg, Rand grew up surrounded by a sizable Jewish clan.

Anna was also more broadly, and proudly, educated than her husband was. She read and spoke English, French, and German, and until the Belgian governess arrived she taught Rand and Natasha to read and write in French. Though Rand made good use of these advantages as she grew older, she viewed her mother as hypocritical and shallow, an opinion not entirely borne out by the evidence. She once characterized Anna as an aspiring member of the St. Petersburg intelligentsia whose main interest in life was giving parties, and she suspected that Anna enjoyed books and plays less than she enjoyed the appearance of talking about them at her frequent gatherings of family and friends. Anna subscribed to foreign magazines, including children's magazines, which Rand read and was strongly influenced by as she began to write her own early stories. Still, until the 1917 Revolution changed everything, Anna seems to have been an artistic social climber (though a remarkably intelligent and resourceful one, as we shall see) who wanted her daughters to rise in the city's Jewish social hierarchy—a project for which Ayn Rand was particularly unsuited.

In *We the Living,* Rand's autobiographical first novel, written when she was in her twenties, the heroine, Kira Argounova, views her mother as an unprincipled conformist. Rand's childhood clashes with Anna were often focused on her refusal to play with other children and her solitary, even antisocial nature. But Anna seems to have had a cruel streak, too. She told her eldest daughter that she had never wanted children, that she looked after them only from a sense of duty, and pointed out how much she sacrificed for them. Once, she got angry and broke the leg of a doll that Rand was fond of. When Rand was five or so, she recalled, her mother came into the children's playroom and found the floor littered with toys. She announced to Rand and Rand's two-and-a-half-year-old sister, Natasha, that they would have to choose some of their toys to put away and some to keep and play with now; in a year, she told them, they could trade the toys they had kept for those they had put away. Natasha held on to the toys she liked best, but Rand, imagining the pleasure she would get from having her favorite toys returned to her later, handed over her best-loved playthings, including a painted mechanical wind-up chicken she could describe vividly fifty years later. When the time came to make the swap and Rand asked for her toys back, her mother looked amused, Rand recalled. Anna explained that she had given everything to an orphanage, on the premise that if her daughters had really wanted their toys they wouldn't have relinquished them in the first place. This may have been Rand's first encounter with injustice masquerading as what she would later acidly call "altruism." Her understanding of how power can be acquired by a pretense of loving kindness would grow only more acute with time.

Perhaps it's little wonder, then, that from the age of four or five onward, Rand developed a keen sense that anything she liked had to be *hers,* not her mother's, the family's, or society's, an attitude that readers of her 1943 novel *The Fountainhead* will recognize in the perverse and complicated character of Dominique Francon. As a corollary, she claimed not to care about being approved of or accepted by her family and peers. Since she generally *wasn't* accepted, the proud, intelligent child appears to have learned early to make a virtue of necessity. In her twenties and thirties, she would construct a universe of moral principles built largely on the scaffolding of some of these defensive childhood virtues.

One of the things Rand claimed fiercely as her own was a certain kind of turn-of-the-century music heard in popular theaters and park bandstands, music that included light Viennese waltzes, Western military marches, and "The Drinking Song" from Verdi's *La Traviata.* She remembered pleading with her grandmother Kaplan to play this music on the grandmother's brand-new Victrola, one of the first in St. Petersburg, Rand later said. Her mother and aunts disapproved of her musical taste, but this made the music all the more alluring. She would pick out songs at first hearing and immediately decide, That's mine, or That's *not* mine. For the rest of her life, in moments of happiness, she would dance around the room to period recordings of this music, which she called her "tiddlywink" music.

She also collected popular postcards of famous Western paintings that were sold in dry-goods stores. But she chose only the ones with human forms; she wouldn't touch the landscapes or the still lifes. Some of these postcards were found after her death, along with newspaper clippings and sketches of clothes she liked, in a file folder marked "Pictures I Like." "I always collected things," she said, adding that her mother regularly complained about how much rubbish she acquired. Happily, her grandmother Kaplan "retaliated" against her mother's complaints by buying Rand a chest of drawers in which to store her collections.

The great exception in her somewhat alienated childhood affections was her handsome father, Zinovy, known to the family as Z.Z. and to Rand as Zakharovich. Presenting him as Kira's Uncle Vasili in We the Living, Rand noted his "thick hair, powerful body, [and] sunken eyes[,] like a fireplace of blazing coals." Like Vasili, Zinovy was, for the most part, silent, but he was immensely proud of his accomplishments as a self-made businessman. He admired his eldest daughter's proud spirit and original, razor-sharp mind. An avid reader of Russian literature, he encouraged her efforts to write her first stories and, later, her drive to craft a fiction of ideas.

Zinovy had once wanted to be a writer, too, but took the more practical, if difficult, route of getting a degree in pharmaceutical chemistry from the University of Warsaw in 1899. Warsaw, 120 miles east of Zinovy's hometown of Brest-Litovsk in the Russian Pale, was popular with the Jewish residents of the region because it had a relatively lenient admissions policy for Jews. Since non-Christians couldn't matriculate but were confined to being "listeners," or auditors, however, Zinovy's degree was a two-year certificate rather than a baccalaureate. Rand believed that he had chosen the field of chemistry because there had been an opening in that department for a Jew. Since he didn't begin his course of study until age twenty-seven, it seems likely that his parents couldn't afford to pay his tuition and that he worked and saved for years to pay his own way. Later, Rand recalled, he helped all but one of his eight brothers and sisters to get training in the medical trades and leave the Pale. Those who moved to St. Petersburg became physician's assistants, dentists, midwives, and masseurs.

Zinovy's father's extended family were tradesmen and professionals in Brest. Exactly how his parents earned their living is not known, but they were probably medical practitioners, too, since, like Zinovy and his siblings, Zinovy's paternal uncle Aron Rosenbaum and a number of Aron's children were physicians, midwives, pharmacists, and dentists in and around Brest and in St. Petersburg. Anna's family originally came from Brest, too, and dozens of her Kaplan relatives remained behind there. Factory owners, community leaders, and tradesmen, some lived or worked on the same streets where Rosenbaums lived and worked and would certainly have known and been known to Zinovy's parents. Indeed, it is possible that Anna and Zinovy were engaged to be married *before* Zinovy reached St. Petersburg—that is, that Rand's parents' marriage was arranged. One clue: On Zinovy's arrival in St. Petersburg in 1902, he immediately took a managerial job with Anna's sister Dobrulia Konheim and her husband, Iezekiil. That a newly licensed pharmacist was hired not as an apprentice or assistant but as a manager suggests that his position was preferential and prearranged.

In any case, up to the years of the revolution, Anna and Zinovy's marriage was peaceable and conventional rather than ardent. He worked long hours and didn't spend much time in the apartment; she managed the girls' social activities, education, health regimens, and religious training until they entered school at eight or nine—since, like most boys and girls from the Russian middle and upper classes, the Rosenbaum sisters were educated at home until relatively late in childhood. According to Rand, her father, who wasn't religious, tolerated her mother's Sabbath and holiday celebrations with a "better safe than sorry" shrug. Rand herself, later a strict atheist who rarely spoke about her Jewish ancestry, believed in God and accepted her mother's religious observances as a natural part of life—until she made a conscious decision to become a nonbeliever during the second year of the revolution, at the traditional male bar mitzvah age of thirteen.

Rand's first conscious memory of experimenting with the idea of God took place at age six, she recalled, when she and a maternal cousin decided to pray for a little white kitten belonging to their grandmother Kaplan. The kitten was sick and dying, and Rand's cousin proposed that if they "prayed sincerely" God would hear their prayers and save the kitten. They retreated to a corner of the room and prayed, but the kitten died, and though Rand still halfheartedly believed in God, she wasn't surprised by the ineffectuality of prayer; she hadn't really believed that it would work, she said. Later, in the terrifying year of 1918, she must often have heard the kind of fatalistic Russian Orthodox talk of God's will and the necessity to follow Christ's example of suffering that would infuriate her all her life. She decided to cast her lot with man—that is, with her own observations and sense of entitlement and justice—rather than with an oppressive, inscrutable, unjust, and alien deity.

Although her parents tried to protect her from the political and ethnic strife all around her during childhood, they could hardly have been successful. From the age of five or six, Ayn Rand took everything in, including the ugly and nonsensical pieties and prejudices of neighbors and official spokesmen who treated Jews as, at best, second-class human beings. Often, their pretext for such treatment was that the Jews were the greedy entrepreneurs, rabid industrialists, and ruthless bankers who were spoiling Russia's "pure" Slavic traditions and fomenting labor unrest. In such circumstances, Rand's love for her self-made father was strongly roused. The results would be seen in her pro-individualist, pro-industrial novels, which more than one commentator has also viewed as an impassioned defense of gifted, productive Jews.

Rand received attention and praise from her family and later, from her teachers and classmates, primarily, if not only, for being a startlingly intelligent child. (Judging by her lightning-quick logic and depth of insight as an adult, she must have been *frighteningly* intelligent, observed Rand acquaintance Robert Bidinotto.) Yet her actual ideas and feelings were of little interest to anyone, including her extended family, except her youngest sister, Nora. The household was busy with her father's growing business and her mother's and middle sister's comings and goings, and the women, especially, had little patience with Rand's odd musings. In her first novel, *We the Living,* she writes that Kira's family "shrugged impatiently at what they called Kira's feelings. . . . They were not *feelings* to [Kira's sister Lydia] but only *Kira's* feelings [italics added]." When Rand entered school, the same was true of her classmates. The intensely thoughtful child was not only solitary, but she was also awkward and offbeat. She remembered being aware that her extreme shyness and violent intensity put people off, but she was sure that such social awkwardness was merely a technical fault and that other people were wrong not to understand and appreciate her. She was self-consciously different from others, as if by choice. But she was painfully lonely.

Little Nora trailed after her eldest sister, providing a worshipful chorus for Rand's enthusiasms and dislikes. Because they favored the same books and pictures, Rand thought Nora was *like* her, with an almost identical natural bravery, sensibility, and style. In this, she mistook Nora's

imitation of her for the girl's authentic inner self. Eighty years later, the
sister would say bitterly that she was merely Rand's "shadow and yes-
man." In all of her most crucial relationships, Rand would see others favorably largely to the degree that they mirrored her unusual self.

That's where stories—both those she read and those she was beginning to write—came in. At the age of eight or nine, just before creating
her own first stories, she read two children's books that electrified her
hopes and helped to set her course; one of them would become a kind of
template for some of her most famous work. The first, a mini-biography
belonging to her sister Natasha, recounted the lonely girlhood of Catherine the Great, the late-eighteenth-century czarina who, half a century
after the reign of Peter, brought the ideas of the European Enlightenment to Russia. It presented Catherine as an unusually bright little girl
who was overlooked and underestimated by her aristocratic family and
friends because she was odd and homely: "something between a misfit
and an ugly duckling," as Rand remembered the character. Yet Catherine was destined to outshine all her prettier rivals and bring a culturally
backward Russia closer to the industrially advancing West. In the story,
a fortune-teller at a party sees Catherine's future greatness in the shape
of an invisible crown engraved on her brow, much to the envy and disbelief of the other girls and their mothers. Young Rand was sure that
she, too, was meant for an exceptional fate, and wished that, like the
fortune-teller in the story, someone would notice the special mark on
her brow. She was a child of destiny, she told herself. Nobody knew it
yet, but everybody would find out. Like many of Rand's predictions
about her future, this one would come true.

Later in the same year, 1914, she encountered a boys' serial adventure story called *The Mysterious Valley* in one of the French children's
magazines her mother subscribed to. Written by Maurice Champagne,
an author of children's books, and illustrated by René Giffey, it was set in
British-ruled India in 1911—contemporaneous with Rand's time, but set
in an exotic place, so the story's heart-stopping action may have seemed
plausible to her. As the tale opens, a dashing British infantry captain
named Cyrus Paltons and four of his fellow officers have been snatched
from the field by trained Bengali tigers and carried to a clique of bloodthirsty Hindu shamans in a hidden valley in the Himalayan Mountains
of West Bengal—a beautiful valley with noticeable resemblances to the

hiding place of the striking businessmen in Rand's 1957 novel, *Atlas Shrugged*. Cyrus, imprisoned with his peers deep in a cave beneath the valley floor, is brave, purposeful, and, according to Bill Bucko's translation, "arrogant," a characteristic that will become a marker for Ayn Rand's future heroes. He is also handsome. The original pen-and-ink illustrations show him as, in Rand's words many years later, "my present kind of hero: tall, long-legged, wearing soldier's leggings but no jacket, just . . . an open-collared shirt, torn in front, open very low, sleeves rolled at the elbows and hair falling down over one eye." Gripping the bars of a bamboo cage, he shouts defiant threats at the death-goddess-worshipping Hindus who surround him, while his friends cower in a corner. Meanwhile, a rescue team made up of two junior officers and a supremely rational French archaeologist track Cyrus and the others to the cave. After many brushes with gruesome forms of sacrificial death, Cyrus escapes and leads his friends, rescuers, and a beautiful young British woman (soon to be his wife) safely out of the valley. As they stand looking back from above, fires and a flood consume the valley and erase its bloodthirsty inhabitants from existence.

There are some remarkable things about *The Mysterious Valley*. Like Rudyard Kipling's stories of the same period, it is a romance about civilization and its adversaries. But these are specifically death-worshipping adversaries, a theme Rand was to visit again and again. In her mature fiction and essays, death worship, or "whim-worship," as she sometimes called it, is associated with antirationalism, anti-individualism, fascism, and collectivism of all kinds—most pointedly, in *We the Living*, with soul-destroying Russian Communism. The tale can also be read as subtly (but, to a Jewish child, compellingly) anti-Christian, since Kali, the death-dealing Hindu deity the shamans worship, demands a grisly and pointless living sacrifice of noble men. That these men, the story's heroes, are members of the British upper class would have made it all the more enthralling to Rand. All things British were in fashion with Russians at the time, and Rand had additional reasons for admiring England. On vacation near the Black Sea a year or two before, she had found the perfect model for her lissome future heroines in a tall, fair, slender, tennis-playing older British girl she developed a crush on from afar. She never forgot this girl, whose name was Daisy, or lost her admiration for the girl's type of long-legged beauty and fair-haired Anglo-Saxon glamour, which she later compared to that of a movie star. In the years before she had yet learned much about America, Britain came to symbolize the heroic virtues of her inner universe. It was her "ideal country" at the time, she later said.

Then, too, the British officers and the French archaeologist in *The Mysterious Valley* are unusually analytical for characters in a boy's adventure story. At every impasse—in the face of terrifying perils—they pause to ask themselves and one another what is the most logical way to proceed. Their insistence on examining every alternative before unerringly deciding on the right one slows down the action comically at times. But the result is swashbuckling punctuated by practical puzzles, which the reader solves alongside the captives and their friends. It is unusual, and one can imagine the nine-year-old Rand—the person who would later describe reason as "one's only source of knowledge" and "one's only guide to action"—being as much engrossed by the logical conundrums as by the action itself.

But it was the sexually charged character of Cyrus who fixed the story permanently in her mind. She probably spent hundreds of hours poring over the drawings and descriptions of the dashing hero who for her became the equivalent of an adolescent heartthrob. He was her "exclusive love," she said, from the age of nine until the age of twelve—that is, until the horrors of the October 1917 Revolution put an end to everyone's daydreams. He provided an aspirational remedy for her sense of isolation. With Cyrus as her secret lover and perfect soul mate, she successfully moved outside the circle of others' conventional reality. The parties and social successes that preoccupied her mother, sisters, and cousins were no longer a concern of hers, she later said. She had something better, something higher, something that none of them could see or share. In homage, she would name Kira Argounova, the protagonist of *We the Living,* for Cyrus, "Kira" being the feminine version of "Kirill," which is the Russian variant of "Cyrus." As a mature writer, she patterned her most explicitly erotic male characters after Cyrus, including Howard Roark in *The Fountainhead* and John Galt in *Atlas Shrugged.* In 1929, working at odd jobs in Hollywood, she married a studio actor who looked almost exactly as Cyrus did in the 1914 illustrations she remembered. As she approached adolescence, started school, and began to write, her feeling for Cyrus was of "unbearable intensity" and practically all-consuming. She worshipped Cyrus—and she also identified with him, just as she did with Catherine the Great. Her tendency to identify with men and male characters would have interesting implications for the adult Rand's ability to write more persuasively from a male point of view than any female writer since George Eliot.

It appears to be no coincidence then that, like Catherine and Cyrus—and like Rand's father during the impending revolution and like Jews throughout Russian history—her most famous fictional characters would be ostracized and even hunted down and punished, not for their faults but for their virtues.

In the summer of 1914, when Ayn Rand was nine and still reading *The Mysterious Valley,* a series of momentous events occurred, for her, for Russia, and for the European continent. As she and her family set out on their very first trip "abroad"—a word that soon would stir an echo of longing in middle-class Russians trapped by the revolution—the Austro-Hungarian emperor-in-waiting, Archduke Franz Ferdinand, was about to ride into an assassin's sights. His politically motivated murder would propel Europe into World War I. His killer was a Serbian nationalist who, maddened by the Austrian empire's annexation of parts of the Slavic Balkans, ambushed and shot the archduke in Sarajevo, Bosnia. Russia was closely allied with its fellow ethnic Slavs in Serbia, and by the end of July 1914, Germany, Austria's ally, had declared war on Serbia and Russia. Russia reciprocated. France and England entered the conflict on Russia's side, and Turkey, Russia's ancient enemy, eventually joined with Austria and Germany. Europe quickly became impassable, and, before the year was out, would be the scene of slaughter such as the world had never seen.

Of course, the Rosenbaums knew none of this in late May or early June, when they set off. With their governess in tow, they embarked on the kind of six-week idyll that every St. Petersburg family who could afford it took: the European tour. They traveled first to what was then the intellectual capital of Europe, Vienna. There, as it happened, they might have glimpsed some of the giants of the age who were in residence that summer: Sigmund Freud, Carl Jung, Ludwig Wittgenstein, Rainer Maria Rilke, Arnold Schönberg—and also Lenin and Leon Trotsky, the architects of the coming revolution. Even Archduke Ferdinand was on hand, conducting official business before he headed off to

Sarajevo. From Austria the Rosenbaums moved on to Switzerland and Paris. In a resort in the Swiss Alps, Rand found a rare playmate, an intelligent boy whose family was staying in the same hotel. Setting aside her aversion to exercise, she climbed hills with the boy, picked wild berries, and generally discovered a freedom in the outdoors that forty years later she would commemorate in her descriptions of the happy childhood of Dagny Taggart in *Atlas Shrugged.* As with everything Rand responded to passionately as a child, she remembered this boy; he later contributed to the character of Dagny's childhood playmate, the copper scion Francisco d'Anconia. In Paris, Rand and her mother and sisters probably shopped for the season's fashions, including clothes for Rand's approaching first school term. Later, she would remember this summer abroad before the war as being what she had always thought existence would be like. This was where real people, intelligent people, lived. The trip confirmed her childish hatred of Russia.

While still on the Continent, the Rosenbaums learned that Russia was at war. They made a dash for London, where, since land travel had now become impossible, they and thousands of other stranded European travelers waited for ships to take them home.

In the few days Rand spent in the city on the Thames, the small, dark Jewish child glimpsed other willowy, fair-haired girls like Daisy, and one day, the story goes, strolling in the West End with her governess, she saw a poster for a theatrical production featuring a chorus of blond girls in plucky English pageboy haircuts. By her account, she went back to her hotel and began to write adventure stories about the girls—her first endeavor at writing. That evening, pencil to paper, she decided to become a writer. Although this memory may be apocryphal, in the service of the adult Rand's legend, it has the ring of truth. The girls, pictured as bold, modern, beautiful, and vaguely Aryan, were the female counterparts of Cyrus, and his proper consorts. At the time, of course, wanting to be a writer wasn't unusual for a girl of nine—especially a girl from St. Petersburg, where poets, novelists, and polemicists were celebrated. Whatever the timing, Rand's decision lasted a lifetime; she very rarely changed her mind about anything important to her.

From the moment she began to regard herself as a future writer, Rand's life had a purpose. Writing became an idée fixe that would see her through the next tumultuous years in Russia and feed a growing and finally passionate determination to escape and emigrate to America—like Britain, a free society that historically tolerated Jews.

The Rosenbaums sailed on a packed ship through the North Sea, but their fate would have been kinder had no ship been found to take them home. After 1914, the war created unimagined hardships for all Russians, but especially Russian Jews, and its toll in lives and penury led directly to the revolution. Among her family members on both sides, with a very few exceptions, only Rand would ever again leave Russia. By the time she did, she and those closest to her would be battered and starving. "The war marked the end of the world," she told a friend much later.

By early August the family was safely home. But their home was in an altered city renamed Petrograd. The czar, mistakenly believing that St. Petersburg was a Germanic name, had ordered the official change to an eastward-looking Slavic variation, ending two centuries of proud, and productive, openness to the developing West.

That fall, as the imperial regime was hastily mobilizing its huge but badly prepared army to go to war against the modern, well-trained Germans, Rand entered school. Natasha and Nora stayed at home with the governess, while Rand began a classical course of study at a famous private girls' gymnasium, or primary school, called Stoiunin. The choice of Stoiunin has all the earmarks of Rand's mother's preferences. It was fashionable with the city's elite families, and its curriculum promised to encourage both intellectual and athletic development in girls. Off and on, for the next three and a half years, Rand profited from it and hated it.

The school was progressive and well run. Founded in 1889 by Madame M. N. Stoiunina, a renowned educational thinker and a friend of Fyodor Dostoyevsky's wife, and by her husband, V. J. Stoiunin, a noted teacher of Russian and a member of the scholars committee of the Ministry of Public Education, it was conceived as an exemplary school for the Stoiunins' daughters and the daughters of their literary friends. Its purpose was to balance academic, artistic, and hygienic development. The tuition was steep, but money wasn't enough to secure entry. Applicants had to pass rigorous entrance exams, and so the small student body was alert, well connected, and affluent—typically, better connected and more affluent than Rand's family. The school had an extraordinary faculty, including, during Rand's years there, the well-known literary critic V. V. Gippius, who had earlier been the headmaster of the Tenishev boys' school, where Vladimir Nabokov was a student, and the famous philosophy professor N. O. Lossky, with whom Rand would later take a memorable class at the University of Petrograd. They tended to be prominent liberals who favored a democratic middle way between the czar and the burgeoning revolutionaries. The school was liberal, too, in its admission policies: Thanks to the Stoiunins' government contacts, it sidestepped official quotas on Jewish students. Almost a third of Rand's second-year class of thirty-nine girls was Jewish at a time when most Russian secondary schools were legally constrained to limit Jews to no more than 2 to 5 percent of students. By a decree of the academy's governing council, each year two or three bright girls from very poor families were admitted and allowed to study at the expense of the trustees, though Rand wasn't among them.

Stoiunin was renowned for an equally high level of teaching in the humanitarian disciplines and in the natural and mathematical sciences, which Rand was good at and liked. She remained a student there from 1914 until 1918, and she received a general education such as few American middle school students today can dream of. She studied French and German, mathematics, natural and physical science, European history, Russian language and literature, drawing and painting, and possibly music, medical hygiene, jurisprudence, gymnastics, and needlework. Russian Orthodox religion classes were mandatory and conducted by a priest; Jewish girls had to attend but didn't have to participate. Although sitting through lessons in this "revoltingly dark," "secret, superstitious, and unhealthy" doctrine must have been torture for her—especially in light of the horrific anti-Semitic violence that was then occurring throughout Russia, avidly supported by the church—in middle age she could still amaze her friends by correcting a mistaken recitation of a well-known Russian Orthodox prayer.

In 1958, while discussing the eponymous hero of Sinclair Lewis's *Arrowsmith,* she wrote, "Any man [who has] a serious central ambition is more of an outsider in his youth than in later years. It is particularly in his youth that he will be misunderstood and resented by others." A poignant remark, considering how much of an outsider Rand would remain.

By the time she entered Stoiunin, she was proudly and painfully conscious of her difference. She recalled having "a tremendous sense of intellectual power," a conviction that she "could handle any [idea or task] I wanted to." In one early experience at school, she remembered taking a field trip to the city's zoological museum, a dusty repository of stuffed animals, snakes, and birds. The teacher asked the class of girls to choose a bird or an animal about which to write a story. Rand chose a stork perched on a sliver of rooftop with a hint of a chimney poking through and wrote her story about a girl who lived in a house that just happened to have a stork on top, "merely mentioning the stork." The teacher was tickled, Rand recalled, and gave her a high grade. Later, the teacher confided to Rand that she had created the assignment because she thought the girls were too young to write convincingly about people. But as evidenced by her postcard collection, Rand's eye was always focused on her fellow man.

In another school assignment, the girls were asked to write a few paragraphs about why being a child is such a joyous thing. Rand didn't agree that it *was* joyous and shocked her classmates with "a scathing denunciation" of childhood, she recalled. At the top of the page, she copied quotations out of an encyclopedia from Descartes ("I think, therefore I am") and Pascal ("I would prefer an intelligent hell to a stupid paradise") to make her point, which was that children couldn't think as clearly as they would be able to once they had grown up and learned more. And what use was it, she asked, to play boring games and read silly books while waiting? This memory formed the basis for a revealing flashback in her third novel, *The Fountainhead* (1943); there, a brilliant and exuberant little boy named Johnny Stokes humiliates the book's archvillain, Ellsworth Toohey, by composing a masterly, rebellious gradeschool essay on hating school, while Ellsworth sucks up to the teacher by pretending to love school. Toohey ends up envying and hating Stokes, as perhaps Rand felt that her fellow students envied her.

Rand was known as "the brain" of her class. But she had no friends. There was one girl, however, who struck her as interesting and whom she liked to observe. Self-confident, independent, and intelligent, the girl was a very good student and was also universally popular with the other girls. How did she do it? She didn't seem to be making an effort to win people over. Rand imagined that she and the girl might become friends and was also curious to know what made the girl different from herself. Were social graces perhaps not a sign of shallowness or mediocrity? One day, she marched up to the girl and asked, awkwardly and

bluntly, "Would you tell me what is the most important thing in life to
you?" The girl, startled but willing, answered, "My mother." Rand nodded and walked away. In her view, this was a ridiculous thing to say, and
it disqualified the girl from further interest.

This was "the first most important event in my life socially, which
made me see that it's not significant why some people, who seem to be
individualistic, get along with the crowd, and I don't," she later said. "I
had thought she was a serious girl and that she was after serious things,
but she was just conventional and ordinary, a mediocrity, and she didn't
mean anything as a person. It was really like a fallen idol."

Rand wasn't antisocial; she would have liked to have a friend. But
her quick dismissals of people based on what she saw as fatal flaws in
character or thinking would form a pattern in her life. In the face of disappointment, she was unable or unwilling to ask herself why a girl she
had admired, for example, would give a silly or sentimental answer to a
serious question. Could the girl have misunderstood what Rand was
after? Could she simply have been startled? Could she have had an interesting reason for what she said? Rand did not ponder the context
of the girl's response, nor did she dig deeper to see what she could
learn. People were either exceptional or ordinary, her kind of people or
nonentities. Later, she would call herself a hero-worshiper, and it's no
accident that she spoke of this girl as "a fallen idol." Her romantic tendencies caused her to overestimate some people and underestimate others. She rarely reconsidered. Her readings of people who disappointed
her would only harden and darken over time.

Her ambitions were set. By her tenth birthday, she was writing novels at home and in school. At Stoiunin, she sat in the back of the class,
a book propped in front of her to disguise what she was doing, and
wrote. She finished four novels by the age of eleven, each of which featured a heroine who was exactly her own age. The surface similarities
stopped there. Foreshadowing Dagny Taggart and Dominique Francon,
these first heroines were tall and long-legged, with bobbed hair and blue
eyes. One was named Thunder ("Rpom"). Another, from the same
year—1915, the gruesome second year of World War I, when Russian
military losses had already exceeded a million men and England was in
danger of being invaded by Germany—was an English girl who argued
her way into the British Royal Navy and single-handedly machine-
gunned down the entire German fleet. Such lone heroism and unflinch-

ing use of violence are more familiar in boys' stories than in girls', but this was to be Rand's pattern: to assume the preferences and prerogatives of the men of her time.

Cyrus's influence can be seen in this story, of course, but so, perhaps, can that of Joan of Arc, whom Rand considered the most heroic woman in history. Why? Because she "stood alone against everyone, even to the point of death," explained a longtime friend of Rand's. Whenever necessary, so would Ayn Rand.

The child was aware that these early stories were "just for her"; she didn't expect to publish anything until she was grown up, she said. But she did expect to publish. So by the age of ten she was pursuing what she already thought of as her future career. As her mother wrote to her many years later, "You [always] planned to be greater than Columbus."

If Anna hoped that young Rand would make friends among the hand-picked students at Stoiunin, she was for the most part disillusioned. Rand stood on the outside of her peer group, proudly, bitterly, self-consciously alone. She hated the stocky shape of her developing body, which she felt didn't accord with her essence, but she was proud of her mind. She told herself that she took life and ideas more seriously than the other girls and that her values, especially her all-consuming passion for Cyrus, were superior to theirs. She was "left strictly alone," she said. In spite of her proud defiance, she was again desperately lonely. She longed to find *her* kind of people, and, for now, to do so meant she had to make them up in stories. And so emerged the three-dimensional world of Ayn Rand, where idealized characters take the measure of reality and often find it needs correcting.

TWO

LOOTERS

1917 – 1925

There is a fundamental conviction which some people never acquire,
some hold only in their youth, and a few hold to the end of their days—
the conviction that ideas matter. . . . And the radiance of that certainty,
in the process of growing up, is the best aspect of youth.
　　　　　　　　　　　　　　—"Inexplicable Personal Alchemy," 1969

oward Roark, the flame-haired architect-hero of *The Fountainhead*, has often been compared to the famously willful American architect Frank Lloyd Wright. Both were professional rebels; both were "faithful to the truth, though all the world should stand against" them, to quote Wright. But Roark's original prototype may well be Peter the Great, the early-eighteenth-century Russian czar who, harnessing his own unbending will and limitless power, built the improbable city of Ayn Rand's birth.

Some of the best-known lines in Russian poetry, memorized by Russian schoolchildren for the last 150 years, were written by Aleksandr Pushkin and describe Peter at the moment of his decision to raise St. Petersburg on a collection of frigid, barren islands on the Baltic seacoast near Finland: "On the shore of empty waves he stood, filled with great thoughts, and stared out." Perhaps it's no coincidence that the opening

lines of *The Fountainhead* read, "Howard Roark laughed. He stood
naked on the edge of a cliff. A frozen explosion of granite burst in flight
to the sky over motionless water."

In Rand's first novel, *We the Living,* she describes St. Petersburg as a
"city of stone," which it is. Like her rock-jawed hero Roark's sculpted
glass and granite buildings, the city Rand grew up in was "not acquainted
with nature," she wrote in the early 1930s. "It is the work of man" and,
moreover, "the work of man who knows what he wants." The adult Rand
admired, even lionized, men who knew what they wanted, though few
she ever met would understand their objectives as well as she understood hers. And all her life she loved cities that were "not acquainted
with nature," especially New York, her home for her final thirty years.

The willful Peter paved the way for Catherine, his granddaughter by
marriage, to embrace and celebrate everything European. What Peter
wanted was "a window to the West": a new capital city that would turn
its back on the Mongol and Slavic traditions of central Russia and look
toward Europe and its technical achievements. In building St. Petersburg as close as possible to Europe, his aim was "to astonish Russia and
the civilized world" and to rival Paris, Amsterdam, and Venice. This he
did: In the course of just twenty-five years, beginning in 1703, he created an astonishing eighteenth-century port city entirely of imported
granite, marble, slate, and travertine. For Peter, as one historian has observed, "St. Petersburg was . . . a vast, almost utopian, project of cultural
engineering to reconstruct the Russian as a European man." To this end,
he commissioned peasant workers from all over the empire; tens of
thousands of them died of starvation, disease, and exposure to the cold.
Even today, residents of St. Petersburg speak of their city as having risen
on the bones of the dead. As Ayn Rand would demonstrate, though less
violently, the utopian strain in the Russian imagination was harsh and
rarely found expression without inflicting damage.

Peter's project failed to Westernize Russia. Although generations of
inhabitants of St. Petersburg, including Rand, learned to value Western
attitudes and culture, Ukrainians, Turkmen, Mongols, and Russian yeo-
men and peasants remained uneducated and stubbornly provincial. An
intractable tendency lay embedded deep in Russia's heart: to hold fast
to its semi-Asiatic, feudal, Byzantine Christian, anti-Western past. For
the most part, Peter's city remained an island of Western values in a sea

of illiteracy, abject poverty, and daunting superstition. This was the Russia that Ayn Rand hated and that the Bolshevik Revolution would appeal to with promises of potatoes, collective power, and revenge.

In February 1917, the month of Rand's twelfth birthday, statues and symbols of Peter still stood everywhere among the domed churches, granite palaces, and broad squares of St. Petersburg. But the capital's neoclassical architecture could not mask a society in tatters. This was the third long winter of World War I, and the coldest winter on record in many years. Temperatures stood at twenty or thirty degrees below zero Fahrenheit for days at a time. The war was going badly. Six million Russians had been killed, captured, maimed, or wounded. Lacking uniforms, guns, ammunition, and rations, thousands of deserters poured into the city, looking for food and work. Even there, shortages of food and fuel were reaching a crisis point, especially for the lower and working classes, who lived on bread and stood in bread lines for hours, sometimes only to be turned away empty-handed. Because the nation's railway system had long since broken down under the strain of troop transport, grain lay rotting in the southern provinces. Crime was rampant; curfews were set, but prostitutes, robbers, and murderers prowled Nevsky Prospekt after dark, making it unsafe for the Rosenbaums and other families to venture out.

Meanwhile, in the south and the Pale of Settlement, anti-Semitic bloodshed was on the rise. Czarist "Black Hundreds" groups roamed the countryside, spreading rumors that Yiddish-speaking spies and Jewish profiteering were responsible for war losses and shortages of goods. As the Russian army retreated from the advancing Germans, Russian troops were ordered to round up residents of Jewish villages in the Pale and herd them, under the lash, eastward to the Ukraine or Siberia. Many of these villages, including Brest, where the Rosenbaums' extended family lived, welcomed temporary German occupation as "salvation."

But scapegoating of Jews could no longer head off a political showdown. Given the nation's battlefield losses, Czar Nicholas II, Peter's great-great-great-great-grandson, was widely viewed as militarily and mentally incompetent, possibly traitorous, even insane. Revolution was in the air; the only question was whether it would be a relatively democratic revolution or one made brutal and tyrannical by the Bolsheviks.

The comfortably middle-class Rosenbaums probably didn't go cold or hungry in the early months of 1917, though in years to come they would, but privation was all around them. For this reason and others, it was natural that Anna, Zinovy, and their daughters were hoping for a democratic change of government, as were most Russian Jews. For the first time in three hundred years, the reign of the Romanovs was poised to end. St. Petersburg's European-educated liberal elite—a category that included many of Rand's teachers as well as the father of a new friend she made that winter—were ready to take the reins of government. For in spite of the terrible hardships of war, the Bolsheviks had gained only a small, if concentrated, following among urban workers and the nation's land-hungry former serfs and peasants. To the Rosenbaums' relief and joy, the reform-minded liberal intelligentsia, whom Anna so admired, were leading the call for the czar to share power or step down.

Rand, at twelve, was just entering adolescence. Short for her age and squarely built, she was highly animated when excited and became fidgety, standoffish, and sullen when her family's conversation turned from ideas and significant events to small talk. She already wore a look of luminous penetration in her large, dark, exquisite eyes. Stimulated by outward events and impatient to grow up, she assigned herself a new task: to examine her own ideas and beliefs just as rigorously as she examined those of others. This is what I think, she remembered saying to herself. *Why* do I think it? If her answer didn't measure up—if it was based on what others believed or on a mistake in logic—out went the idea.

Later, after achieving fame as a novelist and a largely self-taught metaphysician, she called such thinking "pre-philosophy." The job of the adolescent, she explained, is to integrate the likes and dislikes of childhood into a coherent if subconscious "sense of life," which she defined as an implicit appraisal of the nature of the world. Is the world understandable or incoherent? Do people have the power of choice, or are they servants of destiny? Can a person achieve his goals, or is he helpless against the designs of an all-powerful God or a malevolent universe? Depending on how the child answers, he will become a self-assured creator or a passive social parasite. That Rand answered her questions with such an insistent affirmative, and devoted so many years to proving that lack of credence in the power and efficacy of individual will equals moral cowardice, provides a clue as to just how great she felt were the obstacles to having "what I want" as a child. Russian tradition and her family provided some of the resistance. The politics of the Russian Revolution produced the rest.

Now in her third year at the Stoiunin school, she got one thing she wanted very much: her first close friend, a slightly older girl named Olga Nabokov. Olga, also a student at the school, was one of five children of a wealthy and distinguished family that was known throughout Russia and Europe even before Olga's older brother, Vladimir, began to publish poems and novels, including, in English, *Lolita.* Olga's mother was a cultured heiress. Her grandfather had been the minister of justice under Czar Alexander III, and though a gentile, was asked to resign partly because of his outspoken advocacy of political rights for Jews. Olga's father, V. D. Nabokov, was a jurist and a statesman, a member of the Russian army's General Staff, and a founder of the Constitutional Democratic Party, which favored a parliamentary form of government and emancipation of the Jews. In 1917, he had a bird's-eye view of the unfolding revolutionary drama from his ranking seat on the Duma, St. Petersburg's on-again, off-again national legislative assembly whose power the czar periodically stripped away and then restored. In February 1917, the Duma was in session.

Olga had been a member of Rand's class since 1915, but the girls seem to have become well acquainted only in their third tumultuous year. Olga lived with her family in a massive Florentine-style pink-granite mansion on Morskaya Street, not far from the czar's Winter Palace and about a mile from the Rosenbaums' store and apartment. To Rand and her mother and sisters, the Nabokovs' glittering life, seen up close, must have been a revelation. In their mansion and at their estate at nearby Vyra, Olga and her siblings were looked after by footmen, coachmen, chauffeurs, a concierge, cooks, maids, butlers, governesses, and tutors. Many of Russia's most admired poets and statesmen came and went as family friends. According to Helene Nabokov Sikorski, Olga's younger sister, Rand paid many visits to the family home in 1917. Rand appears to have been thinking of the Nabokovs when, in *We the Living,* she gave Kira Argounova, her semiautobiographical heroine, a prerevolutionary home that was a "vast" . . . "stately granite mansion" . . . where, at night, "a maid in black fastened the clasps of [Kira's mother's] diamond necklaces" in preparation for parties "in sparkling ballrooms." The fictional Argounovas' former summer estate, set amid acres of well-tended gardens, near a fashionable resort, recalls the Nabokovs as well.

The unusual friendship between Rand and Olga must have pleased, if somewhat mystified, Anna, whose frustration with her daughter's gracelessness didn't diminish as Rand entered her teen years. And the friend-ship was a boon to Rand. In Olga's company, the solitary girl probably felt as she did in Switzerland and Paris: This was where real people lived and where existence was exciting. She and Olga "conversed endlessly" about political ideas and events, Helene Sikorski remembered, with Olga bringing political bulletins from the family dinner table and Rand exercising, even then, her gift for ironclad analysis. Olga, echoing her fa-ther's conviction that Russia wasn't ready for a pure democracy, argued with Rand in favor of a constitutional monarchy, like that of England; Rand wanted a republic, she remembered, in which the head of state would be chosen for merit and there wouldn't be a king. The future afi-cionado of the U.S. Constitution hadn't yet studied American history (that would come in secondary school). But she had gathered impres-sions of America from family conversations, including the naming of the family cats, and from stories about a branch of Anna's family that had moved to Chicago in the 1890s. With Olga, Rand's tendency to argue "violently" and "at the slightest provocation," which she knew to be so-cially "not right," seemed to make no difference. If anything, her pas-sionate opinions enhanced Olga's and her pleasure in each other.

Though political change was in the air, it came as a shock to almost everyone when, during the final week of February 1917, history gal-loped past its gatekeepers to a point of no return.

The February 1917, or "liberal," Russian Revolution began with a shortage of bread. On February 23, several St. Petersburg bakeries ran out of flour and closed their doors. That afternoon a planned Interna-tional Women's Day march turned into a bread riot. The next day, male workers left their factories and joined the women in the streets. Before long, one hundred thousand hungry, war-weary workers, students, and soldiers collected at points outside the city and marched down Nevsky Prospekt, recklessly shouting "Down with the czar!" As in 1905, the Rosenbaums heard the insurrection from their windows; Rand later said that she and her sisters stood on their apartment balcony and watched as a line of mounted Cossacks fired warning shots above the crowd. Un-like in 1905, however, the czar didn't react quickly or decisively. By Feb-ruary 28, his St. Petersburg garrison, haphazardly led and sympathizing with the protesters, turned their guns on their commanders. The next day, thousands of munitions workers armed themselves for combat. That's when the Duma demanded, and got, the abdication of Czar Nicholas II. On March 3, Nicholas's younger brother Mikhail ceded his right of succession, quietly signing an abdication letter written by Olga's father. The Duma immediately installed a liberal Provisional Government, with V. D. Nabokov as its chancellor and Aleksandr Kerensky as its minister of justice, soon to be prime minister. For a brief period, the dashing and rhetorically gifted Kerensky became Ayn Rand's second hero, after Cyrus.

All Russia cheered the fall of the czar. In the streets, shops, and cafés of St. Petersburg, people spoke jubilantly of coming political freedoms, economic revival, and an end to the war. Much later, Rand would remember this as a period of unparalleled excitement, hope, and happiness, both for her and for the country. It was the only time in her life, she said, when she was "synchronized with history."

A few people, including the popular writer Maxim Gorky, took a dimmer view. He predicted that the "dark instincts" of the Russian people would "flare up and fume, poisoning us with anger, hate, and revenge. They will kill one another, unable to suppress their own animal stupidity." He was prescient, as the nation would soon learn.

Another skeptic emerged during the national celebration: Zinovy Rosenbaum. Beginning in February 1917, Rand's father quietly began stockpiling cash and family jewelry against the day when the revolution would turn ugly. He didn't have long to wait. On the heels of the czar's defeat came the Bolshevik leader Vladimir Lenin, an archenemy of the propertied classes and of all the privileges that come with money. He, too, had a utopian plan: to marshal the forces of poverty, envy, and anger, built up over hundreds of years of economic inequality, in pursuit of a classless society. In April, he arrived at the Finland Station from European exile, red banners flying from his train.

In the summer of 1917, the Rosenbaums and their extended family took a final carefree summer vacation in Terijoki, today called Zelenogorsk, a leafy resort town on the Russian-Finnish coast about thirty miles from St. Petersburg. This was one of the happiest summers of Rand's childhood. For one thing, she was reading *Ivanhoe,* Sir Walter Scott's historical romance set among twelfth-century English knights and ladies.

The book follows the adventures of the gallant young Ivanhoe, home from the Crusades and in love with the mild-mannered Lady Rowena. Ivanhoe, in turn, is loved by Rebecca, a gifted Jewish healer whose father, the wealthy merchant Isaac, sponsors Ivanhoe's chivalric exploits.

Amid a tangle of plots and subplots, Scott proposes that capitalism (as represented by Isaac) and character (which charming Rebecca has in spades) will be the defining values of the coming modern world. But the heraldic universe of *Ivanhoe* is not yet ready for modernity, and the hero finally spurns the beautiful Rebecca in favor of Rowena. Rand never remarked on this turn of the plot in a favorite novel, but the rejection of a superior girl for an insipid one and the second-class status of Jews were all too familiar to her. Robin Hood also makes an appearance in the book as the altruistic spokesman for popular resentment against the Norman nobles. This was probably Rand's first encounter with the legendary English outlaw who takes from the rich and gives to the poor—which also happened to be the stated objective of the Bolsheviks. For Rand, Robin Hood immediately became a villain, a symbol of the cowardly, destructive idea that "need, not achievement, is the source of rights," as she wrote in 1964. Readers of *Atlas Shrugged* remember the character of Ragnar Danneskjöld, an anti–Robin Hood who takes back from the poor and gives back to the rich.

When Rand returned to school that fall, the city's mood had darkened. The Provisional Government's first official act had been to confer equal rights on Jews, an unpopular move with most Russians. While the government also rapidly granted basic freedoms of speech, press, and assembly to the people at large, the lower classes were unmoved by abstract freedoms; they wanted bread, fuel, land, and jobs with a living wage. These were not forthcoming. In fact, shortages were such that the government began to ration bread.

Equally important, Kerensky didn't end the war; through a blizzard of speeches, he tried to rally the army for a push to victory. This shifted popular sentiment leftward. In legislative elections in September, the Bolshevik candidates, running on a promise to end the war, nationalize factories, and confiscate landowners' fields, made gains. Unfortunately, this didn't alarm Kerensky. In early October, when V. D. Nabokov asked him whether an armed Bolshevik attack on the new government was now possible, the prime minister answered that he hoped so; he was sure his troops could defeat the radicals once and for all.

Then, to worldwide dismay, on October 25, 1917, Lenin and his Bolshevik followers struck. Simply by occupying a few key buildings, cutting telephone lines, and winning over a handful of strategically placed soldiers, they gained control of the capital and overthrew Russia's fragile republican government. A bloody civil war for command of the rest of the empire followed, but this one-day coup was the unspectacular beginning of the dictatorship of the proletariat, whose ensuing brutalities Rand would one day brilliantly detail in fictional form. Kerensky, who fled the country, spent the rest of his life explaining why he shouldn't be blamed for the failure of his nation's single great moment of political opportunity. Russian parliamentary democracy had lasted exactly eight months.

Rand kept a diary during this period, where she wrote down her ideals and, on her thirteenth birthday, noted her decision to be an atheist. Later, she remembered her reasoning this way: Since no one had ever been able to prove that God exists, God was obviously an invention, and even if God *did* exist and was perfect, as reputed, then man would necessarily have to be imperfect and "low" by comparison, an idea she said she rejected then and never reconsidered. She may have been more deeply influenced than she remembered by anger at the seeming lack of justice, divine or otherwise, in the events taking place around her.

A few years after starting her diary she burned it; by then, keeping a written record of ideals that clashed with the official Bolshevik party line was perilous, even for a child. Much later she said that she used this diary to work out her views on popular ideas and maxims of the time, such as that people should "live for the state" or "live for others," specifically for the poor. It will come as no surprise to Rand's readers that, even then, she didn't like the sound of living for someone else. She remembered picturing her beloved heroes—Cyrus, Thunder, perhaps Kerensky—being forced to set aside their noble ideals and dashing temperaments to serve and obey proletarian "non-entities," as she called them, simply because those nonentities were illiterate and poor. Never! People have a right to live for themselves, she decided, transforming her native sense of entitlement into an integrated "sense of life." The unique rights of individuals, especially gifted individuals, would become a fundamental building block of—and point of contention about—her novels of ideas, starting with *We the Living*. Later, she would often say, "Whoever tells you to exist for the state is, or wants to be, the state."

Long before she began making notes for *We the Living,* she reached another conclusion: that political and philosophical ideas, especially those that are heroically clothed and set in large-scale social novels, have the power to shape perceptions and change the world. As scholars have noted, novels and poems have been a surrogate for banned political speech in Russia. Literature as a subversive force is a peculiarly Russian notion, one that was widely celebrated during Rand's youth. As Lenin was consolidating power in 1917, he invoked not only Karl Marx but also, more tellingly, the works of Ivan Turgenev (*Fathers and Sons*), Fyodor Dostoyevsky (*Poor Folk*), Maxim Gorky (*The Mother*), and especially Nikolai Chernyshevsky (*What Is to Be Done?*) as inspiration and grounds for action. Lenin said that Chernyshevsky's novel, a nineteenth-century tale of superhuman sacrifice in the service of a coming revolution, converted him to Communism at age fourteen, and he named his own seminal revolutionary tract *What Is to Be Done?* in tribute. It's little wonder, then, that Rand once referred to her own novels as anti-Communist propaganda, or that she henceforth viewed national politics as a morality play whose theme is individual freedom in contest with overt or hidden mob force.

She continued to write stories, though no copies and few accounts of these exist. She would have needed the company of her heroes that fall and winter, because she was losing her only friend. In late November, Olga's father, who was plotting a final legislative challenge to the Bolshevik usurpers, sent his wife and children south, to the Crimea, near Yalta, an area that was still free of Communist control. Within weeks, he and his liberal colleagues were rounded up, briefly jailed, and threatened with death. He escaped and joined his family. In 1919, the Nabokovs immigrated via Constantinople to Europe and the West. Rand never saw any of them again.

The worst was yet to come. In a campaign of class warfare waged by an ascendant Lenin against the middle class to pacify the poor, Rand's father's pharmacy, along with many of the city's factories, banks, shops, and offices, was raided, stamped with a red seal, and shuttered. Lenin called this "looting the looters." By encouraging acts of proletarian plunder and retribution against the city's bourgeoisie, Lenin's new government consciously initiated the Red Terror. Twelve-year-old Rand was in the store on the day Bolshevik soldiers arrived, brandishing guns. The anger, helplessness, and frustration she remembered seeing in her father's face remained with her all her life; the tenacity she bestows on her American businessman-hero Hank Rearden as he confronts the U.S. government's bureaucratic "looters and moochers" in *Atlas Shrugged* can be seen as her extended version of getting this scene right. Her father was out of business, and out of work.

Although Lenin and the early Communists weren't overtly anti-Semitic, Jewish merchants were targeted as scapegoats of the new regime, just as they had been in the old one. The government inflamed popular envy of Jews by euphemistic references to the "bourgeoisie," and Jews were left especially vulnerable to robbery and violence. It's likely that Zinovy's and Anna's St. Petersburg relatives, including the Konheims and Rand's grandfather Kaplan, also lost their businesses, livelihoods, and life's work at this time. Still, like others, the Rosenbaums couldn't believe that the Bolshevik regime would last. In spite of nationalizations, economic conditions didn't improve for the poor and working class, and support for Communism was eroding quickly in the city. Armies were massing against Lenin in the south. The Rosenbaums decided to wait it out, believing that the Bolsheviks would be routed, although with each passing week mob justice became more ruthless and food and other necessities more difficult to find.

The Stoiunin school continued to hold classes. Rand attended until the end of the 1917–18 term. Without Olga, however, she was again alone, with no one to talk to about the excruciatingly painful events going on around her.

It was at about this time that she began to read the novels of Victor Hugo, the only novelist she ever acknowledged as having influenced her work. Her mother made the introduction; in the evenings, Anna would read aloud from Hugo's works, in French, to Rand's grandmother Kaplan, while Rand listened from her bed. Hugo, the foremost Romantic writer of the nineteenth century, was a master of epic melodramas featuring solitary, larger-than-life heroes and psychologically misshapen villains in what were typically scorching critiques of French society and government. The first one of his novels she read was *The Man Who Laughs,* then *Les Misérables.* In these and her other favorites, including *The Hunchback of Notre Dame* and *Ninety-Three,* the author excoriated kings and queens, the French Revolution and street violence, while also projecting emotional nobility and human grandeur. His preoccupations could hardly have been more pertinent to Rand's situation, and his insights must have deepened her understanding of revolution. She relished his intricate plots, inspiring themes, and outsized characters, and she fell in love with one of his most radical inventions: Enjolras, the high-minded, again implacable young revolutionary leader in *Les Misérables,* who would serve as a model for both the handsome aristocrat Leo Kovalensky and the Communist Party hero Andrei Taganov in *We the Living.* In each of her published novels except *Anthem* (1938), she retained traces of the plotting techniques and stylistic sleights of hand she learned from Hugo. Her love of his work stayed with her. At age fifty-seven, after everything else in her life had radically changed, she called him the "greatest novelist in world literature."

By late summer of 1918, the Rosenbaums had had enough. Under threat of a new order compelling them to share their living space on less than equal footing with former servants, factory workers, and soldiers; with whole days now spent in search of rationed millet, peas, and cooking oil; and with the terrifying knowledge that what the revolutionaries regarded as their and their neighbors' "hoarded" savings had become the object of systematic official searches, they gathered their belongings and departed. Still expecting the regime to collapse, they thought they would be away from home for six months; they were gone for three years.

As *We the Living* opens in 1922, the Argounov family is wearily returning to a dreary, disease-ridden St. Petersburg from the Crimean peninsula, now also in Bolshevik hands. But in 1918, when the Rosenbaums fled south, the Crimea was a bustling center of White Russian resistance to the Communists and was full of transplanted czarist military officers, aristocrats, statesmen, manufacturers, and merchants from the north. Rand later told a friend that she and her family were forced to walk all the way from Leningrad (as St. Petersburg came to be known in 1924) to Odessa, a journey of nine hundred miles. This is unlikely, especially as she told another friend that the railroad train in which the family traveled broke down in the Ukraine and that they and other passengers hired horse-drawn carts to continue their journey, adding that the carts were robbed by a gang of bandits. In this story, Zinovy managed to safeguard his savings of several thousand rubles by burying them in the straw that lined a cart. It may be that the family was forced to walk after the robbery, though Rand recalled climbing back in the cart, or that the family walked during another leg of the journey and the child recalled the ordeal as being longer than it was.

In any case, Rand remembered rocky terrain, broken shoes, hunger, darkness, terror, defiance. If she was going to die, she remembered thinking at the time of the robbery, she would die on her own terms, picturing Hugo's young hero Enjolras. Her last thought would be of his steadfastness and courage, "not of Russia nor the horrors." Later in life, she would prove herself gifted at focusing on distant ideals in the face of unpleasant realities. Yet another quality comes to light here: a propensity for imagining characters as more real than the people around her. As an adult she would ask friends, "But would you want to meet" the characters in a novel they were reading? If the answer was no, she considered the discussion finished. Fictional heroes and villains lived and breathed for Rand, and her own larger-than-life characters came to define the limits of an imagined world so compelling that many admirers who entered it never left.

Rand and her parents and sisters lingered briefly in the Ukraine, where a number of Zinovy's cousins practiced medicine and where Zinovy might have expected to find work. The Bolsheviks were making military inroads there, too, however. So the Rosenbaums moved on, as originally planned, to the Crimea. For the next three years, they lived in Yevpatoria, a resort town near the southern tip of the Crimean peninsula, on the Black Sea. The town stood only one hundred miles from Yalta, where the Nabokovs were staying, but Rand didn't know this; she believed that Olga and her family had left the country in 1917. Since the Rosenbaums had taken summer vacations on the Black Sea in better days, Yevpatoria may have been familiar to them. Side by side with thousands of other refugees from the Red Terror, they searched for shelter, paid work, and food. They found a small, damp, unheated house in which to live. Zinovy eventually opened a pharmacy, but this was looted and shut down, either by renegade White Russian soldiers, invading Reds, or the staunchly anti-Semitic local Orthodox peasants who rampaged against the Jews whenever the Whites were in retreat. The town changed hands four or five times. Fifty-five years later, Rand remembered the terror of the Red Army and the empty, "smelly," "Holy Russian" religious bromides of the Whites with almost equal loathing. The family lived "on a battlefield," she said.

During the years in Yevpatoria, she and her sisters, Natasha and Nora, attended a private girls' school. Here, in the last remaining corner of Russia not permanently occupied by Reds, the schools were free of the Communist curriculum that had taken hold elsewhere. Among other subjects, Rand studied math, which she loved, Russian language and literature, which she claimed to have hated, and Aristotelian syllogistic logic, which taught her to prize rigor and strive for consistency. At the time, she recalled, she knew little about Aristotle except that he was supposed to be an archenemy of Plato, whom she took to be a virtuous idealist, as opposed to a vulgar Communistic materialist, and so she expected to "be against" Aristotle. In one of her first college courses, she would change her mind about Plato, fall in love with Aristotle, and passionately align herself with Aristotle's empiricism for the remainder of her life. She also studied political economy, which fired her imagination. The class was her introduction to the Declaration of Independence and America's constitutional guarantee of individual rights, and these deeply impressed her. Henceforth, the United States would replace Britain as the focus of her hopes and plans. She read Edmond Rostand's *Cyrano de Bergerac,* a romantic fable about a witty, proud French soldier and poet with a disfiguring nose whose love letters on behalf of his rival, Christian, win the heart of his cousin Roxane; when Roxane discovers who wrote them, she pledges her love to Cyrano, but only as he is dying from a wound. On reading about the trials and triumph of the ugly, honorable misfit, "I cried my eyes out," Rand said. She learned the play by heart, and it became another of her lifelong literary touchstones.

There is a picture of Ayn Rand from this period, posing with her high-school graduating class of about twenty somber-looking girls and almost as many teachers, all artfully arranged on a period Turkish rug outdoors, in the schoolyard. Rand's hair is bobbed and caught in a barrette, and she wears a white broad-collared shirt and skirt, both fresh and crisp. She must have made a special effort to look neat that day, for her usual disarray often caused her mother to complain that she didn't care how she looked. In the picture, she peers out intently, almost defiantly, toward the camera, while the other girls just stare. This was in the late spring of 1921, and Rand's class was smaller by a third than it had been six months before. During the previous November, retreating White Russian military officers had evacuated 150,000 soldiers, civilians, and families—anyone who wanted to leave Russia—while the Red

Army massed for its final, conclusive assault on the Crimea. The Whites loaded everybody into French and British ships and sailed them across the Black Sea to Constantinople, whence passengers could travel on to Europe. Some of the ships set sail from the docks at Yevpatoria, but the Rosenbaums were left behind. Anna had pleaded with Zinovy to let the family emigrate, but Rand's father was as certain as Kerensky had been that Communism couldn't last. One day, he promised, they would reclaim their business and property in St. Petersburg. By spring, the Bolshevik victory was complete and uncontestable; with a few far-flung exceptions, all of Russia was under Red control.

The Communist victory meant that Yevpatoria and nearby towns were overrun by an army of ragged, hungry, illiterate Red soldiers, many of whom had also served in World War I. As a group, they were looking for booty and eager to exact revenge and spread terror—they were a classic mob. There were mock trials, burnings, and hangings, and Rand later recalled that one classmate's father was summarily and publicly shot. Zinovy's old-style rubles were now worthless; the Bolsheviks issued their own inflated rubles, which became the legal tender in the south. By 1924, five billion of these rubles would buy what one had bought in 1914. This was a decisive blow in the campaign of economic devastation against the former middle class.

In this setting, the sixteen-year-old Rand composed what she later called her "first adult novel." It was inspired by Hugo and set in medieval France, where battling groups of feudal lords fought for and against an evil king in an epic civil war. (According to one researcher, the teenaged Rand admired feudalism because it represented "a pyramid of ability," with noble, if not necessarily gifted, men and women at the top.) She completed about a third of the novel's planned chapters, then halted—in fact, stopped writing plays and novels altogether. She was aware, she later told a friend, that she was simply too young to write the way she now wanted to write—presumably, with some of the urbanity and passion of Victor Hugo—and that the stories she longed to tell could not be told in Russia. Instead, she made lists of plots and themes for future projects. By age thirty, she said, she intended to be famous.

Rand graduated from secondary school on June 30, 1921. She and her mother, both desperate for work, timidly signed on to teach illiterate Red soldiers to read and write. To Rand's surprise, she found the men eager to learn and polite in the classroom. She was unusually gifted at teaching, as her friends and followers would later remark with almost universal awe, and she enjoyed making a misunderstood or murky concept exquisitely clear. But by midsummer she and her family no longer had any reason to stay in the Crimea; they had lost their gamble, and their confiscated real estate and remaining relatives were in St. Petersburg. While they struggled to feed themselves, they waited for seats on one of the antiquated trains that were taking Red soldiers, peasants, black marketers, and everyone else who could leave the region north. After weeks of waiting, they found a train and squeezed on.

There's no better description of the Rosenbaums' journey home than the opening pages of *We the Living*. What had formerly been a three-day train trip took two weeks. The third-class compartment the family rode in was packed with men and women who had been waiting trackside, for days or weeks, without a bath or change of clothing. The train was filthy. Everyone was hungry. Scraps of food and the relics of old valuables had to be secreted, out of sight, and guarded. When a few of the passenger cars broke down, the Rosenbaums scrambled for cramped space aboard a boxcar. The teenaged Rand observed every nuance of timidity, pretentiousness, callousness, and greed among her fellow passengers, including her family, and recorded it all with Dostoyevskian precision in her semiautobiographical novel a decade later.

The train stopped in Moscow before completing its journey to St. Petersburg. She briefly left the boxcar and stood in a city square just outside the railroad station. Moscow, which had become Russia's capital city in March 1918, was enormous, she remembered thinking, and was only one city among hundreds or even thousands in the world. She had something to say to people in all of them, she reflected with a thrill; the audience for her plays and stories would be immense.

By late summer 1921, the permanent population of St. Petersburg was smaller by two-thirds than it had been at the outbreak of the world war. Even so, workers, the unemployed, and roaming hordes of demobilized Red soldiers occupied almost every square foot of habitable housing. Back in their native city, the Rosenbaums settled into a single room of their old apartment on Nevsky Prospekt, now inhabited by a sign painter and his family, who let them use some of their old furniture. There was no electricity or hot water. Nor was there food for those who didn't work or study, since government-issued ration cards, the only way to lay hands on what meager and often rotten food there was, were distributed in workplaces and schools. Finding work was a priority. Under a brief amnesty for private merchants called the New Economic Policy (NEP), Zinovy obtained a position in a cooperative pharmacy, but such semiprivate businesses were soon closed down and their wares impounded. Like Uncle Vasili in *We the Living,* he refused to work for the Communists, the only work there was. Later, Rand explained, her father "wouldn't do anything. To begin with, he wouldn't have been accepted, as a former owner, into any Soviet job, and he didn't want to do it. . . . He was enormously on strike." Zinovy's attitude made a strong impression upon Rand; to her it seemed heroic. Similarly, in the 1940s, she began to refer to her husband, the unemployed actor Frank O'Connor, as also being "on strike." The original title of her third major novel, *Atlas Shrugged,* was, unmusically, *The Strike.*

It was Rand's mother who kept the family financially afloat after returning to St. Petersburg. Anna, the former dentist and literary lady of the house, applied for and got a Soviet teaching certificate in 1921; for many years thereafter, she traveled the city by tram, instructing impoverished workers and their children in reading, writing, and foreign languages. By the mid-1920s, she was earning much-needed money on the side by tutoring and translating politically correct books and magazine articles for the Soviet state publishing house Gossizdat. Once Rand arrived in the United States, she sent her mother American novels to translate; Anna marveled at her daughter's ability to choose works of proletarian fiction that Gossizdat would readily accept.

Anna was unusually resourceful and seems to have thrived in her new role as the family's breadwinner. At one point, she wrote to Rand in America, "You and I have our love of work in common." In a diminishing turnabout, Zinovy was placed in charge of keeping house, waiting in lines for rationed food, and cooking the millet or, in flush times, peas or potatoes that typically made a meal. Some of these were chores that Rand's husband Frank would also perform.

Rand had left St. Petersburg a girl and had returned a young woman. In August 1921, she was admitted, free of charge, to Petrograd State University as a student in the newly formed Social-Pedagogical Division of the College of Social Sciences. This division combined the old disciplines of history, philology, anthropology, and philosophy under one academic roof. She declared a major in history and a minor in philosophy and began attending classes in October. As a student, as in little else, she benefited from the Bolshevik regime, since Lenin had adopted Keren-sky's policy of offering educational opportunities to Jews and women, while doing away with tuition fees and reducing the full term of study to three years. These changes were meant to help factory workers, but they made it possible for her to get the kind of education, and degree, that her parents could have only dreamed of. By her own lights, she made the most of it, studying as much as she could with the older, classi-cally trained, Western-leaning liberal professors who were slowly being phased out, arrested, and deported. She took ancient, medieval, West-ern, and Russian history; logic; philosophy of the mind, a forerunner of psychology; French; biology; and historical materialism and the history of socialism, which were required courses. She read Hegel and Marx, Shakespeare, Schiller, and the great proto-Nietzschean novelist Dos-toyevsky, whose mystical point of view she said she rejected but whose brilliant integration of plot, theme, and "philosophy of mind" she learned from and found exciting. She later said that Dostoyevsky was the world's best interpreter of the psychology of evil. He "gives me the feeling of entering a chamber of horrors, but with a powerful guide," she wrote in 1971. She was lucky to be admitted to the university when she was; by 1924, the year she graduated, a decree was issued barring admission to students from families who had owned property before the revolution or who had employed one or more servants at any time during the last three generations.

Determinism, the irreducible feature of a Marxist view of history, was on the rise at the university. Rand found the notion offensive, and not merely because "historical necessity" was the battle cry of the Bol-sheviks. She recalled sitting outraged through a lecture in which the in-structor offered proof that individuals act without free will. If a young man, he said, standing at the doorway of his home, could turn either left or right to reach a destination in the same amount of time, but knew that he would see a pretty waitress in a restaurant if he turned right, he would turn right. He would have no choice; his action would be deter-mined by his nature. Rand thought, If you have a reason for what you do, you are making a choice. Later, she would define free will as the freedom to think or to avoid thinking in any particular situation.

During her stay in the Crimea and as a university student, she grew closer to her silent and usually inexpressive father, who was almost al-ways at home while her mother worked. It was only after she and he began to be allies in opposition to the Bolsheviks, she later said, that she felt real love for him, a love that meant something beyond family affection and abstract respect. She and he shared a disgusted contempt for Communist ideology, which was perhaps best summarized by the slogan "from each according to his ability, to each according to his need," and their contempt grew deeper and more acrid as "need" was increasingly revealed to be a euphemism for the demands of those in power—those exerting "pull," as Rand would memorably write in *Atlas Shrugged.* Somewhat unreasonably, both father and daughter considered Anna much too eager to defend and appease her Communist employers, just as she had once been pleased to emulate the city's intellectual elite. In fact, Zinovy severely disapproved of his wife's working for the Communists at all, and Rand's sister Nora once remarked that Anna was a little "pink." Young Rand and her father proudly endorsed individualism and free will.

Most important, the father was openly supportive of his daughter's brilliant analytical intelligence, drive, and vocation as a writer. He must often have encouraged her as he did in the late 1920s, when he wrote to her in America: "You must see clearly that you are not like everybody else and be proud of it. Eschew all doubts and continue firmly and with assurance to walk toward your goal." She clearly returned his love and admiration. "She spoke about him with more respect than I can recall her ever speaking about anybody," said a friend who knew Rand in the 1950s.

There was one area of conflict between the girl and her father: He opposed her chosen course of study at the university. Without asking her to give up writing, he wanted her to apply her math training and love of the scientific method to a more remunerative occupation, such as engineering. This would have been an unusual profession for an early-twentieth-century Jewish father to urge on any daughter other than Rand, who was to make it Kira's frustrated calling in *We the Living.* Having grown up in the Russian Pale, he was more aware than Anna or the children of the crucial role that work and money played in protecting against the onslaughts of anti-Semitism. As Rand and her sisters grew older, he urged them to choose occupations that would always allow them to earn a living. All three chose to be artists. Natasha studied piano at Petrograd Conservatory, the nation's most distinguished school of music, along with fellow students Igor Stravinsky, Sergei Prokofiev, and Dmitri Shostakovich and former student Pyotr Tchaikovsky. Anna

approved of Natasha's choice, unlike Rand's, because music was a properly ladylike career. Nora, the youngest, studied to be an artist, though
she later became a teacher like her mother and, finally, a graphic designer. Rand argued with her father that, as a future writer, she had to
study history in order "to have a factual knowledge of man's past" and
understand philosophy in order "to achieve an objective definition of my
values." She promised him that she would one day make a living as a
writer, and, as always when hard work and force of will were the deciding factors, she was right.

In her first two years at the university, a number of events took place
that solidified her "sense of life" and influenced her for years to come.
The first was taking a course called Ancient World Views, probably the
last class taught by the distinguished professor N. O. Lossky before he
was deported. The course surveyed the pre-Socratic philosophers, Plato,
and Aristotle. This may sound innocuous, but not for Rand; by now,
ideas of every kind and vintage earned her passionate assent or disapproval. In Lossky's class she was dazzled by Aristotle, particularly his
logical starting point of the axiomatic existence of objective reality and
his belief in human reason as the only means to understand the world;
for him, as for Rand, man was a rational animal. She learned to detest
Plato and his mysticism, which is how she regarded the Platonic belief
that the observable world is a mere shadow of ideal forms that can't be
seen; she associated this, rightly, with mystical Christianity. And she
learned from Lossky an intensely dialectical method of thinking—
"thinking in principles," she called it—which helped her to construct a
worldview that was radically individualistic and seemingly Western but
in some ways Russian to the core.

Rand described herself in these years as solemn, even grim, and always engaged in serious discussion. She was aware that people often
didn't want to talk to her and that she was sometimes forcing conversations on her family and schoolmates. Where she had once seen laziness,
indifference, or shallow-mindedness, however, she now saw envy: she
grew convinced that she was actively resented, and not for her faults but
for her best qualities, her virtues, as her rebellious heroes Howard Roark
and John Galt would also be.

She had no known friends, but she did spend time with two maternal cousins, Vera and Nina Guzarchik, who lived above the Rosenbaum
apartment. It was Vera who, while reading Friedrich Nietzsche's philo-

sophical novel *Thus Spoke Zarathustra,* remarked that Rand reminded her of Zarathustra, the German philosopher's prophetic outlaw hero, or at least that Nietzsche had "beat me to all my ideas," Rand recalled. The book describes the hero's journey down a mountainside, after the death of God, to teach what he has learned to the people below. From now on, he tells the jeering masses, human beings will determine their own values and their own destinies, free of superstitious reliance on gods, conventional morality, and faith. Furthermore, people must learn to make way for the exceptional individual, the Superman of whom Zarathustra is the first example; through a "will to power" and a talent for "self-overcoming," the Superman will establish a new morality of man.

Nietzsche's work was popular among intellectuals in Russia at the time, especially his descriptions of master and slave psychology and of the absolute right of the superior individual to place himself in opposition to the common herd. The seventeen-year-old Rand immediately seized upon his ideas, including his call to discard old values and create new ones, his condemnation of altruism as a slave morality, and his argument for the inviolate rights of the gifted person, whose only obligation is to refine and use his gifts as he sees fit. One point, in particular, had an immediate influence on her thinking, she recalled. Until reading Nietzsche, she had assumed that in order to defend man against religion, she would have to defend *all* men, no matter how weak or strong; Zarathustra demonstrated "that it doesn't have to be collective. In other words, that the species can be vindicated by one man." She responded to his heightened language, his brilliance, his bold critique of Christianity, and his principled admiration of Jewish thought. From this point on, her major characters would be more or less overtly Nietzschean—and, because of their Superman aura, would often be wrongly seen as fascistic by her critics. It wasn't until she was writing *The Fountainhead* that she was able to begin to loosen Nietzsche's seductive hold on her imagination.

Vera's younger sister Nina Guzarchik was the leader of a group of intellectual young people who called themselves "Uno Momento" and sometimes gathered for parties in the Guzarchik apartment. At one of these Rand met a handsome, brooding boy with whom she fell in love, the third great event of these years. His name was Lev Bekkerman, and not only did he resemble a fictional character (Cyrus), he would also become one (Leo Kovalensky, Kira's dissolute lover in *We the Living*). An engineering student at St. Petersburg Technical Institute, he was four years older than she was, and, unlike the fictional character Leo, he was Jewish. "The first time I saw him, I remember being very startled by how good-looking he was," she recalled when she was fifty-five. "It was his looks that I liked enormously." He had a sharp, intelligent, purposeful-appearing face, a graceful, slender body, a thick shock of hair, and light gray eyes. As with Cyrus, Hugo's Enjolras, and Prime Minister Kerensky, "the quality I liked about him most was arrogance," she later said. He was "like some fantastic aristocrat" in his consciousness of his attractiveness to women, his desirability, and his sense of his own worth. She learned that he shared her political views; he had once hidden in his apartment students who were being hunted by the Soviet police, or GPU, an act of bravery that she would later confer on Kira's cousin Irina Dunaeva in We the Living.

On some of their few dates, they bought cheap seats at operettas in the silver-and-peach grandeur of the Mikhailovsky Theatre, probably including Rand's lifelong favorite, Emmerich Kálmán's Die Bajadere (1921). As the two sat "solemn, erect," the Viennese music seemed to laugh and the settings bring to life a 1920s European bar and the spirit of contemporary German cabaret, as Rand noted in We the Living. Lev Bekkerman was Rand's first flesh-and-blood infatuation, and she fell "madly and desperately" in love with him.

The love affair didn't end happily. Rand was open, possibly too open, about her feelings. She pursued him, and he didn't like it. "I knew he didn't like it," she would later say. He continued to see other girls, and after a few weeks, he stopped asking her out. When they met, usually because the resourceful Rand had found out where to find him on a particular evening, he pointedly ignored her. Still, until she left the country in 1926, she continued to see him at occasional social gatherings. In 1924, he contracted tuberculosis and traveled to the Crimea to be treated in a state-run sanatorium, much as We the Living's Leo would do. In 1933, by which time Rand had established herself as a Hollywood screenwriter and was married, she learned from her cousin Nina that Lev, too, had married, divorced, and married again, each time to an unappealing, frowsy, ordinary woman. She was shocked by this, she said in 1960. "The whole issue [of Lev] . . . is still an unfinished story in my mind. My only explanation [for his choice of partners] . . . would be what I wrote about Leo in We the Living, that it was deliber-

ate self-destruction, deliberately consigning himself to mediocrity, because [whatever] higher values [he possessed] were not possible there,"
amid Russian Communist repression. In May 1937, during the height
of the Stalinist Terror, Lev was put to death under a Soviet statute that
mandated the execution of black marketers and perpetrators of terrorist
acts against the state; he had been accused of plotting to blow up tanks
in the Leningrad factory where he worked. She never learned of his
death, but it's not hard to imagine the fictional Leo Kovalensky ending
his life in much the same way, had Rand's heroine Kira only survived to
witness it.

In a haunting irony, Rand herself might have been present for Lev's
death if, in 1922 or 1923, he had reciprocated her feelings for him;
much later she said that she would almost certainly have remained in
Russia had her first love loved her, too. "I would have stayed . . . and I
would have died there," she told a friend.

Exactly how this early romantic disappointment affected her life and
work is hard to gauge. By the time she spoke about it with someone who
recorded her remarks, she had been married for thirty years and was engaged with a much younger man in a long-term love affair. But in a letter from 1927, her mother reminded her that during those years she had
spent hours in her bedroom, "yelling in despair." In a chronological list
of music she loved, her favorite piece for the year 1924 was "Simple
Aveu," by French composer Francis Thomé, the only melancholy music
on the list. Lev's rejection may help to explain why, after We the Living's
Kira, Rand's heroines would tend to be romantically and sexually submissive hero-worshipers, while Rand herself remained aggressive in pursuit of anything she wanted, including men.

Just as she loved military marches and light Italian opera, Rand developed a passion for the elaborately staged Viennese and German operettas that, for a brief period, the Bolshevik government made available
and affordable in state-run musical theaters such as the Mikhailovsky.
She waited in line for hours each Saturday morning to buy cheap tickets
for the back row of the fourth and highest balcony. During her first two
years at the university, "I was there every Saturday," she recalled. But
soon an even more alluring opportunity arrived: to see the masterful,
thrillingly melodramatic new silent films directed by D. W. Griffith,
Fritz Lang, Ernst Lubitsch, and Cecil B. DeMille. She and her family
had been attending Russian-made movies since 1913. As a nine- or ten-

year-old, she had even composed two childish film scenarios, one of them about a woman who has to choose between her husband in prison and her child; in a decision that reverberates eerily down the years, precocious young Rand's heroine chooses the husband. (The child lived anyway, she said, so there was "a happy ending.")

Starting in 1923, however, during the NEP period, sophisticated American and European films began making an appearance in small, inexpensive, privately run theaters on the outskirts of the city. She took full advantage of them, seeing more than one hundred movies, some three or more times, in the years before she emigrated. "It was almost as if I had a private avenue of seeing the world outside," she later said. She loved the tangled plots, glamorously costumed stars, and exotic settings of movies like *Intolerance, Lucrezia Borgia,* and *The Isle of Lost Ships.* Her favorite film was Joe May's 1921 melodrama *The Indian Tomb,* starring Conrad Veidt as Prince Ayan, a nefarious Bengali maharaja who bribes a yogi to capture and kill his wife's lover, a British army officer played by Paul Richter. A British architect (Olaf Fønss) and his wife (Mia May) track Prince Ayan and foil his murderous scheme. The film ends with an elaborate, triumphant chase scene in the Bengal mountains. If this sounds suspiciously like the story line from Maurice Champagne's *The Mysterious Valley,* Rand never noted the resemblance and perhaps was never conscious of it.

Veidt, a German Jew, became her favorite movie actor until she encountered Gary Cooper in the late 1920s. Veidt was a screen idol in Russia, and Rand's infatuation with him brought out a trait that was present from early childhood: intellectual possessiveness. When people she didn't know or like spoke admiringly of Veidt, she felt anger, she recalled. *She* had chosen him; other people weren't worthy of him. Not for her was "a heart like a pavement, trampled by many feet."

Rand's introduction to American silent films was the fourth defining experience of her university years. There, she got her first glimpse of the New York skyline, which would become for her an emblem of creativity and liberty in the capitalist free world. Although Soviet government censors always added absurd subtitles to the films, she said—turning an ordinary American family dinner scene into a portrait of greed, for example, by labeling it "A capitalist eating well on profits wrung from his starving workers"—she and other Russians understood this to be nonsense, or "applesauce," as she called it. Her enthusiasm for America was forged in movie theaters. The films she saw inspired her to picture it as "Atlantis": the ideal existence for intelligent, purposeful, ruggedly individualistic men and, presumably, women. America, she decided, was the place on earth where she would find real people and the country in which she wanted to live and work.

Meanwhile, in spite of new cinemas and state-sponsored operettas, 1923 and 1924 saw the city under renewed political and economic siege. For the previous two years, Lenin had been preoccupied with quelling far-flung rebellions and a nationwide famine. Now, as he and his deputy Joseph Stalin focused on the cities, the repression grew harsher. Food rations were cut to one thousand calories a day. Diseases of dirt and poverty such as cholera, typhoid, rheumatic fever, and tuberculosis swept the city, exacerbating Rand's and Anna's fear of germs. Russia officially became the Soviet Union, and the regime began busily rolling back the NEP—eliminating the jobs it had created and the useful products and services it brought to market—while intensifying its attack on the remnants of the middle class. Workplaces and schools were purged of political undesirables, which meant that becoming an informant against fellow students or workers and attempting to join the Communist Party were among the few strategies to try to stay alive. Candid speech was dangerous and dissent was deadly. The light of academic discourse was quickly going out.

In 1923 the Rosenbaums found an apartment of their own at 16 Dmitrovski Lane, a few blocks from their prerevolutionary home. Grandfather Berko Kaplan and Rand's cousin Leonid Konheim joined them there. Though the family had more space, their lot was dreary. In a city festooned with fraying Red banners, they cooked their thousand calories a day on a smoky kerosene stove called a "Primus" and at celebrations ate cakes made of potato peelings, carrot greens, coffee grounds, and acorns. When there was fuel, they read by kerosene. Rand recalled that her one party dress was refashioned from an old summer coat of her mother's, which Anna must have carefully packed, repacked, and carried to the Crimea and back again.

There had been a number of purges at the university since Rand arrived there in 1921. In the fall of 1922, for example, her eminent professor N. O. Lossky, along with his wife, his mother-in-law Mme. Stoiunina, and 220 other famous Russian academic philosophers and intellectuals were arrested for so-called anti-Soviet activity and deported on what came to be known as the "Philosophy Ship." (On Mme. Stoiunina's arrest, Rand's alma mater the Stoiunin school closed its doors forever.) A year later, while she was in her third and final year, the university announced the largest purge yet of "socially undesirable elements" among the students. She was one of four thousand students expelled, a third of the student body, some of whom—"young boys and girls I knew" she later said—were sent off to die in Siberian prison camps. She was officially charged with "not fulfilling academic requirements," but this was merely code for belonging to a prerevolutionary middle-class family and not being an ardent-enough Communist. (In her first year, she, like Kira, made "all kinds of anti-Soviet remarks" before realizing that she was endangering her family and herself.) The purge and its chilling, academically stifling aftereffects are unforgettably portrayed in *We the Living*. Rand, however, unlike her heroine Kira, got an unexpected reprieve. When a group of visiting Western scientists heard about the student purge and complained to their Communist hosts, she and other third-year students were reinstated and allowed to graduate.

She received her diploma on October 13, 1924. Her university records show that she had passing grades in all her subjects. Later, she would claim that she had finished "with highest honors"—an impossibility in a system that had been converted to "pass," "fail," and "retake." Her followers would repeat this story and other questionable anecdotes about her prowess as a student, although scholarship was never her strong suit and by that time she didn't need anyone to bolster her claim to genius.

While still at the university, Rand joined local writers' clubs, but members were supervised and turned out little other than pat political treatises. Still, she constructed outlines for plays and stories and wrote an interesting short novel in this period. The text of the novella seems to be lost, but as she described it in 1960, it involved a meteorological disturbance that causes a gigantic airplane to spin out into space and begin to circle the earth. The passengers are a mixed group of scientists and Communists. Luckily, the plane is loaded with supplies. Using these, the scientists create a self-sustaining miniature economy that benefits all on board, even allowing them to grow food, while also devising a plan to get the airplane back to earth. Then the Communists gain the upper hand. In a chapter called "Humanity in a Teaspoon," she showed the Communists gradually picking apart and destroying everything the scientists have accomplished. Soon everyone is starving. The Communists beg the story's hero, a leading scientist, to take charge. He agrees. As the story ends, he begins to re-create his earlier work, with the implication that all will be well and the plane will return to earth. This, of course, echoes the ending of *Atlas Shrugged,* except that there the novel's hero, John Galt, refuses to help the socialistic villains and instead flies his plane to a self-sustaining miniature world hidden in the Rocky Mountains; there he waits for the incompetent "looters and moochers" to perish of their own incompetence. Although Rand used many of the same ideas and motifs in both narratives, by the 1950s she appeared to be less hopeful that minds can be changed, villains converted, and mankind in general saved; a sealed world became her only answer.

It's remarkable that this story is set aboard an airplane, let alone one that orbits the earth. If Rand's memory is correct, she wrote it four years before Charles Lindbergh crossed the Atlantic Ocean. The explanation may lie in an influence she never publicly spoke of: the stories and novels of a few then-famous Russian futurist and surrealist writers who lived in St. Petersburg in the early 1920s and made their names by envisioning the utopian, and anti-utopian, potential of the decade's new machines. Rand's 1938 novel, *Anthem,* clearly reflects their influence, and so, perhaps, did this early effort. She almost surely encountered their work, both published and unpublished, in an underground network connected to one of her writers' clubs.

Aircraft always fascinated Rand, although until late in her life she was too fearful to fly in a plane. In *Atlas Shrugged,* Dagny Taggart and John Galt both fly solo through Colorado. In a 1969 essay, Rand described watching in "exaltation" as Apollo 11 streaked skyward from Cape Kennedy. And in "Philosophy: Who Needs It," her famous speech to the 1974 senior class of West Point, she narrates a parable of an astronaut whose spaceship veers off course and crashes on a strange planet. The astronaut, who doesn't understand his craft or its instruments, merely waits passively, hoping that something will intercede to save him, as aliens approach. The unstated moral: Airplanes, like skyscrapers, are the domain of the intelligent hero.

While still at the university, she outlined another novel foreshadowing her masterwork, *Atlas Shrugged.* This novel concerned a beautiful, spirited American heiress who lures Europe's greatest men to follow her to America. The Europeans are quickly becoming Communists, and the heiress wants to entice all men of ability to withdraw to a better world. A Frenchman is appointed by the Europeans to conquer and collectivize America. Our heroine offers him a million dollars to join her instead; he, in turn, offers her two million to come to work for him. They fall in love. The plot, though complicated, ends in the collapse of the Europeans. The heiress's assistant in the novel is named Eddie Willers, the name Rand would also give to her heroine Dagny Taggart's assistant in *Atlas Shrugged*—where John Galt lures all men of ability to withdraw to his mountain hideout.

In October 1924, diploma in hand, the nineteen-year-old Rand enrolled in a new performing-arts school called the State Technicum for Screen Arts, founded with Lenin's explicit support in 1922 as a training camp for aspiring actors and cinematographers. The Bolsheviks viewed motion pictures as a promising new weapon in the international propaganda war between Communism and capitalism, and they offered free tuition to any ideologically qualified student who applied. (Rand probably would not have been admitted had her mother Anna not joined the Communist teachers' union in February 1923, very likely to Rand's and Zinovy's disapproval.) She hoped to learn the techniques of screenwriting, and had a special reason: By now, she was determined to find a way to immigrate to America and work in the new and rapidly growing movie industry. This would be a manageable prelude to writing publishable plays and novels, which she knew would require English-language and literary skills she didn't yet possess. The only alternative to emigration she could fathom, she later said, was to remain in Russia and oppose Communism by writing satirical films attacking it. She and her mother both foresaw that this road would be short and lead to death. Anna supported her dream of emigration; her father, fearful and perhaps dependent on her intellectual companionship, did not.

By spring, the way to America found her, through Anna's relatives in Chicago. In the late 1890s, one of Anna's aunts, Eva Kaplan, had immigrated to the United States and settled in Chicago with her husband, Harry Portnoy, and their eight children. Eva had borrowed part of the money for the family's passage from her brother, Rand's grandfather Berko Kaplan, and felt indebted to him. The Rosenbaums hadn't heard from the Portnoys during World War I and the Russian Revolution, because mail service from the West had been interrupted. Now they received a letter, and Rand begged Anna to ask Eva's grown daughters

Minna Goldberg, Anna Stone, and Sarah Lipton to sponsor her for a visit to America. The Chicago cousins had brought over other Russian Jews, both inside and outside the family, and they readily agreed and sent the necessary affidavit of support. What's more, Sarah Lipton owned and operated a Chicago movie theater, and she promised that Rand could work there if she liked. With affidavit in hand, in the spring of 1925 Rand applied for a Soviet passport, with the declared intention of visiting the United States for six months and of returning to Russia to make propaganda films. Luckily, a tiny window of opportunity remained open for Russians to go abroad; within two years, that and almost every other window of escape would slam shut.

While Rand waited anxiously for passport permission to be granted or denied, she wrote a long essay for the State Technicum Institute on the subject of her favorite movie actress, the Polish-American silent-film star Pola Negri. In the essay, which was discovered in a St. Petersburg library after Rand's death, she characterized Negri in terms that suited her as well. Whereas "Francesca Bertini is a prizewinning beauty," she wrote, "Pola Negri is unattractive. Gloria Swanson dazzles the eye with . . . the originality of her outfits; Pola Negri has no taste in clothing. Mary Pickford conquers hearts with her childlike tenderness . . . ; Pola Negri is a gloomy, intense, cruel woman." What was the secret of Pola Negri's success? She was "a proud woman-conqueror." After a "difficult, joyless childhood," Rand continued amiably, the actress was "insolent" on screen and in life. Once, when she had been confronted by a Polish border guard who refused to let her pass until she handed over her jewelry, she proved "ready to crush the man who dared to stand in her way." That Negri had immigrated to America and become one of the earliest foreign-born Hollywood studio stars added to her allure; the dark-eyed actress had "been able to conquer Americans' cold distrust of Europeans, their patriotism," wrote the Russian girl who had not yet been to America. In 1925, the essay *Pola Negri* was published in Moscow as one of a series of pamphlets about popular actors. It was Rand's first published work.

She was granted a passport in the fall of 1925. She and her mother sent away for French passenger ships' brochures, and when the pamphlets arrived the whole family gathered to look at them. Alissa might soon be embarking on an odyssey into this fantastically colorful world of shipboard cafés, well-dressed men and women, laughter and gaiety. Passage was booked for late January; Harry Portnoy, Eva Kaplan's widow-ered husband, and his daughter Anna Stone helped to pay the fare. At Anna Rosenbaum's suggestion, her daughter arranged for English lessons from a British expatriate who had remained in the Russian capital after the revolution, perhaps paying the woman out of her small salary as a part-time tour guide at the Peter and Paul Fortress, a former czarist prison.

But there was still one hurdle to be faced. She would have to travel three hundred miles by train from St. Petersburg to the American consulate in Riga, Latvia, to apply for a U.S. student visa. Since U.S. diplomatic personnel all over the world—and especially in Eastern Europe, through which tens of thousands of White Russians were trying to flee to freedom every year—rigorously enforced immigration quotas and guarded against "visitors" who really planned to stay, the visa might well be denied. Many of Rand's acquaintances expected this to happen and looked forward to seeing her back home again before the next snowfall. But Rand never wavered.

Anna is said to have sold the last of the family jewelry, most of which had long ago been bartered for food and firewood, to help fund Rand's journey to "the freest country on earth," as she once called it. The daughter packed her few clothes and her typewriter in a suitcase her grandmother had given her, slipped on her mother's old Persian lamb jacket, and buried the equivalent of the epic sum of three hundred dollars deep inside her purse. On the afternoon of January 17, sixteen days before her twenty-first birthday, she said good-bye to her mother and father, her grandfather Kaplan, sisters, aunts, and cousins at the Moscow Railroad Station in St. Petersburg. She had asked Lev Bekkerman to be there, and for the first and last time he kissed her hand. As the train began to move, she shouted, "By the time I return, I'll be famous!" Her family waved until the train was out of sight. Later, Zinovy told Anna, "Just you wait! [Alissa] will yet show the world who she is."

Rand did show the world who she was, and the world took notice. She never returned to Russia, but in many ways, she never really left.

THREE

FREEDOM TO THINK

1926–1934

❧

When I am questioned about myself, I am tempted to say, paraphrasing Roark: "Don't ask me about my family, my childhood, my friends or my feelings. Ask me about the things I think."

—"To the Readers of *The Fountainhead*," 1945

The old-style Soviet train took Anna and Zinovy's gifted eldest daughter from St. Petersburg to Riga, and a newer, faster train took her from Riga to Berlin. There, on January 30, 1926, she met her cousin Vera Guzarchik, who had also received permission to study abroad and was now a medical student at the Institut Robert Koch in Germany. The two young women were photographed together, looking cold but happy in their flapper hats and secondhand finery, outside Berlin's grand Old National Gallery. They celebrated the new arrival's twenty-first birthday by going to the movies; they saw *Der Wilderer* (*The Poacher*), a romantic idyll starring Carl de Vogt, a German silent-screen Adonis whom Rand adored. From Berlin, she traveled on to Paris and to the port city of Le Havre, from which, on February 10, she sailed for America aboard the French liner S.S. *De Grasse*. She had a first-class cabin, but the passage was cheap, because winter weather made the Atlantic crossing slow and rough. The voyage took ten days.

When the ship carrying the five-foot-two, dark-eyed Russian girl lowered its anchor in New York Harbor on the afternoon of February 19, dusk had set in and a light snow had begun to fall. Rand and the other non-Americans on board were held back by U.S. immigration officials, who boarded the ship, examined their visas, and double-checked their travel plans. By the time she reached the open air, the Statue of Liberty was invisible behind her, wrapped in a bank of snow and fog. Looking up, she could see the lower Manhattan skyline, whose stone towers and copper spires pierced the sky in celebration of the American era's busy faith in commerce. This was the dollar decade, when Americans believed that a talent for achievement and acquisition could and would create a second Garden of Eden on earth, and skyscrapers were the proof and symbol of that faith. For Rand, the brilliantly lighted windows of J. D. Rockefeller's Standard Oil Building, the Singer Tower, and the ornately Gothic Woolworth Building, then the tallest and, Rand thought, the most beautiful skyscraper in the world, represented an astonishing display of American inventiveness, energy, economic aspiration, and engineering talent. They were "the will of man made visible" and "the finger of God," she thought. In a rare display of emotion, she began to cry at the sight of them. Her tears were "tears of splendor," she recalled in middle age.

The documents she carried conveyed the important facts about her at the time: she was Alice, a.k.a. Alissa, Rosenbaum, a twenty-one-year-old unmarried Russian female of the Hebrew race. Her immediate destination was Chicago. The ship's manifest noted that she had promised to return to St. Petersburg, now Leningrad, when her temporary American visa expired. But she had no intention of returning. In order to qualify for the visa in Riga, she had told a U.S. consular official that she was engaged to marry a Russian man with whom she was in love and to whom she would unfailingly return. The truth was that from the moment her mother's cousins agreed to sponsor her, she had decided to resettle in the United States. She was conscious of the new, draconian U.S immigration quotas enacted in 1924, largely to impede the wave of Eastern European Jews trying to enter; if she couldn't get visa extensions, she had decided to cross the border to Canada or Mexico and wait to re-enter the United States under the Russian permanent-resident quota, which could take many years.

It's worth noting that in the 1960s she would become famous for celebrating honesty and integrity as indispensable virtues of her capitalist heroes. "One must never attempt to fake reality in any manner," she would write in her famous description of the ethical man. That she could sometimes invent, exaggerate, or hide events in her own life in order to advance her hopes or bolster her public image may be partly due to her experience in Russia, especially as a Jew; for generations, small deceptions were a matter of safety or survival for Russian Jews. She made this point explicit when, in middle age, she told friends that an obligation to be truthful ends where the immoral behavior of others makes truth telling damaging to one's own interests. Surely, she viewed Russia's closed borders as unjust and immoral, but in later life she would give herself other reasons for moral leniency as well.

She stayed in New York for four days, the guest of relatives of Mandel Stone, who was the husband of Anna Stone, one of Aunt Eva and Harry Portnoy's five daughters. These relatives, the Rosens, lived in a new, stately enclave on Sutton Place, near the East River, and so Rand began her American sojourn in style. She later told friends that by then she had only fifty dollars of her travel money left. She must have roamed the bustling city by streetcar and on foot. She would not have easily been able to ask directions, for her spoken English consisted of about a dozen words, "all mispronounced," she said.

In 1926, New York, like much of the nation, was reveling in unparalleled prosperity. The miracles of capitalism were visible everywhere: in the Model T cars on the street, the streamlined diesel-electric locomotives roaring into and out of Grand Central Terminal, the automatic traffic lights, animated neon signs, radios, telephones, loudspeakers, electric refrigerators, tickertapes, and pop-up toasters. By day, airplanes buzzed overhead. By night, men and women in formal clothes walked arm in arm to restaurants, Prohibition-era speakeasies, arcades, and Broadway theaters. "I'll never forget it," Rand said of her first experience of New York. "It seemed so incredibly cheerful and frivolous, so non-Soviet!" Photographs from this period show her in a 1920s Louise Brooks haircut, a style she would keep until she died. Similarly, her enthusiasm for this free-wheeling, wildly optimistic, largely unregulated pro-capitalist time and place remained a lifelong touchstone of her expectations and her art.

As in Riga and Berlin, she went to the movies, which then cost thirty-five or fifty cents. In four days in New York, she saw four silent films, including *The Girl Who Wouldn't Work*, a courtroom melodrama of the same general type that would bring her early fame as a playwright in 1934. She kept a journal, ranking each movie from zero to five, according to her assessment of its plot, theme, actors, and level of romantic action. Even here, she remained intensely focused on pursuing her long-term professional goals.

By the time she boarded a New York Central train to Chicago, Alice Rosenbaum had chosen a new name: Ayn (pronounced "ein" or "eye-in") Rand. Because she was determined to move on to Hollywood as soon as she could improve her English, she knew she would need a professional name. A pseudonym would also provide camouflage, if needed, against American immigration officials who, should her visa expire, might try to track her down.

The name she picked has stirred the curiosity of readers and fueled speculation among fans for half a century. Not particularly American, or Russian, or Jewish, its clipped, mannish syllables are ethnically hard to place and gender neutral; many of her more casual readers have assumed that she was male. When asked in the 1930s and 1940s about her pseudonym, she offered different explanations, sometimes saying that "Ayn" was a Finnish female name or that she borrowed it from a Finnish writer, and at least once claiming that she made it up herself. As to "Rand," her second cousin Fern Brown, who was eight years old when the older girl came to live with her family in Chicago, remembered Rand's lighting on it one afternoon while the two of them sat at the family dining table, gazing at the Remington Rand typewriter Rand had brought with her from St. Petersburg. Rand repeated this story, but it can't be true; for one thing, the Remington Rand was not yet on the market in 1926. For another, her family seems to have been aware of her new surname before she wrote to them from America. Ten years later, in 1936, she told the *New York Evening Post* that "Rand" was an abbreviation of her Russian surname, and in 1961 said something similar to *The Saturday Evening Post*. By the late 1990s, a number of followers believed that they had spotted the word "Rand" in a slightly altered version of the first six letters of the Cyrillic spelling of "Rosenbaum" (*Розенбаум*) and the word "Ayn" in the last three letters of the name. However, the visual evidence is flimsy, and Rand never claimed to have adapted "Ayn" from "Rosenbaum."

The origin of "Ayn" may be more sentimental—and more ethnic—than the creator of a philosophy based on the self-made soul would be

likely to admit. In the 1960s, a habitué of lectures on Randian Objectivism remembered asking her whether her father, like the woman's
own, had ever called his daughter by the pet name "Ayin." Rand smiled
and nodded yes, this admirer recalled. The woman explained that her
own father had used "Ayin" as an affectionate Jewish diminutive meaning "bright eyes," derived from the Hebrew word for "eye." Adding substance to this theory is a letter from Anna Rosenbaum to Rand in the
early 1930s, making fond reference to her eldest daughter's childhood
nickname "Ayinotchka"—a perfect Russian-inflected endearment for a
little girl with bright, bold, hypnotizing eyes. If, in facing a new world,
she adopted a childhood nickname that was a token of her father's love,
the choice is poignant. The derivation of the surname "Rand" remains a
mystery.

In any case, with only two or three exceptions, she did not reveal her
birth name to American acquaintances. Some friends and relatives ascribed this oddity to a concern about the barriers then confronting Jews
in the United States, who were banned from certain neighborhoods,
professions, social organizations, and clubs. Mimi Sutton, Rand's niece
by marriage, who came to know and love her in the 1930s and remained
her friend until she died, recalled, "She didn't want anyone to know that
she was Jewish at first. No, she *did not*. There was a whole period, up
until the [Second World] war, when she did *not* want that known."
Mimi, whose maiden name was Papurt, recalled Rand's warning her not
to reveal that her father's clan had originated in the city of Berdychiv in
the Ukraine. "That's terrible, Mimi! That's a Jewish ghetto!" the émigré
told her. "She would introduce me as [her husband's] niece," said Mimi.
"She didn't use my last name." Another relative who knew Rand less
well, a great-granddaughter of Anna Rosenbaum's cousin Anna Stone,
explained that, in general, the extended family "was very secretive. They
all changed their names." The most important reason for Rand to have
changed her name, this woman's great-grandmother and other family
members told her, was that "since she wanted to be a philosopher and
have a best-selling book, she could not be a Jewish woman. People
didn't listen to Jewish women." Although the novelist later said that her
primary purpose had been to protect the Rosenbaums from any association with her public persona, for other reasons, discussed later, this
explanation seems unlikely. Whatever the rationale, her reluctance to

disclose these basic facts about her family of origin was so extreme that not a single one of her close friends or followers knew her real name when she died.

As Ayn Rand's train moved west through Pennsylvania, Ohio, and Indiana, she sat gazing at the wintry fields, dozing or practicing her English, perhaps by reading an American translation of *Thus Spoke Zarathustra,* the first book she purchased in America. When the train pulled into the LaSalle Street Station in Chicago, her mother's hospitable and hardworking cousins were on hand to welcome her. Practiced as they were at sponsoring sometimes disorientated Russian-Jewish "greenhorns," as the family called new immigrants, the Portnoy women buzzed with ideas about what their cousin's daughter might like to see and do. But they had never sponsored anyone quite as independent as Ayn Rand. She had her own agenda. She even persuaded them to let her see *Ben Hur,* a silent film about a captive charioteer who outwits his Roman captors, on her first day in Chicago. She liked it; she gave it a rating of four out of five in her journal.

She had been invited to stay with Anna and Mandel Stone, who were in the dress business. But after some difficulty about the family schedule, she moved in with Fern Brown's parents, Minna and Sam Goldberg, who owned a small grocery store on Chicago's North Side, near Lincoln Park, and lived in a neighboring five-room, ground-floor apartment. The parents slept in the front bedroom with their five-year-old son, Harvey. Harry Portnoy, the widowed husband of Anna Rosenbaum's aunt Eva and the family patriarch, occupied a back alcove. Fern moved to the living-room couch, and Rand slept on Fern's cot in the dining room. From the first, she focused on her near-term goal, which she half-jokingly referred to as "conquering Hollywood." She stayed awake and worked at night, as she would periodically do for the rest of her life. She wrote or typed drafts of her screenplays, or movie scenarios—silent-film story lines that were relatively easy for her to compose because they didn't require dialogue—at the dining-room table. She wrote these in Russian, and a Stone or a Lipton cousin translated them into English. In the middle of the night, she took breaks for long baths, young Harvey Portnoy recalled years later; but first she let the hot water run as long as possible, to kill any germs. Baths were a forgotten luxury in the Russia she had left behind, but cholera and typhoid fever, which thrive in filth, were all too common. The Goldberg family slept fitfully and woke bleary eyed. In the daytime, their guest walked around the apartment singing "I'm Sitting on Top of the World" at the top of her voice, in a Russian-accented contralto that substituted "z's" for American "th's." When Minna Goldberg couldn't take the noise, she appealed to her sister Anna Stone to resume her share of hospitality, and the newcomer began shuttling between the Goldbergs' and Stones' apartments.

Oddly, Fern Brown recalled, Rand didn't take any special interest in family meals or food in general, although in middle age she would recall being constantly hungry after coming to America, where she was able to eat as much as she wanted for the first time in years. She spoke little to the adult members of the family and, most strikingly, rarely mentioned her own family or the political situation in St. Petersburg unless she was asked. Even then, she tended to answer in monosyllables, "as though the subject didn't interest her." This could not have been because she didn't care about the welfare of her parents and sisters. Over the next ten years she would write to them often, sending her sister Natasha American sheet music (including period favorites, such as "Yessir, That's My Baby"), Nora movie memorabilia and clothes, and Anna American proletarian novels to translate for extra income, including Theodore Dreiser's *An American Tragedy.* She would make at least one serious attempt to bring them all to America. But when she did talk, "all she talked about was what *she* was going to be and going to do," said Minna Goldberg—in other words, about her future. From the very beginning, her psychological stance toward her personal past seemed to be: Don't look back. Later, she would say that neither her family of origin nor the country she was born in had any determinative meaning for her, because they were accidental, not chosen by her own free will. She was a "being of self-made soul," a point of pride.

As to Chicago, it wasn't New York or Hollywood, and she viewed it as a stopping-off place en route to the West. ("I felt I was not yet in an American city," she remarked stiffly, years later.) She did not know that to the north and west of the city lay a scattering of iconographic Prairie houses by Frank Lloyd Wright, who would become her chief model for *The Fountainhead*'s protagonist, Howard Roark, or that downtown Chicago was seeded with important buildings by Louis Sullivan, a founding father of the skyscraper and, later, one of her inspirations for Roark's mentor, the architect Henry Cameron. (Like Cameron, Louis Sullivan died in alcoholic poverty and obscurity, just two years before she arrived in Chicago.)

She spent her time in movie theaters, especially in the South Side theater owned by Sarah Lipton, called the New Lyric. She saw 138 movies between late February and August 1926, largely thanks to passes furnished by Sarah. Sitting in red-plush seats, watching her then-favorite film director Cecil B. DeMille's *The Road to Yesterday* and *The Volga Boatman* (ranked five and five plus, respectively, in her journal), Lon Chaney in *The Phantom of the Opera* ("not even zero"), King Vidor's *La Bohème* (only three), and dozens of other now famous classics of the silent screen, she was learning the American vernacular from the films' title and dialogue boxes and absorbing film vocabulary and style.

The tutoring she'd had in English allowed her to read and sometimes even think in her new language. But her speaking and writing skills were undeveloped. She made remarkably swift progress, but she also picked up period words and phrases like "lazy bum" and "bootlegger's joint" and employed them in her first professional writing efforts. In fact, she would always retain an idiosyncratic, sometimes jarring habit of mixing elevated diction with somewhat tin-toned 1920s slang, both at least partly attributable to movies.

She stayed in Chicago for six months. Just before she left, she recorded her impressions of America in a letter, written in Russian, to her unrequited love Lev Bekkerman. "I am so Americanized that I can walk in the streets without raising my head to look at the skyscrapers," she told him. "I sit in a restaurant on very high chairs like in futuristic movie sets and use a straw to sip 'fruit cocktails.' " Americans joke a lot and take almost nothing seriously, she observed gaily, but her own sense of purpose was fixed. "The only thing that remains for me is to rise," she wrote, "which I am doing with my characteristic straight-line decisiveness." She hoped that Lev would find a way out of Russia and come to visit her someday; she promised to meet him at the station "even if you arrive in 1947; even if I am by then the greatest star in Hollywood." It is not known if she received an answer to her letter.

Meanwhile, before she left for California, the Stones and Goldbergs were able to arrange for a six-month extension of her visa, and good-natured Sarah Lipton inveigled a film distributor who did business with her, and also with Cecil B. DeMille, to supply Rand with a letter of introduction to someone in the glamorous DeMille organization. The family put together one hundred dollars ("a lot of money in those days," said Fern Brown) to cover Rand's train fare and initial living expenses in Hollywood. By late August 1926, she was ready to go. Tucking four completed scenarios into the suitcase her grandmother had given her, and carrying her typewriter in its case and a score of other ideas in her mind, she bade her relatives good-bye and began the three-day railway journey west.

One of the scenarios she carried was called *The Skyscraper,* a kind of distant, whimsical forerunner of *The Fountainhead.* Its hero is "a noble crook" who jumps from skyscraper to skyscraper by means of a parachute, enacting some of the familiar antics of her Russian science fiction stories. But here, for the first time, she traded the dashing heroes of her childhood for the figure of a persecuted outsider. Rock-ribbed defiers of law and convention and solitary geniuses would now populate the foreground of many of her stories, from an unpublished 1928 novella called *The Little Street* all the way to *The Fountainhead.* From haughty crooks to Howard Roark, her new protagonists display qualities of ambition, audacity, arrogance, ability, pride, and passionate self-esteem against the "heavy, hopeless stupidity" and mediocrity of most people, whose lives, she wrote in 1928, are "a rotten swamp, a sewer." Her heroes are offspring of Nietzsche's Zarathustra, with his buoyant superiority to the herd of men.

When Rand left Chicago, she left mixed feelings behind her. On one hand, the Portnoy women felt familial pride in their cousin's daughter's brilliant mind, intrepid spirit, and determination to make something of herself. Like Zinovy and Anna, they believed she would be famous, because *she* believed it. Yet their guest had behaved in a manner so manic, incurious, and seemingly inconsiderate that tart stories were still being told about her seventy-five years after her stay. She wrote to them regularly until the middle 1930s and afterward sent copies of her books and tickets to her lectures. Minna and Anna Stone assumed, probably mistakenly, that the success of her first play, *The Night of January 16th,* lifted her sense of self-importance above family ties. According to Minna Goldberg, Fern Brown, and others, she also failed to repay—or even to offer to repay—small amounts of money she borrowed during her first difficult years in Hollywood. Minna recalled Rand's telling her, "I'll never forget you. I'll get you a Rolls-Royce and a mink coat." "I didn't get five cents," said Minna. On return visits—one in 1949 and one or two in the 1960s—she struck them almost as a stranger. By that time, the general impression among her relatives was that she was closer to members of her husband Frank O'Connor's family than to her own. When she died in 1982, her remaining acolytes told newspapers that she had no family in America.

Most important to the Goldbergs, Liptons, and Stones, they thought in retrospect that she did not adequately communicate to them the calamitous circumstances her parents and sisters were confronting in St. Petersburg. "She never talked about her family or the things that were going on in Russia," recalled Minna Goldberg. Said Anna Stone's great-granddaughter, "The [extended] family had enough money. They could have saved [her parents'] lives if they had known. She didn't tell them." She was in her own world, thinking of what she was going to do and be.

There is a famous story about Ayn Rand's first meeting with the great film director Cecil B. DeMille. On her second day in Hollywood, the story goes, she was standing forlornly in the sunbaked parking lot of the DeMille Studios, having just been turned down for a job, in spite of the letter of introduction that she carried in her purse. Suddenly, a long, low, open-topped touring car pulled to a stop beside her, driven by DeMille. He asked her who she was. When she answered that she was a recent Russian immigrant looking for a job, he told her to get in. She did, and the two drove off to the Culver City set of *King of Kings,* DeMille's epic drama of the life and death of Christ. There, over the next few weeks, he instructed her in the fundamentals of filmmaking technique—the proper angle of the camera, the dramatic focus of a set— while employing her as an extra in the teeming Palm Sunday and crucifixion scenes. Within days, she had picked out a toga-clad Roman legionnaire who looked uncannily like Cyrus and whom she made up her mind to marry.

There are several versions of this story. In one, the Russian girl accepted a ride with the great director without knowing who he was, and found out only when, on the road, she worked up the nerve to ask his name. In another, she saw him before he saw her; she recognized him from publicity photographs she had seen in movie magazines in Russia and stared at him in wonder until he pulled up in his car and offered her a ride. People who knew her imagine that the episode may have unfolded in yet another way. "She stalked him," Fern Brown exclaimed, only half in jest, adding, "She never left a thing to chance." "That *would* be like her," said an acquaintance from the 1960s.

In any case, during her first few weeks in Hollywood she met with exceptional good fortune, both through her encounter with DeMille and in other ways. Her Chicago relatives had suggested she stay at the YWCA, and on the day of her arrival she rode a streetcar to the Los Angeles branch. When she explained to the duty clerk that she had come all the way from Russia to be a screenwriter, she later said, he steered her to the much more proper and delightful Hollywood Studio Club— an inexpensive Y-sponsored residence created specifically to shelter aspiring actresses and other young women away from home for the first time. Regularly oversubscribed, the club had recently moved into brand-new quarters on Lodi Place, in the heart of Hollywood. There, residents had use of a well-stocked library, a small rehearsal theater, a gymnasium, and a beautifully planted courtyard for the Tuesday evening tea dances that were a club tradition. Even in its new, larger quarters, however, there was typically a waiting list. Since Mrs. Cecil B. DeMille sat on the board of directors and had led the five-year building drive, it's possible that DeMille helped Rand secure a room a day or two after they met, as he later claimed he did, although why she would want to obscure this fact, if true, isn't apparent. The Studio Club, a palace of safety and ease compared to her family's cramped rooms in St. Petersburg, became a haven. She remained there for two and a half years, paying ten dollars a week for her room, with breakfast and dinner included.

Thus comfortably settled, and employed by DeMille, she wrote to her parents for the first time and told them her new first name. The family was immensely pleased to hear of her progress. Her mother wrote back to say that she had read Rand's letter describing her remarkable meeting with Cecil B. DeMille aloud to gathered relatives and got a standing ovation. She and the younger girls were practicing English at home, in preparation for someday joining Ayn. Nora sent a separate letter, rejoicing in her belief that Rand's new name would one day be "the embodiment of the world's glory and glamour."

In 1926, the Hollywood film studios were still housed in ramshackle buildings scattered among sweetly scented orange groves, but they were expanding quickly. Midwestern homecoming queens, fraternity boys, former dock workers, foreign film stars, and New York writers and stage directors poured into the small city, taking jobs as actors, producers, script writers, and technicians. In this sun-struck frontier boomtown, whose most famous entrepreneurs were also Russian and Polish immigrants, a socially shy, dark, Russian-speaking child of Victorian-era Jewish parents would not have been as strange a sight as elsewhere in the country. Still, she was most certainly foreign, and she must have found the variety of manners confusing and even daunting. During her first day on the set of *King of Kings,* she was hungry but too shy, or proud, to take part in the lavish lunch set out for the cast and crew. Yet she was always willing to stand up for herself and was assertive when it came to reaching her objectives. When she was assigned to work as an extra, a wardrobe clerk tried to dress her in dirty sackcloth to play the part of a beggar woman in a crowd; rather than meekly do as she was told, she complained and was sent to a young wardrobe designer named Adrian Greenberg, known as Adrian, who made her a patrician. Later, Adrian became a commercial dress designer, and she wore his suits and gowns for many years. In the 1940s, he and his wife, the actress Janet Gaynor, became her neighbors, political allies, and friends.

It wasn't long before she informed DeMille that she had brought a stack of movie scenarios with her from Chicago. The director turned her over to the head of his story department, a woman named E. K. Adams. After reading the scripts, Adams told her outright that her story lines were too far-fetched and her characters not human enough. Nothing could have been better suited to incite Rand's anger, then or ever; as the soul mate of Cyrus and the aspiring heir of Victor Hugo, Fyodor Dostoyevsky, and Nietzsche, she was acidly scornful of stories that read "like last year's newspaper," as she put it, and indifferent to characters who resembled the folks next door. On the spot, she decided that the story chief was not only a hardened anti-romantic but had also taken a personal dislike to her. More than thirty years later, she told a friend, "I still hate [that woman] to this day." Reconsidering the sound of this, she corrected herself and said, "No, I don't hate her. I dislike her intensely."

Later, Rand spoke of her early days in Hollywood as "grim." By then, she had come to dislike the movie capital of America and its "barbarians." She remembered feeling as though she were "an intruder with all the world laughing at [her] and rejecting [her] at every step," as she wrote to the head of the Studio Club in 1936. Yet for the most part—given that she was a stranger and penniless in a culture that even then thrived on power and personal connections—she received a courteous, even a warm, reception. For five and a half months, DeMille, who appreciated her drive and was flattered by her admiration, kept her working as an extra, earning $7.50 a day—enough to pay her room and board and put something aside for future expenses. Early on, she was able to borrow from the Studio Club kitty to take shorthand classes at a secretarial school, although she never worked as a stenographer.

Once filming had ended on *King of Kings,* in January 1927, DeMille hired her—presumably over the objections of his story chief—as a junior screenwriter. Her initial assignment was to do background research on movies that the studio had scheduled for production. At the same time, as a test of her writing ability in English, DeMille asked her to try her hand at converting a short story the studio owned into a film scenario. She set to work on a maudlin tale called *His Dog,* apparently her first professional effort in English. As she rewrote it, the story describes the fortunes of an ex-convict whose affection for a wounded dog helps him to recover from a life of crime and win the hand of his childhood sweetheart. The scenario is a roughly rendered but competent set piece, with flashes of originality and just a hint or two that someone may have helped her with her word choice and spelling, and it already demonstrates a gift for tight, elaborate, fast-paced plotting, one of the hallmarks of her later work.

His Dog must have met DeMille's minimum expectations. By May, she was earning twenty-five dollars a week to evaluate the film potential of fictional works by outside writers and to synopsize them for possible screen treatment; if her synopses proved worthy, she was told, they would be turned over to a more experienced writer for development into actual working scripts. In her first few assignments, as in *His Dog,* she had to set aside her dislike of sentimental stories and all-too-human characters to master the craft of typical Hollywood writing. In *The Angel of Broadway,* completed in midsummer 1927, she fine-tuned the character of a cynical cabaret singer who finds her better self through caring for—and praying for—a former criminal turned Salvation Army worker. In *Craig's Wife,* based on a Pulitzer Prize–winning play by George Kelly, she dramatized a series of small, cowardly betrayals by a wife resulting in her innocent husband's arrest for murder; the loving testimony of a treacly young woman saves the day. She was frustrated by the second-handedness of the work and, no doubt, the banality of the stories. Still, in each of these early efforts it is possible to find signs of her peculiar "sense of life," including her fascination with social outsiders and taste for twists of plot that turn on the envy of ordinary people for anything outstanding. The apotheosis of this peculiarly Nietzschean kind of envy would be, of course, *The Fountainhead*'s magnificent villain, Ellsworth M. Toohey.

Rand's fingerprints are especially evident on *The Skyscraper,* written late in 1927 and based on a story by Dudley Murphy, not on her earlier Chicago effort. Here, she transforms the original story's hero, one of a pair of tough construction workers, into an architect named Howard Kane. Kane's dedication to the skyscraper he is building furnishes a jealous colleague with the means to try to ruin him and steal his girlfriend, the world-famous singer Danny Day. Partly through the loyalty of his workmen, Kane foils the plot against him. Like *The Fountainhead, The Skyscraper* ends with a triumphant architect named Howard perched atop his tall building; his head is thrown back in joy. Rand's journal entries on the intended theme of *The Skyscraper* also echo *The Fountainhead.* "Plotline: victory over obstacles," she wrote. "*Achievement is the aim of life,*" she noted, in no-nonsense italics. "Achievement is life," she added, to clarify the point. Sixteen years later, in *The Fountainhead,* her first mature hero, Howard Roark, would so perfectly embody this rigorous code of living that he would become, for millions of readers, the consummate enemy of mediocrity and the anti-Babbitt of his age.

If her screenwriting work took her far from Victor Hugo's medieval Paris and Scott's courts of Ivanhoe, her private world at last achieved real romance when she met and fell in love with an aspiring actor named Frank O'Connor, who was playing a Roman legionnaire in the cast of *King of Kings.* Born Charles Francis O'Connor in Lorain, Ohio, in 1897, the DeMille extra was one of seven children of a hard-drinking Catholic steelworker and a strong, artistically ambitious housewife, who was, in some respects, a double for Rand's mother. Until Mary Agnes O'Connor became ill with breast cancer in 1910 or 1911, Frank had been groomed by her to rise above the laboring class. He was stunningly beautiful, as anyone who ever met him agreed: tall, slender, with a classic profile and great natural elegance. At age fourteen, after his

mother's death, he had dropped out of his Catholic high school and became a lifelong atheist. (He was "even more of an atheist than I am,"
Rand once said.) Although he had little education, spelled phonetically,
and possessed almost no independent curiosity about books or ideas, he
was exceptionally witty, perceptive, well mannered, and kind. By 1926,
he had traveled from coast to coast, seeking a vocation. He had been a
rubber worker in the tire mills at Akron, a film extra for D. W. Griffith in
New York, a furniture deliveryman on Long Island, and a steward on a
freighter that took him through the Panama Canal to Hollywood, where
his two elder brothers had settled and where he felt he had the best
chance to gain a foothold as an actor. He may also have worked as a
dancer, a circumstance that, if true, he and Rand later suppressed.
"Frank had some feminine tendencies," said a friend of the time. "I
think Ayn preferred not to have any of that more noticeable than it had
to be." His role in *King of Kings* was his first part in Hollywood.

There is no doubt that Ayn Rand did stalk Frank O'Connor. She later
told the tale of their meeting and courtship. When she first saw him on
the set, he was dressed in a short tunic, with sandals laced to his knees
and a long scarf tied jauntily around his head. He was Cyrus's twin
brother. "What I couldn't forget [was] the profile," she recalled. Each
day, she looked for him among the Romans and Jerusalemites, and one
day she spotted the lanky twenty-nine-year-old Roman legionnaire
preparing to join a crowd scene. She ambled over to his side, stuck out
her foot, and tripped him. He apologized for stepping on her toes, and
they exchanged names.

Later that day, she waited for him on the weekly payroll line, and
they spoke to each other again. And then he disappeared for nine long
months.

Rand was heartbroken, and obsessed. As with Lev Bekkerman four
years earlier, she daydreamed about him, watched for him everywhere,
wept over him in her room at the Studio Club, and talked guardedly
about him to the young women she lived with there. Although she had
spoken with him only twice, "it was an absolute that this was the man I
wanted," she declared. Some of her housemates offered to help her find
him, but Rand wouldn't disclose his name. Like Cyrus, he was *hers*; like
The Fountainhead's heroine, Dominique Francon, she wasn't about to
taint the purity of her feeling for him—or, perhaps, give someone else

the chance to find him first—by speaking his name aloud. She was terrified that he had gone for good. She was certain she would find him.

She saw him again in the Hollywood branch of the public library, in May 1927. She was visiting a nearby construction site as research for her adaptation of *The Skyscraper* and had an hour to fill before meeting with a building foreman. O'Connor was sitting at a table, reading a book. He saw her, remembered her, greeted her. Later, he confided to her that he had told his brothers all about the "very interesting and funny" Russian girl he had met on the set of *King of Kings,* including the amusing fact that he couldn't understand a word she said. That afternoon in the payroll office had been his final day with DeMille; the crowd scenes in which he figured were finished.

Ayn and Frank walked out of the public library reading room together and began to see each other in the evenings and on weekends. He picked her up at the Studio Club—where eighty-odd young women took note of his good looks—and accompanied her to the movies, on walks, and to inexpensive meals with his brothers, Joe, also an aspiring actor, and Harry, who called himself Nick Carter and found occasional work as a newspaper reporter. Perhaps for the first time in her life, Rand was transparently, completely happy. She had earlier shunned the dances and amateur theatricals at the club—for the most part, she appeared "grim and remote," one of her housemates recalled—but now she joined in, banging pots and pans to produce sound effects, participating in civic-minded field trips, and giving the general, incongruous impression of an excited child on her birthday. At one point, having received an unexpected windfall from a Studio Club donor, she bought black silk lingerie, an extravagance she would later confer on Kira Argounova in *We the Living,* as a gift from Andrei Taganov. O'Connor probably gave her her first kiss; he was her first and, for a long time, only lover. She was an ardent, hungry lover in return.

By early 1928, however, her professional momentum was slowing. Of the half-dozen scenarios she had written for DeMille in 1927, none had been used as the basis for a final working script, and by spring, the studio had stopped providing her with full-time work. At the same time, the introduction of talking pictures was causing frantic realignments in the industry. Partly in response, DeMille closed his studio in August 1928 and joined the better-financed, technically more proficient Metro-

Goldwyn-Mayer. He didn't take Rand with him, and she was left without a job. Although in years to come she would again earn a comfortable living as a screenwriter—and be well known, even notorious, among her peers in 1940s Hollywood—she was never entirely successful at writing for the movies. Persuasive screen characters were not her strong suit, and Hollywood did not know what to do with the increasingly iconoclastic themes and highly stylized characters that were.

From mid-1928 until the summer of 1929—the last summer of the nation's long, carefree era of prosperity before the Great Depression—the girl with the sign of a crown on her forehead worked as a waitress, a department-store clerk, and a door-to-door saleswoman. It was an embarrassing and probably a frightening time for her. At age twenty-two, she was without dependable employment in what was still to her a foreign country. She had half-jokingly boasted to family and friends that she would be famous within a year of reaching Hollywood, but for the moment she stood outside the golden circle of that city's opportunities. She had to borrow small sums from her Chicago relatives, and, according to unpublished letters from her parents, depended for a time on a twenty-five-dollar monthly subsidy from them, in order to pay her Studio Club rent. Worst of all, her legal standing in the United States was in jeopardy. While she had been working for DeMille, the director presumably sponsored visa extensions for her with the immigration service, as was the custom in the movie industry. Without a permanent job or a powerful sponsor, she had reason to fear that her time in the United States was running out. At one point, things looked so bleak that Anna actually urged her to come back to Russia, or at least to return to her relatives in Chicago. Rand, of course, refused.

Pride was not a defect of character in Ayn Rand's universe. She concealed her menial jobs from industry acquaintances by working in the suburbs, and she disguised her dire financial condition from O'Connor, who was making ends meet by working in a restaurant alongside Nick and Joe. She wanted her suitor to see her at her best—that is, to see the woman in Ayn Rand. She already believed, as she would later write, that romance should never be mixed with suffering or pity. Echoing her mother's Victorian maxims, she also thought that a woman should avoid cooking or cleaning in the presence of her lover and steer clear of becoming her lover's pal. O'Connor had materialized as "an answering voice, an answering hymn, an echo" of her inner world and deepest longings. Surely, her vocation as a writer would also materialize if she could learn to conquer the problem that constrained her. It was her old problem: the world did not yet understand or appreciate Ayn Rand.

She looked to herself for solutions. At night, in the mornings, and on weekends, she practiced her new language in journal entries and in letters to her parents and sisters. When she was discouraged, Anna and Zinovy tried to cheer her up. In one letter, Anna reminded her that, even as a child, she had considered bad things to be unimportant. She was a true child of her father, Anna remarked, because both he and she "put so much weight on success and so little on failure." Zinovy wrote to say that everyone in the family "worshiped" her drive, purposefulness, and unfaltering march toward her goal, which was to write novels that would be important to the world. In an echo of a phrase Rand later used when offering high praise, he called her "my kind of person."

Some of the stories she was writing were practice drills, imitating what she was reading: Sinclair Lewis's *Main Street, Babbitt,* and *Elmer Gantry,* detective stories ("for the plots"), and short stories by her new favorite writer, O. Henry. (She even signed two unpublished stories from that period "O. O. Lyons.") She was also absorbing the civil-libertarian iconoclasm of H. L. Mencken, Albert J. Nock, Gouverneur Morris, and, perhaps, *Saturday Evening Post* columnist and novelist Garet Garrett. She read and reread a charming turn-of-the-century novel of engineering prowess and conventional anti-unionism called *Calumet "K,"* which DeMille gave her as a present and which became her lifelong favorite novel. She was careful to make note of books she didn't like: Ernest Hemingway's *A Farewell to Arms* ("mushy, morbid") and Thomas Mann's *The Magic Mountain* ("pointless conversations about the meaning of life"). There was no use in looking for heroes there.

The topics and narrative strategies she chose in these early stories cast long shadows; she would visit them again and again. In "The Husband I Bought" (circa 1926), she dramatized something she would later call "man worship," which involves a woman's placing a heroic male lover above everything else in her life. Sometimes, man worship results in a female character's having to renounce the man she loves in service of an ideal version of her love. In "The Husband I Bought," for example, a wife leaves a "beautiful, too beautiful" husband so that he may guiltlessly marry another woman with whom he has fallen in love; the wife, now a pariah in her town, prefers to deify the "maddest, wildest" joy of

her husband's early love for her than save her reputation and her hum-
drum marriage. Interestingly, the story attempts to turn the tables on the
old fictional formula of a wife's self-sacrifice; this wife, far from giving
up her own happiness in favor of her husband's, claims to be preserving
what she values most: her memories, her fantasies, her inner world.
Written before Rand found O'Connor again, it reads like an exercise in
grieving for Lev Bekkerman.

Other stories reveal surprisingly critical views of American life and
character. Rand seemed to be encountering the same essential envy,
conformity, and mediocrity in Americans that she had seen and loathed
in Russians. In unfinished notes for a stunningly harsh and antisocial
novella called *The Little Street* (1928), based on the actual trial of a notorious killer named William Hickman, she took a page from Sherwood
Anderson and Sinclair Lewis and presented a cast of small-town jurors
and spectators who were fat, stupid, and placid: "human herds . . . who
have but one aim: to ruin all individuals and individuality."

In spite of the novella's hateful tone, it formulates her great theme:
the exceptional individual against the mob of men. Of the protagonist
in her story, a murderer, she wrote, "He doesn't understand, because
thankfully *he has no organ for understanding,* the necessity, meaning, or
importance of other people. Other people do not exist for him and he
does not understand why they should." (This, by the way, is practically a
diagnostic description of narcissism, and also a description of Rand herself.) As to the actual Hickman, whose highly publicized crime had
been to strangle and dismember an eight-year-old Los Angeles girl, she
spends pages describing his admirable qualities, including his "disdain-
ful countenance," "his immense, explicit egoism," and the fact that he
is, in her estimation, a "brilliant, unusual, exceptional boy," although she
does not condone his gruesome crime. In a message to herself in her
notes, she observed, "A strong man can eventually trample society
under his feet. That boy [Hickman] was not strong enough."

At the time she drafted *The Little Street,* she had been out of Russia
for just two years—too little time to form a reasonable critique of the average American citizen. Her loathing for the mob was partly literary,
based on Dostoyevsky and Nietzsche, and partly a memory she carried
with her: of rioters and lynch mobs during the revolution and, perhaps,
of generations of anti-Semitic peasants and priests who had led pogroms
against undefended Russian Jews. "All the crimes in history have always

been perpetrated by the mob," she wrote to a friend in 1936. As a Russian Jew, she would have had to be wary of a single-minded crowd or even a political majority. That her remedy was not to understand "the necessity, meaning, or importance of other people" suggests a powerful defensiveness. "Psychologically, she never acknowledged that she experienced fear or self-doubt," said a former friend, the psychiatrist Allan Blumenthal. "She hated being afraid." Not Hickman, not even *The Fountainhead*'s Roark, but she herself would become strong enough to trample—intellectually, in any argument—the mob that might have wished to trample her.

In any case, the novella, intended to revolve around a trial, is so unrelenting in its fury that it produces a slightly comical effect; it is as if H. L. Mencken were guiding Nietzsche along *Main Street.* Yet it also discloses how deeply alienated and undervalued Rand must have felt in the late 1920s—and how desperate she was to gain the recognition she wanted. At the end of her notes on *The Little Street,* she added a personal resolution: "From now on, [you will permit] no thought about yourself, only your work. You don't exist. You are only a writing engine." The "secret of life," she added, is that "you must be nothing but will. [You must] know what you want and do it. . . . All will and all control. Send everything else to hell."

Ayn Rand and Frank O'Connor were married in the Los Angeles City Hall of Justice on April 15, 1929, either just before or just after Alice Rosenbaum's visa officially expired. Two weeks later, she and her husband took a borrowed car to Mexicali, Mexico, and re-entered the United States at Calexico, California. She recrossed the border with a new name, Mrs. Charles Francis O'Connor, and a new legal status as the wife of an American citizen. As such, she was entitled to a rapid evaluation to become a permanent resident, and, eventually, a citizen. By June, having proved that she wasn't wanted for crimes in Soviet Russia, she received a permanent visa, the equivalent of a green card. With only one exception, she never left the United States again.

Her wedding was "a shotgun wedding, with Uncle Sam holding the gun," she later said, humorously. For weeks beforehand, O'Connor and his brother Nick Carter had joked about which of them would marry her and rescue her from deportation. But there was no real question about who would be her husband. Months earlier she had moved out of the Studio Club and into a furnished room, so that she and O'Connor could become lovers; given the conventions of the time and O'Connor's natural gallantry and early Catholic training, he would have felt obliged to marry her even if her immigration status hadn't made the issue urgent. As for Nick, his and O'Connor's niece Mimi Sutton, née Papurt, would later say, "He loved Ayn better than [he loved] any woman. Ayn and Frank could not have happened nor have lasted without him. He wrote the script, directed it, and chose the cast. He fed them their lines and told them how they were to view each other. What he did lasted forever."

The newlyweds settled into a small apartment at 823 North Gower Street in Hollywood, not far from the famous intersection of Hollywood and Vine. From the beginning of their marriage, she was jealous of Frank's attention. "Ayn didn't allow too much closeness between Frank and anyone else, even Nick. Frank was all hers," recalled Hollywood friend Millicent Patton. "Just after the wedding, Ayn said, 'I married Frank because he is so beautiful.' Frank went along with her. He respected her."

With no more possibility of hiding their financial difficulties from each other, they took odd jobs and worked together to make ends meet. Then, in July 1929, Ivan Lebedeff, a White Russian actor—at one time, an officer in the czar's army—who had played in the production version of *The Angel of Broadway,* helped Rand to get a full-time clerical job in the women's wardrobe department of the newly formed RKO Radio Pictures, where she worked for the next three years and eventually became the department boss. She started at a salary of twenty dollars a week and earned rapid raises to forty-five. Now or a little later, she began to send money to her parents, apparently telegraphing or mailing it to a semiprivate St. Petersburg store, where Anna and Zinovy used it to buy food and other necessities. This was dangerous, as the Soviet government was desperate for foreign currency and habitually arrested and extorted anyone who had access to money from abroad.

In October 1929, the stock-market crash shook the nation out of its high spirits and into what would become the longest economic depression in U.S. history. Rand's permanent job was not only a stabilizing force in her marriage but also a precious commodity at a time when hundreds of thousands of Americans were losing their jobs. "I loathed [that job] and hated it," she said in 1961, but "it was a godsend." As a new wife, she also tried to keep house—"to cook, and wash dishes, and such"—at night, but she soon gave up and let Frank organize the household. He decorated their new apartment—the first sign she had seen of his ability as an artist, she said. She devoted what little spare time she had to writing. "I came to America to write, and I [have] not forgotten that. That's something I'll never give up," she wrote to her mother's cousin Sarah Lipton. With worries about her immigration status and money largely behind her, she began to compose another original movie scenario, a theatrical play, and a novel, each of which would help to put her on the map—at last.

The film scenario, called *Red Pawn,* gathered many of Rand's current themes, preoccupations, and literary strategies and set them down on a remote prison island off the Siberian coast in the early 1920s. The story begins with the arrival by boat of a slender, beautiful, haughty American woman called Joan, who is secretly the wife of the prison's most defiant inmate, a Russian engineer arrested for displaying too much "ability" while managing a Soviet factory. Joan, hoping to free her husband, has come in response to an advertisement placed by the stern Bolshevik prison warden, Commandant Kareyev, who is seeking a mistress to relieve his loneliness and boredom. Joan immerses herself in the job of seducing Commandant Kareyev and dazzling him with her Western clothes and values; he, in turn, falls passionately in love with her and with the brand-new idea she gives him that every person, including himself, has "a right to the joy of living." When he discovers Joan's identity as the inmate's wife, the author stages a psychological coup de grâce in which neither the proud Communist nor the imprisoned rebel husband can be sure of whom Joan loves—until she betrays one of them in the story's final moments.

There are a few notable things about *Red Pawn.* The prison, built on the site of a former monastery, provides Rand with her first opportunity to compare mystical Russian Orthodox Christianity with muscle-bound Communism and point out the similarities. One of these, an implicitly repugnant assumption that people have a duty to sacrifice their own interests and ambitions to those of others—others often inferior to themselves—forms the story's core idea: that no religion or ideology may legitimately deprive a man of his absolute right to exist for his own sake, to have "what I want." Also, in a letter explaining the finished scenario to a producer, she summarized her new method of "building a story in tiers," starting with a plot that's gripping enough to carry both the characters and a deeper philosophic meaning; in this way, she explained, an audience can choose to ignore the philosophic content and still enjoy the story. (That audiences and critics would actually *do* this—ignore her ideas—would become a sore point, but she apparently hadn't yet thought of that.)

Most strikingly, *Red Pawn*'s characters form exactly the kind of romantic triad that Rand was now elaborating at length in her novel *We the Living,* which she had begun to outline soon after her marriage in 1929. In fact, *Red Pawn* is the first example of Rand's famously overheated, sometimes roughed-up sexual triangles, in which a man-worshipping woman juggles two or more male lovers, typically in service of a high ideal. Once she and O'Connor were married, such triangles were never far from her mind, her work, or her life.

With the help of a well-connected neighbor in her North Gower Street apartment building—a young woman named Marcella Bannert, who would later provide a model for the character of Peter Keating in *The Fountainhead*—Rand sent *Red Pawn* to an agent who worked for the powerful Myron Selznick agency. The agent, coincidentally named Nick Carter, submitted the scenario to the story department at RKO, to Universal Pictures, to Marlene Dietrich, and to Paramount Pictures, which had Dietrich under contract. According to the author, the sultry thirty-one-year-old German star liked the screenplay, but her director and handler, Josef von Sternberg, turned it down. At the same time, Rand dispatched a carbon copy to Gouverneur Morris, a well-known politically conservative short story and screenplay writer who was on staff at Universal. He later said, "In all my life, [*Red Pawn*] was the first script sent me by an unknown youngster which showed positive genius." Morris became her advocate at Universal. In September 1932, the studio paid her seven hundred dollars for the story and hired her for a fee of eight hundred dollars more to turn the scenario into a working screenplay for the studio's new Austrian star, Tala Birell. Rand was "burning with ambition, just burning," said Marcella Bannert. "From that point on, you couldn't stop her."

All the studios "were interested in Russian stories," Rand wrote to Sarah Lipton that November, "but have had trouble finding any, so that helped me." The subject also helped her to attract press attention. In one newspaper interview about *Red Pawn,* headlined "Russian Girl Jeers at Depression Complaint," she belittlingly compared the hardships of the American Depression with the unending drudgery of life in Communist Russia. "The high-priced executive in Russia does not have the physical comforts of the laborer in America," she sniffed. The lump-sum payment and the script-writing contract established her as a writer. When she finished the screenplay, Universal hired her to rewrite an unrelated project. *Red Pawn* was never produced, as it turned out, but its sale helped her to make a small name for herself and let her escape the RKO wardrobe department and write full-time. She and O'Connor moved into the stately new Trianon Apartments, designed by Leland Bryant.

O'Connor, too, was doing relatively well. He had resumed work as an actor, at first sporadically and then with greater regularity. He was landing small parts in early talking pictures: *Shadow of the Law* (1930), *Cimarron* (1931), *Ladies' Man* (1931), *Arrowsmith* (1931), *Three on a Match* (1932), and *Handle with Care* (1932). He was earning enough to buy his young wife her first portable American typewriter, a radio, and a beautiful second-hand walnut desk. He presented her with a brand-new copy of *Webster's Daily Use Dictionary*, inscribed with a love poem he wrote, based on the letters of the alphabet: "Ayn; adorable; angel; / Beloved; / Cupid; / Darling; / Everything; / Friend," until he got to "Zenith." Together, they purchased their first car: a used Nash, bought on time, which Rand would never learn to drive. He decorated their new apartment, giving his wife another glimpse of his artistic talent. They were happy.

While working on *We the Living*, "a real big novel . . . about Russia," she also drafted her first stage play, a stylized murder mystery that was eventually known as *The Night of January 16th*. (Rand originally called it *Penthouse Legend* but changed the title, first to *Woman on Trial* and then to *The Night of January 16th*.) Many years later, she referred to it as a "sense-of-life" play, by which she meant that the events were less important than the characters' attitudes toward them, and hence toward life. This may have been her way of deflecting attention from her protagonists, who once again were criminals and, because the play was later published, eventually became an embarrassment to her.

The Night of January 16th is an engaging, if stilted, courtroom melodrama, inspired by the public uproar over the 1932 suicide of Swedish Match King and con man Ivar Kreuger and largely modeled on a popular 1927 play called *The Trial of Mary Dugan*. In Rand's play, a secretary is on trial for the murder of her ruthless boss and lover, a bankrupt Swedish financier named Bjorn Faulkner, who at first appears to have committed suicide. Evidence presented at the trial points in two other, mutually contradictory, directions: Either the secretary, Karen Andre, hurled Faulkner off a penthouse balcony in a fit of jealous rage over his recent marriage, as one eyewitness suggests, or else Miss Andre and Faulkner conspired to stage his suicide in order to give themselves a fresh start with his father-in-law's money—a ruse that would have succeeded had the father-in-law not discovered the plot and killed the financier. The play's chief innovation, which proved popular, was to leave the verdict to a jury chosen each night from the audience. What members of the jury had to decide, Rand said, was whether they were romantics who believed in the passionate devotion of Karen Andre to the domineering, antisocial, but fiercely attractive rascal Faulkner or whether they were predisposed to accept the mewling, self-righteous testimony of the witnesses against Andre, who portrayed her as a jealous viper and the father-in-law as an upstanding citizen. If they chose the latter, she implied, they were judging their own "sense of life" and finding it unheroic.

The Night of January 16th was the culminating expression, to this point, of her growing preoccupation with the envy and ill will she saw around her and with the nobility of Nietzschean outsiders. She later renounced her romantic fascination with criminals, explaining that characters such as Bjorn Faulkner had been her youthful symbol for the man who stood alone against conventional society. But she remained passionately attracted—at least in her imagination and her work, if not in life—to ruthless, defiant, potentially violent figures who could easily dominate not only conformists and milksops but also powerful and brilliant women like herself. It must have surprised her, and perhaps not entirely pleased her, that when the play opened in Hollywood, audience juries overwhelmingly found in favor of Karen Andre.

She wrote *The Night of January 16th* in a few months' time, hoping to make money, as *The Trial of Mary Dugan* had lavishly done for its author, Bayard Veiller, and for a first theatrical effort, it was remarkably successful. The play opened as *Woman on Trial* at the Hollywood Playhouse in October 1934, in a production by sometime actor E. E. Clive and featuring former silent-screen actress Barbara Bedford. Critics and a star-studded first-night audience, including Rand's Polish idol Pola

Negri, Frank Capra, Jesse Lasky, Mary Pickford, Gloria Swanson, Marlene Dietrich, three members of the White Russian aristocratic diaspora, and Rand's friend Ivan Lebedeff, among other film celebrities, praised the plot and were beguiled by the volunteer jury.

Afterward, at a party Lebedeff threw for the young writer and her handsome husband at a stylish Hollywood café called the Russian Eagle, the stars toasted her literary debut. Ever shy, she later told a friend that she had felt uncomfortable at the party. The public attention and critical acclaim didn't wholly please her, either, although years earlier she must have imagined that they would. When reviews appeared the next morning, she was disappointed to find that critics had missed the point of her play; diverted by its resemblance to *Mary Dugan* and focused on what they saw as its principal improvement, the jury "gimmick," they failed to note its theme, Rand's heroic "sense of life." They also overlooked what, to her, was its chief virtue, its underlying force as a drama of ideas— specifically, the Nietzschean idea that the heroic individual must resist ordinary people in order to live as a free man.

In spite of her conscious use of tiers of meaning, Rand found this critical oversight hard to bear. From her teenaged years onward, if not from childhood, she had expected "superlatives or nothing," she later confided to a friend. "I wanted raves that raved about the right things. The reviews [of the play] were not intelligent."

It is baffling to discover that Rand's predominant feelings at the moment of her earliest public triumph were of discontent. She had wanted to leave Russia and become a famous writer in a culture and language she hardly knew. In a mere eight years, she had taken a big first step, while some of her favorite movie stars looked on. Why couldn't she celebrate? For this deeply driven woman, who paid tribute to human achievement and worked ceaselessly to be its avatar, her own triumphs were never quite enough. This was the nature of her drive, and the stakes kept getting higher.

Woman on Trial had a limited though successful run. In October 1934, MGM bought an option on the film rights and paid Rand an unspecified amount to write the screenplay for Loretta Young. MGM wanted the script to be funny in places, and Rand, who could occasionally crack an uproarious joke, wasn't able to write comedy to order. When the work was finished, she wasn't happy with the result; perhaps the studio wasn't, either, because the screenplay was ultimately shelved.

Film rights to *The Night of January 16th* would later be passed, at rising valuations, from MGM to RKO and finally to Paramount. The play would not be filmed until 1941 and would be based on a new treatment commissioned by Paramount and created without Rand's participation or approval.

Meanwhile, she began to contemplate moving to New York as the next logical step in her career. She had come to despise Hollywood's taste for overly sweet stories and its intellectual timidity in pursuit of commercial success. After a few years, she had even lost her high regard for Cecil B. DeMille, who she said was a box-office chaser. Living in the publishing capital of the nation would be advantageous to her as a writer, she wrote to a New York literary agent in the summer of 1934, especially as she was nearing the completion of her Russian novel.

At the time, O'Connor's acting career was slowly gaining momentum. In 1933 and early 1934, he had small parts in six or seven films, including the sequel to *King Kong*. But he wasn't earning much money, and he wasn't getting major roles. Rand began to chafe under the impression that he was being passed up for the romantic leads she thought he had been born to play. She later described as heartbreaking the experience of seeing her handsome husband portraying characters who were clumsy or foolish. That she communicated her distress to O'Connor is likely, since years later she spoke of it openly, in his presence, usually adding soothingly that he was very good in the parts he got. If O'Connor had another view of his work, he didn't publicly express it.

Woman on Trial closed in late November 1934. As she was looking around for what to do next, her prospects for a move to New York brightened considerably. An offer came from a well-known East Coast theatrical producer named A. H. Woods to take her play to Broadway. That he was the man who had successfully produced *The Trial of Mary Dugan* made the offer especially compelling. The contract he offered permitted him to make script changes, and he demanded a new title, *The Night of January 16th*. Somewhat warily, she agreed: here was her ticket to New York, and possibly to fame and fortune.

Later, she often proclaimed that O'Connor was at least as happy to leave Hollywood and the film industry as she was. The poor quality of movies in general and of the roles he was being offered in particular "killed his ambition to work as an actor," she said, and gave him "enormous contempt" for the whole movie business. But it's hard to imagine this mild, adaptable man expressing enormous contempt for anything, and he himself seems never to have openly articulated a negative view of the movies. He was reserved in his opinions and modest in his aspirations. With her magnificent way of marshaling arguments, she no doubt found it easy to persuade him to move. "His downfall was his enormous respect for her," said his niece Mimi many years later, "just as [his father] Dennis respected [his mother] Mary Agnes: a cut above." Besides, his beloved brother Nick Carter was already in New York, working off and on as a reporter.

Preparations for the Broadway production would begin immediately, A. H. Woods told her; she had to depart for New York quickly. Within days, she and O'Connor packed up their belongings, including her new typewriter and walnut desk, piled some of them into their car and had others shipped, and bade their friends good-bye. They were going off to live in "the greatest monument to the potency of man's mind" in human history. It was another dream come true.

Before the dream lost any of its sweetness, she mailed a copy of *The Night of January 16th* to her family in St. Petersburg. Nora, proud and possessive of her older sister's glamour and success, locked up the play and wouldn't let anyone see it. Anna pried it loose and translated it into Russian so that Zinovy and the non-English-speaking members of their extended family could read it. Afterward, her father wrote to her that he was in awe of her achievement. He compared the beauty and economy of her language, even in translation, to that of Shakespeare. Nora sent a sketch of a theater marquee with the name "Ayn Rand" emblazoned in lights. Anna rhapsodized about the radiance, human suffering, and hope that the play projected and commemorated MGM's purchase of the play by writing, "Hollywood with its caprices at last used common sense and is forced to admit that white is white"—a fascinating forward echo of Rand's later philosophical rallying cry that "A is A." But she also conveyed a warning. On the basis of her daughter's previous letters, she foresaw that the young writer would soon be surrounded by jealous competitors and gatekeepers who would resent her intelligence, originality, and drive. It didn't matter whether or not the play was a success in New York, Anna wrote. What mattered was to retain her belief in her talent. Weak people give up easily and lower their heads in defeat, she admonished, but "the strong who grow strong in battle grow ten times as strong." What everyone was proudest of were Rand's optimism, her iron will, and her determined belief in her abilities.

Clearly, Anna had been won over to the side of her daughter the writer—but not without foreseeing struggle or giving a small competitive jab suggestive of troubles to come.

FOUR

WE ARE NOT LIKE OUR BROTHERS

1934–1938

Men have been taught that it is a virtue to agree with others. But the creator is the man who disagrees. . . . Men have been taught that it is a virtue to stand together. But the creator is the man who stands alone.
—*The Fountainhead,* 1943

A yn Rand and Frank O'Connor left Los Angeles in their secondhand Nash on November 24, 1934. The actor drove the drafty old convertible across the southern half of the country, replacing worn brake linings and a dying battery along the way, until on a back road in Virginia the car hit a pothole in the rain, rolled over, and refused to budge.

The car was towed to the nearest town. The travelers, unhurt, followed behind, taking in the landscape of the as-yet-undeveloped rural South. At one point, they glimpsed an antebellum plantation house on a broad lawn, with a convict gang working on the road outside. With an instinct for Gothic drama, Rand committed the sight to memory. It gave her the idea for Dominique Francon's Connecticut country mansion and the nearby granite quarry in *The Fountainhead,* where the heroine first sees the lean, muscular, half-naked Howard Roark perspiring as he breaks rock. She had already begun to make mental notes for what would be her third novel and needed a point of conflict to ignite the love affair between cool, aristocratic Dominique and working-class Roark. The car was wrecked, but the author spent the day in an ecstatic mood, waiting for a bus to carry them north in the rain.

They arrived in New York City during the first days of December. Almost immediately, her new producer, A. H. Woods, put her to work preparing *The Night of January 16th* for its Broadway premiere. Woods was hoping for an early January opening, and while she trimmed lines and polished scenes, he laid out his ambitious production plans, whose intricacy and scale Hollywood could never match, he told her. Rand was naturally elated. The producer was wonderfully easy to work with, she wrote to her former Hollywood agent Mary Inloes, and so far had sought few changes. She also got on well with her new theatrical agent, Sidney Satenstein, who struck her as an able businessman.

Almost as soon as she handed in the hastily revised script, in mid-December, and while she and her husband were still arranging their belongings in a one-room furnished apartment they had rented at 56 East Sixty-sixth Street, Woods informed her that the play would not open in January after all. His funding had fallen through. New funding was needed. Casting and rehearsals would have to wait.

Rand accepted the bad news with unusual equanimity. Still, she needed money. Her cash advance against the play's New York box office royalties had been $250, plus $100 traveling expenses; this was enough to get her to New York and let her live for a few weeks, but not enough to weather a delay, even in the cut-rate fifth year of the Great Depression. Fees from her recent screenwriting projects had apparently been spent, perhaps partly in support of her parents. Yet with her small but growing reputation, she was in a good position to get whatever contract work there was. Her theatrical agent, Satenstein, found her a freelance job as an East Coast reader for RKO, her former Hollywood employer, although she complained in a letter to Mary Inloes that her hours were long and her pay small, on average about ten dollars a week. To help keep her household going until the play opened, she borrowed money from her Hollywood friend Millicent Patton, who had relocated to New York. "She was very direct," said Patton. "She said, 'I'm going to [produce] this play and make some money, and then I'm going to write what I please.'" Patton and her husband made the loan, and Rand repaid it. But she never acknowledged that Patton's help had made a difference to her. "I don't think it entered her mind," Patton said years later. "It was just a matter of what she had to do" to survive and reach her goals.

She and O'Connor had to economize on everything, including the food they heated on a hot plate in their room. She didn't like the hardship, but she was resolute and hopeful. She lived in the greatest city in the world. Her play might eventually attract the kind of sophisticated intellectual attention she craved. And her new East Coast literary agent, a woman named Jean Wick, was circulating the completed manuscript of *We the Living* to some of New York's most prestigious publishing houses.

She had been introduced to Wick by her Hollywood admirer Gouverneur Morris, who, like Ivan Lebedeff and a few others who took the time to read her work and talk to her, was deeply impressed by her personal history, the quality of her mind, and her passionate intellectual commitment to individual achievement. After reading a draft of *We the Living* ("the *Uncle Tom's Cabin* of Soviet Russia," he called it), he sent sections to the famous libertarian newspaperman H. L. Mencken. Mencken, an avid defender of American civil liberties, pronounced the work "excellent" but warned that its anti-Communist message might hurt it with publishers. Whatever the demand for Russian stories such as *Red Pawn*, Mencken's letter implied, receptivity might not extend to open criticism of the Soviet state.

This was Rand's second explicit warning that the Depression was beginning to produce political monsters of a kind she thought she had left behind in Russia. The first warning had come in the form of a casual remark by a White Russian acquaintance in Hollywood, who offhandedly suggested that certain film-industry Communists might try to prevent the studios from buying *Red Pawn*. Rand's response was disbelief and indignation. There couldn't be more than a handful of Communists in the United States, she averred. This was the home of capitalism, where competence, not rhetoric, earned rewards. And didn't the Declaration of Independence proclaim the right to life, liberty, and the pursuit of happiness—the very foundation of individualism? She took Mencken's letter more seriously but remained convinced that the American public had no real understanding of Communism and that even liberal Americans would "scream with horror" if they knew what was happening across the Bering Strait. "No one has ever come out of Soviet Russia to tell it to the world," she declared in a letter to Jean Wick. "This [is] my job."

She had not yet begun to follow American party politics, apart from somewhat naively casting her first vote as a U.S. citizen for Franklin Delano Roosevelt in the election of 1932. Roosevelt had campaigned against Prohibition, which she opposed as an abridgment of individual rights, and had promised to balance the federal budget and support a business revival. (He later changed his approach to almost everything but Prohibition.) In Hollywood, she had been intimate with relatively few people and was largely unaware, she later said, of the degree of "pink" penetration in America or of the growing appeal of Communist battle cries to screenwriters and directors and to some of the nation's bankrupt farmers, miners, and unemployed industrial workers. In New York, the leftward trend was more evident, especially among the cultural elite; she gradually became aware that many literary celebrities, such as Mencken's old friend Theodore Dreiser, Heywood Broun, Edmund Wilson, Langston Hughes, John Dos Passos, and critics Malcolm Cowley, Matthew Josephson, and Granville Hicks, were members of or sympathizers with the Communist Party of the United States. At the literary cocktail parties and events that were covered in the gossip columns, they endorsed Stalinism as a noble experiment and drank toasts to the coming of America's "Red Dawn." Their message was that capitalism had been tested and had failed; the time had come to try Marxism on the Soviet model. It was only after living in New York for a year or two that Rand began to see the extent of the pro-Communist bias on the American intellectual left. A nineteenth-century Russian at heart, she believed that ideas have the power to change history and that intellectual leaders are the engines and agents of change. It was American intellectuals whom she eventually decided she would have to target and fight.

Now, however, she was exhilarated by Mencken's praise of her work. Answering his letter to Gouverneur Morris directly, she hailed him as the world's greatest exponent of the philosophy of individualism, to which she planned to dedicate her life. She vowed to confront the messengers of collectivism wherever she found them. She began a program of extensive reading to educate herself in American history and politics. To some extent, then, she was prepared to meet resistance to the plot and message of her first and most autobiographical novel.

We the Living is the least popular of Rand's four novels—regrettably so, since it is the most lyrical, the most straightforward, and, in some respects, the most persuasive. Legend has it that writing the novel was the fulfillment of a promise she made just before leaving St. Petersburg. At a farewell party given by her parents in late 1925, the story goes, a man she barely knew pleaded with her, if she ever got out, to tell the world that "Russia is a huge cemetery" and that "we are dying here." She vowed that she would tell them. In *We the Living,* she did.

The setting is St. Petersburg, or Petrograd, in 1922 and 1923, years when Rand was a student at the university. The plot is simple. Eighteen-year-old Kira Argounova, returning from the Crimea with her now-impoverished bourgeois family, dreams of becoming an engineer and building American-style skyscrapers and aluminum bridges. Although her parents and sister think she is crazy, she enrolls in the city's free State Technical Institute to learn engineering. One bitter winter night, walking in the city's red-light district, she meets young Leo Kovalensky, the proud but world-weary son of a slain aristocrat, and his severe countenance reminds her of her childhood hero, a Viking. Seeing that he is in search of a prostitute she pretends to be one. This is an apt preamble, for Kira's primary task now becomes to serve as a mirror for Leo's noble qualities and to try to save him from himself. To her parents' dismay, she moves in with him. He is a part-time student of philosophy and history at the University of Petrograd, just as Rand was during the same years. Because of his aristocratic background, he is barred from government office work—that is, from almost all work. He sweeps streets for kopeks to support Kira and himself and then, humiliated and defiant, joins a ring of black marketers and begins to drink heavily. When he shows symptoms of tuberculosis, Kira trudges to government offices, pleading with sullen workers-turned-commissars to send him to a state-run hospital; turned away by all, she devises another plan. She seduces young Andrei Taganov, a Bolshevik civil-war hero and campus GPU leader who has fallen in love with her during their heated ideological arguments at school. Richly paid by the Bolsheviks, he showers her with gifts and rubles, unaware that she is using the money to pay for Leo's treatment at a private sanatorium in the Crimea. When Andrei finally learns the truth, the proud, honest, and until-now idealistic Communist is left to yearn for a love he cannot have.

To this point, the novel resembles the creaky movie scenario *Red Pawn.* But *We the Living* is, in a broad sense, a political novel. Like all of Rand's books, it is about power. In her journals, she wrote that it was written to demonstrate "the rule of brute force and what it does to the best [people]" within a culture. "The individual against the masses— such is the real, the only theme of the book," she noted to Jean Wick. Faithful to her monumental theme, she measures each of her characters against the backdrop of totalitarianism and an absence of personal power. Kira's ex-socialite mother quickly joins a Red teachers' union to achieve better living conditions for her family. Kira's uncle Vasili—once a prosperous merchant, like Rand's father and grandfather—proudly goes on strike and lets his capitalist skills dwindle with his spirit. Kira's cousin Irina Dunaeva, an artist like Rand's sister Nora, endures arrest and Siberian exile for the crime of hiding her anti-Communist boyfriend in her room. Irina's brother, a villainous upstart named Victor, gains political power by turning his sister in. Irina's crime is a clear remembrance of Rand's Russian flame Lev Bekkerman's youthful act of courage. In fact, *We the Living* can be partly seen as her attempt to come to terms with Lev, as well as a meditation on the psychological roots of the Russian Revolution.

In most respects, the beautiful, arrogant, sexually talented Leo Kovalensky is the fictional alter ego of the real-life Lev. In Rand's notes for the novel, she describes him as "too strong to compromise but too weak to withstand pressure, [the kind of man] who cannot bend but only break." When Kira first meets him, she finds him irresistibly "implacable" and spiritually defiant: he has a mouth "like that of an ancient chieftain who could order men to die" and eyes "such as could watch." To the lovesick young woman, his haughty indifference to everything, including her, suggests his potential greatness had he lived in a free society— meaning, of course, all that he cannot become in Bolshevik Russia. Once free of tuberculosis, he sinks deeper into the criminal underworld and succumbs to alcoholism and despair. At the novel's climax, he has become a gigolo, the paid companion of a florid, jewel-encrusted middle-aged Communist whore. For Rand, his character solves the riddle of the real-life Lev Bekkerman's preference for mediocre women over her: both men opt for spiritual self-destruction in the absence of any other kind of personal choice. In writing *We the Living*, Rand discovers that, for her, this is an indefensible and unacceptable solution; upholding values, even in the airtight atmosphere of a dictatorship, is the only way to go on living. When Leo decides to return to the Crimea with his lusty paramour, Kira and Rand both let him go.

We the Living is Rand's only novel to be set in Russia and the only one to portray a collectivist—meaning a Communist or a socialist—character, Andrei, sympathetically. In the future, anyone who barters individual rights for enhancement of "the state," "the public," or "the common good," that is, who uses power to serve some men's interests at the expense of others, will be a villain. It is also her only novel to end in tragedy. Leo gives up on himself. Andrei commits suicide. As to Kira, the girl who cannot be broken, she abandons her proximate dreams and dies of a gunshot wound while trying to crawl across the border to the West. Rand once told a friend that she, too, would have chanced death by walking to the border if the American consular officer at Riga had not let her board a train.

Over the years, *We the Living* has been revised and somewhat attenuated. She finished writing it in 1935. At the height of her fame in the late 1950s, perhaps mindful of her legend, she re-edited it and removed some of its shriller and less republican elements. She toned down her heroine's cool indifference toward the masses. In the original edition, Andrei tells Kira, "I know what you're going to say. You're going to say that you admire our [Bolshevik] ideals, but loathe our methods." On the contrary, Kira responds, "I loathe your ideals. I admire your methods. If one believes one's right, one shouldn't wait to convince millions of fools, one might just as well force them. I don't know, however, whether I'd include blood in my methods." Her argument echoes the Nietzschean view that the lower social orders are often impediments to the advance of society's Supermen, and, if necessary, need to be herded by their betters. By the 1950s, she had reconsidered and tempered this view. Conscious of the controversy over her approach to sex, she also muted the novel's gauzy sadomasochism, excising a love scene in which Kira imagines that Leo is whipping her. Interestingly, at the same time, she subtly altered erotic encounters so that Kira and other female characters never initiate sex, as they often do in the original edition of the novel; by then she had formulated a strict hierarchy of sexual roles for her male and female protagonists. In spite of such revisions, there is no mistaking the strong bond between Kira's active pride and her pleasure in being sexually dominated by her lover. This is man worship at the level of erotic arousal and suggests another, more personal, layer of Rand's interest in power.

Touchingly, the mature writer didn't disguise the many passages that

pay tribute to her mentor, Victor Hugo—especially the long, lush description of the history of St. Petersburg at the beginning of part 2, which
so closely resembles Hugo's miniature essay on Paris in *The Hunchback
of Notre Dame*. Frank O'Connor recalled that, at the time she wrote the
book, the St. Petersburg section was her favorite. That was then, she
gamely answered him. In the intervening years, she had come to be
proudest of the beautifully understated passage in which Andrei destroys
his few reminders of Kira before putting a gun to his head.

In early 1935, as the novel was circulating to publishers, Rand's mood
continued to be optimistic. Here, at last, she seemed to have found
people—Woods, Wick, Mencken, others—who could understand her.
O'Connor appeared to be settling in. Nick Carter, her favorite O'Connor
brother-in-law, was writing for newspapers and lived in a hotel room
within easy visiting distance. Her acquaintance Ivan Lebedeff was in and
out of town, and she was meeting a few prominent political conservatives:
Melville Cane, a distinguished poet, former journalist, friend of Sinclair
Lewis, and copyright attorney who became her guide in literary legal matters, and Cane's partner Pincus Berner and his wife, who would become
important friends and allies in years to come. She met and corresponded
with Ethel Boileau, the wife of a British baronet and the author of *A Gay
Family* and *The Clansmen*, who described her own literary mission as a
defense of individualism. "Is it still possible to stop collectivism," Lady
Boileau asked Rand in a letter, "or is it too late?" Rand responded by artic-
ulating one of her developing core themes: "All achievement and progress
has been accomplished, not just by men of ability and certainly not by
groups of men, but by a struggle between man and mob"; the struggle, she
seemed to suggest, would be won by individuals.

She also met an impressionable twenty-two-year-old aspiring playwright named Albert Mannheimer, a graduate student at the Yale School
of Drama and a junior theater critic for the *New York Enquirer*. Mannheimer, tall, fair, and curly haired, was an earnest Marxist who had interrupted his studies to make a pilgrimage to Moscow with his friend
the future novelist and screenwriter Budd Schulberg and others, including an eventual member of the Hollywood Ten, Ring Lardner, Jr. Mannheimer, an aspiring playwright, happened to be living in Rand's apartment
building, and a mutual theatrical acquaintance introduced them. When,
during their first conversation, he announced that he would convert her to
the Communist ideology, she countered by predicting that it was she who

would convert him, and do it within a year. It didn't take that long. He became her first proselyte and unofficial follower. Mesmerized by her intellectual charisma and the logical precision of her thinking, and probably also flattered by her gestures of friendship, he met her often for coffee and intense debate. He became a vehement advocate of capitalism and would grow closer to her in the 1940s.

Perhaps best of all for Rand, as she awaited word on her play and her novel, was the fact that she was living in New York. She never enjoyed walking, but she saw the sights, and there were many. In the years between her first brief visit and 1935, a construction boom had heightened and beautified the city skyline. On the former site of the Waldorf-Astoria Hotel, on Fifth Avenue and Thirty-fourth Street, the steel-faceted Empire State Building had risen like a jagged needle, replacing the Woolworth Building as the tallest structure in the world. As a symbol of the wonders that human reason could perform, this building thrilled her; once she began to earn money, she would always try to have a view of its spire from her apartment windows. Meanwhile, the Waldorf-Astoria had been reinvented as an Art Deco masterpiece on Park Avenue and Fiftieth Street and had tripled in size; she would one day draw on its grandeur for the fictional Wayne-Falkland Hotel in *Atlas Shrugged*. In spite of the collapse of New York's economy in the Depression, Times Square and the theater district were thriving. Lillian Hellman's first play, *The Children's Hour,* and Clifford Odets's *Awake and Sing!* were two of more than a hundred theatrical productions lighting Broadway. Although Rand and her husband probably couldn't afford to see many plays, she would have known of both. Odets was a founding member of the nation's first theater collective, modeled on the Russian Moscow Art Theatre, and he had recently staged a play by John Howard Lawson, president of the Hollywood Screen Writers Guild and an early Communist organizer in Hollywood, later blacklisted, whom she would come to know. Hellman was her own age, thirty, was Jewish, and had been a script reader for MGM while Rand was adapting *Red Pawn* for Universal. A vocal Communist sympathizer, in 1937 Hellman would travel to Republican Spain and to Moscow on behalf of left-wing causes. Bizarrely, she and Rand would later briefly share the spotlight as star screenwriters for the Paramount-affiliated film producer Hal Wallis. At this point, Rand may have viewed Hellman's phenomenal theatrical success with a little bit of envy.

For her own play was idling. All winter and spring, Woods kept promising that casting and rehearsals would begin any day. Funding finally
came through in midsummer 1935, when the hard-nosed theatrical mogul
Lee Shubert agreed to underwrite the project. That should have been
a cause for celebration. Almost immediately, however, pitched battles
began. Woods, now reporting to Shubert, turned out to be a good deal less
accommodating than he had at first appeared. He and she argued over
everything: his demands that she abridge her "highfalutin" courtroom
speeches (arbitrarily, she maintained); his insertion into the play of extra-
neous props (a gun) and characters (a floozy in furs, reportedly Shubert's
mistress); and his tirades about how ponderous ideas had no place in popular entertainment. In her view, he was rapidly dismantling the story she
had carefully constructed to test theatergoers' "sense of life" by removing
elements of the motivation of her characters through cuts. When she objected to his changes, he would shout, "But this is your first play! I have
forty years of experience in the theater!" Experience meant very little to
her; she wanted logic. In exasperation, she reportedly told him that if an
elevator operator suggested a change and could explain his reasons, she
would happily consider it, but if a literary genius dropped in to propose an
alteration without a valid explanation, she would reject it out of hand.

Given that her greatest gift was, perhaps, as a translator of unfamiliar and counterintuitive ideas into the vernacular of popular melodrama,
she must have found Woods's point of view particularly vexing. Their
most furious quarrels, however, were reserved for his decision to hire
two hack collaborators, named Hayes and Weitzenkorn, to implement
script changes she refused to make—and, incidentally, to siphon off
one-tenth of her royalties, set at 10 percent of box-office receipts. With
the help of her friend and attorney Melville Cane (and the support of
Mrs. Vincent Astor, who was appointed arbiter), she fought the royalty
reduction and won. She also managed to install the incomparable actor
Walter Pidgeon in the role of tough-guy gangster Guts Regan, Karen
Andre's and Bjorn Faulkner's accessory in crime. But though she could
walk away from Woods's harangues, she could not prevent his meddling;
the contract she had signed gave him the right to hire new writers,
change the script, add props, and more. The experience of watching
him dilute her work with commercial pap was "miserably painful," she
said. In the end, she came to hate him, her agent, Satenstein, and the

adulterated play. Years later, when a friend noticed a published copy of it on her coffee table in California and asked to borrow it, Rand snatched it away and cried, "Don't read that! I'm going to destroy it."

Meanwhile, *We the Living* was being read with serious interest by some of New York's best editors, but was also gathering rejection letters. Some turned it down because they couldn't imagine who would buy and read a novel about 1920s Russia. Others were wary or skeptical of the anti-Soviet theme. Jean Wick didn't always pass their comments along to Rand, and when she did, the agent seemed bewildered as to how to answer. Gradually, the author realized that her agent didn't understand the novel, let alone how to sell it. She wrote detailed explanations for Wick to refer to when talking to editors. *We the Living* wasn't merely about postrevolutionary Russia, she pointed out, although it did possess the sales advantage of being, she claimed (apparently accurately), the first novel on the subject written in English by a Russian writer. Nor did the narrative need an infusion of more emotion, Hollywood style, as Wick took to arguing it did. This was not a love story—at least, not one that made sense without reference to its totalitarian setting. It was a novel of crucial topical importance, exposing as both thoughtless and corrupt the liberal-collectivist dream of stripping prerogatives from the wealthy to enhance the welfare of the poor. Such a dream always ended in the destruction of the best—in other words, of those who asked for no help and simply wanted to be left alone, and therefore had the greatest claim to life. This was a theme the American public, now more than ever, needed to hear. Defining collectivism as a system of thought or action in which the individual person is subordinated to the common interests of a group, she told Wick that its worldwide growth was "the greatest problem of our century." Later, in a foreword to the 1959 edition, she wrote, "*We the Living* is not a story about Soviet Russia in 1925. It is a story about Dictatorship, any dictatorship, whether it be Soviet Russia, Nazi Germany, or—which this novel might do its share in helping to prevent—a socialist America."

Wick thought all this sounded much too intellectual, and said so. By this time, Rand had heard the word "intellectual" used pejoratively once too often. By summer, with the help of friends, she found a new literary agent, the highly respected Ann Watkins. Watkins began to circulate the manuscript again.

Then suddenly, after nine months of delays, *The Night of January 16th* was scheduled to open in mid-September. On September 8, Rand, O'Connor, and Nick Carter headed to Philadelphia by train to attend the weeklong tryouts at the Chestnut Street Opera House. These began badly and descended into chaos; with opening night on Broadway scarcely a week away, collaborator Weitzenkorn was summoned to make yet another round of last-minute changes. Rand, furious, exhausted, and fearful for her nascent reputation and her novel, felt as if she were about to go under the knife of a surgeon who hadn't been told which of her vital organs to remove. Walking in the street one day, she burst into frustrated tears. She was without any power to control her written words or her created world, never a tolerable state for Ayn Rand.

A telegram from Watkins saved the situation from utter heartbreak. Macmillan, at one time the publishers of Henry James and H. G. Wells, had made an offer to publish *We the Living.* The company would pay a $250 advance against royalties and bring the book out in April 1936. The author and the O'Connor brothers, spirits suddenly high, celebrated in a Philadelphia hotel room. Selling the novel was the most wonderful thing to happen in her life to date, she wrote to Gouverneur Morris.

The Night of January 16th premiered at the Shubert-owned Ambassador Theatre in New York on the unusually chilly evening of September 16, 1935. The theater was packed and so, said Brooks Atkinson of *The New York Times,* was the jury, with Jack Dempsey, the fighter, serving as foreman and Sidney Satenstein's brother and other insiders filling jurors' seats and meting out justice from the stage. The celebrity jury acquitted Karen Andre, but Atkinson wasn't able to acquit the play of corny devices and "hokum." The *Wall Street Journal* gave it a respectful nod, recommending it to theatergoers as adroit and amusing entertainment, and that view prevailed; the play quickly started earning money at the box office. Once again, though, reviewers overlooked the playwright's underlying theme, the do-or-die contest between the Nietzschean-heroic outsider and the safe, conventional "sense of life" displayed by witnesses for the prosecution. That said, Rand's message must have been hard to find amid Woods's clumsy changes. The embarrassed playwright and her husband sat in the back row of the theater on opening night, adjusting themselves to the disturbing reflection that this was no longer Ayn Rand's work.

Three days later, she signed a contract with Macmillan. *We the Living* was set to run to an immense six hundred printed pages, but the publisher did not ask for cutting or any other alterations, the author happily reported to Gouverneur Morris. She left unsaid what she soon learned: that there had been a heated battle about whether to publish the book at all. As she recounted the story in the early 1960s, a Macmillan editor and poet named Stanley Young had championed the book on literary grounds; Granville Hicks, a well-known critic who read manuscripts for Macmillan, opposed it, taking issue with Rand's dark portrait of Soviet Russia. Hicks had recently joined the U.S. Communist Party and, in that fall of 1935, was completing his own book for Macmillan, an admiring biography of the American Communist John Reed. Twenty-two years later, to Rand's horror, Hicks would also be assigned to review *Atlas Shrugged* for the influential *New York Times Book Review* and would like it less, if possible, than *We the Living*.

Luckily, Hicks lost the argument, and Macmillan published *We the Living* on April 7, 1936. Rand, immensely proud, mailed copies to her Chicago relatives, her Hollywood acquaintances, and a few friends. Cecil B. DeMille received a copy. So did Sarah Lipton, dedicated "with profound gratitude for saving me from the kind of hell described in this book." She inscribed a copy to Ivan Lebedeff, her "Dear Old Man," thanking him for his help and for his faith in her, and to O'Connor's father, Dennis, whom she had not met but addressed as "my American father."

For a first novel, *We the Living* received an impressive amount of attention, especially since novels by Rebecca West, Daphne du Maurier, Sinclair Lewis, and, in translation, Charles Baudelaire appeared in the same week, and the impending release by Macmillan of another first novel, Margaret Mitchell's *Gone with the Wind*, was already creating a whirlwind of anticipation. In late April, Rand told a *New York Times* reporter that she was proud ("as well she might be," the reporter noted) of the fact that her first film script, her first stage play, and her first novel had all found immediate buyers. This is important to note, because later she would brood over and often exaggerate the difficulties she encountered in finding sponsors for her books and plays and the injustices she met with at the hands of prejudiced or malevolent editors and others. Her followers would believe and repeat these tales of hostility and neglect as though they were true talismans of Rand's secret, superior world.

Indeed, the reviews were mixed, as they were bound to be in a culture deeply divided about its capitalist past and future. Yet many reviewers demonstrated remarkable perception. Conservative periodicals, those that looked back longingly to the freewheeling culture of the mid-1920s, found much to admire. The book section of the *New York Herald Tribune* hailed the novel's "wild cry for the right[s] of the individual" and its "subdued fire and intensity." The neutral *Washington Post* remarked on Rand's beautiful writing and provocative love scenes, which "would cause Boccaccio . . . to writhe with jealousy." Rand told one interviewer that she was pleased to have been told that she wrote like a man and to have her work compared with that of Joseph Conrad; she volunteered the additional information that she detested the "inherent sentimentality" that permeated women's writing. The major jibes came from the practitioners of the 1930s radical vogue. The liberal *New York Times* marveled at the Russian émigré's command of English and her narrative power but dismissed her theme as "slavishly warped to the dictates of propaganda"—*whose* propaganda it didn't say. The Marxist-friendly *Nation* mocked the author's infelicities of style to show that she was "out to puncture a bubble—with a bludgeon." Though both the *Times* and the *Nation* might have known that Soviet Communism was not a bubble, especially in 1936, when its henchmen were systematically slaughtering hundreds of thousands of Stalin's perceived political enemies, the *Nation* did have a point: now and in the future, the author's rhetorical pitch and tin ear for American diction caused more than a few influential readers to be deaf to her demands for intellectual respect. Unfortunately, even here the *Nation* wasn't on completely firm footing; as an example, it cited a passage describing Bolsheviks as "crippled, creeping, crawling, broken monstrosities" but failed to mention that the alliterative excess was enclosed in a speech by Andrei Taganov, signaling his change of heart about Bolshevism and marking him for demotion and ultimately death.

Whatever their merits, the reviews ended Ayn Rand's expectations of receiving literary "justice," she later said. *We the Living* sold about two thousand copies, a respectable sale for the time, and appeared on a few regional best-seller lists. But Macmillan didn't support the book with advertising or promotion, which wasn't unusual for the time but which surprised and angered the first-time novelist. Still, even after the publicity storm stirred up by *Gone with the Wind* had carried off most of the book-buying public, readers quietly continued to buy and read *We the Living*.

And she was earning money. In a decade when average American incomes were well under $1,500 a year, *The Night of January 16th* was bringing her royalties of between $200 and $1,200 a week. By the time the play had closed on April 4, 1936, three days before the publication of her novel, theatrical rights had been sold to producers in London, Vienna, Budapest, Berlin, Switzerland, Poland, and elsewhere. A return engagement was already filling seats in the El Capitan Theatre in Los Angeles, and a road show was about to open in Chicago. Somewhat ironically, Watkins had negotiated a contract with Franklin Roosevelt's new federal Works Progress Administration to bring performances of the play to local theaters across the country. Although by 1936 Rand strongly disapproved of Roosevelt and his New Deal programs, the WPA provided her with royalties of ten dollars per performance, a small fortune, throughout the later 1930s. And because the play's single courtroom setting made for easy staging, it also became a favorite of privately run summer-stock companies, generating a sometimes larger, sometimes smaller stream of income until her death. Meanwhile, *We the Living* was experiencing an afterlife: British publisher Cassell & Company planned to distribute a U.K. edition in the fall of 1936, and Rand and Jerome Mayer, a theatrical producer and director, opened discussions about taking the novel to Broadway as a play.

Financially prudent, Rand decided to earn extra money by returning to her old trade, screenwriting, and working as a contract writer based either in New York or Hollywood. Well established as a novelist and playwright, she took it for granted that the film industry would now offer her good-quality writing projects and more money; with this in mind, Watkins got in touch with a Hollywood associate, who contacted executives at the major movie studios. None of them would hire her. Rand was certain that she was being ostracized because of her anti-Soviet stance, both in *We the Living* and in public speeches and print and radio interviews, and the Hollywood associate apparently confirmed her suspicions. "She talks too much about Soviet Russia," the associate told

Watkins. She saw this as retaliation—as, in effect, blacklisting by the Hollywood intellectual Left. Later, she said, "This [blacklisting] lasted until *The Fountainhead*." She began to take the American Communist threat very seriously indeed.

It's hard not to conclude that Ayn Rand sometimes lacked good judgment, or at least good timing.

She called herself shy, and she was shy in social situations, but when speaking before an audience, teaching, or discussing serious ideas, she was animated, inspiring, and charismatic. In the spring and summer of 1936, after the publication of *We the Living*, she was in demand as an anti-Soviet speaker. She lectured at the then-famous New York Town Hall Club on "Whitewashed Russia," where she asked the audience to imagine being ruled by a group of men who have not been elected and cannot be recalled, who control all public information, who distribute all food, housing, and employment. They cannot be criticized; they dispatch political adversaries to dungeons or death without a trial or hearing. They claim that individual rights do not exist. Would her listeners wish to live under the thumb of these "two million snow-white [Stalinist] angels," as she characterized the Left's view of them? She gave dozens of radio and print interviews in which she described her bourgeois Russian background, elaborated on her hatred of the Bolsheviks, and mentioned the approximate date and circumstances of her escape to the United States. In one New York newspaper interview in late spring, titled "Only High 'Ransom' for Passports Opens [Soviet] Border, Says Miss Rand," the interviewer observed that the Russian-born author, whose first remark was, "If the [Soviet] borders were ever opened there would be a migration like that of the early Middle Ages," was also known as Mrs. Frank O'Connor. A picture of the author and her husband seated in their living room appeared above the text of the interview, with a caption explaining that they lived in an apartment on Park Avenue.

At the same time, Rand was making a determined effort to rescue her parents from their life of hardship in Russia. Although the Rosenbaums no longer remained in danger of starving, they, like much of the rest of Soviet Russia, had settled into an underfed, fearful, precarious, and dreary routine that she considered inhuman. She appears to have been deeply in earnest about bringing them to America. Since becoming a citizen herself in March 1931, she had kept up an intermittent correspondence with the U.S. State Department and other agencies, in hopes of obtaining immigration visas for all four members of her family, but she and O'Connor were thwarted by the requirement that they show sufficient income to get an affidavit of support. Now they had the income, from her royalties.

There is a mystery here. Even as she renewed her efforts to get her family out of Russia, she was publicly presenting herself as an anti-Communist activist. That she wasn't aware that Soviet agents might be watching her—and might easily confirm that Alissa Rosenbaum, Mrs. Frank O'Connor, and Ayn Rand were different names for the same woman—is hard to believe. She took normal, recommended precautions, such as using only her legal, married name in government correspondence and not sending her parents a copy of her book. But in the 1930s, there was a Soviet government agency whose specific job it was to read correspondence from abroad, and Russian agents at home and in the United States and Europe were notorious for their ruthlessness and skill in tracking and spying on Russian émigrés. Her Chicago relatives were sure that she was conscious of the risk she took in publishing *We the Living* and in giving interviews. Said Fern Brown's cousin Roger Salamon, "The fact that [her parents] never came out of Russia was due to *We the Living*. My grandmother [Sarah Lipton] and mother [Beatrice Collier, daughter of Sarah Lipton and her second or third husband, Harry Collier] used to talk about it. She had an agenda, and if she wanted to do it, she did it." Perhaps the task of "telling it to the world," though more impersonal, was more compelling. That she later felt uneasy about the danger in which she may have placed her family can be guessed from the fact that, in 1961, she told her friend Barbara Branden that she had never revealed her new name to her family in Russia. "She lied," said Branden. After her death, hundreds of letters from her parents and sisters were discovered among her papers, many mentioning her pseudonym and applauding the soon-to-be-famous "Ayn Rand."

By this time, Nora had fallen in love with an engineer named Fedor Drobyshev and was married and teaching in a Soviet school. Natasha no longer wanted to come to America. But Anna and Zinovy, in ill health and in need of medical care not available in Russia, were willing to make the journey, and she redoubled her efforts to have them join her.

At first she was optimistic, even excited. In June 1936, she wrote to her mother's cousin Sarah Lipton (by now remarried and named Satrin) that she hoped to get word of their date of arrival any day. One of the reasons she may have looked for work in Hollywood was to care for her parents there, where it was warm.

The Rosenbaums' prospects would have been precarious in any case. For the next few months, telegrams flew back and forth between Leningrad and New York. In the end, the official Soviet answer was no. "Cannot get permission," read the Rosenbaums' final telegram in May 1937. Whether the result would have been different had Rand kept out of the public spotlight is debatable, but her timing didn't help. Shortly afterward, the U.S. government warned that communicating in any manner with acquaintances in the Soviet Union could endanger their lives. The letters between Rand and the Rosenbaums ceased, and all was silence.

Rand wasn't interested in luxuries; her focus was on producing and earning, not on spending. But she began to use her royalty income for goals she had long deferred. One of these was to move out of the tiny furnished room she and O'Connor had shared for more than a year. They left Sixty-sixth Street and rented a larger room at 129 East Sixty-first Street and then moved into a sunny seventeenth-floor apartment in a handsome Art Deco residential hotel at Park Avenue and Thirty-eighth Street, where the newspaper photograph was taken. With more space to fill, they bought a set of blond Art Deco bedroom furniture and a sleek modern sofa. She shopped for needed clothes—unfortunately tending toward faddish or frilly outfits—and began to wear the sculptural black cape that became her trademark in the 1940s. That was all; the rest of the money would be saved and applied to future projects.

Her greatest objective was to gain time to work on her new novel. She had been musing about its theme since her late teens and had made her first extensive notes about it in December 1935. It would tell the story of a rough-hewn American architectural genius named Howard Roark and his quest to create a new kind of architecture. At its heart would stand a great American skyscraper, a symbol of America, of human achievement, and of life on earth. In *We the Living*, she had focused on young people and on events she had actually lived through because she knew she wasn't yet ready to create a world; now she was ready. Her first novel had been a practice drill, a preparation for this one. By the summer of 1936, she said, she had earned the right to put her affirmative vision of what it meant to be an individualist—i.e., a champion of the sovereign, self-determining individual—down on paper. She began to construct an outline of characters and events that she thought were intrinsically important. The novel's working title was *Second-Hand Lives,* but it would become famous as *The Fountainhead.*

As she pondered the egoistic, single-minded, hot-blooded character of Howard Roark, whom she was consciously molding into her ideal man, the first notes of marital discord between her and O'Connor sounded. He was far from sexually dominant, or even highly sexed. He had limited ability to discuss ideas with her. By all accounts—and there were many people who knew and loved him—he was sweet, gallant, stoic, funny, emotionally inexpressive, easily led, and profoundly passive. Professionally, he had found little to occupy him in New York and was dependent on Ayn. Although he auditioned for parts in plays, the only roles he is known to have been offered were parts in his wife's productions and related dramas. He took odd jobs but quit them, apparently at her behest; selling shoes, for example, which he did for a few weeks in 1943, didn't fit her romantic image of him. He decorated their apartments inexpensively and, according to visitors, imaginatively and beautifully. As teenagers, he and his brothers had cooked meals and done housework during their mother's illness, so it didn't seem unnatural that he and Nick should now take over many household chores to give her time to write. As she became better known, he joked that he was "Mr. Ayn Rand." But it was not a joke. Without paid employment, his working-class values sometimes troubled him. If the situation had occurred four or five decades later, "there would not have been so much hurt pride," his niece Mimi later said. It's difficult to know whether his financial dependency troubled her, since now and in the future she did not complain. Neither did he. He seemed to lack the drive and focus to begin a new career, and by 1936 she was the sole breadwinner.

For the first time, they began to lose their tempers with each other. A quiet man in the best of times, he withdrew from conversation. She was brimming with new ideas about the psychology of individualism, Americans' sorry slide toward collectivism, and the many political and, now, architectural texts and periodicals she was reading. She craved intellectual companionship. For relief, she turned to Albert Mannheimer, the curly-headed young convert to capitalism, and to Nick, who joined the O'Connors for dinner almost every night. Nick was charming, funny, well read, intelligent, a good critic, and a gifted storyteller, although he seemed as lackadaisical about his writing career as his younger brother was about acting. He and Joe O'Connor had both served in World War I, and he had been wounded in a chlorine gas attack. He collected disability payments for lung disease, later diagnosed as tuberculosis. He often had free time.

Nick became Rand's own first Commandant Kareyev, the man who stands between the heroine and her hero and so preserves their union. "He supervised," said Frank and Nick's niece Mimi, who visited Nick and the O'Connors twice in the middle 1930s and more often after that. "He was Noel Coward." Like Rand's later young male protégés, he talked with her about ideas and her current work in progress late into the night, while O'Connor dozed in a chair, but he differed from them in important ways. He didn't flatter her, and he acted as her practical guide in matters of dress and entertaining. In the 1930s, Rand had a "peasant" face and figure and no clothing style at all, said Millicent Patton. Typically, she wore a housedress all day long, remembered Mimi, and went around wiping her hands on it. ("My father was appalled," said the niece.) But she had rococo tastes when dressing up. Once, Mimi recalled, her aunt by marriage gaily modeled "a small white Dutch hat with a starched peak and a blue netty veil," which couldn't have looked worse. While Frank tactfully hemmed and hawed at the sight of the whimsical headpiece on the logical head, Nick told her to take it off. He steered her—not always successfully—to simpler, more tailored clothing and a conventional entertaining style. This was important, because she was meeting influential people at political events and cocktail parties and beginning to give dinners. Also, in contrast to the younger men who came later, he was never a candidate for seduction. He was a homosexual, although Rand probably did not know it. ("She would have been the last person on earth to realize that Nick was gay," said a 1960s friend, even though by then Rand condemned homosexuality on philosophical grounds.) The good-looking husband, the lively brother-in-law, and the diminutive dark-haired Russian woman with hypnotizing eyes now made a threesome.

For most of the summer of 1936, Ayn, Frank, and Nick, with the occasional addition of Mannheimer, remained in the broiling heat and humidity of New York City. In August, O'Connor left to play Guts Regan in a Connecticut summer-stock production of *The Night of January 16th,* while Rand remained behind. They had never before been parted. In spite of whatever tensions may have existed between them, she missed him terribly; for much of their marriage, she would feel safe only when he was by her side. They exchanged love letters, hers alternating between news—of an overnight houseguest named Marjorie Hiss (the wife of a cousin of Alger Hiss whom Rand had met at the Studio Club), the impish behavior of their housecats, the contract she had finally signed with producer Jerome Mayer—and a startling, incongruous baby talk they reserved for each other. (She called him Cubbyhole; he called her Fluff.)

She had spent the spring and early summer poring over architectural texts as background material for *The Fountainhead,* but now she set aside her books and musings to tackle what soon became a months-long effort to turn *We the Living* into a stage play for Mayer's expected 1937 production. At Ann Watkins's urging, she also rewrote a novella she had completed but not published in Hollywood in 1934 as a play; both agent and author were eager to strike again on Broadway while *The Night of January 16th* was remembered as a hit. Called *Ideal,* the novella-turned-play featured a Greta Garbo–like movie star named Kay Gonda who quotes Nietzsche and, with tragic demeanor, seeks one fan from among her millions who will agree to risk his life for what he claims to be his ideal: her. Finding only a lonely drifter named Johnnie Dawes, a less violent version of the murderer-hero of the unpublished 1928 novella *The Little Street,* Kay Gonda reflects that most of her audience really hates her, because she embodies a commitment to romantic ideals that they are afraid to live by. As she flashes back to the original source of her exalted expectations of life—the sight of a very young man standing on a rock, his slender body like "a string trembling to a note of ecstasy no man had ever heard"—the reader of the play has his first glimpse of Howard Roark. *Ideal* is about fidelity and unfaithfulness to values, a theme that foreshadows the preoccupations of *The Fountainhead.* Watkins couldn't find a producer for it, and although Rand's Russian-American friend Ivan Lebedeff's wife, a gifted German-born actress named Wera Engels, tried with Rand's encouragement to interest European producers in the play, negotiations broke down. While *Ideal* didn't find a home, either as a novella or as a stage play, Gonda's ultimate problem, the conviction that she is morally superior to her audience, is one that both Roark and Rand would soon confront. (As a clue to how much Rand identified with Roark and other male figures in her fiction, in a Freudian slip during this period she referred to Kay Gonda as a "truly heroic man.") When Jerome Mayer, like A. H. Woods before him, ran into funding problems, the stage adaptation of *We the Living* was put on hold.

In July 1937, Rand moved with her husband to Connecticut for his second season in summer stock. They settled in shady Stony Creek, on the Long Island Sound, where, she told friends, she was soon doing her best work. While O'Connor rehearsed the role of Guts Regan and parts in other plays ("It will be very good experience for him," she wrote somewhat condescendingly to a Hollywood friend), she walked on the beach with visitors Albert Mannheimer and Nick Carter and mused on the evolving shape of *The Fountainhead*. She was within two miles of the town's famous pink-granite quarries, which she may have visited as research for the all-important quarry scene in which her heroine, Dominique, meets Howard Roark. But plotting the novel was complicated—"I was going crazy" trying to tie the characters together in a climactic scene, she said—so, as a rest, she composed the short, futuristic novel *Anthem* while propped on a rubber raft in the sand. A mannered but still entrancing story, *Anthem* envisions a primitive world in which the word "I" has been erased from human memory and replaced by the collective "we." Characters repeat things to "ourselves" and intone mottos such as "We are nothing. Mankind is all. We exist through, by, and for the State." After the hero, a subversively inquisitive figure called Equality 7–2521, falls in love with Liberty 5–3000 in an act of individual choice that is punishable by death, he finds himself investigating other secrets, including the key to electricity, a lost art of the "Unmentionable Times," and the use and meaning of "I." Although it is written in an approximation of Nietzschean aphoristic English, with biblical overtones, it neatly exposes the ultimate logic of totalitarianism: perfect conformity for perfect control. Rand's purpose was to demonstrate that brainwashed slaves of the state cannot produce technological achievement—a theme she would revisit—and that only autonomous selves can fall in love. The choice of electricity to stand for individual accomplishment is interesting. In the Bible, God commands, "Let there be light." With Thomas Edison's invention of the electric lightbulb, the power of light was placed in human hands. In a sense, then, electricity made human beings deities, as Professor Bernice Rosenthal has pointed out. In fact, electricity was highly controversial in Russia during Rand's childhood; people "either condemned or exalted it" for the reason that light belonged to God, observed Dr. Rosenthal. To seal the connection between God and the individual self, Rand makes her primitive society dimly aware of an "Unspeakable Word," which in Jewish tradition is "Yahweh" and in *Anthem* is "I."

That Equality 7–2521 happens to be twenty-one years old when he and Liberty take flight and give themselves new names—Prometheus (bringer of firelight) and Gaea (mother of the gods)—is interesting, given that that was the age at which Rand left Russia and adopted a new identity. In fact, she had conceived *Anthem* as a four-act play during her university years. Like Aldous Huxley's *Brave New World* and George Orwell's *1984* (published in 1949), it appears to have been strongly influenced by Russian writer Yevgeny Zamiatin's little-known dystopian novel *We,* written in St. Petersburg in 1920. *We,* the tale of D-503 and his forced choice between love for a female and loyalty to the all-powerful "One State," was constructed as a series of diary entries, as was *Anthem.* It was censored by the Communist government, but it circulated samizdat style among artistic groups throughout the city. Rand would almost surely have encountered it in meetings of one of her writing clubs. *Anthem* also echoes H. G. Wells's *The Time Machine,* popular in turn-of-the-century Russia, and Stephen Vincent Benét's "The Place of the Gods," a short story that tracks a primitive future man as he stumbles upon a glittering twentieth-century city, which Rand read that summer in *The Saturday Evening Post.* This was the first time she had seen a science fiction or fantasy story in a mainstream American magazine, let alone a widely circulated, highly respected conservative magazine that paid authors exceptionally well. She wrote *Anthem* start to finish in three weeks, hoping to sell it to the *Post.*

Anthem has most often been compared to *1984,* in which the hero, Winston Smith, also attempts to rediscover the lost world of the pretotalitarian past. But unlike Equality 7–2521, Smith is captured and succumbs to torture. Rand admirers point out another, related difference. Although Orwell hated totalitarianism as both stultifying and evil, the novel treats it as a system that is practical and *works;* Oceana stands as a hyperindustrialized society containing such advanced technology

that individual citizens cannot fight back against it. Rand concluded—
long before most others—that totalitarianism *doesn't* work, because the
independent motivation indispensable to economic and social progress
cannot survive in an atmosphere of intimidation, coercion, and lack of
individually earned rewards. She regarded totalitarianism as both immoral and impractical and would go on to explain exactly in what ways
the two are bound together in her fast-paced masterpiece of anticollec-
tivism, *Atlas Shrugged*. Her insight was predictive, at least in the case
of the former Soviet Union. When it came unglued in 1991, Western
countries were surprised to discover in its fearsome military and industrial might a case of the emperor's new clothes. Not much economic or
technological progress had been made during Communism's seventy-
five year reign.

Watkins couldn't place *Anthem* in *The Saturday Evening Post* or in
any other magazine, and Macmillan and two other publishers rejected it
as a book. (One of Macmillan's readers, perhaps the ubiquitous Granville
Hicks, imprudently observed that the author of *Anthem* "does not understand socialism," Rand wryly recalled in the early 1960s.) The novella
was published in 1938, when Cassell & Company brought it out in England under the title *Ego*. Eight years later, in the wake of the immense
commercial success of *The Fountainhead*, she revised it, added a preface,
and let a political ally's small West Coast press publish and distribute it
in pamphlet form. A beautifully illustrated magazine version appeared in
1953. And when a paperback edition became available in the 1960s,
some high schools made it mandatory reading. To date, a total of three
and a half million copies have been sold. Rand loved this story, perhaps
more than her later, celebrated work. It was "more precious to me than
anything I have ever considered writing," she revealed in a 1938 letter to
Cassell.

Rand was fond of Watkins, whose rescue at a low moment in her career she never forgot. But the agent's inability to sell *Anthem* and *Ideal* disturbed her. Then, in the fall of 1937, she accidentally discovered that the
agent had neglected to keep an eye on Macmillan's postpublication handling of *We the Living*. She had run out of author's copies of the book, and
when she made a routine request to the publisher for more, she was
dumbfounded to find out that the novel was out of print. Macmillan, in
violation of its contract, had failed to reprint the book when inventory ran

low. Far worse, it had destroyed the type the novel had been set with and *couldn't* reprint it. For Rand, this calamity was compounded by the fact that *We the Living*'s sales had actually been rising in 1937, not falling, as typically happens in the second year after publication. She agreed to meet with a Macmillan editor, James Putnam, who—not especially contrite—offered her a deal: He would arrange to have the type reset and to issue a new edition, at considerable cost, if she would sign a contract with Macmillan for the publication of *The Fountainhead*. Furious and heartsick as she was, this sounded attractive. She decided to accept the offer on one condition: that along with a $250 advance against royalties, payable now, the publisher would guarantee a $1,200 budget for promotion of the new book. The editor refused. Rand walked away, taking the copyright to *We the Living* with her. Not until the late 1950s would readers again be able to buy and read her arresting first novel. Her trust in Watkins was wearing thin.

The O'Connors moved again—in fact, they moved twice between autumn 1937 and autumn 1940—and again settled on the Upper East Side of Manhattan. By early 1938, with Nick's help, Rand was feeling socially at ease enough to throw a party in Town Hall for her aristocratic British friend by mail, Lady Boileau. Boileau was visiting America to promote her new novel, *Ballade in G Minor*, to give conservative political speeches, and to meet with such luminaries as Eleanor and Franklin Roosevelt in Hyde Park and Washington, D.C. J. Edgar Hoover arranged for a special tour of FBI headquarters for her, where, Boileau gaily reported, she shot a Tommy gun. She pronounced the FBI director "charming." Years later, Rand herself would try, and fail, to see him.

The year 1938 brought rumors of impending war in Europe. It also brought a welcome burst of economic activity after a short but devastating recession in the midst of the lingering Depression. Rand's own financial condition improved that summer when RKO made an offer of ten thousand dollars to acquire the long-expired MGM film rights to *The Night of January 16th*. The studio intended to cast Claudette Colbert or, even less plausibly, Lucille Ball as the solemn Karen Andre. The fee would have to be split with the detestable A. H. Woods, but five thousand dollars was better than nothing. This was especially so because Watkins had found a publishing company that was enthusiastic about bringing out *The Fountainhead* but refused to pay the author an advance on royalties until the novel was completed. The publisher was Alfred A. Knopf, Inc., one of New York's best and most reputable firms. Rand's editor would be the founder's stylish wife, Blanche Knopf, whom Rand later came to think of as "a phony." Even without payment, there was both promise and protection in consigning her unfinished book to a well-regarded publisher. On June 27, 1938, the thirty-three-year-old novelist and playwright signed a contract with Knopf. Blanche Knopf gave her a year to finish.

FIVE

THE FOUNTAINHEAD

1936–1941

I do not recognize anyone's right to one minute of my life. Nor to any achievement of mine. No matter who makes the claim, how large their number, or how great their need. I recognize no obligations toward men except one: to respect their freedom and to take no part in a slave society.

—*The Fountainhead,* 1943

The story of *The Fountainhead,* Rand once explained, is the story of how a moral man can live in a corrupt society.

Howard Roark is *The Fountainhead*'s moral man, of course, and also Ayn Rand's first full portrait of an individualist hero. By vocation, he is a gifted young architect beginning his career. He wants to create bold new buildings, but he is surrounded by frightened conformists and envious schemers who conspire to stop him. When he persists, his most relentless enemy, Ellsworth M. Toohey, an architecture critic and the novel's archvillain, tries to destroy him. But Roark prevails. He takes his case for the inalienable rights of the creative individual into court, where a jury of twelve thinking Americans takes his side. He goes on to design and erect the most original skyscraper in New York. As the novel closes, the flame-haired hero perches atop the building's pinnacle, the world—and his beautiful new wife—at his feet.

The first and last words of *The Fountainhead* are "Howard Roark," and Howard Roark is the novel's embodied message. In the opening scene, the reader meets him as a gaunt nineteen-year-old, standing naked on the edge of a cliff, high above a lake, with his hair—"neither blond nor red, but the exact color of ripe orange rind"—blowing in the wind. He laughs, just as Rand remembered Cyrus laughing in his cage, mocking his enemies. He has been expelled that morning from the architectural school of the prestigious Stanton Institute of Technology. His offense: refusing to follow the school curriculum and spend months designing Tudor-style chapels and Renaissance villas. He has been drawing his own unprecedented buildings. His defiant laughter echoes from the rocks that surround him as he dives into the lake. These rocks are there for him, he thinks: "waiting for the drill, the dynamite and my voice; waiting to be split, ripped, pounded, reborn; waiting for the shape my hands will give them." Who will let you design buildings without an architectural degree? the dean asks him in an exit interview. "Who will stop me?" he asks in return.

In one form or another, Ayn Rand had been daydreaming about Roark all her life. In figure, he is tall, thin to the point of gauntness, and almost always rigid with creative tension, although in repose he can be as supple as a cat. He possesses Cyrus's moral certainty, self-confidence, and even insolence. Like Zarathustra, he welcomes difficulties that propel him beyond ordinary, drab humanity to the formation of new values. Like Enjolras, he is single-minded in pursuit of his goal. He differs from Leo Kovalensky in that nothing can shake his self-esteem, and from Andrei Taganov in that he has no desire to convert others to his creed. He would "walk over corpses" to be an architect, one of the characters says about him. No matter what inducements or penalties he faces he won't compromise his architectural vision by a single pilaster. He is not afraid of disappointment or of pain. In her notes, Rand calls him "the noble soul par excellence," paying homage to Nietzsche's definition of a hero as "a soul that has reverence for itself." He is the archetype of the creator in a dissipated world. As he leaves Stanton for New York to pursue his career, he soon discovers that almost everyone will try to stop him.

Familiar to Rand as his character was, not least because it resembled her own, Roark did not provide the first germ of the idea for *The Fountainhead*. His glossy, callow schoolmate and opposite number, Peter Keating, did. Rand liked to tell the story of how she conceived of Peter Keating, who gave the novel its original title, *Second-Hand Lives*. In 1931 or 1932, while she was still living on North Gower Street and clerking in the wardrobe department of RKO, she became fascinated by her next-door neighbor, Marcella Bannert, the young woman who had helped her to place *Red Pawn* at Universal Pictures. Marcella was an executive assistant to David O. Selznick, at that time RKO's chief of production, and she was ambitious. Every day, the Russian émigré observed the American go-getter, admiring her obvious drive but disliking almost everything else about her, including her choice of a career and the impression she gave of being a Hollywood climber. One day, to pin down the differences between them, she asked the young woman to explain what she wanted to achieve in life. Marcella had a ready answer. If nobody had an automobile, she would not want an automobile. If some people had an automobile and others didn't, she would want an automobile. If some people had two and others had only one or none, she would want two automobiles, and so on. And she would want people to know that she had more than they did.

The conversation was a revelation to Rand. By her standards, Marcella seemed not to want anything for herself. Rand's goal was to create a fiction of ideas out of her experience and extraordinary gift for imagining and reasoning. Marcella merely wanted to outstrip the Joneses. The prickly young moral philosopher's judgments about people were based on whether they shared her values and "sense of life." Marcella appeared to have no values except those derived from other people; she prized what they prized and wanted more of whatever they had, evidently to fill an emptiness inside. Although some people might have called Marcella selfish because she set her sights on luxury and status, Rand didn't look at it that way. On reflection, she saw that the young woman was actually "selfless," in the sense that she had no authentic self with which to desire or create anything that was hers alone. Marcella's quality of selflessness, or lack of passionately held ideas and values, explained why she and so many other people Rand knew conformed to apparently meaningless conventions. It gave her the key to a problem that had puzzled her since childhood: why people who were so much less intelligent and passionate than she was treated her with such unfriendly indifference or even malice, seemingly because of her gifts. Pondering her conversation with Marcella, she concluded that her resolve to do and think what *she* wanted, so different from what others seemed to want, challenged the

premises of their existence. Not only was she a genius surrounded by
mediocrities, as her mother had often reminded her in letters. She also
possessed a moral independence and integrity that the others did not. To
some degree, she, like her 1934 character Kay Gonda, shamed them
merely by living.

Marcella's admission stirred a broader revelation. It explained the
psychological source of what she called "the collectivist motivation," by
which she meant the drive to seek the meaning of one's life outside oneself. Collectivists hunger for an all-knowing deity, an altruistic purpose,
or a dictator to tell them what to do as a fig leaf for their own inadequacy
and emptiness; they love what is average and "selfless" and fear what is
exceptional, original, and has to be created by the self. Such people live
by others' choices. They exist at second hand. The absence of an authentic selfishness—that is, a desire to live according to one's own principles,
based on the action of one's own mind—this, she decided, was what the
Bolshevik mobs, Russian Orthodox votaries, and ordinary Americans had
in common.

And so Peter Keating was born, with the soul of a second-hander.
Vain, affable, dependent on his popularity for self-respect, and without
specific talent, he enters the book in a mild state of adolescent self-
inflation and ends in a frightening and irreversible moral decay. Unlike
his college housemate Roark, he graduates from the Stanton Institute at
the top of his class, amid a sea of envious admirers, yet he has no gift for
architecture. He leans on Roark for help with his most difficult assignments and cheerfully stabs competitors in the back. He hates Roark's
asceticism, talent, and purpose, as well as the fact that Roark knows
that Keating is a fraud. Rand describes him this way: "He was great;
great as the number of people who told him so. He was right; right as
the number of people who believed it. He looked at the faces, at the
eyes; he saw himself born in them." As she began to outline *The Fountainhead,* Keating became the emblem of all that Roark is not.

There was another probable source for the character of Keating,
however, one that Rand may not herself have been aware of. A year or so
after talking with Marcella, she received a letter from her mother describing a seeming change of personality in her sister Nora. Nora had
won a prize at school for being the most socially active teacher, the letter said, and the young woman was positively jubilant about it. Anna
chafed at this, fretting that Nora had grown far too concerned with what

other people thought of her; she seemed to live to make others jealous, Anna wrote. That Nora may not have changed as much as Anna and Rand imagined didn't occur to either of them, since until then it had been Rand whose preferences Nora had mimicked and admiration she had wanted. It isn't known how Rand answered, but she surely identified one influence that she may have believed was at work on her favorite sister, for she hadn't forgotten Anna's social climbing in the years before the revolution or her constant nagging to be nice to other people. (Late in *The Fountainhead,* for example, Roark chuckles at people who attend a lecture only in order to tell their friends that they heard a famous person speak, echoing Rand's memories of her mother.) Thus she had an old, embittering, and ready model on which to fit her new insights into second-hand lives.

Once in New York, the penniless Roark goes to work for the great Henry Cameron, a grizzled genius and an alcoholic outcast whose character is based on Louis Sullivan. Cameron is the only living architect from whom Roark is sure that he can learn the fine points of his trade; the old man is famous for having built the first skyscrapers that looked like skyscrapers and not like Gothic castles curling into the clouds. Keating, too, heads for New York, but he joins the high-society architectural firm of Francon & Heyer. Through mild (at first) duplicity, imitation, and flattery, Keating quickly rises in the firm. Meanwhile, Roark and the out-of-favor Cameron sit day after day, without paid commissions, in a dim studio in lower Manhattan. Eventually, Cameron dies, and Roark survives in poverty on a few small commissions his admirers send his way. He is beginning to develop a reputation.

One day Keating comes to ask a favor. Will Roark help him enter a global competition to design and build the new Cosmo-Slotnick movie studio headquarters in midtown Manhattan, just as he used to help him with thorny school assignments? Keating is desperate: Unless he can win the contest, he fears public humiliation and the loss of a prospective partnership in Francon & Heyer. Out of enthusiasm for a chance to design a tall building, Roark agrees and overnight devises an elegant and innovative plan for a skyscraper. Yet even with Roark's blueprint in hand, the talentless Keating can't quite believe he'll win. So one afternoon he pays a visit to the firm's ill, elderly partner, Lucius Heyer, and tries to blackmail the old man into stepping aside in favor of himself. Heyer falls to the floor and dies of fright. A few days later, Keating learns that Heyer has left him a small fortune. Furthermore, he has won the Cosmo-Slotnick competition. With cameras rolling and lights blazing, he is hailed and feted by New York's glittering architectural fraternity, while the brilliant, self-directed Roark, now destitute, rides a train from the city of his dreams to a Connecticut granite quarry, where a job awaits him breaking rocks.

It is while laboring in the quarry that he meets—and notoriously "rapes"—the tall, slender, elegant heiress Dominique Francon. Dominique is the daughter of Peter Keating's now-partner Guy Francon and of a mother who was very rich and left Dominique a fortune. She happens to be spending a quiet summer at her father's Connecticut estate, although she usually lives and works in the city as a home-decorating columnist for the *New York Banner*. When she first glimpses Roark, at work, he wears a thin cotton shirt that clings damply to his chest, his shirtsleeves are rolled at the elbows, and a strand of hair falls into his face: He is Cyrus with an orange cap of hair. She instantly understands that he is the ideal man, not only for herself but abstractly, absolutely. Against the considerable force of her concentrated determination to care for no one, she becomes consumed with love for him.

Sex permeates *The Fountainhead*. In various scenes, Roark's construction blowtorch becomes a flame he holds on a leash, shuddering with violence; Dominique sees skyscrapers as molten fire that thrusts and shoots through the earth's crust to freedom and release. And sadomasochism permeates the sex. The most celebrated scene in the novel is the so-called rape scene. Having once seen Roark, Dominique fights to keep herself from going back to the quarry to peep at him while he hacks and drills in the blistering sun. She goes anyway, and he becomes aware that she is watching him. The first time he looks at her she experiences his contemptuous gaze as a slap in the face. She feels a "convulsion of anger, of protest, of resistance—and of pleasure." She doesn't yet know who the orange-haired young worker is, but she already hates him, this dusty, lowly creature who is performing a convict's labor, yet he is the only man she has ever lusted after. Later, she returns on horseback with a whip and intercepts him as he walks to his boardinghouse. When he mockingly signals that he understands why the proud Miss Francon has followed him there, she whips him across the face and gallops away. This is a wonderful silent-film-era melodramatic set piece, except that Dominique's attraction to Roark and his to her have a deeper—a philosophical—meaning.

He is "a first cause, a fount of energy, a life force, a Prime Mover," as Rand says of him late in the novel. And it is through him that Dominique will find her own real, passionate, active self, a somewhat second-handed strategy that is somehow all right for the novel's heroine though not for the novel's men.

Roark's slashed face is the only invitation he needs. What follows is sexual assault—or consensual sadism and masochism, depending on how you look at it. Rand thought of the sex as consensual and, indeed, provoked by Dominique. Late at night, Roark lets himself into the heroine's expensively scented bedroom through a terrace window. He stands in his dirty work clothes, hands on hips, legs astride, and lets her look at him. She crouches in terror beside her dressing table. He is laughing. He picks her up and throws her on the bed. Although she is in her mid-twenties, she is a virgin. She fights "like an animal," Rand informs us. As she fights, she thinks that if he were less detached, less cruel, she would not want him. But he is even colder and crueler than she thought. He ravishes her "as an act of scorn," the author writes in a famous passage. "The act of a master taking shameful, contemptuous possession of her was the kind of rapture she had wanted." After waiting for so many years for Leo Kovalensky—and possibly O'Connor—to brandish *his* whip, Ayn Rand has finally made and met someone who does.

Dominique has to be one of the most contrary characters in twentieth-century fiction. Her love for Roark ignites both her sexuality and her malice. Before she sees him again, he is called back to Manhattan to design an important building. At summer's end, she, too, returns to the city, and after a week or two she finds out who he is. She discovers that she loves his buildings and, as a result, sets out to deprive him of commissions and destroy his reputation through her popular newspaper column. She does this not from anger, jealousy, wounded pride, or even rebelliousness; her motive is a contorted form of hero worship that drives her to protect what she loves from the desensitized gaze and dirty hands of the world. Rand once said that Dominique is "myself in a bad mood." Like Rand as a child, the heroine wants what she values to be hers alone; others aren't worthy even to admire it. Like Kay Gonda, she lives in a permanent state of gloom over the lack of heroic standards in the ordinary world. She tries to sabotage the hero's work in part to save him and his beautiful prospective buildings from contamination by the "soot-stained" mob. To add to her contrariness, her belligerence and sexuality are tied together: on nights when her column has been particularly damaging to his ambitions, she goes to his room and lets him sleep with her. They both find ecstasy in their struggle with each other. But even this ecstasy is unacceptable to Dominique. On the night she tells Roark that she loves him, she also announces that she has married Peter Keating. "When I think what you are," she says to Roark, "I can't accept any reality except a world of your kind." She adds, "They'll destroy you, but I won't be there to see it happen. I will have destroyed myself first."

The mob emits a kind of muffled roar in *The Fountainhead*. The novel opens in 1922 and ends in 1940, but most of the action takes place during the Red Decade of the 1930s. The *New York Banner*, a mass-market newspaper that publishes Dominique's column, specializes in maudlin stories about the hardships and religious piety of slum dwellers, single mothers, subnormal children, and the poor. On that note appears the novel's fourth major character, Ellsworth M. Toohey, the *Banner*'s spindly, power-hungry architecture critic and a collectivist malefactor; he has a concave chest, lacquered hair, and a Hitler mustache. He is almost Dickensian in his malicious genius for undercutting his superiors' achievements and for striking becoming poses on behalf of the downtrodden. His purpose is to undermine the social importance of integrity and originality, in order both to conceal his own lack of creativity and to flatter the lumpen mass of men and women who are the *Banner*'s readers. He and Dominique join forces, albeit with different motives, to bring down the now slowly up-and-coming "Mr. Superman," Howard Roark.

By the spring of 1937, Rand had outlined most of the book, along with a number of subplots she would later cut. In order to provide authentic details of the characters and settings, she now needed a thorough introduction to architecture. She turned for help to the legendary reference librarians at the New York Public Library on Fifth Avenue and Forty-second Street. They supplied her with stacks of expertly vetted materials on architectural history and theory. Looking for clues to the design philosophy of Cameron and Roark, she began by studying the masters of early skyscraper design and of clean, fluid modernist styling. This led her directly to Sullivan and Frank Lloyd Wright. In fact, one of the first books she read was Wright's 1932 masterpiece of American iconoclasm, *An Autobiography*. She later said that she had barely heard of Wright before encountering the book, but she couldn't have chosen a more suitable self-made creator, or a more useful model for Roark, without reviving Thomas Edison. As she fine-tuned her hero's professional experience and mission, she borrowed Wright's organic architectural style, his emphasis on "Truth in Architecture," his contempt for imitation and mediocrity, his transcendent indifference to clients' good opinion, and even his famous "temple to man," turning Wright's Unity Temple in Oak Park, Illinois, into Roark's Stoddard Temple in New York. Although Rand would later deny it, whole scenes from the novel are modified from or inspired by Wright's account of his life. Roark's rebellion against the dean of Stanton, for example, echoes the young Wright's argument with his patron, his uncle Dan, against learning to work in traditional styles. A Mr. Austin is an early admirer of the fledgling Wright; Roark's first client is named Austin Heller. (At one point in her notes, Rand substitutes the name of H. L. Mencken for that of Heller, suggesting that he was another model for the civil-libertarian Austin Heller.) Wright describes the nights he spent in a wooden shanty he constructed while supervising the creation of a nude female sculpture for his Midway Gardens project; Roark stays late into the night in a shack on the grounds of the Stoddard Temple while sculptor Steven Mallory creates a magnificent nude statue of Dominique Francon.

Twice Rand wrote to the curmudgeonly old midwesterner, asking to interview him. Her first letter was answered, "Dear Mr. Rand," by a secretary who explained that Mr. Wright was traveling; in fact, Wright was in the midst of planning Taliesin West, his retreat in Arizona. In the fall of 1938, she arranged to be introduced to him after a lecture he gave at the National Association of Real Estate Boards in New York. "I spent three hundred and fifty dollars out of my savings to buy a black velvet dress and shoes and a cape, everything to match, at [the expensive Fifth Avenue department store] Bonwit Teller, which I had never entered before," she later told a friend. "I felt this would be an unrepeatable occasion, because I was to meet a man who was really great." According to Wright's biographer, he felt no immediate rapport with her and was suspicious of her intentions. Still, in November 1938 she wrote again, enclosing a draft of the first three chapters of the novel. He replied that "no man named 'Roark' with flaming red hair" could possibly be an architectural genius or hope to "lick" the building-trades conspiracy. She responded to this by telegram, imploring him to see her. Wright's secretary again informed her that the architect had gone away. Once *The*

Fountainhead was published, she and Wright would become acquaintances, briefly and tempestuously.

Meanwhile, she scoured the works of architectural and social historians and compared their attitudes to those of Wright. She found most of them to be conventional thinkers, unwitting collectivists, or worse. She gave her villain, Ellsworth Toohey, the pretenses and mannerisms of those she especially disliked: the elegant theoretician Lewis Mumford, who cast a cold eye on technology and praised the architecture of communal life; Heywood Broun, a popular syndicated columnist, champion of the underdog, and founder of the pro-Communist Newspaper Guild; Clifton Fadiman, *The New Yorker*'s book critic and host of the popular radio show *Information Please,* from whom Toohey received his encyclopedic memory; and British socialist Harold Laski. At the urging of her friend Pincus Berner and his wife, in 1937 she attended one of Laski's guest lectures at the New School for Social Research and hated him; the following year, she went back to look him over in greater detail. She committed his elegant slouch and air of snide superiority to memory. She said, "You could sense the bared teeth behind [his] smile." He was Toohey in the flesh.

In early notes for *The Fountainhead* in 1935, she had briefly sketched the novel's fifth main character, the New York *Banner*'s owner and publisher, Gail Wynand. Now she elaborated Wynand's role in her intricate drama of good and evil. Wynand is a self-made millionaire who owns a vast empire of real estate holdings and newspapers and employs Dominique and Toohey to add a touch of culture to his flagship paper. A combination of William Randolph Hearst and a Horatio Alger character, he is a poor boy from Hell's Kitchen whose overriding ambition has been to gain power over the illiterate brutes who once used to beat him up by giving them the pablum they want and growing rich. In Dominique, he gradually recognizes a kindred spirit and decides to marry her. Wishing to humiliate her new husband, Keating, she agrees to marry him. The newspaper magnate offers Keating a plum architectural assignment in exchange for divorcing Dominique. Keating, in moral free fall, takes the deal.

Like Dominique, Wynand cares for no one, with the possible exception of Dominique herself. He hates both his own pandering and the mob his newspaper serves. Then, while searching for an architect to design a dream home for himself and his new wife, he meets Howard Roark. Unaware of Roark's history with Dominique, or that Dominique and Toohey have been using the *Banner* to discredit the young architect, he hires and befriends Roark. By the time he understands Roark's immense moral and aesthetic value, however, it is too late to save his paper or himself. Toohey has mobilized popular resentment against Roark, and against Wynand's patronage of Roark, into an advertising boycott and a strike by the newspaper's reporters and editors. In a failed effort to preserve his business, Wynand also forfeits what remains of his self-esteem by denouncing the one person he respects, Roark. Rand intended Wynand to be the book's great tragic figure: a Nietzschean antihero who allows the weakling Toohey to destroy his empire because he misunderstands the nature of power. In fact, his character was partly her critique of Nietzsche's will to power; although she, like Nietzsche, still held the masses in contempt, she no longer believed in dominating or forcing them. "You were a ruler of men," Wynand famously tells himself. "You held a leash. A leash is only a rope with a noose at both ends." Because rulers are dependent on their subjects for their power, they also live at second hand. Wynand "rules the mob only as long as he says what the mob wants him to say," Rand noted. Roark, on the other hand, needs no power other than his own dynamic drive to create and build. Never does he suggest that the masses are there to serve him, as both Kira and Nietzsche do.

Toohey, whose sole aim is power and is therefore the incarnation of collectivist evil, can destroy the *Banner,* but his plans to take it over and run it are thwarted by Wynand's simple last-minute remedy of halting the presses and closing the paper. This was Rand's trial run of an idea that would become a major element in *Atlas Shrugged* and in her vision of utopia: the impotence of evil to produce anything or prevail against creators, unless good people cooperate with evil and give it strength.

In her notebooks, she defined *The Fountainhead*'s theme as "individualism versus collectivism, not in politics, but within a man's soul." Apart from the heroic theme and the sex, and notwithstanding the seemingly implausible events of the story, what makes the book phenomenally compelling is her remarkable ability to tie her ideas about individualism and the proper use of power to her plot and characters, and then tie her characters to one another. Thus, in her notes, Roark is "the man who can be [an individualist hero] and is [one]." Dominique, who in spite of her combativeness actually yearns for Roark's eventual triumph, is a priestess and "the woman for a man like Roark." Wynand is "the man who could have been [a hero] but isn't." Cleverly, passive Peter Keating is "the man who never could be [a hero] and doesn't know it," while Toohey is "the man who never could be [a hero]—and [does know] it." Because Toohey is aware of his fundamental lack of generative power and wants to recast the world in his image, he is the embodiment of evil: a collectivist avenger who acts as the Lenin of *The Fountainhead*.

By the early fall of 1937, Rand had outlined everything but the novel's climax. She wanted to organize the plot so that Roark would not only be sued in civil court for his unorthodox design of the Stoddard Temple but would also undergo a criminal trial in which he would expound the author's views on the rights of the creative individual. The trouble was, she couldn't come up with a crime to get him there. Meanwhile, she needed to invent or elaborate dozens of secondary characters, from the *Banner's* staff of reporters and editors to a chorus of draftsmen and minor architects, and to learn how a contemporary architect ran his office.

She decided to go to work for Ely Jacques Kahn, a well-known Art Deco architect and an admirer of Swiss modernist Le Corbusier. Kahn had a successful New York commercial practice. He instantly understood what she was after, and was intrigued by her description of her novel in progress as a vindication of modern architecture. He hired her, incognito, as a clerk in his office at Park Avenue and Thirty-third Street. He proved immensely useful to her. She studied his drafting techniques and the pecking order in his workmen's rooms. He brought her along to professional seminars and parties. She pumped him for gossip and stories, and he complied. She assiduously collected background information about his colleagues, whom she later turned into a gallery of roguish minor characters. He even helped to engineer her introduction to Frank Lloyd Wright at Wright's National Association of Real Estate Boards lecture. He contributed his own traits to the figure of Guy Francon, Peter Keating's socially connected mentor and partner. Francon is portrayed as the most successful and least industrious architect in New York—the last part definitely not an attribute of Kahn's.

Here and elsewhere she picked up and deployed the finer points of well-known New York buildings and 1930s personalities, which makes *The Fountainhead* an amusing parody as well as a juggernaut of romantic ideas. The inspiration for Henry Cameron's landmark Dana Building, for example, was probably Louis Sullivan's gemlike Bayard-Condict Building, the only Sullivan structure in Manhattan, and its name seems to have been chosen in honor of Frank Lloyd Wright's Dana House in Springfield, Illinois. Peter Keating's winning entry for the Cosmo-Slotnick competition closely resembles the 1926 Paramount Building; it, too, was built as the result of a public competition, which was won by a firm called Rapp & Rapp. A real architect named Gordon Bunshaft, a pioneer of the boxy International Style, provided the model for the pompous, tweedy Gordon Prescott, and the famous architect Cass Gilbert served as inspiration for the Renaissance-loving character of Ralston Halcombe. In creating the novelist and Toohey protégé Lois Cook, Rand parodied Gertrude Stein and added a Russian touch; not only is Cook an American cubist, like Stein, but she is also an early 1920s Russian futurist who, in the words of Russian historian Bernice Rosenthal, "valorizes [that group's] cacophony, disharmony, and even a kind of crudeness" in her home and work. The debauched old *Banner* theater critic, Jules Fougler, may well be Brooks Atkinson, the reviewer who so brashly condemned *The Night of January 16th* as "hokum." Toohey's millionaire patron Mitchell Layton seems to have been based on the department-store magnate Marshall Field III, and his nonsense-playwright sidekick, Ike the Genius, on William Saroyan, a client of Pincus Berner's. When at the end of *The Fountainhead,* newspaper mogul Gail Wynand commissions Roark to build a skyscraper in Hell's Kitchen, he is completing a dream announced by William Randolph Hearst in 1921.

Most important, Kahn gave Rand the key to the novel's climax. Chatting with him one day, she asked what was the biggest problem in architecture at the time. "Low-cost housing," he answered and went on to explain how lack of adequate funding limited the quality of public construction for the poor. At lunchtime, she rushed downstairs, sat at the counter at Schrafft's, and furiously scribbled notes. With a flash of irony, she imagined Roark designing a star-shaped public housing project that is both cheap and beautifully engineered—not because he believes in publicly funded housing, but because Keating has again come to him and begged for help and he is intrigued by the challenge. In exchange for the glory that Keating will receive as the nominal creator of the prize-winning Cortlandt Homes, Roark imposes one condition: His old classmate must swear to protect his blueprints from the slightest design alteration. Weak willed and by now habitually amoral, Keating does not keep his promise. He permits Toohey and a band of out-of-work hangers-on to disfigure and mar every element of Roark's cluster of six asymmetrical buildings. Roark, acting on the premise that a creative individual has the right to confer or withdraw the products of his own mind as he sees fit, gets some dynamite and blows up the almost-completed project. He is arrested and put on trial. The prosecution argues that he is a monster for placing his ego above the need for shelter by the city's Depression-battered poor. In his own defense, Roark delivers an eight-page speech, which can be summed up as a passionate plea for egoism "in its real meaning," as Rand phrased it at the very beginning of her notes. "All that which proceeds from man's independent ego is good," Roark declares in court. "All that which proceeds from man's dependence on men is evil." Collectivism and altruism (collectivism's religious twin) are the second-handers' best tools for yoking the creator to their own aims, which they need to do because they can't create anything new or worthwhile themselves. Witness Peter Keating, who testifies for the prosecution against his benefactor Roark; in the last throes of a "selflessness" that has devoured his soul, he leaves the stand and creeps home, permanently ruined and disgraced.

Here, as elsewhere in the novel, Rand is channeling the ideas of Albert Jay Nock, who argued that members of a society can be grouped in one or the other of two opposing camps: either they are "economic man," those who produce what they need to survive, or "political man," those who use charm or coercion to live off the productivity of others. Rand's fascinating contribution to this formulation is her depiction of its psychology: Nock's political man is her psychological second-hander; his economic man is her individualist hero, reliant on his own ego as the fountainhead of productivity and value. In Roark's self-defense at trial, he says, "The creator's concern is the conquest of nature. The parasite's concern is the conquest of men." Roark refuses to be conquered. Expecting no help, he asserts his right to deny his help to others. The jurors—and millions of Rand's readers throughout the years—may find his crime shocking, but they also find his logic eloquent, his pride compelling, and his notion of individualism peculiarly American. They acquit him.

In fact, in his own way, Roark is as American as Huckleberry Finn or Holden Caulfield. Self-determination, originality, defiance of authority, hard work—these are qualities Americans prize in themselves and in the national character. Yet, as a few perceptive readers have pointed out, in certain ways Roark is also an exquisite portrait of a nineteenth-century Eastern European Jew. The rights he claims for himself would, if universally acknowledged, create a perfect barrier against the anti-Semitic violence and thievery Rand knew at first and second hand in Russia; for centuries Jews' special contributions to banking, manufacturing, trade, and capital formation had been punished by Christians even while they used them for their own ends. When Roark dedicates his destruction of the Cortlandt Homes "to every tortured hour of loneliness, denial, frustration, [and] abuse [that every creative individual] was [ever] made to spend," and "to every creator who was destroyed in body or in spirit," he speaks for Rand's father and grandfather, not only as Russians but also as Jews.

Russian history and temperament also figure not so subtly in the book. In Roarkland, as in Russia, productivity is prized far more than its Western cousins accumulation, acquisition, and pleasure; no good character in *The Fountainhead* wants anything material or relational for himself, and even the bad characters' deepest ambitions are spiritual. Keating wants adulation so that he can have the illusion of a self. Toohey wants to make use of his only gift: manipulation. "Enjoyment is not my destiny," he tells Keating. "I shall find such satisfaction as my capacity permits. I shall rule." Much of the novel's thrilling intensity comes from the dangers posed by Roark's insistence on spiritual integrity—his unwillingness to compromise any aspect of his vision. Compromise is said to be an insult in Russia; in America—a functioning democracy—it is a way of life. Finally, Roark feels no sexual jealousy, even when his beautiful mistress sleeps with and marries first Peter Keating and then Gail Wynand. In fact, he seems to feel closer to Wynand because he knows what the mogul doesn't know: that the two men share a knowledge of Dominique's body. Free love and sexual equality were standard notions in Russian intellectual circles from the middle 1800s onward. They certainly weren't standard in America in the 1930s and 1940s; and Rand's hard-breathing fantasies and blithe acceptance of serial sexual affairs were to create as much surprise and buzz among readers of the time as did her hero's pride in blowing up a housing project.

In later years, when Frank O'Connor took up painting, Rand would say that she envied him his simple pleasure in applying paint to canvas. As she left off outlining and began to write, her work proved slow and grueling. Although she had mastered her story line, finding the proper nuances of style and an emotional vocabulary that fit her theme took more time and energy than she expected. As with *We the Living*, these matters had to be worked out sentence by sentence, almost word by word, in her adopted language. She wrote and rewrote, cut and restored, bending over her walnut desk every day and deep into the night. For inspiration, she gazed at the publicity photograph of an ethereal young O'Connor she had hung above her desk. The portrait of Frank "makes John Barrymore look like an office boy," a visitor once remarked. By mid-1939 she had only about a third of the novel in first draft.

She missed her deadline with Knopf. Blanche Knopf gave her an extension of one year, until June 28, 1940. For a number of reasons, she missed that deadline, too, and couldn't say with certainty when she would finish. By mutual assent, then, her contract with the publisher was canceled. As Watkins once again began to circulate her outline and early chapters, Rand grew alarmed about money. Her theatrical royalties were slowing and her savings were slipping through her fingers. She could look forward to no advance or sales. But her inner world was richer and more luminous than ever, and the moral ideas she and Roark were testing "in man's soul" would soon also be tested in the political sphere and begin to harden into code.

SIX

THE SOUL OF AN INDIVIDUALIST

1939–1942

Renunciation is not one of my premises. If I see that the good is possible to men, yet it vanishes, I do not take "Such is the trend of the world" as a sufficient explanation. I ask such questions as: Why?—What caused it?

—Introduction to *The Romantic Manifesto*, 1969

My research material for the psychology of Roark was myself."

In the four and a half years it took her to write *The Fountainhead*, from late June of 1938 through Christmas of 1942, her psychology was increasingly volatile. All around her, in news about the impending war in Europe and among the top players in political and literary circles, she thought she saw Keatings and Tooheys triumphing in matters of policy and popular opinion. Her own professional setbacks—the collapse of a theatrical venture, renewed difficulty in earning a living as a writer—stung more than ever. The perception that she was being passed up, even undermined, as a result of her courage in speaking out against Communism grew more acute. The period was not all darkness, but she remembered it as if it were. About her life at this time, she wrote, "Frank was the fuel. . . . He helped me to maintain [the "sense of life" that I was trying to capture in *The Fountainhead*] over a long span of years when there was nothing around us but a gray desert of people and events that evoked nothing but contempt and revulsion." Hollywood, New York, America—these might not be Atlantis, after all.

Her husband returned her idealized love with loyalty, support, and a strong sense of protectiveness. He enjoyed meeting people and attending movies and plays. She had lost her interest in movies and preferred to stay at home, and so they did. "I have no hobbies," she proudly noted in an open letter to readers of *The Fountainhead* in 1945. "I have few friends. I do not like to 'go out.' . . . Nothing [besides writing] has ever mattered to me too much."

Nothing except him, that is. He mattered a great deal, though not in an ordinary way. Everyone who knew them believed she loved him passionately. But she possessed little or no empathy, a useful and maybe a necessary tool for intimacy. She sometimes didn't seem to know who he was. She conflated him with her heroes; she insisted that he shared all her convictions, her desires, her tastes, and her propensity for moral outrage and contempt. "He's on strike," she would later tell friends who wondered why such a powerful woman had chosen to marry such a sweetly unambitious man. The only time his temper flared was when he saw Ayn being badly or unjustly treated—and sometimes when they argued. Even then, the larger issues between them remained unspoken.

She wanted to know everything about him, however, and when his father died in late December 1938, at the age of seventy-four, from the effects of arteriosclerosis on the heart, she went with him to the funeral. She was curious to see Lorain, Ohio, the small Lake Erie steel town where her husband had been born and raised, and to view Dennis O'Connor's body at the wake, she told Mimi Papurt. She wanted to know whether Frank had inherited his willowy beauty from Dennis, a retired steel roller. By all accounts, he had. She was less curious about the rest of the O'Connor family, most of whom she was meeting for the first time. No doubt she disapproved of the Roman Catholic funeral ceremony and felt uncomfortable amid family small talk; small talk remained something she didn't do well and often didn't try to do. The Ohio O'Connors, in turn, did not entirely take to her. With her Russian accent, mesmerizing gaze, and air of being intellectual but also bored and fidgety, she struck them as aloof, high-handed, and too "drab and homely" for Frank, said Mimi's younger sister Marna Papurt, later Wolf. Marna, then eleven years old, thought her new aunt's clothes and shoes were dark and "junky." She also objected to the way the woman "mothered" Uncle Frank, telling him what to eat and not to eat. During one dinner, Marna recalled, Rand warned him not to drink a glass of cold water and then eat ice cream; he might get a chill and come down with polio. The polio virus that had crippled Franklin Roosevelt in the 1920s was a source of dread throughout the 1930s and 1940s, but the disease could not be caught as the result of a chill. She had an ongoing phobia about germs, however, perhaps a vestige of an adolescence in which waves of typhoid and cholera rolled through her native city. Still, Frank didn't eat his ice cream. Marna's mother Agnes Papurt, Frank's younger sister, and other relatives were wary, lest one of their family favorites become separated from them by marriage to an exotic stranger. This didn't happen; Rand was immensely fond of Nick and Joe, kept in touch with other members of the family, and became good friends with Mimi. Later in the marriage, however, acquaintances recalled, Rand did increase the distance between her husband and his family, even if unintentionally. She grew more possessive of him as time went on.

In late 1938 and 1939, Ayn and Frank were living in a large, modern red-brick apartment building on East Eighty-ninth Street in New York. Rand's second cousin Fern Brown, now twenty years old and in college, came to see them one evening in June of 1939, on her way home from a summer job in Pennsylvania. Fern hadn't set eyes on her Russian cousin in thirteen years, since Rand left Chicago for Hollywood. She remembered being profoundly impressed by Rand's literary conversation and accomplishments, her lovely apartment, and her welcoming, handsome husband. To Fern's astonishment, O'Connor cooked and served a Russian dinner, dressed in a smoking jacket. ("The man cooking was something I'd never *heard* of in those days," she said.) Rand remained at the dining-room table talking with Fern and chain-smoking through a long cigarette holder. After dinner, they attended the ballet. Fern eventually decided to become a writer herself and went on to publish more than twenty young-adult biographies and novels.

That summer, the 1939 New York World's Fair opened in Flushing Meadows, Queens, to crowds from all over the nation and the world. Twenty million visitors came to New York to tour the World of Tomorrow pavilions, where they could see early prototypes of a Xerox machine, a jet-propelled airplane, RCA's first television set, a speech synthesizer, and many other engineering triumphs in Art Deco shapes and colors. The architectural exhibition, labeled "Pacifica" for its Far Eastern theme, probably provided Rand with some details for her fictional March of the Centuries exposition in *The Fountainhead,* a massive project in which Roark refuses to participate because it is "architecture by committee" (a phrase coined by Frank Lloyd Wright) and of which Peter Keating then takes leadership.

Mimi, also twenty and an art student, came to stay with the O'Connors that summer, perhaps to visit the World's Fair. She was attractive, high-spirited, and (unlike her mother and sisters) full of awed admiration for her aunt by marriage, whom she had first met and idolized while visiting her uncle Nick in December 1934. She was on hand to witness the many ups and downs of her aunt's long summer. Rand, having missed her first Knopf deadline and with only a year left to finish *The Fountainhead* and meet her second deadline, had just agreed to set aside her work on the novel and concentrate on what she hoped would be a money-making proposition: a new production of her 1936 play rendition of *We the Living.* On the recommendation of a Russian-born actress named Eugenie Leontovich, the well-known director George Abbott had offered to produce the play after cash-strapped Jerome Mayer backed out. Abbott, who later shared a Pulitzer Prize with Jerome Weidman for the musical *Fiorello!,* was then best known for jovial Rodgers and Hart musicals, including the previous year's hilarious Shakespeare spoof *The Boys from Syracuse.* The cast he chose was a wild assortment of types. Leontovich herself, thirty-nine years old and a veteran of the Stanislavskian Moscow Art Theatre, took the role of twenty-year-old Kira. Actor John Davis Lodge, the brother of Henry Cabot Lodge, Jr., and a future governor of Connecticut, tried but failed to bring to life the character of Andrei Taganov; Abbott replaced him with an up-and-coming young midwesterner named Dean Jagger, later to be famous as a high-school principal in television's *Mr. Novak.* Broadway hand John Emory played a lackluster version of Leo. Frank O'Connor understudied the part and also earned Actors' Equity pay as a GPU deputy commissar. Rehearsals began in June.

This time, Rand retained script control, and she asked for and received a one-hundred-dollar-a-month stipend while rehearsals lasted. She assumed that any rewriting of the play would be quick and straightforward. She was wrong. Once the production was under way, Abbott, like A. H. Woods, wanted extended revisions.

Having once mapped out a complex plot in novel form, Rand later said, her mind rebelled against reshaping it in another genre. As a result, her stage adaptations, like some of her screenplays, tended to be literal, stiff, and nakedly melodramatic, and it was partly these theatrical defects that Abbott wanted to correct. Before long, he asked her to work along-side another contract writer, the respected playwright S. N. Behrman, and she agreed. She liked Behrman and was fond of Abbott but was im-patient with what she thought of as their "unstylized" sense of the dra-matic. Like Woods, they advised and cajoled her to soften her characters' hard symbolic edges and, as she saw it, give Leo, Andrei, and Kira the fla-vor of "the folks next door." This, of course, she could not do. If form fol-lowed function, as she believed it did in literary art as in architecture, then the special, the exalted, the highly stylized was her medium and her message. She did her best to make the play commercially viable, but *The Unconquered,* as Rand titled it (invoking the designation Liberty 5–3000 had given to Equality 7–2521 in *Anthem*), tottered woodenly toward its opening.

In many ways rehearsals that summer were a repetition of *The Night of January 16th,* with two important differences. One was that she made a fast, close friend of her majestic leading lady, Eugenie Leontovich, who had escaped from Russia four years before Rand. Mimi remem-bered being in the O'Connors' apartment, listening as the two re-doubtable expatriates chatted on the phone for hours, mixing Russian with English. Then one day, Mimi recalled, the friendship was over. The actress hadn't been adapting well to the role of Kira or to the mixed ap-proaches of her fellow actors. In any case, Leontovich's husband, Greg-ory Ratoff, apparently convinced her that performing the lead in an overtly anti-Communist play on Broadway might hurt her nascent Hol-lywood career, and she quit. Rand was furious, and probably wounded and worried. Abbott replaced the Russian diva with a tepid American actress named Helen Craig, and, according to Mimi, Rand never saw or spoke to Leontovich again.

There were other ruptures with friends in the 1930s, Mimi recalled, although she never knew exactly what had caused them. When she asked about people whom she had seen and no longer saw during her vis-its, her uncle Frank explained that they and the O'Connors had not seen eye to eye on some subjects, so "we don't see them so much." These peo-ple included actor Robert Shayne, who had played a small part in *The Night of January 16th,* and his wife, Elizabeth, who couldn't or wouldn't understand Rand's concept of selfishness; Ivan Lebedeff; and a newspaper publicist named Frank Orsini. "Almost everybody," Mimi said.

This was an example of an emerging trend in Rand's personality that is characteristic of both ideologues and narcissists: sudden and acrimonious breaks with friends. Leontovich may have defended her acting by criticizing the character of Kira or may have disagreed with Rand about Russian or American politics. Whatever she did, she broke the spell of consensus Rand increasingly required.

The second notable event was a romantic flirtation she carried on that summer with Dean Jagger. She was fascinated by the handsome thirty-six-year-old Jagger's bald pate, and he went out of his way to be warm and courtly to her during rehearsals and cast gatherings. As close acquaintances pointed out, men were often drawn to Ayn Rand's brains and intellectual conviction but almost never to her physical womanhood. Jagger was. Mimi, who attended rehearsals, noticed that her aunt's eyes lit up whenever she and Jagger met. One day, the niece said boldly, "I bet you'd like to have an affair with him, but you'd be afraid to take a chance, because you'd be afraid of losing Frank." Rand smiled genially and said, "You're absolutely right."

O'Connor was also working on the set, and it's likely that he was aware of his wife's mild flirtation. He may have been uneasy but may also have felt relief that she had found a source of pleasure. At home, her fear of running out of money and her growing anxiety over time spent away from *The Fountainhead* gave rise to changeable moods of depression and irritation. Mimi witnessed Rand's angry outbursts at O'Connor, fast-rising storms that he weathered without protest. He was proud of his brilliant and courageous wife, he confided to his niece. But Mimi thought he appeared less guarded and more at ease when Rand wasn't present. At one point he told her that he would have liked to have children but that "it wouldn't fit with Ayn." Mimi may already have known of her aunt's decision to have an abortion earlier in the 1930s, since Mimi's father, A. M. Papurt, had loaned O'Connor the money to pay for it. It is interesting to note that children do not figure much in Rand's fictional universe, with the exception of a few flashbacks and the character of eight-year-old Acia Dunaeva in *We the Living*, who behaves like a spoiled five-year-old. Some of her closest followers would also forgo having children.

Beginning with *We the Living*, Rand wrote the first drafts of her nov-

els in longhand, and after completing a scene or a section read it aloud
to Frank and Nick. So it is also likely that she and her husband discussed her fictional sexual triangles in both *We the Living* and *The
Fountainhead.* Based on material in her journals, at least one commentator has argued that her basic model for male sexual psychology in her
novels was Frank O'Connor and that he enjoyed her three-sided sexual
fantasies and, perhaps, her first and subsequent flirtations.

At that time, O'Connor had a mischievous sense of adventure. One afternoon, he took Mimi around to modeling agencies for tryouts, as a lark.
Another day, he brought her to the Town Hall Club, on West Forty-third
Street, where he drank Scotch at the bar. They were away from home for
five hours, and Rand was frantic when they returned. Frank remained
calm when she cried, "Where have you *been*? I thought you were dead!"

The curtain of Broadway's Biltmore Theater finally rose on *The Unconquered* on February 13, 1940, six weeks later than announced. The
first-night audience was packed with theatrical and film-world celebrities in tuxedos, evening gowns, and furs. Jagger gave an elegant opening-
night party while the cast and crew awaited the reviews. But the reaction
of critics was anything but festive, withholding from the play even the
faint praise that, at a minimum, they had bestowed on *The Night of January 16th*. The conservative *Herald Tribune*, which had applauded the
novel, called the play "one of the season's mishaps" and observed that it
was so clumsy as to confuse the audience about whether it might be *advocating* Bolshevik propaganda. *The New York Times* complained that it
did not delve deeply enough into the individual rights of man, where, the
reviewer wrote, "there would be a play." It's easy to imagine Rand's anger
and humiliation. She came home that night in tears and spent the next
two days in bed, despondent.

The Unconquered closed abruptly after a five-day run. It had not produced new royalties for her to live on and had in fact cost her money in
car fare, restaurant meals, and other out-of-pocket expenses. It had further damaged her literary reputation. And it had led the nation's premier
newspaper to blame her for neglecting the very message she had been
trying to deliver, one that she believed grew more urgent every day: safeguarding the individual against the majority, the mob, the collective, the
church, the state, the Soviet.

On February 18, the day after the final curtain fell and the cast dis-
banded, she resumed her work on *The Fountainhead*. For unknown rea-

sons, she left off again in May, a month before her second and final
Knopf due date. She may have been discouraged or depressed. One night
in early June, she recalled, she "felt so profound an indignation at the
state of things as they are that it seemed as if I would never regain the energy to move one step farther toward things as they ought to be," in the
shape of Howard Roark. "Frank talked to me for hours that night. He
convinced me of why one cannot give up the world to those one despises.
That night, I told Frank that I would dedicate *The Fountainhead* to him
because he had saved it."

At some point in 1938, Rand had written a letter, in Russian, to the
short-tenured former prime minister Aleksandr Kerensky, who was living
in exile in Paris and New York. Russia's last republican had not yet earned
her enduring enmity by publicly supporting Stalin during the Nazi invasion of Russia in 1941. She sent him a copy of *We the Living,* expressing
the hope that he would find in it a worthy portrait of his homeland at its
turning point. (Whether he responded is not known.) Now, in mid-1940,
she decided that she must take direct political action to prevent a similar
calamity at a crucial moment in the history of her adopted homeland. In
July, FDR won the Democratic Party's nomination for an unprecedented
third term in office, breaking an uninterrupted tradition of American pres-
idents serving for no more than two terms. A few weeks later, the Republicans nominated Wendell Willkie to oppose him, and she signed on to be
a foot soldier in the Republican presidential campaign. That fall, she took
to the hustings for Willkie. It was the beginning and end of her active political career.

Among conservatives in the late 1930s, FDR was viewed as a madman,
a traitor to his class, a warmonger maneuvering America into World
War II, and worse. It would be impossible to exaggerate how bitterly he
was hated. Many on the Right had voted for him in 1932, when he appeared to be fiscally conservative and friendly to business. Once in office, he declared a need for extreme measures to lift the nation out of the
Depression. He assumed large new presidential powers, transforming
the economy from a minimally regulated free-for-all into a federally regulated system that his adversaries regarded as European-style socialism.
He kept his promise to repeal Prohibition, but to the fury of some business interests and the political right, and the relief of many unemployed

and working people, he also established the first minimum hourly wage, guaranteed unions the right to bargain collectively, created Social Security and unemployment insurance, and enacted 550 separate regulatory codes that capped industrial production, set wages and prices, limited competition, and gave rise to government-backed manufacturing cartels, all of which Rand would parody to the verge of surrealism in *Atlas Shrugged*. Most threatening of all, perhaps, to her, he prohibited the private ownership of gold, which made it possible for the U.S. government, like the Bolshevik government of her teens and the Nazi regime then ruling Germany, to inflate the currency and, she thought, arbitrarily redistribute wealth from the rich to the poor. For her, the rise of the welfare state and a managed economy smacked of Fascism. It looked very much like a covert transfer of power from the old free capitalist class to a new all-powerful government elite.

It is debatable what influence the New Deal's economic policies had on any trend toward socialism in America; they may have helped to save capitalism from its hungry dependents, its doubters, and its organized adversaries by compromising with a mild form of collectivism. (Rand apparently never considered that one of Roosevelt's accomplishments may have been to stave off a Russian-style insurrection.) Still, the intrepid president was so deeply, if narrowly, hated that country-club Republicans swore he possessed every vice from Stalinism to syphilis (rumored to have been transmitted to him by the first lady, who got it "from a Negro").

When he ran for a third term, those who believed in minimal government and laissez-faire capitalism saw totalitarianism in the making. If he were to win, Rand and others believed, there might never be another federal election. America might turn to dictatorship, a notion that was not as fanciful then as it seems now, given that Hitler and Mussolini had risen to power through popular movements and were overrunning the free nations of Europe. By the summer of 1940, Nazi Germany and the Soviet Union, allies for the moment, had already invaded France, Poland, Norway, Belgium, the Netherlands, Finland, Lithuania, Estonia, and Latvia. As Rand knew, the next target was England, which was already being bombed by the Luftwaffe; Londoners were donning gas masks "against the worst madman the world has known," Lady Boileau wrote to her. Rand's childhood heroine, the little English girl who gunned down the German navy, was needed once again; although, since much of Europe had by now embraced a diluted form of socialism and because war always enhances governmental powers, Rand and other right-wingers also opposed the entry of the United States into the European conflict. They preferred to let Hitler march unimpeded into Russia and then enter the war against whichever dictator was left standing.

Wendell Willkie was not against American participation in the war, but he was an outspoken, clean-cut, and popular defender of business interests against the New Deal. An electric-utility holding-company president raised in Elwood, Indiana, he was a self-made businessman who inspired hope in the anti-Roosevelt forces. They especially admired his stirring speeches on the rights of property owners and the importance of industrial freedom to the continued prosperity of the country. Against Roosevelt's chilling declaration that "the old reliance on the free action of individual wills" was a relic of the past, he insisted that "only the strong can be free. And only the productive can be strong." Rand couldn't have agreed more. She seems not to have taken in his oft-repeated calls "to strike a balance between the rights of the individual and the needs of society."

While Ann Watkins and Blanche Knopf were working out an agreement to nullify her book contract, Rand and O'Connor reported each day to the National Willkie Clubs headquarters on West Fortieth Street, overlooking Bryant Park and the New York Public Library. She told a friend that working as a volunteer there wasn't a sacrifice but was an act of "pure selfishness," because she was fighting for her own ideas and the right to express them. At first, she typed while the dutiful O'Connor rang doorbells, but soon she was leading a political-research action team and making speeches. During much of the month of October she campaigned on street corners and in coffee shops; often, she manned the stage of an old, boarded-up East Fourteenth Street movie theater that Gloria Swanson, a fellow conservative, had rented to run Willkie campaign films. Following each of seven shows a day, she and sometimes Swanson spoke out against the New Deal and answered the audience's questions. "I was a marvelous propagandist," she later said. By all accounts, she mesmerized her audiences. She was especially good when challenged by hecklers. Once an onlooker shouted, "Who are you to talk about America? You're a foreigner!" to which she replied, in her raspy Russian accent, "I *chose* to be an American. What did *you* do, besides having been born?" She loved the give-and-take, and, as always, excelled at making abstractions understandable and complicated notions simple.

She met a larger number of interesting men and women during the campaign than she had ever met before, she told a friend, among them important members of the Old Right establishment. Gloria Swanson became a friend and political ally. Through Channing Pollock, an anti-Communist playwright and theater critic whom she met and liked, she got to know Albert Jay Nock, H. L. Mencken's eccentric friend, whose highly cultivated and unapologetically elitist books and essays had already given her several of the key ideas she was incorporating into *The Fountainhead;* Frank Chodorov, a staunch proto-libertarian magazine editor; George Sokolsky, a well-known conservative opinion maker and the son of Russian immigrants; John C. Gall, the chief attorney for the National Association of Manufacturers and, later, Big Steel; and the distinguished economist and public lecturer Ruth Alexander, who became Rand's lifelong friend and once called her (undoubtedly to her delight) "America's Joan of Arc." Through their influence, she read Carl Snyder's *Capitalism the Creator: The Economic Foundations of Modern Industrial Society* (1940), which set out to prove that free markets were the chief way societies moved from "barbarism and poverty to affluence and culture," and began to think more deeply about economics.

When Willkie lost the election in November, Rand experienced "violent" indignation. At first she blamed Willkie. She and her new associates perceived him as having knuckled under to Roosevelt's liberalism and backpedaled his way to defeat. No doubt they had overestimated his commitment to a program of free-market conservatism. In her disillusionment, she berated him. "Willkie was the guiltiest man of any for destroying America, more guilty than Roosevelt, who was only a creature of his time," she said, with a contrariness that would mark her developing public style.

Coming as it did on top of other serious setbacks, the Willkie loss proved a subtle turning point in her life. In the previous four years, after many early signs of success, her disappointments had mounted. She and Watkins had not succeeded in finding a producer for *Ideal* or an American publisher for *Anthem. We the Living* was out of print. *The Unconquered,* her first novel's unsightly stepsister, had gone from hoped-for moneymaker to critical fiasco and professional embarrassment. Her advanceless book contract had been canceled. All the while her subliminal awareness of her own, if not her husband's, slight restlessness in marriage was increasing. The years 1940 and 1941 ushered in a perma-

nently more severe, less open Rand. The adherent of reason acquired a
habit of turning weak or irresolute allies into enemies and doing so un-
flinchingly, with Russian flair.

For the time being, however, she thought of her fellow former Willkie
supporters as men and women of strong convictions. She and others
formed the Associated Ex–Willkie Workers Against Willkie and wrote
broadsides and letters to the editor ridiculing the luckless utilities executive and accusing him of aiding the U.S. Communist Party agenda.
What the country needed now, before it was too late, she told Channing
Pollock, was an organization of conservative intellectuals to frame and
promote a full-fledged ideology, or moral justification, of laissez-faire
capitalism—to do what Willkie had refused to do. She asked Pollock to be
its leader. He agreed. The first few meetings were held in offices around
town or in the O'Connors' most recent apartment, tucked into a slightly
scruffy building on East Forty-ninth Street and First Avenue, near where
the United Nations headquarters later rose. She and her husband had
moved there from the Upper East Side during the campaign, to save
money, and the following fall they would move again, this time to a sun-
less ground-floor apartment on East Thirty-fifth Street near Lexington Avenue. They were down to less than nine hundred dollars of her savings.

It was within this framework that Ayn Rand met Isabel Paterson, the
brainy, quirkily Christian fifty-four-year-old novelist and libertarian chief
book-review columnist for the *New York Herald Tribune*. Or, rather, how
she remet Paterson, for as soon as the columnist's name was mentioned
as a potential member of the group, Rand remembered having been introduced to her at a literary cocktail party in the spring of 1936, shortly
after the publication of *We the Living*. According to Paterson's biographer, Stephen Cox, the older woman didn't remember the encounter, although soon after it took place she mentioned Rand in her column.
Through a publicity handout, she had learned that the émigré author
had survived the Russian Revolution and had come away believing that
suffering was anything but noble and had no redeeming value. Paterson
casually but firmly disagreed. She thought that hardships could be instructive, especially for writers.

Cox describes Paterson as the literary world's most outspoken critic
of Roosevelt's policies. Her column of literary and political commentary
was widely read, and she was politically well connected. (For example,
her boss, the *Herald Tribune*'s stylish books editor Irita Van Doren, was

Wendell Willkie's longtime lover.) When she didn't respond to a printed invitation, Rand telephoned and made an appointment to see her at the *Herald Tribune*'s offices on West Forty-first Street. Paterson never joined organizations, she explained. But Rand impressed her. A couple of weeks later, Ann Watkins called to report that the older woman had been asking for Rand's phone number, and they met again. Rand liked her "enormously." Before long she was attending Paterson's regular Monday-night get-togethers in a dingy eleventh-floor cubbyhole at the *Tribune,* where half a dozen literary and political essayists and pundits, including *Time* magazine's Sam Welles and *Fortune*'s John Chamberlain, typically gathered to proofread the paper's weekly books section before it went to press. Between sets of proofs, Paterson led discussions on subjects ranging from books and gardening to capitalist economics and the American Articles of Confederation. Participants thought of these sessions as a conservative Round Table, comparing themselves to an earlier group of literary wits led by Dorothy Parker, Heywood Broun, and Alexander Woollcott that met at the Algonquin Hotel, a few blocks north of the *Herald Tribune.*

Rand tended to behave with old-world formality among political and professional acquaintances, but when Paterson invited her to spend a weekend in her rural Ridgefield, Connecticut, country house, without O'Connor, Rand uncharacteristically accepted—remarking later, after the two women had fallen out, that it was rude of Paterson not to have included Frank. Both night owls, they talked nonstop until dawn about philosophy and politics. Paterson had grown up among pioneers in the Canadian West and was widely and deeply acquainted with American history and theories of free-market economics. Her guest was less broadly read, and was fascinated by Paterson's views. Setting aside a hazy presentiment that Paterson might have a buried mystical streak (after all, who but a religious mystic would argue that suffering had an upside?), she was captivated and exhilarated by the older woman's explanations of judicial process and the measures the Founding Fathers took to protect minority rights against the will of a potentially tyrannical majority. Paterson had a theory about capitalism, that it operates like an expanding circuit of energy whose generating plant, or dynamo, is the individual who produces what he is best at and trades with other individuals who do the same; money acts as a signaling system that allows people to transmit their desires around the world and expand the circuit. Much of what

Rand learned from Paterson would find its way into the essays she was beginning to write, into the last two-thirds of *The Fountainhead,* and, in the use of energy circuits, motors, and power as metaphors for human action and achievement, into the structural motifs of *Atlas Shrugged.*

Rand later remarked that, at her best, Paterson exhibited a magnificent ability to make rapid-fire abstract associations, ferret out philosophical meanings, and, in contrast to almost everybody else, instantly understand what Rand was talking about. She had a "marvelous mind," Rand said, and Paterson returned the compliment by declaring that her new acquaintance was a genius, a word she rarely used, according to her friend and executor, Muriel Welles Hall. Paterson became Rand's closest friend since Olga Nabokov had abruptly left St. Petersburg and was her first and only living mentor. On scores of Monday nights, in phone calls, over dinner, and on many subsequent weekends in Connecticut (*with* O'Connor), Rand "sat at the master's feet," as Monday-evening habitué Sam Welles (Muriel's brother) later recalled. Mimi, on her summer sojourns with Rand and O'Connor in New York, was often present during her aunt's late-night conversations with Paterson. She recalled that the women would stay up talking until four or five o'clock in the morning. Rand asked the questions and Paterson answered them. It was as if the older woman were Rand's "guru and teacher," Mimi said, "and Ayn *didn't do that.*"

Paterson also learned from Rand, although partisans of both women debate what and how much. In one early discussion, they were affably arguing about how far it is possible to extend the ethical limits of Rand's philosophy of anti-altruism, or selfishness. Paterson asked the younger woman her opinion of a riddle she recalled from Boswell's *Life of Johnson.* Imagine that you are in a castle tower with a newborn baby in your arms, Paterson proposed, and only one of you can escape alive. Would you save your own life or that of the baby? Rand shocked Paterson into momentary silence by declaring that she would most certainly let the baby die. How could you ethically do that? Paterson demanded. Don't human beings have a moral obligation to care for the young? No, Rand answered. She held no such view, although she did concede that her analysis might be different if the baby were her own. When Paterson suggested that such an attitude could be considered depraved, Rand declared, Very well, then, I am depraved. For the time being, that ended the discussion. Later, Paterson brought it up again. What would you do if the baby *were* your own? Reflecting, Rand answered that she still would choose to save herself, on the premise that without an adult to feed and care for it, the baby would die anyway. Aha! replied Paterson, who evidently found this point of logic persuasive. Rand later claimed that by means of such instruction, she converted Paterson from an entrenched secular Christian ethic to a morality of anti-altruism. Paterson thanked Rand for the clarification of parental ethics but insisted that she had always believed in enlightened self-interest, and the preponderance of evidence is on her side.

If the women loved to debate, they also loved to laugh. They were both entertained by Rand's occasional malapropisms in her adopted language. Once she lamented "an ungulfable bridge." Another time she asked, "Will you write my autobiography? I can't do myself justice." Paterson adorned her columns with witty drawings of herself and friends or authors and once printed a sketch of Rand dashing across a street, hat ribbons flying, dragging behind her a man who looks a lot like O'Connor. "She is afraid of traffic," Paterson observed in the adjacent text, "because she was hit by a taxi once; and the way she shows it is to stand a minute at the crossing, viewing the stream of vehicles with alarm, seize the hand of her escort with a gesture of feminine terror, and then march ahead across the street, hauling her protector after her." Paterson was droll, and a shrewd judge of Rand's character.

Oddly, post-Willkie, Rand was getting a lot of writing done, though not on *The Fountainhead*. She produced three interesting items. In late 1940 or early 1941, she composed a bad-tempered open letter to conservatives who she thought were sitting on their hands and whom she hoped to persuade to join the active campaign she and Pollock were waging. She called it "To All Innocent Fifth Columnists." If conservatives didn't take immediate steps to oppose Roosevelt's war of socialist propaganda and halt his expansion of executive powers, she wrote, they, like Willkie, would be to blame for the coming totalitarian dictatorship of America. "Of such as you is the Kingdom of Hitler and Stalin," she added. The letter was far too rancorous to be used as a recruiting tool and was put away in a drawer. She also wrote a play, *Think Twice*. And she composed her first extended work of philosophical nonfiction, "The Individualist Manifesto," which she drafted as the organization's in-house mission statement. With it, she wanted to do for free-market capitalism what *The Communist Manifesto* had done for Communism.

Rand later said that *Think Twice* was written in three weeks, during the month of January 1941. An earnest, well-plotted whodunnit of ideas, the play is set in the Connecticut country house of a world-class "altruist" during a Fourth of July weekend party. His guests, all current beneficiaries of his largesse, hate him for the unacknowledged power he wields over their lives. One of them, hiding in the bushes, shoots and kills him. A local detective arrives to solve the crime. But the culprit, a physicist and business associate of the dead man, has planned a perfect murder: he's arranged all the evidence to point so obviously to himself that the detective in charge can't believe he's really guilty. The physicist's motive for killing: to stop the altruist from bestowing a potentially earth-destroying invention, a forerunner of Dr. Robert Stadler's apocalyptic sonic device in *Atlas Shrugged,* as a gift to a world filled with power-maddened dictators. Rand wanted to dramatize the bad intentions and dreadful effects of a second-handed humanitarian such as Roosevelt, but the murdered character also recalls her marginally sadistic mother, the woman who once donated her daughter's favorite toys to charity. The play renewed her old interest in science fiction. "You may be amused to note how prophetic I was," she wrote to an acquaintance in 1948. At the time of writing the play, "I had not heard or dreamed of the atom bomb." Again, the play did not find a publisher or a producer, but it helped the author to refine some of the "altruistic" stratagems that Ellsworth Toohey employs to blackmail and entrap characters such as Peter Keating.

Two months later, in April, she wrote "The Individualist Manifesto." The thirty-three-page polemical essay presented her moral philosophy in the fullness of its development at that time. It echoed and amplified *Anthem*'s closing cry for the sovereignty of the individual mind—"I am. I think. I will"—and anticipated the author's famous moral and political tracts of the 1960s.

The first thing right-thinking people must understand, she explained in the manifesto, is that man is an independent entity, an end unto himself, and never a means to an end. Since this is so, he has certain inalienable rights. These are not granted by any state, society, or collective, but rather they shield *against* all governments and societies. They constitute "Man's protection against all other men" and are absolute. They include the right to life, liberty, and the pursuit of happiness. Bloodthirsty tyrants throughout history have tried to strip men of their rights or lure them into giving up their rights on behalf of the poor, the fatherland, enhanced security, or the common good. Never has a despot confessed to seeking power for himself; he always claims to be serving some nobler purpose. *Caveat civis:* Those who tell you to give up your rights for the sake of someone or something else typically want to *be* that someone or something else.

Second, the government exists to protect your rights, and *only* to protect your rights; you do not exist to obey or serve the state. (In fact, citizens owe the government nothing, not even taxes; government funding should be by voluntary means.) As Communism proved, primary allegiance to the state was a recipe for slavery and stagnation. In fact, taking a leaf from Albert Jay Nock, Rand and Paterson both argued that governments have rarely contributed anything material or spiritual to humankind's development. Most governments have hounded geniuses to martyrdom. The sole affirmative function of the state is to safeguard individuals from one another so that they may create and work in peace.

Third, there is "and ever has been" one fountainhead of progress: the individual person in a state of political and economic freedom. This was the source of the wheel, the steam engine, the electric lightbulb, and all great music, art, and literature. Laissez-faire capitalism is the only system ever evolved to operate solely on the basis of individual human reason juxtaposed against an opportunity or a need, and as such must be thanked for 150 years of industrial creativity and material progress such as the world had never known.

Perhaps most important, capitalism, unlike Communism, doesn't demand the impossible. It doesn't ask people to turn themselves inside out and twist their desires into halos to serve its ends, as Communism does. Although free markets do benefit most men as a consequence of the phenomenal productivity they make possible, that is a side effect, she argued. Capitalism gives man's "natural, healthy egoism" the scope and freedom to allow him to enrich himself, if he so wishes—and as a result enriches others. "Selfishness is a magnificent force," she declared, arguing that not a single great genius has ever been motivated by a desire to help others or by anything other than a perfectly natural selfish commitment to his own ideas and vision. While this is debatable—later, even Rand sometimes seemed driven by a desire to guide others—it is an emotionally powerful rebuttal to the tenets of the dark, punitive Christianity and cynical Stalinism she abhorred.

Finally, capitalism doesn't serve the strong at the expense of the weak, as liberals claimed, for two reasons. First, the weak would never be able to create an equivalent level of progress or prosperity on their own, and they benefit from its creation by those more competent and motivated than themselves. Second, capitalism is a system of free and voluntary trade. Theoretically, no one is compelled to sell his labor or goods at, say, a fixed state price or to buy another's goods based on force. The flaws and abuses of capitalism are a result of the introduction of collectivist premises in the form of government regulation and favoritism, such as tax favoritism, as she would argue dramatically and in detail in *Atlas Shrugged*.

Although she had been intimate with Paterson for only a few months when she wrote the manifesto, the older woman's influence shows in the milder language and the egalitarianism of the essay. Two months earlier, "To All Innocent Fifth Columnists" had bullied and belittled almost as much as it had argued from principle. The manifesto proceeds in relative sweet reasonableness. She was clearly modifying her early Nietzschean belief in the native superiority and proud birthright of the best relative to ordinary men, which permeates her writing of the 1920s and 1930s. In the 1936 edition of *We the Living,* for example, the masses are "mud to be ground underfoot, fuel to be burned" for the sake of those who are gifted, according to Kira. In the manifesto, as in the last two-thirds of *The Fountainhead* and in *Atlas Shrugged,* heroes—i.e., the creators and producers of useful new goods and ideas—are to be judged by what they make and do, not by their station or native gifts. In late-night chats with Paterson, Rand was refining her understanding of a uniquely American brand of individualism, based on a commitment to the natural and equal rights of men. The heart of Americanism, she wrote, is the principle that "Man, each *single, solitary, individual man,* has a sacred value which [we] respect." In America, heroes are made, not born.

While Rand and Pollock were recruiting for their unnamed organization, Ann Watkins was doing her best to find a new publisher for *The Fountainhead*. She sent the author's outline and first few chapters to eight publishers, including Simon & Schuster; Harcourt Brace; Dodd, Mead; and Doubleday. This time there were no offers, although, as with *We the Living,* there were close calls. At Doubleday, after an encouraging luncheon with editors, Rand and Watkins returned to the agent's office to learn that a Mr. Thompson had vetoed the editors' consensus to publish the book—a "bad" disappointment for Rand, she said. At Simon & Schuster, an executive tried to prove the firm's conservative credentials by boasting that it had published the work of Leon Trotsky, Lenin's more "democratic" former sidekick. With his love of democracy thus established, he rejected *The Fountainhead*. Rand found this episode funny, akin to being spurned by a cartoon character, she said.

But Watkins was losing patience. Like Jean Wick, she began to display some peevishness. The book might sell if only the characters were more human, she complained to Rand. Why couldn't they *do* something, instead of talking all the time? And why did Roark have to be so stiff and unsympathetic? Poor, exasperated Watkins, a link in a long chain of doubters past and future, may have been right about Roark but sadly missed the point. The tale of the architect is fundamentally an allegory of good and evil; it takes place in a sealed world where ethical and psychological ideas, not plausible characters, serve as glue. What Watkins was trying to say was that Roark is a character without inner conflicts, a fact that makes him seem two-dimensional and at times inhuman. As the ideal man, Rand would have answered, Roark can have no doubts or conflicts. For her, mixed emotions were a sign of faulty thinking. Her hero's values, emotions, and actions flow in a unified stream from the fountainhead of his creative values. Here, moral integrity is forceful, ruthless, and erotic.

Rand, in turn, had come to doubt Watkins's reliability. She had not forgotten the debacle of *We the Living* at Macmillan, nor the time spent on projects her agent had encouraged her to write but couldn't sell. As for *The Fountainhead*, at first Watkins had been enthusiastic—so much so that before the Knopf contract came along she had gaily promised that she could get an advance on the book anytime Rand ran out of money. That promise had turned out to be unfounded. Now Rand conjectured that Watkins was embarrassed by it and wanted to find someone else to blame for her inability to fulfill it—namely, Rand. She also guessed that the agent was talking about her behind her back, secretly criticizing her to others.

The showdown came one day when Watkins mused aloud that there was simply something wrong with the novel. She didn't know what. Name it, Rand demanded. Watkins couldn't name it and, furthermore, was fed up with being asked to give reasons for things she knew by instinct to be true. She added that Rand's inflexibility about the book was making it impossible to sell. At this point, the women hung up on each other and the relationship was severed, either because Watkins resigned in protest, as Rand suggested in a letter, or because Rand abruptly broke off with her, which is what Rand later told a friend. The letter, written to the agent on the afternoon of the dispute, was conciliatory but not apologetic. "Even *instincts* have reasons behind them," she pleaded. "Words, thoughts, reasons—if we drop them we will have nothing left. . . . If you really meant what you said, 'Let us try to clear up [our differences]'—let's try to do that," she concluded. Watkins didn't respond by letter, and it's not clear whether she responded at all. Although she continued to handle business transactions concerning *The Night of January 16th* and *We the Living,* Rand had lost a champion and a friend as well as her sales representative for *The Fountainhead.* She had no publisher, no agent, no money.

In truth, there weren't many business transactions for an agent to handle. Royalties from *The Night of January 16th* had slowed to a trickle. *We the Living* was out of print. Even with a cheaper apartment and pared-down expenses, Rand urgently needed money. Before the rupture, Watkins had sent the completed chapters of *The Fountainhead* to Richard Mealand, the head of the New York office of Paramount Pictures, who sometimes bought unpublished stories for the screen. Mealand couldn't persuade his Hollywood bosses to buy the novel in progress, but he was electrified by what he read, according to Rand. In the late spring of 1941, she went to see him. Still unable to find screenwriting assignments, she asked for work as a freelance reader. He hired her on the spot. Her job was to evaluate the film potential of about-to-be-published books and stories—the same work she had done during her early months with Cecil B. DeMille. Her pay ranged from six dollars for a short evaluation to twenty-five dollars for a long one. She was a slow reader and worked twelve hours a day, seven days a week, to earn as much as she could. Mealand and his assistant, Frances Hazlitt, wife of the distinguished free-market economist and journalist Henry Hazlitt, were touched to see that she was not in the least above her job but was unusually conscientious and hardworking. They took her under their wing, into their social circle, and gave her all the work they could find.

Although she and Pollock continued to try to stitch together a conservative advocacy organization, meetings tapered off and the recruiting slowed. To her astonishment, many potential members reacted to her

manifesto as if it were written in an unfamiliar language. Her placid definitions of individualism (a political philosophy that holds each man to
be "an independent entity" who cannot be deprived of his rights for any
reason) and of collectivism (the subjugation of the individual to a group)
proved surprisingly controversial. She began to see that Willkie wasn't
the only cloudy thinker on the Right. While she wasn't ready to dismiss
all self-styled conservatives as hopeless traitors, the way she later did, the
right-leaning, post-Willkie journalists and businessmen she was meeting struck her as anti-intellectual and smug. She faced the prospect of
educating them before they could educate the public. The thought was
wearying. She lost interest.

Ever after, she remembered the 1940 campaign and its aftermath as
harsh, exhausting, and gloomy—her own real-life descent into the granite quarry to hack out a livelihood from stone.

It was also a frightening moment in world history. In September
1941, the Nazis, having invaded Russia, launched a nine-hundred-day
bombardment and blockade of Leningrad (as St. Petersburg was then
called), in which as many as a million people died of gunshot wounds, illness, and starvation; she had no way of knowing whether her parents and
sisters were alive and able to feed themselves. At the end of September,
when the Nazis occupied Kiev in the Soviet Ukraine, soldiers slew almost thirty-four thousand Jews in the massacre at Babi Yar; in the same
month Germany began constructing the gas chambers at Auschwitz.
New tyrants were reenacting old atrocities, and no one knew whether
they could be stopped. Personally, Rand felt powerless, although she
characteristically expressed her powerlessness in anger and self-pity. "If
I were a defender of Communism, I'd be a Hollywood millionaire by
now, with a swimming pool and a private orchestra to play 'The Interna-
tionale,'" she wrote to a businessman acquaintance in September. She
referred to herself as a proletarian capitalist. Mostly, she yearned for the
resources to return to work on *The Fountainhead* as another person
might long for a vacation.

Then, seemingly out of nowhere, hope appeared. According to the
account she later gave to friends and followers, she had purposely not
told Mealand that her literary agent had decamped or that the chapters
he had read were gathering dust on her desktop. She didn't want him to
think she was desperate for help. But he found out and insisted on introducing her to a few of his Paramount publishing contacts. After a

false start with Little, Brown and Company, he and she decided to approach a bright young man who had just been hired as chief editor in the New York office of the Indiana-based Bobbs-Merrill Company. Earlier that year, Bobbs-Merrill had published a now-classic book-length exposé called *The Red Decade: The Stalinist Penetration of America,* by United Press's former Moscow correspondent Eugene Lyons. It had kicked up a storm of angry controversy on the Left. That impressed Rand. Mealand made a phone call, and she dropped off the manuscript of *The Fountainhead* at the Bobbs-Merrill office on Park Avenue and Thirty-first Street, where she met the new young editor, Archibald Ogden. She noted, skeptically, that his dress was collegiate and his manner overly "palsy." He reminded her of Peter Keating.

Just as with Rand's first encounter with Cecil B. DeMille, there is another version of this story. The estimable Muriel Hall, Isabel Paterson's executor, who worked for decades as a research editor at *Time* and *Life,* recalled Paterson's having told her proudly that it was she, Paterson, who provided Rand with an introduction to Ogden at Bobbs-Merrill. "Pat had contacts there, and she could bludgeon people," Hall said. "She told [Ogden] that he *had* to publish that book, and he did. I don't think Rand ever credited her with that." Perhaps Rand didn't know of Paterson's efforts, or perhaps both accounts are true; Mealand and Paterson may each have helped to propel the book to print. In any case, in letters and biographical interviews from 1960 and 1961, Rand didn't mention receiving support from her friend. Hall was certain that Paterson could not have made it up. "She was not given to bragging. She was absolutely straight arrow, factual," Hall said.

Within a week of receiving the manuscript, Ogden telephoned. He had read her chapters. He thought they were "great writing in the tradition of real literature," he told her. He listed the things he liked most: the ambitious theme, the emblematic characterizations, the brilliant writing, the heroic sensibility. Since it was for exactly these qualities that she most wanted to be admired, she prized Ogden's compliments for the rest of her life. He went to bat for the book with his boss, D. L. Chambers, the president of Bobbs-Merrill in Indianapolis. When Chambers wired him to reject the book, he wired back: "If this is not the book for you, then I am not the editor for you." Chambers responded: "Far be it from me to dampen such enthusiasm. Sign the contract. But the book better be good."

Ogden's second congratulatory phone call came at ten o'clock one wintry morning when Rand had been up all night typing a rush report for Paramount. She listened, breathless, and hung up the phone. Then she left the apartment on East Thirty-fifth Street to deliver the report to Paramount. Mealand and Frances Hazlitt were on hand to congratulate her. Since Ogden hadn't been able to talk his famously frugal boss into paying the full $1,200 advance she had requested to meet expenses, they also pledged their continuing support; they promised to give her weekend reading assignments until the book was finished.

At home that evening, she probably danced around the living room with Frank and Nick to one of her old-world recordings; the German march song "Marionettes at Midnight" was her favorite at the time. All her adult life, whenever she was happy, she put an old 78 rpm disc on the record player, waved her arms, and stomped about, pretending to be conducting an orchestra—typically, to the beat of a light-hearted waltz, a European operetta, or a march remembered from her childhood, recordings of which she had carried with her from St. Petersburg to Chicago, to Los Angeles, and back to New York. During celebrations she also liked to place funny hats on her pet stuffed lion cubs, Oscar and Oswald, a gift from O'Connor soon after their marriage. Friends often remarked that she seemed startlingly childish in her pleasure. But then, in many ways, she remained a demanding and entitled child.

On December 10, 1941, three days after the Japanese bombed the American naval base at Pearl Harbor and catapulted the nation into World War II, she signed a contract with Bobbs-Merrill. She promised to deliver *The Fountainhead,* two-thirds of which remained to be written, in a little more than a year's time. She received an advance of one thousand dollars. Her new due date was January 1, 1943.

In spite of the war, now began the happiest year of Ayn Rand's life, she later said. This time, she was determined to meet her deadline; the more vehement and explosive parts of the story were yet to be written, and she didn't want to give her new publisher an excuse for backing out. If she did, there might not be another chance. She set to work like "a writing engine" on a tour de force that would change the American cultural landscape.

All her life, Rand displayed a mental capacity for work that few could equal. But her youthful physical inertia never left her; she avoided exercise, gained weight easily, and lacked the bodily stamina to keep pace with her penetrating mind and her ambitions. In 1942, with a pressing deadline before her, she began to take amphetamines, probably Benzedrine, which was still relatively new on the market and was easily available in pill form with a doctor's prescription. In mild doses, amphetamines improve temper and self-confidence, enhance energy and mental acuity, reduce appetite, and stave off sleep. Over time or in larger doses, they can lead to mood swings, irritability, uncontrolled emotional outbursts, impaired judgment, and paranoia, all of which Rand was susceptible to without chemical assistance. During the final months of composing her breakthrough novel, the drug seems to have worked well for her; allied with an indomitable will to succeed and renewed hope, amphetamines made it possible for her to write both day and night. She sometimes didn't go to bed at all; for two or three days running she would take catnaps on the couch in her clothes, then get up and resume writing. For appointments outside the apartment, she would make herself "clean and respectable." Once she worked for thirty hours straight, pausing only to eat the meals that Nick and Frank prepared.

Rand continued to write in longhand and to read aloud to the O'Connor brothers, who would sometimes suggest American expressions or idiomatic bits of dialogue. Then she would expertly type her new pages, making alterations based on how they sounded. She regularly consulted Paterson, too, particularly about her characters' speeches. Among other suggestions the older woman made was one to eliminate explicit references to Hitler, Stalin, Fascism, Nazism—to all contemporary history. "The theme of your book is wider than the politics of the moment," Paterson told her. "You are really writing about collectivism—any past, present, or future form of it." This was excellent advice, and Rand took it, not only in *The Fountainhead* but also in *Atlas Shrugged*. The novels' timeless, almost mythical atmosphere is surely one of the reasons for their enduring popularity.

Rand depended on Nick to help proofread pages as they rolled from her typewriter. When working hours ended, he sat into the night and discussed the day's progress with her. Although she cherished Frank's intuitive and sympathetic grasp of her viewpoint and intentions, she valued Nick's more nuanced reaction to developments of plot, character, literary technique, and, most importantly, style. Rand's grasp of the American idiom was still spotty. According to the O'Connors' friend Millicent Patton, Nick claimed that he had even written some of the novel's dialogue—

the light party banter and repartee; Patton added that Nick would occasionally stop by and show her draft pages with his contributions. What seems at least equally likely is that Frank and Nick suggested or corrected her dialogue and pointed out opportunities for humor.

In the first draft of *The Fountainhead* on file at the U.S. Library of Congress, her handwriting changed in 1942; as the year progressed, where it had been fairly large, loopy, and legible it became rushed and cramped, possibly as an effect of the amphetamines. She stayed in, chain-smoked cigarettes, and sped through complex scenes illuminating Roark's setbacks and victories, his friendships and betrayals, his contorted love affair, and finally his acquittal at trial. She dated her chapters, and her velocity and precision seem almost unbelievable. Whereas it had taken her years to plan and compose the first third of the novel, over the twelve months of 1942 she averaged a chapter a week. When her scrawled sentences were typed, the pacing flew and there were few corrections.

On July 4, 1942, she began part 4, the final section of *The Fountainhead*. It opens with a boy who has recently finished college and wants to compose music happening upon a beautiful summer resort in the grassy Monadnock Valley of Pennsylvania. The resort has not yet opened and is uninhabited and lovely. Roark has designed and built it. The boy, gazing at the small, gemlike glass houses and gardens falling over natural fieldstone ledges, sees that architecture can be a kind of music in stone and gains courage from its perfection to pursue his own vocation, much as Rand had once found inspiration in Victor Hugo. Of the months Roark and his workmen have spent building the resort—which has been financed by swindlers hoping to lose money—Rand wrote a description that must also have characterized her own experience in 1942. "The year at Monadnock Valley remained in [Roark's and the workers'] minds as the strange time when the earth stopped turning and they lived through twelve months of spring. . . . They remembered only the feeling which is the meaning of spring—one's answer to the first blades of grass, the first buds on tree branches, the first blue of the sky—the singing answer, not to grass, trees and sky, but to the great sense of beginning, of triumphant progression, of certainty in an achievement that nothing will stop." In the resort's first season, it becomes a phenomenal success, to the shock and ruination of its crooked backers.

Her work with Channing Pollock placed indefinitely on hold, her admirer Albert Mannheimer having left New York to pursue a screenwriting career in Hollywood, she saw almost no one that year, apart from the O'Connor brothers and Isabel Paterson. Paterson, too, was finishing a book, her first and only work of nonfiction, an eccentric individualist history of America called *The God of the Machine;* now largely forgotten, it was influential in its time. Like *The Fountainhead, The God of the Machine* was scheduled for publication in the spring of 1943. The two friends, who talked by phone most nights, entered into a good-natured competition to see who could finish first. Paterson appears to have won by a week or two. Her prose recalls the somberness of a moment when America was not yet assured of winning World War II. "Whoever is fortunate enough to be an American citizen," she wrote in her final paragraph, "came into the greatest inheritance man has ever enjoyed. . . . If Americans should now turn back, submit again to slavery, it would be a betrayal so base the human race might better perish."

The human race had no need to perish yet, for Rand had also finished *The Fountainhead* on time. The principle of individual freedom was alive and well, with a new hero for freedom-loving people to emulate. On the novel's closing page, Roark's almost-completed skyscraper rises as an emblem of the independent mind in action. To both Rand and her heroine, Dominique, who stands at the building's base, the sight is as thrilling as the male principle itself. The tower springs and thrusts. It "breaks through the clay, the iron, the granite" of the earth and, carrying the earth's fire to the surface, "shoots out to freedom." As Dominique boards a construction elevator and rides skyward to join her new husband at the pinnacle, she floats above the world's greatest city's busy merchant banks, gaudily decorated movie theaters, and solemn church spires until "there was only the ocean, the sky, and the figure of Howard Roark." So ends *The Fountainhead.* So began Rand's life of fame.

SEVEN

MONEY

1943

Many words have been granted me, and some are wise, and some are false, but only three are holy: "I will it!"

—Anthem, 1938

Sales of *The Fountainhead* got off to a slow start. The 754-page novel was delivered to bookstores on May 7, 1943. Much of the first printing of 7,500 copies remained unsold on bookstore shelves throughout the summer.

Reviewers were hostile or, at best, bewildered. The first important review of the novel appeared in *The New York Times* on May 12, five days after publication, and was written by the *Times*'s acid-tongued daily book critic, Orville Prescott. Prescott appeared to be battling his own fascination with the author's "concentrated intellectual passion" (for the profession of architecture, he thought), flair for melodrama, and "grotesquely peculiar characters" in what amounted to a giddy denunciation of the book. "Miss Rand must have a hidden dynamo of superhuman energy purring inside her head," he offered. "Her book is so highly charged it seems to vibrate and emit a shower of sparks." Unfortunately, he continued, the sparks lighted up a fictional world of such "dirty, crawling" malice, animal lust, lechery, and twisted conspiracies that the Marquis de Sade, Cesare Borgia, and Adolf Hitler would all feel at home there. In the end, he declared, the plot and characters were on a par with a grade-B Boris Karloff movie. The best that could be said for the book was that its setting suggested a path for new and better novels about architecture.

Rand never commented publicly on this review, but it must have kindled both fury and fear, especially because positive prepublication buzz had led her to expect intelligent, or at least intelligible, commentary. More cause for distress quickly followed. The *Chicago Daily Tribune,* among many out-of-town newspapers, endorsed the novel but also mistook it for a story about architecture. At Isabel Paterson's paper, the *New York Herald Tribune,* a mysterious unnamed conservative female writer refused to review it, Paterson told Rand, and Irita Van Doren assigned the book to Albert Guerard, later a celebrated professor of English at Stanford University. He angered Rand by identifying Roark with Nietzsche's Superman and by placing himself warily on either side of the fence, as she colorfully put it. (Whoever the mysterious female refusenik was, Rand exclaimed to Paterson, she deserved to be damned for letting Guerard get his hands on *The Fountainhead.* Some years later this review would become a bitter point of reference in an escalating quarrel between the women.) Diana Trilling, writing for *The Nation,* was positively indignant, calling the book "an orgy of glorification" of the building trades and of their ten-foot-tall, flame-haired, capital-G Genius Howard Roark. Mrs. Trilling spoke for many reviewers when she wrote, "Anyone who is taken in by [*The Fountainhead*] deserves a stern lecture on paper rationing."

Unknown to Mrs. Trilling, a scarcity of paper, if not actual wartime rationing, had played an active part in the publication of *The Fountainhead.* Shortly after the Japanese attack on Pearl Harbor, which took place three days before Bobbs-Merrill signed Rand's contract, the U.S. government warned of coming civilian shortages of everything from gasoline to wood fiber as it mobilized the army. If the book contract had been delayed by a week, Rand's editor, Archibald Ogden, later confided to her, the company would have canceled the contract; it couldn't have guaranteed access to the paper to print such an unusually long novel, given its other publishing commitments. As it was, shortages partly explain a riddle of the novel's structure: why the alluring Dominique Francon doesn't appear until late in chapter 9, when, as Rand well knew, the rules of melodrama call for a love interest to be present from the start. To save paper, she had voluntarily cut out about a third of the manuscript before it went to press, eliminating, among other things, an early sexual liaison between Roark and a young stage actress named Vesta Dunning. Dunning's hunger for adulation mirrored Gail Wynand's drive for popular influence, she decided, and so was thematically repetitive. Besides, she reflected, Roark's affair with Dunning—which also included a "rape" scene—diluted the intensity of his relationship with Dominique. Yet because there had been no time to rewrite chapters 1 through 9, the disappearance of the stage actress left a romantic gap. As a result, Rand always thought that the first quarter of the novel read more slowly than the rest.

Paper scarcity may also have contributed to the slow pace of the novel's climb to best-sellerdom. Until the war in Europe ended in the spring of 1945, Rand regularly protested that Bobbs-Merrill was assigning too much paper to other books and not enough to hers and that the policy of allotting equal proportions of paper to all books slowed shipments of *The Fountainhead* to bookstores, sabotaged sales, and kept her off the regional best-seller lists. "What about our other authors?" Bobbs-Merrill's production department exclaimed. That was their problem, she replied. *The Fountainhead* was *her* book, *her* chance, and she wasn't going to let it slip by out of an ill-conceived concern for others, whose books, she conjectured, were less important and had less potential than her own. At one point, she hired an attorney and hinted that she might sue. As often in these matters, her reasoning made sense if you accepted her assumptions—in this case, that the practice of rewarding (others') need rather than (her) excellence was tantamount to socialism and exemplified a second-hander's way of avoiding making a literary or a business judgment. But her manner did not win her friends.

The single most perceptive review of *The Fountainhead* appeared on May 16, 1943, in the Sunday edition of *The New York Times*. Archibald Ogden telephoned Rand in her apartment on East Thirty-fifth Street to read the review aloud to her. She didn't want to hear it, she told him; she had already seen and heard enough. He answered that she would be happy to hear this. The reviewer was Lorine Pruette, a psychologist, a former Smith College professor, and an early feminist writer. She not only praised *The Fountainhead* as a masterful and thrilling tour de force;

she predicted that it would cause all thoughtful readers to re-evaluate their basic attitudes about the pressing issues of the day. Calling the prose brilliant, beautiful, and bitter, she wrote, "Good novels of ideas are rare at any time. This is the only novel of ideas written by an American woman that [I] can recall." Unlike Prescott and others, she understood the theme. It was not architecture. It was the inherent nobility of the autonomous individual as he defies collective power. "Rand has taken her stand against collectivism, 'the rule of the second-hander, that ancient monster,' " Pruette wrote. "She has written a hymn in praise of the individual." The psychologist identified Ellsworth Toohey as an illustration of the Fascist mind in action. She cited key passages from Roark's defining courtroom speech, which deeply pleased Rand. Most important, she was not afraid to call attention to a controversial political and philosophical issue, collectivism, risking disapprobation by the outspoken left.

Rand later said that Pruette's review had saved her world. It was the first to refer to individualism, a concept she passionately wanted to see discussed in print. Only by explicit reference to it could she hope to reach "my kind of readers," she told a friend, echoing her father's phrase in tribute to her. At that historical moment—after the Hitler-Stalin Pact had come apart and Stalin was marshaling millions of men to fight German troops on Soviet soil—the Soviet Union was an official military ally of the United States and the Roosevelt administration had taken to promoting it as a freedom-loving friend. To criticize collectivism or publicly advocate capitalism or even civil liberties was at best to commit a social gaffe, she said, and chronicles of the period bear her out. To her mind, a fear of retaliation or rebuke was the only plausible reason for reviewers to be silent about her theme. Her message was so overstated, she remarked to a business acquaintance ("it's practically in every line"), that critics had to make a deliberate decision to ignore it. All the more reason to laud Pruette.

Once *The New York Times* had identified the novel's theme, other publications gradually took it up. By the end of the war, all forms of government collectivism had permanently lost much of their popular appeal and would, in fact, become a political taboo, and "individualism" would re-enter the language of respectable discourse—chiefly, Rand suggested, as a result of her efforts and Paterson's to keep the word alive.

She was not a timid propagandist. Nevertheless, it took half a decade before most readers of *The Fountainhead* consciously noticed that it was a tract as well as a story.

What drove demand for the book, at least at first, was the titillating sex, along with the contrarian spectacle of a red-blooded American hero serenely blowing up a Depression-era public housing project. At lunch counters and cocktail parties, in beauty parlors and at bridge games, Dominique's masochism and Roark's triumphant selfishness became topics of electrified debate among both men and women. Not since Theodore Dreiser's *Sister Carrie* had bad behavior been so gleefully rewarded by an author.

While sales still stalled, however, Rand was understandably irritated with her publisher for the few small, conventional ads it took out for the book, and Ogden lacked the power to persuade the ad department to take a bolder tack. So she decided to raise private money for an ad campaign focused on her *ideas*. The day after Pruette's review appeared, she mailed a copy of it to DeWitt Emery, president of the Pittsburgh-based National Small Business Men's Association and an early supporter of her suspended political organization. She asked him to endorse her cause with potential donors, since, she argued, greater sales of *The Fountainhead* would benefit all political conservatives. The public mood "is going our way," she argued, but the nation's influential intellectuals had imposed a blockade against the dissemination of conservative ideas. *The Fountainhead* provided the heavy artillery to overpower the blockade. Novels moved people emotionally first and intellectually second, she explained to Emery, and this made them the most compelling kind of propaganda. She knew this because she had witnessed the power of nineteenth-century novels to transform her native country and provoke revolution. American Reds also knew it, she argued, which explained why they were so "savagely" bent on maintaining their hold over the creators and purveyors of ideas in Hollywood and New York. In case anyone suspected that she was trying to line her pockets through accelerated sales, she offered to turn over a share of her royalties to all donors until every dollar spent had been repaid.

She couldn't fund the campaign herself because she was again out of money. Her thousand-dollar advance from Bobbs-Merrill had long since disappeared into rent, groceries, and an occasional cafeteria dinner. Although by midsummer *The Fountainhead* was already moving toward the black side of the ledger, she would have to wait to collect any royalties until a six- to nine-month accounting period had passed. At the invitation of Richard Mealand and Frances Hazlitt, she went back to work full time at Paramount.

In her spare hours, she set up luncheon meetings with Emery's friends and others who could, if persuaded, give or lend her the ten thousand dollars she estimated she needed to advertise the book. Despite the power of her arguments, her lunch companions were hard-pressed to believe that a novel—especially, perhaps, one written by a woman—could advance their cause against the monster Roosevelt. After months of crusading, including arranging for an intermediary's approach to the du Pont family, her only prospective donor was a Kalamazoo, Michigan, fishing-tackle manufacturer named Monroe Shakespeare. This first experience with fund-raising added a crust of bitter personal disappointment to her disenchantment with Republican conservatives.

During this period, O'Connor was determined to help out. He found a job as a sales clerk in a cigar store, probably earning the New Deal–mandated minimum wage of thirty cents an hour, and another job selling shoes. Able, self-effacing, charming, and droll, he endeared himself to the shoe-store owner, who asked him to stay on as a manager. He might have accepted and excelled at the job had Rand's fortunes not quickly changed. At the moment, however, financial hardship, anxiety over the fate of *The Fountainhead,* and embarrassment at (as she saw it) hawking her book to anti-intellectual businessmen reinforced her feeling of living in "a gray desert." For a time, she practiced lowering her expectations. She told Isabel Paterson that if *The Fountainhead* stopped selling—if it went the way of *We the Living*—she would resign herself to working at a dead-end job and writing only at night, for future generations. That would be her life. When Paterson, herself the author of eight moderately successful novels as well as *The God of the Machine,* asked why Rand was placing so much emphasis on a single book, the younger woman replied that she considered *The Fountainhead* to be so good that if *it* didn't sell she could hope for nothing further from this culture in her lifetime.

Paterson mulled this over and followed up, perhaps during a vacation she persuaded Rand and O'Connor to take at her Connecticut country house in July; Rand had been working much too hard and needed a rest, Paterson told her. The novelist was grateful. In her fifties, she would tell an admirer that those two weeks were the only formal vacation she had ever taken; she didn't mention her childhood trips to the Baltic Sea or the Black Sea in summer, as, by that time, she avoided mentioning anything about her Russian past. Paterson asked what it would take to convince her that *The Fountainhead* was a success. "A sale of one hundred thousand copies," Rand immediately replied, watching as a look of disbelief crossed Paterson's face. No doubt the more experienced writer thought the younger woman's expectations bordered on lunacy and invited further disappointment. Very few books sell that well, Paterson pointed out.

But the determined novelist, who had clearly given the issue some thought, insisted that nothing short of such a sale could guarantee that she had reached the right minds in the country—a group very much resembling Albert Jay Nock's famous concept of "the Remnant," a model of political deliverance he introduced in a famous essay called "Isaiah's Job," published in 1936. Nock, doubtful that pandering to the public at large would ever win large numbers of people over to his conservative viewpoint, conjured a conservative Remnant made up of a scattered, chosen few in every generation who would stand fast against the fickle masses and build a new society when the old one crumbled. This, of course, is practically a summary of Rand's next novel, *Atlas Shrugged*. In any case, Rand eventually won the argument. One hundred thousand copies of *The Fountainhead* would be sold in 1945 alone.

By now, in spite of occasional bickering, Rand and Paterson had designated each other "sisters" in a figurative family of shared values and personal grit. "Really, those women were enormously brave," Paterson's old friend Muriel Hall reflected in 2004. In the 1940s, "they were given the cold shoulder by almost everyone they met—they were *scorned*" by the great majority of liberals, she said. So they championed each other. During the year 1943, Paterson favorably mentioned *The Fountainhead* and its creator eight times in her weekly *Herald Tribune* books column. She advised her "little sister [from] St. Petersburg" how to manage business disputes with Bobbs-Merrill over delayed press runs and paperback reprint rights, especially after the summer of 1943, when Ogden left the company to lead the Council on Books in Wartime. Rand, in turn, praised *The God of the Machine* to every influential conservative she met, even sending a long letter to Paterson's editor, Earle Balch, at G. P. Putnam's Sons, urging him to get behind what she assured him was the most important book in centuries. Sounding like the nineteenth-century Russian intellectual she essentially was, she wrote, "It takes a book to save or destroy the world." Putnam might well have filed her letter under "agitator" or "eccentric," as her own publisher was beginning to be inclined to do.

In late fall, 1943, sales of *The Fountainhead* began to rise dramatically. Readers had begun to tell one another about the tale of lust and defiance they had read, and other readers bought the book. By Thanksgiving, after two hurried new printings by the Bobbs-Merrill Company, eighteen thousand copies were in readers' hands, an impressive sale for a novel by a little-known author.

D. L. Chambers, Bobbs-Merrill's budget-conscious president, in town from Indianapolis, phoned and asked Rand to meet him for lunch. Observing that sales had gained momentum, he proposed a deal. If she would agree to waive a scheduled increase in her royalties, from 10 percent to 15 percent after the ten-thousandth copy had been sold, he would match the money she gave up and use the entire sum to fund a new, more dramatic ad campaign. The Bobbs-Merrill ads would run for a month or two, he told her, after which time the company would restore her higher royalty rate. She agreed. This was what she wanted—to increase advertising of her book.

A day or two later, a Warner Bros. story editor phoned her at home. Earlier in the week he had been in touch with Bobbs-Merrill, he said, and when he inquired who was in charge of movie rights for *The Fountainhead* he had been referred to her. She immediately passed him along to her new literary agent, Alan Collins, president of Curtis Brown, Ltd. But a suspicion that Mr. Chambers had known about a possible movie deal when he invited her to lunch and had calculated the advantages of proposing a joint effort before she found out about it, too, arose and took hold. She made a note to add this possible deception to a growing list of grievances against Bobbs-Merrill.

Grievances, however, were not much on her mind in late 1943. Mr. Chambers was preparing bold new full-page ads for placement in newspapers, she wrote happily to Paterson, who was on vacation. More surprising, Warner Bros. seemed to be serious about making an offer for the book. Alan Collins, who had demonstrated his good judgment by approaching her to initiate a business relationship after reading an advance copy of *The Fountainhead,* was conducting negotiations. The sticking point was Rand's asking price: $50,000. This, Collins told her, was an unrealistic—a fantastic—sum. True, the great Ernest Hemingway had recently been paid $150,000 for movie rights to his best-selling novel *For Whom the Bell Tolls.* But Dashiell Hammett, the author of *The Maltese Falcon, The Thin Man,* and other box-office hits, got only $25,000 for *The Glass Key.* Six months after publication, there were not likely to be any competing offers to drive up the price. He advised her to ask for $25,000 and settle for $20,000.

Although $20,000 represented years of living expenses at the O'Connors' current rate of spending, Rand staunchly told him no. She explained her reasons. In the 1930s, Universal Pictures and MGM, respectively, had bought and then traded or resold the rights to *Red Pawn* and *The Night of January 16th.* Both studios had made a hefty profit. She had been pleased to discover that her work was worth so much. But she was a mature writer now and did not want to put too small a price on *The Fountainhead.* She was sure that it would soon be worth much more than she was asking.

Ten days later, to everyone's amazement, except Rand's perhaps, Warner Bros. made the hoped-for offer: $50,000. As part of the purchase price, the studio wanted her to travel to Hollywood to write the preliminary screenplay from the novel. It would pay round-trip fare, for both her and O'Connor, and estimated that the job would take a month. In the event it took longer, the studio would pay her $500 a week for every additional week she worked; this was a good rate for a largely untested screenwriter, and she was impressed with Collins for negotiating it into the contract. If Hollywood had earlier blackballed her as an outspoken anti-Communist, it was pursuing her now. The hitch was that Warner Bros. had no obligation to use her preliminary screenplay, and it could assign the writing of the final script to anyone it chose. It could cast Margaret Dumont as Dominique and Gabby Hayes as Roark. It could do anything it pleased. Rand, knowing how bad it could become, agreed. If she did a good job, she hoped the studio would hire her to write the final script. At worst, the publicity from the movie would help to sell the book.

Collins delivered the good news early one afternoon while Rand was at lunch with a proper old businessman who had no intention of writing a check to raise advertising funds for her continuing campaign. When she got back to the apartment, tired and downcast, her husband was waiting in the dimly lit living room, a peculiar look on his face. "Well, darling," he said, after a dramatic pause, "while you were at lunch you earned fifty thousand dollars." That evening, the two celebrated with dinner at a local cafeteria where they had eaten many times before. As they studied the menu's right-hand column, where the forty-five-cent meals were listed, it suddenly occurred to them that they were no longer poor. They could afford to order whatever they wanted from the sixty-five-cent side of the menu, and so they did. That meal made real the issue of her wealth, she later said. They stayed awake all night, "gloating" together, until the sun rose over 139 East Thirty-fifth Street.

A few weeks later, on their way home from signing the official Warner Bros. contract, they stopped for a champagne cocktail at the Roosevelt Hotel. They were as happy as they had ever been. The hard work, the single focus, and the courage not to compromise had all paid off. To reflect on the money she had earned was exhilarating. To experience the momentary assurance of a sought-after success was deeply satisfying. She did not regret the past. If she had achieved financial success and recognition in a gentle upward line, over time, she and O'Connor told each other, this moment would not have been as sweet. She had become a capitalist overnight, she jested to her friend the economist and writer Ruth Alexander.

Of all her hard-won accomplishments, why did this one finally touch her? She had no more respect for the judgment of Hollywood than for the New York publishing world; indeed, she had less. And she most emphatically did not believe that wealth alone signals worth. A clue may be found in the dazzling speech she would later write for Francisco d'Anconia, one of three capitalist heroes in *Atlas Shrugged*. "Money is the root of all good," Francisco famously announces to a group of hypocritical politicians and professional humanitarians assembled at a wedding party. "Money is the barometer of a society's virtue." Francisco goes on to deliver a virtuoso defense of the profit motive; in all of history, he tells his listeners, the free exchange of money has been the only nonviolent, orderly, and socially transparent means of calibrating the value men place upon one another's work. Without money, and particularly money backed by gold, force decides, Rand argued.* Perhaps it was natural, then, that after many disappointing encounters with politicians, businessmen, theatrical producers, and literary rainmakers, money pleased her more resoundingly than praise. At best, praise could be marred by errors of understanding; even the admirable Lorine Pruette had tarnished an otherwise perfect review by comparing *The Fountainhead* to Thomas Mann's *The Magic Mountain,* a novel Rand considered both ponderous and ludicrously mystical. Most important, money gave Ayn Rand the time and the freedom to write.

In her ebullience, the thirty-eight-year-old author must sometimes have turned her thoughts to her parents and sisters, from whom she had heard nothing in six long years. From the 1920s on, the Rosenbaums had lived primarily to applaud their eldest child's achievements in America; now that she had what for her was real wealth, she must have wished that she could share it with them and relieve their hardship. But communication with Russia was still impossible. Even if Stalin had permitted mail to flow freely from the West, Europe's transportation infrastructure was in tatters. Absent the power to contact them or even find out if they were alive, she may simply have avoided dwelling on thoughts of them. She did not mention them in letters or in published working journals. She did, however, send a signed copy of *The Fountainhead* to her mother's cousin Minna Goldberg in Chicago. Minna's daughter Fern Brown remembered the book, and also remembered her mother's caustic asides about the fact that their celebrated young relative did not then or later repay the money she had borrowed from the family in 1926. She most certainly did not send Minna a mink coat—an oversight that was not forgotten by the Goldbergs, Stones, and Liptons.

Surprisingly, Ayn Rand did purchase a mink coat for herself. On learning of the Warner Bros. deal, her first thought was, Now I can pay

---

*Rand's views on money, which influenced her disciple Alan Greenspan, are particularly interesting in light of the 2008 financial meltdown. Francisco's speech continues: "Whenever destroyers appear among men, they start by destroying money, for money is men's protection and the base of a moral existence. Destroyers seize gold and leave to its owners a counterfeit pile of paper. This kills all objective standards and delivers men into the arbitrary power of an arbitrary setter of values. Gold was an objective value, an equivalent of wealth produced. Paper is a mortgage on wealth that does not exist, backed by a gun aimed at those who are expected to produce it. Paper is a check drawn by legal looters upon an account which is not theirs: upon the virtue of the victims. Watch for the day when it bounces, marked, 'Account overdrawn.' "

for my own extended ad campaign. That notion quickly gave way to an anxious resolve to save every penny so that she would never again have to work when she needed time to write. But she didn't foresee a friendly conspiracy to add a touch of glamour to her wardrobe. With Paterson's encouragement, Frank persuaded her to go with him to Saks Fifth Avenue, on a jaunt to replace her worn-out winter coat. Once inside the store he told her sternly, "You can choose any kind of coat you want—as long as it's a mink." He led her to the fur salon. The coat she chose cost $2,400. Later that day, she went up to Paterson's office to show her friend her prize; Paterson wasn't there, so she modeled the coat for the secretaries and assistants and passed it around for them to try on. Her pleasure in it was later captured in a speech by Hank Rearden, the self-made steel magnate in *Atlas Shrugged*. Rearden tells his lover Dagny Taggart, to whom he's just presented a fur coat, that he had never before paused from his work to enjoy his wealth. "I couldn't find any purpose for it," he says. "I've found it now," in the realization that "it's I who produced that wealth, and it's I who am going to let it buy for me every pleasure I want." Rand had become a proud, conscious producer of wealth—a capitalist—and she would never be poor again.

EIGHT

FAME

1943 – 1946

I decided to become a writer—not in order to save the world, nor to serve my fellow men—but for the simple, personal, selfish, egoistical happiness of creating the kind of men and events I could like, respect, and admire. I can bear to look around me levelly. I cannot bear to look down. I wanted to look up.

—"To the Readers of *The Fountainhead*," 1945

The weeks she expected to spend in Hollywood turned into months and then years.

The O'Connors arrived in high style in early December 1943. Warner Bros. had sent them to Chicago aboard the New York Central Railroad's luxurious Twentieth Century Limited, where they slept in a paneled private compartment and ordered two impossible-to-get government-rationed steaks in the formal dining car. They continued on to Hollywood aboard the streamlined Santa Fe Super Chief, world famous for its elaborate meals and celebrity passengers. The fact that they had earned this modish treatment was what made it seem so marvelous, Rand said, adding, "The only advantage of poverty is that you can get *out* of it. The contrast is wonderful."

Apartments were hard to come by in wartime Hollywood, and the cat the O'Connors had brought with them on the train didn't help in the hunt. After a few days' search, they smuggled Tartalia, Russian for "Tur-tle Cat," into a furnished flat not far from Hollywood Boulevard. (When the landlady inquired if they had any pets, Frank charmingly answered, "Only my wife.") In the meantime, she reported to work at Warner Bros. studio in Burbank and was astonished to be given an office the size of a living room, with an outer vestibule occupied by two personal secretaries—one hers and the other assigned to a writer named Howard Koch, who worked in an adjacent office. To her delight, her secretary announced visitors and screened calls. These were the "mink-coat" con-ditions of a screenwriter's life in Hollywood, she wrote playfully to Archibald Ogden, now living in Washington, D.C. So far they hadn't tempted her to "go Hollywood," she assured him, or to forget the rap-tures of writing exactly what she pleased.

Rand wasn't especially interested in meeting those actors and studio luminaries she called "Hollywood people." In Koch's memoirs, he re-called that she was almost always hard at work in her office and seemed to keep her distance from the bustle of studio life. One day, before he had found time to introduce himself, her secretary knocked at his door and informed him that Miss Rand did not wish to be disturbed—a pro-phylactic measure presumably taken because, in 1943, he had written the script of a movie called *Mission to Moscow*. The movie was based on a book by the same name, written by Roosevelt's former ambassador to Soviet Russia, that presented Stalin as a defender of justice and a brave opponent of the Nazi onslaught. Unknown to her, and possibly to Koch, the movie had been made at the behest of the Roosevelt administration and on behalf of the war effort—a fact apparently not taken into ac-count when Koch was blacklisted for Communist sympathies later in the decade. He didn't meet her until one stormy evening when her sec-retary knocked again and asked if he would give Miss Rand a ride home in his car. She didn't drive and couldn't get a taxi. They chatted warily as they rode. When she opened the door to get out of the car, she re-marked, "I didn't know you were this way at all," and dashed out into the rain. She was slightly friendlier after that.

One person she met immediately was her new boss, Henry Blanke, the Warner Bros. producer in charge of filming *The Fountainhead*. Blanke was small, dapper, and animated, a German immigrant who, in 1920s Berlin, had worked under two of her favorite silent-film directors, Ernst Lubitsch and Fritz Lang, before going on to assist in the production of movies such as *The Maltese Falcon* and *The Treasure of the Sierra Madre*. He loved *The Fountainhead*. "It's *magnificent*," he told her during their first meeting. Barbara Stanwyck had brought him the book, he told her, and he had demanded that Warner Bros. buy it. He thought of it as the tale of a great man fighting injustices—a story line that may have had special meaning for him, since he had won a 1937 Academy Award for *The Life of Emile Zola*. This was only roughly congruent with Rand's own view of her novel. But as she began to write the script he encouraged her to retain as much of the original story and tone as possible, to test how well the novel in its entirety would translate to the screen, and this reassured her. All in all, she was pleased. Blanke "is almost an Archie Ogden," she wrote to the real Archie Ogden, adding, "Of course I know that it is too early for me to judge." Still, the producer's advocacy at Warner Bros., like Ogden's at Bobbs-Merrill, had convinced her that "it will be my fate, like Roark's, to seek and reach the exceptions, the prime movers, the men who do their own thinking and act upon their own judgment."

By early February, she had completed the preliminary screenplay, a 179-page treatment (later to grow to 283 pages) that preserved all the novel's major characters and events, including both of Roark's jury trials. According to her, Blanke and the studio bosses were very pleased with her work; the producer especially appreciated her impassioned love scenes and her stylized dialogue. Unfortunately, the studio executives soon concluded that building the sets for the movie would consume unacceptably large amounts of rationed wood, cement, and metal. They put *The Fountainhead* on hold, presumably until the following year, but it remained unproduced until 1948.

In January, Blanke had briefly taken her off *The Fountainhead* and loaned her to his friend and mentor, Hal Wallis, the Warner Bros. producer of *The Maltese Falcon, The Man Who Came to Dinner,* and *Casablanca*. Wallis was shooting an ill-conceived sequel to *Casablanca* called *The Conspirators* and needed a writer to add heat to the romantic scenes between Hedy Lamarr and Paul Henreid. On the set one day, hoping to learn more about the leading lady, she invited Lamarr to lunch. She later said that she immediately understood why the film's director had asked her to keep the dark-eyed beauty's dialogue to a few lines at a time; rarely had she met a less intelligent woman. Rand told this story without rancor, but she seems to have been mistaken. In

1941, Lamarr, an Austrian émigré whose first husband had been an arms manufacturer, co-invented and patented a radio-controlled torpedo guidance system that the U.S. Navy at first derided and then impounded as a state secret, and that Sylvania refined, built, and deployed after the war.

After four months in California, Rand hated Hollywood as both shabby and vicious and longed for New York, she wrote to Ogden, adding, "Frank says what I love is not the real city, but the New York I built myself," a shrewd remark. Still, when Blanke offered her a permanent job, she was tempted. The movie-industry pay scale and the accoutrements of studio life were irresistible after years of watching every dollar. She proposed a compromise: If the producer would allow her to work six months of the year and take an unpaid leave of absence for the remaining six, to pursue her own writing, she would stay on. Alas, he answered, Warner Bros. would never agree to such a contract. Hal Wallis, however, would. The prize-winning producer had argued with Jack Warner, a co-founder of Warner Bros., and had walked off the set of *The Conspirators* to launch his own production company in partnership with Paramount, and he invited Rand to join him as his first employee. (His second was Lillian Hellman, whom Rand "lost no opportunity to run down," recalled a Hollywood acquaintance of the time. Hellman didn't much like Rand, either, and later caricatured her as an anti-Communist puppet in her memoir *Scoundrel Time*.) In early April, her new West Coast agent, Bert Allenberg, met with Wallis and they drew up an attractive five-year contract. Her starting salary would be $750 a week, with rapid raises to $1500. From roughly July through December of every year, with the exception of 1944, her time would be her own; from January through June, she would work five-day weeks on projects chosen by Wallis. The first year, she was scheduled to begin in July and work through May 1945.

The timetable was important to her, and so was the money and the industry prestige. She was eager to begin her next novel, whose working title was *The Strike* and which would become her controversial magnum opus, *Atlas Shrugged*. She also had a minimum and a maximum set of expectations for her film work. At worst, the money she earned would protect her savings; at best, she would achieve a position of influence in Hollywood such that the "pictures [I write] would be done *my* way," she wrote to Isabel Paterson. "This last is not impossible," she added optimistically—and also prophetically, although five years would pass before her prediction bore its fruit.

The theme of *Atlas Shrugged* had come to her one evening during the previous summer, soon after the publication of *The Fountainhead*. She was on the phone with Paterson, expressing her frustration with slow sales and inane reviews. Paterson pointed out that readers might be confused by encountering serious ideas in a novel, and why didn't she write a nonfiction book explaining her individualist philosophy? "No!" she said. "I've presented my case in *The Fountainhead*. . . . If [readers] don't respond, why should I wish to enlighten or help them further? I'm not an altruist!" Paterson stuck to her guns. People *needed* to hear Rand's ideas; the author had a duty to present them clearly. Oh, no she didn't, Rand exclaimed, temper rising. Then she said, "What if I went on strike? What if all the creative minds in the world went on strike?" As an aside, she added, "That would make a good novel," and moved on to other subjects. When she hung up the phone, O'Connor remarked, "That *would* make a good novel." At once she saw the extended possibilities of a story line she had first conceived at the University of St. Petersburg: the story of the heiress who persuades a group of brilliant men to withdraw their talents from an increasingly evil world and go into hiding. The new novel would dramatize the consequences to society if all the best artists, inventors, and businessmen refused to exercise their skills. The novel's theme would be "the mind on strike."

She and O'Connor were still living in their cramped rental apartment. They had bought a 1936 Packard car (it was "magnificent looking—black, half-a-block long, and drips with chromium," she gloated to Ogden), and on the strength of the Wallis contract, he began searching for a house and land to buy in the San Fernando Valley. The national inflation rate was high—wavering between 5 and 7 percent, and at that rate, he explained, the money they were saving in the bank was losing buying power. He also had a theory that proved to be correct: after the war, when gas rationing ended and people increased their driving distances, land values in the still-undeveloped valley would rise. A house would be a good investment, he told her. She was hesitant. She didn't drive, and the San Fernando Valley was a twenty-mile commute from Hollywood. Then one day their landlady caught sight of Tartalia and issued an ultimatum: Choose the animal or the apartment. The cat was placed in a pet hostel while the O'Connors arranged to buy an astoundingly Roarkian house on thirteen acres of fertile farmland that Frank had discovered amid miles of orange groves in the rural town of Chatsworth in the valley. The four-thousand-square-foot house had been designed in 1935 for director Josef von Sternberg and his mistress Marlene Dietrich by Richard Neutra, a Viennese architect who had been an apprentice of Frank Lloyd Wright. It was a swan-shaped structure made entirely of glass, steel, concrete, and aluminum alloy, with a soaring two-story living room, an immense master bedroom lined with floor-to-ceiling windows, a large and airy study opening into a walled garden, a rooftop pool, and a moat encircling the house. It cost them the fantastic sum of $24,000. They asked Frank's brother Nick to pack and ship their New York furniture and moved into 10000 Tampa Avenue in July, a week before she started work for Wallis.

O'Connor, a born landholder, it seemed, fell in love with the San Fernando Valley ranch. He tended its fruit trees, gardens, and meadows; he experimented with raising peacocks, chickens, and rabbits and grew gladioli and alfalfa as a paying business. With her salary, they could now afford to hire a cook, a maid, and a handyman. She was pleased that her husband had become "chronically and permanently happy" in his outdoor life and she liked the roominess of the ranch. But she confided to a few friends that she still missed her spiritual home base in New York.

Frank persuaded Nick to visit them in the fall of 1944 and, with fresh air and oranges, nursed him through a serious spell of active tuberculosis. Nick went back to New York in late fall. He died in January on an operating table in a veterans' hospital, and was buried on Long Island. Tuberculosis had weakened his heart, and his heart had stopped under anesthesia. A few weeks earlier, Rand had sent him a long, affectionate letter from the ranch. She must have mourned his death but didn't refer to it in any of her published notes or letters.

Meanwhile, sales of *The Fountainhead* continued to be brisk. By Christmas 1944, fifty thousand copies had been sold. Every two or three weeks, for no apparent reason, it climbed to the top of a handful of regional best-seller lists and then fell back again. This occurred twenty-six times through the end of 1945. Fan mail was pouring in to Bobbs-Merrill, coming from lawyers, teachers, librarians, bookstore owners, chemists, engineers, housewives, active-duty military personnel, artists, and musicians. The letters would continue to come for as long as she lived. Soldiers wrote from battle zones to say that they had been reading parts of the book to one another as a way of bolstering morale. Many readers thanked her for giving them the courage and inspiration to flout the stultifying expectations of their families and communities and to act according to their hopes and dreams; or they asked her advice on how to become more like Howard Roark; or they timidly inquired who Ayn Rand *was,* anyway. A Hungarian-American musician named Erwin Nyiregyházi, whose performances Rand had enjoyed in the mid-1930s, thanked her for her "great and exceptional" stand on the importance of the individual ego and called her the greatest satirist since Oscar Wilde. Most of the writers were men. Roark, a passionate woman's erotic rendition of a rugged male hero, spoke to American men. Rand tried to answer every letter, assuring worried readers that if they understood and liked *The Fountainhead* they weren't second-handers and politely declining the occasional "compliment" of being addressed as "Mr. Rand." Much later, she said of these early admirers that she mistakenly assumed that their enthusiasm for Roark implied their agreement with her philosophy, since her ideas followed so meticulously from the novel's characters and action, and since *her* mind was so quick to grasp implications. She hadn't counted on the number of logical contradictions most people could sustain at any given time, she said. In the meantime, the passionate public response to the novel's themes was earning her a reputation as a kind of novelist-guru.

She was famous now. Ely Jacques Kahn boasted to colleagues and the press that he had helped her; he invited her to speak before gatherings of architects in New York and California. (In her New York speech, in 1943, she told the group of architects that her book was not about the structure of buildings but about the structure of man—the girders and supports, the rotten beams and shoddy foundations of man's spirit.) Gossip columnists reported on the progress of her movie and employment deals, and her presence in Hollywood produced a flurry of social invitations. Even after *The Fountainhead* had been delayed, actors and actresses were vying for the parts of Dominique and Roark. Joan Crawford gave a dinner party for her in which she dressed as Dominique, in a flowing white gown decorated with green-blue aquamarines. Barbara Stanwyck, a political conservative and the godmother of Warner Bros.'s purchase of *The Fountainhead,* befriended Rand and lobbied Blanke for the part. Making reference to Dominique's helmet of pale-blond hair, Veronica Lake let it be known that the part had been

written for her. Rand preferred Garbo. As to Roark, she had always pictured Gary Cooper in the part but read in the gossip columns that Alan
Ladd and Humphrey Bogart hoped to be considered. Clark Gable, then
a volunteer lieutenant in the Army Air Corps, was rumored to have read
The Fountainhead on a transcontinental train heading east and to have
hopped off during a stop to call MGM, his employer, and demand that
the studio secure the part for him; MGM reportedly responded by offering Warner Bros. $425,000 for the movie rights, vindicating Rand's
prediction that the book would be worth more than she was paid for it.
(She did not forget to call Alan Collins to tell him about the offer.)
When she signed on with Hal Wallis—"*the* big man in Hollywood," as
she called him in a letter to Ogden—Hedda Hopper and *The New York
Times* covered the event, and Cecil B. DeMille, now heading his own
independent production company at Paramount, tried to pry her away
from Wallis, though nothing seems to have come of it.

She was even invited to spend an evening with the elusive Frank
Lloyd Wright at the home of his son Lloyd, in Santa Monica. The two
paragons of American self-reliance spoke cordially of individualism, integrity, and, in relation to creativity, their own personal suffering. Wright
expressed the courtly opinion that she was too young to have suffered.
She told him wryly that she had certainly suffered over his 1938 letter to
her ridiculing Roark. He had forgotten the letter and hadn't yet read the
published book. She sent him a copy. He read it and professed to be an
admirer. "Your thesis is the great one," he wrote. "The Individual *is* the
Fountainhead of any Society worthwhile." He hailed her for her portrait
of Ellsworth Toohey but didn't mention her hero, except to say that
Howard Roark should have had a mane of white hair, like his own. Hoping to learn more, she wrote to Gerald Loeb, a mutual friend, begging
him to tell her "*everything* that Wright said to you about *The Fountainhead* and about me." Loeb demurred, taking the stance that Wright's
comments to him were confidential. Still, she was gratified by the famous architect's apparent approval. His letter was "like the closing of a
circle for me," she wrote to him. As for his single serious criticism of her
book—that it "sensationalized" the quest for truth—she suggested that
his own buildings were equally sensational. They were not made for
homey living or "flopping around in bedroom slippers," she wrote, but
for heroic individuals who stood up straight and made every minute

count. Like her book, his houses were an expression of life as it *should* be lived, not as it was. When Wright wryly remarked that he supposed she would now be "set up in the marketplace and burned for a witch" for writing in praise of individual conscience, she replied, "I think I am made of asbestos."

She and Henry Blanke were both eager to get Wright to design the sets for *The Fountainhead,* whenever it should be scheduled for production. The novelist and the architect would tussle over this issue until 1948, when his demand for prior approval of the costumes, sets, and script and a fee amounting to 10 percent of the budget of the movie ruled him out. At some point, she also asked him to design a house for her, on land that she eventually hoped to buy in the suburbs north of New York City. He enlarged a set of plans created for one of his never-built 1937 All-Steel Houses and converted it into a flowing four-tiered concrete-and-stone mansion featuring a large fountain, in honor of *The Fountainhead,* and a rooftop study. Altogether, it was reminiscent of his 1935 masterpiece, Fallingwater. When he told her the price, $35,000, she winced. "My dear lady," he reportedly remarked, "that's no problem. Go out and make more money." The land was not bought and the house was not built, but Wright's sketches remain in his library at the Frank Lloyd Wright Foundation in Scottsdale, Arizona.

Wright, in turn, invited her and O'Connor to visit his legendary summer residence, school, and architectural studio at Taliesin East, in Spring Green, Wisconsin. They went in 1945 and were horrified by what they saw. The beautiful 1911 buildings were in a state of disrepair. ("He had a theoretical mind with no concern for how one would actually live," she remarked, amusingly anticipating what cultural commentators would say of her.) She long remembered her indignation over the attitude of hero worship and servitude that Wright was famous for instilling in his "Fellowship," made up of tuition-paying students. They cooked, served meals, and cleaned. They ate at tables set a step or two below the dais on which Wright and his guests and family dined, and they consumed a plainer diet. Their drawings, she noted, were undistinguished and imitative of Wright. "What was tragic was that he didn't want any of that," Rand told a friend in 1961. "He was trying to get intellectual independence [out of] them during the general discussions, but he didn't get anything except 'Yes, sir' or 'No, sir' and recitals of formulas from his writing." She compared them to medieval serfs. At the time she made these comments, in the early 1960s, the charge that she required hero worship from *her* young followers was swirling around her in newspaper and magazine accounts.

For some reason Wright, who had warmed to her after their meeting in Santa Monica, was disappointed by the visit, his son-in-law recalled. Wright's biographer, Meryle Secrest, speculates that prolonged exposure to her dogmatism would almost certainly have irritated him, especially since he was sympathetic to socialism, a fact that Rand was unaware of. So would her need for admiration, strong tendency to moralize, imperiousness, and inability to find any fault with herself, which the two powerful personalities had in common. On this trip or another, she smoked so heavily that the curmudgeonly old architect reportedly grabbed her cigarette, threw it in the fireplace, and ordered her to leave the lodge; afterward, he imposed a permanent smoking ban at Taliesin. When later asked if he was the model for Howard Roark, he answered, "I deny the paternity and refuse to marry the mother."

Rand's self-confidence as a writer was at a peak. From her office in Paramount's Art Deco–style studio lot in Hollywood, Hal Wallis became her affectionately nicknamed "Boss" and she his jocular "loyal wage-slave." She worked for him uncomplainingly on a series of B movies that the Oscar-nominated producer now, for some reason, chose to produce in the company that bore his name. During her first work term, extending from summer 1944 until late spring 1945, she wrote three screenplays. The best known is *Love Letters,* adapted from a novel by British writer Christopher Massie. Rand's lifelong fondness for Edmond Rostand's *Cyrano de Bergerac* came in handy here; the plot features an American soldier who writes a second soldier's love letters and eventually marries the woman to whom they are addressed (although she is an amnesiac and possibly a murderess). The movie starred Joseph Cotten and Jennifer Jones and was a box-office hit but a critical failure. She also co-wrote *You Came Along* in collaboration with its original author Robert Smith. A wafer-thin wartime romantic comedy, the script is interesting for its characterization of a government agent as a "wet nurse" (a term she later deployed as Hank Rearden's nickname for a heart-warming minor character in *Atlas Shrugged*) and for the four distinctly different endings that Smith supplied and Rand polished and presented to Wallis, demonstrating the plotting proficiency and by-the-yard ingenuity of writers for the movie industry that would come in handy in the composition of her most celebrated work. She drafted a third screenplay, based on a novel called *The Crying Sisters* by mystery-crime writer Mabel Seeley, which she had read on the recommendation of her old friends, the attorney Pincus Berner and his wife, and brought to Wallis. The movie was not produced. She also tried unsuccessfully to interest Wallis in acquiring her 1932 screenplay *Red Pawn,* still owned by Paramount. She and Wallis worked well together and even flirted mildly now and then.

She entered her initial sabbatical period in June of 1945. The first thing she did was to buy the collected works of Aristotle, which she had wanted to read since her university years, and three new outfits by Adrian, the former DeMille wardrobe assistant who, upon her 1926 arrival in Hollywood, dressed her for a walk-on role in the movie *King of Kings.* He was now a modish dress designer and her nearest neighbor at the ranch. Then she scrambled to finish a short nonfiction book she had promised to Bobbs-Merrill. Called *The Moral Basis of Individualism,* it was an attempt at a brief, orderly explanation of the ethics of *The Fountainhead,* exactly the kind of book that Isabel Paterson had urged her to write in 1943. In notes, she explained the moral necessity of Howard Roark's defiantly independent stance and contempt for the opinions of others. Among man's inalienable rights, she noted, the right to life is the most fundamental. Yet an individual can survive only through the use of his rational ability. To prove that reason is man's only tool of survival in a world he cannot understand instinctively, she began to elaborate the nature of human existence itself, as she wrote to Paterson. In her notes, she described what she knew for sure: that humans exist; that the world around them is real; and that the faculty of "rational consciousness" is the only way for humans to know and control the real world. How else but through meticulous reasoning could Roark have built grand new structures that did not fall down? How else could Peter Keating have failed so bitterly, except by letting others do his thinking for him? Roark's unspoken code is a morality of reason. He is the Active Man, the creator, producer, egoist, life-giver; Keating and Toohey are examples of the Passive Man, the parasite, the imitator, the collectivist, the "altruist," the mediocrity, the death-carrier. Severely condensed, an early draft of the book appeared as "The Only Path to Tomorrow" in the January 1944 issue of *The Reader's Digest,* where Eugene Lyons, whose *The Red Decade* had first attracted her to Macmillan and who was now her friend, was working as an editor. She found expository writing boring and difficult at this stage in her career and never finished the book.

Two years earlier, she had written an inscription in Paterson's copy of *The Fountainhead* that quoted Roark's tribute to Gail Wynand: "You have been the one encounter in my life that can never be repeated." This was a warm commendation, conveying affection and respect. Yet it also carried a subliminal, elegiac note, one that echoed Roark's mixed sympathies for Wynand. Rand was beginning to think of Paterson as stubborn, even stifling. On first moving to Hollywood, she had traded long, fond letters with Paterson. But by 1945, her side of the correspondence had cooled. In the midst of sisterhood, conflicts had opened a narrow rift between them. God the father was one sore point. Rand had always known that Paterson believed in God, although she also knew that the crotchety individualist did not endorse any organized religion and thought that the Christian morality would one day be replaced by something better. Rand held faith of any kind to be inconsistent with rationality; she particularly despised Christianity, with its insistence on suffering and brotherhood, as "the best possible kindergarten of communism." The women had punted and dodged this issue for years. But in their letters it rose acrimoniously to the surface, with Rand at one point writing that "an omniscient being, by definition, is a totalitarian dictator. Ah, but he won't use his power? Never mind. He has it." The two also conducted a fascinating, though highly charged, argument about the limits of Aristotelian deductive reasoning. Paterson thought that Rand's use of logic sometimes resembled the arid arguments put forward by the philosophers Rand most disliked. When such philosophers "had strung some words together, in the form of a syllogism or other logical construction, they thought that [the formulation] had to be so—without asking if the facts which constitute the necessary premises are so," Paterson wrote. Take, for example, the logic of, "All men are mortal; Socrates is a man; therefore Socrates is mortal. That is a good syllogism," she wrote, "but its truth depends on the premises being true—that men are mortal, that Socrates is a man. Logic is an instrument for dealing with whatever you can get into its measure." The older woman thought that God and men were both to some degree immeasurable. She argued that Rand trusted deductive reasoning too much and overlooked matters that reason might identify as being worthy of investigation but that were illogical, or inexplicable, at least for now. Rand thought that the alternative to a morality of reason was "the fiat of revelation," and that to hypothesize entities and spheres that the human mind was by its nature inadequate to understand was at best perverse.

More personal matters also troubled their friendship, or at least disturbed Rand. Later, she would describe how, in 1942, Paterson had made a point of asking permission to paraphrase some of her arguments against altruism in *The God of the Machine,* including the gist of her argument about Boswell and the baby. In the chapter on "The Humanitarian with the Guillotine," Paterson had adapted Rand's insight, that a baby cannot survive in a tower without an adult to care for her, to make a case that professional humanitarians will sooner or later halt production by turning everyone into a needy person—a dependent baby—in an effort to increase their own sense of power. If the baby lives and production ceases, whither the baby? At the time, Paterson had explained that she didn't want to mention Rand's name in print because she disliked footnotes; and the inexperienced writer was pleased and flattered that her older, better-known friend wished to mention and publicize her ideas. She was reassured by the fact that Paterson had privately described her basic insight—that human reason, not an impossibly good deity, is the basis of morality—as the most important ethical discovery since Christianity. But after the publication of the book, Rand became increasingly suspicious of Paterson's motives. In the published copy, the older woman had acknowledged the contributions of a number of prominent people. Why not Rand? Was it because she was not yet famous in 1942 and 1943? Because Paterson wanted to present the younger woman's ideas as her own? As Rand brooded on the matter, Paterson's decision not to give her credit struck her as enormously improper. That she hadn't yet confronted her friend in person or in writing was a mark of how deep were her deference and attachment.

If Rand's final dismissal of Paterson's musings on God as a creative force offended the older woman, so did the lengthening intervals between Rand's letters. Paterson felt neglected. Rand felt harassed. The correspondence between them became more frequent again in the summer of 1945, and they carried on a kind of epistolary lovers' quarrel. In one letter that July, Rand boasted that *The Fountainhead*'s sales had now topped 150,000 copies, injudiciously reminding Paterson that she had set a goal of one hundred thousand copies. Paterson remembered, all right. She replied that "sometimes I [think] you might [be] more tactful" in proclaiming the triumphs of *The Fountainhead,* since she, Paterson, had to see the book displayed in bookstore windows all over New York, while *The God of the Machine* "could not sell at all."

Most inflammatory, perhaps, were Paterson's repeated attempts to browbeat Rand into giving up "the dope you take." "Stop taking that benzedrine, you idiot," she wrote in July 1945. "I don't care what excuse you have—stop it." Rand's reply is missing from the archived correspondence, but she seems to have defended herself by insisting on the pressure she was under to produce good work on deadline, her exhaustion, low spirits brought on by the spread of Communist influence in Hollywood, and her doctor's willingness to write prescriptions. Paterson responded, "I am seriously vexed with you for believing such nonsense as that the dope you take won't hurt you because a doctor told you so." She added, "Don't take that stuff to work on. If you persist, believe me, you are running into a perfectly hellish time within a few years." At one point, she issued a mock warning: "If you take any more of that benzedrine I will come out there and spank you to a blister." Paterson didn't visit until 1948 and probably wouldn't have made any headway if she had. Rand would continue to use amphetamines for the next three decades.

Late that summer, Rand and O'Connor made the first of two or three trips back to New York to confer with her agent and publisher. She looked forward to seeing Paterson, but the two women must have argued, for after that their correspondence stopped abruptly and didn't resume for many months. She also visited Eugene Lyons of *Reader's Digest,* who invited her to a party in his apartment, where she encountered the political idol of her early adolescence, the former Russian prime minister Aleksandr Kerensky. He was now in his sixties, immaculately dressed, with thick glasses and a slight stoop. Introduced, they spoke in Russian. As they discussed their native land, she wondered if he would express second thoughts, or possibly regret, about his government's failure to take seriously enough the Bolshevik threat in 1917. Instead, she listened, appalled, as he prattled on about how much Russians hated Stalin and how much they had loved Kerensky. Worse, summoning a mystical fatalism she deplored in her native culture, he insisted that the soul of the Russian people would one day set them free. He was a typical Russian sentimental fool, with a fat Russian smile and no capacity for analytic thought. He was a mere zero, she said afterward.

One of Paterson's earlier letters had mentioned the successful novelist's bloom in middle age. "You can knock the world for a loop now," Paterson declared. And there is no doubt that Rand was glamorous. At the age of forty, she wore expensive, elaborately tailored suits and gowns by Adrian. She chain-smoked through a long cigarette holder, wore her dark hair short and straight in 1920s flapper mode, and carried her fame regally, like Catherine's invisible crown. She was conscious of her power and achievement and loved to hear her writing praised, but—apart from basking in a compliment when especially well dressed—was largely without conventional vanity. Ruth Ohman, the daughter of Morrie Ryskind, a Pulitzer Prize–winning playwright, remembered, as a little girl, watching Rand at parties in her parents' living room. All the men in the room would cluster around her, listening, rapt, as she discoursed on politics and economics. The other women hung back, talking among themselves. "I admired her. She gave me confidence and hope," said Ohman. Rand had not yet learned, and never would learn, the despised art of small talk and got "furiously nervous" before every social occasion. To Paterson, she had written, "I am becoming more antisocial than I was—and the reason is the same as yours. I can't stand the sort of things people talk about." Her conversation about political trends in Hollywood and the importance of individual rights, however, was more scintillating, brainier, and more original than ever. Men, especially young men, noticed, and were attracted.

She began to collect the most interesting young men she could find, those who appealed to her for reasons of merit or like-mindedness. An early example was Thaddeus Ashby, who came to live on the ranch in the spring of 1945. An irrepressible twenty-one-year-old fan, he had written to her from New York, calling her the most important philosopher living and suggesting that, because he understood the character of Howard Roark better than Warner Bros. ever could, she should appoint him producer of *The Fountainhead*. He held an entry-level job at the McCann-Erickson advertising agency on Madison Avenue and typed his letter on company stationery. Was he important? Rand and O'Connor apparently wondered. Later, Ashby discovered that they had sent Frank's older brother Joe, who happened to be in New York, to the advertising agency to check him out. "I was just a flunky, a clerk," Ashby said, "and I couldn't really help her."

Rand didn't answer his letter. Nevertheless, he quit his job, hitch-hiked to Hollywood, and phoned her through Hal Wallis's office at Paramount. Impressed by his persistence, she invited him to lunch on the Paramount lot. The attractive young man was working on a novel and wanted to be a writer, he said, and regaled her with passages from *The Fountainhead* that he had learned by heart. "I could quote it the way fundamentalist Christians quote the Bible," he remembered. That night, Rand invited Ashby to supper at the ranch. When she learned he lacked sufficient money to continue writing, she invited him to stay. He moved in the following day and remained for between five months and a year.

Rand's friend and former neighbor in New York, Albert Mannheimer, the tall, curly-haired former Yale Drama School student and Communist apostate, was already living and working in Hollywood. He took to spending long weekends at the ranch, both during Ashby's stay and afterward. Now a moderately successful young screenwriter, he still wanted to write for the theater and was working on a play called *The Bees and the Flowers*. According to Rand's part-time secretary during those years, June Kurisu, Mannheimer looked more like a "sports hunk" than a standard-issue intellectual. Although Rand usually wrote seven days a week, all day long, especially after she started intensive planning of *Atlas Shrugged* in the spring of 1946, she deviated from her schedule when Mannheimer was with her. On those occasions, she spent her weekend afternoons and evenings closeted with him in the study, discussing his play and other writing projects, developing her ideas, exchanging Hollywood political gossip, and, as time went on, offering him emotional counseling and support. "They spent an awful lot of time in there," said Kurisu, then an eighteen-year-old college girl whose Japanese-American parents worked as the O'Connors' live-in housekeeper and handyman. During the summer of 1947, and on weekends afterward, Kurisu typed the author's handwritten manuscript pages and her personal letters and sometimes typed for Mannheimer at Rand's request. She worked and slept on a balcony overlooking the double-height O'Connor living room. Mannheimer slept on the study couch. "I never saw them touch, but I always wondered. Frank O'Connor never went in" the study while Mannheimer was in there with his wife, but he never seemed to mind the time they spent together, either. During the two years Kurisu worked at the ranch, Rand referred to Mannheimer as her "intellectual heir," the typist recalled. Another frequent guest, Hal Wallis's personal assistant Jack Bungay, similarly remembered, "She was terribly, terribly fond of him. They were very close friends. I thought he was going to be her heir then." But "intellectual heir," that odd honorific, which Rand seems to have made up, would not belong to Mannheimer for long.

In 1945, another young man named Walter Abbott, a playwright whom Rand and Mannheimer had befriended in New York, began to show up at the ranch. Abbott had met her in late 1935 or early 1936, shortly before *The Night of January 16th* closed on Broadway. A theatrical producer who knew them both gave her one of his plays to read; she was crazy about it, she told an interviewer, and she and Mannheimer had pooled their money to buy an option to produce it. They couldn't raise the additional capital to bring it to the stage, and the project withered. But when Abbott arrived in Hollywood in the mid-1940s, he joined Ashby and Mannheimer in a threesome of regular weekend votaries to Rand. Although she eventually came to think of him as an "emotionalizer" and the kind of ne'er-do-well writer who works only when "inspired," she lobbied Hal Wallis to give him a job as a junior screenwriter at $150 a week. His first, or nearly first, mission was to collaborate with her on a script about the life of the Russian composer Pyotr Tchaikovsky, a celebrated alumnus of the St. Petersburg conservatory where her sister Natasha had studied. Leonard Bernstein, then twenty-seven, tried out for the composer's role. But the film was not produced, probably because a company called Monogram announced plans for its own Tchaikovsky movie. Abbott took to writing B-grade screenplays, such as *Scared to Death* (1947), with Bela Lugosi, in which a murdered woman narrates dark deeds from a slab in the morgue.

Rand saw a lot of Jack Bungay, who sometimes joined the male trio and their intellectual guiding light in all-night philosophical discussions. For a period of months in 1946, he, too, lived at the ranch. In the evenings, he and O'Connor enjoyed watching her perform a little two-step, with a cane, to radio music, à la Marlene Dietrich. "She was a very sensual woman," Bungay recalled. "Beautiful eyes, black hair, and very beautiful lips, very prominent lips." She encouraged him, as she did the others, to write. "You must, you must, you must," she told him. He didn't, but he and the others adored her and during that period were her only regular visitors, she later told a confidante.

Her fondness for young men was apparent to her friends. Geologist and ethnographer Ruth Beebe Hill, who, with her husband, a biochemist named Dr. Borroughs ("Buzzy") Hill, became close to the O'Connors in the late 1940s, witnessed one of the writer's mild flirtations. At a formal Books and Authors Club luncheon in the Beverly Hills Hotel, featuring Rand as a speaker, Hill noticed a striking young blond man approach her to request an autograph on his copy of the recently reissued *Anthem*. In the car on the way home, "she said, 'I'd like to meet him,' " Hill remembered. So Hill gave a party and invited the young man, whose patter quickly bored the brilliant writer. "The whole attraction was his looks," said Rand's friend. "He looked like John Galt," the ultimate hero-to-be of *Atlas Shrugged*. "He looked like Frank O'Connor."

Young men were aware of her sexuality, too, perhaps for the first time in her life. Bungay recalled observing "a lot of sex in her face." Evan Wright, a young ex-marine whom she hired to proofread her typescripts in 1951, said that she once stood silently by his side while he worked, exuding a powerful sexual magnetism that was far from disagreeable. She stood there for a long time. "I don't know what would have happened if I had looked up," he said. "Yes, perhaps I do know." He was young and shy and didn't look up, and she walked on.

At the same Books and Authors Club luncheon, Rand uttered one of her occasional uproarious, and revealing, bon mots. During a question-and-answer period, a white-gloved matron asked where all those wonderful sex scenes in *The Fountainhead* had come from. Were they based on Rand's own experience? Hill, knowing well that her friend could be prickly, winced, but Rand responded with perfect poise. "Wishful thinking," she said, and smiled. Hilarity ensued among the audience of mostly wealthy women.

At this early juncture, she was just beginning to set conditions for public appearances, in order to screen out disputatious hosts and potentially hostile audiences. "She will not speak with liberals," Hill remembered warning the club's president, a Mrs. Helen Guervin. Mrs. Guervin was required to call on Rand in Chatsworth before the author would commit herself to speaking to the group. The club president passed the test, as Hill herself had done before being welcomed into the circle of Rand's acquaintances.

There were additional, more-or-less permanent houseguests who came to stay at the ranch in the middle 1940s. She provided sanctuary to at least two European refugees fleeing the postwar Soviet occupation of central Europe. The first was a woman who, Ashby recalled, developed a paranoid fixation on him and eventually was evicted. The second was Marie von Strachow, Rand's long-lost former English tutor from St. Petersburg. Von Strachow had been a close friend of Rand's mother and, in 1925, had helped to prepare the young émigré for life in the United States. She seems to have fled Russia for Western Europe before the onset of the Stalin Terror. In early 1946, she managed to locate Rand through the American delegation to the Intergovernmental Committee on Refugees in Austria, where she was living as a displaced person. She wrote to tell her former pupil of the elder Rosenbaums' deaths. Zinovy had succumbed to heart disease in 1939, she reported. Anna had perished from cancer during the siege of Leningrad, in November 1941. Rand later learned that her sister Natasha and her childhood friend and cousin Nina Guzarchik also had died, Natasha during a Nazi air raid and Nina on a ship in the Caspian Sea that was bombed. A year or two later, she discovered that Nina's sister Vera was alive and had made her way from Berlin, where Rand had last seen her in 1926, to Paris to take a medical position at the Pasteur Institute. Vera had married and given birth to a daughter, Lisette, then moved to Lyon. Rand sent Vera's family packages of food and clothing. No one knew what had happened to Rand's lively and much beloved youngest sister, Nora.

Rand's reaction to the shock of her parents' deaths was muted, but she declared herself anxious to bring her mother's former friend to safety in the United States. Evidently, as a person carrying a Russian passport, von Strachow was in danger of being extradited to the Russian zone in Austria and from there to the Soviet Union. It took two and a half years of legal maneuvering for Rand to gain permission for "Missis," as she called her former teacher, to travel to the United States, but in late 1948 von Strachow arrived in California and moved into the Neutra house. She lived there for six or nine months, June Kurisu recalled, until the women's political disagreements created friction. Although Missis tried to be agreeable and avoid arguments, she "wasn't a quiet lady,"

Kurisu said appreciatively. "She would speak up at the dinner table. She would say just what she thought." This made for an intolerable strain on Rand as she was working on a difficult and important section of *Atlas Shrugged*. Eventually, the writer arranged for von Strachow to live elsewhere in California and saw the woman no more.

Assorted friends and family members also came and went. Two of Rand's Chicago cousins stopped by to see her and were amazed that she was living in Marlene Dietrich's former house. One of them, Jack Portnoy, the twenty-three-year-old son of Rand's mother's cousin Mandel Portnoy, marveled at the moat, the bright gardens, the rooftop pool, and the tree that grew straight through the foyer floor, reaching for the roof. Late in the afternoon, when Rand had finished her day's work on *Atlas Shrugged* and joined Jack and his traveling companion, her favorite cousin, Burt Stone, in the living room, Jack noticed that she had a needle wrapped around her thumb; it looked like a ring, except that the point stuck up and out. What was it for? he asked. When she was writing, she answered, she sometimes pricked herself "to keep my thoughts alive." He also noticed that O'Connor supervised the care of the house as well as the property and did the shopping for their dinner. Like other relatives, he found the arrangement odd.

Frank's brother Joe O'Connor, now an itinerant actor with a small theatrical troupe based in Los Angeles, visited when he was in town. As a young man in Lorain, he had hoped to marry a woman named Millie. Millie married someone else, gave birth to a daughter, got divorced, and, in the 1920s, moved to California. Joe became the godfather of Millie's daughter, whose name was Rosalie Fitzgerald. In the late 1920s, the small girl often visited the O'Connors in their apartment on North Gower Street. Rand kindly appointed herself Rosalie's godmother, and Rosalie was very fond of her.

Fifteen years later, Millie and Rosalie enjoyed driving out from Los Angeles together after church on Sundays. On one such Sunday, Ayn revealed a facet of her background and character that took Rosalie and her mother by surprise. The four were talking about a newspaper article concerning a federal investigation of American Communists when Millie said, apropos of the conventional wisdom that most Communists were Jewish, that she didn't approve of Hitler but agreed that "he should have incinerated all those Jews." Dead silence ensued. Then Rand said quietly, in a voice that Rosalie remembered as beautifully modulated,

"Well, Millie, I guess you've never known, but I am Jewish." (On hearing this story, a longtime acquaintance of Rand's commented that she didn't believe Rand's reportedly mild response: "I guarantee that her reaction would have been rage," the acquaintance remarked.) Rosalie was horrified, ashamed of her mother's bigotry, and frightened that she would lose Rand as a godmother and friend, but Millie wouldn't apologize. "I'm sorry it has to end this way," Frank told the women as he walked them to their car. That Sunday was one of the few times Rand disclosed her Jewish background to anyone other than Frank, Nick, Mimi, and possibly Joe. On this day, her principled abhorrence of anti-Semitism, and, indeed, of any collective, group-based bias, trumped whatever generalized fear of humiliation or of tactical disadvantage she may have had. By then she would almost certainly have seen photographs of liberated Nazi concentration camps. A few years later she would tell a friend, "But they [the Nazis] were killing *me*."

O'Connor's niece Mimi Papurt, now married and called Mimi Sutton, hadn't made her way to California. But she and Rand wrote letters to each other. Mimi's father, A. M. Papurt, the man who had once loaned the O'Connors money for an abortion, had died a few years earlier, leaving the young woman's mother and two younger sisters impoverished—so much so that the elder of the two, Marna, had quit high school to help support them. Mimi had been badgering Marna to finish school, and in the spring of 1946 she asked Rand for help in bringing Marna to Boston, where Mimi and her husband lived, to earn her high-school diploma. She and Frank agreed to pay fifty dollars a month, plus the cost of transportation from Ohio, plus school clothes.

The arrangement led to a misunderstanding. Marna had dropped out during the second semester of her junior year. To graduate, she had to complete three semesters. Rand was under the impression that the girl was supposed to graduate in one year. Marna re-entered school in April and finished her junior year in June. But she was forced to leave school again the following April, because Rand stopped sending money. The writer, who didn't understand, or wouldn't make allowances for, the traditional school-year calendar, was furious with Marna. "She said, 'You *promised* me you'd finish,'" the niece recalled. Marna found a job with a traveling magician, whom she married, and eventually earned an equivalency diploma and attended college. But a strain developed on both sides.

Readers familiar with Rand's disapproval of institutionalized altruism often assume that she frowned on private charity. This is not so. She seems to have had a fairly conventional approach to helping others and was personally generous in the years before a cult following increased her tendency to be self-protective and suspicious. She made small gifts and loans and offered professional help and hospitality to relatives and friends whom she saw as deserving—that is, as competent, energetic, and capable of getting on their feet. But she did not see it as a moral duty, and her style of expressing her views on the subject could seem self-serving as well as immoderate and harsh. Charities focused their attention on the old and the lame, she complained in a letter to the director of the Studio Club in 1936, rehearsing a theme that she developed richly in *The Fountainhead*. Why didn't anyone help the ambitious and gifted people? Who deserves help, the above average or the "subnormal"? Who is more valuable to humanity? she asked. In early notes for *Atlas Shrugged*, she observed, pithily, "Charity to an inferior does not include the charity of not considering him an inferior." Years after the high-school misunderstanding, when Marna asked her why she had contributed to her education, Rand answered, "I considered it an investment." Similarly, when discussing Thaddeus Ashby's long residence at the ranch, she explained that she had been trying to spare a promising writer the hardships she had faced. Whatever her rationale for helping, she was often disappointed.

If O'Connor was bothered by the dustup over aid to his niece or by the comings and goings of younger men, he didn't show it openly. Ashby remembered him as placid, unconcerned, cheerful, and friendly. On warm afternoons when Rand had spent a productive morning writing, she would sometimes walk outside to find him in the fields and call him in for sex. "She had a certain tone of voice when she called him for sex," Ashby recalled. O'Connor, he added, always came. The young man was aware that they were having sex because "they made a lot of noise." But Rand wasn't fully satisfied, he thought. "Frank was an undersexed person. He was very sexy in the sense that he was one of the most handsome men I ever knew. He could just look at you and project sex. But he never initiated anything." Once, Ashby asked Rand if she wished O'Connor would be rougher with her in bed, and she admitted that, yes, she did.

Ashby himself was madly in love with her, he claimed, but too timid and polite to try to seduce her. He said she gave him ample opportunity. She would lie on the divan in her study and invite him to sit beside her. They would talk about ideas deep into the night, while O'Connor slept upstairs. "We'd stop talking and stare into each other's eyes, for sometimes a couple of hours," he recalled in 2005, at the age of eighty. When O'Connor was away from the ranch, which wasn't often, she would figuratively "leave the door open," he said. "When I didn't follow up, she would be mad at me." She began to tease him about his shyness, even though he thought of himself not as shy but as careful. One day she told him the plot of a story she had read at the studio. As he remembered the story sixty years later, a male houseguest finds that he is attracted to his married hostess, who sleeps apart from her husband. One night, the houseguest dresses up as a Revolutionary War soldier whose ghost is rumored to haunt the house. Wearing his uniform, he enters his hostess's bedroom. She wakes and gazes at him. He wants to make love to her but is too shy. Nothing happens. "Ayn said that I reminded her of him," said Ashby. When the teasing became too frequent and intense, he said he moved out of the house. Like Mannheimer, Abbott, and Bungay, he took to visiting her once a week or so until he left Los Angeles to enroll in Harvard in the fall of 1946. During the 1950s and 1960s he worked for tiny libertarian magazines and became a devotee of Robert Heinlein, as well as of the effects of magic mushrooms.

Rand remembered their falling-out very differently. In 1961, she told an interviewer that when she and Frank traveled to New York during the summer of 1945, she had left the ranch jointly in the care of Ashby and Mannheimer. Home again, she discovered that Ashby had broken his promise to remain in the house during the day while Mannheimer was at work in Hollywood. The young man had also driven, and dented, O'Connor's Packard and then tried to cover it up, she said. In her recollection, he left the ranch that fall, having lived there fewer than five months, and sent her a long letter regretting his lies and errors and wishing he were more like Roark. Yet six weeks earlier, Rand had written lovingly about him to Isabel Paterson, calling him her adopted son and describing him as the image of herself at the same age. In search of reflected images of herself, she would say much the same about another favorite young man in 1950.

When they were alone, Rand and Frank were again becoming impatient with each other. The admirer of skyscrapers and airplanes had never learned to drive a car; a friend later speculated that this was her way of ceding control in one small area of life to Frank. In practice, it meant that during her working months at Paramount he had to drive her back and forth to town each day, an hour each way, leaving behind his flowers, animals, and fields. Friends of the period sometimes heard him snap at her—not about her control of the household purse strings, although that sometimes bothered him, or about young men, but about her nagging him to watch out for germs, her tendency to wear snagged stockings, and occasionally her rudeness or her temper. Once, she had a tantrum because Frank was engaging in too much small talk with guests. Another time, on Thanksgiving Day in 1945, she had a public screaming fit because a Christian minister showed up unbidden at the door and, when Frank invited him in to join the small group assembled at the dinner table, began to lecture her about her heartless view of the poor. Frank, visibly angry at his wife's vehement reaction, reminded her that it was an American custom to offer hospitality to anyone who stopped by on Thanksgiving. Few other people saw them argue in public, but O'Connor was apt to make deprecatory jokes. "Frank is the power behind the throne," Rand sometimes told acquaintances. "Sometimes I think I am the throne, the way I get sat on," a friend heard Frank reply. Another acquaintance recalled that Rand had once confided in her that this period was a bad one for their marriage. Exasperated by Frank's intellectual and sexual passivity, she considered divorcing him, she said, but decided to put it off until she finished writing *Atlas Shrugged*. She couldn't bear to interrupt her work.

In her public statements, O'Connor was still at the center of her emotional life. Passive or not, he had believed in her when she was almost without hope, and he had always put her writing first. He was "the only exception" to the rule that "nothing has ever mattered to me too much" other than creative work, she wrote in an open letter "To the Readers of *The Fountainhead*." He was Howard Roark, she claimed, "or as near to it as anyone I know."

NINE

THE TOP AND THE BOTTOM

1946–1949

The average man doesn't have the strength to do what is right at any cost, against all men. Only the genius can do that. The genius clears the way for the average man.

—Journals of Ayn Rand, 1946

To the Readers of *The Fountainhead*" began the building of Ayn Rand's public legend. This small pamphlet self-consciously depicted a woman who had been a prodigy from childhood, whose ideas were entirely her own, and whose primary values were intelligence, ambition, ideas, and achievement. It was here that she first confided her decision to be a writer at the age of nine. From that time forward, she declared, "I had in my mind a blinding picture of people as they could be," suggesting that real people held little meaning for her. With memorable self-assurance, she added that her reason for creating the character of Howard Roark was not to "serve my fellow man" or to "save the world," but to obtain the purely private pleasure of writing about a kind of man she could admire; she didn't add: in a world she could control.

The Bobbs-Merrill Company commissioned "To the Readers of *The Fountainhead*" in the fall of 1945, when the novel was again climbing the best-seller lists. It was mailed to thousands of fans who continued to write to the author, care of the publisher, with questions concerning her background and the character of her hero. It communicated as much about her self-concept as about her life. "When I am asked about myself," she wrote, "I am tempted to say, paraphrasing Roark, 'Don't ask me about my family, my childhood, my friends, or my feelings. Ask me about the things I think.'" Except by searching in old newspapers, readers could not know that she was born outside the United States, let alone in Russia; most never learned that she was Jewish, a background she did not bestow on any of her scores of characters. "I have no hobbies," she continued. "I have few friends. I do not like to go out." When she declared that twelve publishers had rejected *The Fountainhead* before Bobbs-Merrill had agreed to publish it, her tone contained a note of pride at being a triumphant outsider. She included Knopf in her count, although it hadn't rejected the book so much as refused to extend her deadline for a second time. She also included two or three publishing houses that had seen only an early, incomplete outline, not the text, and she didn't mention that her first publisher, Macmillan, had offered her an advance that she turned down. Her disciples would accept and repeat the story of *The Fountainhead*'s twelve rejections hundreds of times over the years, both as a symbol of the hardships she had endured at the hands of timid or imperceptive editors and as an implicit compliment to her independent-minded readers. Likewise, they would cite the struggles she listed here: working as a waitress, an office clerk, and a reader for film companies before she could earn her living as a writer. In a rational world, she seemed to say, she would have been spared such experiences. Perhaps she felt this more deeply because some of the menial jobs she held would have been unthinkable in the world of her childhood. In any case, she was not of the view that these experiences had helped her with her writing or the development of her ideas. She was not writing about the folks next door, in offices and diners. "I am interested in men only as they reflect philosophical principles," she declared, and "in philosophical principles only as they affect the actual existence of men." Later, in discussions of *The Fountainhead* and her other novels, she memorably amplified this point. "An abstract theory that has no relation to reality is worse than nonsense; and men who act without relation to principles are worse than animals. Those who say that theory and practice are two unrelated realms are fools in one and scoundrels in the other."

"Do not underestimate the admirers of *The Fountainhead*," she warned Warner Bros. producer Henry Blanke in December 1945. "[They are] becoming a kind of cult." This was true, although she would later angrily reject the use of "cult" when it was used to describe the political and cultural movement that grew up around her in the 1960s. Although the movie was still on hold, the book's success was attracting other keen-eyed marketers. In early 1944, a digest-sized magazine called *Omnibook* had condensed the novel and offered it for sale to members of the armed forces. A year later, the popular book club the Literary Guild issued its own edition as a dividend book, or bonus, to its members. Most surprisingly, beginning on Christmas Eve in 1945, the comic-strip giant King Features began syndicating a handsomely illustrated, condensed, serialized version of the novel in Hearst-owned newspapers across the country. Rand had been upset about the *Omnibook* publication, because Bobbs-Merrill had sold the rights without a guarantee that she could read the shortened text beforehand. This time, she read and approved every sentence of the King Features condensation and endorsed, and adored, the hand-drawn, Art Deco–style illustrations. "The artist has done a wonderful job of making Roark look like Frank," she wrote to niece Mimi. In fact, the artist had done a wonderful job of making Roark look like Cyrus in *The Mysterious Valley*, right down to the rolled-up sleeves and the lock of hair that fell over his forehead. Amusingly, in one drawing Dominique is a passable replica of Rand, except that she is taller and wears shoulder-length, 1940s-style blond hair. The serial ran weekly through midsummer 1946.

Just as the serial was starting, Rand left the relative isolation of the San Fernando Valley ranch and returned to work at Hal Wallis Productions, on the Paramount lot. She found the atmosphere dramatically changed. The war was over. The larger-than-life Franklin D. Roosevelt had died of a cerebral hemorrhage. The previous August, Harry Truman, the new president, had ordered American planes to use the world's first two atomic bombs on the cities of Hiroshima and Nagasaki, forcing a Japanese surrender but also killing tens (and eventually hundreds) of thousands of civilians and setting off a nuclear arms race with the Soviet Union. The Cold War had begun. In Hollywood, most wartime rationing had ended and a postwar boom was under way, but exhilaration was mixed with a new anxiety. Most Americans had never imagined the existence of such a destructive weapon as the atomic bomb until it was exploded. As *Time* magazine put it, Americans were proud that their resourceful scientists had been able to coax tiny atoms to reveal their mighty secrets. But they were also frightened—by the power of the new weaponry, by the magnitude of the damage to Japan, and by the prospect that the Soviet Union might develop its own bomb and deploy it against the United States. Still, theoretical physicists such as Albert Einstein, J. Robert Oppenheimer, and Enrico Fermi, whose work had helped create the bomb, became new American heroes.

In this respect, popular opinion caught up with Rand, who from adolescence had loved the luminous rationality of science, engineering, and technological invention. For a few days, Wallis assigned her to a silly gangster movie called *I Walk Alone*. In early January 1946, however, he asked her to plan and write an original screenplay documenting the development of the atomic bomb. The assignment, coming barely five months after the war had ended, was a vote of confidence from Wallis, a challenge, and, as she saw it, a unique opportunity to communicate the virtues of the American way of life. To her, the fabrication of the bomb stood for man's greatness and his salvation, as she put it in a memo to Wallis, primarily because it had been created, and could only *be* created, by rational, free men living in a free society. Nazi Germany had tried and failed to build a bomb, she reminded Wallis. Even the toughest tyrant can't coerce a mind to work. That's why, in a fair fight between dictatorship and freedom, freedom will always win. This was the message she wanted the movie to deliver.

The lengthy memo, written on the very day she accepted the assignment, is remarkable for revealing layers of meaning within a categorically new event. Always quick to discover large, original themes among steel girders and diaphanous evening gowns, she pitted liberty against tyranny as the core principle at stake in any discussion of the weapon. The memo also suggests an apparent, and potentially disturbing, disregard of the suffering brought on by the deployment of the bomb. No doubt, use of the weapon saved hundreds of thousands of American lives, and possibly as many Japanese lives, by making unnecessary an American land invasion. But this was not Rand's point, and the theme she chose to illustrate took no account of ordinary civilians, even in this real-life calamity. To Wallis, she joked that "if there is a God, He" might have planned the successful development of the bomb as proof of the superiority of American capitalism. Urging Wallis to adopt her approach, she wrote, "The responsibility of making [this] picture [with the proper moral lesson] is greater than that of knowing the secret of the atomic bomb."

One wonders: Did she really mean that framing an idea is more important than possessing the power of life and death over an entire population? There is nothing in her work to suggest she didn't. Three months earlier, she had answered a confused fan by noting, "If there is such a thing as an average man, who cares about him or why should anyone care? What I am interested in is the great and the exceptional." At times, the unexceptional simply wasn't real to her. Perhaps the first half of her famous formulation—her interest in men as they reflect philosophical principles—meant more to her than the second half, her interest in principles as they affect the lives of men.

She set to work immediately. She scheduled interviews with General Leslie Groves, the army's senior commander at Los Alamos National Laboratory, where the bomb was built, and J. Robert Oppenheimer, the former scientific director of the Manhattan Project at Los Alamos, who had returned to his teaching post at California Institute of Technology in Pasadena. She visited Dr. Oppenheimer twice, winning his cooperation and goodwill through her respect for his scientific achievement. He endorsed her interpretation of Germany's failure to produce a bomb and told her, thrillingly, that the ethos at Los Alamos precluded giving or taking official orders. In other words, the device was created by free men and free minds. She found Oppenheimer enormously intelligent and fascinating but also slightly bitter and apparently tormented by moral doubts. He certainly became bitter: Within a few years federal agencies, angered by his public opposition to the American-Soviet nuclear arms race, would accuse him of having been a Communist and strip him of his security clearance. Perhaps because of his political liberalism, otherworldly air, and battered pride, she made him her primary model for the character of Dr. Robert Stadler in *Atlas Shrugged,* a vain, weak, and progressively evil-minded physicist. She even borrowed the details of his office to use for that of Stadler.

The story she was outlining for *Top Secret,* as the film was called, became a rehearsal for *Atlas Shrugged* in other ways as well. She introduced into the film script a purely fictional character named John X., a young soldier she invented as a guard for Dr. Oppenheimer at Los Alamos. John X., influenced by his fictional father's Depression-era defeatism and his teachers' unseemly moral relativism—a growing complaint of Rand's about postwar culture—is resigned to a world without heroism or meaning. While witnessing the accomplishments of Oppenheimer, however, he gains perspective and courage—just as a tragicomic character called "the Wet Nurse" will gain courage in *Atlas Shrugged*. At the end of the script, John X. enunciates the movie's message: "Man can harness the universe, but nobody can harness man." The unhappy fate in store for a society that dares to try to harness man was to be magnificently elucidated in *Atlas Shrugged*.

Like the Tchaikovsky movie, *Top Secret* was never produced. In March 1946, after she had completed her outline and written about a third of the shooting script, Wallis sold the rights to MGM, which was on the verge of filming its own movie about the bomb and wanted to quash a competing project. She was furious, not only because Wallis sent a secretary to give her the bad news but also because she figured out that he must have begun the project with a sale in mind. She wrote a second memo to the Boss, suggesting a moral (as opposed to a legal) agreement between them. From now on, she wanted greater up-front control in choosing her assignments and greater say-so in executing them. And she wanted Wallis to phone her directly, not through a functionary, if he thought she was behaving badly, unreasonably, or arrogantly. Whatever the reply was, she left the studio a week later. Although her contract called for her to work until the end of June, she signed off on March 25 and didn't return until late September.

During her six-month leave at the ranch, she made her first extensive notes for the characters and plot of her fourth novel, her magnum opus, and drafted its first chapter.

Atlas Shrugged, Rand's tour de force in support of American capitalism, has been described as a literary masterpiece, a philosophical detective story, and a prolonged tantrum against Neoplatonism, Christian brotherhood, and government regulation. It tells the story of a group of industrial titans who go on strike against an anticapitalist and increasingly totalitarian society. The time is a hazy version of the 1930s, and the mood is apocalyptic. The government, and the nation, are sliding toward collectivism. Industrialists are publicly derided as selfish fiends who grow rich off the labor of the poor. Washington bureaucrats manipulate industries by fiat and have begun to appropriate the capitalists' products and profits—always "for the good of the people." As the novel opens, the nation's industrial titans have been vanishing slowly for twelve years. Now the pace of their disappearances is picking up. No one knows where they are going, or why. They are abandoning their mines, banks, and factories, which cannot go on functioning without their leadership and brains. As a result, industrial America is shutting down, and the nation is running short of coal, oil, steel, manufactured goods, electricity, and transportation. People seem eerily resigned to the economic collapse all this forebodes. As an expression of hopelessness, people ask one another, with a shrug, "Who is John Galt?" Where the question came from and what it means are a matter of indifference to those who ask it.

Amid the impending crisis, the novel's high-spirited heroine, Dagny Taggart, strives to save her family's great ancestral railroad, the New York–based Taggart Transcontinental Railroad. She is the vice-president of operations; her peevish, whining older brother James Taggart is nominally the president. While Dagny tries to keep thousands of miles of railroad track repaired with pieces of scrap metal and stretches the capacity of years-old diesel engines, James ingratiates himself with a clique of high-powered Washington officials, who bestow favors in return. He is a kind of inverse rendering of Peter Keating: having been born to money and position, he attempts to acquire self-esteem by giving them away. He hates and envies his competent younger sister but secretly depends on her to safeguard enough of their inheritance so that he has something left to trade among the "aristocracy of pull."

"The social welfare" is the motto behind which the bureaucrats and lobbyists grab for privilege and power. Under this banner, and as a diplomatic favor, James arranges for the railroad to build a spur into a barren stretch of the socialist state of Mexico. This proves financially disastrous. As a countermeasure, Dagny announces plans for her own new spur line, which she sardonically names the "John Galt Line," to run through the nation's last stronghold of free enterprise, the booming state of Colorado. Raw materials being impossible to come by, she calls on her colleague, a tough, self-made steel magnate named Hank Rearden, to sell her large quantities of his new invention, Rearden Metal, so that she can build the track. Rearden Metal is a superhard alloy that the "looters and moochers" in Washington (Rand's unforgettable phrase) have been trying to impound on behalf of a government-backed steel cartel that hasn't produced anything in years.

Dagny and Rearden miraculously complete the John Galt Line in record time. Hurtling through the Rocky Mountains on the line's first run, with Dagny at the throttle and her friend Rearden beside her, and with crowds of Coloradoans cheering at each stop, the two trailblazers realize that their admiration for each other has turned to molten desire. This sets the stage for another of Rand's power-driven sex scenes. Having completed their run, the two are gazing at a field of oil derricks from a balcony in the Colorado moonlight when Rearden first embraces her. The embrace is "like an act of hatred, like the cutting blow of a lash encircling her body," Rand writes. Yet Dagny is conscious of surrendering something of far greater import than her body. Leading her into his guest room, Rearden throws her on the bed while she thinks, "Whatever pride of person I hold . . . *that* is what I offer you for the pleasure of your body." Rearden, married to a monstrously cold and delightfully spiteful villainess named Lillian, at first despises both Dagny and himself for their animal lust. Gradually, he comes to understand the philosophical necessity of their sexual appetite for each other. This is especially true after Francisco d'Anconia, a courtly South American copper-mining heir who was once Dagny's friend but now presents himself in the guise of a debauched international playboy, incongruously explains that sexual desire in a rational man is an expression of his highest values. Soon Rearden learns that years before, Francisco was also Dagny's lover. But Rand makes it clear that neither man is Dagny's ideal man.

Among its many strengths, *Atlas Shrugged* is a uniquely intricate thriller, with a dozen hair-raising, idea-driven subplots radiating from the main story line, reinforcing its characters and themes. Dagny and Rearden, two of the last titans remaining at the helm of their businesses, play the part of the novel's philosophical detectives. Why does the stately, omnitalented Francisco, the chosen son of a proud aristocratic family, boast of being a dissolute playboy and yet speak like a sage? Why are "the men of the mind," as Francisco calls his fellow industrialists, disappearing? Who is the copper-haired stranger seen talking solemnly to each of the titans before he disappears? And what is going wrong with the world? In order to find out, the pair of heroes—like the brainy French anthropologist in *The Mysterious Valley*—must reconcile contradictory information at every step. About his own seemingly divided identity, Francisco says to Dagny, "I'll give you a hint. Contradictions do not exist. Whenever you think that you are facing a contradiction, check your premises. You will find that one of [your premises] is wrong."

The John Galt Line proves a commercial success, and Dagny and Rearden celebrate with a cross-country driving vacation. But the national landscape is not a pleasant sight. It has lapsed into a series of barren farms and desiccated towns, some of which have reverted to barter, recalling Russia in 1920 and 1921. The two stop to investigate a ruined factory called the Twentieth Century Motor Company. Amid the rubble they find discarded pieces of the prototype of a revolutionary motor designed to convert static electricity into usable power. Dagny is enthralled and also horrified: This pioneering motor could theoretically produce an inexhaustible supply of cheap energy to fuel the next generation of innovation. Who invented it? Why did he leave it here, in pieces?

When Dagny and Rearden return to New York, collectivist Washington is busy wresting the John Galt Line from Dagny by means of an "Anti-Dog-Eat-Dog" directive that prohibits "vicious competition" among railroads; the profitable line gives Dagny too much independent power. Once the line is closed, all that's left in the region is an old, broken-down railroad, and it stops running. Without transport, the new industries founder. Their leaders, too, begin to disappear. That's when Dagny decides to pursue the mystery of the vanishing titans, find the inventor of the motor, and discover why "the motor of the world" is poised to stop.

In the midst of unrelenting action, *Atlas Shrugged* is also an eleven-hundred-page deconstruction of the Marxian proposition "From each according to his abilities, to each according to his needs." The failure of the transportation system, the collectivization of industries, and the resulting economic atavism all broadly reproduce the Russian transition period under Lenin from a primitive capitalism to a brutal Communism in which human energy, far from being a creative force, was no more than "a raw commodity which the state could use to 'build socialism,' " wrote Orlando Figes. The novel is full of detailed parallels with the Russia of Rand's youth, including the Communists' failed attempts to force deposed capitalists to run their old businesses for the benefit of the state. It is surely also the only page-turning critique ever written of the Rooseveltian welfare state, the bureaucratization of the altruistic impulse, and the transformation of America from a culture of self-reliance to one of entitlement.

Midway through the novel, Dagny meets an old hobo who tells her a parable that deftly encapsulates this theme. Dagny is on a Taggart train, rushing west to find a talented young scientist before he, too, disappears—only to be stranded in the Kansas prairie when the train's crew bolts in the night, in defiance of a new law forbidding any worker to leave his job. The hobo is dressed in rags not because he doesn't want to work, he assures Dagny. For twenty years, he held a job as a skilled lathe operator at the very same Twentieth Century Motor Company where Dagny found the prototype motor. Dagny is startled but says, "Go on." About twelve years earlier, he says, Jed Starnes, the founder of the company, died, leaving the business to his three rich, idle children. The Starnes heirs had noble ideals, or so they announced to an assembly of the company's six thousand employees when they took over. "We're all one big family," they said. On a mass vote, the employees adopted the Starneses' progressive plan, in which work would be assigned according to ability and rewards would be doled out based not on merit but on need. Within a year, previously productive employees suddenly developed incapacitating needs—they had crippling accidents, became alcoholics, gave birth to broods of hungry children. As the needy segment grew, the active workforce shrank, quality dropped off, and customers went elsewhere. The industrious ones who did their jobs were expected to work long hours for less money. Usually, they either hid their ability or quit. Workers spied on one another to make sure that no one was working more slowly or less effectively than they and destroyed equipment out of laziness or malice. Within four years, the company was bankrupt. One man had foreseen the evil of this system from the start—a tall, copper-haired engineer who kept to himself and was known only by name. After the vote, he had stood and said, "I will put an end to this once and for all. I will stop the motor of the world," and strode out of the factory and disappeared. The Starnes heirs and the employees never saw or heard from him again. But after the company failed and thousands of other businesses also began to close their doors, the hobo often wondered if the engineer *had* exercised some awesome kind of retributory power. He took to asking people about the man, whose name was John

Galt, and now he wonders if he might be responsible for initiating that apparently meaningless question, "Who is John Galt?" Dagny, electrified by this new information, begins to understand the concept that the author calls "the sanction of the victim." If capable people would only reject the second-handers' calls to altruism and refuse to cooperate, the looters and moochers, the expropriators, and the "needy" would all perish.

Dagny hires a private plane to resume her journey west. Near Colorado, she spots another plane carrying the gifted young scientist she seeks. She follows and crash-lands in a camouflaged mountain refuge reminiscent of *The Mysterious Valley*. This is Galt's Gulch, where the great titans of the era have been hiding. Here reside the preeminent industrialists, financiers, builders, jurists, scientists, composers, and artists who have vanished over the previous twelve years. They are hard at work at their trades, constructing a capitalist utopia and using a reconstructed version of the Twentieth Century Motor Company's revolutionary engine to power their endeavors.

Dagny wakes from the crash in John Galt's arms. *He* is the inventor of the engine and the organizer of the titans' strike. The strikers—including Francisco d'Anconia, whom Dagny now spots—intend to prove that minds, not muscles, are the source of all prosperity. Their plan is to bring down the collectivist system by means of its own inherent weakness: its members' inability to think clearly enough to produce what they need to survive. Dagny gazes at Galt's features and, like Kira meeting Leo, sees the image of her ideal man. "This [Galt's face] was the world as she had expected to see it at sixteen," Rand wrote. But Dagny cannot stay in paradise. She will not stand by while the nation self-destructs in an orgy of altruism and decay, as Rand put it in her journals, or let go of her beloved railroad.

At this point, *Atlas Shrugged* veers ever more sharply toward the utterly implausible, and with the appearance of the protonuclear device designed by Galt's evil former physics professor, Dr. Robert Stadler, and delivered into the hands of the government, it borders on science fiction. As an apocalypse approaches, John Galt commandeers the radio airwaves from his hidden mountain valley and delivers a sixty-page speech to the battered nation, anatomizing the evils of the welfare state and prophesying the victory of Rand's now-mature philosophy of individualism, freedom, rationality, and capitalism. The speech is popular among the frightened masses. The looters and moochers decide to find John

Galt and make him economic czar. But the ideal man has no desire for power; and he has a surprise in store for the enemies of freedom.

With a railroad map above her desk and a furnace foreman's manual for steelmaking by her side, Rand wrote hundreds of pages of preliminary notes for *Atlas Shrugged* in the spring and summer of 1946. She started with a statement of the novel's theme as she and O'Connor had discussed it two years earlier: the mind on strike. She was setting out, she wrote, to show the world how badly it needed its creators and producers and how it mocked and martyred them at its peril. At this stage, she didn't foresee Galt's long speech or the painstaking work of giving a formal structure to her free-market philosophy. She thought the message of the novel would echo that of *The Fountainhead,* except that, instead of demonstrating individualism within a man's soul, it would dramatize the importance of individualism within the sweeping social, political, and moral realms of what was basically a panoramic nineteenth-century novel.

In this initial stage of note making, before the plot and characters were fully formed, she was imagining her heroes and villains as new variations on earlier characters or as aspects of her acquaintances and friends. John Galt, like Howard Roark, had always been in her mind, she said. She was basing Dagny Taggart largely on her own temperament but endowing the railroad heiress with more physical skill and courage. Dagny's "hunger for her own kind of world," like Rand's, she noted, is why "she works so fiercely. . . . She knows she can have her world only by *creating* it." As for the strikers, she developed their traits by analyzing the people closest to her. Her husband was the sort of finely tuned man who simply stops functioning, or functions only minimally in an occupation not his own, when forced to live in a morally corrupt society, she noted; the nondescript blue-collar jobs that many of the heroes regularly work at while on strike from their real professions are based on this view of O'Connor and his working life. Of Walter Abbott, her young playwright protégé, whom she would later remember as a ne'er-do-well, she now wrote, "[He is] the sensitive, poetic kind of writer who spends his time writing bloody thrillers" for the movies. "He thinks this is all he has a chance at. That is his form of being on strike." (No particular character in *Atlas Shrugged* seems to have been modeled after him.) She cast a cooler eye on the attributes of Frank Lloyd Wright and Isabel Paterson. Although she continued to view Wright as "a Roark" in his work, she thought his "desire to be a 'god'" among the lesser mortals who surrounded him undercut his integrity and placed him squarely in the camp of the new novel's parasites. Paterson's mistake was of a different kind. Loving justice and finding it nowhere, Rand observed, the older woman had given up all hope of living in a rational world or of gaining any valid recognition for herself. As a result, Rand wrote in a passage that would have been breathtaking had she written it about herself, "She knows that she cannot reach her enemies, the irrational ones, by her proper weapon, the mind; so she turns upon her friends, wreaking upon them the very thing she should hate, the thing which has hurt *her*—*the irrational*." (Interestingly, Galt, too, will battle his friends and allies, such as Dagny, by targeting the producers who continue to work and benefit the looters.) While contemplating the attributes she had in common with John Galt, she wrote, "I think I represent the proper integration of a complete human being."

She was also going out and entertaining. During her two and a half years in Hollywood, she had collected a sizable group of politically conservative friends. They were interested in her evolving ideas about capitalism and government and offered help in promoting her ideas and her work. One of these friends was Leonard Read, who headed the Los Angeles Chamber of Commerce until 1945, when he left to manage the National Industrial Conference Board in New York City. Shortly after Rand's arrival, in the winter of 1944, he had given a dinner party in her honor, introducing her to a dozen prominent West Coast businessmen who, by the evening's end, were favorably impressed with her originality and fervor. One evening in the spring of 1946, while Read was visiting Los Angeles from New York, he and William Mullendore, one of the dozen businessmen, dined at the ranch. A former special assistant for commerce to President Herbert Hoover, Mullendore presided over the Southern California Edison electric company and was highly regarded among free-market champions as a brilliant and accomplished speaker. The two men and their hostess were enjoying a rousing conversation about economic liberty, Read recalled, when Mullendore announced that he wanted to write a book about how a 100 percent collectivist society would, in practice, make most ordinary economic activity impossible. Rand responded, "I have written such a book. It is called *Anthem*. It was written in 1937. It was published in England" but not in the United States. Surprised to hear of a book by Rand he hadn't read, Read told her that he had recently founded a tiny publishing company, called Pamphleteers, Inc., whose purpose was to print and distribute libertarian monographs. It had already issued one by the Austrian economist Ludwig von Mises and one by Isabel Paterson's friend Rose Wilder Lane. He and Rand agreed that Pamphleteers, Inc., would publish *Anthem* as its first, and only, venture into fiction. The resulting ninety-eight-page booklet appeared in July 1946 and sold for a dollar a copy; ironically, it had as one of its distributors a one-man organization called the Pro-American Information Bureau, described by the liberal newspaper *PM* as the U.S. purveyor of *The Protocols of the Elders of Zion*. The *Protocols* was a famous, forged document purporting to reveal a Jewish conspiracy to dominate the world. It had been written by an anti-Semitic Russian secret policeman at about the time of Ayn Rand's birth. Of course, Rand and Read didn't know this.

Rand reworked the original 1938 British edition for American publication, and her revisions became standard in all subsequent editions. Although they weren't as self-conscious or as radical as those she would make for the 1959 republication of *We the Living,* they were extensive and revealing. To simplify and streamline the narrative language, she lessened her hero Equality 7–2521's reliance on biblical turns of phrase and echoes of Nietzsche's stern poetry of contrasts. The nineteenth-century German philosopher remains a forceful presence in the fable, however. "What can be loved in man is that he is an overture and a *going under,*" Nietzsche's hero Zarathustra says to an assembled crowd in *Thus Spoke Zarathustra.* "Man is a rope between beast and [Superman]." "We shall go down," Equality 7–2521 announces to his friend International 4–8818 when they come upon an underground tunnel, the contents of which eventually lead him to reinvent electric light. Rand's symbolism is her tribute to Zarathustra.

Although by this time everyone acknowledged that "Ayn Rand is a phenomenon in literature," as Rose Wilder Lane put it in a review of the reissued *Anthem* in the *Economic Council Review of Books,* the lyrical novella padded very quietly into the literary marketplace. Two or three additional reviews appeared in small publications, such as the *Columbia Missourian,* but the individualist parable did not become a popular success until a commercial publisher released a paperback edition in 1961. Still, Rand was fond of this short work, which she considered the parent of *The Fountainhead*. She mailed gift copies to Cecil B. DeMille, to *The New York Times* reviewer Lorine Pruette, to her Boss, Hal Wallis, to Henry Blanke at Warner Bros., to Walt Disney, and to Barbara Stanwyck, who continued to campaign for the part of Dominique. She also sent Stanwyck a copy of her 1932 script *Red Pawn,* hoping that the star of *The Strange Love of Martha Ivers* would see a role for herself in Joan, the story's American wife and mistress, and that Wallis would produce it. Stanwyck wasn't interested, and Wallis turned it down.

Rand remained an active opponent of Communist sympathizers wherever she went, particularly in postwar Hollywood. Along with her friends Sam Wood, John Ford, Ginger Rogers's mother, Lela Rogers, the producer James McGuinness, King Vidor (the future director of *The Fountainhead*), Walt Disney, and Morrie Ryskind, she helped create an organized opposition to left-leaning craft guilds and unions such as the Conference of Studio Unions and the Screen Writers Guild. With the rumored silent backing of Louis B. Mayer, these "campaigners for freedom" set up the Motion Picture Alliance for the Preservation of American Ideals, or MPA, whose mission it was to push back "the rising tide" of Communism in movies and promote the American way of life. Members met weekly at MGM Studios, and MGM executive Robert Vogel remembered that Rand attended almost every meeting.

Rand sat on the MPA executive board, and in 1946 she contributed a series of short articles to the organization's newsletter, *The Vigil.* Each was framed as an answer to a civics question. "What Is the Basic Issue in the World Today?" she asked rhetorically (individualism versus collectivism, she answered) and "What Is the Proper Function of Government?" (to protect individual rights against encroachments by other individuals and groups. It must never initiate the use of force but may use force in response to attacks from violent criminals or foreign powers). These little lessons served as a crash course in libertarian political thought for uninitiated members of the MPA and, later, as a rough foundation for some of her post-*Atlas* nonfiction. She may have attended a few free-for-all evening sessions in which MPA stalwarts debated with leaders of liberal Hollywood groups and which usually ended in shouting matches and "smears" (a favorite word of the time) in the next day's trade papers. "Reds!" exclaimed the MPA. "Fascist anti-Semites!" returned the Screen Writers Guild, using 1940s code for anti-Communists. Unintended slapstick notwithstanding, the depth of animosity, fear, and bad faith that existed between Left and Right during this period is hard to capture. At one point, Rand suspected her own treasured literary agent, Alan Collins, of acting on behalf of the "Communist spark-plugs planted around [Hollywood and New York]," whose assignment it was to recruit and use "literary agents and publishers . . . as stooges." Her suspicions were somehow allayed, because Collins and his associate, Perry Knowlton, remained her New York agents until her death. According to Robert Vogel, "we were all seeing ghosts, no question about it."

In the fall of 1946, the political friction intensified. The crime novelist and screenwriter James M. Cain, author of *The Postman Always Rings Twice* and *Double Indemnity*, got a brainstorm for an "American Authors Authority" that would own, license, and tax all literary copyrights belonging to members of the Screen Writers Guild, the Authors Guild, and other writers' unions. Because the guilds were immensely powerful and could influence producers and publishers to buy or not buy authors' works, Rand and her conservative colleagues saw this as a naked ploy to loot every American writer of his ownership rights and impose a Communist monopoly over the nation's literary output. Side by side with the unlikely trio of John Dos Passos, James T. Farrell, and Dorothy Thompson, Rand and her fellow MPA members formed the American Writers Association to fight the Authors Authority and the guilds. At the invitation of the New York newspaper columnist Benjamin Stolberg, she joined the board of the new organization, too. Meanwhile, Albert Mannheimer, who sat on the Screen Writers Guild committee that had proposed the plan, fought it from within, while left-wing committee members tried to "chop his head off." He and Rand gossiped about Hollywood's fractious politics on weekends, when they weren't talking about his plays or her progress on *Atlas Shrugged*.

At the same time, the U.S. House Committee on Un-American Activities (HUAC) announced its intention to investigate Communist infiltration of the movie industry. The committee—led by its publicity-seeking chairman, J. Parnell Thomas of New Jersey, who was assisted by Representative Richard M. Nixon of California and the volubly anti-Semitic Representative John Rankin of Mississippi—planned to descend on Hollywood in the spring of 1947, to gather information for public hearings scheduled for the following October in Washington, D.C. The MPA went into action. That winter, Rand and the executive board met as often as three times a week, selecting emissaries and discussing tactics for the spring preliminary hearings. As Rand's special contribution, she composed the "Screen Guide for Americans," addressed to movie producers and executives who wanted to avoid the appearance of left-wing influence. She warned them not to "smear" success, the profit motive, or wealth, and not to "glorify" the common man. "Don't spit into your own face," she added, "or, worse, pay miserable little [Communist screenwriter] rats to do it." As for Communists' right to free speech, she argued, rather persuasively, that the principle of free speech requires "that we do not [pass laws or] use a police force to forbid the Communists the expression of their ideas." It did *not* require privately owned and operated movie studios to offer jobs to Communist writers or give them the means to "advocate our own destruction at our own expense." This sensible distinction lost its sharp edge when, some months later, she publicly testified before HUAC to help police what she believed to be Communist content in some films.

On September 2, Ayn Rand wrote the first sentence of the first formal draft of *Atlas Shrugged*—which happens to be the date (minus the year) displayed on a lighted calendar that seems to float ominously above New York City's skyline at the beginning of the novel. Three weeks later, she rejoined Hal Wallis for what would turn out to be her last few months of work for him.

By now, the Boss was in a slump. The films he was working on for Paramount were fewer and far less distinguished than those he had produced for Warner Bros. in the early 1940s, where he had received twelve Oscar nominations. Rand's projects were no worse or better than the others. From September 1946 through mid-January 1947, and then again briefly in the fall of 1947, she worked on a movie called *House of Mist*, a tepid love story adapted from a novel by Chilean writer Maria Luisa Bombal. Like *The Crying Sisters, Top Secret,* and the Tchaikovsky movie, *House of Mist* was never filmed. But a draft found among Wallis's papers bears distinct marks of her thinking at the time. The story's heroine, Helga, like the developing heroine of *Atlas Shrugged,* "looks like a young girl who has never known any sorrow." Orphaned and poor, Helga tells her cousin Teresa something that a younger Rand may well have said or thought. "I don't believe in unhappiness," says Helga. "I won't let [unhappiness] make me bitter and ugly. I will think of things as they should be . . . even when they aren't." The film was finally shelved in October 1947. Without resigning, Rand left Wallis, never to return.

By then, she had finished seven chapters of *Atlas Shrugged* and was steering Dagny and Hank Rearden into their once-in-a-lifetime adventure on the John Galt Line. As the main plotlines unfolded without much difficulty, she thought that the book would be shorter and quicker to write than *The Fountainhead* and predicted that she would soon be finished. But when she began to consider the philosophic underpinnings of her plot and characters, she realized that she would have to probe more deeply. Asking herself, "Why is the mind important? What specifically does the mind do in relationship to human existence?" she decided that "my most important job is the formulation of a rational morality of and for man, of and for his life, of and for this earth." It would take her a total of thirteen years to complete the intricate and sweeping web of *Atlas Shrugged*.

On Thursday, October 16, 1947, she and O'Connor boarded a train for the nation's capital, where she had agreed to testify as a friendly witness before HUAC. The hearings opened on the following Monday, as into the marble caucus room of the old House Office Building strode Rand and a crowd of film celebrities, some wearing sunglasses against the glare of klieg lights. Looking for seats behind them were hundreds of newspaper reporters, photographers and cameramen, spectators, and a television crew. Outside, fans fought police for a glimpse of their favorite stars. It was the hottest show in town.

By prearrangement, the MPA supplied most of the twenty-four friendly witnesses expected to appear, including Ginger Rogers, Clark Gable, Robert Taylor, Adolphe Menjou, Walt Disney, and Ayn Rand. The nineteen unfriendly witnesses—those suspected of Communist Party ties or sympathies—had been subpoenaed to appear against their will. Ten of them would be sentenced to prison for refusing to answer the infamous question that introduced an era: "Are you now, or have you ever been, a member of the Communist Party?" Cited for contempt of Congress as a result of their refusal to answer, each of the "Hollywood Ten," as they came to be known, would serve between six months and a year behind bars. They would be blacklisted by the major studios and would be a liberal cause célèbre for decades. They were Alvah Bessie, Herbert Biberman, Lester Cole, Edward Dmytryk, Mannheimer's former friend Ring Lardner, Jr., John Howard Lawson, Albert Maltz, Samuel Ornitz, Adrian Scott, and Dalton Trumbo.

Rand was sworn in and testified on the first afternoon of the hearings. She didn't name names or inform against her colleagues, though others did. As the only individual present who had lived in Russia, she answered questions about the misleadingly cheerful impression of Russian Communist life conveyed by a 1944 wartime romance called *Song of Russia.* In the movie, an American symphony conductor, played by Robert Taylor, tours the USSR and falls in love with a Russian pianist named Nadya, who invites the conductor, John, to attend a music festival in her native village. The village peasants are pictured as strong, prosperous, happy, musical, and free—they ride state-of-the-art tractors, seem to own the land they farm, and excel at playing orchestral instruments. When the German army invades, the peasants fight valiantly but lose. John and Nadya flee to America, where they assure large audiences that the liberty-loving Russian people will soon defeat the Nazis. With U.S. government encouragement (if not actual arm-twisting), *Song of Russia,* like Howard Koch's *Mission to Moscow,* was produced by MGM as war propaganda, to help persuade Americans to support Russia's post-invasion conversion to the Allied side.

Rand was offended by *Song of Russia,* incensed by it, even pained by it. She explained to the committee that the country she came from was a land of frozen borders, omnipresent GPU (or NKVD) agents, meager food, prison camps, and constant, purposeful terror waged among average, ill-fed people, who didn't smile gaily and make music, as they did in the film. She pointed out the obvious and less obvious elements of propaganda. In one scene, a Russian band plays "The Star-Spangled Banner" while the camera lingers on a Soviet flag. In another, John's hard-boiled American road manager tells Nadya that, although her determination to fight the Germans personally makes her a fool, "a lot of fools like you died on the village green at Lexington," during the American Revolution. "I submit that that [speech] was blasphemy," Rand announced to the committee. She did not discuss the film's screenwriters, Paul Jarrico and Richard Collins, both of whom later identified themselves as members of the Communist Party.

Rand's remarks directly followed the much-publicized testimony of Jack Warner, Sam Wood, and Louis B. Mayer. Warner repeated testimony he had given the previous spring, in Hollywood, naming sixteen

Warner Bros. screenwriters whose views he considered to be un-American. One of them was Koch, Rand's old office mate, who, though not a Communist, would nonetheless not be able to secure work for the next seven years. Independent producer Wood, who was the president and founding member of the MPA, had been keeping a "little black book in which he jotted the names of radicals," according to Hollywood historian Neal Gabler; Wood accused seven screenwriters of being Communists, including four of the Hollywood Ten. MGM studio boss Louis B. Mayer took a more cautious position; he simply denied that there was any Communist influence exerted on or radical propaganda produced by MGM. It was then that the committee, prepared to prove him wrong, called Rand to talk about MGM's *Song of Russia*.

Rand later said, quite credibly, that she had been promised an opportunity to make a full statement of her views on the dangers of Communist propaganda in the movies and to read aloud from her "Screen Guide for Americans." Instead, the committee used her for its own purposes. Not listed in the schedule of speakers for that day (or any other day), she was called upon ad hoc, primarily to discredit Mayer's testimony. Her function was to demonstrate that in making *Song of Russia* MGM had, in fact, engaged in Communist propaganda. Had Mayer not taken what the committee considered an evasive stance, Rand would not have been called as a witness. She remained on hand throughout ten days of hearings, encouraged by Chairman Thomas to believe that, from one day to the next, she would be allowed to complete her statement. When she wasn't called, she remembered having a "violent scene" with the chairman in his office. He tried to placate her with promises of a "whole [new] special hearing devoted to nothing but ideology," where she could bring out "all the facts." She told him that, if she came back to testify at all, it would be on her terms. "What terms?" he asked, visibly nervous. Why, philosophical terms, of course, she answered. Relieved, he said, "Oh, I thought you meant money." "That gave me an insight into [his] psychology," she later told a friend, adding, "You know, in Washington, if you talk about terms, it's not philosophy." She was quite right. The following August, Thomas was convicted of taking kickbacks for favors and sent to a federal prison in Danbury, Connecticut, where Lester Cole and Ring Lardner, Jr., two of the Hollywood Ten, were also jailed. Cole and Lardner would sometimes pass ex-chairman

Thomas in the prison yard, where inmates tended chickens. "Still handling the chicken shit, I see," Cole is said to have remarked to him.

The HUAC hearings ended abruptly ten days after they began. Thomas told the press that there were rumors of planned Communist street demonstrations and that he wanted to thwart them. The real reason seems to have been that press coverage had turned negative.

In order to deliver a fresh scandal on the final day, the committee arranged for provocative testimony about, of all people, J. Robert Oppenheimer. Chairman Thomas called to the stand a HUAC investigator who claimed that, five years earlier, in 1942, the physicist had been approached by an American Communist agent seeking atomic secrets; this had taken place, the investigator said, with the help of a prominent Hollywood hostess, who had extended hospitality both to the alleged agent—a colleague of Oppenheimer's named Haakon Chevalier—and to two members of the Hollywood Ten, albeit *on entirely different occasions.* "The connection with the motion-picture industry was little more than incidental," *The New York Times* mildly observed. As for the motion-picture industry itself, studio flacks hailed the curtailment of the hearings as an exoneration of Hollywood. But the inquiries would go on.

For Rand, HUAC was "nothing but disappointments," she said. It was also a publicity disaster. Liberal newspapers mocked her and her novels and treated her as a certified member of the right-wing "nightshirt fringe" and as someone whose opinions on politics and social issues could not be taken seriously. For the next fifty years, almost every book written about Hollywood and HUAC, including Lillian Hellman's *Scoundrel Time,* presented her as a semihysterical reactionary who condemned *Song of Russia* strictly because it pictured Russians smiling. Unjust as this was, it made her fair game in the political as well as the literary press. Moreover, it was reported that she had annoyed Louis B. Mayer by contradicting him about the issue of Communist influence at MGM and irked Jack Warner with her initial intention of criticizing not only *Song of Russia* but also *Mission to Moscow, The Best Years of Our Lives,* and Hellman's *Little Foxes.*

Although she later admitted that the hearings were "a disgusting spectacle," she never changed her mind about their legitimacy. Far from conceding that a U.S. government agency had no business investigating citizens' political affiliations in the absence of a crime, she insisted that belonging to the Communist Party *was* a crime; that is, to be a member of a closed, secret, though legal political organization that advocated the overthrow of the American government and engaged in acts of espionage, sabotage, and murder was on its face to participate in a criminal conspiracy. This boils down to guilt by association—an odd stance for a radical individualist and admirer of the U.S. Constitution. It suggests a limited understanding of American jurisprudence, notwithstanding the teaching of Paterson, and, perhaps, a trail of ideological crumbs from her insurrectionary homeland.

Before leaving Washington, she tried to see J. Edgar Hoover, who turned her down. What she wanted from him is not known. En route to California, she and O'Connor stopped for a few days in New York, where she focused on collecting background material for the railroad scenes in *Atlas Shrugged.* She toured Grand Central Terminal (the inspiration for the Taggart Transcontinental Railroad Terminal) and interviewed half a dozen executives of the New York Central Railroad, including the male vice-president in charge of operations, the real-life equivalent of Dagny Taggart. She showed Archibald Ogden the first six chapters of the novel and met with editors of *Cosmopolitan, Reader's Digest,* and *Life,* presumably about assignments. She finally met Rose Wilder Lane, and she and O'Connor treated Marna Papurt, then twenty years old and back in Rand's good graces, to an expensive dinner at the Essex House, where the O'Connors were staying. In their hotel room after dinner, she, Marna, and Frank acted out scenes from her script for *House of Mist.* She spent her final evening in New York with Paterson. Albert Mannheimer, who was also in New York and was present on that evening, recalled that Paterson told her, "I love you." Mannheimer murmured, "I love you, too," but the following day, he bolstered his statement in a letter: "You are the ultimate in human beings I have known: free emotionally, with a full natural ability to love and hate (and to be loved)." He added that the abundance of her love of life was an enduring inspiration to him. This is a rare spontaneous tribute to a personal warmth and charm that Rand most assuredly possessed but that few people described in writing.

Mimi Sutton also visited her uncle and aunt by marriage in their room at the Essex House and witnessed an argument about money. O'Connor, always a stylish dresser, had been out shopping, and Rand objected to something he had bought. He told her, "Goddamn it, I will not account for anything I spend, buy, or do!" "She shut up," said Mimi. "I think it was because I was there. She had embarrassed him." In fact, she often backed down when Frank got angry. "She was afraid that she would lose him," Mimi said.

Back in Hollywood, she put the best face on the hearings. The studios moved immediately to conciliate the powerful committee, excising so-called un-American and overtly egalitarian content from their films and firing screenwriters whose loyalty to the country had been questioned. She took a measure of credit for these developments. "The 'Screen Guide for Americans' did it," she told friends. Two weeks after the hearings ended, the guide was published in a conservative magazine called *Plain Talk,* whose editor Rand had met while in New York. The Sunday *New York Times* picked up the story and reprinted the guide's itemized recommendations. Requests for reprints began pouring into the MPA from studios. Because of HUAC, she said in 1961, "all the points I made in [the guide], particularly about the attacks on businessmen as villains, disappeared" from Hollywood movies. "Watch old movies on TV [and] you'll see."

Another immediate outcome of HUAC was that producers began looking for *pro*-capitalist, anti-Communist screen material. She and her Hollywood agent, Bert Allenberg, seized the opportunity to bring her 1936 novel *We the Living* to executives' attention. She preferred to sell screen rights outright, Allenberg told trade reporters, but was willing to strike a deal with an American studio to distribute a two-part, six-hour Italian film version that had been made in Rome in 1942, at the height of the war, without Rand's permission and without payment. When she was finally able to get hold of a print of the film and saw it, she loved its stark, old-fashioned beauty and was especially pleased by Italian actress Alida Valli's superb performance as Kira. From Valli, now in Hollywood and under contract to David O. Selznick, she claimed to have learned a detail about the film's Italian release that struck her as wonderful in itself and as excellent publicity. Two months after the movie opened to packed theaters, Valli told her, Mussolini ordered the film to be withdrawn and prints and negatives destroyed, on the grounds that it was anti-Fascist as well as anti-Communist. This proved the kinship of Communism and Fascism, "which even Mussolini recognized," she wrote to her attorney. Luckily, an Italian producer had managed to preserve the master negative, and a print had been smuggled out of Rome by Rossano Brazzi, the actor who played Leo and who was also now in Hollywood. In February 1948, while post-HUAC fever still ran high, Rand contacted Jack Warner and offered to screen the print for him. Warner—perhaps still smarting over her planned testimony against *Mission to Moscow*—told her no. In the early 1950s, the Italian government paid her $35,000 in compensation for the unauthorized use of *We the Living*. Still angry at the theft, she was pleased with the payment and used part of the money to buy a new mink coat. It was not until 1972 that an artful splicing together of the film segments, *Noi Viva* and *Addio, Kira!,* with English subtitles, became available to art-house audiences, thanks to the efforts of three of her admirers. An American movie of *We the Living* has never been made.

Jack Warner was on her mind for another reason. In January or February 1948, she came upon an item in a Hollywood gossip column announcing that *The Fountainhead* was about to go into production, with Gary Cooper as its star and King Vidor as director. The hiring of Cooper was welcome news, of course. But that the producer, Henry Blanke, had notified a gossip columnist and not Ayn Rand about the project was *not* good news—and was angering because, at the time the studio had suspended production of *The Fountainhead,* Blanke had promised to keep her informed. With no assurance that she would be hired to write the final script, she fired her Hollywood agent Bert Allenberg and took to phoning Blanke directly. Awaiting word, she "went through hell." Then she remembered that one of the dozen businessmen at Leonard Read's 1944 dinner party was employed as the studio's chief legal counsel. She called him to report that someone (she thought Vidor, the director) was trying to keep her off the movie. Two days later Blanke phoned and offered her the job. The front office didn't dare to hire someone else, she later told a friend. It didn't understand the book's popularity and was scared to death that it would blunder and inadvertently offend the fans.

By March, she was back in a Warner Bros. office, with a secretary, and was working on the screenplay. Blanke and director Vidor were casting the remaining roles, and competition intensified for the part of Dominique. Hedda Hopper hinted that Lauren Bacall had accepted the part; Margaret Sullavan said she wanted it; Vidor had his eye on Jennifer Jones. Rand, who lobbied for the forty-three-year-old "Swedish Sphinx" Greta Garbo, was ordered by Blanke to tell their long-suffering mutual friend Barbara Stanwyck that the studio thought she was too old at forty. In early June, a month before the filming started, Vidor hired Patricia

Neal, a twenty-two-year-old ingenue who had only once before appeared on screen. When Rand heard Neal's Kentucky-bred voice on a screen test, she was horrified. So, the story goes, was Gary Cooper. He swore he'd have her fired; then, over dinner with Vidor, he met her and they fell in love. "They went for each other right away," the director told one of Cooper's biographers. "After dinner we never saw the two of them again except when we were shooting." The love affair between Cooper's Roark and Neal's Dominique was genuinely searing and continued offscreen until 1951.

Rand completed the screenplay in late June. As the shooting began in a quarry near Fresno, she remained on the lot to fine-tune the dialogue and explain her characters' motivations to the actors. In letters, she sounded euphoric. She had turned in her script in a blaze of glory, she wrote to Ogden, and Blanke and Vidor had promised not to make any changes unless she approved and wrote them. Vidor, in whose hands the project rested, was an excellent director. She seemed even more delighted, if possible, in late September, when the filming ended with her plot and theme intact. "For the first time in Hollywood history," she wrote proudly to Paterson's friend John Chamberlain, "the script was shot verbatim, word for word as written." When the first trial screening of the film took place in front of a live audience in January 1949, it went so well, she told her literary agent Alan Collins, that the studio executives decreed that additional screenings would not be necessary. When she suggested a few cuts that could be made during prerelease editing, the executives positively forbade her to touch a single line. They were in an uproar of excitement, she informed Collins. The front office expected *The Fountainhead* to be the most talked-about movie of 1949.

A decade later, Rand told a dramatically different story about the making of *The Fountainhead*. In an early 1960s interview she said, "The whole thing was an enormously miserable experience." Producer Blanke meant well, she said, but constantly caved in to pressure, especially when it came to casting Patricia Neal. Director Vidor was a vegetable, a frightened has-been whom no other studio wanted and whose career was hanging by a thread. Fired from his previous job because of cost overruns, he was concerned only with getting this movie in on time and under budget. She recalled endless unpleasant conferences with the production staff and continual arguments with Vidor over ideological and stylistic issues. Her most nightmarish moment took place during the filming of Roark's trial. Arriving on the set one day, she found Vidor shooting an abbreviated version of her hero's speech—the soliloquy that gave the book and the movie meaning, in her view. She rushed to Blanke's office, "screaming at the top of my voice," she said. She threatened to take her name off the movie and publish ads telling her millions of readers not to see it. Blanke, speaking for Jack Warner, overruled Vidor, and the scene was shot as written. Warner issued an edict: There were to be no more changes made to the script on the set. Her troubles didn't end there, though. The Hollywood censorship authority, the studio's business office, even Gary Cooper's personal attorney all badgered her to water down her central philosophical theme of the morality of selfishness. Making good use of her aptitude for calling the bluff of duller wits, she defied them all. To the business manager, who fretted that Roark's declaration that man is not "a sacrificial animal" would alienate (presumably Christian) audiences, she said, "So you think man *is* a sacrificial animal?" He backed down. Speaking to her interviewer, she explained, "That's how one should treat all underground pressure that doesn't dare come out into the open. Make it open. Name what they are implying." This was good advice, and she used it brilliantly for the better part of her career. Still, after a day of shooting, she recalled, she came home and pounded the arm of her favorite chair in frustration, enraged at being forced yet again into battle with the agents of conformity and pointless compromise. Worse, she knew that the movie was "no good" as soon as she saw a rough cut, long before the supposedly triumphant early screening. The script wasn't long enough to showcase the characters and theme, she said. The people involved were unworthy of the project. Then and there, she told her interviewer, she decided to wash her hands of the movie industry and never write another movie. The last trace of her youthful love of Hollywood as a utopia of beautifully costumed, strong-willed, dashing men and women was gone.

What explains the disparities between her account at the time and her recollections twelve years later? For one thing, when she finally attended the movie's gala opening night at the Warner Theatre in Hollywood in late June 1949, she discovered that one line *had* been cut in final editing, the sentence that summarizes Roark's self-defense at trial: "I wished to come here and say that I am a man who does not exist for others." The front office had demanded the cut, she later discovered, but no one seems to have had the courage to tell her in advance. For another, *The Fountainhead* was not a hit, either with film critics or at the box office. "High-priced twaddle" was the verdict of Bosley Crowther of *The New York Times*, who, not satisfied to condemn the movie, wrote a second article reproving Warner Bros. for its role in helping to promote her doctrine of the Superman. A newspaper syndicate distributed an article facetiously headlined "Cooper in Race for Longest-Speech Oscar." Though dramatically set and beautifully shot, the movie was stiff, and most reviewers said so.

But the larger explanation for the disparity lies within Rand's character. She would not admit that she had written a flawed script. From adulthood, if not before, she positively refused to consider that she bore significant responsibility for any of the conflicts, failures, or disappointments in her life. "In all the years I knew her, I never heard her say anything remotely to the effect that she had acted badly, mistakenly, or unfairly," recalled a former friend. As her fame increased and she became conscious of her own iconic stature with readers and audiences, she tended increasingly to fuse her life with the lives of her characters, whose mistakes, if any, arose from ignorance of others' bad intentions and not from a lack of objectivity, diplomacy, or wisdom. She remembered obstacles and disappointments less as ordinary, if infuriating, setbacks than as episodes in a tug of war—like Roark's, like Equality 7–2521's—with evil. People and events appeared as black or white. She minimized to the vanishing point the help she had received, failed to mention thinkers who had influenced her, and presented herself as an almost wholly self-created soul. Nowhere is this trend more apparent than in the aftermath of her final falling-out with Isabel Paterson in June 1948, while she was still trying frantically to finish the screenplay of *The Fountainhead*.

To some degree, Rand and Paterson seemed to have repaired their friendship during Rand's visit to New York after the HUAC hearings in the fall of 1947. And no wonder: Paterson had taken the trouble to arrange a special treat for Rand on Rand's way back to Los Angeles. This was a favor the younger woman was not likely to forget.

It was the trip of a lifetime, Rand wrote to Paterson in February 1948. The aging columnist, on learning that Rand wanted to ride in a locomotive to gather background details for Dagny's triumphant run on the John Galt Line, had contacted her good pal Colonel Robert S. Henry, a railroad executive and historian, and together they made arrangements for the novelist to travel partway home in the locomotive engine room of the Twentieth Century Limited, while Frank rode in a compartment car behind. When the Limited had pulled out of the underground tunnels beneath Grand Central Terminal, Rand wrote to Paterson, "Everything I thought of as heroic about man's technological achievements was there concretely for me to feel for the first time in my life." At Croton-Harmon, New York, the train exchanged its coal-burning engine for a faster diesel engine, and outside of Elkhart, Indiana, she took the throttle and drove the train at eighty miles an hour. After touring Inland Steel in Chicago, she and Frank resumed their trip to Hollywood as passengers. They were treated like royalty, she wrote. But she didn't exactly thank Paterson and afterward didn't mention her former mentor's help when describing the experience to others.

Rand had taken a train during almost every important journey of her life. Yet she admitted to Paterson that, as an adult, at least, she had often felt a nagging dread of railroad accidents. "I have seldom enjoyed anything concrete or in the present tense," she wrote. "That locomotive ride was one of the very few times when I enjoyed the moment for its own sake." This is a startling statement and provides an insight into Rand's enormous drive and habitual placement of all real joy and satisfaction in the future. In *Atlas Shrugged,* she leaves it to Dagny to explain the connection between anxiety and the uncharted present moment. At the throttle on the John Galt Line, "she [Dagny] wondered why she felt safer here, where it seemed as if, should an obstacle arise, her breast and the glass shield [of the front window] would be first to smash against" the looming obstacle. Then Dagny understands: "It was the security of being *first,* with full sight and full knowledge of one's course. . . . It was the greatest sensation of existence: not to trust, but to *know.*" Alone in command of a powerful machine, not unlike her mind, Rand and her character were most alive.

As they exchanged letters in early 1948 they traded compliments—until they started trading barbs. In response to something Paterson wrote, which has been lost, Rand mailed off a terse tract against Catholics ("those people") and the emphasis they placed on suffering. The older woman asked how Rand could indict all "those people"—hundreds of millions of Catholics—without risk of indicting the entire human race. Easily, Rand replied, echoing Nietzsche: even if every person in the world other than she became a Christian, a socialist, or any other kind of collectivist "altruist," the greatness of man would be vindicated by the lone remaining rationalist. In another letter, Paterson unwisely mused that she, Paterson, might well be the only person "alive or dead" who really understood capitalism. Rand answered testily, "Does it really seem to you that I haven't been born yet?" Still resentful over the perceived failure of her former elder "sister" to give her credit in *The God of the Machine*, she reminded Paterson that, until she had explained that altruism asks the impossible of men, Paterson believed that altruism was an ideal to which to aspire. Paterson denied that she had ever said such a thing and then moderated the argument with a jest: Altruism was like sawdust, she wrote, in that both were indigestible to humans. Rand became conciliatory. She conceded to having learned the practical aspects of capitalism from Paterson, and apologized in case she had wrongly remembered their conversation. Never in her life had she doubted her memory, which added a note of grace to the concession.

Rand was midway through her screenplay when Paterson phoned to say that she was coming to California. The reason for her visit was to raise money for a new magazine, which would be edited by their common friends John Chamberlain of *Fortune* and Henry Hazlitt of *Newsweek*. The magazine was to be called *The Freeman* in honor of Albert Jay Nock's 1920s libertarian weekly and would advocate free-market politics and economics. Rand liked the idea; since Willkie's defeat, she had believed that serious conservative thinkers needed a serious public forum. If she would furnish introductions to her high-powered conservative friends in Hollywood, Paterson proposed to do her best to win their financial backing for the magazine.

Rand seemed genuinely pleased by the prospect of a visit from her friend. She paid Paterson's plane fare and invited her to stay for ten days at the ranch. Rand's affection for Paterson at this point is unmistakable. She wrote to the older woman that she hoped to be finished with the screenplay by the time Paterson arrived. If Paterson could be on the set when the first camera shot was taken, "it will be a wonderful philosophical omen," she wrote. As it happened, the shooting didn't begin until Paterson was back in New York, but Rand had rarely paid such a solemn compliment to anyone.

Paterson arrived on May 28. Irascible by nature, she was in an especially irritable mood, according to her biographer Stephen Cox. She had not enjoyed the flight and regarded the entire fund-raising expedition as a tedious necessity. At sixty-two, she was battle-weary. She was also probably aware that Irita Van Doren and her other ideological adversaries at the *Herald Tribune* were on a campaign to have her fired. The following January, she would lose the job she had held for twenty-seven years. She would never really work again. Rand, too, was under pressure; one of her more minor complaints about Paterson's visit was that her guest's constant chatter made it hard for her to write.

Rand behaved generously in her role as fixer, staging a series of parties with wealthy conservatives. The first hint of trouble came at the end of a small party attended by Rand's friend the playwright Morrie Ryskind and his wife. After Ryskind left, Paterson apparently said to Rand, "I don't like Jewish intellectuals." Paterson's biographer Cox surmises that this was merely an awkward joke, an attempt to disguise her boredom and discomfort with many of Rand's friends, who were by no means New York–style literary intellectuals. Naturally, it struck Rand as an insult. In another example of her response to anti-Semitism, she asked, "Then why do you like me?" and answered herself sarcastically, "Of course! I'm not an intellectual." Paterson apologized.

The next incident took place at a large gathering of members of the Motion Picture Alliance. There, a peevish Paterson spoke rudely to one of Rand's colleagues at Warner Bros., a screenwriter named Gordon Chase, and he and his wife walked out. A night or two later she told six or so anti-Communist luminaries, seated around the dinner table at the home of Rand's neighbor and friend Adrian Greenberg and his wife, the actress Janet Gaynor, that they knew nothing, *nothing,* about politics. (Years later, a repentant Paterson told a friend that Gaynor had said that night, "[That woman] ought to be kept out of sight and produced only on special occasions." Paterson admitted that she had to agree.) Finally, during a party at the ranch, hosted by Rand in honor of the man she called her best conservative ally, William Mullendore, the sexagenarian had a public temper tantrum. When Adrian suggested producing a promotional dummy issue of the new magazine, with real articles by Paterson, she went into a fit. Hadn't she worked hard enough in her lifetime? she shouted. Why should she write without pay? Why didn't someone else do something for a change? Turning to Mullendore, who could have been helpful to her, she cried, "None of the businessmen do anything! *None* of them!" In other circumstances, with a businessman other than Mullendore, Rand might have agreed. Now she attempted to quiet Paterson, but the tirade continued. Mullendore left. That was *it* for Rand, she later told a friend.

Paterson behaved badly, but the trouble between them was older and more personal than that. In addition to their dispute over who had taught what to whom, and who had received proper credit, Rand suspected that Paterson had not really liked *The Fountainhead*. For five years, Rand had resented the fact that Paterson had not openly praised the novel in the *Herald Tribune* or publicly defended her against the Left's attacks. Of the many references Paterson had made to the book in print, most were gossipy or anecdotal, she complained. One day during the visit, Paterson, probably inadvertently, revealed that she was the mystery woman who had refused to review the novel for the *Herald Tribune* in 1943. According to Rand's later account—the only one there is— when the novelist demanded to know why, Paterson gave an evasive answer. She didn't agree with everything in the book, she muttered vaguely. She didn't like the sex and was particularly uncomfortable with the fact that Dominique didn't bathe after the "rape" by Roark because she wanted to keep his scent on her skin. She hadn't wanted to attack her friend in print. Anyway, she added, by that time her literary influence was waning and a review by her would not have helped the book. Rand wanted to throw her out of the house right then and there but considered Paterson's age and distance from home and let her stay. "I forgive you, but God won't" was a favorite expression of Paterson's. Rand gazed at her former friend with her laser-beam eyes and said, "God may forgive you, but I won't," and returned to her work.

On the night of the Mullendore incident, Paterson offered to go home early. Rand and Frank didn't plead with her to stay. The next morning, Paterson made a show of not knowing how to change the date of her airplane ticket. If she was hinting that she wanted to stay, her hostess didn't take the bait. O'Connor chauffeured Paterson to the airport, Rand sitting silently up front while Paterson chatted from the back about books and authors and New York literary life. Listening to but not answering the kind of small talk she had always hated, Rand decided that Paterson was "gone" psychologically. She was "no good."

Rand and her first and only mentor saw each other once again, in February 1959, shortly before Paterson's death. Paterson, then seventy-three and down at the heel, came to Rand's New York apartment to ask her former friend for help in finding a publisher for her final novel, *Joyous Gard*. Isolated and regretful about the past, she also hoped to reignite their friendship, according to her biographer. Rand was not interested. She went right to the point, explaining without rancor that the novel was too dated, too old-fashioned, to be published. Then she gradually turned the conversation to what Paterson had thought of *Atlas Shrugged*, which had been published in 1957. The undiplomatic Paterson admitted that she had reservations about the novel's treatment of man as a purely rational being—their old dispute. One of Rand's disciples was in the room when Paterson said good-bye. She appeared burned out, sour, and defeated, he recalled. Rand was at the pinnacle of her fame. He couldn't imagine what Rand and the older woman had ever had in common.

Neither could Rand. When she later spoke of Paterson—infrequently, according to acquaintances—her comments were derisive. Close friends had no idea that Paterson had once been Rand's most intimate friend, let alone her mentor. By 1959, the novelist seemed to have forgotten that Paterson had taught her anything or helped her in any significant way. As time went on, "she could not say that she had been crucially helped by anybody," said Barbara Branden, a close friend from the 1950s and 1960s. She was grateful to her parents for freeing her from Russia, but she never mentioned the hundreds of supportive letters she had received from them in the 1920s and early 1930s or the gifts and loans extended by her mother's relatives in Chicago. When she spoke of her neighbor Marcella Bannert, she recalled her as the social-climbing paradigm for Peter Keating, not as the woman who had helped her to find a home for *Red Pawn*. "No one helped me, nor did I think at any time that it was anyone's duty to help me," she would write in her author's note in *Atlas Shrugged*.

However decidedly Paterson was to blame for the final falling-out between the two women, Rand's demotion of her friend to the status of a minor player in her life was a template for broken relationships to come. In large measure, her partings from people were based on principled complaints about those people's premises (philosophical beliefs) and behavior, but once banished, they had as little reality for her as Ellsworth Toohey had for Howard Roark. "If she didn't love it," or *still* love it, "it couldn't be great," said a friend. "She was not interested in process," said another, mildly. Yet she never stopped recommending the *books* she loved, including Paterson's *The God of the Machine*.

The price of being her friend went up. From these years onward, she required at least fundamental agreement with a system of political and moral ideas that would finally enter the world at large with *Atlas Shrugged*.

TEN

THE MEANS AND THE END

1950–1953

❧

*"I have nothing to sell. But myself. And no one wants that," said
Leo Kovalensky.*

"I might," said Kira Argounova.

*The scornful arc [of his eyebrow] rose slowly. "Want to reverse our
positions? Well, what price have you to offer?"*

[Kira] raised her face to a ray of light.

"Look into my eyes," she said very seriously. "What do you see there?"

He bent close to her. "They're beautiful."

*"I have no other mirror to offer you." She asked again: "What do
you see there?"*

"My own reflection."

"That's the price I'll offer you."

—From the first draft of *We the Living*,
written in April 1933

B y the time the movie of *The Fountainhead* opened in July 1949, to
moderate box-office success in theaters across the country, Warner
Bros. was boasting that ten million Americans had read the novel.
"Monumental Best-Seller! Towering Screen Triumph! The Love
Fire That Blazed on Every Page of the Novel!" shouted the display
posters. As the movie arrived in theaters in New York, Philadelphia, Mil-

waukee, Des Moines, Dubuque, Detroit, Gulfport, and Galveston, the Bobbs-Merrill Company had ample books waiting in local bookstores. In three weeks, fifty thousand copies were sold. Notwithstanding the movie, in years to come *The Fountainhead* would continue to be promoted primarily by excited readers, and it gradually became a publishing legend. "It was the greatest word-of-mouth book I've ever been connected with," said a Bobbs-Merrill sales manager named William Finneran in 1968, on the novel's twenty-fifth anniversary. That year, total sales reached two and a half million copies. By the mid-2000s, the audience for the book was expanding again at a rate of 150,000 readers a year, with six million copies circulating. Although three generations of critics could hardly believe it, Ayn Rand's newly patented fictional formula of "metaphysics, morality, politics, economics and sex," as she described her novel in progress to an interviewer in 1948, clearly worked with readers.

Of all the readers and viewers of *The Fountainhead,* however, only one had personal meaning for her, she later said. This was a nineteen-year-old college freshman named Nathan Blumenthal. A few years after meeting her, he would legally change his name to Nathaniel Branden.

Like Thaddeus Ashby, Nathaniel Branden sent his favorite author a youthful fan letter. That was in the summer of 1949, the summer before he entered college. He was living in Winnipeg, Manitoba, twelve hundred miles from his home city of Toronto, and was working as a clerk in his uncle's jewelry store while taking a year off between high school and college. He was trying to write a novel. The first time he had read *The Fountainhead* he had been fourteen. He had read the book forty times since then, and parts of it a hundred times. Hearing a sentence from any section, he could summarize, if not quote verbatim, the sentence that came before and the sentence that came after. With its lofty view of life's possibilities, its elevation of independence and creative work, and its rejection of dreary conventionality, it had inspired him and given him a program for living. Its author had become the heroine of his teenaged years. He was planning to start college in California in the fall. He was writing to Rand to say that he would like to know more about her political and philosophical opinions, and particularly whether or not she believed in capitalism. Like Thaddeus Ashby, he received no answer.

In the late fall of 1949, near the end of his first semester at the University of California at Los Angeles, he tried again. This time, in reply to a question he asked, she mailed him a note listing her three published novels. Awestruck and hopeful, he sent another letter, a long one, praising *The Fountainhead,* posing questions about atheism, socialism, and free will, and pointing out what he thought might be inconsistencies in *We the Living.* Instead of being offended by this, she was so favorably impressed by his intelligence that she answered at length. She ended her letter with a short reading list on the strengths of capitalism. Although just starting a difficult chapter of *Atlas Shrugged* and ducking new social obligations, she asked for his telephone number and hinted that they might arrange a meeting. Looking back on the series of events that led to their first encounter, she always said that it was Frank O'Connor who encouraged her to answer Branden's letters and to call.

She phoned the Hollywood apartment the young man was sharing with his older sister Elayne, a nurse, one night in February 1950, waking him from an early sleep. A week or so later, on March 2, he drove out to the ranch at her invitation and they met. Dapper, genial O'Connor answered the door and escorted him into the double-height living room, where he watched as the forty-five-year-old novelist crossed the room to greet him. She was wearing a plain skirt and blouse, her dark-brown hair arranged in her usual 1920s forward-slanting bob. Branden, well scrubbed, with sharp, strong features and on his best behavior, was good-looking. He was immensely in awe of her, though, as he recalled, not intimidated by the aura of power she most definitely projected. She took his hand in greeting. Before they spoke, she gazed into his eyes. He later described the sensation as one of standing in the direct path of the beam of a searchlight. He liked being the object of such scrutiny, and she saw he liked it. She interpreted his lack of fear as a sign of strength of character—and a mark of the arrogance that was a stamp of heroes.

Once they had introduced themselves and taken seats, he noticed that the room was peacock blue and filled with objects in green-blue, Dominique's favorite color in *The Fountainhead.* (Although he didn't know it then, it was also the color of Hank Rearden's miracle alloy, Rearden Metal, and Ayn Rand's favorite color.) He saw that his literary idol was shorter, stockier, and less poised than he had expected, given her descriptions of Dominique and the glamorous photograph that appeared on the back cover of his favorite book. She smoked heavily through a cigarette holder and spoke with a surprisingly thick Russian accent. Still, he felt that he had entered the ennobling world of *The Fountain-*

head. She sensed that she had made a discovery and that this young man would be a significant person in her life.

Many years later, Branden remembered what they talked about. She inquired politely about his background, and he explained that he had grown up as the only son of immigrants in a family of six in Toronto. His Russian-Jewish parents had never fully assimilated themselves into life in Canada, and he, too, had always felt out of place, unpopular, and awkward. For guidance and companionship, he had turned to characters in books, especially to Howard Roark. Was that weak? he asked. "Oh, foolish child!" she answered. "We all need that fuel. That's what art's for." She mentioned Aristotle's distinction between history and fiction: history represents things as they are, whereas fiction presents things as they might be and ought to be. That's the reason people turn to novels for inspiration, she told him. Her agreement with Aristotle was why she called her form of writing "romantic realism." By "realism" she meant that her plot and characters were not fantasy but a projection of what might be, and by "romantic" she meant that she infused her writing with a moral vision of what ought to be and wasn't yet. In Roark, she had created an ideal man in a stylized version of the world. Her view of man as the achiever of heroic deeds through the use of his own judgment in creative work and in life—*this* was what she had brought to life in Howard Roark. This was what Branden loved about the novel.

She asked him a series of philosophical questions, which she had also asked Ashby and other young admirers. What did he think of the faculty of reason? What did he think of man? Did he imagine the universe as a malevolent place where men were doomed to be defeated or a benevolent place where, by means of reason, they could accomplish whatever they set out to do? Of course he supported reason, Branden answered, hardly daring to believe that this brilliant woman was interested in what he thought. While O'Connor listened from a nearby chair or padded back and forth from the kitchen with coffee and sweets, she amplified her ideas. The basic issue in all her writing, she explained, was not so much individualism versus collectivism as reason versus mysticism—the conflict between objective thinking on the one hand and irrational subservience to a deity, a tyrant, or a group of people on the other. Capitalism was the only economic system in history to operate on the basis of independent reason; furthermore, without capitalism's underpinnings, the right to own private property and to work for one's own profit, no other political rights could be guaranteed. If the state could seize the wealth and property a person had acquired through hard work and the use of his own mind, why would anyone bother to invent new things? Glancing at Frank, who nodded, she revealed that she was working on a new novel that would explain all this and more.

When Branden rose to go, it was 5:30 a.m. He and Rand had talked for nine and a half hours. She handed him her phone number so that he could call with additional questions. He drove away from the ranch at dawn, with an exhilarating conviction that the world really did make sense and that he could master it. He also had an invitation to return.

Branden was involved in an on-again, off-again romantic relationship with a slightly older girl whom he had met while working for his uncle. She had been a sophomore at the United College in Winnipeg, where she had grown up. The two were introduced by a mutual friend who thought they would like each other because they both talked nonstop about *The Fountainhead.* The girl's name was Barbara Weidman, and she, too, had read Rand's novel in her early teens. That she happened to look like a Rand heroine was serendipitous; tall, blond, willowy, and lovely, she had delicate features and a diffidence that could easily be mistaken for cool reserve. Men found her attractive. Like Branden, she saw herself as different: for one thing, she was an intellectual; for another, in Winnipeg, where she grew up, she was the only Jewish child she knew until high school, and she was aware of anti-Semitism all around her.

She and Branden started a sexual relationship in Winnipeg—Branden's first. It didn't go well. She liked him and admired him as a brilliant young thinker on philosophical and psychological subjects. But she was uncomfortable with him as a lover, and by summer's end she was dating other boys. They both enrolled at UCLA—he as a freshman studying psychology, she as a transfer student majoring in philosophy, and they maintained a close friendship on the basis of their shared love of *The Fountainhead,* which at that time few students at liberal colleges admired. But Branden continued to want more.

"Ayn Rand is fascinating," he reported to Barbara on the morning after his visit. "She's everything I could have expected from the writer of *The Fountainhead,* and more. She's Mrs. Logic." This brief encounter with the famous author had made him feel appreciated, understood, competent, and psychologically *visible* in a way that nothing else ever had, he told Barbara, and Rand had given every appearance of liking him, too. He promised to ask if he could bring the young woman along on the following Saturday evening, when he planned to visit Rand again.

He phoned on Sunday evening, and five times more that week, and on Saturday evening at eight o'clock he and Barbara drove up the long, birch-lined driveway to the house. This time, both Frank and Ayn greeted them at the door. Although Rand wasn't pretty "by any means," her eyes were dark and magnetic and "seemed to be staring right down to the bottom of your soul," Barbara would recall. Her face was square, but her mouth was sensual. Her exceptional intelligence was apparent even before she spoke. O'Connor appeared vaguely aristocratic, with a gaunt beauty and a charming grace, and was welcoming and warm.

When they all sat down, Nathaniel explained that he and Barbara had met because of *The Fountainhead*. Rand seemed charmed. "It's a wonderful fiction event!" she cried. There the evening's small talk ended. The thinker and her new pupil dove into a discussion of economics, religion, ethics, epistemology, and the vast potential of the human mind. Somewhat bashful, Barbara didn't say much but was exhilarated by the rapid stream of ideas that were new to her. Here, she thought, with this woman, in this room, ideas *matter*, with a life-and-death importance that both she and Branden seemed to have been waiting all their lives to find. She was also impressed by Rand's obvious regard for Nathaniel.

Like Mannheimer and Bungay before them, they began to visit every weekend, and then, by appointment, on weekday afternoons and evenings, too. Rand and Frank were always gracious; in fact, Rand spent hundreds of hours with them over the next several months. They were astounded by her energy—she wrote all day and stayed up talking with intoxicating inventiveness all night—and by her generosity with her time. She almost always took Branden's daily phone calls from the city; their conversation could go on for hours, explaining why the young man's phone bills ran to a stupendous thirty or forty dollars a month. When he asked why she indulged an undergraduate who hadn't yet accomplished anything with so much of her time, she answered, "You will!" The gap in their ages and levels of achievement mattered very little, she said, in light of their shared ability to think.

What Nathaniel couldn't have guessed was that, once again, Ayn Rand was lonely. She was glad to meet an intelligent young man with the time and inclination to conveniently divert her from her unsatisfactory marriage. In 1949, she had worked for days and sometimes weeks in a row without leaving the ranch or, at best, the town of Chatsworth. Her prized Hollywood conservatives, who sometimes came to visit, were loyal political allies but uninterested in philosophical ideas. Paterson had written two or three letters after her disastrous visit, but Rand had answered coolly and the letters stopped. O'Connor, although always ready to listen to her work in progress, was now fully occupied and often tired; he went about the property, looking after the alfalfa, gladioli, fruit, and farm animals, including brightly colored peacocks, peahens, and caged white pigeons, with a pleasure and satisfaction that almost amounted to self-sufficiency. He created a modestly profitable business selling flowers to Beverly Hills hotels. When a friend came upon him dipping mums into buckets of colored dye, he laughed and said, "Not the sort of thing Howard Roark would do!" He was happy.

He had also made an independent friend. A local woman who raised flowers and sold them from the front porch of her house, this woman was "the joy of Frank O'Connor's life" at the time, said a mutual friend, although there appears to have been nothing sexual in their friendship. Her name was Aretha Fisher. She and her brother Bill lived about a mile from the ranch, and O'Connor got in the habit of ambling over to see her in the early afternoons. Out of earshot of the Neutra house, he chatted amiably with her about the weather and flowers and usually fell asleep in a chair on the porch until late afternoon. Aretha told their mutual friend that she would wake him at four, so that he wouldn't be late for dinner at the ranch. More than once, she said, he sighed as he rose and headed home. Rand never met Aretha and may not have known where Frank spent his afternoons. It was another one of the many satisfactions he found in his life as a gentleman farmer.

In any case, Nathaniel's looks and manner reminded Rand of the dynamic and determined Howard Roark. Like Frank, the young man had her "kind of face," she later said. She also quickly concluded that he possessed the best mind of anyone she had ever met. From his first visit, she ranked him as a genius, she told Barbara in 1961, "and I really mean *genius*." To earn that title, she explained, it wasn't enough to grasp ideas rapidly or be able to manipulate abstractions. One had to have "a creative intelligence, an initiating intelligence," and she thought she had finally found one in the nineteen-year-old psychology student. But she was wary, wanting to be sure that *this* intelligent young man shared her ideas and "sense of life." She had a horror of being fooled or disappointed again, as she believed she had been by Ashby and Abbott.

Gradually, she and O'Connor took to referring to Nathaniel and Barbara as "the children." They didn't mean anything parental by it, Rand insisted. She often repeated her dictum that birth families are unimportant. An acquaintance of the period heard her say that she was "absolutely, *violently* against" them. She believed in "relatives through choice, not blood." When another acquaintance asked whether she thought of herself as the young people's mother, she answered sharply, "Certainly not. They are not *my* children. They are the children of *The Fountainhead*."

Branden shared her view of families. Nonetheless, he was aware that his mentor's geographic and ethnic origins were very similar to those of his biological parents. He sometimes thought that his literary idol looked very much like one of his mother's cousins. And though he and Barbara weren't her actual children, they began to come to her for motherly advice. How should they deal with the left-wing professors and students at UCLA who treated them as pariahs when they argued for her point of view in class? How should they respond when a popular philosophy professor, a logical positivist, insisted that perception is unreliable, logic is arbitrary, and nothing is universally true? Rand responded more protectively than she later would to similar dilemmas, warning "the children" against risking their academic careers by deliberately espousing her ideas. She also trained them to be alert to the implications of all that they were hearing and being taught. "Check your premises!" she would call out in conversation, meaning make sure that the assumptions you argue from are true. She astonished them by skimming a few pages of their college texts and accurately construing the authors' starting points, arguments, and conclusions. "One could not encounter a human being in whom the psychological attribute of rationality was more pronounced," Barbara wrote in 1986. Added Nathaniel, in 2008, "She had a Sherlock Holmes ability to ferret out implications that other people might miss," as well as a prophet's pleasure in guiding her young fans in mastering her ideas.

Meanwhile, she also learned from them, especially from their encounters with professors. In *Atlas Shrugged*, Lillian Rearden's pseudo-intellectual friends the satirical Balph Eubank, a pretentious literary scholar (whose name translates as "barf"), and Dr. Simon Pritchett, a pompous purveyor of a "nothing-is-anything" philosophy, are partly based on Rand's young friends' university experiences. The novel's good professor is a philosopher named Hugh Akston, who taught both John Galt and Francisco at Patrick Henry University. As Francisco tells Dr. Pritchett at a party, Akston holds that "everything is something." This phrase neatly captures Rand's emerging view of metaphysics, the study of what's real. Following Aristotle, she argued that reality is absolute: that A is A and facts are facts, independent of feelings, wishes, hopes, or fears. Furthermore, every entity's existence is also its identity ("everything is something"). To *be* is to be something in particular. Finally, reason—defined as "the faculty that identifies and integrates the material provided by the senses"—allows the formation of concepts. Therein lies the rational foundation of all knowledge, she contended in *Atlas Shrugged*.

She especially enjoyed talking to Nathaniel about psychology. Universities then favored Freudian psychoanalysis and behaviorism. Rand furiously disagreed with both. Freudianism seemed mystical to her; behaviorism was mechanical; and both lacked respect for the human will and the conscious mind. In conversations with him, she began to articulate her own theory of mind, based on her confidence in objective reality and her reverence for reason. She started with the concept of free will, which she defined not as freedom of decision and action, the usual definition, but as "the choice to think or not to think." Thinking is tied to survival and is volitional, she argued; unlike animals with instincts, people must make the effort to think in order to obtain a steady supply of food, build shelter, make tools—and, eventually, create skyscrapers and trains. People can choose not to think, not to face facts, not to make rational choices; like James Taggart and the other evil characters in *Atlas Shrugged,* they can decide instead to wish, dream, whine, stamp their feet, or bury their heads in the sand to avoid reality. If they do so, however, they have only two remaining choices going forward: to live off the productivity of others or to die.

In light of this, she argued that psychotherapy should take aim at the removal of mental contradictions and moral defects, which result from a failure to think. Looking to the emotions—fear, elation, guilt—for information about conflicts with the world outside is foolish. "Emotions are not tools of cognition," she liked to say. At best, they are clues to whether a person's philosophical premises and "sense of life" are in accordance with reality or need adjustment. In 1961, she wrote that her view of human psychology was that "the head has its reasons which the heart must learn to know."

To treat neuroses, then, ought to be as simple as recognizing and banishing unrealistic, repressed, or contradictory ideas. As for her own psychology, she claimed that she could account rationally for every emotion she had ever had, a claim more dazzling to Barbara and Nathaniel than any professor's wall of framed degrees.

Partly as a consequence of these conversations, Branden began to construct a theory he called "the psychology of self-esteem" in which he exalted rationality, productivity, and achievement. Achievement is the most important source of a person's pride in self, and pride in self is a requisite for independence. Books and papers on this subject would later make him well known as the father of the self-esteem movement and as a significant contributor to the development of cognitive psychology, which holds that by changing one's thinking one can change one's feelings and behavior.

As their friendship grew, she and Branden talked of more personal matters. He confessed that he was unsure of himself with the opposite sex. Girls had never liked him, and he, in turn, had almost always found them shallow. In Barbara he had found both intelligence and a shared love of Roarkian values. If he was looking for reassurance, he received it. She said she bet he wouldn't even notice if a girl *did* like him and predicted an illustrious future for him, both as a psychologist and as a communicator of ideas. If she could make his life's path any easier, she would. She also praised Barbara. She could see that Barbara was very intelligent, she said.

In sunlit walks around the ranch, Barbara, too, confided in the older woman, describing her mixed feelings for Nathaniel. On one hand, she said, she admired him immensely. He was brilliant and charismatic. She knew that their dazzling mentor regarded him very highly. He still wanted *her*. And yet she wasn't strongly romantically or sexually drawn to him, and she couldn't understand why not. Lately, she had been worrying that she had some kind of mind-body split. It bothered her, she said, that she was strongly attracted to other boys and had even slept with one or two. What was wrong with her? Why didn't she love him completely? As Rand walked by her side, collecting small stones—sorting them helped her organize her thoughts about the novel, she said— for once she was unable to offer insight. She couldn't comprehend that a girl as bright as Barbara, with Barbara's love of the heroic, wasn't madly, passionately, sexually in love with Branden.

Barbara's concern about a mind-body split came directly from Rand's discussions of romantic love with them while she was writing the chapter of *Atlas Shrugged* in which Dagny and Hank Rearden have their first sexual encounter. For just as she had devised a theory of the emotions emphasizing reason, so, through the character of Francisco, she proposed a theory of sex based on rational self-interest, the keystone of free-market economics. What she came up with is best illustrated by the predicament of Rearden, the novel's most complex and sympathetic character.

Like Roark, Rearden has a strong sex drive; unlike Roark, he has a wife, Lillian, who has reinforced an old idea, that sex is an animal function that only degenerate males want or need. Interestingly, like Rand's mother prior to the revolution, Lillian's greatest pleasure lies in giving parties and playing hostess to fashionable intellectuals, such as Balph Eubank and Simon Pritchett, who are amusingly skewered in Rand's dialogue. Lillian's sexual scorn sends Rearden into throes of agony over his desire for Dagny. Francisco, seeing him suffer later in the novel, sets him right. "Love is our response to our highest values," he explains. "Tell me what a man finds sexually attractive and I will tell you his entire philosophy of life." For the hero, then, there is no conflict between the desires of the body and the convictions of the mind. A productive man wants to celebrate his accomplishments and self-esteem in sexual ecstasy with a worthy woman. Moreover, women such as Dagny—and Kira, and Dominique, and presumably Rand—hardly dislike sex. They long to be man worshippers with their bodies *and* their souls and to mate with the highest possible types of men. Hearing this, Rearden begins to set himself free from his wife's malignant grasp and to see how the novel's other villains use his most praiseworthy moral strengths and values against him.

Much later, an older Barbara told a journalist that Rand's doctrine of man worship made her "want to crawl under a rug." By then, Barbara had concluded that it was personal longing that had prompted Rand to identify femininity with hero worship: Because she almost always saw further and penetrated more deeply than others did and thus was painfully alone, she longed to find and to yield to a strength greater than her own. As much to the point, perhaps, Rand's theory of sex seemed to require any man who was rational, in her definition of what was rational, to be in love with her, since she was the worthiest woman of them all.

In this context, twenty-year-old Barbara became convinced that her ambivalence about Branden was, at best, a sign of confused thinking and a lack of self-esteem. At worst, it was a moral failure. She made a promise to herself to change her thinking.

Meanwhile, for months the two students had been pleading with Rand to tell them more about the novel. Late in the summer of 1950, she gave them eighteen completed chapters to read and watched as they sped through them, page by page. Then she began reading aloud to them from the chapters she was working on. Once a week, in the evening, she, they, and O'Connor—who had already heard each new section as it was being written—gathered in the living room. The young people listened, spellbound, as Nick Carter had once listened to *The Fountainhead.*

Entering into Rand's epic narrative of principled resistance to the destruction of the American spirit by small-minded collectivists was like landing on another planet whose bedrock was individual achievement. Describing the power of the book for Branden and herself, Barbara wrote, "We were hearing, on each page, a command to rise to heights of greater nobility than we had ever conceived. We felt that we were now citizens of a world in which man's mind was efficacious and the human potential was unlimited." As for the author of this world, Barbara said, "I can't fully communicate the exhilaration of being in intimate contact with so great a mind and spirit."

Still, away from the book a few things puzzled and disturbed them. One was a thin edge of anger they sometimes glimpsed in Rand. Two or three times, Barbara experienced the sting of Rand's displeasure—once, when she mentioned her love of the mountains and the ocean, which the writer interpreted as a rejection of "man," and another time when she praised the work of Thomas Wolfe, which, in Rand's view, was chaotic and philosophically vacuous. Rand commented harshly on Wolfe's neglect of the very elements of fiction that Barbara had already agreed were essential—"plot, theme, characterization, style"—and so overwhelmed the young woman with her logic that Barbara renounced Wolfe on the spot. Years later, in a series of private seminars that were transcribed and collected posthumously in Rand's *The Art of Fiction,* the author selected some of Barbara's favorite passages from Wolfe's works to illustrate how *not* to write, asking Barbara to read the passages aloud; Barbara naturally assumed the harsh critique was aimed at her. For Barbara—admiring, self-doubting, and intimidated by Rand's seemingly unassailable logic—the stifling of her response to Wolfe was remembered as a step in what she thought of as a forced march "into a destructive vise" of repression of real feelings and opinions, as she wrote in 1986. "I was to continue along that path for many years."

In an era when grooming counted, the Brandens also noticed that Rand was personally untidy. She wore short skirts to showcase her shapely legs, but her stockings were often torn, her skirts were stained, and her hair might be unwashed or uncombed. Frank occasionally snapped at her about such carelessness, Barbara recalled. In this respect, as in others, Rand hadn't appreciably changed from the quixotic child her mother used to nag.

Most intriguing to them was her marriage. O'Connor, who could have posed for an *Esquire* ad and who exuded warmth, gentility, and wisdom, was unresponsive to philosophical discussion and even to most books, yet Rand, who usually placed the highest premium on analytical intelligence and self-assertion, called him her "top value." Seated, she would glance around to be sure he was nearby; she continuously touched him and held his hand. "Frank is my rock," she told Barbara. To Nathaniel, she said, "He believed in me when no one else did," and, "We have the same sense of life." He was silent because he was "too disgusted with people to share what he is with the world," she told them. In their memoirs, both Brandens would declare that a few years after meeting Rand, the author would confide that her marriage had been in trouble at the time and that she had contemplated divorce; she didn't divorce Frank primarily because she didn't want to upset her life while her book remained unfinished. She even confirmed Thaddeus Ashby's observation that Frank never initiated sex and never *had* initiated sex in the history of their marriage. In any case, since Barbara and Nathaniel could find no trace of disgust in Frank O'Connor, nor of the energy and conviction that powered Rand's heroes, they shrugged off their questions and gradually stopped thinking about the nature of this marriage.

In the fall of 1950, Rand began touching Nathaniel, too. She sometimes held his hand as they strolled the grounds and talked about their ideas and her work. Barbara saw nothing odd in the older woman's affection for Nathaniel. If Nathaniel did, he was not troubled. His feelings bruised by Barbara's rebuffs, he enjoyed this mild, seemingly safe flirtation. After evenings spent reading *Atlas,* Rand compared him to the talented, irresistible Francisco, whom she had modeled on swashbuckling heroes such as Zorro and the Scarlet Pimpernel and on memories of the childhood summer she had spent climbing in the Swiss Alps with a boy. "I could never love anyone but a hero," she told him more than once. Later, he admitted that he sometimes found these assertions and comparisons confusing. For how, at twenty, was he a hero? How was O'Connor one? At the time, however, Branden basked in her approval. He had been raised by a doting mother and grandmother who had prepared him for life as a young prince, said friends who knew him well. He stepped into the role of Rand's favorite with a minimum of discomfort.

It was as her protégés that she presented Barbara and Nathaniel to her California acquaintances: Adrian and Janet Gaynor, a young libertarian activist named Herbert Cornuelle and his eighteen-year-old brother Richard, William Mullendore, Lela Rogers, and Morrie Ryskind. Along with the last two, Rand was a defendant in a $2 million lawsuit filed by Emmet Lavery, a playwright and the former president of the Screen Writers Guild, who alleged that Mrs. Rogers had defamed him by calling his latest play, *Gentleman from Athens*, "communistic" during a *Town Hall Meeting of the Air*, and that Rand and Ryskind had counseled her to do so. Lavery eventually settled for $30,000, but for a while Rand saw a lot of both Rogers and Ryskind.

The young pair sometimes encountered Albert Mannheimer at the ranch. He flirted pleasantly with Barbara and joined in evening conversations. But his friendship with Rand was waning. The stage play she had spent many hours helping him to finish, *The Bees and the Flowers*, had been produced at the Cort Theatre in New York in the fall of 1946 but had lasted for only twenty-eight performances. Its lackluster success effectively ended Mannheimer's theatrical career. Although he was working on a film adaptation of Garson Kanin's successful Broadway play *Born Yesterday*, for which he and Kanin would share an Academy Award nomination, he was discouraged by the inanity of most of his Hollywood assignments. This was especially true in light of his idealization of Howard Roark's uncompromising drive and Rand's own larger-than-life example of mixing high-voltage creative work with commercial success. When a girlfriend committed suicide in his Los Angeles apartment, his sense of despair increased. Rand tried to convince him that he was not at fault—that the girl was responsible for her own unhappiness and death—but to little avail. After that, their relationship consisted of little more than her helping him with his psychological problems, she later said. When she realized that he wasn't going to resolve his emotional conflicts, she drifted away from him, and by the end of 1950 he stopped coming to the ranch.

When Barbara and Nathaniel asked about him, Rand told them that his anxieties had affected his rationality and had destroyed his commitment to philosophy. "I think we replaced him in Ayn's life," Barbara said in 2006. Ten years after their parting, Rand would deny that she and Mannheimer had ever been close. Their relationship was really only something that "could be called—should have been a semi-friendship," she said, while also declaring that Mannheimer and Paterson had been her only friends of any duration from her arrival in the United States until the end of the 1940s. They were "the only two . . . which I consider serious relationships or semi-friendships or potential friendships," she said, demoting them in importance even as she spoke. Barbara thought differently, remarking, "She was very, very close to Albert. He was important to her, and the rejection of him was total."

Altogether, Branden was disappointed by the people in Rand's social circle. They weren't good enough for her, he thought. When he hesitantly told her this—and confessed to feeling awkwardly possessive of her—she did not seem to mind. "That's the Dominique premise," she explained, "not wanting to share your values with anyone." It was a precept she had lived by since before encountering Cyrus at the age of nine.

Other than Nathaniel and Barbara, the O'Connors most often saw Ruth Beebe Hill and her husband, Buzzy, who were transplanted midwesterners and avid *Fountainhead* enthusiasts. Buzzy, a medical doctor, conducted cancer research at the new Harbor-UCLA Medical Center in Torrance. Ruth, a crisp, high-spirited woman of thirty-six, was an ethnographer, a mountain climber, and yet another person who had memorized long passages from *The Fountainhead*. Because she loved its celebration of creativity and independence, she asked a college friend—Rand's then-current typist, Jean Elliott—to arrange an introduction. Rand agreed and invited the two women to visit her one evening in late summer 1949.

What happened next reveals Rand's mixed reaction to her fans in the 1940s. After introductions and a few eager exchanges about *The Fountainhead*, Hill disclosed that she had not only memorized *The Fountainhead* but had also memorized *Anthem,* and that she liked to give dramatic recitations from the novels to garden clubs and civic groups. Rand was astounded. "What else have you memorized?" she asked. "Plato," Hill answered, dishonestly, and then realized that she had made a big mistake. The author narrowed her eyes and asked, "Plato? The father of Communism?" In truth, Hill had only wanted to impress her hostess and had racked her brain for the loftiest writer she knew. O'Connor broke the menacing silence. He said, "What Ruth probably means, Ayn, is that she was required to memorize passages from Plato and other philosophers in college." Then he walked over to Hill, who was sitting on the floor, took her hand, drew her to her feet, and led her to a chair near the fire.

Rand accepted this explanation, and the two women quickly hit it off. Since Hill had grown up near Lorain, Ohio, and her husband, Buzzy, loved to garden almost as much as Frank did, the Hills and O'Connors became friends. During the next two years, until October 1951, the transplants often drove seventy-five miles from their house in Newport Beach to Chatsworth to dine and converse with the O'Connors.

Ruth Hill glimpsed Rand in moods and postures few others did. Rand rarely dressed up, but when Hill invited Ayn and Frank to dinner shortly after the couples met, Ayn wore a black silk evening gown designed by Adrian, embossed with planets, moon, and stars and trailing a twelve-inch fan-shaped train. Over cocktails she twirled and posed, laughed and showed off, as she had done with her new mink coat at the *Herald Tribune*. Hill sometimes spotted a radiant little girl inside the formidable writer—when she found Rand listening to her "tiddlywink" music, for example, and once, during a conversation Hill no longer recalled, when Rand made such a sweet remark that Hill rose and patted the novelist on the head. One night Rand spilled salt on a restaurant table and surprised the Hills by throwing a pinch of it over her left shoulder, an ancient rite to blind the devil. Most uncharacteristically, Hill also observed her in the role of witness to a UFO. One Saturday afternoon, Rand greeted the Hills by beckoning Ruth upstairs, into the immense master bedroom, where tall glass windows lined a wall to the left of the bed. "Do you see those junipers?" she asked, pointing to a row of twelve-foot bushes about half an acre from the house. "A UFO came by there last night." Stunned, Hill asked for details. "It was hovering just above the junipers and then flying in slow motion," she said. It was round and its outer edges were lighted, she continued, and it made no sound. By the time she woke Frank and led him to the window, it had moved out of sight. "Did you really see this?" Hill asked. "I saw it," said

Rand. The story seems to demonstrate her confidence in the ability of her mind to interpret the evidence of her senses. As the years went by, this particular confidence would not always serve her well.

Then, suddenly, Barbara and Nathaniel were leaving. The philosophy major earned her bachelor's degree in the spring of 1951 and enrolled in the master's degree program at New York University. Nathaniel, about to be a college junior, decided to go with her and study psychology at NYU. In later years, he could hardly reconstruct his reasoning, so astonished was he at his readiness to leave the most significant relationship of his life. But with Rand's encouragement, Barbara and he had become lovers again and were committed to making it work.

In late June, the two stood in the O'Connors' driveway and told their older friends good-bye. Everyone promised to call and write. Ayn, her arm entwined in her husband's, vowed that when *Atlas* was completed she and Frank would join "the children" in New York. As the young couple waved and drove away, she was surprised to find herself crying. She had not anticipated the emptiness she felt when they were gone, she said, or just how much they had come to mean to her.

Ruth and Buzzy were on hand to witness some of the phone calls that took place during that summer and fall of 1951. "It's the kids!" O'Connor would call, and Rand would hurry to the phone. Always a phone enthusiast, she talked to Branden for hours at a time—about New York, about his classes and the relatively advanced intellectual atmosphere at NYU, about her day's work on the novel. They discussed Barbara; Branden reported that during a summer trip to Canada Barbara had again been involved with an old boyfriend. She seemed to be full of confusion about her behavior, he said, but didn't add, and perhaps didn't need to add, that he was frustrated, humiliated, and enraged by it. Rand and he also exchanged letters. The aspiring psychologist wrote to the thinker that he looked at her photograph on his mantel every day, and every day he found her more attractive. "I don't know whether it's love or what," he wrote. To Frank, he joked, "My offer is still open to trade the picture for the real thing. What do you say?" He recalled thinking that his letters were funny. He wasn't aware that he was behaving seductively, he later wrote.

It had to be obvious to O'Connor that his wife and Branden were flirting, and had been for months, although she, too, professed not to know it at the time. "I suppose it was a kind of suppression or repression or something," she later told Branden. "I was so cautious in the beginning. And yet, wasn't I already feeling . . . almost everything?" Barbara, too, claimed that none of them was conscious of what was rising to the surface. "If Ayn had designs on Nathaniel," she said, "it wasn't Nathaniel at age nineteen. He was [only] a kid." To a retrospective observer, it appears likely that she did.

In late September 1951, Rand completed the twenty-first chapter of *Atlas Shrugged,* the first chapter of what would become the third and final part of the novel. It was called "Atlantis." In it, 640 pages into the book, Dagny meets Rand's ultimate hero, John Galt. "The shape of his mouth was pride," Rand writes of Galt. Like Leo Kovalensky's face in *We the Living,* Galt's is ruthless and certain; like Nathaniel Branden's, it is "a face with no fear of being seen or of seeing." For Dagny, and for Rand, "This was her world . . . this was the way men were meant to be." Although in the next chapter the heroine turns back to the world to try to save it, the author, elated by her days and nights in company with the "real people" of Galt's Gulch, decided to pursue her own Atlantis, now.

On the evening after she finished "Atlantis," she phoned Branden and announced that she and Frank were moving to New York. "I can't stand California any longer, darling!" she cried, breathless with excitement. She repeated a comment O'Connor had made, as though it were a joke: "He says . . . I can't live without you!" Frank felt the same way she did about leaving California, she assured him; Frank, too, couldn't wait to arrive in New York. Pincus Berner, her old friend and lawyer, was searching for a suitable apartment. They would pack, drive across the country, and arrive within three weeks.

On the long drive in Frank's new Cadillac convertible, they stopped for a day or two in Ouray, Colorado, an old gold-mining town a few miles east of Telluride, whose surroundings contributed to the topography of Galt's Gulch. As they continued east, they may have passed the former site of Nikola Tesla's scientific laboratory, which had stood on a mountaintop near Colorado Springs in the early 1900s; the experiments the eccentric genius had made in harnessing electricity from the atmosphere and transmitting it wirelessly through earth and air may have provided a model for the revolutionary new motor invented by Galt. (Tesla also invented a fantastical but possibly workable "death ray" that

Rand may have borrowed, in part, for Dr. Stadler's terrifying weapon, Project X.) Along with Edison, Tesla became one of Rand's models for her hero. She and O'Connor stopped in Cleveland, where they took Frank's sister Agnes Papurt and her youngest daughter, Connie, out to dinner. Connie recalled that her exotic aunt by marriage wore a modish blue sharkskin pantsuit, its glamour undercut by brown ankle socks in black pumps, and puffed on a cigarette holder that seemed "as long as my arm." Rand explained that Uncle Frank was in charge of safeguarding the manuscript of *Atlas Shrugged*, which he took with him to the delicatessen where they ate. It was in a case attached by a chain to his wrist, like a handcuff, Connie recalled. "He uncuffed it for dinner, I think with a key. We ate. They paid. He locked it to his wrist again, and left."

Berner had leased them an apartment at 36 East Thirty-sixth Street, across a tree-lined street from the beautiful McKim, Mead and White–designed Pierpont Morgan Library. On October 24, they took occupancy of apartment 5-A. Their furniture had preceded them by a day, but the apartment was small, and much had been left behind in care of the Hills, who were to live at the ranch while they were away. Because they didn't plan to drive in New York, they gave their convertible car to Branden.

The younger man later claimed that he felt nothing but pleasure on learning that this middle-aged celebrity was coming to join him in New York. Although Barbara told him that she, too, was delighted, she was aware of having reservations. She had enrolled at NYU with a desire to start a new life, on her own. First Branden had followed; now Rand. She knew that her lover had spoken to Rand about her flirtations and infidelities, and she anticipated personal pressure on Rand's arrival—about Branden and about her inner conflicts. "Part of me wanted to be free. To find out what my own way was and to go that way. I wanted it desperately," she said in 2006. But that was not to be.

Frank O'Connor didn't write many letters, but when he and Rand were settled in New York he wrote to Ruth and Buzzy Hill. The letter was written in ink on lined notebook paper, Hill remembered, and was wittily titled "The Fountain Pen, by Frank O'Connor." He asked for news of the crops, especially the gladiolus pips that had been harvested for planting in the spring. He thanked them for moving in on such short notice and asked Ruth to say hello to Aretha Fisher for him.

He was expecting to live in New York for five years, seven at most, he reminded the Hills, which was the amount of time Ayn now believed she would need to finish *Atlas Shrugged*. Before leaving, he had told them that her writing had been going slowly and that she was tired of country life. "She wants to write her novel in the shadows of skyscrapers," he explained. The Hills had promised to keep everything just as it was for their friends' return. And like good anti-altruists, they insisted on paying rent: eighty-five dollars a month.

From Rand's first burst of enthusiasm for moving to New York, Hill thought that her beloved friend was acting rashly. She didn't believe the explanation about writing in the shadows of the skyscrapers. It was not the skyscrapers that motivated her, Hill later said. "It was one hundred percent 'the kids.' They were the *only* reason she went to New York, and I knew it at the time." The main attraction was Branden, she added. Barbara was a side issue, though an important one.

Hill, like Frank, was sure they would return to 10000 Tampa Avenue. "You see, Ayn had told Frank that they would be back," she said, "and Frank had told Buzzy. I thought so, too. But I believe Ayn knew that they would *not* be back." As it turned out, the Hills stayed on as tenants for twenty years, during which time Ayn and Frank visited just once, in the fall of 1963. In 1962, the O'Connors arranged for the sale of the ranch to one Katharine Houchin for a price of $175,000, a 700 percent gain on the $24,000 they had paid in 1944, confirming Frank's prediction that real estate values in the San Fernando Valley would rise. The Hills remained as Houchin's tenants until 1971, when they bought a house in the San Juan Islands, north of Seattle. Ayn and Frank would remain in New York for the rest of their lives.

No one who knew O'Connor believed that he willingly left the San Fernando Valley ranch. "That property was his business and his world," said Hill. "Ayn knew it. There was no way she didn't know how badly she was hurting Frank." Over the years, acquaintances noticed her uneasiness with the subject of the move. Years out of California, she would talk about how much she hated the place, adding, "You feel the same way, don't you, Frank? Don't you?" "She said it too often," observed Barbara. "She said it too insistently." Hill, defending her friend, urged, "Please do stop and think who Ayn Rand was. She was the brightest and most determined person anyone had ever met. Who did she put first? Who did she advise all of us to put first? She knew what she had always known, that she would be important to the world. Frank knew it, too, and gave her what she wanted. Not because he was submissive or because she made the money, but because he recognized her talent and ability."

He made the best of the move. Within a year or two, he found a part-time job working for an East Side florist, arranging flower displays in the lobbies of buildings. He had a business card that read, "Francisco, the Lobbyist." A few years later, he began to paint—figures, cityscapes, and still lifes with flowers. When Buzzy visited on business in the middle 1950s, Rand showed him her husband's paintings. "It just broke Buzzy's heart that Frank, who had been working on acres of beautiful gladiolas— here he was in [the apartment in New York] painting the damned flowers instead of growing them," said Hill. "I asked, 'But what about Frank's work itself, Buzzy?' Buzzy hesitated. 'It's not that good, Ruth,' " he told her. Some others thought him gifted, though untrained.

Interestingly, before the Hills lost regular contact with Ayn and Frank, which—except for mailing off their monthly checks—they soon did, they discovered that *both* O'Connors were indifferent housekeepers, to put it mildly. At the ranch, Ruth found drawers filled with unopened fan mail, business letters, circulars, and bills. In Rand's study, the floor was littered with railroad magazines, research material for her novel. There were more than two hundred grocer's cartons, each divided into sections and filled to the brim with colored stones Rand had collected and sorted. In the kitchen, empty cottage cheese cartons, the remains of Frank's favorite lunch, were heaped from countertops halfway to the ceiling. The servants evidently had been busy making their own collections; apart from whatever they may have taken with them, they had hidden jars of jams and jellies, bottles of artichoke hearts, and other delectables under chair cushions in their rooms. In the New York apartment, the trend continued. Visitors remembered that the cats sharpened their claws on the upholstered furniture, leaving tattered edges, and left a foul smell in the air; and that bill collectors sometimes showed up at the door. It was Frank's job to pay the bills. Some saw his casual approach to these duties as a passive form of protest, but others viewed their absentmindedness in practical affairs as natural and charming.

The apartment Berner had rented for them was not only relatively small but also plain. First-time visitors, expecting Roarkian grandeur along the lines of the Neutra house, were surprised by its modesty. An entrance foyer doubled as the dining room, with a black-lacquered table, designed by O'Connor, pushed against a mirrored wall. Formal dinners were eaten there; otherwise, the table served as a work surface for a series of manuscript typists. A small kitchen opened off the foyer. The living room was small, with windows on the far wall, and was decorated by Frank with mid-century modern chairs and a black tweed sofa, glass-topped tables, and green-blue pillows and knickknacks strewn around. There was one bedroom and a tiny study facing an air shaft, from whose single window she could see the Empire State Building if she leaned out and peered west. She preferred it to her airy California study, just as she preferred her new, compact quarters to the sunshine, space, and architectural distinction of the ranch, which had been O'Connor's discovery and reflected his taste. A preference for productivity over luxury: She kept this aspect of her Russian heritage.

On their very first evening in the apartment, Nathaniel and Barbara came to call, and the familiar mingling of texts and subtexts resumed. The young couple tore through the latest chapter of the novel. While O'Connor unpacked and puttered, the other three launched into a spirited discussion of John Galt, whose chief trait is that, like Roark, he lives without marked emotional conflicts. But Roark experienced pain; Galt does not. In general, this aspect of the writer's view of heroes had remained the same since *The Little Street* in 1928, when she wrote that "other people do not exist [for the protagonist] and he does not understand why they should." In the new chapter, "Atlantis," an absence of emotion is one of the qualities Dagny prizes in John Galt's face and manner as he gives her a tour of the beautiful and bustling valley called Galt's Gulch.

Branden found this quality in Galt unsettling. On that first evening, he asked whether the hero might be too cold or too abstract to be compelling to readers. Rand answered succinctly, "One does not approach a god too closely," a remark which Branden never forgot. The subject wasn't raised again. But over the years many readers have rightly complained that the character of Galt is featureless and wooden and is thus the least compelling in the book.

Rand was diplomatic enough not to mention Nathaniel's concerns about Barbara, and she wasn't aware that Barbara felt anxious about her relationship with Branden. As it happened, the insecure boyfriend had been responding to Barbara's summer flirtation by pointing out what was wrong with her and finding deep psychological flaws in her defenses. He had persuaded her to write a letter to their mentor explaining that she was a "mystic," and instead of laughing out loud Rand had written back to tell Barbara that she must keep working with Branden to fix her errors. This was the state of affairs when, a few weeks after the O'Connors had settled in, Barbara raised the subject of their troubled romance. There ensued a mild version of a style of inquiry that would come to characterize the author's response to followers from the middle 1950s on.

Frank was out on the evening Rand and Barbara set aside to talk about Barbara's relationship with Nathaniel. Oddly, Branden was present, too, sitting in an armchair on the opposite side of the living room, letting his mind drift, he later wrote, while Barbara and Rand murmured to each other. When Rand inquired about a second boy whom Barbara had told Branden she liked but hadn't slept with during the summer in Winnipeg, Barbara responded vaguely and let the subject lapse. A few minutes later, Rand asked again, her tone clipped and purposeful. This brought Branden to attention across the room. When Barbara admitted that, yes, she *had* had a brief affair with the young man, Branden experienced a "pain that . . . was excruciating." Rand's manner grew gentle, he recalled, as she probed Barbara's motives and offered reassurance. "Given the moral ruthlessness that was more typical of Ayn," he wrote in his memoir, *Judgment Day,* "this was unusual." "Everything is going to be all right," she told Barbara soothingly. "We're going to solve this, once and for all."

Barbara remembered Rand's manner differently, as probing and harsh, especially considering that she was not married to Nathaniel and had no obligation to be faithful to him. She felt humiliated. Yet, as the apparently guilty party, she decided she couldn't ask the man who had by now become her "moral mentor" and, "worst of all," her psychological counselor to refrain from seeking *his* mentor's advice again. As for Branden, looking back he thought that he and Barbara should have ended their relationship that night, in the late fall of 1951. Instead, with Rand's encouragement he became her unofficial psychotherapist. "He was going to help me reach the exalted state where I would be fully in love with him," Barbara told an interviewer in 1990. "Confessing to a man who flayed me alive each time I confessed was supposedly in the interest of my self-esteem." They hardened their resolve and became engaged in the summer of 1952. Six months later, they were married.

In the intervening period, they introduced a dozen of their brightest relatives and friends to Rand. Wishing to "expand our circle," Branden

Ayn Rand, age four, and her extended family in
St. Petersburg, Russia, 1909. Center row, from
left: Rand's parents, Zinovy and Anna
Rosenbaum; Rand's maternal grandmother,
Rozalia Kaplan; Rand's cousin Nina Guzarchik,
Rand's maternal grandfather, Berko Kaplan; and
Rand, leaning against her grandfather's knee.

Rand's Russian passport photograph,
dated October 29, 1925, when Rand was
twenty years old.

Rand, fourth from left, with other Studio Club residents during "Cleanup Week" in Hollywood, May 1927.

An original illustration of Cyrus, the hero of *The Mysterious Valley* by Maurice Champagne and Rene Giffey, first published in serial form in 1914. Cyrus was Rand's "exclusive love" from ages nine to twelve.

Rand's husband, Frank O'Connor, circa 1920. "It was an absolute that this was the man I wanted."

Nick Carter, Frank O'Connor's brother. "Ayn and Frank could not have happened nor have lasted without him."

Isabel Paterson, 1939.

(Above)
Rand at her desk at the ranch in Chatsworth, California, in 1947. The house was designed by Richard Neutra for Josef von Sternberg in 1935 and was purchased by Rand in 1944.

(Right)
Rand with friend and fellow anti-Communist activist Lela Rogers, mother of Ginger Rogers, in Hollywood, 1951.

(Facing page)
Ayn and Frank on the long driveway to the Chatsworth house, lined with birch trees presented to von Sternberg by Marlene Dietrich.

(Facing page)
Rand listening to testimony presented to the House Un-American Activities Committee, October 1947, in the marble caucus room of the Old House Office Building in Washington, D.C.

(Left)
Rand being sworn in as a friendly witness at the House Un-American Activities Committee hearings.

(Below)
Frank O'Connor, neighbor Janet Gaynor, and Rand outside the Chatsworth house.

(Above)
O'Connor and Rand, dressed in protective gear, visiting Inland Steel, in Chicago, 1947. She watched steel being poured and met with a metallurgist and a plant superintendent, as preparation for the creation of Rearden Steel in *Atlas Shrugged*. Unidentified Inland Steel executive at left.

On the set of *The Fountainhead* with Gary Cooper and Patricia Neal, 1948.

In a Hollywood courtroom, 1951, as one of six defendants in a slander suit brought by Emmet Lavery. Other defendants included screenwriter Morrie Ryskind (first row, second from left) and Lela Rogers (talking to Ryskind).

wrote, he deliberately set out to convert those close to him to Rand's ethos of radical individualism in a conformist world. During the summers of 1950 and 1951, he persuaded his three older sisters, Florence, Elayne, and Reva, to read or reread *The Fountainhead* and share his enthusiasm for it. He patiently proselytized his first cousin, Allan Blumenthal, an intelligent, soft-spoken young medical student and pianist. Barbara introduced her college roommate and best friend since childhood (and Dr. Blumenthal's future wife), NYU graduate art student Joan Mitchell. Joan, in turn, brought along a friend, Mary Ann Sures, and the future chairman of the Federal Reserve Board, Alan Greenspan. (In 1953, Joan and Greenspan were briefly married. They remained on excellent terms after dissolving their marriage in 1954. Joan married Allan Blumenthal in 1957.) Barbara also enlisted her bright, bespectacled seventeen-year-old first cousin Leonard Peikoff, young for his age, who shortly after meeting Rand dropped out of a Canadian pre-med program and, to his parents' horror, enrolled at NYU to study philosophy. This familial group formed the core of Rand's later band of followers, with no one more devoted to her than Peikoff.

Beyond family ties, these young people had a lot in common with one another and their new leader. They were passionate about ideas and courageous enough to go against the political and religious temper of the time. Everyone but Mary Ann Sures was Jewish. With the exception of Sures and Alan Greenspan, all were the children of first- or second-generation Russian immigrants whose religion they rejected, and all were seeking an ethical system and a moral worldview to replace it. Most had grown up in Ontario or Manitoba, where they were outsiders, if not outcasts, in the prevailing Anglican culture. Greenspan, a German and Polish Jew born and raised in Manhattan, proved less susceptible than the others to the convert's classic evangelistic fervor. "Alan had his own relationship with her, which was dignified," recalled Erika Holzer, a lawyer who joined the circle in the early 1960s. "He kept somewhat aloof from everybody. He was older and smarter."

Both men and women tended to be intellectually serious, and all but one or two of the women were tall, slender, fair, and beautifully groomed. Because it was the 1950s, they dressed with care, as if for dinner or a formal office, the men's dark suits pressed, shoes shined, the women's dresses full and tightly cinched around the waist, hair coiffed in the manner of Grace Kelly. Since they had gravitated to Rand because of their admiration for *The Fountainhead,* she nicknamed them "the Class of '43," in honor of the novel's year of publication. With cheerful irony, the eight or nine most intimate members—Nathaniel and Barbara, Joan Mitchell and Allan Blumenthal, Leonard Peikoff, Alan Greenspan, Mary Ann Sures, and Nathaniel's sister Elayne and her future husband Harry Kalberman—called themselves "the Collective."

Rand came to like them all, to a greater or lesser degree. At first, she disapproved of Alan Greenspan, whom she found so somber and uncommunicative that she called him "the Undertaker" behind his back. Once, during a philosophical exchange with Branden, Greenspan reportedly declared that he didn't believe that objective reality, including his own existence, could be proved. Hearing of this, she took to asking others in the group, "How's the Undertaker? Has he decided he exists yet?" At the time, the economist was working for the National Industrial Conference Board, studying steel inventories, and so was able to shed valuable light on the economics of steel for *Atlas Shrugged.* As she began to appreciate his mastery of economics, not to mention his surprising keenness as a reader of her novel in progress, she gave him a new nickname, "the Sleeping Giant," and rightly predicted that he would achieve great things. Another favorite was Leonard Peikoff, who asked scores of eager questions for which she had clear and satisfying answers, a quality that still endears her to the young. (For example, "Is Roark idealistic, or is he practical?" Peikoff asked her. She answered, "If your ideals are rational, and your moral principles are based on reality, there's no conflict. The moral *is* the practical," a cornerstone of her developing ethics.) Peikoff said that in her presence he felt "total awe, as though I were on a different planet," and she found his curiosity and boyish devotion endearing. Yet it seems unlikely that she would have entertained Leonard or many of the others for more than an evening now and then if it hadn't been for her deepening interest in Nathaniel Branden. She confirmed this later when she said, "I've always seen [the Collective] as a kind of comet, with Nathan as the star and the rest as his tail."

Nevertheless, their devotion offered important compensations. They were an unusually talented group of students and young professionals. They provided her with a comforting sense of being understood and appreciated at a pivotal point in the writing of *Atlas Shrugged,* when Dagny, returned from Galt's Gulch, begins to discover the unpleasant psychological motives of the left-wing bureaucrats who are marshaling their forces against her. When the author met with other acquaintances and colleagues—as she often did, either at gatherings of political conservatives or over drinks and dinner—the strain could cost her two or three days' work. "When I'm writing I'm living in the world of the novel, not 'ordinary reality,' " she explained. It was difficult for her to find her way back after an interruption. Surrounded on most Saturday nights by this group of captivated young people, she didn't have to leave her fictional world or risk having its premises challenged. When she passed around or read aloud her week's work, she saw not two but eight or nine rapt young faces beaming at her as they devoured the latest installment of a book they knew to be a masterpiece. She watched them, asking, "What? What is it?" when one of them smiled at a passage, raised an eyebrow, or showed confusion or excitement. They were astonished by the intricacy and originality of her work and so respectful of her that they politely raised their hands to ask a question or listened quietly as she, Nathaniel, and Barbara commented on the book, current events, politics, music, and theater late into the night. "The world we were living in wasn't just the world of California or New York or UCLA or NYU," recalled Branden in 2004. "It was the world of *Atlas Shrugged*." The young people were her ideal readers, and she knew it.

One snowy night in January 1953, Rand and O'Connor climbed into the backseat of a limousine and rode north to White Plains, a suburb of New York, to act as matron of honor and best man at Nathaniel and Barbara's wedding. The ceremony took place in the home of one of Barbara's aunts. In photographs, Frank stands beside the groom, looking thin, handsome, and paternal in a dark suit and a white boutonniere. Rand stands next to Barbara, in profile appearing glamorous and young. She wears a black-and-white gown designed by Adrian (*tsked* at by some of the relatives, who considered a black dress inappropriate), and on one side her dark hair is slicked back, revealing a sweet expression on her face. As she looks on, the newly married couple kisses. That night, after a reception, the Brandens returned to their new studio apartment to discover that O'Connor had filled its single room with fragrant flowers.

That night, too, some of Nathaniel's relatives noticed that his mother, herself a formidable woman, was jealous of Ayn Rand. Dinah Blumenthal had raised her son to be a young prince, *her* young prince, and wasn't pleased when she saw firsthand his strong attachment to his best man's wife. "She was so offended, so mad, so very jealous" of the rela tionship, said a family member, that she never afterward liked or approved of Rand. Even then, she knew that "he liked Ayn better than he liked her."

The apartment was at 165 East Thirty-fifth Street, two blocks east and one block south of the O'Connors' apartment. In months and years to come, some members of the Collective and an assortment of other young enthusiasts would find and rent apartments in the surrounding blocks. Many would later reflect that this was the infant geography of the Ayn Rand cult.

ELEVEN

THE IMMOVABLE MOVER

1953–1957

Only the man who extols the purity of a love devoid of desire, is capable of the depravity of a desire devoid of love.

—*Atlas Shrugged*, 1957

I n the 1960s, new young acolytes would be surprised to find that Rand had few close friends of her own age or level of ability. But in the early 1950s, she was a legend in the tiny world of the New York intellectual Right. *The Fountainhead* had almost single-handedly renewed popular interest in the cause of individualism. Rumor spread quickly that she was finishing a massive new novel that would do the same for capitalism. Few knew her, and everyone wanted to meet her.

New York was such a politically liberal city in the 1950s that Saul Bellow described it as an intellectual annex of Moscow. The Right was very small, but vibrant and unified; it hadn't yet splintered into Old Right libertarians and cold warriors, as it would do later in the decade. Members had a few favorite gathering places, and one was the Upper West Side penthouse apartment of J. B. Matthews, a reformed Communist fellow-traveler who, by 1953, was serving as Wisconsin Republican senator Joseph R. McCarthy's head of research and the executive director of the senator's Permanent Subcommittee on Investigations. Among active anti-Communists, Matthews was known for his large collection of files on suspected Communist sympathizers in federal agencies and elsewhere; these were proving helpful to McCarthy as he tracked down supposed traitors in the U.S. government. When visiting New York, McCarthy often stopped in at Matthews's, enjoying a drink with anti–New Deal newspaper columnist Westbrook Pegler, Rand's friend Eugene Lyons, William F. Buckley, Jr., Russell Kirk, and others; Rand first met McCarthy there. Buckley, a high-spirited partisan and writer then in his twenties, was leading the youthful postwar wing of hard-Right Republicans who wanted government to support traditional Christian values and actively defend those values around the world. A Catholic from a privileged Connecticut family, he had gained early fame with a controversial book called *God and Man at Yale;* in 1955, he would found and edit *National Review,* the soon-to-be oracle of conservative orthodoxy.

Rand attended a number of Matthews's parties, one of the few places where her 1947 HUAC testimony was regarded as a badge of honor. As in California, she was often at the center of a powerful male throng, taking on all comers, and she left an indelible and largely favorable impression. "Tell me your premises," she would say on greeting new acquaintances, and having placed her serve would launch a volley of ideas. Contemporaries, including Buckley, remembered her as "singular." Recalling the first time he met her, he mimicked her Russian accent as she declared, "Mr. Buckley, you arrrr too intelligent to believe in Gott!" ("That certainly is an icebreaker," remarked Buckley's friend Wilfrid Sheed on being told the story.) The future host of *Firing Line* took it in good grace, and they became friendly acquaintances—until the publication of *Atlas Shrugged* in 1957, when many of her relationships changed or perished. She invited him for cocktails in her apartment, with her husband; he arrived with his mother-in-law in tow, and they all had a lively time talking about McCarthy. "She was a McCarthyite," Buckley stated, "and so was I. I had just written a book about him." The young man-about-town thought she possessed "an instantly communicable charm" and "glamorous hair." For the next few years, he sent her postcards written in liturgical Latin, as a joke.

The postwar Right tended to view McCarthy's Senate hearings as not only necessary on their face but also as payback for earlier leftist allegations that the antiwar, pro-capitalist Old Right conservatives were Nazis and Fascists. Rand's support for McCarthy, as for HUAC, may have had as much to do with her fragile understanding of American due process as with her principled abhorrence of Communism. But it may also have been a result of the trust she tended to accord to those who shared her views and, as she saw it, had the courage to express them against liberal opposition. Toward the end of the 1950s, soon after the senator's death from alcoholism, an acquaintance named Joan Kennedy Taylor ran into her at a National Book Awards ceremony. "Tell me," Taylor recalled her saying, "what did people have against McCarthy?" Taylor told her, "Well, Ayn, it's primarily because he wasn't truthful. He said all these things and couldn't back them up." And she said, "Oh, I see. The Big Lie." In later years, she told a young friend that McCarthy's mission had been right but that he had lacked the moral courage to pursue it into the highest reaches of government. She also supported the larger-than-life, forcibly retired army chief of staff General Douglas MacArthur during his brief flirtation with presidential politics, presenting him with a copy of *Anthem*, admiringly inscribed, "From an author who voted for him for President of the United States in 1952—with profound respect and admiration." Of course, this was a joke. MacArthur didn't run in 1952—Robert Taft and Dwight D. Eisenhower competed for the Republican nomination—and Rand, disgusted with the choices, reportedly didn't vote either then or in 1956.

Like Buckley and other anti-Communists, she liked McCarthy and detested Eisenhower as a conservative lacking in principles and backbone. Branden recalled her indignation over a 1957 *Time* magazine article recounting a 1945 meeting between General Eisenhower and his Russian counterpart, Marshal Georgy Zhukov, in Berlin. The two had been debating the strengths of their respective forms of government. The article quoted Eisenhower as saying, "I was hard put to it when [Zhukov] insisted that [the Soviet] system appealed to the idealistic and [that ours appealed] completely to the materialistic, and I had a very tough time trying to defend our position because he said: 'You tell a person he can do as he pleases, he can act as he pleases, he can do anything. Everything that is selfish in man you appeal to. . . . We tell him that he must sacrifice for the state.'" The fact that Eisenhower couldn't defend "the noblest, freest country in the history of the world" as a matter of principle against a puppet of "the bloodiest dictatorship in history" infuriated her. "That's why, without a morality of rational self-interest, capitalism can't be defended," she told Branden. By then, she had delineated such a morality in *Atlas Shrugged*.

Rand was also a regular guest at dinners and parties given by Frances and Henry Hazlitt in their apartment on Washington Square. Frances had been Richard Mealand's assistant and Rand's boss in the New York office of Paramount Pictures' story department in the early 1940s. Henry, an economics journalist who championed laissez-faire capitalism to generations of readers of *The New York Times, The Nation,* and *Newsweek,* was the newly appointed editor of *The Freeman,* the magazine for which Paterson had been raising money in 1948. Both were longtime friends and admirers of hers. Through them she met East Coast acquaintances of her California political allies William Mullendore and Leonard Read, such as Frank Meyer and Willie Schlamm, and renewed her acquaintance with the now canonical Austrian economist Ludwig von Mises.

Mises, as he was known, was a Jewish refugee from Nazi-occupied Austria whom Hazlitt had helped to bring to the United States in 1940. An author and prewar chief economic adviser to the Austrian government, he was considered one of the period's great economic and social theorists in Europe but was known by only a handful of free-market intellectuals in the United States. Rand had met him soon after he arrived in New York. The two had much in common. They agreed that the future of political liberty lay with unregulated markets and limited government. They avidly supported private property, deregulation of industry, and a fixed gold standard to prevent governments from expanding state power by inflating the currency, the terrible consequences of which both had experienced at first hand. Throughout the 1940s and later, she consistently recommended his books to her friends, along with Hazlitt's *Economics in One Lesson* and Paterson's *The God of the Machine.* But Rand and Mises didn't see eye to eye on the essential importance of individual rights, among other subjects, and legend has it that they got into an impassioned argument the very first time they met.

Hazlitt had introduced them at a dinner party he and Frances gave in 1941 or 1942. As he later recalled the incident, they and his other guests were gathered in the living room after dinner. He took drink orders, and when he returned from the kitchen with a tray in his hands, he heard Rand saying to Mises, "You treat me like an ignorant little Jewish girl!" Without knowing exactly what had happened between them, but assuming that they were arguing about the doctrine of natural rights, he tried to make peace. "Oh, I'm sure, Ayn, that Lu didn't mean it that way," he remembered telling her. Mises, who was famously dapper, self-disciplined, and charming, jumped to his feet and shouted, "I did mean it that way!" Since the Austrian sexagenarian was already hard of hearing, Hazlitt surmised that he had not heard what Rand had said. In any case, peace was restored.

Rand and Mises probably didn't see each other again until the early 1950s. But during one of Hazlitt's trips to Los Angeles, the well-known journalist delighted her by confiding that "Lu Mises and I were talking about you the other day, and he called you 'the most courageous man in America.'" "Did he really say *man*?" she asked him. "Yes," said Hazlitt, and she beamed. Within limits, she and the old-world economist liked and respected each other. But ideas trumped compliments. Years later, Nathaniel Branden discovered a set of angry margin notes she had penned in her copy of Mises's most famous book, *Human Action*. "Bastard!" he recalled that she wrote on one page, irritated by Mises's rejection of a moral, as opposed to a practical, argument for capitalism. (Her devotion to her own ideas sometimes "allowed normal human considerations to fall by the wayside," Branden remarked mildly.)

A second clash with Mises occurred in 1952 or 1953. It ended in a falling-out indicative of Rand's diminishing tolerance for intellectual opposition. Again at the Hazlitts', with the Brandens in attendance, the two eminences argued over the government's right to impose a military draft, which was ongoing after World War II. Mises, who had a purely economic aversion to state power, supported it. Rand considered it an utter violation of individual rights, beginning with the right to life. The morning after their argument, she phoned Richard Cornuelle, the younger brother of her California acquaintance Herbert Cornuelle and a regular attendee at Mises's weekly NYU economics seminar. Twenty-three, strapping, and handsome, Cornuelle knew both Mises and Hazlitt and had become fascinated by Rand. He liked to stop by her apartment whenever she had time to sit and talk with him. "I thought she was a most remarkable person, exerting a huge influence for liberty," he said. But when she called and asked him to take sides in her dispute with Mises, he pled neutrality. "That's not possible," she told him. "You're either with me or against me." He refused to choose, and she ended the conversation and never spoke to him again. She remained friendly with Mises, however, for another decade and helped him to promote his books.

Cornuelle was half relieved by the break, he later said, because his relationship with her had gotten a little "creepy." "She was very magnetic, and you didn't want to argue with her. You wanted her to like you, and you sensed that it wouldn't take much for you to [be shown] the door." Besides, "she was a terrible flirt. My brother Herb and I used to try to count the guys she'd told were models for her heroes. It was more than one but less than twenty." Although he had met both O'Connor and Branden, they were rarely at Rand's apartment when he was invited to drop by. "She kept her boyfriends separated," he said, laughing. "Branden was then just beginning to be her protégé." She had started to question Cornuelle about his sex life. "That scared me to death," he said. For him, the shy younger son of a Protestant minister, the flirtation "was becoming a problem," and so he didn't try to reconnect with Rand.

The earlier argument with Mises, and the older man's apparent agreement that she was "just a silly little Jewish girl" (as the story came to be told, with the added embellishment that she wept), became a perennial item of gossip on the Right. William Buckley, Russell Kirk, and other right-wing Christian intellectuals repeated it with relish, for decades, without evidence that it was true. Her young friends, on first hearing the story in the 1960s, peremptorily denied that the incident had happened. In 1962, Branden wrote directly to Mises, requesting a written denial, and Mises, then in his eighties, complied. Yet, as Rand knew, the story was true. Hazlitt told it privately, to friends, a number of times over the years, and immediately after Rand's death he wrote to correct an inaccurate account included by Buckley in his *National Review* obituary of the author.

If the exchange with Mises did take place, as it almost certainly did, perhaps it isn't surprising that at least once in her life Rand reflected something of the poisoned atmosphere of the anti-Semitic Russia of her childhood. That she tended to confront pain and fear by minimizing their importance would surely not have guaranteed a complete escape from the effects of second-class citizenship in her native city. In *Atlas Shrugged,* there comes a revealing moment, before Dagny's crash-landing in Galt's Gulch, when the heroine briefly gives up the battle to save Taggart Transcontinental. She resigns her official position and withdraws to a country cottage that had belonged to her father. She feels immense pain at the prospect of losing her railroad; startlingly, she likens her pain to the howling of a wounded stranger in whose screams she could drown at any moment. "She felt no pity for the stranger, only a contemptuous impatience; she had to fight him and destroy him." Later, in the chapter "Atlantis," Dagny reflects that "all the years of ugliness and struggle [weren't real. They] were only someone's senseless joke." Of course, anti-Semitism was not a senseless joke. Neither were the other traumas and anxieties of Rand's childhood and young adulthood.

In this small world, other friends of Hazlitt and admirers of Mises were drawn into her circle. In the Austrian economist's weekly graduate-level seminar at NYU, academics, businessmen, and activists, including Cornuelle, came to listen and ask questions; many stayed in the seminar for years or even decades. One longtime student and friend of Mises was Murray Rothbard, a quick-witted twenty-eight-year-old intellectual prankster and self-styled "anarcho-capitalist." The Cornuelle brothers had brought Rothbard to visit Rand in 1952, and Rothbard found the experience of paying court to her both fascinating and depressing. In 1954 he tried again. As the leader of a high-octane clique of young Mises students who called themselves the Circle Bastiat, he bowed to group pressure to provide an introduction to her. He arranged for a meeting between members of his circle and Rand's Collective. The date set was for a Saturday evening in mid-July, with a follow-up meeting scheduled a week later. Rothbard and his friends survived to tell the story, and told it many times.

The Brandens were in Canada, but Rand, O'Connor, Leonard Peikoff, Alan Greenspan, and other Rand associates were arrayed on the sofa and chairs in her living room when Rothbard and his young companions George Reisman and Ralph Raico entered. After introductions, she spoke mostly to seventeen-year-old Reisman, a brainy recent graduate of the Bronx High School of Science. Before the discussion got under way, Reisman presented her with a pair of tickets to a dinner event in support of Roy Cohn, who had recently resigned as Senator McCarthy's chief counsel; Cohn had been accused of misusing the power of his office on behalf of a homosexual lover during the recently completed Army-McCarthy hearings. Reisman was on assignment from one of the dinner's organizers to ask the novelist to come, he explained, and mentioned that McCarthy would also be there. Although McCarthy's star was swiftly setting, Rand still supported him. She declined, however, on the grounds that, for her to become involved in a defense of Cohn, she would have to abandon *Atlas Shrugged* and proclaim his innocence as the novelist Emile Zola had proclaimed that of Dreyfus.

At first, Reisman was amazed—not by Rand's comparing Cohn to Dreyfus, but by her grandiosity in likening herself to Zola. After reading *Atlas Shrugged* in 1957, however, he concluded that "a comparison [of Rand] to Zola [was] several orders of magnitude too modest."

Reminiscing years later, Reisman, by then a distinguished economist at Pepperdine University, recalled that his hero Rothbard sat silently and appeared amused as the younger man experienced what the older one had undergone two years earlier: the grim impossibility of winning an argument with Ayn Rand. As the novelist's delighted admirers looked on, Reisman attempted to defend the Misesean proposition that people's values—meaning their judgments and choices—are necessarily subjective, changeable, and often arbitrary. Rand would have none of it. She lured him into admitting the objective fact of his own existence—as Branden had tried to do with Alan Greenspan—then pointed out that human life requires definite, particular resources and actions to keep it going. *Those* were values. From there, she captured all the points. "No matter how hard I tried I couldn't budge her," Reisman recalled when he was in his seventies. "She had an answer and an explanation for everything, including a preference for vanilla ice cream over chocolate ice cream." He never forgot her method of arguing. With irrefutable logic, she transformed what he thought were self-evident propositions into absurdities. Adding to the impression made by her logic was the sheer force of her personality. At some junctures, he became so "frightened of her driving me into some *other* position I did not want to take that I did not even allow myself to recognize what I really believed." When the discussion took a detour into physics, Reisman hypothesized that, since no two objects can occupy the same space at the same time, there must be empty pockets of space, or voids, when objects move from one position to another. That was "worse than anything a Communist could have said!" she thundered. Later, he understood her to have meant that the "existence of *non*existence" was the kind of conceptual gibberish that historically set the stage for priests and tyrants to brainwash people. At the time, however, debating with her was "comparable to being in the presence of the voice of Judgment on Judgment Day." For Reisman, it wasn't a pleasant experience, but that didn't keep him from becoming one of her loyal lieutenants after the publication of *Atlas Shrugged*.

The party broke up at five thirty in the morning. The next week, other members of the Circle Bastiat came along to support their friends in open competition. The evening ended in defeat, and, for Rothbard, in deflation. After that, he decided it was best to keep his distance from the first lady of reason. In a letter to his friend Richard Cornuelle, he reflected on her blind spots and also her charisma. She offered a brilliant argument for the importance of ethics in a time and place that badly underrated them, he noted, and communicated "great truths that we have literally never heard in the classroom." But she was also humorless, puritanical, and gave herself far too much credit for the originality of her ideas. "While I agreed (or thought I agreed) mainly with her position, I found myself rooting like hell for George [Reisman], who found himself under a typical Randian barrage, according to which anyone who is not now or soon will be a one-hundred-percent Randian Rationalist is an 'enemy' and an 'objective believer in death and destruction' as well as crazy." In a leap of logic and intuition, Rothbard divined a flaw in her approach that others wouldn't discover for a decade, if at all: the one-party nature of her philosophical system. The famous individualist "actually *denies* all individuality whatsoever!" he exclaimed to Cornuelle. Given her rejection of the relevance of family background, temperament, and personal preference in the formation of values and ideas, a Randian utopia "would be a place where all men are identical, in their souls if not in their personal appearance." This was an eerily precise forecast of the busy uniformity of Galt's Gulch in *Atlas Shrugged,* where everyone agrees on almost everything. Forewarned as he was, though, Rothbard could not resist her intellectual appeal. In 1957, he, too, would briefly enlist in her growing army of supporters, with unfortunate results for him.

During this period, Ayn and her recently married protégé Nathaniel Branden were neighbors and saw each other two or three times a week. Exchanging greetings at her apartment door, or saying good-bye after a Saturday evening of reading and group discussion, Branden was aware that their embraces lasted a little longer and were a little more intimate than they had been before. He felt "an enhanced sense of male power" when he kissed her good night, he later wrote, and sensed "that she felt a heightened awareness of herself as a woman." Heretofore apprehensive in his relationships with women, even with his wife, he wrote, "I liked knowing I was the cause of what she was feeling." Gradually, they began to hold hands in public and say aloud that they were soul mates. Oddly, no one in the Collective noticed, or acknowledged noticing, anything overly familiar in their behavior with each other or in the effusive compliments they traded. Later, Branden would claim that he and Rand were still unaware of what was coming.

In private moments, she asked him about the state of his marriage. Had the sex problem been cured? Predictably, the answer was no. When he attempted to make love to Barbara, she often turned away. Rand, acknowledging that the situation was frustrating, advised him, and also Barbara, to be patient and persevere. One evening, he told her that he sensed in himself a capacity for sexual passion that had never been fully aroused or released with his wife. To drive the point home, he compared himself to Dagny at a low ebb in the story, feeling downcast and yearning for an ideal lover at the very moment when the anonymous John Galt happens to be passing in the shadows outside her office window. Was Branden suggesting that Rand was *his* John Galt, or that he was willing to be hers? In either case, the analogy must have served to remind her that she was sexually lonely, too. Branden was throwing down a gauntlet. He later said that he did not know that she would pick it up.

From his teenaged years onward, Branden had wanted to be a writer as well as a psychologist. As it turned out, his first published piece of writing had been a letter to the editor of the UCLA newspaper while he was still a student there, in protest of an editorial that was sympathetic to a Communist professor who had committed suicide. He gave a copy of the published letter to Rand on Father's Day of 1951, signing it, jokingly, "To my father—Ayn Rand." In the spring of 1954, he applied to New York State to change his legal name from Nathan Blumenthal to Nathaniel Branden, which is a perfect anagram of the common Hebrew formulation for "son of Rand": "ben Rand." "Nathaniel," in addition to being a variant of Nathan, was the first name of Dagny's idealized ancestor, the self-made railroad tycoon Nathaniel Taggart in *Atlas Shrugged*. In September 1954, the courts approved the change. Now Rand and he were father and son, mother and child, romantic heroine and—grandfather. They were also sons and lovers. A few days after the official name change, the first act in their love affair began.

They were riding together in the front seat of a car alongside O'Connor, who was driving, with Branden's sister Elayne and Barbara in the back. They were returning to New York from Toronto, where the group had been visiting Elayne and Nathaniel's parents and sister Florence and her husband. In Florence's living room one afternoon, Rand and Branden had been explaining some of her ideas when they found themselves performing a spontaneous duet, jointly fielding questions from the family and several acquaintances and laughingly completing each other's sentences. They felt a degree of spiritual unity that was intoxicating.

The trip was Rand's first outside the United States since O'Connor and she had gone to Mexico in 1929 to establish her permanent residency. Driving home, she was in a gay mood, laughing and cavorting with Branden. Wasn't he a genius, a great psychologist, a man of destiny? she cried to Barbara and Elayne. Somewhat wryly, they agreed. As dusk fell, she rested her head on his shoulder and took his hand. He put his arm around her, and they murmured to each other. Their voices were low, excluding the others, and their glances were "too personal and lasted too long, as if they were gazing deeply into each other and could not bear to look away," Barbara wrote in 1986. During that long car ride, Barbara couldn't ignore the pitch and tone of their voices and finally realized that her twenty-four-year-old husband and his forty-nine-year-old mentor had moved beyond the bounds of mutual admiration and familial affection. "She's in love with you!" she shouted angrily at her husband, once they were alone in a motel room. "And you're in love with her!" Branden denied it, both to his wife and, he claimed, to himself; he insisted that the twenty-five-year age difference between them and the fact that they were both married made a romantic liaison impossible, outlandish. What O'Connor thought or said is not known.

Two days later, back in New York, the sexually ardent older woman invited the young man to come to her apartment in the afternoon. Frank was on duty at the florist's shop; Barbara was in Midtown, working in her first job as a receptionist for *Woman's Day*. With a note of caution and, possibly, an eagerness that had the tone of a demand to Branden, she asked, "Do you understand what happened to us two days ago?" As Branden recalled the scene, he faltered, and she said, "In the car . . . what we said to each other. It sounded like love. Or have I misunderstood everything?" Now at the height of her mental and emotional powers, she had been rehearsing just such a moment of triangulated passion for at least half her life. Branden, as flattered and incautious as he may have been, was out of his depth. For all his flirtatiousness, he had never really contemplated an actual affair with his literary and intellectual idol, he later said. Nor would he have raised the subject of the car ride if she had not.

Nonetheless, he felt an unfamiliar sense of elation, power, even mastery. The woman with the magnificent eyes and the penetrating mind was looking to him for romance; and when he looked back at her, "the image [of myself] I saw reflected [in her eyes] was that of a god," he later wrote. "I am in love with you," he said aloud. It was a fiction that would last for fourteen years.

It wasn't a conscious fiction, not at first. That they had fallen in love struck them both as philosophically inevitable and romantically and morally correct.

That first afternoon, they told each other that whatever they did they would not hurt each other or their spouses. Rand suggested that the affair be "nonsexual, in the ultimate sense," meaning that their lovemaking would stop short of intercourse. Branden agreed, disappointed but also relieved, he recalled. As crusaders for integrity and honesty, they prepared to present the facts to Frank and Barbara. They decided to ask for permission to meet by themselves twice a week. "I'm sure they'll agree to that. We have a right to something," Branden recalled Rand declaring. He heard anger in her voice and recognized it as a response to the presence of potential impediments. "It was not named but it was felt, and it was in our eyes as we looked at each other in silent understanding," he wrote in 1989. "We would not be stopped."

A few days later, Rand opened the fateful discussion. As recounted by both Brandens, she and Nathaniel were already seated on the living-room sofa, holding hands, as first Barbara and then Frank came in at the end of the workday. According to Nathaniel, Frank appeared calm and expectant; the nervous young suitor gathered that he and his wife had already discussed the situation. Not so Barbara, whom Branden had not informed. Rand said simply that she and Nathaniel were in love. "There is nothing in our feeling [for each other] that can hurt or threaten you," she assured them. "There's nothing that alters my love for my husband, or Nathan's love for his wife. It's something separate, apart from our normal lives." Barbara sat, frozen, not surprised by what she heard but stunned into silence nonetheless. As Rand talked, Frank turned pale and looked downcast. "We're not Platonists," she continued. "We don't hold our values in some other realm, unrelated to the realm in which we live our lives. If we mean the values we profess, how can [Nathan and I] not be in love?" She talked for a long time. Once—so Barbara reported—the young wife jumped to her feet and shouted, "No! I won't be part of this!" at which point, she recalled, Frank also raised *his* voice, saying, "And *I* won't be part of it." Rand remained calm. They weren't proposing a sexual union, she explained. The twenty-five-year age difference ruled that out. No, they wanted only to spend a little time together. Wasn't that a reasonable request? Thirty years later, Barbara told an interviewer, while trying to explain her agreement to such a request, "With Ayn's mind, once you accepted her premises she'd spin out a deductive chain from which you just couldn't escape." Ensorcelled by the older woman's authority and theories of love and value, Barbara assented. So did O'Connor.

Two months later, in November, the curtain rose on the second act of the affair. The philosopher and her protégé could not stick to their original agreement to abstain from sex, they informed Frank and Barbara. They defended the rightness and rationality of a full-throttle sexual affair in a series of conversations with their spouses that went on for weeks. Each was the embodiment of the other's highest values, they pointed out in the language of *Atlas Shrugged,* and because neither suffered from an irrational mind-body split, they naturally felt sexual longing for each other. Surely Frank and Barbara, both of whom subscribed to Rand's value theory of sexuality, could understand and accept this new development. In making her case, Rand invoked her years of deprivation. "You both know how little I've had in my life, by way of personal reward," she told them. "This is the very last period in my life when I can think about or permit myself" the pleasure of a passionate sexual affair outside of marriage. "I'm a realist about age," she added. "What we're asking for is temporary. . . . Just to have had it for a little while."

A month before her fiftieth birthday, she and Nathaniel received their partners' permission to meet for sex twice a week. Barbara, to whom Rand had shown both personal kindness and an example of "the epitome and standard of the human potential," acted on a mixture of gratitude to the writer and guilt over her inability to respond sexually to her husband. Why O'Connor went along with the scheme is not known, but speculation among Rand aficionados divides in two camps. Some, including the Brandens, surmise that he was so devoted to his wife's well-being, including her sexual well-being, and so conscious of his limitations that he quietly waived his marital rights. Others contend that Frank, who knew and approved of his wife's fantasies of sexual triangles in her novels, also approved of the affair. As evidence, they cite passages such as this one from her 1949 notes for *Atlas,* written six months before she met Branden: "[Hank Rearden] takes pleasure in Dagny's greatness," she wrote, and this "arouses his sexual desire; he [also] takes pleasure in the thought of Dagny and another man, which is an unconscious acknowledgement that sex, as such, is great and beautiful, not evil and degrading." A few pages later, she continued, "On the right philosophical premise about sex, *my* premise . . . a husband would feel honored if another man wanted his wife; he would not let the other man *have* her—his exclusive possession [of her] is the material form of her love for him—but he would feel that the other man's desire was a natural and proper expression of the man's admiration for his wife, for the values which she represents and which he saw in her." In this view, Rand changed her mind about whether a husband would "let" another man "have" his wife, but the husband's arousal remains the same. That she wrote these passages without reference to O'Connor is another possibility, of course.

Rand swore everyone to silence, not yet imagining that the affair would "involve all four of us in a life of deception," as Barbara later said. Because of her concern with privacy, she dismissed Nathaniel's suggestion that they lease a separate apartment or book hotel rooms for their meetings rather than use the O'Connors' apartment. She couldn't risk their being seen together in a hotel lobby or entering a strange apartment and becoming the subject of a scandal. Though proud of her love for him, she said, she drew the line at furnishing gossip to malicious detractors. Like Dagny in her first ecstatic encounters with Francisco as a teenager, she wanted to keep their intimacy "immaculately theirs," locked away from prying eyes and prurient minds. Frank agreed to leave the apartment twice a week, while the two made love in his bed. Thus, like Hank Rearden after Dagny meets John Galt, the older man stepped aside to make way for a more ideal man.

The matter settled, Rand comforted the spouses. The affair would last only a year or two, she promised. She would not allow herself to become that ludicrous figure, "an old woman pursuing a younger man." She decreed that they would all continue to tell the truth to one another. If anyone in the world could handle such a situation, they could. They were superior people; like the characters in her novels, they lived on an emotional plane far above the irrational jealousies and fears of ordinary men. "If the four of us were of lesser stature, this would not have happened," she assured them. "And if it somehow had [happened], you would not accept it." Interestingly, her remarks contained echoes of a twenty-year-old letter from her father, who after reading *The Night of January 16th* wrote to her, "I'm amused that you condemned Karen for her disreputable behavior, as you called it. Don't you see that words like this do not apply to people like Karen? For those who surround them are of so little stature that they [Karen and her lover Bjorn] cannot be held to the same standard."

In any case, the once-lonely Russian girl with a crush on a storybook hero now had the power to win the handsome young prince for herself.

Ayn and Nathaniel began sleeping together in January or early February of 1955. He later recalled the pleasure he took in playing the role of sexual aggressor with a woman who was ravenous for the experience of sexual surrender. "Ayn frightened most people," he reflected in 1989. "What she wanted was a man whose esteem would reduce her to a sex object." He added, "Her progressive loss of control in our encounters disclosed the depths" of her desire to be ravished and submit. Like Dominique, she seems to have found both pleasure and release in "the act of a master taking . . . possession of her." The difference was that *this* master was younger than Roark and that his self-esteem was tied to her approval of him. If Rand was sexually vulnerable, she also had control. Her lover was not an emotional threat. Seen from a certain perspective, he made an ideal mistress, even as Frank had become an ideal wife.

The affair provided excitement and deep fulfillment at a crucial, and essentially pleasureless, moment in her writing life. By early 1955, she was stuck on the now-famous fourth-from-final chapter of *Atlas Shrugged* called "This Is John Galt Speaking," in which Galt presents his radio speech explaining what has gone wrong with the world and what must be done to fix it and giving the first complete account of the history and purpose of the strike. It lays bare Rand's argument that the evils of altruism—by which Rand meant the proposition that men have no right to exist for their own sake—are at the root of America's deterioration into a pre-Jeffersonian, potentially preindustrial era in the book, and, in life, into a communistic trap, and it summarizes the values and virtues that make for a purposeful life. When, a decade later, tens of thousands of followers joined Rand study clubs and packed large lecture halls to hear her speak, it was to the radical individualist vision of this speech that they were drawn.

She had drafted the first line of the speech in the summer of 1953. Having allotted roughly three months to its completion, she was frantic in early 1955, when she had already devoted eighteen months of nonstop effort to it and was not yet finished. She would require an additional eight months before she wrote the final sentence: "I swear by my life and my love of it that I will never live for the sake of another man, nor ask another man to live for mine." That declaration, repeating the theme of Howard Roark's courtroom speech and emphasizing the reciprocal nature of individual rights, was important to Rand. The oath is "a dramatized summation of the Objectivist ethics," she explained in a *Playboy* interview in 1964, using a term she coined for her system of ideas, and it is the oath taken by each of the strikers on entering Galt's Gulch. Similarly, Galt tells the millions of people listening to their radios, "Just as there are no contradictions in my values and no conflicts among my desires—so there are no victims and no conflicts of interest among rational men." Although she was living with others' silent conflicts, Rand intended no irony. She was removing the teeth from reality's harsh bite.

For nearly ten years, off and on, she had been promising Alan Collins and Hiram Haydn, who was Archibald Ogden's replacement at Bobbs-Merrill, that the completed manuscript of the novel was only months away. During the two-plus years she spent constructing John Galt's speech, she gradually stopped going out into the city she loved. By the start of her affair with Branden, she was seeing few of her distinguished New York friends. She settled into the kind of grueling schedule that had earlier yielded two-thirds of *The Fountainhead* in twelve months' time. That year, 1942, had been the happiest of her life. She was not happy in 1954 and 1955, apart from the time she spent with her lover. In place of *The Fountainhead*'s colorful scenes of adventure and conflict, she was wrestling with the logic of a system of abstractions, laboring to tie together her theories of metaphysics (that reality is objective and cannot be altered by wishes or emotions), epistemology (that knowledge comes through reason and never through feeling), morality (rational self-interest), politics (individual rights), economics (free-market capitalism), and sex (the erotic response to intellectual values). Closing every loophole and presenting the finished doctrine in the form of a dramatic speech by the novel's leading hero was the most difficult task of her life, she confided to Barbara. It was while working on this famous section of *Atlas Shrugged* that she began to speak of herself not only as someone with a philosophy of life but also as a philosopher.

With a few exceptions, none of the ideas contained in the speech were new to her. But shaping them felt like "drops-of-water-in-a-desert kind of torture." She often worked all day, and sometimes all night, dressed in her favorite nightgown: a floor-length, blue-green cotton tunic trimmed with Hollywood-style rhinestones at the neck. At one point, she stayed inside the apartment, working for thirty-three days in a row, seeing no one but her husband, Barbara, and Nathaniel, and, on Saturday nights, members of the Collective. The amphetamines she took helped her to stay awake, but she grew so tired that her body sagged. At times she couldn't eat, sleep, or even talk. She complained of tension in her neck and shoulders. She nagged at O'Connor, who sometimes snapped at her, and she exhibited unpredictable mood swings with the Brandens. Finishing John Galt's speech pushed her to the limits of her endurance, Barbara wrote, and shortened the distance between intensity and rage. If she had sometimes been self-absorbed, or incurious about others' points of view, or grandiose, those tendencies became more marked.

Her love affair with Branden helped to relieve her crippling anxiety and its symptoms, bitterness and anger, as she pushed to finish the difficult expository section of the book. "You are my reward for everything," she told him—"for my work, for my life." As the writing dragged on, she depended on him more, both as a companion in her fictional world and as a mirror for the sexually desirable woman she was discovering in herself. "You're turning me into an animal," she sometimes told him, playfully. "Really?" he remembered answering with a grin. "What were you before?" "A mind," she replied, believing it. He was vitally aware of his admiration for her and was amazed that he could bring her so much pleasure, even joy. But something—was it her age? her expectations of him?—disturbed him, he later noted. And he felt uncomfortable about both Barbara and Frank. Once he recalled entering the apartment to find Ayn quarreling with Frank over the older man's lack of interest in helping her shop for clothes. Branden went shopping with her against her will, she was saying loudly to her husband, and he and Barbara both gave her advice on what to wear. Why couldn't Frank be less passive? O'Connor didn't seem to mind the comparison to Branden or the scolding and even gave the younger man a conspiratorial wink. But Branden

felt both too large and too small for the role he was playing, and his uneasiness increased. He also thought that Frank must be suffering, even
if he didn't show it.

There were other early signs of trouble. Once they began meeting
for sex, she protected their time together fiercely and became impatient,
to say the least, if anything interfered. This included Branden's occasional preoccupation with Barbara, who had recently begun suffering
from panic attacks and night terrors. One night, Barbara called Rand's
apartment from a pay phone, choking with anxiety and pleading to come
over for a little while. She had been walking for hours in a state of panic,
an image that brings to mind the haunting scene in which James Taggart's young wife, Cherryl, commits suicide after wandering the streets.
She needed their help, Barbara told Nathaniel. In a rage, Rand took the
phone and railed: "Do you think only of yourself? Am I *completely* invisible to you?" The older woman refused to let her join them, pointing out
that no one had helped *her* in times of trouble. "Why should *I* be victimized for Barbara's problems?" she said to Branden afterward, who
though horrified and worried stayed with Rand, an indication of the loyalty and fear she already commanded in him. Amazingly, not until much
later did either of the Brandens connect Barbara's increasingly painful
anxiety to the affair.

Rand became more demanding. She liked to talk to Branden about
their feelings for each other and got angry when the twenty-five-year-old
man squirmed and changed the subject. What's the matter with you? she
asked, again and again. Why are you being emotionally distant? Are you
repressed? "Repression"—that is, hiding your real nature by refusing to
grapple with unwelcome conflicts or with painful impulses and ideas—
became the word she used for her lover's inability or reluctance to discuss
their romance. Yet the one time he tried to talk about his distress over
Frank and Barbara, she instantly displayed a "distant, icy rage," he wrote.
"She became more than a stranger; she became an adversary." She often
phoned him as soon as he had walked the two blocks home at night, "still
angry, scolding, accusing, denouncing him for what she termed his 'emotional distance,' for his periods of coldness and emotional withdrawal,"
Barbara noted in 2007. The young husband, who had felt proud of his ascendant manhood, now sometimes drooped with a sense of failure. Still,
he wanted to succeed as Rand's lover and keep her high regard.

Barbara forgave her friend and mentor for the night of the telephone call and every other apparent act of callousness. She told herself that the writer was under enormous emotional and intellectual pressure, which was true, and that she had earned the right to an undisturbed weekly idyll in Atlantis. But Rand did not as easily let go of the event. She decided that Barbara must have a psychological problem and briefly put aside her work on Galt's speech to draft a paper on the subject of Barbara as an "emotionalist," using a term that Nathaniel had coined to describe a person who understands the world through the filter of his emotions, rather than by reason. Such people tend to recoil from the pain of disappointment, she noted, which distorted their perception of reality. Barbara accepted this hypothesis. So did Nathaniel. From that time forward, he became his wife's officially acknowledged therapist, guiding her to repair her "premises" and "sense of life." He remained in that role for as long as they were married. "You cannot imagine what a nightmare" it became, Barbara told an interviewer in 1991. Branden, by the mid-1950s enrolled in a master's degree program in psychology at NYU, went on to write his thesis on anxiety as a crisis of self-esteem. He considered turning the theory into a book. He also began to offer therapy based on Rand's and his ideas at low prices to members of the Collective.

Rand and her protégé introduced other specialized words and phrases into their daily discussions. To indicate a person's general style of learning and thinking, they referred to his or her "psycho-epistemology." To identify people they thought were overly concerned with the opinions and approval of others, Branden created a category he called "social metaphysics," which encompassed a detailed analysis of the disordered mind of "second-handers" and which became a much-feared diagnosis. People who confused wishes with horses were labeled "subjectivists." Beginning with these terms and a few others, Rand's circle adopted a psychological argot that separated them from other members of their age group and, later, provided defensive characterizations of unfriendly outsiders.

Few knew that "emotionalist" applied to Barbara, let alone that Rand also consigned O'Connor to that type. Apart from his flower arranging, the genial man had found little to do. He and Branden sometimes met in the foyer and shook hands as he left the apartment in deference to his wife. The Brandens later claimed to have discovered that he was drinking heavily in a local bar—an assertion that has been bitterly disputed by Rand's hard-core followers, but that what evidence there is suggests is true.

It didn't take long for Nathaniel to conclude that he was in over his head. As he told an audience of Rand fans in 1989, "I confused loneliness, marital frustration, incredible admiration and hero worship for Ayn with romantic love." Once, he said, he tested the waters of retreat, wondering aloud whether they had made a mistake by introducing sex into their friendship. To his horror, she replied coldly, "This affair is sexual or it's nothing." She added, "If we are not man and woman to each other, in the full sense—if we are merely disembodied minds—our philosophy is meaningless." He naturally heard in this both a warning and a threat and never again raised the subject. Her demands for emotional intimacy, which accompanied the sex ("Where have you gone to? You've disappeared," she'd badger him), would cease when the affair ended, he told himself, within another year or two.

Still the Collective noticed nothing unusual, with the exception of graduate art student Joan Mitchell Blumenthal, Barbara's oldest friend. "One night very early in the game," Blumenthal recalled, "Ayn was posing for me. She had on a filmy nightgown. She was primping, and I asked her what she was looking so self-satisfied about. She said, 'I'll tell you someday, but I can't tell you now.' That was all. And I said to myself, 'Oh.' And then—this will give you some idea of the fear and trembling around this thing—I decided not to tell Allan," her new husband, who was Nathaniel's cousin and a doctor. "I never did, until things started showing at the seams." For most of the circle, Ayn's sexuality was invisible, even inconceivable, perhaps especially as she labored day and night over John Galt's speech. Long after learning the facts of the affair, one follower explained it, in part, by saying, "Ayn wasn't very clean. I couldn't picture Nathan in her bed."

On Saturday nights, Rand and her protégé often sat slightly apart from the rest of the group, at the dining-room table or on a couch, while Barbara, Joan and Allan, Leonard Peikoff, Alan Greenspan, and Mary Ann Sures devoured the latest aphoristic developments in John Galt's code of life. The novel was giving them undreamed-of intellectual stimulation, role models to test themselves against, and, with Rand's progress on the speech, a road map for living. Some recalled these evenings with Rand as a high point of their lives. "In a world that was hurtling toward collectivism and darkness, we were listening to the ideas of a woman who was a strong, bright light that pointed the way toward freedom," said one. "I often felt, greeting her, as though I were entering Atlantis, where the human ideal is not merely an elusive projection but is real, alive, here—seated across the room on blue-green pillows," wrote another. "She wanted us to discuss [her writing], which we did, and those discussions were one of the most exhilarating, exciting, wonderful times of my life," recalled Nathaniel's sister Elayne.

As the manuscript pages piled up, some of the women, including Mary Ann Sures, volunteered to work as part-time secretaries. Using Rand's ancient manual typewriter, "like an old tank," on the dining table in the O'Connors' foyer, Sures typed and retyped sections of the novel. The foyer was about ten paces from the study; sometimes, Sures recalled, when she and another helper were reading freshly typed pages to each other as a proofreading technique, they were aware of the author standing half hidden behind the study door, listening for narrative pace and rhythm. Unlike Frank Lloyd Wright at Taliesin, she was scrupulous about paying her assistants for their work. Sures recalled that she gave them the going wage, down to the quarter hour. As had also been true in California, however, she and Frank sometimes forgot to pay other bills. Some months, sending in the rent check slipped their minds and they received an eviction notice from the landlord. One afternoon, recalled Sures, a man from Consolidated Edison showed up at the door to turn off the electricity after three overdue notices had gone unpaid. It was Frank's responsibility to handle bills, Rand told Sures, but she didn't seem upset about it. The lights stayed on, and she greeted him with "darling"s and "Cubbyhole"s when he came home.

Meanwhile, *The Fountainhead* was far from forgotten. Every few weeks, packets of fan letters arrived from Bobbs-Merrill. Sorting through them, Rand scribbled notes, typically on the order of "very good—to be answered" or "swine—to be damned to the eternal fires of hell." Some of the most irritating or interesting of these letters she showed to the Brandens, who, when they spotted an especially intelligent correspondent who lived within commuting distance of New York, might ask him or her to a gathering of the Collective. In late 1955, they pounced on one such letter writer, a young woman named Daryn Kent. Twenty-two and eager to improve her life, she had left a working-class home against her parents' wishes to become an actress and a dancer in New York. Happening upon *The Fountainhead* in a drugstore, she took it home and was thrilled by what she interpreted as its validation of her right to live the life she wanted. She wrote to Rand and a few weeks later received a phone call from Leonard Peikoff. The two met in a restaurant on West

Fifty-fifth Street, talked for hours about their favorite protagonist, Roark, and agreed that Kent should meet the Brandens. The Brandens liked her. She introduced her friend, Kathleen Nickerson, to them; Nickerson was told to write her own letter to Rand, explaining why she was attracted to the novelist's philosophy. The letter passed muster, and both Kent and Nickerson began to attend parties and other group events. Thus the novelist's base of active followers gradually expanded. As newcomers demonstrated allegiance to the principles of Rand's philosophy, they formed a concentric circle around the original Collective. In this way, an official "junior Collective" grew up. Except at odd times and at parties, new followers typically didn't see much of the philosopher herself. While she remained bent over the manuscript of Galt's speech, Branden stepped in as surrogate, mediator, and "spiritual bodyguard," as they half-humorously called him. He created his own hierarchy, one that would prove helpful in managing the crowds of enthusiasts who he rightly predicted would flock to her after the publication of *Atlas Shrugged*.

Within a few months, Kent and Peikoff had decided they were "in love." She moved in to his apartment and earned pocket money by typing *Atlas Shrugged*. Peikoff hadn't really wanted her to move in with him, Kent later said, but she had wanted to, "desperately," and he eventually agreed. Later, she learned that Leonard, Rand, and the Brandens had together decided that Leonard should phone her. Although he eventually married three times (twice to Rand's secretaries), acquaintances said that the quick, funny, ungainly young philosophy student typically paid little attention to girls. The three Objectivist elders thought he should have a girlfriend, and Kent appeared to be an excellent candidate. Trouble soon erupted. "I was a needy person," she recalled. "I was far too possessive, and I'm sure I made demands on him that he was unprepared to meet." Before long, his unhappiness came to Rand's attention. One day, Kent arrived home from acting class to find a note from Leonard instructing her to come to the novelist's apartment that evening. There she discovered Ayn, Nathaniel, Leonard, Frank, and Barbara already seated. She sat on a corner of the sofa, not yet realizing that she was the person they were waiting for. Branden picked up a straight chair, placed it facing her in the middle of the room, seated himself, and said, "Tonight we're going to have a psychological session, and the patient is you."

The drama that unfolded that evening offered a disturbing glimpse of the imperious underside of Rand's emerging vision. It was "devastating" to Kent, she said, because it represented "damnation by people I worshipped as models of what man could be and should be. Fifty years later, I still find it hard to talk about." Branden launched into a highly personal inquiry that went on for two or three hours. "He dissected every move I'd made and everything I'd done, and ended up concluding that I was an Ellsworth Toohey and a queen bee in sexual matters." At times, when he was making a particularly trenchant point, Rand clapped her hands, applauding like a child. "I had had a lifetime of being told I was nothing and nobody from nowhere," Kent recalled, adding that this was the first time she had believed it. "I felt myself sinking into that sofa and disappearing completely." In the end, she was offered an ultimatum: do everything possible to remedy her thinking and adjust her attitudes or be expelled. Choosing to stay, she entered psychotherapy with Branden. She paid for sessions by typing for him. That night Barbara accompanied her to Peikoff's apartment and helped her to pack and move out.

Rand was arguing the need for unhesitating moral judgment in Galt's speech. Anyone who refuses to judge others, "who neither agrees or disagrees, who declares that there are no absolutes and believes that he escapes responsibility," she wrote, "is the man responsible for all the blood that is now spilled in the world." Without the tacit consent of good people, the world's leeches, looters, and tyrants could not survive, let alone rule. Not to condemn was to consent. Something in this theatrical call to moral judgment appealed to Branden, who gradually became not only Rand's deputy but also her enforcer. After the publication of *Atlas Shrugged,* such mock trials, or "kangaroo courts," as Barbara called them, became increasingly common. At one time or another every member of the original group, and many newcomers, endured at least one such improvised courtroom scene; and from the late 1950s on, younger students were expelled by Nathaniel "and just shattered," said Barbara, who recalled her husband's most bruising interrogations as "savagery." Peikoff was a particular target, since the sweet-natured but nerdish philosophy major sometimes fell under the influence of "non-objective" philosophers, such as John Dewey and Bertrand Russell, or innocently befriended academic scoffers at Rand's ideas. As a result, he was often chastised by both Rand and Branden, and was once harshly rebuked and banished for two years—to teach at the University of Denver. But he always returned to Rand's side. He and others who remained learned to trade occasional humiliation for intimate exposure to Rand's penetrating thought and personal insights. "When she laid out her argument [against you]," said Barbara, "people thought that she was right. When she laid out your flaws, what she said made sense." Her magnetism drew and held them. As Kent recalled, "The six months I had spent [in the group] were like a new world. All my life, I'd wanted to know people who talked about ideas. I'd wanted to find a point of view that made real sense to me. Most of all, I'd wanted to believe that man is good. She was the first person I had ever heard say that man is good and *can* be good, that there is a way to achieve what you want to achieve, and that you should aim high and have a *right* to aim high." Rand's soaring testimonials to individual accomplishment and her consummate ability to make sense of the world were qualities her followers deeply prized. The young actress stayed close to Rand for another fifteen years, then walked away after a final, pitiless deflation of her hopes.

On one Saturday night during this period, Ayn and Nathaniel ducked into the kitchen to fetch coffee and sweets for the group gathered in the living room. Excitement about Rand's progress on Galt's speech was running high. In answer to a question about why so many critics attacked her celebration of individualism and strict justice as cold or cruel, she explained that people often think "pro-reason" means "anti-emotion." The truth, she said, is just the opposite. Among rational men and women, emotion and reason go hand in hand. "If a person tells you that he regards reason and emotion as antagonists, he is telling you that *his* emotions are irrational and that he wants to get away with something dishonest," she told them. As she and Branden prepared the snacks, they were both in a heady mood. So when she whispered, "Darling, there's something I think I was wrong about," he answered playfully, "Impossible. What could that be?" Why, the limited duration of their affair, she answered, beaming, and added, "Can you think of any good reason why we can't go on like this forever?" With his own emotions sounding an inner siren, and a sudden feeling that a gun was pointed at his head, he had no doubt that it was he who "pulled the trigger," he later wrote. "No. I can't," he answered, irrationally, confusedly, and fatefully.

Rand completed Galt's speech on October 13, 1955. She took three weeks off, and then plunged directly into drafting the last three chapters of the book. Here the novel picks up pace. Wesley Mouch, a wily government bureaucrat, and his placid boss, Mr. Thompson, the American "Head of State," kidnap John Galt and torture him in an effort to force him to save the nation from economic ruin. Galt not only refuses to become the despot they want him to be, he helps his incompetent kidnappers to repair a broken-down electrical shock machine to which they have strapped him, all the while mocking their primitive notions, as Cyrus and Roark had laughed before him. Dagny, along with Rearden, Francisco, and an anti–Robin Hood pirate (and former college classmate of Francisco's and Galt's) named Ragnar Danneskjöld, rescue him, but not before the railroad heiress shoots and kills a burly government guard who bars their way, thus demonstrating the legitimacy of using force against those who use force first. (Dagny's predecessor was Rand's girlish English heroine from 1915 who machine-gunned the invading Germans.) As the group of heroes returns in John Galt's plane to their utopia in Colorado, the lights of New York City flicker and go out. This is the sign that Galt and his fellow strikers—that is, Albert Jay Nock's Remnant of right-thinking men—have been waiting for. Back in the valley, Ayn Rand's ideal man and his companions prepare to leave their enclave of justice, independence, and free trade to return to the world, which is now prepared to admit how much it needs the men of the mind, the moralists, and the producers.

While she worked on the final chapters, the Collective prepared for the intellectual sea change they thought the book would bring.

TWELVE

ATLAS SHRUGGED

1957

*If anyone should ask me what it is that I have said to the glory of Man,
I will answer only by paraphrasing Howard Roark: I will hold up a
copy of* Atlas Shrugged *and say: "The explanation rests."*
— "The Goal of My Writing," 1963

I f *The Fountainhead* introduced a new and radical brand of American
individualism, *Atlas Shrugged* resurrected interest in American capitalism at a time when it was under pressure by both the liberal Left and
the Christian Right. Rand didn't praise capitalism as the best of a bad
set of choices, as the Buckleyites did, or even as a means by which the
poor would prosper, although she believed it was. She defined it, lovingly, as the only economic system in history to be rooted in and inextri-
cable from individual rights: the freedom to choose an occupation, to
earn and spend money in a free market of consumer goods, and to own
the fruits of one's own creativity and labor in the form of private property.
Capitalism set the individual, especially the creative individual, free to
invent, produce, and thrive. When reflecting on the novel's theme in a
letter to her friend John Chamberlain, she put it more aggressively.
"Those who are anti-business are anti-life," she wrote.

If *We the Living* had exposed the lethal effects of totalitarian state
power on the best and most spirited individuals in a closed society; if

Anthem had charted an escape from the tyranny of brotherhood; and if *The Fountainhead* had defined the struggle of a free, active, self-reliant individual against a culture of suffocating conformity, then *Atlas Shrugged* extended the perspective to reveal a new ideological and social order, one in which those who are independent, purposeful, creative, and proud no longer have to fight or suffer. It was an oblation to her father and grandfather and a public tribute to her own gifts and strengths.

Minus Galt's speech and the last unfinished chapters, this was the book that she presented to publishers in November 1956. She had decided not to show the text of the speech to interested parties until after the first round of negotiations. Her original contract with Bobbs-Merrill for *The Fountainhead* required her to submit the manuscript of *Atlas Shrugged* to that firm before offering it to others. She did so. But she was determined to keep the firm from buying it. Still angry at Bobbs-Merrill for its failures to support *The Fountainhead,* she was drawing up a list of terms she thought it would refuse to meet when the company's sales director Ross Baker phoned and invited her and Collins to meet him over dinner. "What is it you want to discuss?" she asked on the phone. The book she had submitted was far too long, he replied. He wanted to mention sections that might be trimmed or cut, including, she later learned, to her horror, Francisco d'Anconia's masterful five-page speech about the benefits of a money economy and the profit motive, ending with a paean to America: "To the glory of mankind," he tells the guests at James Taggart's wedding reception, "there was for the first and only time a *country of money,* and I have no higher or more reverent tribute to pay to America, for this means a country of reason, justice, freedom, production, achievement. . . . Americans were the first to understand that wealth has to be created," and thus they invented the felicitous phrase "to *make* money." Even without being aware of specific cuts, however, she declined the sales director's invitation to dinner and told him that the book must be published exactly as written. Baker, presumably speaking for Bobbs-Merrill's president, declared that, in its present form, "the book is unsaleable and unpublishable." Rand had heard that before. She thanked him and set out to find the publisher she wanted for the achievement of her life.

This time, in vivid contrast to 1943, the publishing world tripped over itself to court her. More than a dozen companies phoned or wrote, to Collins or to her, some sending flowers or invitations to a lavish meal.

She and her agent analyzed her many options, and if they experienced a pleasant sense of vindication at having finally bested conventional wisdom, they had earned it.

She made a chart, and she and Collins narrowed the field to four firms. Since Archibald Ogden was now a consultant for Viking Press and would be her editor should Viking buy the book, Viking was placed on the list. So was McGraw-Hill, for its superior promotional resources, and Knopf, where Blanche and her husband, Alfred, were gradually turning the business over to their son, whom she had met and liked. Last, she considered Random House. That's where Hiram Haydn, a well-respected and personable editor who had earlier replaced Ogden at Bobbs-Merrill, had recently signed on as editor-in-chief. She phoned him, gently chided him for being out of touch, and explained that she was wavering about including Random House in her final list because she had heard that the firm's directors, the celebrated Bennett Cerf and Donald Klopfer, were Communists.

Haydn laughed. One of his assignments at Bobbs-Merrill in the middle 1950s had been to take Rand out to lunch every few months, with the goal of gradually restoring her good opinion of Bobbs-Merrill. He failed, but he enjoyed the lunches and the office visits. In his memoir, *Words & Faces,* he remembered Rand as short and square, with a Dutch bob and a tricorne hat, "the exact replica of the one in the famous Bonaparte portrait—the sulky [portrait] in which he pokes around in his waistcoat with his fingers." In cool weather she donned her hallmark short black cape, he recalled, which flowed dramatically in the breeze and which she wore, he remembered that she once confided to him, in imitation of Supergirl. But he had been even more astonished by her style of arguing than by her style of dress. Like Rothbard, he recalled that she would zero in on any inconsistency in her companion's case, exploiting weaknesses with Socratic questions and airtight arguments. Eventually, she always "emerged victorious, whether because her partner finally capitulated or because he lost by default through exhaustion." She was "dialectically invincible." He grew to enjoy watching his peers innocently attempt to argue with her. Invariably they ended up among "the corpses on the Randian battlefield," he wrote. He appreciated her, and she tolerated him.

Haydn pointed out that Random House had published Whittaker

Chambers's *Witness,* a fascinating book-length confession by a right-wing former Communist spy who had fingered Alger Hiss as a Russian agent in a series of congressional hearings and a trial. For once, Haydn wrote, he won an argument with the logician. She agreed that she and her agent would attend a lunch with Haydn, Cerf, and Klopfer a week later.

The lunch took place in the Trianon Room at the old Ambassador Hotel, on Park Avenue at Fifty-first Street, just around the corner from the Random House offices in a magnificent neo-Gothic mansion neighboring on and belonging to St. Patrick's Cathedral. Over eggs Benedict, she asked Haydn, Cerf, and Klopfer "an infinite number" of questions about their approach to publishing and their attitude toward her work. Haydn recalled that Cerf, a wily entrepreneur as well as a best-selling humor anthologist and a popular guest on the television game show *What's My Line?,* answered her question, "What are your premises?" with a bold declaration that he was smarter than other publishers and had built a great company from scratch, without subsidies or special favors. She was delighted with his answer. She explained that *Atlas* represented a moral defense of capitalism and contained a complete, unique, and radically anti-Left philosophy and was impressed when Klopfer, Cerf's distinguished business partner, shrewdly remarked that a moral defense of capitalism would have to be in conflict with Judeo-Christian ethics. The jovial Cerf surprised her by announcing, "I find your political philosophy abhorrent." But, he added, "If we publish you, Miss Rand, nobody is going to try to censor you. You write anything you darn please, and we'll publish it." No one else had dared to tell her this, Cerf remarked in his posthumously published memoir, *At Random.* As a result, "I came out very high" on her grid. When he proposed an auction among her four top choices for publisher, each of whom would read the manuscript and respond with editorial comments on a given date, she was so impressed with his self-confidence that she chose him and Random House almost on the spot.

"They spoke as I would want publishers to speak," she told Barbara Branden after the lunch: They faced ideas openly, heard what she had said, were enthusiastic about her earlier work, and answered all her questions. Barbara had rarely seen her so pleased.

And the men were pleased with her. They appreciated her quick, in-

ventive mind and moral courage. When all three had read the nearly completed manuscript, they arranged for another meeting. As soon as Rand
and Alan Collins seated themselves in Cerf's office, Cerf declared, "It's a
great book. Name your own terms." She and her agent had discussed
what to ask for: an advance of $50,000, a 15 percent author's royalty, a
guaranteed first printing of 75,000 to 100,000 copies, and a $25,000 ad-
vertising budget. To all of these terms the men agreed, adding that the
length of the novel should not exceed 600,000 words. Business settled,
Cerf told her that upon reading part I, chapter 8, "The John Galt Line," in
which Dagny and Rearden ride the rails straight into each other's arms, he
ran out of his office into the hallway, shouting, "It's magnificent!" Klopfer
reported that he had begun to look at factories and smokestacks, and at
his own success, with a new appreciation. Back in her apartment, she exclaimed, "This is life as it should be and ought to be—and, for once, is!"
To Barbara, she said, "They didn't pretend to be converted, but they knew
these were important ideas and they were very affected by the book. And
Bennett was chortling [over] how they'd antagonize their neighbors" by
publishing it. Of course, Cerf could not imagine just how hostile and brutal the antagonism would turn out to be.

She and Cerf quickly became friends. He and his wife, Phyllis, attended dinner parties on East Thirty-sixth Street, where they met the
Brandens and other members of Rand's circle, and the O'Connors spent
occasional weekends visiting the Cerfs in their weekend house near the
village of Mount Kisco in New York. On first meeting Phyllis, who happened to be Lela Rogers's niece, Ginger Rogers's cousin, and a former
Hollywood actress, Rand recognized her; to Phyllis's amazement, the
smoky-voiced writer recalled once having dressed her for a movie role in
the RKO wardrobe department. Rand met other Random House authors and some of Cerf's wide circle of acquaintances. Years later, he remembered the mischievous pleasure he, like Haydn, took in introducing
her to liberal friends. "What I loved to do was trot her out for people
who sneered at me for publishing her. Ayn would invariably charm
them. For example, Clifton Fadiman"—one of her models for Ellsworth
Toohey in *The Fountainhead*—"sat up with her until about three in the
morning one time." George Axelrod, the man who wrote *The Seven Year
Itch*—"he's always being [psycho]analyzed," Cerf noted—"at the end of
a long, long evening disappeared with Ayn into another room. We

couldn't get George to go home. We were at Ayn's for dinner. Later that night he said, 'She knows me better after five hours than my analyst does after five years.' " The worldly Cerf was unruffled, even amused, by the way "she peers right through you. She has . . . a wonderful way of pinning you to the wall." Klopfer, who kept his distance, found her "a remarkable woman," though also "wacky as a fruitcake."

The months immediately preceding the publication of *Atlas Shrugged* brought a spell of bright optimism after a long season of emotional and intellectual exhaustion. The hard work of writing the novel was finished; the remaining chapters involved a pleasurable "cashing in," as Rand put it, of clues and themes already well established. For the first time, she felt secure in having the support of a truly outstanding agent, editor, and publisher, all of whom grasped her ideas, her objectives, and the breadth of her accomplishment. Although she did not delude herself that the cultural elite of the late 1950s—Lionel Trilling, Mary McCarthy, Edmund Wilson—would embrace her work any more cordially than the elite of the 1940s had, let alone undergo a capitalist conversion on the basis of the novel, she did believe that no attentive reader could misunderstand her message or its kinship to the ideals of America's Founding Fathers. Her Enlightenment sense of life (though clearly not the facts of history) assured her that ideas based on human reason would always, eventually, triumph over small-minded schemes devised by the irrational and the power hungry, and that ideas rule the world.

She warned both Cerf and her circle of young friends not to expect too much. "I am challenging the cultural tradition of two and a half thousand years," she explained, with her usual sense of grandeur concerning her work. Cerf knew that the reviews would be mixed, at best. But the others anticipated drumrolls and accolades. Years earlier, Barbara had written to her, "Whether or not the world [deserves; crossed out] to be saved will depend on how they respond to your book." She still thought so. Peikoff, now twenty-four and half hysterical with admiration for his favorite writer, foresaw a renaissance of political liberty and a restoration of an idealized nineteenth-century-style laissez-faire economy. Alan Greenspan, the oldest in the group at thirty-one and by far its most sophisticated member, couldn't shake off the conviction that her arguments in *Atlas Shrugged* were so "radiantly exact" as to compel agreement by all honest men and women. He often said that Ayn Rand put the moral basis under capitalism for him. Until 2008, he never changed his mind.*

As Rand hurried to finish the last three chapters in the early months of 1957, O'Connor was painting. He had taken up painting in 1955, when, as a dare, Joan Blumenthal had offered to teach everyone in the inner circle how to draw and paint. Most who signed up bumbled along, but O'Connor took to painting as he had taken to gardening, avidly and with remarkable focus. Using a corner of the bedroom as his workroom, he sketched and painted constantly and again established a certain degree of independence for himself. After greeting the Collective on Saturday evenings, he would slip away to paint imaginary views of modern towers and tree branches with chiseled leaves. As long as he was nearby, Rand didn't object to his not appearing by her side; she was proud that he was giving visual expression to what she called his "exalted sense of life." She marveled at what she regarded as his talent and often said that she saw a striking similarity between his artistic vision and her own. "There were no historical influences at all in his work," noted Barbara Branden, probably echoing Rand, in 1962. Rand maintained the same about her fiction and philosophy. Yet she decided that he would benefit from professional training and asked Mary Ann Sures, a graduate student in art history, to search for a suitable art school for him, and after the publication of *Atlas Shrugged* he enrolled in the Art Students League on West Fifty-seventh Street. His teachers, portrait painter Robert Brackman and Robert Beverly Hale, an expert in anatomy, praised and encouraged him, and he was popular among the students. The women, particularly, admired his good looks and natural gallantry, recalled Joan Blumenthal, who was also a student at the League. Best of all, for a period of time no one knew that he was Ayn Rand's husband. Branden later hypothesized that his absorption in painting drew his attention away from his wife's affair during these years; he appeared unconcerned about it, Branden wrote in 1989, except, perhaps, for exhibiting "a sense of relief that I had lifted a burden" of wifely demands from his

*In October 2008, Greenspan, then eighty-two, told the House Committee on Oversight and Government Reform, "those of us who have looked to the self-interest of the lending institutions to protect shareholders' equity, myself included, are in a state of shocked disbelief." That testimony constituted his retraction of assertions he'd made in a 1963 essay he published in Rand's *The Objectivist Newsletter*, "The Assault on Integrity," in which he wrote, "It is precisely the 'greed' of the businessman, or, more appropriately, his profit-seeking, which is the unexcelled protector of the consumer."

shoulders. Portraying O'Connor as a beaten man, which he wasn't yet, Branden added, "I did not know about his drinking."

Months earlier, Rand had honored her lover by naming him her "intellectual heir," the mark of distinction she had earlier conferred on Albert Mannheimer, although Branden didn't know that. On one of their intimate evenings together in the fall of 1956, over dinner at the Russian Tea Room, she confided that she would also like to dedicate *Atlas Shrugged* to him, along with her husband. The dedication page would read, "To Frank O'Connor and Nathaniel Branden," the two indispensable men in her life. Again she cautioned him that aligning himself publicly with her might bring him trouble. He didn't care, he answered proudly. "The idea of the greatest literary masterpiece I've ever read being dedicated to me is almost more than I can hold in my brain," he told her. It didn't occur to him until later that such a monumental gesture by Rand might bind him more permanently in his romance with her or otherwise limit his freedom. As they rose to leave the restaurant, she murmured, "Do you ever wonder what people think when they look at us?" He answered gaily that they probably mistook her for his daughter and told her that he loved her.

In her author's note at the end of *Atlas Shrugged,* she explained the double dedication. O'Connor, she wrote, embodied the "values of character I wanted to find in a man. I met such a man, and we have been married for twenty-eight years." While writing *The Fountainhead,* however, she had kept in mind an ideal reader: someone with "as rational and independent a mind as I could conceive of." She had found that reader in a nineteen-year-old fan named Nathaniel Branden, she wrote, adding grandly, "He is my intellectual heir." Then and later, she did not seem to notice the apparent irony of an "intellectual heir" of independent mind.

Rand once called the futuristic novella *Anthem* "my manifesto, my profession of faith, the essence of my entire philosophy." It was the hero of *Anthem* who gave meaning to the honorific, first in the case of Mannheimer and then in the case of Branden. As she explained her thinking to Barbara, the Collective as a whole reflected "what I had once told Nathan about himself—that I was regarding [him] as Equality 7–2521 in *Anthem*," meaning as the progenitor of a new and better world. When she asked herself, "Of what importance is posterity to me?" she answered, " 'It's not posterity [I care about] but the exceptional man, or my kind of man, in the future.' Nathan is that man in the next generation." Thus, as she saw it, the fate of her lover and disciple had already been chronicled in the fantasy world of *Anthem*. In some measure, then, and in some recess of her mind, she preferred to leave the corrupted world she lived in lightless, as in both *Anthem* and *Atlas Shrugged,* and thus prepared to receive her torchbearer and message.

If *The Fountainhead* had released an outpouring of excitement, hope, and yearning among hundreds of thousands of readers, Rand and Branden were aware that *Atlas Shrugged* might well set off an avalanche. As Hiram Haydn noted, the book had best-seller stamped all over it.

They decided they needed a name for her system of ideas other than Randianism, which had occasionally cropped up. They discussed what word would best describe it. She liked "existentialism," Branden said in 2004, because it echoed Aristotle's maxim that "existence exists." But Jean-Paul Sartre and his band of "bad guys" had beaten them to it. They briefly considered "contextual absolutism" and "contextualism" but gave them up for lack of sex appeal. They settled on the only slightly spicier name "Objectivism," which they intended as an homage to the immutability of objective reality and the competence of perception and reason to grasp and understand it. It also conveyed an urgent emphasis on the scientific method, Rand thought; she had become especially concerned with countering the influence of John Dewey and his followers' subjectivist theories of education. She was probably unaware that such ideas partly derived from Oliver Wendell Holmes's eloquent responses to the unintended consequences of the abolitionist movement and the Civil War. Yet she knew that it was Dewey who, in the 1950s, "showed us how to live without truth or any theory of reality [and] made us aware that what we think and believe has no foundation anywhere," as Norman Podhoretz later put it. In many ways still a Russian thinker, she located the origin of this problem in ideas, especially those of Hegel and Kant, rather than in the peculiarities of American and European history.

On the afternoon of March 20, 1957, Joan Blumenthal and Mary Ann Sures were on secretarial duty in the East Thirty-sixth Street apartment. After proofreading a stack of typed pages, Blumenthal timidly knocked on Rand's study door, then cracked it open to announce that she and Sures were ready for more pages. From inside they heard a raspy growl, "If you come in here, I'll kill you!" Nonplussed by her tone, they rode the elevator to the street and called Leonard Peikoff from a pay phone, since the apartment's only phone was in Rand's study, and asked him what to do; and so Peikoff, too, was on hand when she emerged an hour or so later waving a manuscript page that read, "The End." "One word leads to another!" she said gaily. She had met her Random House deadline one day in advance. Trailing her into the living room, Frank said, "Congratulations, darling," and everyone fell to hugging everyone else. Someone phoned the Brandens. Sures ran out to buy pastries at a local bakery. Champagne appeared and coffee flowed. Rand danced like a girl to the turn-of-the-century melodies she called her "tiddlywink" music and led the band with her baton. After thirteen years of work, she had memorialized in words her own music, its intricate orchestration, and her determined march toward its completion. Just as Dagny, listening to the last recorded concerto of Richard Halley, recognizes in the chords "a great cry of rebellion . . . a 'No' flung at some vast process of torture," so Rand now flung her definitive "no" at the despots and conformists who would try to control or exploit such brilliant, creative minds as hers.

She delivered the book. From his earlier reading of it, Haydn was ambivalent, at best, about its ethics and politics. Although he admired her narrative pace and mastery of plot and was pleased to have been able to attract a best-selling author to his new firm, he had doubts about the novel's "drab" prose style and core ideas. Pursuing what he thought was his editorial duty, he, too, suggested a number of cuts, including cuts in John Galt's speech. When Rand refused, he appealed to Bennett Cerf. "You're some editor!" Cerf barked at him. "I'll fix it in no time." The high-spirited founding editor met with the author. "Nobody's going to read that [speech]," he told her. "You've said it all three or four times before. . . . You've got to cut it." Answering with a comment that became publishing legend, she said, "Would you cut the Bible?" With that, Cerf threw up his hands but cagily asked her to forfeit seven cents in royalties per copy to pay for the additional paper it would take to print the uncut speech and other long passages that put her in excess of the word count in her contract. She agreed. Henceforth, Cerf cheerfully acted as her facilitator and supporter. Haydn resigned himself to being an "apprentice copy editor" who helped her search for and remove words within a paragraph that rhymed, "an obsession with her," he recalled in his memoir. Task completed, he turned the mammoth manuscript over to Bertha Krantz, the firm's actual copy editor, who came to know its author well.

The two women worked together in a corner of Haydn's large office, discussing changes in punctuation and wording. Copy-editing discussions with an author normally took a week or two, Krantz later said, but in this case they went on for several months. At first, Rand seriously frightened Krantz. The methodical thinker insisted on a logical reason for every change of period and comma; Krantz's view was that punctuation depends on the eye and ear almost as much as on rules and reason. Often, the author would call across the room to Haydn, "Hiram, is Bert right?" "They were putting a great deal [of money] into the book, and for a long time it was very tense," Krantz recalled in 1983. Gradually, the copy editor came to regard the famous author as "a little lady" much like herself: they were the same height, build, and coloring, and she guessed correctly that they shared a geographical and ethnic heritage. Moreover, working in close proximity with Rand, Krantz slowly concluded that the author herself was a frightened human being—and not just because of the imminent publication of her magnum opus. On visiting the O'Connors' apartment for a working lunch, she was shocked to see the advocate of reason don a pair of heavy rubber gloves and scour the dishes in scalding hot water. "There are germs!" Rand exclaimed when Krantz questioned her. As the two became familiar with the details of each other's lives, Rand nagged Krantz about the dangers of living in a risky neighborhood in the west Bronx, and Krantz noticed that the author, a proponent of the benevolent universe theory of life, sealed herself in her doorman-guarded apartment behind the usual steel locks. "The subway scared the hell out of her," Krantz recalled, and Rand warned the copy editor not to use it. ("She must have thought I could afford to take a taxi to and from the office," Krantz remarked, although Rand more probably had in mind a bus.) For a brief time, Rand attempted to convert Krantz to Objectivism, but Krantz politely demurred and Rand didn't push. She still behaved with old-fashioned good manners, especially in professional relationships.

Like others over the years, Krantz observed that Rand was silent about her Jewish background. "It was funny to me, and to other people. She certainly never denied being Jewish, but somehow or other there seemed to be a certain evasiveness on her part." The Random House staffer also remarked, with remembered consternation, that the O'Connors' apartment was overrun by their unneutered male cat Frisco, named after Francisco d'Anconia. Frisco scratched the upholstered furniture to tatters, beat himself against the walls, and emitted a foul-smelling spray on furniture and rugs. The stench was terrible and permanent, Krantz recalled, as did other visitors to the apartment. When she asked why the O'Connors didn't have the cat fixed, Rand replied that, unlike humans, cats cannot choose to go against nature or mold it to their wishes, and she would not interfere with them or force them. Krantz retorted that she had never heard a more irrational statement. "That made her angry," Krantz recalled, "because I used the word 'irrational.' " The copy editor was equally upset. "It was awful. She was such a brilliant woman. Her rationale was the big things of the world, but it's the little things we live by."

In the end, Krantz felt sorry for Rand. One day, Rand proudly showed Krantz some of Frank's paintings. "I thought they were such schlock," Krantz said. "She put on a front for her husband," but "I thought he was a nebbish. I didn't know how the hell he could live with her."

Not "for one minute," however, did Krantz or any other staff member at Random House doubt the author's sincerity in everything she wrote and preached. The women remained on friendly terms for several years. But the self-made Russian messenger of reason was, in the end, impenetrable to Krantz. Rand "built herself," Krantz said, and became "a slave to the image she built. [I never really knew] what she was like. She wouldn't let you know."

A few months before *Atlas Shrugged* was published, Bennett Cerf invited his "most interesting" new author to address a Random House sales conference. She stood at the head of the room and talked at length about the characters and meaning of her novel. When she finished, one salesman, still puzzled as to how to explain the book to bookstore owners, asked half-jokingly, "Miss Rand, could you give the essence of your philosophy while standing on one foot?" The salesman must have known that his question paraphrased the question asked of the legendary Israelite Rabbi Hillel, who, when challenged to summarize the Torah while standing on one foot, replied, "Do not do unto others what you would not have them do unto you. That is the whole of the Torah. All the rest is commentary." (Interestingly, the Christian Golden Rule is affirmative: Do unto others as you would have them do unto you. The problem with that, as George Bernard Shaw once pointed out, is that your neighbor may not want done to him what you want done to you. Hillel's formulation is elegantly, and, when applied to Rand, suitably individualistic.) She gamely raised a leg and answered, "Metaphysics: objective reality. Epistemology: reason. Ethics: self-interest. Politics: capitalism." The sales staff applauded. Presumably, she was delighted by the classical reference as well as the applause.

As publication day approached, the excitement at the firm was palpable. Alan Collins and Bennett Cerf ordered cigarettes stamped with a gold dollar sign, like those smoked by the novel's striking titans, and presented packages to Rand and guests at a surprise banquet in her honor at the Plaza Hotel. She was pleased when the Random House promotional staff collaborated with Branden and her husband to produce a billboard advertisement in which a glamorous portrait of Frank was overlaid with type that read, "This is John Galt—who said he would stop the motor of the world—*and did.* Meet him in *Atlas Shrugged.*" Advance orders from bookstores were unusually strong. As the initial printing of one hundred thousand copies came off the press, Cerf presented the very first to her. One early autumn evening, just before the book's release to stores, Ayn, Frank, Barbara, and Nathaniel drove up Madison Avenue to see whether the book was in the display window on the ground floor of the Random House offices. It was there, all by itself in solitary splendor, wrapped in a green-blue cover designed by Frank. Barbara cried, "That's us!" and Ayn roared with pleasure.

Atlas Shrugged was published on October 10, 1957. The reviews began to appear three days later, and the celebrations ended. They were not merely critical, they were hateful and dishonest. In *The New York Times,* Rand's old nemesis from the 1930s, Granville Hicks, branded the novel "a demonstrative act rather than a literary novel," a creation of demonic will "to crush the enemies of truth." Without acknowledging the author's nineteenth-century breadth of scope, her jaw-dropping integration of unfamiliar ideas into a drumbeat plot, or the Dickensian keenness of her eye for bureaucratic villainy, Hicks went on: "[As] loudly as Miss Rand proclaims her love of life, it seems clear that the book is written out of hate." He suggested it was nothing more than a clumsy mixture of melodrama and didacticism, a 1,168-page "howl" by a harpy wielding "a battering ram."

Hicks set the tone for the reviews that followed. The writer for *The Washington Post* announced, "This is a story of conflict where it's equally easy to hate both sides." *The Chicago Tribune* compared her ideas on mysticism to those of Hitler. "Is it a novel? Is it a nightmare?" wailed *Time* magazine in the opening sentences of its review. If the *Los Angeles Times* had ever praised her, chief critic Robert Kirsch set out to correct the record. "It would be hard to find [another] such display of grotesque eccentricity outside an insane asylum," he wrote and, perversely, "[John] Galt is really arguing for a dictatorship." *The New Yorker* chimed in with mordant humor. The reviewer, a short-story writer named Donald Malcolm, wrote that, at the novel's end, the heroes return to the world convinced that "the globe's two billion or so incompetents, having starved to death," will finally "know better than to fool around with businessmen." *The Atlantic Monthly* berated the novel as "crackbrained ratiocination." Smaller publications griped that it was wordy and, at $6.95, inordinately expensive.

There were a few public declarations of support from old-line conservative acquaintances. In Isabel Paterson's former newspaper, *The New York Herald Tribune,* John Chamberlain praised the book as a "vibrant and powerful novel of ideas" that, in breadth of ambition and intellectual intensity, rivaled Dostoyevsky's *Crime and Punishment.* Rand's friend the economist Ruth Alexander, writing for William Randolph Hearst's *New York Daily Mirror,* went so far as to assert that "Ayn Rand is destined to rank in history as the outstanding novelist and most profound philosopher of the twentieth century." Some out-of-town newspapers praised her writing style, the novel's clever plot and action, and her ability to unite ideas and suspense. But these tributes were largely lost amid the flood of invective, and in any case they didn't console or satisfy the author or her circle.

Privately, old friends sent letters of appreciation. After making many pages of notes about the novel, particularly about its insistent atheism, which he didn't share, electric company executive William Mullendore wrote, "I am now able to say it: It is a great book," although he added, "I do believe in the spiritual life." Ludwig von Mises was more forceful in his praise. "*Atlas Shrugged* is not merely a novel," he wrote. "It is also— or may I say: first of all—a cogent analysis of the evils that plague our society. . . . You have the courage to tell the masses what no politician told them: you [the masses] are inferior and all the improvements in your conditions which you simply take for granted you owe to the effort of men who are better than you." He told his students, "No one writes about the bureaucrats the way Ayn Rand does." As private affirmations, these remarks were welcome, but they did nothing to counteract the public scourge. And they didn't praise her as a *writer*. She still wanted "superlatives or nothing" and "raves that raved about the right things." She would not receive them until decades later.

Bennett Cerf suffered mild apoplexy. After investing hundreds of thousands of dollars, "we thought that we were going to be hooked," he said in 1971. The worst was yet to come. At Christmastime, William F. Buckley's *National Review* ran a savage critique of *Atlas Shrugged* that has become a model of a successful intellectual ambush. Called "Big Sister Is Watching You," it was the work of Whittaker Chambers, the very reformed Communist spy whom Haydn had mentioned as evidence that Random House was politically evenhanded. Like Buckley, the exceptionally intelligent if eccentric and oracular Chambers was now a devout Christian, a Quaker, and he didn't merely disparage the novel, he set out to destroy it, partly in an attempt to discredit her defense of godless capitalism. "*Atlas Shrugged* can be called a novel only by devaluing the term," he huffed. "I find it a remarkably silly book. It is certainly a bumptious one." Its heroes and villains, he wrote, derived not from Aristotle but from Nietzsche and Karl Marx. "Just as her operatic businessmen are, in fact, Nietzschean supermen, so her ulcerous leftists are Nietzsche's 'last men,' both deformed in a way [that would] sicken the fastidious recluse of Sils Maria," a reference to the summer house where Nietzsche wrote *Thus Spoke Zarathustra*. As to Marx, Chambers wrote, "He, too, admired naked self-interest." More reasonably, he argued that the problem with Rand's godless vision of earthly happiness as man's highest moral purpose was that happiness, as an end in itself, quickly deteriorates into the pursuit of pleasure, "with a consequent general softening of the fibers of will, intelligence, spirit. . . . Randian man," he continued, "has to be held 'heroic' in order not to be beastly," and all deviations from Randian revelation must be viewed as willful immorality so as to prevent debauchery. "There are ways of dealing with such wickedness," he thundered in the essay's most inflammatory passage. "From almost any page of *Atlas Shrugged,* a voice can be heard, from painful necessity, commanding, 'To a gas chamber—go!' " Interestingly, within two years of writing the review, in a series of private letters to Buckley, Chambers moved closer to Rand's position in favor of unrestricted capitalism. He withdrew his support for *National Review*'s brand of religion-

based conservatism and lauded the indispensable dynamism of the nation's economic system, which "is not, and by its essential nature cannot
conceivably be, conservative" in any traditional sense. Rand did not
learn about his change of heart.

She had expected attacks, but she had not expected her worldview
to be confused with Marxism or Fascism, or for herself to be accused
of advocating mass murder. Anguished, she asked Barbara and other
friends why American intellectuals such as Chambers couldn't understand what she was saying. And why hadn't anyone with cultural standing risen to defend, or at least accurately summarize, her themes of
freedom, rationality, no first use of force, and individual rights? "I had
expected *some* kind of better understanding," she told Nathaniel. Instead, critics focused on her adamant atheism and harshly contemptuous passages and finally placed her outside the realm of the reasonable
Right. Wearily, she said, "Historically speaking, [it's] even earlier than I
imagined." To some degree, history would prove her right.

Ironically, perhaps, Isabel Paterson, who though no longer a columnist with the *Herald Tribune* still retained some influence among conservatives, did come to Rand's defense against Chambers, although Rand
probably never knew it. Notwithstanding the older woman's own early
warnings to her former friend about the limits she was placing on her influence by insisting on her atheism, Paterson sent an indignant letter to
William F. Buckley in care of his secretary, Gertrude Vogt, who had once
been Paterson's secretary at the *Herald Tribune*. Chambers's review was
so vicious it could be considered libelous, Paterson wrote, and was absolutely worthless. Because Paterson was now an occasional contributor
to *National Review,* Buckley answered in a vaguely conciliatory manner.
Paterson was not satisfied; she told her friend Muriel Hall that the review was "the dirtiest job imaginable" and "If I ever see Mr. Chambers
again, I won't speak to him." It's hard not to wonder whether a mending
of fences might not have taken place between the two old friends had
Paterson said that in print.

Rand ignored Chambers, but she never forgave William F. Buckley, Jr., for his bad faith. After 1957, she did her best to avoid him. At her
death, he wrote in his *National Review* obituary of her that she made it a
practice to ask potential party hosts whether he was on the guest list; if
so, she refused to go. For his part, he told acerbic stories about her
throughout the 1960s and 1970s and, in 2003, lampooned her as a pon-

tificating, bob-haired, chain-smoking poobah in his novel *Getting It Right*. Yet he insisted that the selection of Chambers to review her book was not a conscious act of sabotage and that no one at *National Review* was out to get her. "I believe she died under the impression that I had done it to punish her for her [religious] faithlessness," he said. "But [pairing Chambers with the book] was a coincidence." Like other former friends with whom she had—and would—cut off contact, he seemed to miss her. In years to come, he sent her *non*liturgical postcards suggesting they make up. He sometimes phoned at night. Rand thought that he had been drinking on such occasions and hung up. Yet a quarter century after her death and just two years before his own, he paid tribute to her singularity. "She was a valiant human being," he told an interviewer.

Years later, in *The Passion of Ayn Rand,* Barbara astutely observed that the foes of *Atlas Shrugged* often confused its author's increasingly authoritarian personality and narrative voice with her philosophy of radical individualism, thus discarding a fascinating baby with the bathwater. "To hear a woman whose main political idea was [that there should be] no first use of force called a fascist—it seemed impossible," recalled Barbara. But Rand's certainty that she alone understood the truth and that people who lived by other convictions, especially liberals, religious adherents, and public intellectuals, were mystics of spirit, savages, looting thugs, beggars, parasites, gibberers, carrion eaters, cavemen, and headhunters did have the ring of Big Sister, even if the ideological content of the novel did not. "Her personal bitterness was at odds with her philosophy," Barbara told an interviewer in 1992. Rand's language, never pitch-perfect, was abusive and becoming more so.

Bennett Cerf's concern that the novel would be a financial calamity proved baseless. It prospered with ordinary readers almost from the start. Within six weeks it had sold almost seventy thousand copies. Jostling for attention amid a weird assortment of old-fashioned and forward-looking best-sellers, including James Gould Cozzens's *By Love Possessed,* Pearl Buck's *Letter from Peking,* Nevil Shute's *On the Beach,* Grace Metalious's taboo-breaking *Peyton Place,* and Jack Kerouac's *On the Road,* it quickly ascended to number five on *The New York Times* best-seller list. The belligerent reviews slowed its rise to fame, but it recovered and remained a best-seller for seven months. Five years after its first printing, it had sold more than a million copies. Decade after decade, readers retained their appetite for it. Fifty years after publication, without advertising or the benefit of appearing on most college reading lists, it was still being sold at an astonishing rate of 150,000 copies a year. In a 1991 poll, sponsored by the Library of Congress and the Book-of-the-Month Club, readers selected it as the book that had most influenced their lives, after the Bible. In a separate 1998 poll by Modern Library, in which readers chose the best one hundred novels of the twentieth century, it and *The Fountainhead* took first and second place, with *Anthem* and *We the Living* following in seventh and eighth place on the list. In other words, readers found all four of her novels among the top eight in a century filled with brilliant work. (Interestingly, in a corresponding list of critics' literary choices, Rand's novels are entirely absent.) Bennett Cerf had been dead for twenty years by 1991, but had he lived he might have laughed merrily to learn that, after all, in one respect at least, *Atlas Shrugged* was like the Bible.

Again, fan letters arrived by the thousands, from readers whom Rand's friend Joan Kennedy Taylor characterized as the intelligent common man and whom journalist Claudia Pierpont described as "the largely abandoned class of thinking non-intellectuals." The letters of thanks and appreciation would continue until her death. The novelist grew wealthy. She achieved fame commensurate with her teenaged dreams. And, for good and ill, she fulfilled the mission she had lived for: to create her ideal man and a microcosmic ideal world in which he and all other "real people" could breathe freely and love passionately—and love most passionately those whose strengths and values most resembled her conception of her own. Nevertheless, the critical backlash in which the novel thrashed and almost sank darkened her outlook and shriveled her spirit, and she had no additional goal to ignite her drive and occupy her mind.

She did her best not to succumb. A month after the appearance of the Chambers review, she began making notes for a new novel, which she called *To Lorne Dieterling* and described as a story of unrequited love. In it, a writer (in later drafts, a dancer) named Hella Maris falls in love with "a man of action," Lorne Dieterling, who spurns her to marry a worldly woman named Gloria Thornton, who is better suited to advance his unspecified ambitions. Dieterling's mistake is to "sacrifice values for the sake of 'living on earth,' " Rand wrote, "for the sake of action, motivated by a passionate pro-life premise [and] an unbreached ('Narcissus'-like) self-esteem, but thrown off by the wrong premise of taking action as a primary." (Ten years later, she would repeat this description of a "wrong premise" while analyzing what had gone wrong with her lover Branden.) Other notes identify the novel's theme in terms of her old preoccupation: "the art of psychological survival in a malevolent world." The essence of the story would be "the universe of my 'tiddlywink' music." After a day or two of work, however, she set her notes aside. She would resume musing on the characters and their relationships intermittently throughout the 1960s, but she never wrote the novel.

Branden and his circle were deeply bewildered and angered by the injustice of the critics' assaults on Rand. Anxious to defend the ideas he believed in and lift her spirits, he organized a letter-writing campaign by her senior and junior confederates, who together now officially numbered twenty-nine. "We were all strongly encouraged," said one follower, "in fact, it was practically demanded by Nathaniel, that we send letters to the editors and the writers of these negative reviews. We were told that after all Ayn had given us, we owed her absolutely full support, and that it would be traitorous not to 'smite' anyone who criticized her." Alan Greenspan and Barbara Branden wrote to *The New York Times*. Murray Rothbard, newly returned to the fold, answered *Commonweal*'s charge that *Atlas* lacked compassion and "proceeds from hate"; he pointed out that its author displayed a lot of compassion—for the heroic individuals who were being eaten alive by society's looters. Leonard Peikoff, Daryn Kent, and Rand's old friend and ally John Chamberlain took on Chambers and *National Review,* though without making much headway against the editors' cozy assurance that they had bested Rand. Branden talked everyone into canceling subscriptions to *Time*.

Like the Willkie campaign, the mostly brutal reception of *Atlas Shrugged* seems to have been a turning point for Rand. Battered by black moods, her sense of estrangement from others deepened. That "wounded stranger," pain, returned and required forceful measures to be stilled, and her hope for literary justice, which she said she had given up after the publication of *We the Living,* permanently died away and was replaced by a taste for loyalty and adulation, at least from the young. Her life's mission to create an ideal man and delineate the ideas and worldly conditions that would allow him to live, love, create, and produce had been completed. But the society outside her study door did not accept her novel as its model. "She had left Galt's Gulch and come out into a rather sleazy world," said Barbara Branden. "She was tired." Perhaps it's not surprising that, to some degree, she continued to inhabit the world of her novel. "Ayn had disappeared into [the] alternate reality [of *Atlas Shrugged*] and was not coming back," Nathaniel Branden wrote. "Something was gone, and gone irretrievably."

Something had changed for Nathaniel as well. "What kind of world is this?" he remembered saying to his wife, and, "Ayn has done enough. She's entitled to rest. It's our turn now." From that point on, "I felt like my job was to protect her from the world, from disappointment, from suffering," he said. For months, he had been making plans for a series of public lectures called "The Basic Principles of Objectivism," combining an elegantly structured and highly detailed description of her philosophy with his own corresponding theories of psychology and the nature and source of self-esteem. He felt certain that "one part of my destiny was to transmit her message to the world." He also wanted to defend and vindicate her art and vision. "With my lecture course, I was her crusader in a sacred cause," he later told an interviewer. The lectures would systematize and amplify her ideas on existence, knowledge, economics, politics, ethics, art, and romantic love in an orderly way that was impossible in a novel.

Like any capitalist, he hoped to make a profit and decided to charge $3.50 for each of twenty lectures, or $70 for the series. Rand had concerns about the venture. Who would pay to hear a young psychologist with no institutional affiliation talk about philosophy? And what would the public association with her unpopular ideas do to his future? Eventually, she agreed, on the condition that he not name the organization after her. More than ever, she was protective of her name and ideas; she didn't want to give her enemies an opportunity to seize on her friends' errors of knowledge and attribute them to her. So the series was designated the Nathaniel Branden Lectures, soon to become the Nathaniel Branden Institute, or NBI.

NBI's twenty-seven-year-old founder immediately began to recruit an audience. He contacted mutual acquaintances. (Bennett Cerf and Hiram Haydn pled a shortage of time; Rand's friend Joan Kennedy Taylor attended.) He also sifted through Rand's fan letters and sent flyers to intelligent-seeming admirers within driving distance of New York. His flyers were addressed to "the readers and admirers of *The Fountainhead* and *Atlas Shrugged*" and, with Rand's permission, mentioned the author's name in the first line of copy. Members of the junior and senior collectives eagerly signed on, but even they didn't foresee the almost

Elmer Gantry–like talent that Branden would bring to the presentation
of her ideas. If she was a "she-messiah," as *Newsweek* called her in
1961, he was the rock upon which her 1960s following was built. Even
those who disliked him—and over the years, there were many—
admired his almost single-handed organization of Objectivism into a
detailed philosophic system, a national movement, and, briefly, a
familiar national brand, and recognized the fact that he set the foundation for Objectivism's better-known stepchild, the 1970s libertarian
movement.

As his famous mentor's bodyguard and philosophical double ("We
[are] like Siamese twins," she once told him. "Our minds work exactly
the same way"), his responsibilities multiplied. At her request, he and
Barbara helped to select the forums for her public appearances, sat in
on her interviews, accompanied her to important appointments, screened
her visitors, and held a presumptively unfriendly world at bay. When he
explained her theory that ethics should be consistent with the requirements of actual human life or issued orders for action to various ranks of
loyalists, he spoke with Rand's authority. In New York, he became the face
and voice of her philosophy. From this time forward, what he wanted, he
most often got.

THIRTEEN

THE PUBLIC PHILOSOPHER

1958 – 1963

My personal life is a postscript to my novels. It consists of the sentence:
'And I mean it.' I have always lived by the philosophy I present in my
books—it has worked for me, as it has worked for my characters. The
concretes differ, the abstractions are the same.

—"About the Author," *Atlas Shrugged*, 1957

ennett Cerf and Hiram Haydn were among the first to notice the change in Rand. In professional settings, their "most interesting" author was a simple, often modest, spellbinding person, even if she was singularly sure of her ideas and impossible to vanquish in an argument. But as Cerf remarked years later, she was also behaving like a movie queen with a retinue, trailing a crowd of followers he didn't especially like. Looking back in 1971, he called Nathaniel Branden and his circle "hangers-on," "brown-nosers," "sycophants," "stooges." Editor Haydn saw them as a group of unattractive malcontents. When she and they were in a room together, he wrote, "the very whining, toadying quality of the camp followers threw into brilliant relief the wholly dedicated, crusading, intrepid nature of the leader." Both men had only a limited view of Rand, but they recognized an important effect on her of her expanding group of admirers: Every time its members told her, one another, and outsiders that she was a genius on a world historical scale, they encouraged her to add a layer of polish to her self-regard. She began to act the part of a Madame de Staël of contemporary philosophy.

Although she always considered herself a novelist above all, in interviews she presented herself as a woman of ideas. Turning the tables on her literary critics, she displayed the elegantly constructed epistemology and ethics of John Galt's speech as proof that the world of *Atlas Shrugged* was not only plausible but philosophically inevitable: the perfect product of impersonal reason. In a *New York Post* interview published two months after the novel's debut, she went further, designating herself the world's best, or at least most consistent, philosopher. Asked, "Are you the most creative thinker alive today?" she said, "If anyone can pick a single rational flaw in my philosophy, I would be delighted to acknowledge him and learn something from him. Until then—I am." At the time of the interview, she hadn't yet published a single line of nonfiction philosophical writing.

As requests for interviews and appearances poured in, Barbara and Nathaniel persuaded her to give a number of public lectures. They predicted that she would be a riveting speaker and that live audiences would energize her after the embittering print reception of *Atlas Shrugged*. Reluctantly, she agreed. Given her popularity among the young, colleges seemed a likely setting. In early 1958, she gave a lecture called "Faith and Force: Destroyers of the Modern World" to student groups at Queens College, NYU, and City College in New York, contrasting the fruit of reason (freedom) with the historical consequences of mysticism and tyranny (the annihilation of independent thought). Although she was anxious about possible hecklers, the lecture went well. Dressed in her trademark black cape adorned with a provocative gold lapel pin in the shape of a dollar sign—a gift from the Brandens, which she would wear until her death— she impressed students with her lucidity and passion for ideas. At Brooklyn College, she gave a talk to the nation's first Ayn Rand Club titled "Zero Worship," her unforgettable name for the altruists' supposed tendency to revere the poor and undistinguished and to hate and envy the productive rich. Here, a crowd of hostile students and teachers *did* come to heckle her, but she found that she relished the give-and-take, just as she had enjoyed debating with passersby on Fourteenth Street during the Willkie campaign. "I was awed by the power of what she had to say," said a member of the audience that day. During the question-and-answer period, "she

didn't take anything personally; she was completely devoted to her principles." There and elsewhere, her meticulous arguments for individual liberty startled many students into taking a fresh look at their assumptions.

At the same time, she was enjoying watching as Branden thoroughly
and deftly systematized the ideas in John Galt's speech into a series
of twenty lectures of his own. These included "What Is Philosophy?"
"The Meaning and Nature of Volition," "God," "The Psychology of Sex,"
and, most characteristically, "Why Human Beings Repress and Drive
Underground Not the Worst Within Them but the Best." For the initial
series, which began in January 1958 and was held every week in a
meeting room in the small, elegant Sheraton Russell Hotel on Park Avenue, only a block or two from the O'Connors' and the Brandens' apartments, twenty-eight people signed up. Branden was a natural showman:
handsome, virile, articulate, young, impassioned, even poetic. He was
passionate about Rand's ideas and he loved to perform. Word spread
that the NBI lectures were mandatory for New Yorkers interested in
Rand's books or in a life of individualism, and during his second season
in the fall of 1958, forty-five people enrolled. At Barbara's suggestion, he
began placing small announcements in *The New York Times,* titled "Lectures on Objectivism, the Philosophy of Ayn Rand & Its Application to
Human Psychology." The text promised that Miss Rand herself would
answer questions after every lecture. From that point on, attendance
rose steadily until it peaked at an average of about two hundred people
in each twice-yearly series of lectures—an immense turnout for a private study group. Apart from Rand's growing circle of devotees, participants were much like her core readers: scientists and engineers, college
and graduate students, professors, nurses, doctors, businesspeople, lawyers, artists, and lost souls. They listened, spellbound, to Branden's descriptions of the almost limitless human potential—a phrase she first
used in *Atlas Shrugged*—of lives rooted in a philosophy of reason, purpose, and self-esteem. During the question periods, the famous novelist
was gracious, serene, and thrillingly lucid in these early lectures. One
regular participant, an attorney, remembered that her "every word, every
sentence was magic."

Many enrolled for second and third terms. When they requested additional topics, Branden enlisted Alan Greenspan to give a talk entitled
"The Economics of a Free Society," Barbara to speak on "The Principles
of Efficient Thinking," and Mary Ann Sures and Leonard Peikoff to ex-

plore, respectively, art and the history of philosophy up to and including Rand. By popular demand, the maestro herself launched her own private lecture series, on the art of writing romantic-realist fiction, which also began in early 1958. For six months, she gave informal workshops in her apartment, with about a dozen NBI students ranged in chairs around the living room and a table and microphone set up to record her remarks. By all accounts, the talks were fascinating, if self-referential; she depended mainly on examples from her novels to illustrate the correct principles of character creation, narrative description, and unity of plot and theme.

There were a few disagreeable incidents, two of them involving the wife of her lover. She spent half a session analyzing what she regarded as the overwritten prose and bad plotting of Thomas Wolfe, choosing to critique the very passages that Barbara had praised eight years before. She liked to test her listeners for depth of understanding and, during the final session, called on Nathaniel to read aloud from an anonymous short story, then asked the class for comments. The story was a farcical tale of a small-town reporter who kidnaps the town's richest girl in order to produce exciting news and make his name; the plot thickens when a local gangster named Pug-Nosed Thompson scoops him and collects the ransom. The story ends when the kidnapped girl refuses to go free until the reporter agrees to marry her. The story was full of 1920s tabloid dialect ("My stars in heaven!" the newspaper's editor cries, whereupon a reporter shouts, "Hot diggity dog!"). Barbara was first to raise her hand. She said that the story was competently plotted—almost like an Ayn Rand story!—but awkwardly written and without much point. That made for a surprise ending, because Rand had written the story, "Good Copy," in 1927. Offended by the criticism or by a suggestion of condescension on Barbara's part, "she began to shout in outrage," Barbara recalled. "I knew nothing about literature [she said], I knew nothing about writing, and most of all, I knew nothing about *her!*" The class quickly broke up, but Rand continued shouting at the woman who was by now her closest friend until four o'clock in the morning, when both women were exhausted. "Stop it!" the younger woman cried after one last harangue, and the argument finally ended. Barbara was one of the few people in Rand's life, including Paterson, Frank, and Branden, who could seriously offend her without risking a permanent break.

Even as Rand's moods grew more changeable and dangerous in the months following the publication of *Atlas Shrugged,* her public emphasis on philosophy—"a philosophy for living on earth," she called it—attracted new intellectual seekers. One was a journalist, a former staff writer for *The New York Times Magazine* named Edith Efron, who became intellectually infatuated with the author while researching a New York newspaper interview column that ran beneath the byline of her current boss, Mike Wallace. Soon after, Efron began attending NBI lectures and Rand's Saturday night salons and set out to enlist one of her colleagues, Al Ramrus, a producer and writer for Wallace's late-night TV show, *The Mike Wallace Interview.* Suddenly, recalled Ramrus, Efron started "spouting these strange ideas about the insidious influence of the welfare state" in the office. This surprised him, he said, because she and he had shared a die-hard "nonobservant New York Jewish left-wing" outlook. They clashed with each other until, one evening, she invited him to meet the novelist. The meeting didn't go well, Ramrus remembered, especially after he remarked that maybe *Atlas Shrugged* had received "lousy reviews" because she was "a lousy writer." She asked him calmly if he had read her work and handed him a copy of *Atlas Shrugged.* "Find an example of lousy writing," she said. He riffled through the book and hit on a page he can no longer remember. "Wow, this is pretty good," he said. The night ended amicably. He was certain that he had met a remarkable person and a world-class intellect.

The following week, he devoured *Atlas Shrugged* and sent Rand a letter praising the novel but expressing reservations about the characterization of Galt. "Maybe in my youthful arrogance I thought I would impress her with my critical acumen," he recalled. A day or two later, he received angry letters from Efron and Branden, notifying him that he was not welcome in Objectivist circles. But relations with his colleague were mended when he made it clear that he had been deeply impressed by the life-altering and magisterial message of individualism and achievement contained in *Atlas Shrugged.*

In his second meeting with the author, he was acutely aware of her mental gifts. Fifty years later he remembered the impression she made on him that evening. "Her big, black, glowing, lustrous eyes radiated a *tremendous* energy, and penetration, and focus, and intensity," he said. "And they never left you." With infinite patience and no display of haste or condescension, she teased out buried assumptions in his liberal creed and carefully corrected them. She emanated "universal genius" to a degree he had never before witnessed and never would again. ("The only [other person] who came close," he said, "was Frank Lloyd Wright.") Watching such a great and disciplined mind at work "was inspiring and, by example, empowering" to Ramrus. As with so many others, his next two or three meetings with her revolutionized his political outlook. He, too, enrolled in NBI, and both he and Efron joined the circle surrounding Rand.

At about the same time, Rand received an effusive letter from her former late-night debating partner, Mises student and Circle Bastiat ringleader Murray Rothbard. Rothbard and his friends had obtained early copies of *Atlas Shrugged* from an airport bookstore where one of them worked and had read the novel straight through, pausing only to call one another and rave about its insurrectionary power. Rothbard had avoided Rand since young George Reisman's losing argument with her in the summer of 1954; even at that time, he had recognized the inherent pressure toward rigidity in her thinking. Writing to his friend Richard Cornuelle in August 1954, he observed, "Since [Ayn's followers] all have the same premises, they are all . . . individual parts in a machine." As a consequence, he added, in a flight of whimsy that six months afterward became half fact, "there is no reason whatever why Ayn, for example, shouldn't sleep with Nathan, or Barbara with Frank." Because her followers all seemed intent on evolving into the same kind of person—replicas of Howard Roark or Dominique—"the case [is] really very good for a complete Stalinist tyranny that plans everybody's lives," he concluded, even though he still considered Ayn herself a "wacky" advocate of freedom.

But he and his friends were so bowled over by *Atlas Shrugged* that he forgot or set aside his reservations.

A week before *Atlas* went on sale, Rothbard sent Rand a four-page, single-spaced letter of stunned praise. "I will start by saying that all of us in the 'Circle Bastiat' are convinced . . . that *Atlas Shrugged* is the greatest novel ever written," he began. "For the first time [in history], you have [depicted] persons and their actions in perfect accordance with principles and their consequences." Admitting that he had kept his distance from her for the last three years ("the fault is mine . . . a defect in my own psyche"), he explained that he suffered from depression and had experienced a bout after every long discussion with her. He was convinced that this was due either to the exhausting effort of keeping up with "a mind that I unhesitatingly say is the most brilliant of the twentieth century" or to a subconscious fear that his independence and personality would be swallowed up "by the tremendous power of your own." Rand accepted his apology and asked to see him, and for a few weeks in early 1958, she, Nathaniel Branden, and the "anarcho-libertarian" Rothbard got along together well.

By the early 1960s, Branden would have created a well-oiled assembly line that delivered thousands of young men and women to Objectivism every year. But in the late 1950s he was on the lookout for high-value converts such as Efron and Ramrus. Rothbard, age thirty-one, had a Ph.D. in economics and came with his own circle of five or six Bastiat associates, including George Reisman and a bright Queens College undergraduate named Robert Hessen, who later became a business and economic historian at the Hoover Institution at Stanford University. Rand and Branden welcomed Rothbard and his friends. But intimations of trouble followed.

Rothbard's brief connection with Rand and her circle is a cautionary tale of cult initiation gone awry. Like most New York Rand enthusiasts, he signed up for the NBI lectures. He also entered into a course of psychotherapy with Branden, hoping that Rand's theory of the mind, as interpreted and practiced by her closest advisor, would guide him in overcoming his recurring depression as well as a severe travel phobia that prevented him from taking trains and planes. When he mentioned this, he later noted in a letter, Branden gave him a "ninety-five percent guarantee" that he would be cured of his phobia along with his depression. On the basis of such assurances, he accepted an invitation to speak at an Emory University–sponsored academic symposium scheduled to take place nine months later, in Sea Island, Georgia.

The novelist's protégé was still only twenty-seven years old in late 1957, but, as Rand's followers knew, she considered him to be an established genius in a field she often said she hated to deal with; most psychology was "a sewer" of the irrational, she said, while applauding Branden's skill in bringing her principles to bear on it. By this she meant that, since emotions stem from ideas, a neurotic person is necessarily a repository of wrong, evasive, or contradictory ideas, which didn't interest her. If the person wasn't immoral, however (meaning consciously evading the facts of reality as she saw them), she was confident that Branden could fix what ailed him. When young friends came to her to discuss their problems, she habitually referred them to Branden for either long- or short-term treatment, depending on the nature of their troubles and complaints. Because her suggestions had the force of law, at one time or another "Nathan was everybody's therapist," at least within the Collective, his wife later said. Some worked it off, others paid five dollars an hour, Branden's modest fee.

Impartial observers, however, might not have been so sure that the NBI chief was qualified to treat emotional disturbances at that time. Although he now had an M.A. in psychology from the education department at NYU, he hadn't received any professional training, and he didn't yet have a Ph.D. (He would get one in 1973.) He had applied for but been refused a New York State license to practice therapy on the basis of too few hours of supervised practice; eventually he would obtain certification in New Jersey, Pennsylvania, and Washington, D.C., with privileges to work in New York. In spite of his minimal credentials in the late 1950s, however, his clients took up all of the hours he was willing to devote to therapeutic practice, and those he could not see he passed on to his cousin Allan Blumenthal, a physician, whom he was training in his techniques and who set up a practice largely on that basis.

At first, Rothbard was pleased to be in therapy with Branden. After a few weeks, however, the sessions began to sour. Branden started to pester him about converting his wife, Joey, a practicing Christian, to atheism and Objectivism, Rothbard recalled, in a much-disputed 1989 magazine memoir called "My Break with Branden and the Rand Cult." According to him, one evening when he and Joey were visiting Rand, someone suggested that Joey listen to a recording of Branden's NBI lecture arguing for the nonexistence of God, in Objectivist parlance (since one cannot prove a negative). When she listened but refused to reevaluate her convictions, the pressure on Rothbard intensified. He later reported, perhaps falsely, that Branden urged him to divorce her.

By the spring of 1958, Objectivist events and activities were multiplying. After Branden's weekly NBI lecture, a group gathered at a nearby coffee shop and talked about ideas until closing. The discussion that followed Rand's fiction-writing workshop sometimes lasted into the early morning. Educational events were augmented by gatherings at the Blumenthals' or Brandens' apartment, in addition to invitation-only Saturday nights at Rand's. Everyone lucky enough to be included was expected to attend all or most of these events. ("Why is it you don't see us more often?" Branden once asked Rothbard—ominously, Rothbard thought.) Yet even during socials, there was very little small talk, which Rand, of course, deplored; typically, she, Nathaniel, or Barbara would lead a discussion of politics, books, music, or current events, while others stretched their necks to listen. ("Those parties were very hierarchical," recalled one disenchanted NBI student. "They were roundtables of oratory." "They were absolutely a nightmare," Barbara later admitted. "They were as far from parties as anything you can imagine.") As though spontaneously, guests adopted Rand's opinions, preferences, even gestures. Since she smoked, they smoked. Once, Rand bought a new dining room table, and according to Shelly Reuben, her typist at the time, two admirers who had been in her apartment went out and bought the same table. The musicians in the group pretended to prefer Rachmaninoff—Rand's favorite Romantic composer, a popular figure in the Russia of her youth—to the tragic, "malevolent" Beethoven and the "pre-musical" (meaning, pre-Romantic) Bach and Mozart. Once she described Brahms as "worthless," and Leonard Peikoff, a talented pianist who was perhaps Rand's most reverential follower, rushed to give away his collection of Brahms recordings. When not in his studio painting, Frank sat silently in a corner.

The naturally unruly Rothbard and his prankish friends found some of this funny, and one night they improvised a skit that made fun of the Collective. With George Reisman playing a chain-smoking, thickly accented Rand, Ralph Raico as a pompous Branden, and young historian Ron Hamowy imitating a beleaguered rank-and-file follower named Tina, they blended reasoned demands for lecture fees by Raico with satirical quotes from Francisco's money speech in *Atlas Shrugged*. They taped their hijinks on a reel-to-reel recorder, and when Branden found out about it he demanded the tape. "After all," Rothbard claimed he said, "you wouldn't mock God." The libertarian refused, citing private-property rights and thinking, *Who's God here, buster? You, Rand, or both?*

The beginning of the end of Rothbard's relationship with Rand came when Branden accused him of plagiarizing John Galt's speech, as well as key parts of Barbara Branden's NYU master's thesis on free will, in a paper he had prepared for the summer 1958 Sea Island symposium. Rothbard gave Branden a copy out of "misplaced good will," he later wrote, and was, or pretended to be, stunned when Rand's deputy responded with a six-page list of purloined words, phrases, and concepts. Branden threatened to send a letter to Helmut Schoeck, a well-known scholar and head of the symposium, as well as to initiate legal action, if

Rothbard didn't either retract the paper or credit Rand and Barbara. After an agitated exchange of letters, including one from Rand's attorney Pincus Berner to Helmut Schoeck, Rothbard was summoned to a full court trial in Rand's apartment. He refused to appear and was banished in absentia. That he had revealed himself to be a committed anarchist was another mark against him.

Though overwrought, perhaps, Rand and Branden had a legitimate complaint. The paper, titled "The Mantle of Science," was infused with concepts and terms peculiar to Rand and *Atlas Shrugged* and reflected Barbara's argument, based on Rand's fallacy of the stolen concept, that a defense of philosophical determinism involves self-contradiction. Either Rothbard was unconscious of the echo (which is unlikely) or was reluctant to own up to the influence of a novelist—a *woman* novelist, no less, and one who was either ridiculed by or unknown to most university professors. On the other hand, Branden's allegations were hasty and cold and, when imparted to Schoeck, might easily have ended Rothbard's academic career. As time went on, real or potential theft of her intellectual property became an increasingly troublesome issue for Rand. In the mid-1960s she retained two attorneys who were also followers, Hank and Erika Holzer, to handle most possible infractions; eventually, Branden himself would become an object of their accusations. In his own defense, Rothbard pointed out that none of the disputed ideas had originated with Rand. Rather than admit guilt, he usefully if spuriously listed external sources from Aristotle to Adam Smith and Nietzsche for each one. In the end, he couldn't attend the symposium anyway, because Branden's attempted cure hadn't helped his travel phobia or his intermittent depression.

The Rothbard story has many of the earmarks of the emerging Ayn Rand cult. That someone who had seen danger in her habits of thought so early and so clearly should be drawn into her orbit merely proves the strength of her charisma, the countercultural freshness of her ideas, and the power of her literary formula. As she had pointed out to her Republican acquaintances in the 1940s, great novels first stir the passions and then engage the mind; *Atlas Shrugged* did both superlatively. Whether she knew it or not, she was retailing her philosophy of strict rationality through a primal emotional appeal by characters in a fable. For certain kinds of readers who were romantics or especially methodical, bookish logicians or lonely rebels, organized Objectivism provided at least an illusion of freedom, individuality, integrity, and courage and fostered a pleasurable contempt for bureaucratized parental culture—all based on an imagined world that had yielded a resplendent philosophy for living.

For twenty-five years after the incident, Rothbard ridiculed and satirized Rand and what he called "the Ayn Rand cult" in private and in print. He once compared the group's hierarchical structure and institutionalized veneration of the founder and leader to the cults of Hitler, Mussolini, Trotsky, and Mao. Naturally, Rand also wholly renounced him. "Prior to our break with him," Branden wrote in 1989, "both Ayn and I regarded Murray as highly intelligent. . . . [Afterward] it seemed to me each time she spoke of him she thought him less intelligent than before." This was her old pattern. She did not, however, disparage or even mention him in public or in print.

In fact, unlike some later defectors, Rothbard wasn't seriously injured by his break with Rand. His teacher Ludwig von Mises, Helmut Schoeck, and other conservative thinkers and writers took his side in the plagiarism scandal, perhaps partly because they disliked Rand's habit of self-promotion and Branden's heavy-handed tactics on her behalf. But he lost two close friends, George Reisman and Robert Hessen, both also in therapy with Branden. Flushed with the grandeur of Rand's vision, they sided with their new confederates. In just a few months, Reisman, in particular, had come to worship Branden, describing him to Ralph Raico as "what the best within us [in the Circle Bastiat] started out to be" and explaining that under his care, he had discovered what it felt like to be someone for the first time in his life. He remained loyal to organized Objectivism until well after the author's death. As for Hessen, who later described his single therapeutic session with Branden as a "hideous" episode of bullying and intimidation, during which he watched Branden pace the room like a panther, he left New York for a year of graduate work in history at Harvard. When he returned, he switched therapists to Branden's cousin Allan Blumenthal. In the spring of 1959, he also went to work as Rand's part-time personal secretary. With her permission, while in that position he collected and helped to safeguard archival drafts of her essays. She purged him, too, over a minor disagreement, in 1980.

Even if Rand didn't always initiate what insiders called "denunciations," she established the atmosphere in which they took place and participated. Her daily conferences with her protégé became more fractious as her moods darkened during 1958. After Rothbard's expulsion, she tightened the rules of admission to their philosophical clubhouse. "She was very controversial and feared that others would use the actions of her acolytes to discredit her," recalled Hessen. As a result, she decreed that only she, Nathaniel, and Barbara could call themselves "Objectivists." Everyone else had to refer to himself as a "student of Objectivism." NBI enrollees were not only required to read *Atlas Shrugged* but also to declare their agreement with the major tenets of John Galt's speech, according to a reporter from the *Saturday Evening Post*. Prospective participants were invited to pay for and attend a single introductory lecture but could not ask questions, in part because the crowds at these preliminary events overwhelmed the ability of the principals to answer. ("I went to a [lecture] once and raised my hand," said Bertha Krantz, Rand's copy editor at Random House. "I was told very bluntly, very coldly, 'You don't question.' I got up and left.") In any case, Rand was likely to explode in anger if questions suggested doubt or disagreement.

As NBI expanded, Barbara gave up her job as a junior editor at St. Martin's Press to supervise its daily operations. Seen as a kind of Aphrodite to Rand's imperial Hera and Branden's Apollo, she, too, was an object of awe and admiration among the lesser lights. "If one considers that Ayn was God and Nathan was Jesus Christ, that left me as the Virgin Mary," she once said wryly. Students referred to her as "the most beautiful woman in the world" or as "the Ice Queen," both tributes to her cool, pale, increasingly aloof aura of good looks and regal bearing. "I learned repression, as so many of [Ayn's] young friends did," she later wrote about this period. By stifling unacceptable thoughts, perceptions, and facts—her literary enthusiasms, her mentor's moods, her husband's ongoing affair with the ideology's great parental figure—"I encased myself in a sheet of ice," she wrote.

Years later, Nathaniel bitterly described the program of conformity he implemented on Rand's behalf during the 1960s. The implicit premises the inner circle accepted and that he "transmitted to our students at NBI" included:

- Ayn Rand is the greatest human being who has ever lived.
- *Atlas Shrugged* is the greatest human achievement in the history of the world.
- Ayn Rand, by virtue of her philosophical genius, is the supreme arbiter in any issue pertaining to what is rational, moral, or appropriate to man's life on earth.

- Once one is acquainted with Ayn Rand and her work, the measure of one's virtue is intrinsically tied to the position that one takes regarding her and her work.
- No one who does not admire what Ayn Rand admires and condemn what Ayn Rand condemns can be a good Objectivist. No one who disagrees with Ayn Rand on any fundamental issue can be a fully consistent individualist.
- Because Ayn Rand has designated Nathaniel Branden as her "intellectual heir" and has repeatedly proclaimed him to be an ideal exponent of her philosophy, he is to be accorded only marginally less reverence than Ayn Rand herself.
- It is best not to say most of these things explicitly (excepting, perhaps, the first two items). One must always maintain that one arrives at one's beliefs solely by reason.

To Rand's credit, it must be remembered that she never actively sought this kind of reverence, at least outside the circle of her original loyalists, and, at first, was not overly impressed with the students who flocked to NBI. Most struck her as well meaning, perhaps, but lacking in intellectual depth and quickness. "The lectures attracted a lot of not particularly intellectual people, such as dentists and engineers," recalled Joan Kennedy Taylor. "They loved her vision of a technologically advancing, logical world. But this was the first time many of them had dealt with ideas. They thought that Ayn Rand had invented laissez-faire capitalism." After the Rothbard incident, "I saw her change," Taylor added. "In the beginning she was genuinely collecting data and trying to figure out what people's motives were. She came to the point where she had gathered enough evidence and thought she knew what certain attitudes or questions meant." Having made a judgment, she "wouldn't look closely [at individuals] again." During the first years of NBI, Rand said, "I thought that my fans disappointed and depressed me worse than my enemies."

By the fall of 1958, she was drifting into a clinical depression. At first, no one noticed the intensity of her moods. Sales of *Atlas* were going strong. Fan letters arrived by the hundreds every week. Largely due to the Brandens' efforts, her growing reputation as an abstract thinker and a charismatic speaker was attracting new readers and generating lecture invitations from all over the United States. She was relatively rich. She had a beautiful, kind husband and a bright young lover. And yet she was profoundly unhappy. She began to speak to her friends of the bitter revulsion she felt for the culture. To Frank and the Brandens, she said she could not understand why she and her masterpiece had been vilified, belittled, and willfully misconstrued to mean the opposite of what she had written. She cursed the literary Tooheys and Keatings who she believed were trying to destroy her book. Where were the "raves that raved about the right things"? Where were the men of ability, whom she had always championed? Why didn't the nation's scientists and businessmen stand up for her? Why wasn't there at least one intellectual giant who had the courage publicly to declare the meaning and revolutionary value of her work, as the young people around her did?

Filled with despair and in dread of appearing less than fully in control, she began to refuse social invitations and to stay in her apartment. Again, she complained of physical tension. Gradually, the Brandens realized that her condition went well beyond postpublication letdown. During their visits and on the phone, she lamented and raged against the mediocrity, cynicism, timidity, and malice she saw rewarded everywhere, and, as the months wore on, she wept almost daily out of frustration and grief.

With minor reprieves, she remained depressed from late 1958 until early 1961. She stopped giving lectures on college campuses; she no longer enjoyed the intellectual give-and-take. "I cannot fight lice," she said to Branden. In physical pain from stress, tired to the bone, she spent hours playing solitaire at her desk in her dim, cramped study. The few people who saw her regularly found her short-tempered, prone to demands for praise and reassurance, susceptible to violent outbursts of entitlement and rage, and painfully aware that her attitude and conduct amounted to a mind on strike without a theme or a guaranteed victorious ending. "John Galt wouldn't feel this," she often said. "He would know how to handle this. I don't know." And, "I would hate for him to see me like this."

The amphetamines she took may have aggravated her condition or added to its duration. In memoirs and interviews, some former friends recalled that her amphetamine habit was confined to a steady, continuous low dose, but there is a small body of anecdotal and circumstantial

evidence that suggests she increased her dose at least occasionally—
when she wanted to work all night or lose weight, for example. Roger
Callahan, a Ph.D. therapist who joined Rand's extended circle in the
middle 1960s as one of Branden's professional disciples, recalled seeing
"someone, I won't say who" carrying a jar of Dexedrine pills to her apartment. He inquired about them and was told, "Oh, these are for Ayn."
Libertarian gadfly Roy Childs once said in an interview that Rand's
secretary—he didn't say which one—told him that "she'd take a couple
of five-milligrams" of Dexamyl and if nothing happened after an hour,
"she'd take another two, three, or four. She was taking this on top of pots
of coffee." Said Robert Hessen, "She *was* wired up. She subsisted on
black coffee and cigarettes and very dark, sliced Russian bread and slices
of Swiss cheese or white cheese," as well as Swiss chocolates. Joan Blumenthal recalled that Rand said she needed the pills to get up in the
morning. She didn't complain of hallucinations, as some longtime low-
dose users do. But she "always had a very elevated pulse rate," which "is
very unusual," recalled Allan Blumenthal, a doctor, and she displayed the
telltale symptoms of suspicion, panic, lack of sleep, and volatility. "The
atmosphere was like that of a hospital at times," recalled Branden, who
visited the apartment two or three nights a week, often staying until
dawn, and spoke to her on the phone every day, sometimes for hours. "I
once made the mistake of telling her so, and she went berserk: How
could I make such a statement? Didn't I understand her at all? she
shouted." Most of the time, she was adamant that her emotional condition was a natural response to intolerable circumstances.

Although her kindly husband had always been able to lift her spirits
in moments of distress, he could not help her now. He was supportive
but largely silent during these discussions, and Branden thought he appeared helpless and bleak. Gradually, he withdrew into his painting. She
leaned more heavily on her heir, for aid in untangling her "premises,"
some of which she sometimes conceded must be wrong, as well as for
hours-long doses of emotional support. She was grateful, but also demanding. "You are my lifeline to reality," she told him. "Without you, I
would not know how to exist in this world." She intensified her complaints about his emotional distance. She called it his "disappearing professor" act. She was quick to judge and condemn members of the inner
circle for their motives and "sense of life," and Branden, under strain,
became harsher and more peremptory, too. "He had always been arro-

gant and judgmental in his dealings with people," Barbara wrote in
1986. "Now, attempting to live his own life while finding for Ayn a reason to live, constantly tense . . . he was more coldly arrogant and demanding than ever before."

As to Rand's low spirits, what O'Connor understood but Branden
and the others didn't was that her suffering was new in degree but not in
kind. It was an acute and persistent instance of her old malady of disappointment at the moment of her popular triumph. In her play *Ideal,* the
Garboesque screen idol Kay Gonda can believe in her fans' devotion
only if they are willing to risk their lives for her; the heroine cries out, "If
all of you who look at me on the screen hear the things I say and worship
me for them—where do I hear them? . . . I want to see, real, living, and
in the hours of my own days, that glory I create as an illusion! I want it
real!" Rand wrote those lines in 1934. Kay Gonda spoke for her creator
then, and spoke for her in 1959. Branden, her book sales—these rewards were not enough.

Whatever the catalyst, she was unable to fend off or end the pain
and confusion her depression brought. She played solitaire because she
couldn't write. Except for a few pages of handwritten notes for the
prospective novel *To Lorne Dieterling,* she wrote little. She no longer
knew for whom she was writing, or why, she told the Brandens. She was
paralyzed by disgust and contempt. And yet not writing was a torture.
"Thinking is all I do," she said.

She and Nathaniel continued to say they loved each other, but she
called a halt to sex. In *Atlas Shrugged,* she had written that "no form of
claim" between lovers should ever be "motivated by pain and aimed at
pity." Relief from pain, not sex, was what she needed most and sought
from him, and self-pity was one of her prevailing moods. The suspen-
sion of sex wasn't the end of the affair, she assured him; they would be
able to renew their intimacy with each other as soon as she came back
to life. In the meantime, she wanted him to remain her suitor in every
other way. In the following two years, she alternately complimented him
on his grasp of her psychology and railed against his lack of expressed
romantic and emotional interest in her. When they did sleep together,
about a dozen times, their encounters were stiffer, more ritualized, and
less enjoyable for Branden.

He did his best to bring her hope based on the steadily expanding
popular influence of *Atlas Shrugged* and the rapid growth of NBI. But

he was not sorry for the interval of sexual inactivity. The attraction to Rand had faded further under the weight of her sadness, anger, demands, and increasing neglect of her physical appearance. She was never fastidious, but at about this time her grooming slipped so precipitously that Branden asked Barbara to speak to Rand about bathing more regularly. In any case, he did not want "the burden of a 'romance' for which I no longer had genuine enthusiasm," he wrote. "I needed all of my resources to continue functioning" as the leader of a movement and the caretaker of its faltering fountainhead.

Thus, as the Eisenhower years ended and John F. Kennedy inaugurated an era of unparalleled American prosperity, new cultural freedoms, increased spending on social programs, and the beginnings of a distant, controversial war, Nathaniel and, to a lesser degree, Barbara established a smaller, safer sphere for their benefactor to inhabit. The proud sufferer asked her two friends not to discuss her depression with the others, so most of her followers knew little or nothing about the extremity of her moods. But they understood that she, and they, were almost universally derided as hate-mongering greed-is-good neo-Fascists and social Darwinists, when they knew themselves to be visionaries of freedom and progress. Some lost friends. Some, like Leonard Peikoff, experienced their parents' disapproval or estrangement. "How is it possible that we can be accused of advocating, politically, the exact opposite of what we stand for?" they said among themselves after lectures and on Saturday nights. They concluded that, like Roark, they were being punished for their virtues and that the outside world hated and feared them for trumpeting the moral good. (In sectarian parlance, the "social metaphysicians" hated "the good for being the good.") In their foreshortened frame of reference, they now incessantly compared the state of the culture to themes from Rand's novels. As time went on and Rand and they continued to be ridiculed, they saw themselves as reflections of her heroes and attributed her villains' evil motives to her adversaries. "It was more and more true that we were living inside the world of *Atlas Shrugged*," said Branden.

All the while, her fame increased. Al Ramrus suggested to Mike Wallace that he invite her to be a guest on his half-hour TV interview show, *The Mike Wallace Interview*. He did, and she made her first television appearance on Wallace's show in February 1959. He gave her a forceful introduction as they sat facing each other across a bare table on an empty stage. She was "the founder of a new and unusual philosophy [that] would seem to strike at the very roots of our society," he declared, "a revolutionary creed" that had launched a national movement along the lines of "democracy or Communism." While he spoke, the camera lingered on a small, plain woman, with uncoiffed hair, a changeable smile, and darting, dark, magnetic eyes suggestive of wariness and excitement. Employing his famous stern interrogatory method, Wallace asked, "Miss Rand, would you agree that, as *Newsweek* put it, you are out to destroy every edifice in the contemporary American way of life?" She blinked, then answered good-naturedly. "Yes. I am challenging the moral code at the base" of a great many institutions, and that code is altruism, she replied. Throughout the next twenty-five minutes of give-and-take, the camera caught fleeting expressions of wonder, amusement, anger, and contempt moving across her features. But she explained the workings of her great philosophic engine clearly, gracefully, and with a fiery emphasis on the sine qua non of individual freedom and individual responsibility.

She didn't always tell the truth in answer to his questions. When he inquired, "Whence did this philosophy of yours come?" she gave an answer that, from this point on, became her stock reply: "Out of my own mind, with the sole acknowledgment of a debt to Aristotle, who is the only philosopher who ever influenced me. I devised the rest myself." This, of course, was not only untrue, but also highly unlikely on its face. It worked against her being taken seriously by the influential intellectuals she wanted to persuade. "You have an accent," Wallace observed. "It's—" "Russian," she replied, whereupon the interviewer asked if her parents had immigrated to America with her or had died in Russia. "I came alone," she told him, adding that she had no way of finding out if her parents were alive or dead. (She had learned of their deaths in 1946, through Marie von Strachow, but may have wished to protect her sister Nora, whose status and whereabouts she did not know. On the other hand, she had told the same story to both Brandens.) Was her husband a big industrialist, like the heroes of *Atlas Shrugged*? the interviewer wondered. Oh, no, he was an artist, she told him. The next question must have surprised her. "Is he supported by you?" Wallace asked. "No, by his own work, actually, in the past," she stammered, adding, "By me if necessary, but it isn't quite necessary." This exchange took place in the context of an earlier discussion about whether only strong, independent people like John Galt and Howard Roark are worthy to be loved. (A weak man or woman "certainly does not deserve love," Rand solemnly told Wallace. People "cannot expect the unearned, neither in love nor in money." When the host protested that few people could meet her standard of strength or merit, she proudly admitted, "Unfortunately, *very* few.") The currency in which O'Connor's right to be loved was to be measured, she explained, was the pleasure he gave her, proving that she was not an altruist in love. For O'Connor, this must have been excruciating: to be described as though he were a mistress, on the one hand, and for Rand to deny supporting him, on the other—here was a perfect vise of *un*deservingness.

She also mentioned Branden, whom she identified as "my best intellectual heir, the psychologist." She shyly but proudly confided that his lecture series was becoming very successful. In the previous month of January 1959 alone, Mr. Branden had received six hundred letters of inquiry about his lectures.

Afterward, the show received many letters from viewers, most of them positive. But journalists in general were dumbfounded that Wallace had devoted half an hour of airtime to a woman whom they thought of as a reactionary crackpot. In 1959, when there were no Oprahs and Edward R. Murrow still set the standard for news and interviews, Rand was considered beyond the pale. "It is hard to imagine the hostility directed at her," said Wallace's producer Al Ramrus. "Most of the media treated her like a leper or the Antichrist." Yet Wallace himself, a lifelong liberal, enjoyed the interview and admired her courage, swiftness of mind, and flair, even if he considered her ideas marginal and her style eccentric. ("I remember with amusement her haircut," he told an interviewer in 1998, "which [was] a little like the one that I wore when I was four or five years old—a Dutch cut.") In the mode of William F. Buckley, Jr., and Bennett Cerf, he went out of his way to become her friend. For the next twenty years, he and she dined together, along with Frank and Wallace's wife, every eight or ten months and occasionally attended each other's parties and celebrations. He invited her to appear on his next show, *P.M. East,* this time in tandem with her improbable new literary flame, Mickey Spillane. Again like Cerf, however, Wallace had dwindling patience with Nathaniel Branden (whom he once called a "creature who sat on her shoulder") and some of her "slavish followers," as he called them. Apparently, this didn't include Efron and Ramrus, both of whom continued to work for him for years, or Barbara, to whom he was courtly. He maintained a warm friendship with Ramrus until he was in his nineties.

For the most part, the shy philosopher stayed out of public view during the most difficult months of her depression, but she made a few new friends in addition to Wallace. One was an elderly composer and music critic named Deems Taylor, the father of Rand's friend Joan Kennedy Taylor. The younger Taylor had met Rand a few weeks before the publication of *Atlas Shrugged,* when her mood was still buoyant. A publicity assistant for Alfred A. Knopf, Taylor received an advance copy of the novel and, like Rothbard, wrote a complimentary letter. At Rand's suggestion they met for lunch. Taylor was flattered but also surprised. "Why did you want to see me?" she asked. "Atlantis," Rand mysteriously replied. Taylor, later a writer and editor, guessed that the novelist was auditioning people for her own version of Galt's Gulch; if so, her disordered state of mind soon put an end to the plan. Through Taylor she met Deems, who at seventy-five had largely outlived his fame as the composer of the 1927 opera *The King's Henchman* and as the host of Walt Disney's 1940 masterpiece *Fantasia.* Rand very likely knew his speaking voice, since in the late 1930s and early 1940s he had been the announcer for weekly radio broadcasts of the New York Philharmonic. At a time "when the whole world wanted her attention, she made the time to visit my father and listen to every single piece of music he had written," Taylor said, adding, "I think she was kinder to people who were not students. She didn't expect as much from them." Besides, "she respected creative people."

Naturally, she asked Deems what he had thought of her fictional character, the composer and striker Richard Halley. He must have answered favorably, because she asked him to write an operatic rendition of *Anthem,* using romantic themes to identify the heroes and atonal music to represent the authoritarian social order. Although flattered, the elderly man didn't want to compose atonal music. No opera of *Anthem* was ever created, but Rand befriended Deems until he died in 1966.

In one of the stranger literary love matches of the period, she also developed a professional crush on crime novelist Mickey Spillane, the tough-guy author of *I, the Jury* and other novels featuring Mike Hammer, private eye. Spillane's publisher, New American Library, had bought the paperback rights to *Atlas Shrugged,* and the editors arranged for a lunch meeting between the firm's two best-selling authors. They talked late into the afternoon, until the restaurant closed its doors to prepare for the evening rush, but instead of asking the pair to leave, the staff pulled up chairs and listened to their conversation. Rand loved the fact that Spillane's potboiling plots and gun-toting heroes were dedicated to separating good from evil in a black-and-white world. ("Grays don't interest me," she said, apropos of his work.) She later befriended the rough-edged author publicly, praising his bawdy and often bloody tales of good guys and bad guys in a syndicated column she wrote for the *Los Angeles Times* and in other forums. Spillane, then at the critical nadir of his career, rewarded her with love and loyalty. At a Westinghouse-sponsored party following their joint appearance on Mike Wallace's *P.M. East* in the fall of 1961, he arrived escorting an aging ex–burlesque queen but excused himself at the door and headed straight to Rand. Grinning mischievously, he told her that, if their lives had been different, he would have wanted *her* to be his lady friend. She threw back her head and laughed; she loved flirtatious behavior and didn't get enough of it. They formed a mutual admiration society that pleased them both. After she died, he said, "Ayn Rand and I, we don't have to shrug. We can carry that weight," and, "We were friends. That's the biggest thing I can say."

Her public adoption of the flamboyantly anti-intellectual Spillane— a dashing Irishman who could have doubled for Guts Regan in *The Night of January 16th*—was yet another instance of Rand's combining the courageous with the contrarian. She said she wanted, and for many reasons deserved, to be taken seriously as a novelist and thinker and was surely shrewd enough to know that she did not help her cause by writing in the *Los Angeles Times* that Spillane was a victim of "vicious injustice on the part of the 'intellectuals.' " Like her legend building and her combativeness toward influential critics ("moral cannibals," she publicly called them), her support of Spillane seemed tailor-made to tempt the William F. Buckleys and the Granville Hickses to make fun of her. They rarely resisted.

Privately, she welcomed and assisted a young woman named Lisette Glarner, who was the grown daughter of her first cousin and childhood playmate Vera Guzarchik, to whom Rand had sent food and clothing after the war. When Lisette arrived in New York from Lyon, France, to study English, the novelist dispensed cookies, tea, and small gifts, and when Vera proposed a visit, Rand paid for her hotel. Neither Vera nor Lisette was interested in philosophy, but they were deeply impressed by their American cousin's fame, glamour, and hospitality. She enjoyed them, too. After Vera returned to France, Rand wrote that she missed her. A decade later, Rand's youngest sister, Nora, would locate Rand and also pay a visit, with very different results. Yet until old age, Rand could be warm and gracious when she chose to be.

At the same time, she shied away from meeting more accomplished men and women, particularly authors; her literary mission accomplished, her social reticence returned. In the late 1950s and early 1960s, Joan Kennedy Taylor hosted a radio program called *The World of Books* on an educational radio station in New York. When Vladimir Nabokov's novel *Lolita* shocked the nation in the summer of 1958, Taylor asked Rand for advice about whether to interview the author on her program. To the younger woman's surprise, Rand didn't comment on Nabokov's lurid subject matter or abstract literary style but instead said, wistfully, "Oh, Nabokov! If you do interview him, please ask him how his sister is! She was once my best friend." It was a remarkable moment of nostalgia for the characteristically forward-looking Rand. Yet she made no effort to see Nabokov, although he was a professor of Russian at Cornell and visited New York a number of times to promote *Lolita*. And she never contacted his sister Olga, who was living openly in Prague. "She was very, um, cautious about being identified," said Taylor. "She was afraid of being on some kind of [secret Soviet] list and being found." She remained wary of Soviet surveillance well into the 1970s.

A year or two after the Nabokov incident, Albert Mannheimer turned up in New York, apparently at Rand's suggestion, for the purpose of entering into psychotherapy with Branden. In the previous dozen years, Mannheimer had largely faded from public view. He had written one screenplay (*Bloodhounds of Broadway*) and co-authored an unproduced play (*Stalin Allee,* a comedy about Soviet life). In his view—and, no doubt, Rand's—he was a failure. His emotional troubles had become incapacitating, he confided to his estranged friend in a letter praising *Atlas Shrugged*. In a return letter, she recommended the therapeutic skills of Branden. Mannheimer arrived from Hollywood appearing anxious, stiff, and visibly frightened of his former mentor, and after a number of sessions with Branden he returned to Los Angeles, having seen almost nothing of Rand. He went on to write episodes of the television series *Gidget* and *The Flying Nun*. In 1972, he fatally shot himself, leaving behind a widow and three children. Rand seemed unable to grieve his death. She shook her head ruefully and said, "Too bad," recalled Joan Blumenthal. Mannheimer had long ago ceased to live by her principles or share her point of view. As with Paterson, to her he had practically ceased to exist.

In the ordeal of her own depression, she let other people slip away. She saw little of Frances and Henry Hazlitt, partly because they remained on friendly terms with William F. Buckley, and she broke with them completely after Hazlitt published his classic book, *The Foundations of Morality*, in 1964. The book's defense of utilitarian ethics—"the greatest good for the greatest number"—struck her as a betrayal of both capitalist individualism and herself. She never had a good word to say about him after that. In late 1958, she, Peikoff, and the Brandens dropped in on Ludwig von Mises's celebrated NYU seminar; a regular student remembered the sensation she created with her wide black hat, flowing cape, and trailing entourage. She also accepted an invitation to attend Mises's eightieth-birthday party in the fall of 1961. Otherwise, she saw little of the elderly economist and his wife. Some old friends disappointed or even horrified her: Her "best" California business conservative, William Mullendore, fell under the influence of a libertarian mystic and LSD aficionado named Gerald Heard and, along with Leonard Read, Thaddeus Ashby, and others, took psychedelics and frolicked at Bohemian Grove. ("LSD steps up our voltage and frequency," wrote Mullendore, the electric-company president. "To use the new vision thus made available one must be able to 'plug in.'") Ashby, having returned to California with a degree from Harvard, was editing a quasi-religious libertarian magazine called *Faith and Freedom;* no doubt that sealed his fate with Rand. Yet he continued to think of her as the twentieth century's most important philosopher. "Whenever I wrote anything" in the following decades, he said in his eighties, "I tried to slip in her name." She never joined the influential Mont Pelerin Society, an annual free-market think tank, and she shunned the old J. B. Matthews crowd, many of whom now wrote for *National Review.*

Even as old bonds loosened, however, professional good tidings continued to arrive. In the spring of 1958, *Atlas Shrugged* was nominated for a National Book Award, along with a dozen other distinguished novels of 1957, including James Agee's *A Death in the Family,* John Cheever's *The Wapshot Chronicle,* and Nabokov's second novel in English, *Pnin,* about an awkward but endearing Russian émigré professor teaching in an American college. Although she lost to Cheever, she attended the awards ceremony and enjoyed herself amid a thousand other literary guests, recalled Joan Kennedy Taylor, who was with her on that evening. In December 1958, Random House published a handsome new hardbound edition of We the Living, with an introduction by the author and her extensive revisions, which muted both her youthful Nietzscheanism and her master-slave eroticism in service of her mature image. In 1960, New American Library (NAL) published We the Living in paperback, and by 2004 her first novel had three million copies in print. The same year, NAL issued Atlas Shrugged as a triple-sized paperback, complete with a bound-in advertising reply card for NBI lectures. The book, at that time the most expensive paperback ever sold at ninety-five cents, went through seven printings in its first eighteen months. There was now no fully developed work by Ayn Rand that wasn't in demand, and in the fall of 1961, NAL republished Anthem.

The NBI reply cards in Atlas Shrugged worked. Requests for information about the lecture series came pouring in from all over the United States and Canada, and even from abroad. Demand reached such a pitch that in 1960 Barbara and Nathaniel launched what he called the NBI tape-transcription service, which distributed reel-to-reel recordings of the New York lectures to remote locations, beginning with Los Angeles and Chicago, then expanding to Philadelphia, Boston, San Francisco, Seattle, and elsewhere. In Toronto, Branden's sister Florence Hirschfeld ran the program from the finished basement of her home. Like other far-flung NBI tape representatives, she gathered friends and, through local newspaper ads featuring Rand's name and the titles of her books, recruited interested strangers. Participants arrived once a week to sit in straight chairs in front of a large tape player; in Toronto as elsewhere, between thirty and one hundred people showed up to listen, each paying half the New York rate, or thirty-five dollars per course of lectures. The physical tapes and a percentage of the money went back to the New York office, at that time located in the Brandens' apartment on East Thirty-fifth Street. NBI also published and distributed pamphlets and books, furnished speakers and material to Ayn Rand clubs, gave readings of Rand's plays around the country, and distributed recordings of the plays. Later, Branden wrote proudly of having aided Rand's transformation from an undervalued novelist to a systematic philosopher, adding that the repeated appearance of their names in NBI newspaper ads across the country added to her fame while initiating his. For him, and for Barbara, Objectivism became a full-time occupation as well as a personal mission.

In the end, Rand later said, it was the buzz and growing influence of the NBI organization, along with Nathaniel's attentions and his optimism, that fueled her recovery from depression. As little as she had believed in the value of a formal lecture service, or seen much promise in Branden's early students, two things about NBI surprised her. First, she noticed that students, even the dull ones, were profiting from her books and Branden's instruction to become "infinitely more rational" than they had been. Second, she saw that her protégé and his wife were creating an unexpected new avenue by which, she thought, ideas could infiltrate a corrupt culture: from the middle class upward, instead of from the intellectual class down, as in Russia and, indeed, among leftists in the United States. With NBI, she saw her philosophy taking root "in a way I did not know." The "whole enormous response to Nathan gave me a preview of what can be done with a culture," she said in 1961. "Seeing [him] start on a shoestring, with the whole intellectual atmosphere against him, standing totally alone and establishing an institution: that was an enormous, crucial, concrete example of what can be done."

By the spring of 1961, she had emerged from her depression. She began to look outward again and to see issues and causes to which she wanted to apply her knowledge and her gifts. But in some ways she never fully recovered—either her sense of purpose or her control over an unstable emotional life. "I hate bitterness," she said to Branden, but she remained bitter. "If only I didn't feel such loathing," she said. "If only there was someone to respect and admire." But there was no one, and aside from Cyrus, Victor Hugo, Cyrano de Bergerac, Frank, Branden, Aristotle, and the Founding Fathers, perhaps there never had been.

Fifty years after Rand had quieted the ache she felt following the critical reception of *Atlas Shrugged,* an interviewer asked Branden whether she would have been satisfied by recognition from a group of literary and philosophical equals, as she had said she would. "I'm inclined to think, in the end, no," he answered, reflecting. "It is inconceivable to me that I would have said this twenty or thirty years ago—I wouldn't have said it— but to me, looking back, I think she felt too sorry for herself in certain ways." After a silence, he added, "I find myself thinking about certain actors and actresses who have received just about every award it's possible to receive from the entertainment industry and who remain self-doubting and feel underappreciated. And you wonder what it would take to make them feel adequately appreciated." In this, too, Rand predicted her own future in the character of Kay Gonda, in *Ideal*.

Perhaps now not even Branden could make her feel fully "visible." But she turned to him, certain that he could.

FOURTEEN

ACCOUNT OVERDRAWN

1962–1967

It does not matter that only a few in each generation will grasp and achieve the full reality of man's proper stature—and that the rest will betray it. . . . The rest are no concern of mine; it is not me or The Fountainhead *that they will betray: it is their own souls.*

—Introduction to the twenty-fifth-
anniversary edition of *The Fountainhead*, 1968

As her vigor returned, so did her fighting spirit. She went back on the college lecture circuit and took the Brandens with her. Speaking in opposition to most of the political and ethical ideas of the day, she became a symbol of contrarian idealism and defiance to student audiences across the country.

In February 1960, she was invited to give the annual lecture in the Yale Law School's prestigious Challenge series. In a car on the way to New Haven, she scribbled the final details of a slightly expanded version of "Faith and Force: Destroyers of the Modern World," her speech for the evening. She was nervous. By chance, the New Haven Symphony Orchestra was performing elsewhere on campus, and the Yale Bulldogs hockey team was playing a home game. Since she thought of Yale as a breeding ground for liberals, she was afraid she would be speaking to an empty auditorium. To her surprise, and Yale's, the flyer tacked to the law-school bulletin board attracted the largest audience in the history of the Yale series; the overflow was so great that the school placed loudspeakers in the building entryway and on two upper floors. During the question-and-answer period, one member of the audience shouted from the balcony, "Under your system, who will take care of the janitors?" She sang out, "Young man: the janitors!" and the hall erupted in laughter. She spoke to the students in the same encouraging tone she had taken with Nathaniel and Barbara in 1950. "Don't give up too easily," she told them. "Don't sell out your life. If you make an effort to inquire on your own, you will find that it is not necessary to give up and [that] the allegedly power-ful monster[s] of collectivism and convention will run like rat[s] at the first sign of a human step." She was several times interrupted by ap-plause and each time smiled shyly and raised her hand to wave. *Time* summarized her thesis but left out some of her most provocative state-ments ("Do not confuse altruism with kindness, good will or respect for the rights of others. These are not primaries, but consequences . . . The issue is whether you *do* or do *not* have the right to exist *without* giving [a beggar] a dime," she declaimed) and omitted a revealing anecdote about a fracas that broke out between Barbara Branden and a law-school student. At a ceremonial dinner before the lecture, the student, a mem-ber of the reception committee, had asked Barbara if she represented "a photographic ideal" of *Atlas Shrugged,* presumably implying that her slender figure and bearing were a purposeful evocation of Dagny Taggart. After the lecture, when the student asked Rand a question from the floor, Barbara jumped from her seat in the front row and publicly ac-cused him of having insulted her at dinner, *Time*'s reporter noted in an unpublished draft. "The bantering back and forth was getting nowhere when the chairman of the event broke in and suggested the dispute be settled privately," he wrote. Not surprisingly, perhaps, some of Rand's ad-herents had begun to emulate her irascibility and pride.

Notwithstanding *Time*'s irreverent report, intermittently, at least, Rand said she enjoyed speaking in front of mixed and liberal audiences. (At other times, she said that she hated speaking and "did it only for the cause.") She told one large gathering in Boston that in the 1930s she had envied the socialists' and New Dealers' ability to argue from principle; the conservatives of the day did nothing but mouth worn-out bromides from an earlier era. "As an advocate of reason, freedom, individualism, and capitalism," she announced, "I seek to address myself to men of the intellect—wherever such may still be found—and I believe that more of them may be found among the former 'liberals' than the present 'conservatives.' " At Princeton, in a lecture called "Conservatism: An Obituary," she took on the Right directly. Identifying herself not as a conservative but as a "radical for capitalism," she spoke scornfully of the Buckleyites who, she said, were moral traitors for refusing to admit that free-market capitalism, not God or religion, had caused a century of American progress and prosperity. In November 1960, she was invited back to Yale for a second lecture. She called her speech "For the New Intellectual," a name that would become the title of her first nonfiction book. This time, Yale thought it was prepared for a large crowd, but nearly twice as many students, professors, and visitors tried to crowd into her lecture as the hall could hold. She addressed an overflow audience in Ferris Booth Hall at Columbia University, which the copy editor Bertha Krantz attended. Krantz later told an interviewer, "That's when I was struck by the number of students who were—just *worshipped* her. You could see it."

Largely as a result of her speeches, the 1960s solidified her fame as a quixotic, tenacious, theatrically inflammatory social thinker. She traveled the country, lecturing to large, often unruly audiences. She gave major addresses at the University of Michigan, Boston University, Brown, Purdue, Johns Hopkins, West Point, Hunter, Adelphi, Syracuse, Sarah Lawrence, and MIT. In 1961 at the University of Wisconsin, she gave a lecture entitled "The Objectivist Ethics." "What is morality, or ethics?" she asked the crowd. "It is a code of values to guide man's choices and actions," she answered. Quoting Galt's speech, she listed Objectivism's three cardinal values, which together provide the means for human beings to live and thrive independently. These are reason, purpose, and self-esteem. Reason—or more broadly, consciousness—is man's "only source of knowledge," she told the audience, but is a matter of free will; people can choose to engage it or turn it off. Purpose is the choice of the kind of happiness a person decides to pursue. And self-esteem is the "inviolate confidence that [a man's] mind is competent to think and that his person is worthy of happiness." She listed corresponding virtues, which she explained were behavioral traits needed to achieve a life of independence: rationality (knowing that nothing can alter the facts), productiveness (the means by which thought and work sustain life), and pride (seeking to earn the right to hold oneself as one's most important value, which she also called "moral ambitiousness"). She defined happiness as the consciousness of having achieved one's values. As for the pursuit of heedless pleasure, which her critics frequently accused her of promoting, she scoffed at it as a negative value—an unthinking person's way of finding momentary relief from a chronic state of terror, à la Lillian Rearden in *Atlas Shrugged*. Other individualistic, entrepreneurial virtues included integrity, justice, and honesty, the last of which she described as the consciousness that "one must never attempt to fake reality in any manner."

A few weeks after the Wisconsin speech, she presented the first of eighteen annual lectures at the Ford Hall Forum, a famous stronghold of free speech on the Northeastern University campus in Boston. The speeches typically began at seven thirty in the evening, but fans who had traveled from around the world to hear her—from as far away as Africa— would line up starting in midmorning (or, as the decade progressed, even the night before) and exchange ideas, news, and gossip all day long. Followers met future spouses, employers, and business associates in line and at postlecture parties. Because, beginning in the mid-1960s, the event took place in April, it became known as "the Objectivist Easter." Meanwhile, Ayn Rand clubs sprang up on campuses from Harvard and MIT to Stanford. She hosted regular syndicated talk-radio programs on WKCR-FM at Columbia University and on WBAI-FM, New York's quirky "free speech" station. Some of her university lectures were carried live on the National Educational Radio Network, the forerunner of NPR. In all cases, her cool intelligence and passionate commitment to ideas as a life-and-death matter turned young adversaries into grudging admirers. Throughout the 1960s, students came to jeer but stayed to listen, then bought her books and joined her movement.

While her underlying message assailed the communitarian spirit that took hold in the 1960s, her specific positions on issues of the day were often classically liberal, as well as farsighted and brave. As an extension of her commitment to individual rights, she consistently championed minority civil rights and equality of opportunity between the sexes (stopping short of the idea of a woman as president, since she believed that every woman should properly worhip a man, or men). Condemning the first use of force in any context, she opposed the Vietnam War long before her contemporaries did. And she spoke plainly and forcefully against state governments' bans on abortion. "Abortion is a moral right—which should be left to the sole discretion of the woman

Nathaniel Branden at age eighteen,
a few months before Rand met him.

Rand and O'Connor,
Chatsworth, 1951.

O'Connor, Barbara
Branden, Nathaniel
Branden, and Rand at
the Brandens' wedding
in New York, February
1953.

The Collective at the wedding of Nathaniel Branden's sister Elayne and Harry Kalberman, April 1955. From left: Joan Mitchell, Alan Greenspan, Nathaniel Branden, Barbara Branden, Leonard Peikoff, Elayne Kalberman, Harry Kalberman, Rand, O'Connor, and Allan Blumenthal.

Rand and Branden in the mid-1950s, during the early years of their affair.

Barbara Branden, late 1960s.

Publicity photograph for *Atlas Shrugged,* taken in Bennett Cerf's Random House office on Madison Avenue, 1957.

Rand greeting admirers at the National Book Awards ceremony, 1958. That year, *Atlas Shrugged* was nominated for a National Book Award in fiction.

Barbara, Nathaniel, Ayn, and Frank at Lewis and Clark College in Oregon, 1963.

Rand, Nathaniel, and Barbara at the 1962 wedding of Larry Scott and Patrecia Gullison. A year or so later, Nathaniel and Patrecia began an affair.

Standing in front of the New York Federal Reserve Bank, wearing her gold dollar-sign brooch, in 1967.

(*Above*)
Mrs. Rose Greenspan, Gerald Ford, Alan Greenspan, Rand, and Frank after Greenspan was sworn in as chairman of the Council of Economic Advisers, 1974.

(*Right*)
One of several cartoons of Rand by Edward Sorel, this one from *The New Yorker,* February 14–21, 2005.

In New York, 1970s.

On the balcony overlooking the central hall in Grand Central Terminal, photographed by Theo Westenberger for *Look*, 1979.

A recently discovered 1961 portrait by Frank. "Her eyes might say, 'Come to bed and dominate me,'" wrote Nathaniel Branden when he saw the portrait in 2007. "But of course if you obey her, who is the master of whom?" Speaking of Frank, another acquaintance said, "So he knew her after all."

involved," she told an audience of fifteen hundred people at the Ford Hall Forum, five years before the Supreme Court decided *Roe v. Wade* in 1973 and in a state, Massachusetts, in which abortion was then illegal. "An embryo *has no rights.* Rights do not pertain to a *potential,* only to an *actual* being," she declared. When she opposed popular movements, her reasoning was original and often, in its peculiar way, progressive. She condemned the Free Speech Movement at Berkeley in 1964 as much for its threat and use of force in taking over administration buildings and its attempted subversion of countervailing opinion (that is, free speech) as for its original goal of overturning a prohibition against political organizing on campus. She was always worth hearing.

In January 1962 Branden persuaded her to launch a four-page monthly bulletin called *The Objectivist Newsletter* (later, in a digest-sized format, *The Objectivist*) to spread her message to all those students and others whose curiosity had been aroused by her books and speeches. It was remarkably professional looking, and it published most of her original nonfiction throughout the 1960s. She and Branden incorporated it as a jointly owned business venture outside the NBI umbrella, which was held and controlled by Branden alone. By contractual agreement, they co-wrote and co-edited the publication in equal shares and split the profit; at a minimum, each was required to write one serious article or essay for every issue, although Branden later denied it.

Rand had never enjoyed expository writing. In the 1940s, she wrote in her journals that such work bored her, primarily because its purpose was not to create a world of her own but to help others to learn. But after thirteen years of shoehorning ideas into the thoughts and speech of characters in dramatic situations, she was finding it difficult to work on a new novel. She wasn't convinced "that there's a human race out there and that the struggle is worth it," she told Branden. Writing for her ideal fiction reader was hard; writing for the newsletter turned out to be surprisingly pleasurable. Compared to constructing a novel, composing essays was child's play. All she had to focus on were clarity and logic. Thus she entered into a new career as a cultural polemicist, almost against her will; without the pages of the newsletter to fill, she might have written less. Throughout the Kennedy and Johnson years, the civil rights movement, the Vietnam War, and all the social tumult of the late 1960s, she published scores of both cranky and brilliant essays, many suffused with the anti-war, old libertarian spirit of the Isabel Paterson–

era American Right: she wrote on the absolute nature of individual rights, on the proper limits of government, on the virtues of capitalism and the evils of economic control by a coercive state. Her often bitter rhetoric notwithstanding, many of these are worth reading decades later, if only for their clarity of language and purity of point of view. In "The Ethics of Emergencies," for example, she warns against defining national emergencies too broadly or, worse, making them permanent, so that everyone is expected to sacrifice his liberties all the time. In "Man's Rights," "The Nature of Government," "The Anatomy of Compromise," and "The Roots of War," she combined her old, defiant dedication to radical individualism with shrewd demonstrations of how to deconstruct political speech and uproot hidden agendas—in other words, how to think one's way through government propaganda.

Branden's essays for the newsletter and its successor publications helped him to refine his core ideas on psychology, especially on the nature of romantic love and self-esteem, which would form the backbone of his future best-selling books. Alan Greenspan and Martin Anderson, later a member of the Nixon administration and an advisor to Ronald Reagan, occasionally added their views on economic issues, including a defense of the gold standard by Greenspan that, in combination with his lifelong admiration for Rand, came back to haunt him when he was named chairman of the Council of Economic Advisers under Gerald Ford and chairman of the Federal Reserve Board under Ronald Reagan. (Nixon had divorced the dollar from the gold standard in 1971, completing a separation begun by FDR.) He never lost his respect for gold. "I have always harbored a nostalgia for the gold standard's inherent price stability," he wrote in his 2007 memoir, *The Age of Turbulence*. Other scholarly young Rand devotees, including Peikoff, Hessen, Reisman, and Barbara Branden, contributed essays on problems in philosophy and history, book reviews, and commentary on current events. There were few or no outside contributors.

She, her supporters, and *The Objectivist Newsletter* campaigned for Senator Barry Goldwater's presidential bid in 1964, hopeful that the most conservative candidate since Calvin Coolidge might at last acquire the authority to roll back FDR's social-welfare legislation. After Willkie, she had never publicly supported a political candidate, but she endorsed Goldwater on a number of occasions, both during the Republican primaries (where he was running against Nelson A. Rockefeller) and in the general election against Lyndon B. Johnson. Inspired by her, two dozen of her friends and admirers formed the New York Young Republican Club to support him and launched a magazine, *Persuasion,* to explain his anti–New Deal views to voters. "We thought he wasn't doing a good job of explaining himself," said Joan Kennedy Taylor, who helped to found the club and magazine. On the night before one famous Goldwater rally in Madison Square Garden, Rand even wrote an unsolicited, reportedly masterful speech for him. "It made his points in his voice, but it was tremendously clear, and even used the concept of God as he would have used it," said an NBI staff member who typed the speech. On the day before the rally, Barbara took the document to Goldwater's temporary office at the Garden and handed it to a campaign staffer. Either Goldwater didn't receive the speech in time to use it, or he preferred his own rhetoric, whose generalities frustrated Rand. The imprecision of his language, Rand thought, made his enemies' attacks easier. In November, he lost to Johnson, in part because of the infamous "Daisy" television ad, which more than hinted that the outspokenly anti-Communist Arizonan might start a nuclear war with Russia. To the readers of *The Objectivist Newsletter* Rand wrote, "In former campaigns Republicans [have] been guilty of compromise, evasion, cowardice, 'me-too-ism.' Barry Goldwater was not; he had courage, frankness, integrity—and *nothing to say.*" She compared his public speeches to headlines running above blank newspaper columns. What he needed was what every other conservative politician and every citizen and businessman had always needed: a consistent philosophy.

More surprising, perhaps, is that Rand, through the activism of some of her closest acolytes, helped to end the military draft that she so hated. Her mid-1960s legal watchdog, Hank Holzer, and his wife and law partner Erika Holzer, along with Robert Hessen, Leonard Peikoff, Martin Anderson, writer David Dawson, and other Young Republican Club members filed legal briefs, wrote plays and essays, and held conferences to raise public opposition to the draft as an infringement of the right to life. Anderson, already a young star in the academic world, joined Richard M. Nixon's 1968 presidential campaign and persuaded him to include a promise to end the draft in his platform. Nixon, a Quaker, agreed. Once elected in the race against Hubert Humphrey, Nixon appointed Anderson to serve on a commission to study an all-volunteer army, and a volunteer army became law in 1973, two years before the American withdrawal from Vietnam. It was the first time the nation had been without a draft since FDR reinstated one in 1940, in preparation for America's entry into World War II. Rand never wrote about her indirect role in this achievement, but she did endorse Nixon in 1968, partly on the basis of his opposition to the draft.

Perhaps the purest, least rhetorical, and hardest-hitting public statement of her views appeared in a March 1964 *Playboy* interview. With Alvin Toffler, who in 1970 would publish *Future Shock*, asking the questions, the text crackled with maverick intelligence. Explaining her choice of the dollar sign as an emblem in *Atlas Shrugged* and a trademark decoration on her person, she said, "As the symbol of the currency of a free country, [it] is the symbol of a free mind." Asked whether she thought of the cross as a symbol of torture, as she had been quoted as saying, she replied, "I do regard the cross as the symbol of the sacrifice of the ideal to the non-ideal. . . . That is torture." Tacitly critiquing Nietzsche, she explained that Objectivist ethics required not only that a man not sacrifice himself to others but also, and equally importantly, that he not sacrifice others to himself. The interview, which, in a departure from usual magazine procedure, Rand was permitted to edit and rewrite, reached two and a half million people, mostly men, and brought countless new readers to her novels and nonfiction.

Her speeches and essays were eventually collected in half a dozen slim volumes that have never been out of print. In the spring of 1961, Cerf published the first of these, *For the New Intellectual: The Philosophy of Ayn Rand*. The material wasn't new: it was a collection of monologues from her four novels, including Kira's speech to Andrei on the value of individual life in *We the Living* and John Galt's radio address, along with a title essay based on the lecture she had given at Yale. The essay is a mixture of historical parable and madcap fairy tale. In it, she attributed the suffering of mankind to two eternally recurring archetypes she called Attila and the Witch Doctor. At different points in history, she wrote, a Witch Doctor might present himself as a shaman, a priest, a popular demagogue, a medicine man, a professor, or a self-serving literary critic who weakened a nation's spirit by dispensing self-sacrificial bromides and promises of a better life to come. After the Witch Doctor had prepared the way with sermons, Attila, or the tyrant, swept in to pillage and enslave the faithful. And this had been the pattern in every age and culture until the establishment of the American Constitution. The essay announced her almost fanatical crusade against the eighteenth-century

German philosopher Immanuel Kant, whom for the rest of her life she blamed for the end of the Enlightenment and the triumph of moral relativism over reason. (Henceforth, she would refer to Kant as a monster and "the chief destroyer of the modern world.")

To stop the nightmare, she offered a new morality, that of the "Producer," and a "New Intellectual," modeled on the philosophical businessmen she had tried and failed to mold in the post-Willkie 1940s. If only everyone would embrace reason, self-reliance, and unregulated markets, she implied, the West could usher in an age of freedom, individualism, productivity, wealth, and peace—and do so without relying on religious faith or the use of force except in self-defense, Rand's basic formula for defeating tyranny.

By now, a new book by Ayn Rand, even a small book, created a stir. *Newsweek* sent a reporter to inform readers about a typical night at NBI. One hundred or so "new intellectuals stalked solemnly into [an assembly room at] the Hotel Roosevelt," NBI's new and larger New York meeting place, wrote the *Newsweek* reporter. These well-groomed men and women listened "raptly," for three hours, to Branden "droning" on, before Rand arrived onstage to answer questions, when the energy level rose with a rush. She didn't coddle the audience. When a brash young man asked a question the reporter couldn't hear, she labeled him "a cheap fraud" and moved on. Her admirers remained calm, the reporter wrote, taking it for granted that anyone who misconstrued or disagreed with her ideas "must be motivated by villainy alone." He likened her to the early twentieth-century preacher Aimee Semple McPherson in her power to "hypnotize a live audience" and quoted one of her adherents sounding particularly loopy: "Her books are so good that most people should not be allowed to read them." Finally, "although she had a glare [that] would wilt a cactus," the reporter hailed her as "a welcome streak of color in the world of authorship." There exists "no label for Ayn Rand," he concluded, "unless it is the valuable and honorable one of born eccentric." He saw little that was colorful in her "foremost apostle" or her band of "militantly non-beatnik" admirers.

Not to be outdone, later that year *The Saturday Evening Post* published an unusually lengthy profile of her and her movement called "The Curious Cult of Ayn Rand." The opening photograph showed the literary lion standing in front of the twin lions at the Forty-second Street entrance to the New York Public Library, her eyes huge, bright, and probing, a cigarette holder in her hand. In a photograph on the next page, an unidentified NBI student stood cradling a massive open copy of *Atlas Shrugged* as reverently as if it were a hymnal. Like *Newsweek*, the *Post* took Rand and her large following with a helping of irony, but without the usual venom. The writer, John Kobler, merely wondered how she had charmed so many young people into quoting John Galt as religiously as "clergymen quote Matthew, Mark, Luke and John." She was "the free enterprise system's Joan of Arc, with a Yankee dollar [for] her Cross of Lorraine." It was a description she might have relished a few years earlier, but by now she made it a point never to read what was written about her in the press.

In *Esquire*'s review of *For the New Intellectual*, the wryly subversive Gore Vidal called her philosophy "nearly perfect in its immorality." But what really galled him was the same issue that had captured the attention of *Newsweek* and the *Post*: the size of her audience. "In my campaign for the House [of Representatives in 1960]," he grumbled, "she was the one writer people knew and talked about." The *Wall Street Journal* echoed the alarm, warning upper-crust parents and corporate executives that their sons and daughters were sitting around "in booths in college-town snack shops" arguing about her work with the same seriousness that earlier generations had brought to discussions of Thorstein Veblen and Karl Marx.

Unfortunately, Rand did read Sidney Hook's review of *For the New Intellectual* in *The New York Times Book Review* on April 9, 1961, and for a number of reasons it provoked a weeks-long fit of rage. One was Professor Hook's allegation that she had misread Aristotle. The distinguished philosopher and historian at NYU was making a point that Isabel Paterson had tried to make years earlier: "A is A" implies nothing, he wrote, other than a logical method to test the consistency of philosophical observations and ideas and cannot be used as the basis for a code of ethics. He disagreed that free minds cannot exist without free markets and surmised that her rhetoric drove her into corners she did not really wish to occupy. For example, if "all the evils popularly ascribed to capitalism" had actually been caused by government interference, as she asserted in the book, then what accounted for the horrors of nineteenth-century child labor, which the government had remedied? (Rand answered that if it weren't for the jobs that capitalism had created in the first place, the children would have starved to death.) As to her blanket rejection of altruism, he wrote, "I am confident that even at some danger to herself Miss Rand would not rush out of a burning building and leave a helpless child behind. She refuses to call such an action unselfish because she falls back on the truism that every voluntary choice is a choice *of* the self, which she mistakes as an act *for* [the] self." He ended with a gibe: Although a writer need not be a professional philosopher to write an interesting book about philosophy, substituting indignation for analysis was not the way to do it.

Another reason Rand was incensed by this review was that Hook had once been a protégé of John Dewey, who had provided a model for the slippery Dr. Simon Pritchett in *Atlas Shrugged*. Hook also was a Marxist, though an unequivocal opponent of Russian Communism. He had been Barbara Branden's master's-thesis advisor in the early 1950s and at the time of the review was supervising Leonard Peikoff's progress toward his Ph.D., which examined Aristotle's law of noncontradiction in classical philosophy. Both Barbara and Peikoff were extremely fond of Hook, and he of them. Recognizing this, Rand exempted them from challenging him in the tumult that followed. But the rest of the inner circle and the NBI network were expected to denounce him as dishonest and corrupt.

Nathaniel Branden led the way. After the *Newsweek* profile, he had used his large NBI mailing list to call on all students of Objectivism to write rebuttal letters to the editor and cancel their subscriptions. In response to Hook's review, he constructed a point-by-point refutation in the contemptuous tone and percussive rhythms of his mentor. Because the finished piece was far too long to appear in print as a letter to the editor, he raised money to run it as a full-page ad in *The New York Times Book Review* of May 28. In three dense columns, he upbraided Hook for even trying "to state what Miss Rand's ideas are," let alone argue against them, and suggested that the highly respected scholar go back to school to study the history of ethics. Rand loved this kind of intellectual combat, especially when she was being aggressively defended by Branden. "It was almost worth Hook's review," she told Nathaniel, to watch him go to war on her behalf. And he was proud of his ability to drive enemies from the castle gates.

Branden later said bitterly that since she, too, had come to expect him "to protect her from the world," his "failure was that I was not in my fifties." By this he meant that he was not experienced or strong enough for her to lean on without damage to himself. But even as he helped her, he also benefited. In 1962, Bennett Cerf agreed to publish a small book adapted from a series of radio talks Branden had given on the art of *Atlas Shrugged*, which he called *Who Is Ayn Rand?* in homage to "Who is John Galt?" in the epic novel. Barbara contributed a biographical essay that revealed, for the first time since the 1930s, that Rand had been born and grew up in prerevolutionary Russia. Not surprisingly, both parts of the book presented the author exactly as she saw herself: as a unique creative force compelled to struggle against a crass, corrupt, unthinking, and indifferent world in order to write and guide her masterpieces into print.

Astonishingly, even this modest volume, so adulatory that the Brandens later disavowed it, sold well, going through several printings and proving that popular interest in Rand was practically unlimited. On a personal note, preparing the book allowed the maestro to spend months working with Branden to fine-tune the texts of his radio scripts for publication, and she grew closer to him, happier, less critical, and more satisfied than she had been in years. It was the first of a number of honeymoon periods that occurred between them. "She could hardly complain that I was neglecting her when her rival was this book," he later wrote.

If like-mindedness and personal loyalty had always been important to the strong-willed émigré, they positively preoccupied her in the years following her depression. During Saturday-night socials with members of the Collective and their spouses, friends, and younger guests, "enormous enthusiasm was expected for every deed and utterance," Branden told an audience in 1996. She discouraged the kind of probing or "invalid" questions she had been happy to answer in the early 1950s. "Right and wrong, rational and irrational, moral and immoral—those were the words being used all the time," recalled Joan Blumenthal. Rand increasingly judged her votaries' merit on the basis of their "sense of life," or subconscious attitude toward the grandeur and perfectibility of man, and encouraged them to do the same with one another. The correct moral stance, she wrote at about this time, wasn't "Judge not, lest ye be judged" but "Judge, and be prepared to be judged." Said a longtime NBI staff member, "Moral judgments were *required* if you were a moral person. It was terrible." The new emphasis on "sense of life" placed devotees' longings, fears, tastes, sexual impulses—anything—on the table for approval or condemnation. "Most people were walking on eggshells," recalled Henry Holzer, who joined the inner circle as Rand's "intellectual bodyguard," or copyright attorney, in 1962 or 1963. "If you said something that was unknowingly immoral you'd be devastated. She'd look at you with those laser eyes and tell you that you had a lousy 'sense of life.' " Recalled Branden, "Her idea of encouraging a person to be independent is to tell him, in effect, 'Go and think it over—until you see things my way.' " Everything was a matter of philosophical importance, and everyone was morbidly afraid of her disapproval.

True to Rothbard's 1954 prediction, a pallid kind of Stalinization set in. Whenever the leader took a position—against naturalism in novels, abstract art, or, a little later, the student rebellions at Berkeley and elsewhere—her young friends followed suit. A slip of the tongue by an Objectivist who liked Alfred Hitchcock's *Psycho* or secretly didn't like the paintings of one of her favorite (and also, she told people, one of her husband's favorite) contemporary artists, Spanish superrealist José Manuel Capuletti, could bring accusations of mysticism, whim worship, malevolence, or an attitude of "anti-life." If a transgression suggested disloyalty or simply that someone was "not my kind of person," often no amount of prior goodwill made any difference. "She was the Evel Knievel of leaping to conclusions," said Hessen, who himself went through a number of painful episodes. Although she typically forgave isolated lapses, tantrums and purges became more common in the late 1960s.

It was most often Branden who took charge of the denunciation of followers who had strayed, and sometimes he revealed information from his therapy sessions with them. "There was very little psychological privacy in those days," he offered as an explanation to an interviewer in 1999. "Everything that was wrong with anybody or was thought to be wrong was publicly discussed. It was like public knowledge in our whole group." By the early 1960s, he "was constantly denouncing," Barbara recalled, and because he was "everybody's therapist, his denunciation was much more damaging than Ayn's." Those who survived learned to juggle the explicit messages of the Objectivist subculture with the unstated rules: They were expected to practice obedience in the name of reason and embrace loyalty as a road to independence.

The story of Rand's brief friendship with a forty-year-old Brooklyn College professor of philosophy named John Hospers is a poignant case in point. She and he, a rising academic thinker, met during the spring of 1960, when she gave the lecture titled "Faith and Force" at Brooklyn College. Unfamiliar with her work, he was thunderstruck by her speech

and invited her to lunch on campus. She enjoyed the lunch and reciprocated by inviting him to a lecture at NBI. In the meantime, he read *Atlas
Shrugged* and was "bowled over" and "wiped out" by the book. She asked
him to visit her at her apartment, and he began to do so every two or
three weeks, usually arriving at eight in the evening and staying until four
or five in the morning. The two talked endlessly about *Atlas Shrugged,*
which Hospers praised in depth and in detail, and about politics, literature, and art, her opposition to the draft, her withering disapproval of
government intervention in a market economy, and her strong views on
determinism and free will. They analyzed traditional ethical conundrums, such as, "If you had a choice between driving over a stranger or
your own dog, what would you do?" (He didn't remember her answer, except that it wasn't to hit the stranger.) On the night before he was to turn
in the manuscript of his first book, *Human Conduct,* he carried it to her
apartment and they talked until morning. As the clock struck eight, she
made him breakfast and waved him off to his publisher's office, calling,
"Good premises!" instead of "Good-bye," which deeply touched him, he
recalled. Hospers, who became the first Libertarian Party candidate for
president of the United States in 1972 and was the author of the classic
primer *Libertarianism,* liked to recall that he learned free-market principles at the great woman's knee. He fell in love with the "uncompromising
rigor" of her arguments, her piercing eyes, and her deep Russian voice,
"which could warm you and freeze you by turns," he wrote.

He wasn't always able to make clear to her how her ideas fit in a historical context or introduce her to new concepts. At that period, "She
read almost no philosophy at all," he said, and she gave the impression
that her ideas "had come full-blown from her head, or from the head of
Jove." They had political differences. He, a methodical thinker with
a social conscience, expressed doubt that the freedom to think gave a
majority of people the freedom to shape their lives; a cripple can't will
himself to walk, he argued, or a poor person transcend a lifetime of risk-
averse or self-defeating habits in a day. (She ceded the point about walking but reminded him that with determination people do overcome
seemingly impossible odds and even rise to leadership positions—not
adding, "as I did.") He also argued that truth and falsehood, or good and
evil, cannot always be established with certainty by reason: Additional
facts are sometimes needed to draw conclusions. For example, "All
swans are white" remains true only as long as no one discovers a black

swan; afterward, a new truth must be constructed. Rand agreed that new facts may sometimes create new truths but insisted that fundamental concepts, such as, "A thing cannot act in contradiction to its nature," remain permanently and self-evidently true. Their spirited exchanges resembled those she'd had with Paterson in the 1940s, except that, by this time, Rand's conceptual framework was set and nothing would alter her thinking.

Hospers had the unusual privilege of meeting with her alone. But he also sat in on a number of NBI lectures and even gave one or two himself. At one lecture he attended, on aesthetics, which was his academic specialty, he was almost shouted down when, speaking from the floor, he tried to defend the artistry of William Faulkner and Pablo Picasso, which the speaker had casually "relegated to the scrap-heap." After a few such experiences, he concluded that Rand's movement was overrun with sheep, "shivering, scared children who dared not say the wrong thing lest they incur her wrath," he wrote in a memoir. He said as much to her in a 1961 letter. What do you gain from your followers' "undigested agreement" with you? he asked. Her reply was revealing. " 'Undigested agreement' does not interest or concern me," she answered coldly. "Through all the years I spent formulating my philosophical system, I was looking desperately for 'intelligent agreement' or at least for 'intelligent disagreement.' I found neither. . . . What I am looking for [now] is 'intelligent agreement.' " If she didn't find it, she could go into a rage.

As their friendship entered its second year, Hospers noticed that she lost patience with him quickly. This was especially true after he politely refused to issue a public condemnation of his friend and colleague Sidney Hook. For her, this was disloyalty; she saw the realm of ideas as a battlefield, he observed, where people must continually put their lives and livelihoods at risk. He knew he was supposed to want to join the ranks of the converted; the more time she expended on a person, the more agreement and allegiance she expected. "Any hint of thinking as one formerly had, any suggestion that one had backtracked, was treated with indignation," Hospers later wrote. Even mild criticism—say, about the philosophical imprecision with which she sometimes used important words like "must" and "will"—could send her "to the stratosphere in anger."

The breaking point came at an academic conference held at Harvard

University, at which Hospers arranged for her to speak. She had frequently complained to him that university philosophers paid no attention to her; the annual meeting of the American Society for Aesthetics,
of which he was the program chair, seemed a perfect occasion on which
to begin to remedy the situation. She agreed to speak on the condition
that Hospers be the person appointed to deliver comments on her presentation afterward, in the academic manner. She gave a formal twenty-
minute paper titled "Art as Sense of Life," which was an interesting
meditation on the sources of art in the creator's subconscious evaluation
of the nature of man and his place in the universe. When she sat down,
he rose to perform his part, which was to point out strengths and weaknesses in her argument. According to Barbara, who was present, some
of his comments were sarcastic, "probably out of nervousness at [having
to criticize] her publicly, while she sat listening." To his horror and his
colleagues' outrage, she responded to his remarks by lashing out with a
coarsely worded personal attack on Hospers. In an especially severe instance of cultural tone deafness, perhaps, she assumed that her friend
had deliberately ambushed and betrayed her. She and her retinue of followers swept out of the room and went off to a planned party at her
hotel. Hospers had been invited, too, but when he arrived no one would
speak to him. He had been excommunicated, just like that. He had seen
it happen to others, but never so swiftly, silently, or crushingly, he
thought. He left the hotel and never saw her again. But he mourned her
loss for many years. Three and a half decades after their parting, he remembered his evenings with her as among the most intellectually exhilarating of his life. The memory of her early-morning send-off, "Good
premises!" brought him close to tears every time he thought of it.

  She was far from finished with discarding friends. In late September 1963, she returned in style to Chicago, the city that had introduced
her to American life. A fan named Ed Nash, who managed the Chicago
NBI tape-transcription business, rented a hall at McCormick Place,
then the world's largest exposition center, as the forum for a speech
called "America's Persecuted Minority: Big Business." On a cool, cloudy
Sunday evening she spoke to twenty-five hundred fans, many of whom
had traveled hundreds of miles to hear her. Mimi Sutton and her sister
Marna were there, along with Frank, representing the O'Connor clan.
On Rand's mother's side, Fern Brown, Fern's parents Sam and Minna
Goldberg, Rand's second cousin Burt Stone and his wife, daughter, and

granddaughter were also present, at Rand's invitation. Shortly after she began to speak, there was a bomb scare. Luckily, it was a hoax. But during intermission in the dressing room, she had a moment of panic. Barbara and Nathaniel were busy in an adjacent hallway, and Frank was elsewhere, so Mimi and Marna were soothing her when the Chicago relatives came in. In the hubbub, Burt Stone's granddaughter noticed that Rand's black dress was on inside out, seams and label showing through a sheer chiffon overdress. She wondered if she ought to mention it. But there was no time. Rand greeted Fern, the Goldbergs, and the Stones by holding out her hand: "It was polite but formal, and not warm," Mimi recalled. "She was like a queen on a throne," said Fern. She returned to the stage to a roar of applause and went on to inveigh against political interference in business, specifically the 1890 Sherman Antitrust Act and other antitrust laws. Afterward she, Frank, Frank's nieces, and the Brandens left for a small reception given by Ed Nash and NBI. Although her Chicago relatives disapproved of her philosophy by then, Minna Goldberg still felt slighted at not being asked to the reception. When Burt Stone died two years later and Rand didn't come to the funeral, family communication ceased. Rand never again saw her mother Anna's American cousins.

That weekend, Mimi met the Brandens for the first time. "He was very rude," she said. From her aunt's manner when she spoke about him, Mimi thought she detected a hint that Branden had become "a slave—something she would like," Mimi recalled, without malice, shortly after her aunt's death.

After the following week, Rand did not see Ruth Beebe Hill again, either. The author and the Brandens left Chicago by plane for Portland, Oregon—Rand's first flight. They led two days of campus-wide discussions of her novels at Lewis and Clark College, which was celebrating her work by awarding her an honorary doctorate of arts and letters. Then they headed south to San Francisco and Los Angeles, where Branden was set to deliver the opening lecture of "The Basic Principles of Objectivism" series. His frequent out-of-town appearances were always popular events, but when students learned that Rand was joining him for a question-and-answer session, the response was overwhelming. In Los Angeles, seats in the five-hundred-person lecture hall sold out quickly, and an hour or so before the start of the event another six hundred people tried to push their way into the lobby. The place was so crammed that a janitor called the fire department; the chief, instead of dispersing the crowd, created aisles and kept order, on the condition that he could meet Ayn Rand after the event. The commemoration of her work in Portland, the reverence and raw emotion of the crowds in Chicago and California—these were heady experiences, even for an author accustomed to a following.

A day or two later, she, Frank, and the Brandens drove northwest to the Chatsworth ranch, which none of them had seen since 1951. Their visit was unannounced. Ruth Hill, puttering on the second floor of the Neutra house, heard Frank's voice through an open window, talking to her husband, Buzzy. She rushed downstairs. "Is that really you, Frank? Happiest day!" she called to O'Connor. "Is Ayn with you?" O'Connor looked pained as he said, "Yes. She's coming now." Hill ran to embrace her old friend and burbled, "Are you half as happy to see me as I am to see you, Ayn?" To her surprise, Rand answered stiffly, with her thick Russian accent, "Why should I be?" The problem, it turned out, was that Hill was guilty of an unintended slight. Months earlier, Branden had asked her to become the NBI representative in the San Fernando Valley. Instead of saying yes immediately, she had asked to hear a sample tape. She had not heard Branden lecture, and she didn't believe in asking her acquaintances to pay for something she couldn't personally recommend. Rand viewed this as a betrayal. "You turned down Nathaniel," she shouted at Hill. "You turned down the tapes. You turned me down!" She and her companions walked into the house and remained there while Buzzy talked to Frank about the fields and flowers. By this time, it had long been clear to everyone that the O'Connors were not coming back to live at the ranch. The Hills continued to mail their monthly rent checks to New York, but the friendship was at an end. Hill stuck to her guns: "To this day," she said, forty years later, "I would not sell something I had not sampled." Yet for the rest of her life the spirited ethnographer, writer, and mountain climber missed her friend. Well into her nineties, she continued to give copies of *Anthem, The Fountainhead,* and *Atlas Shrugged* as holiday gifts to people she especially liked.

Rand also broke with Bennett Cerf. She had regarded his public defense of *Atlas Shrugged* as weak, at best, and for years had been displeased by reports that he didn't always take her side in private conversations. As a result, she considered him "a chicken and unloyal," recalled Perry Knowlton, an associate of her agent Alan Collins. When Cerf suggested pub-

lishing a second collection of her essays in October 1963, timed to stimu-
late discussion and book sales during the 1964 election season, she assembled a dozen articles from *The Objectivist Newsletter* along with some
of her major speeches and handed in a manuscript. Cerf was thrilled. Apparently, he hadn't read it yet. When his editors read it, they hit the roof
over an essay that was intended to give the book its title, an inflammatory
critique of the Kennedy administration called "The Fascist New Frontier."
Outrageous by the standards of the day, it likened the economic policies
of Kennedy—for example, increasing the minimum wage and funding
public housing—to Fascism in the 1930s, and Kennedy to Hitler. Her
purpose was to remind Americans of the distinction between socialism
(government ownership of industry, capital, and property), of which she
thought the electorate might approve, and Fascism (government control
of industry and private property for the benefit of favored groups), which
she saw as a hallmark of the New Frontier. Cerf's editors demanded that
Random House refuse to print the essay. Three weeks after heralding the
arrival of the manuscript, Cerf dejectedly told Rand and Perry Knowlton
that the author would have to remove the essay and change the title of
the book.

"He made his decision not to publish without even consulting me,"
Rand complained to Barbara Branden. One day in mid-October, she
marched into his office and reminded him of his promise not to be political, never to censor her, and to publish anything she wrote. He had
been talking about fiction, he pleaded, and asked her, at a minimum, to
remove the passages from Hitler's speeches and change the title of the
essay to something not implicating Kennedy, such as "America's Drift
Toward Fascism." She was adamant in her refusal; her whole point was
to show that the Kennedy Administration's ideology wasn't socialistic, as
people might think, but fascistic.

As he recalled a few years later, she followed him down to the street
from his office, arguing with him while he hailed a taxicab to take him
home to change for dinner. As he climbed into the taxi, she cried,
"You're going to print every word I've written, or I won't let you publish
the book!" He called back, unhappily, "That's that. Get yourself another
publisher."

She did.

She liked New American Library's spirited founder and editor-in-
chief, Victor Weybright, who, in addition to being her paperback pub-

lisher, had contracted to pay an astonishing quarter of a million dollars for the right to publish *To Lorne Dieterling*, the new "unrequited love story" she had begun to outline in late 1957, without ever seeing a proposal or her scanty notes. He agreed to publish the collection. A year later, in December 1964, he released it as an original paperback with a new, almost equally provocative title, *The Virtue of Selfishness*. It sold well, and in 1965 he reissued it in hardback. The firm became Rand's primary publisher and went on to publish and republish her nonfiction collections, the paperback editions of her novels, and her plays until industry mergers finally put an end to the NAL imprint. Until then, year in and year out, from the 1960s to the 1980s, the huge sales of Rand's books paid many of the bills at NAL.

In spite of her friendship with Weybright, NAL wasn't in the same publishing league with Random House, and after Weybright's death in 1974, things went rapidly downhill for Rand. Perry Knowlton had to nag and coax the editors into paying proper attention to her books. His best leverage was the unwritten *To Lorne Dieterling*; because of this and her financial clout, an NAL staffer was, at minimum, always "delegated to Ayn Rand duty," as one editor recalled. "That meant that every nine months to a year you'd have lunch with her—let her know how important she was and listen to her drone on." A second editor added, "She asked me at lunch if I'd be interested in being cast" in a planned TV miniseries of *Atlas Shrugged*. "I thought, 'She's pretty old to be flirting,' but I said, 'That sounds great.' " A senior editor who grew extremely fond of her recalled his anger when a group of his colleagues, including the president of NAL, told him about their having gone together to a dinner party in her apartment without having bothered to read any of her books. When she asked them which of her books they liked best, the president tried to fake it, with predictable success. "That's not funny," the editor told his colleagues. "You've been living off the woman for years!"

By its title alone, *The Virtue of Selfishness* summarized a lifetime of original thinking on the subject of "what I want." It included five essays by Nathaniel Branden as well as fourteen essays and speeches by Rand, of varying degrees of insight and common sense. She had formed the habit of quoting John Galt as an independent authority who proved her points, and she opened and closed her most important essay, "The Objectivist Ethics," which was based on her Wisconsin speech, with his words. In half a dozen other pieces she set out to establish such self-consistent but eccentric ideas as that "there are no conflicts of interest among rational men," a notion that could have meaning only inside the moral world of *The Fountainhead* and *Atlas Shrugged*.

Ironically, *The Virtue of Selfishness* did not include "The Fascist New Frontier." On November, 22, 1963, five weeks after her climactic meeting with Bennett Cerf, John F. Kennedy was assassinated in Dallas, Texas. Her critique of his administration was instantly obsolete. A few days after the assassination, as the entire nation grappled with its shock and grief, Cerf wrote to her, imploringly, "I hope you will agree with me that the appalling events of the last week make all our previous discussions academic." She didn't agree. "She said the assassination had nothing to do with what she had to say," Cerf recalled. "It didn't change her opinion one iota." Yet he, too, often thought of her fondly. "I think you are one of the most wonderful people I have ever met in my life," he wrote to her in 1965, "and this decision of yours [not to publish any future books with Random House] will not change my feeling in that respect in the least degree." She also wished him well, assuring him that she would always give him credit for publishing *Atlas Shrugged*.

Cerf blamed her followers for having flattered her into greater dogmatism and obstinacy than was natural to her. But she abandoned old acquaintances when they crossed her not just because she was buffered by her devotees, although their adulation surely made this easier to do. A friend of John Hospers's, trying to console him after their falling-out, explained it this way: "Well John," the friend said, "you were a scholar. She was a revolutionary."

An old friend of hers put it another way: "She could be immensely empathetic if she saw things in you that were like her. But if she didn't see herself in some aspect of you, she didn't empathize at all. You weren't real to her."

It was at about this time that Rand began to hint to Branden that she wanted to resume their sexual affair.

She was fifty-eight. He was thirty-three. They were joined together in overlapping business and creative ventures. They collaborated on the monthly newsletter, pamphlets, promotional presentations, lecture tours, and speeches. In an expansion of NBI, Branden started a small publishing venture to reissue Rand's favorite books, including Merwin and Webster's turn-of-the-century novel *Calumet "K"* and Victor Hugo's *The Man Who Laughs,* and established a book service to sell these and other books that might interest Rand's readers. He launched a bicoastal NBI film series called "The Romantic Screen," sponsored NBI dances and formal-dress balls, and created NBI Art Reproductions to sell mail-order copies of Frank O'Connor's and Joan Blumenthal's paintings, as well as a soft-focus portrait of Rand by Ilona Royce-Smithkin, one of O'Connor's mentors at the Art Students League. ("This is exactly how I feel about myself," Rand said on seeing the Joan Fontaine-esque portrait for the first time.) At least twice a year, Rand delivered NBI lectures to jam-packed audiences on the aesthetics of romantic writing and on Objectivist epistemology, and she not only answered student questions at the lectern every week but also tape-recorded answers to questions sent in by off-site tape-transcription groups. Thus she aided NBI's growth— and, presumably, sales of her books—without accepting any remuneration from NBI, although Branden repeatedly offered to pay her. (NBI "was certainly profitable," Barbara told an interviewer in 1990, though "nobody got rich.") Rand backed Branden's first published book and gave his writing on Objectivist psychology a boost by including his essays in *The Virtue of Selfishness* and in her third collection, *Capitalism: The Unknown Ideal* (1966), where she also reprinted essays by Alan Greenspan. Sales of these books presumably generated royalties for Branden, fortifying his income from NBI and *The Objectivist Newsletter,* as well as his psychotherapeutic practice. Every month or two, they traveled together for public appearances. He had her unqualified public sanction: "You can speak for me anytime you wish, on any subject whatsoever," she called out to him from the audience one evening at NBI. She let it be known that he, and only he, would be permitted to write the screenplay for a movie of *Atlas Shrugged.*

Finally, in late 1963, they more or less moved in together. The Brandens traded their set of rooms at 165 East Thirty-fifth Street for a two-bedroom apartment in a brand-new high-rise at 120 East Thirty-fourth Street at Lexington Avenue, where they settled on the ninth floor and where Branden set up an office for writing and conducting therapy. On the second floor, Barbara transformed a studio into administrative headquarters for NBI and *The Objectivist Newsletter,* with a separate office for herself. She oversaw editorial and business operations, and a Canadian friend of hers named Wilfred Schwartz took charge of NBI's financial affairs, while Branden's sister Elayne Kalberman managed the newsletter staff. The O'Connors followed a few months later, choosing an apartment on the sixth floor. It was new and spanking clean but again ordinary, with an L-shaped living room windowed at one end, a galley kitchen, a standard-size bedroom, a bathroom, and a small separate study just large enough to hold Ayn's desk and files. O'Connor, who had been working in a rented studio on East Twenty-eighth Street, transferred his paints and canvasses to a one-room apartment on the fourth floor. After a while, others, including Leonard Peikoff and psychologist Roger Callahan and his family, moved into the building, while rank-and-file followers continued to fill rentals in neighboring streets. An intercom joined the O'Connors' apartment with the Brandens'. Ayn and Nathaniel spoke on the phone two or three times a day. Often, the Brandens were awakened by late-night calls from Rand to Nathaniel. Except when traveling separately, they were barely out of each other's range of hearing.

After the move, the writer liked to visit her husband's fourth-floor art studio and sit quietly and watch him paint. His dedication to his work elicited her deep admiration, remembered Barbara. Yet she tended to have fixed ideas about drawing and painting, as about other things; some were apparently inherited from an art class she had taken as a teenager in Russia. Once, for example, she told NBI students that all curved lines should be drawn not as freehand swoops but as the intersecting planes of the straight lines that define the curve. Sometimes, while watching Frank, she made suggestions. She might point out that his colors were running together or that the perspective in a painting was off. When worried about his progress, she phoned her favorite painter, José Manuel Capuletti, and then relayed to Frank what Capuletti recommended, or she asked knowledgeable friends to buy books for him on aspects of technique. He took pleasure in her pride in him and was typically good-natured about her advice. Once, when she whispered to a guest, "He is a tiger at the easel," he replied, "Well, just don't grab me by the tail." Occasionally, however, he reacted with anger. One evening, while he was making a study of a model's face, she put a hand on his shoulder and pointed out that one of the eyes was lower than the other in the painting. He brushed her hand away and muttered, "Leave me alone." "It was the only time I ever saw him lose his temper," said another artist who happened to be present. Rand apologized profusely, but she didn't change her behavior. "Smoke used to come out of my ears," recalled Joan Blumenthal, who over the years became convinced that Rand's interference in her husband's artwork was partly motivated by fear. "You've heard about the issue of a 'malevolent universe premise'?" she asked. "That was Rand's term for not really believing that happiness is possible on earth. That's what she was concerned about: that some sadness or malevolence would show." She had reason to worry. In a 1961 portrait O'Connor painted of her (a strong likeness that demonstrates his ability to communicate in paint), the huge eyes are not only slightly out of alignment with each other but also radiate different messages: anger, sexuality, and power on the left and wariness and sorrow on the right. It's a striking image. Although she forbade him to sell his paintings while he lived—she said she could not bear to part with them—she was discovered throwing this one in a trash bin after his death in 1979. None of her inner circle had ever seen it.

At first, Rand's hints to Branden about resuming their affair were muted. "I'm coming back to life," she told him, adding, "Can you imagine what these past years would have been like if you did not exist?" or, "You saved my life." Her grateful remarks rattled Branden; he thought they hinted at continued dependency and a new set of expectations. She often asked whether he still loved her, and at one point she stammered, "Do you think . . . ?" He understood her meaning and answered yes—yes, they would go back to being lovers. He later wrote, "It was the only answer [I could give] that would not have precipitated an immediate crisis, the end point of which would have been the annihilation of our relationship." This statement of Branden's has been a subject of disagreement among Rand's surviving disciples; those who later turned against him claimed that he wasn't worried about excommunication as much as about being demoted from his glamorous and gainful role at *The Objectivist* and NBI. Those who took his side pointed out that he had dedicated himself to her and her ideas from his freshman year in college, was intensely protective of her self-image, and was naturally frightened of her volcanic temper and allegiance to a black-and-white moral universe. In any case, he later admitted that he didn't love her, not in the romantic sense she meant, and hadn't since before the publication of *Atlas Shrugged*. If she appeared to forget her original horror of being "an old woman pursuing a younger man" and was maneuvering to get what she wanted, he was procrastinating. He also told her something that was true: that she was the most important person in the world to him. He said he needed time to work out the problems in his ten-year marriage to Barbara before resuming a romantic relationship with her. During that early conversation she replied, sighing, "I don't feel fully ready yet, either. I was just testing your attitude for the future." She offered to counsel the unhappy couple. He accepted. For the moment, he was off the hook.

He knew, if she didn't, that it was far too late to begin again. During the years of her depression, he had behaved toward her as a good son behaves to an ailing mother, except that they occasionally slept together. Yet he had also distanced himself from her. He had discovered an interest in hypnosis, a therapeutic technique that she categorically rejected. In this respect and others, he resented what he later characterized as her narrow-mindedness, intellectual rigidity, and "appalling moralism." Yet he largely hid his resentment from her and continued to moralize prodigiously himself. In *The Objectivist Newsletter,* he stressed that holding any idea that contradicted any other was to "kill one's capacity to be certain of anything." In the department of rendering judgments, said Barbara, "Ayn sometimes seemed like a pussycat in comparison" to him.

He was an unmistakably gifted (if occasionally "droning") speaker, displaying a seductive mixture of self-assurance, poise, and wit, as well as a tone of moral seriousness and a hint of moral threat. Like Sinclair Lewis's famous two-fisted evangelist, he "was so strong on purity and the virtue of womanhood," so to speak, that disagreeing with him was tantamount to admitting one's own moral weakness. He even had an Elmer Gantry–like maxim to describe his speaking technique: "Omnisciate and inflamminate," he used to call it, meaning, "Act as if you know everything, and stir up the emotions of the audience." He dressed the part of an impresario, in good suits and monogrammed shirts. His business style was manic, adrenaline filled, abrupt. To relieve stress, "he would go off on shopping sprees," remembered Robert Hessen, who pinch-hit as NBI's bookkeeper in the 1960s. "He came in one day and [showed me] a bill for five hundred dollars worth of Sulka ties." In general, he treated staffers brusquely. "Nathan had a theory about 'men as tools,'" recalled a secretary who worked for both him and Rand. "These were [people] who weren't particularly worthy but could aid in the cause in certain limited ways. That was his view of the staff." Rand agreed with this theory and deemed it "brilliant," according to Barbara, but in spite of this her secretaries and typists found her exceptionally fair, scrupulous, and considerate. "She didn't know how he'd been treating us," the secretary recalled in 1983. To the contrary, she knew more than anyone thought she did.

In New York's East Thirties, where many young adherents lived and others milled about before and after NBI events, Branden and Rand were celebrities. Whether from shyness or a fear of being buttonholed, the novelist tended to shrink from unexpected public recognition. Shelly Reuben, a typist for *The Objectivist Newsletter* in 1965, remembered seeing her in the street one day, flagging down a taxi. As Reuben approached, Rand frowned, but when she explained that she just wanted to say hello, Rand "broke out into the most beautiful smile." Wow, thought Reuben, she thinks people always want something from her.

More difficult, perhaps, from her point of view, was that people often wanted the same things. She was a remarkable teacher, but after six or seven years of answering questions at NBI and at college lectures she could become bored and frustrated when required to repeat herself. Asked for the umpteenth time during an NBI question-and-answer session how she expected people to be rational in an irrational society, she shouted, "*I* did it myself! No one taught *me* how to think!" Her steadfast follower and one of her attorneys, Hank Holzer, typically spent hours a week fending off possible copyright and intellectual property violations by fans who wrote to announce, say, the founding of a John Galt line of curtains; so when an ingenuous NBI student from Texas asked, "Miss Rand, would it be an infringement of your rights if I painted a picture of my ideal man and called it *John Galt*?" she exploded, perhaps with some justification in view of the fact that the woman didn't have enough imagination to create a hero of her own. To some degree, then, she found herself in the same position as Kay Gonda and Gail Wynand, dependent for admiration and support on people she didn't respect. Because she now tended to see everything as a moral issue, she sometimes lost her patience in public as well as in private and harangued a naïve or dim-witted stranger about his motives and his moral condition. "She had a huge number of young people hanging on her every word," reflected Joan Kennedy Taylor. "It was almost as if she developed what she thought was a psychological analysis of certain questions and then applied it to everybody who asked." When displeased, she had a habit of beginning to speak in an angry tone, then pulling out a cigarette and her Zippo lighter, inserting the cigarette into a holder, flipping open the lighter's metal lid, and producing a huge flame to light the cigarette before continuing. "The expression on her face was something not to be believed," said an admirer—"nostrils flaring, the anger and the flame [making] her look like a dragon. The image was unforgettable." Students were finding her unpredictable and "frightening, really frightening," said one.

Branden seemed to enjoy the attention. "In those days, people worshipped the ground he walked on," recalled an acquaintance of the time. "He ate it up. He loved it." In the early and mid-1960s, he liked to travel, make appearances on radio and television shows, give speeches, make new friends—a constellation Rand later referred to disapprovingly as "going Hollywood" and being "a man of action." Together with Allan Blumenthal, he conducted day-long seminars on the techniques of what had become known as "Objectivist psychotherapy," which aimed at correcting wrong or conflicting thoughts and beliefs as a cure for emotional problems. There, too, he won disciples who adhered to his theories and prospered from his and Blumenthal's referrals. He kept his honorary position as John Galt's avatar ("except for a few blemishes," Rand sometimes added wryly) in front of friends and students. He made it clear that if a woman weren't half in love with him, and if a man weren't half in love with the creator of *Atlas Shrugged,* they were suffering from a lack of self-esteem. "He was the one who made a crusade out of her theory of sex," Barbara recalled. "She didn't." In this, perhaps, he was doing to others what had been done to him.

He flirted with danger. An hour before a telephone interview with a Washington, D.C., radio station, he dialed in to change the number at which he wanted to be reached. Chatting with the production manager, an idealistic young member of the Washington Objectivist club who had booked his appearance, he mentioned that he was calling from Ayn Rand's telephone—yes, and that right now he was lying on Ayn Rand's bed. "This was before anyone knew about the affair," said the woman, Lee Clifford. "But his manner was so familiar, so intimate, it was as if he were telling me. I *knew.* He communicated it." When students at NBI asked whether it was really possible to be in love with more than one person at a time (apparently, a common question, given Rand's steamy literary triads), he answered that only moral giants could possibly pull it off. ("It sounded like bullshit at the time," recalled a member of the audience who knew him well.) Rand sometimes said much the same thing, but at other times answered, "No, but you can be half in love with two different people at the same time," a kind of confession of her own.

What she didn't know was that, beginning in late 1963, Branden was juggling a new romantic triangle, or rather a parallelogram. At just about the time she decided that she was fully ready to resume sleeping with him, he fell in love with a younger woman—a willowy twenty-three-year-old fashion model and aspiring actress named Patrecia Gullison. He had first noticed Patrecia two years earlier, watching him, openly spellbound, from the third row of seats at NBI. After lectures, he and she had talked, then flirted. In the summer of 1962, the young woman, assuming that Branden was happily married and unavailable, had married a tall, good-looking advertising account executive and NBI regular named Larry Scott. Branden attended the wedding, but he continued to think about her. Before her marriage, he had encouraged one of his male students to date her as a strategy for keeping her close at hand; afterward, perhaps with a similar purpose in mind, he offered her and Larry Scott free marriage counseling when they told him they were having marital problems. When she entered his ninth-floor office, he later wrote, she behaved "as if she were entering a temple." Inevitably, one afternoon they found themselves alone together and fell into each other's arms. She was impish, eager, and full of life. She hadn't gone to college but was saving her money to go, and she was attentive in his lectures. Unlike Rand and Barbara, she didn't ask him to check his premises or overcome his flaws. Unconditional female admiration was a thrilling new experience for him, and he was starving for an extraphilosophical experience of sex. She was "what Nathan had never had in his life," said Barbara in 2005, "someone who wasn't trying to save his soul."

Before he slept with the young woman, he told her that he and his wife still had strong feelings for each other and were trying to repair their marriage. He also told her the history of his nine-year affair with the towering figure at the center of their lives. This was the primary obstacle to a love affair with her, he warned her: Ayn's needs came first. Also, if Ayn ever discovered that the man to whom she had dedicated *Atlas Shrugged* had not only lost his desire for her but had also fallen in love with a beautiful young rival, it would mean the end of NBI, of *The Objectivist Newsletter,* and of "everything I've been trying to build since Ayn and I started." He made a decision that would prove fateful. "I can't let it go," he told her. "I don't want to. I love it." Why couldn't they be honest with Ayn? Patrecia asked. Wasn't the older woman the very soul of reason and reality? Branden answered, "You would see an explosion such as you cannot even begin to imagine."

He had another strong motive to keep the affair secret. By the standards of *The Fountainhead* and *Atlas Shrugged,* the choice of this lovely, lighthearted, reflexively self-sacrificing girl in preference to Rand revealed in him an inner Peter Keating. "The man who is proudly certain of his own value will want the highest type of woman he can find," Francisco tells Rearden in *Atlas Shrugged.* Nathaniel was sure that, in his and Rand's cosmology, at least, Patrecia was not the highest type of woman. (To allay Rand's initial suspicions about the meaning of his friendship with Patrecia, he described her as an "Eddie Willers," i.e., an average person who has good premises but no special gifts.) Francisco's speech continues with a kind of curse on any man who only pretends to love the highest type of woman or who tries to love her out of duty or charity. His body "will not obey him, it will not respond," the striking copper baron warns, "it will make him impotent toward the woman he professes to love and draw him to the lowest type of whore he can find." Branden evidently believed this. Aside from his indebtedness to Rand and the mission they shared, she represented his worldview. The thought of being without her was intolerable to him. He anxiously told himself that his attraction to Patrecia would pass and that his life would return to normal.

Patrecia agreed to keep their affair concealed, even from her husband, and never to say a word about Branden's clandestine relationship with Rand. The psychologist and Patrecia met for trysts in his office or in the Scotts' nearby apartment, while Larry Scott was at work or traveling on business. She turned down modeling jobs to be available to him. He learned "to lie expertly," he wrote, "as I became a master at inventing reasons to be away from the office."

In early 1964, he reluctantly gave his wife permission to conduct her own affair with an NBI colleague she had grown fond of. (In addition to every other complication, Branden "really cared for me," Barbara recalled. Consenting to such an affair was "agony," he told her.) He didn't reveal his affair with Patrecia until three years later, when he needed her help in keeping his secret from Rand. Meanwhile, however, she noticed his giddy, almost obsessive, often public banter about Patrecia and his frequent absences from home and NBI and reached the correct but, to her, incredible conclusion that he was deceiving both her *and* Ayn with Patrecia. She asked him outright if he and the young woman were having an affair. He denied it, assuring her that such suspicions were a symptom of her old demons: emotionalism, insecurity, and a lack of self-esteem. She took him at his word. Thus the new math of this real-life romantic triangle left one woman questioning her perceptions, another reluctantly faking reality, and a third waiting and hoping for something that would never come.

In his affair with Patrecia, too, Branden gradually lost discretion, dancing with his young mistress at formal parties and annual balls, driving her around town in his convertible car, appearing at a Los Angeles NBI event with her and her lovely identical twin sister, Liesha, also a model, on either arm, while employees and students gaped at his glamour. No one seems to have mentioned these sightings to Rand or, at first, to Barbara. But rumors swirled, and at last "the truth was evident [to me]," Barbara later wrote. The knowledge that she was being lied to led her, in the summer of 1965, to ask Branden for a separation. He moved out, into a temporary apartment on the third floor, explaining to friends and students that he needed extra office space; after the separation became final, Barbara settled in a one-bedroom penthouse apartment on the twentieth floor. In spite of Patrecia, he was not ready to publicly end a marriage he half hoped to save and whose conflicts "operated as a shield" against his older lover's desires and expectations. He and Barbara continued to appear together in public, and they continued to meet with Rand for the marital counseling sessions she had initiated almost as soon as he mentioned that his troubled marriage was a barrier to sex with her.

In fact, at intervals from 1964 until 1966 and later, Rand spent many hours trying to help the Brandens repair their shattered "psycho-epistemology" (method of thinking) with respect to each other and their marriage and thus free her lover to return to her. For the first few months, before the two officially announced their separation, she treated them with a kindness and tenderness "that had long seemed absent from her personality," Barbara later wrote, and appeared to be genuinely disappointed to discover that their personal relationship had dissolved into such an angry shambles. With Patrecia waiting offstage, Branden knew from the start that Rand's efforts had very little chance of success. Barbara, who attended the sessions under protest, nevertheless did not tell

Rand about her own ongoing affair. When the couple finally informed their unofficial therapist that the marriage was irreparable, she seemed relieved. "Now, darling," she said to Branden, "perhaps there will be a chance for us to be in love again."

Branden stood on a precipice: Should he tell the truth, risking Rand's anger and his own disinheritance, or take up his duties as Rand's lover? He chose a third way, finding other real but incidental ailments to complain of: exhaustion from overwork, trauma from the end of his marriage, fragile self-esteem because of Rand's history of rebuking him, depression, "a sense of [emotional] deadness that made it exceedingly difficult to think of resuming a romance with her," and, somewhat astonishingly at this point, anguish over his second-fiddle status in the triangle with Frank, which had caused him pain in the past, he said, and almost surely would again. "Are you asking me to leave Frank and live with you openly?" she asked him, shocked. No, no, he hastened to answer. Still, he said, her allegiance to Frank was difficult for him. Later, when trying to explain his persistent refusal to talk about their emotional and sexual relationship, he unearthed another, deeper problem to explain his "deadness." He told her that "if the ability to think of people [read: Rand] in relation to himself was a special sense, it feels to him as if he were born without that sense." She was appalled by this remark— reasoning that, if it were true, he had *never* had an authentic romantic attachment to her—but apparently did not recognize it as an almost verbatim quote from her. Writing of the murderer-hero of *The Little Street* in 1928, she had noted that the real murderer, Hickman, "doesn't understand, because thankfully *he has no organ for understanding,* the necessity, meaning, or importance of other people." Of course, this was also a characteristic of Howard Roark—and of Ayn Rand. Even in Branden's attempts to break away from her, he inhabited the psyches of her characters.

She asked directly, and not for the first time, "Is it my age? I could accept that." Oh, no you couldn't, Branden remembered thinking, and gave her the answer he thought she wanted. "You will always be a sexual being," he told her, and, "You have no equals at any age."

Naturally, the man's passion for Patrecia didn't fade; it grew stronger, bringing him "happiness of a kind I had never known before." The way out without hurting anyone, he madly imagined, was to encourage Rand to get to know Patrecia and so discover her virtues and potential to be a good Objectivist—even if, like Eddie Willers, she didn't meet their highest standards. Only then, he thought, might Rand recover her reason and give her blessing to a sexual union between the lovely young woman and her own intellectual son and heir, while remaining his patroness, promoter, and friend.

As daffy as this was, at first it appeared to work. The celebrated author initially liked the ingenue, especially her physical type, so similar to that of Dominique and Dagny. "She's very American looking," she remarked, and once, having seen Patrecia perform in a play, startled both the young actress and Branden by declaring, with her usual air of excited self-absorption, "What is magnificent is that you have taken the philosophy of Objectivism and applied it to the art of acting!" The young beauty charmed most members of the inner circle. She and her twin sister, Liesha, volunteered as artist's models and posed for Frank, Joan Blumenthal, and other painters and sculptors in the group. She offered suggestions about clothing and makeup to Rand and some of the other women and once showed the novelist and thinker how to cross her legs for a television interview. (Rand, assuming that she was supposed to *keep* her legs crossed, complained after the interview that she had developed a leg cramp.) Joan Blumenthal said to Branden, with amazement, "When you're with Patrecia, you like the way you feel about yourself!" "I hated the calculations and manipulations this strategy entailed," he wrote in 1989, "but I felt that my back was to the wall and my survival was at stake."

As Rand more closely observed Branden and Patrecia, however, she changed her mind. She thought that the young woman was "roleplaying," as she noted in a 1968 summary of her impressions of Patrecia over a two-year period. ("I cannot stand people with 'acts,' *particularly women* with 'acts,' " she wrote; "it is too clear to me that such acts come from dreadful premises.") Of course, Patrecia *was* acting, as were Branden, Barbara, and possibly Rand herself. When Branden swore to Rand that he had no sexual interest in Patrecia—that his feeling for her was strictly playful, protective, and paternal—Rand claimed to believe him. She was disturbed by their friendship, she later confided to her journal, not because it was a sexual flirtation but because it was "a disturbing and incomprehensible sign" of a seeming change in her protégé's tastes and priorities, away from philosophy and toward a " 'consumption' (or 'pleasure') 'emotional' world." When he tried to convince her that Patrecia reminded him of her, including the younger woman's "man-worship" and "sexual view of the universe," she balked. To the contrary, she wrote; watching Patrecia, she saw "only a faintly pretentious empti-ness and fear."

Gradually, his evasions, inconsistencies, and "drift" became intolera-ble to the woman for whom logic was tantamount to truth. They began to have explosive arguments. How could he be so out of focus about his reasons for not resuming his romance with her? Where was his mind? Why were his proclaimed values—his love for her and all she stood for—so evidently in conflict with his emotions? What was he repress-ing? What was he hiding? As to sex, "When, if not now?" she asked. When Branden didn't answer, she took to making extensive notes on his psychology and discussing them at length, first with him and then with Barbara, whom she recruited as an ally in deciphering his state of mind. Starting in 1967, she kept a personal journal of her talks with him and her insights into their long history together. The truth was hidden in plain sight, but the aging visionary wouldn't or couldn't allow herself to see it. She tormented herself, and him, by trying to untangle his half-earnest rationales and shifting confusions, which she did by writing, as she always had.

Without providing a truthful explanation, Patrecia asked her hus-band for a separation in December 1965. Branden's cousin Allan Blu-menthal, acting as Branden's proxy, passed the word that they should keep their separation secret until the Brandens announced theirs, which they finally did a few weeks later. "We don't want people to think the two events are related," Blumenthal told the Scotts. "You know how gossip and rumors start."

The news of the Brandens' impending divorce sent shock waves through the concentric circles of Rand's New York, Los Angeles, Boston, Washington, D.C., Toronto, and Chicago organizations. Insiders couldn't believe that Objectivism's "ideal couple," as Al Ramrus described the pair, was divided, and dividing. No, there was no one else involved, the Brandens told their family, friends, admirers, and students. "We're just incompatible," they said. "We're just not able to be happy together." Soon other Rand-centered marriages began to sever, as Roarks and Dominiques took a second look at the Brandens and each other.

In late 1966, almost three years after Branden and Patrecia began sleeping together, the harrowed psychotherapist finally told his estranged wife that he was about to *begin* a sexual affair with the beautiful young woman. Although he lied about the timing, he was evidently seeking relief from lies; he later wrote that he could barely tolerate the strain of carrying on his double life. Once separated and living apart, he and Barbara fell into a pattern of joining together as allies only when under duress. She urged him to tell Rand—if not about Patrecia, then at least about the impossibility on his part of reigniting a twelve-year-old flame. But when he begged for time, she agreed.

The stakes were high. He was working on his first book in his field, to be published as *The Psychology of Self-Esteem.* With it, he hoped to make an independent reputation. Rand had introduced him to editors at an NAL affiliate, World Publishing, and they had offered him a contract for the book, sight unseen. She had praised the almost-completed book as a work of genius and had promised to describe it as such in a signed introduction. But the manuscript was running late. "Just wait until [Ayn] writes the introduction," he implored Barbara during one of their discussions.

On behalf of NBI, he had also assumed a surprisingly large new financial obligation. In summer 1967, a few months after his partial confession to Barbara, he signed a lease on eight thousand square feet of office space one floor below the lobby of the Empire State Building, still the tallest example of engineering prowess in the world. The lease ran for fifteen *years,* and over that period of time it was likely to cost NBI at least a quarter of a million dollars. Given that the combined income of NBI and its offshoots now exceeded four hundred thousand dollars a year, the lease was affordable on paper, and it struck the business manager of NBI as a good price for the space. But the organization was experiencing its annual summer cash-flow shortfall. Each year, before the arrival of revenues from autumn lecture fees, NBI typically borrowed small amounts from the independent account of *The Objectivist* to pay for advertising and promotion of fall courses. Although the finances of the magazine, owned by Rand and Branden jointly, and of NBI, owned by Branden alone, were kept strictly separate, Rand didn't object to these annual interest-bearing loans, which were always paid back in the fall. This year, however, in order to finance a year's rent in advance, plus furniture and additional staff, a larger amount was needed. Rand had told Nathaniel not to bother her with business matters and was only mildly put out to be told about the loan after the fact, but she didn't know its size, approximately $25,000. Meanwhile, in the view of at least one member of the staff, Branden was not paying adequate attention to the money-making part of the operation: the lectures themselves. "I felt we were really in trouble here," said a longtime staffer. "But nobody would listen."

One additional source of distraction for Branden was a brand-new venture he was then recruiting investors to finance: NBI Theater, Inc., a small corporation to be devoted to the production of romantic drama. "Patrecia's involvement in acting had reawakened my early love of the theater," he later wrote, "and I wanted to produce a series of plays and write for the theater myself." Since an effective way to begin was to appeal to Ayn Rand's audience, the first project was to be a dramatization of *The Fountainhead,* adapted by Barbara and approved by Ayn. The Brandens expected it to open in a community-based theater in the Jan Hus Church on East Seventy-fourth Street in the fall of 1968. Casting lay ahead, but at one point Branden considered Patrecia to play the part of Dominique. (Strangely but aptly, Patrecia had recently taken the stage name Patrecia Wynand.) Rand gradually cooled to the project. The involvement of Patrecia would not have increased her enthusiasm.

The lies and conflicts were piling up. By 1967, carefully guarded secrets, rampant gossip, and paranoia were the order of the day. And still Rand hoped for her lover to return.

FIFTEEN

EITHER/OR (THE BREAK)

1967–1968

Pity for the guilty is treason to the innocent.

—*The Romantic Manifesto,* 1969

n early 1967, Rand completed a book-length essay called *Introduction to Objectivist Epistemology.* Never among her popular works, it laid out her theories of how man thinks and acquires knowledge and contains what some admirers regard as her seminal contribution to Western philosophy, a theory of concept formation.* Aside from this, and a fiery, farsighted speech against the Vietnam War in April 1967 at the Ford Hall Forum, and a few short essays for *The Objectivist,* her mental life was now almost entirely focused on what and how Nathaniel Branden thought. Marital counseling having ended, she assumed the temporary role of his personal psychotherapist, even though she had no training in psychology and had little appreciation for therapy's methods and objectives. More or less adhering to traditional ethical practice, she placed their active relationship on hold "in every sense or aspect" while she probed his psyche. Yet the subtext of their verbal dueling was always

---

*In Ayn Rand's view, concepts are formulated by looking for similarities among perceived objects (i.e., seeing that all tables have legs and tops), setting aside differences in measurements of shared qualities (such as the differing lengths of two tabletops), and retaining the essential conceptual similarities.

their relationship. Over the next several months, they met hundreds of times at all hours of the day and night. In most of the sessions, he took to playing a gloomy child who mutters, "I don't know," while she alternated between obsessed scientist and spurned lover. He rationalized, improvised, planted clues, and followed up by denying their significance; she moralized, intimidated, and threatened even as she drilled for answers. She was determined to find out what had happened to her virile young lover "with the sovereign mind of a genius" and the moral courage to love Ayn Rand. In spite of the Brandens' withholding of important facts—and her own naïveté or purposeful blindness—the thinker gradually pieced together some of Branden's motives.

She began by analyzing apparent contradictions between his proclaimed values and his behavior. For example, he often said she was important to him. Yet he knew "years ago," she wrote in her journal, that his apparent inability to be emotionally intimate with her or to discuss their romantic relationship had hurt her. The hours of marriage counseling she had devoted to him and Barbara, along with months of analyzing *his* problems, had made her feel depersonalized and invisible, she both told him and wrote. And yet even after the breakup of his marriage he had taken no corrective steps. "I feel real *fear* when he tells me 'I don't know' in regard to his feelings and desires in our relationship," she wrote. "It is as if everything pertaining to his own emotions is that kind of vague, helpless 'I don't know.'" Also, although he said he wanted to live exclusively according to his—and her—highest values, he let their relationship drift while he filled his time with practical activities he claimed not to value or enjoy: "business, theatrical business, lunches (and worse)," the "worse" apparently a reference to his "friendship" with Patrecia. The pace of these activities, culminating in the real-estate deal, furnishing the Empire State Building offices, and the planned production of *The Fountainhead,* was increasing, not diminishing. Such obvious contradictions were not believable "in a man of Branden's rationality and intellectual development," she wrote in the fall of 1967. *"He is hiding something here. What?"*

As yet, she had been unable to "project" his psychology, she noted. As an aid, she tried to focus on what he wasn't saying—although she, too, avoided any mention of Patrecia. She looked for things he had repressed. For example, in his perpetual turmoil and indecision, she wrote, she sensed that he was afraid. Afraid of what? One hypothesis: He was a second-hander, a social metaphysician, and feared showing it. She looked squarely at this possibility. If valid, then his underlying premise would be that he wanted to be loved ("or, rather, admired," she wrote) more than he wanted to love; he wanted to be seen more than to see. Such an attitude would betray not only her but also the important principle of selfishness (defined by her as the pursuit of rational desires and one's highest happiness) and of everything he admired in John Galt. But it would explain his years-long neglect of her needs and his chronic inability to decide what he wanted, she wrote. It would also account for his often frantic activities in the social and business realms, where he earned admiration, and for his apparent dependency on her to affirm his tottering vision of himself as a hero. She didn't believe this theory, she noted, but should it prove true, the following would be her conclusion: "Here is a man who, for some reason unknown to me, was unable to live up to his own greatness and mine, and ran from it (particularly mine)," and who, by refusing to grant her visibility in his emotional life, "killed me before my time."

Although her language might be theatrical and her perspective skewed by self-absorption, in one respect her reasoning was sound. Branden did approach her as a mirror. But she had positioned herself as such through endless, extravagant compliments to him. Inner-circle member Edith Efron later commented that Rand had urged him to think of himself as a genius "on the same level as Kant and Hegel," a seemingly double-edged compliment, given her hatred of these philosophers, but apparently spoken admiringly, since Efron went on to say that he was "murdered by flattery." If he was even partly driven by "vanity, flattery-seeking, and, ultimately, glamorizing and reality-faking," as Rand suggested in her notes a few months later, she had cultivated these qualities in him for seventeen years.

In the fall of 1967, in spite of their therapy sessions, he was still complaining that he felt depressed and hopeless about their relationship. Disgusted, for the first time she considered the possibility of a break with him. In her notes, she imagined such a rupture differently from the cataclysm both he and Barbara feared. To "break with him entirely," she wrote, would mean "not to see him except 'functionally,' on business." At this stage in what was left of their relationship, she seems to have been willing to end the affair without speaking out against him or terminating their professional and business bonds. Neither Branden believed this, and it would have been a first.

Perhaps her happiest moments that fall came during three guest appearances on *The Tonight Show* with Johnny Carson. Extremely popular as a late-night TV talk-show host, Carson wasn't known for inviting controversial guests, but she and her ideas apparently appealed to him. She was his first guest on the night she initially appeared, and during the first commercial break he reportedly canceled the other guests who were waiting backstage and kept her on alone. He was deferential and, even better, asked thoughtful questions and listened to the answers. By the late 1960s, her media appearances had become so potentially fraught with conflict that she and her legal bodyguard Hank Holzer insisted that producers sign a twenty-point contract before she would go on. It required her agreement in writing to any introductory remarks and proscribed surprise guests, debate, quotations from her enemies, etc. "You won't attack me?" she asked Carson sweetly and disarmingly on being seated on the set. He laughed and they engaged in a lively discussion of her third collection of nonfiction, *Capitalism: The Unknown Ideal,* which NAL had published. Carson's broadcast reached as many as fifty million viewers, and Rand was a massive hit. Many baby boomers remembered first hearing of her "morality of reason" there. The show received a record number of letters, all but twelve of them positive. Carson invited her back twice before Christmas 1967.

At year's end, she and Branden entered one of their honeymoon periods. He became "more openly, romantically expressive toward me than he had been . . . since the beginning," Rand recorded in her journal. In fact, he was effusive. He told her that he couldn't live without her. He kissed her in a sexually arousing way. Only later did she call to mind two anomalies that marred her sense of a hopeful new beginning with him: His eyes were lifeless when he professed his love for her and, on New Year's Eve at the Plaza Hotel, in a party that included Nathaniel, Patrecia, Patrecia's sister Liesha, Alan Greenspan, Rand, and Frank, he danced too often with Patrecia. At the beginning of 1968, he again grew moody and retreated from emotional discussions. In late January, he shocked her with a new disclosure, which she accepted on its face: for the last ten years, he had secretly suffered from a "sex problem" or "sexual freeze" (suggesting impotence). His explanation, recorded by her, was as shocking as his statement. Early on, he had learned to repress his sexuality in response to his rejecting wife, he said. The affair with Ayn had acted as an antidote, but when she first made demands and then withdrew into rage and depression after the publication of *Atlas Shrugged,* he experienced a "subconscious *total renunciation of sex,*" he told her, as a result of this second and mortal blow to his sexual self-esteem.

Setting the stage for the artful introduction of Patrecia into the discussion, he talked wistfully about "a hypothetical 'Miss X' of his own age." Surprisingly, Rand didn't react angrily, at least in her journal notes. She asked him what he would want from such a woman. He would want to travel with her, spend his growing income on her, and go to nightclubs, he replied—all things he couldn't do with Rand. Her notes suggest that he and she also discussed how such a "Miss X" might help to thaw his "sexual freeze." And just where would she, Rand, fit in? she asked him. Ideally, they would conduct a very secret, very private, and very spiritual romance, he answered, sleeping together five or six times a year. From her notes, she seems briefly to have considered this impossible scheme, provided it was the only way to solve Branden's sexual problem and she would never have to meet the woman. She soon changed her mind. In such a triangle, "I would be the only remnant of the [heroic] ideal" remaining to Branden as he went about his pleasurable activities, she reflected. "Therefore, our relationship would be consigned to unreality." Also, of course, any hypothetical Miss X would be intellectually and morally inferior to her; thus, if Branden succeeded in such an affair, it "would destroy his mind." Both practitioner and patient pretended not to know that they were talking about Patrecia.

Later, Nathaniel and Barbara reported separately that during face-to-face discussions of these issues Rand was almost unrelentingly suspicious, resentful, and bitter—and no wonder. She was assembling puzzle pieces in the dark, even if the dark was partly self-imposed. The missing piece was Patrecia. It was always on the table, but she couldn't pick it up. She referred obliquely to the actress. "Don't ever let yourself think, even for a minute, that Patrecia or some equivalent is going to cash in on my ambition, mind, and achievement," she reportedly told Branden during one conversation, and, "You have no right to casual friendships, no right to vacations, no right to have sex with some inferior woman! Did you imagine that I would consent to be left on the scrap heap?" By way of contrast, her journal entries were methodical and calm, although entirely lacking in an ordinary grasp of reality. As always, her mind was well disciplined when she was writing, her discourse fiery and impulsive when she spoke in anger or distress. And while she still did not directly connect Miss X with Patrecia in her journal, on Valentine's Day of 1968 she ended a diary entry with the note, "As far as I am concerned I will not be Cyrano to a brainless Christian." It's hard not to read this sentence as a double entendre: In Rostand's play, Cyrano's good-looking, dim-witted rival is named Christian, of course, but Rand also knew that *her* rival, Patrecia, had grown up in a family of Christian fundamentalists; Patrecia's twin sister, Liesha, remained a true believer. Later, Liesha would join an evangelical television ministry.

Meanwhile, Rand's husband of thirty-eight years was ill.

In the fall of 1967, Frank was seventy. Two or three years earlier, he had been diagnosed with a chronic condition whose symptoms included painful contractions in the tendons of his hands, making it difficult for him to hold a paintbrush. The source of the problem seems to have been Dupuytren's syndrome, a disorder often associated with alcoholism and cirrhosis of the liver, as well as with arteriosclerosis. O'Connor suffered from two of these three conditions: he drank heavily, and he had incipient arteriosclerosis, or a hardening of the arteries, which gradually reduces blood flow to the brain and body. His father had also had arteriosclerosis. Neither condition was apparent at the time, when hints of his failing health were limited to thinness, pallor, silence, and the problem with his hands.

He had surgery, which was temporarily successful. Although he constantly had to squeeze a rubber ball to flex his tendons, he returned to his classes at the Art Students League, where his popularity had won him a seat on the school's executive Board of Control. The League was a world apart—its large, old, turpentine-smelling classrooms and informality were so dear to him that when Joan Blumenthal unwittingly let slip to a group of admiring women artists that Frank was married to Ayn Rand, he told her, "I wish you hadn't said it. This is the one place where people know *me*."

Beginning in the painful years when Rand was writing John Galt's speech, painting had diverted and protected him from full immersion in his wife's affairs. Through Joan Blumenthal, it also introduced him to other artists, including a young sculptor named Don Ventura. Bright and friendly, although shy, Ventura had been working as an electrologist when Allan Blumenthal discovered him. Allan introduced him to Joan, who took him to NBI lectures and parties and encouraged him to pursue his vocation as a sculptor. Like Daryn Kent, he was attracted by the group's emphasis on individualism and intellectual attainment. When he met Rand herself, he thought that she was wonderful. "When there was no public around," he later said, "she was very easy to be with, very reassuring." He also found her endearingly unpretentious. "Once, I told her that Frank Sinatra, in Hollywood, had his bread flown in from New York every day and that it cost a fortune. Her eyes widened and she let out a long, low whistle. The way she reacted was very funny."

Frank and Ventura liked each other. On Monday nights they, Joan, and an actor named Phillip Smith attended Robert Beverly Hale's lectures on artistic anatomy at the League. Afterward, they went to the Russian Tea Room for cocktails. When Frank learned that Ventura couldn't afford to rent a studio, he occasionally invited the younger man to work in his small studio on Thirty-fourth Street. During breaks, he told Ventura stories about the early days of his marriage to Rand. "He loved nostalgia," Ventura recalled, "loved to talk about his relationship with Rand when they were poor." He described rides on the Staten Island Ferry and laughed about the first time Rand had heard herself on the radio and realized she had a heavy Russian accent. Why hadn't Frank told her about it? she had asked indignantly. Because he thought her accent was cute and he didn't want her to change it, he had teased her. By the time Ventura met them, "Frank was very subordinate to Ayn Rand," he said. "In the days he was nostalgic about, he seemed to have been with her more. Their life was simpler."

Rand's distress about Branden gradually spilled over and affected Ventura, his friends the Blumenthals, and many of the followers they knew. For the sculptor, Frank became "an anchor in a turbulent sea" filled with shifting hierarchies and rampant gossip about who was rational and moral and who was not. "More and more, people were operating from the outside in," said Ventura, "judging [each other's] actions in terms of good and evil. For [Rand], that was part of the way she operated. It was integrated, consistent." For those around her, it was often a matter of hiding supposed flaws or jockeying for position. "I became one of [the people] functioning from the outside in," Ventura said. "I was playing such a game [of mimicking the convictions of others] I couldn't see straight."

For a period of weeks, Ventura was in O'Connor's studio working on a small statue of the Greek hero Icarus, who fell to earth when his wax wings melted in the sun. Frank was making a painting of the same subject. He called his painting in progress *Icarus Fallen,* and Ventura began referring to his statue as *Icarus Fallen,* too. One evening, Rand visited and announced that when Ventura's statue was finished she would like to buy a copy; two other visitors chimed in that they wanted to buy copies, too. This was a momentous endorsement, and word of it spread quickly. "From then on," Ventura recalled, "I began to receive telephone calls and letters from people who wanted to see my work. Overnight, I became 'the Objectivist sculptor.' " He decided to look for a studio of his own. He found a rent-controlled unit in a nearby building, but lacking the required proof of income from his art, he solicited official orders from a few friends. Then he flew too close to the sun. He wrote to Rand, explaining his predicament and asking for a small deposit on *Icarus Fallen,* whose price he set at three hundred dollars. Rand reportedly flew into a rage. She raved that the sculptor had stolen the title of Frank's painting and was a plagiarist and had revealed his immorality by trying to exact a price she hadn't agreed to in advance. He should keep *Icarus Fallen* as a "skeleton in his closet" for the rest of his life, she reportedly told the Blumenthals. They relayed her message to Ventura, who was stunned. As quickly as many of Rand's minions had sought him out, so they snubbed him when they heard that he was out of favor. Without being invited to explain himself, he, like John Hospers, was suddenly outside the circle.

For Ventura and other outcast followers—including, in the summer of 1967, Edith Efron, the former writer for Mike Wallace who was by then a well-known staff reporter for *TV Guide*—being expelled from the Randian subculture was traumatic. Efron, who had been close to Rand for a decade, was tried in absentia and purged, for gossiping, or lying, or refusing to lie, or flirting; surviving witnesses couldn't explain what exactly she had done, except that it was related to the many rumors by then circulating about Branden and Patrecia. Since she had occasionally written for *The Objectivist,* the magazine published a notice informing readers that she was no longer associated with Objectivism or Ayn Rand and canceling her fall 1967 nonfiction-writing course at NBI. Afterward, in a familiar pattern, Rand spoke disparagingly of Efron and at least once denied that she had ever respected Efron's writing, and an NBI-affiliated therapist counseled the woman's eighteen-year-old son, Leonard, that his mother was "a horrible woman, that she was evil, and that I should have nothing to do with her," Leonard recalled years later. When he refused, he was made to feel awkward and unwelcome. (On the other hand, Efron's brother Robert, a distinguished neurologist who also occasionally wrote for *The Objectivist,* sided with Rand and temporarily disowned his sister.) As for Ventura, he was so mortified that he moved out of the neighborhood. "I had been seeking an identity, and [instead] I lost myself," he said in 2004.

Frank didn't phone him, nor did Ventura try to call or see his friend. "I thought I was too bad a person to contact him," said the sculptor. But one day, Ventura ran into Frank on a street corner. "I can't tell you how sorry I am about what happened," Ventura told him. Frank looked sad. "It's not the end of the world," he answered, and turned away. He no longer had the power to argue for restraint at home, as he had in the 1940s.

After a recurrence of the trouble with his hands, O'Connor ceased painting in 1968. He resigned from the Board of Control and stopped taking classes at the League. He kept his studio but—so the Brandens and others close to him claimed to have discovered—was drinking there instead of painting. Rand may or may not have noticed his idleness. She was greatly distracted by Branden. In any case, when she brooded aloud over her lover's apparent transgressions, which she did almost continuously, "she insisted that Frank be present for many of the conversations about what was wrong with Nathan," recalled Barbara, to whom Rand increasingly turned for support. "My God, the conversations went on for hours, theorizing, speculating, raging, crying. He was in the room for discussions he *should not* have been present for." If ever Rand's affair had been acceptable to him, her anguish about its approaching end could not have been. His air of absence, forgetfulness, and lethargy were signs of emotional retreat, his friends thought. They were also early symptoms of senility. Month by month, Barbara recalled, he seemed to understand less and less of what Rand said to him. Out of context, he once cried, "That man [Nathaniel] is no damn good! Why won't you see it?" He flew into violent rages against his wife, which left her baffled and hurt. "Frank, darling, are you angry with me about something you haven't told me?" Branden recalled her asking. "They would have interminable talks about his psycho-epistemology," he wrote in 1989. "Ayn did the talking, and Frank listened silently." Privately, she asked her recalcitrant lover for advice about how to persuade her husband to talk to her. When Branden suggested that the reason for his silence might be anger he had stored, she asked Frank about it and reported to Branden, "He says absolutely not. You're wrong." Once, during a vicious quarrel between the O'Connors in the presence of the Brandens, Frank walked out of the living room, into the bedroom. Barbara followed. She found him half sitting, half lying on the bed in an attitude of sorrow and defeat. "I want to leave her," he told Barbara, clutching her arm. "But where would I go?" Rand was the center of his life.

By then, O'Connor had lost his remarkable ability to be both Cyrus and non-Cyrus, Galt and non-Galt, at the same time and in the same respect, an ability that had made his marriage work. But many of the younger people surrounding the sixty-three-year-old guru were finding safety and power in playing roles. While Branden hid whom he loved, for example, he expanded his popular (and prescriptive) twice-yearly lecture "The Psychology of Romantic Love" into a ten-lecture series of its own. With plans to record John Galt's radio speech for national distribution, he was rehearsing the role of the monogamous ideal man on weekends. If he still dressed like a successful young intellectual, his behavior had been altered by the permissive 1960s: On trips to Los Angeles, where he rented an apartment in 1967, he visited Whiskey a Go Go and practiced target shooting. On one occasion, he gathered together a dozen or so Southern California loyalists to listen to a tape of New York followers justifying the excommunication of Edith Efron. As the tape played, "Branden was off in a corner [of the apartment] oiling and polishing a handgun," recalled Al Ramrus. "I moved out of the range of the gun. Afterward, I was sick to my stomach. All these people showing up and passively listening, and [in their minds] that was the end of Edith Efron." About Branden, he said, "I think he was going through a belated adolescence. I think it was destructive for him to have been anointed by Ayn Rand at such an early age." Said Iris Bell, another NBI alumna then living in Los Angeles, "He was having a slow-motion nervous breakdown." Yet he did not cut back his social and professional commitments; because he found his only sense of meaning in action, he told Rand, he continued to ramp them up.

Meanwhile, Barbara was employing delaying tactics to protect him, although he still hadn't told her about the four-year duration of his affair with Patrecia. There was little pleasure in playing the role of middleman with Rand. She lurched between impossible choices, she recalled. "[I

used to race] from my office to Ayn in the middle of the day, or from my
apartment to Ayn in the middle of the night," she wrote, "when she called
to say she had a new idea that might explain Nathaniel. . . . And then I
ran to Nathaniel, to hear him say, tears streaming down his face, 'Barbara, please help me! I don't know what to do!' " She was convinced that
disclosing Branden's secret would, at that late date, place his mental stability at risk. She knew that telling the truth would threaten NBI. And
she feared that the unmasking of Nathaniel might permanently weaken
Rand's desire to live and work—"not [Nathaniel] the person," she told a
friend after the author's death, "but [Nathaniel] the symbol." Yet to go on
comforting the wounded lion as she brooded and raged in ignorance was
cruel, and when Barbara finally understood that Branden was not going
to outgrow or give up Patrecia, it was untenable. Again, she urged him to
confess. He couldn't bring himself to do it.

In this atmosphere of urgent secrets and hushed conversations, other
insiders built small followings of their own, typically acquiring authority
through a false impression of intimacy with Rand, Branden, or Leonard
Peikoff, who was back in favor with the diva. Prescription drugs, including tranquilizers and barbiturates, were readily available to Objectivists
(as they were to many Americans in the 1960s), and some used them
heavily to alter their "only tool[s] of survival," their minds. Male bisexual
and homosexual followers, who understood that by the dictates of Rand's
theory of romantic love they were not only irrational and immoral but
also, as she once declared from the stage of Ford Hall Forum, "disgusting," dated young women in public and hid their same-sex liaisons. "But
of course [in the late 1960s] everybody was having affairs," said a film
producer who hosted NBI's Romantic Screen movie nights. "I was dating
guys and girls. There was stuff going on that was not at all according to
Objectivist rules." Before Patrecia's marriage, for example, this man
dated her sister Liesha while his male lover dated Patrecia. "It was a wild
time," recalled Kerry O'Quinn, a group-therapy patient of Allan Blumenthal's and one of half a dozen artists who attended a painting class given
by Joan. Some followers "knew about us and accepted us," he said. But
the antihomosexual bias expressed by Rand and hammered home by
Branden in lectures and essays took a toll; gay men and women "bit their
tongues and hid their guilt," recalled O'Quinn. Some entered into therapy to rid themselves of unwanted sexual urges. (Rand herself reportedly
once claimed to have "cured" one of her young favorites who admitted to

a preference for men but denied that he had ever acted on his feelings.) They and other followers relied on a small group of therapists who admired Branden, although they didn't necessarily agree with him about homosexuality or other issues, and practiced in New York throughout the late 1960s and early 1970s. This group included Lee Shulman and Roger Callahan, Ph.D.s who migrated from Detroit to work with Branden and quickly built thriving practices, and younger practitioners such as Lonnie Leonard, who was an investor in NBI Theater's planned production of *The Fountainhead* and, later, surrendered his license to avoid prosecution for preying sexually on young female Objectivists schooled in the art of hero worship. Many followers were operating from "the outside in," repeated Don Ventura. "There were those who were extremely hypocritical and those who were less so," and, most probably, hundreds or thousands who simply did their best to apply what they had learned from Rand and her books to their thinking, politics, and daily lives.

Although the whispered phone calls and emergencies didn't escape the notice of NBI staffers or their friends and fellow students, there were still no rumors—not *any*, as far as surviving followers remember— about the romantic entanglement between Rand and Branden. Her preoccupation with Branden rendered her contact with other followers less frequent in 1967 and 1968, and when she did encounter them, she was edgy and suspicious. Her behavior during question-and-answer sessions at NBI was at times so censorious and even abusive that Branden asked students to write down their questions so that he could screen them in advance. When that failed, he and Barbara discouraged her from coming. In May 1967, during a heavily promoted public debate between Branden and the well-known, irrepressibly opinionated psychologist Albert Ellis, she threw an especially dramatic tantrum. The topic of debate was the merits of Ellis's rational emotive behavioral therapy, which emphasized self-acceptance, versus the merits of Objectivist therapy, which aimed at correcting wrong or evil mental premises, though both approaches held that emotions flow from thought. Eleven hundred people had packed a ballroom in the New Yorker Hotel on West Thirty-fourth Street and heard Ellis declare from the podium that Miss Rand's fictional heroes were destructive to the average person's self-esteem because they were "unreal" and "utterly impossible." Enraged, she stood up from the audience and shouted at Ellis, "Am *I* unreal? Am *I* a character who can't possibly exist?" The crowd, mostly Rand's partisans, shouted and booed. It took some time for the moderator, Lee Shulman, to calm them, and the debate ended on a sour note. Ellis, himself a notorious hothead, later described Rand as a full-blown narcissist and a manic-depressive, as well as "a fucking baby" and a fanatical bigot with Nazi leanings. A year after the debate he published a short book intended to prove that Objectivism was a classic religious cult, with Rand playing the role of God.

She and Branden had a reflexive explanation for her anger. They called it "the excess of a virtue" or "the fault of a virtue," meaning that her commitment to a black-and-white moral universe excused, or even required, outsized passion. But the more pressing problem may have been that she was tired of lying, frightened of being lied to, and aware of more than she was willing to admit about the secret of Nathaniel's deeply *un*-Galtish inner conflicts.

Spring 1968 marked the twenty-fifth anniversary of *The Fountainhead*, "one of the most astonishing phenomena in publishing history," as Nora Ephron wrote in a satirical essay in *The New York Times*. (Like the novel's early critics, Ephron had at first missed its deeper point and had spent freshman year in college "hoping I would meet a gaunt, orange-haired architect who would rape me. Or failing that, an architect," she wrote.) The publisher Bobbs-Merrill boasted that two and a half million copies of the novel had been sold, in hardback and paperback. It issued a deluxe anniversary edition, with a new introduction by the author and with Frank O'Connor's painting of a cityscape at dawn, *Man Also Rises*, as the cover illustration. Rand's anniversary introduction touched on the hardships she had faced when trying to publish the book, including the legendary twelve rejections by publishers. She emphasized her continuing commitment to the novel's theme of man worship and chastised all collectivists, religionists, and positivists who still denied man's grandeur. And in four seemingly heartfelt paragraphs, she thanked O'Connor for his years of dedication to her and her work. "He gave me, in the hours of my own days, the reality of that sense of life which created *The Fountainhead*," she wrote, repeating a phrase from Kay Gonda's theatrical cry of longing in *Ideal*, and added, "The essence of the bond between us is the fact that neither of us has ever wanted or been tempted to settle for anything less than the world presented in *The Fountainhead*. We never will." Again, it is impossible to know what Frank thought.

The first shoe fell in early summer. On July 3, Branden telephoned

Barbara in her office and asked her to come to his apartment. When she arrived, he handed her a long letter, or "paper," addressed to his patroness and mentor, explaining that the difference in their ages *had* become a barrier to his sexual response. With an oddly endearing neo-Victorian flourish, he called his loss of sexual desire for her "physical alienation." The letter itself appears to have since been lost, but as Branden recalled its contents, it offered an apology for not telling her the truth, thanked her for all the years of support, affection, and instruction she had given him, and expressed his hope that they would remain good friends. Barbara thought it was as diplomatic as such a devastating document could be. Rand was due for dinner in Branden's apartment at eight o'clock that evening. He planned to hand her the letter, give her time to read it, and then stand by to discuss it with her at whatever length and in whatever way she wanted.

She didn't read the letter. She skimmed the first two pages and construed the rest. Her reaction was manic and alarming. "You *bastard!*" she shrieked, according to Branden's 1989 account. "You bastard, you bastard! You nothing! You fraud! You contemptible swine!" She ran to the telephone to summon Barbara. "Come down at once," she said, "and see what this monster has done!" When the younger woman entered, Rand handed her the sheets of paper, trembling with rage, and went on hurling accusations. "Face twisted in hatred," Branden wrote, she shouted, " 'Everything that you have ever professed to be is a lie! Everything was stolen from me! When did you ever have an idea of your own?' " Bitterly, she lamented, "Everyone else profits from my ideas, but I am punished for them, punished for bringing happiness to others, for initiating and living up to those ideas." His paper was the worst and most depraved instance in a lifetime of being penalized for her virtues, she cried. The best mind she had ever known had rejected her as a person, and there was nothing left to live for.

At some point during the hours of discussion that followed, he offered to make her a gift of his half ownership of *The Objectivist*. She rebuffed the offer as offensive. While he stood by, she swore to Barbara that she would never see or deal with him again. Her reaction appeared to be exactly as he had feared. Although she didn't mention his sexual rejection of her and never so much as hinted that she was wounded and perhaps frightened by it, sexual abandonment was the unspoken accelerant of her rage. She accused him of immorality, irrationality, cowardice, and unforgivable exploitation of her time and her ideas. The relationship was over.

Except that it wasn't. Even in the depths of her rage, Branden was far too important to her to let go of him without a final fight. And while they talked, another thought struck her and put her in a panic. If he had been underhanded enough to deceive her about his feelings toward her for months or years on end, what else might he be capable of? Would he do something terrible to embarrass her in public or discredit her ideas— this traitor whom she had publicly called her intellectual heir and to whom she had dedicated *Atlas Shrugged*? "I can't predict what he'll do, and I'm terrified of what may happen to my name and reputation!" she cried in despair. Growing tired and tearful as the night wore on, she murmured, "My life is over. He took away this earth."

Finally, she began to speak of giving him one last chance. She set conditions: He must do nothing other than prepare his lectures, work on his book, and write for the magazine, activities necessary to earn a living. She ordered him to cancel the planned theater production of *The Fountainhead* and to severely curtail his social life. He must strive to apply Objectivist principles to himself, and he must work with Allan Blumenthal to correct his disordered thinking. To ensure that he would not do anything to damage her reputation, she demanded that he continue to meet with her for help with his psychology. As for the "pretentious, presumptuous" Patrecia ("actually, she is the girl next door," Rand had jotted in her notebook, deploying a favorite insult), she had to be ejected from Branden's social circle; for the sake of Ayn, his therapy with Blumenthal, and Objectivism, he must not see her anymore.

"Appalled by Ayn's terms," Barbara wrote in 1986, Branden nevertheless agreed to all of them. Rand expressed hope that he would "regain his mind." But if he didn't, she would ruin him—presumably before he could ruin her. Their personal friendship was at an end, but if he could prove to her that he was worthy to represent her philosophy before the world, she would consider letting him remain at the helm of *The Objectivist* and would not withdraw her endorsement from NBI, without which it could not survive.

Over the next few weeks, she continued to meet with him, though less frequently. They conducted business, talked about his psychological condition, and, once, reviewed a chapter of his book on self-esteem. ("NB's mind worked excellently on the editing of the book's chapter," she noted afterward.) She gave Barbara the assignment of keeping him mentally on track. All the while, she was making more than one hundred pages of shrewd, if painfully myopic, journal entries about what had gone wrong between them. She did not for a minute accept that her age was the real source of the problem. "I do believe that [his] 'paper' represents something that he is trying to make himself believe," she wrote on the day after their confrontation, when she had read the remainder of his letter. Still under the misimpression that he was sexually "frozen," she added, "Thus he can claim that there is nothing seriously wrong in *him*." At times, her notes expressed an austere affection for the bright young man she had met and mentored; at other times, she struggled with overwhelming revulsion against his "filthy soul." Most often, she displayed remarkable control as she analyzed him from every point of view consistent with her characters and philosophical convictions. At times, she wept in grief. Not once, however, did she ask herself what responsibility she might bear for the harrowing end of one of the two most important alliances of her life. Nor did she attempt to inhabit Branden's point of view—that, say, of a young man entranced and half-consciously seduced by a charismatic, authoritarian mother figure from whom he lacked the courage to break free. Such empathy for the other was outside her range.

Basically, what she found wrong with him was something she had struggled not to believe: that he had an advanced case of social metaphysics, the wound that disfigured the souls of Peter Keating, Ellsworth Toohey, and that chaser after shopgirls, Dagny Taggart's weak and incompetent brother James. Now she returned to the theme, making a fascinating conjecture. Looking back, she thought she could picture Branden as a fourteen-year-old boy first reading *The Fountainhead* and glimpsing similarities between himself and Keating: insecurity, perhaps, worldly ambition, and an appetite for admiration. Terrified, he would have stifled such comparisons and made himself into a Roark by willpower, she speculated. Unlike the architect, however, the young Branden set out in search of what he "ought" to do to be a hero. In Barbara Branden he may have believed he had found a proper Dominique. When she showed no passion for him, his self-doubts festered.

Rand argued with herself about whether he had ever loved her. She concluded that he probably had loved her at first, "at least to the extent to which any love is possible to a man in his psychological predicament."

She was sure of one thing, however, "with the full power, logic, clarity and context of my mind." She was *too much* for Nathaniel Branden—as, indeed, she had been too much for nearly everyone except, perhaps, her father, all her life. The result, she recorded with shocking insight, was that Branden's sexual desire for her "began to grow dim in about a year." Since she was also the mirror and arbiter of the heroic soul he desperately wanted to possess, he couldn't admit this, even to himself, without risking his self-image as "a real Objectivist hero and creative genius." At one time, she wrote, he did have the potential of becoming a hero and a genius, and if he had chosen to pursue Roark's values of independence and integrity she would not have been too much for him, she reflected from inside her world of fantasy. "But I am too much for the role-playing imitation of that hero, which he chose to become instead," she wrote. She didn't pause to consider that her gaudy flattery of a near-adolescent boy had inflated both his vanity and fear, as well as his stake in the enterprise of being a Randian hero—and had also kept him by her side.

She identified two turning points. The first was the publication of *Atlas Shrugged,* whose brutal reception had destroyed his hopes for both his own and her intellectual "visibility," she thought. That's when he had become, like Lorne Dieterling, a man of action for action's sake—although her notes for the novel about Dieterling were made long before she consciously ascribed this trait to Branden. From 1957 or 1958 on, "our relationship became a quiet nightmare," she wrote, with Branden retreating into his disappearing-professor act and her sense of herself as a woman receding out of reach. The second turning point came six or seven years later, during a period she called the "Patrecia-break," meaning, perhaps, Branden's introduction of Patrecia into her social life and her ensuing anger. It was during this period that she became aware of his "wheeling-dealing," which she considered a cheap way of avoiding his problems, and "his peculiar, very subtle or intangible pleasure in giving orders to people," which she called his "big-shot premise, for want of a better name." She described this as "a combination of faint shadings of an autocrat and a show-off," proving she was more observant than those around her gave her credit for. Under the general rubric of role-playing, she wrote that he had probably been "role-playing the part of philosopher-psychologist and [in] the relationship with me" almost from the start.

Inexplicably, she didn't question his claim that he felt only friendship for Patrecia, whose "notary public" soul she imagined offered him relief from the burden of Roark's stern example. Yet she also angrily described him as a man who had forsaken his highest values because of "a sexual urge for the bodies of chorus girls!" For his own sexual "physicality" was surely one meaning of his paper on "physical alienation" and age, she wrote.

In fact, Branden was letting her discover the truth in stages. In mid-July, after the close of a marathon twelve-hour counseling session between the two, he revealed another piece of the puzzle: he (or his acting therapist Allan Blumenthal, or both) informed her that only now had he realized that he *did* have romantic feelings for Patrecia. No, he hadn't made love to the young woman, he insisted, and tried clumsily to comfort Rand, the creator of such second-best female characters as Eve Layton and Betty Pope, by adding, "I know what this must mean to you, to be rejected for a lesser value." The comparison maddened her. "How *dare* you speak to me of lesser values!" she screamed. "The girl is nothing! . . . This situation is obscene!"

After this confrontation, her journal entries apparently halted. So did all communication with Nathaniel Branden. Her attorney and old friend Pincus Berner had died in 1961, but she called his partner, Eugene Winick, and set a date to cut Branden out of her will. "I intend *you* to be my heir," she said to Barbara, who, in a blaze of guilt and apprehension over the imminent change in Rand's will while she, Barbara, was still withholding parts of the truth, rushed to see Nathaniel; he had only recently told her, to her horror, that his affair with Patrecia had been going on since 1964. "It's too late for you to tell her" the whole truth, Barbara recalled saying to her former husband. "*I* have to do it." After calling Allan Blumenthal and soliciting his help, she did.

Joan Blumenthal later said that she intuitively knew about the affair between Rand and Branden but was "afraid to say it, afraid to think it." Her husband, Allan, was aware of nothing of the kind until Barbara told him the story on the afternoon of the evening they visited Rand. The well-mannered psychiatrist at first reacted with indignation on behalf of his cousin. Even when Barbara revealed the details of Branden's secret sexual involvement with Patrecia, he defended Branden. "How could [Ayn] have failed to know where this would lead?" he demanded. "How could she have done this to Frank and you?" He had not yet heard

Rand's side of the story. Within days, he would change his mind and switch allegiances.

The second shoe fell on August 23, a warm Friday evening in New York. Frank answered the door of the apartment to Barbara and Blumenthal, ushered them into the living room, and took a seat in an armchair for the last scene in the drama of Nathaniel Branden. Barbara informed Rand that she and her ex-husband had both been lying about Patrecia. Nathaniel had been involved in a sexual affair with the actress for four and a half years. Barbara said she had known about the affair, but not about its duration, for two years. Rand's face remained impassive as Barbara measured out the truth and falsity in each of Branden's serial explanations for postponing sex with Ayn: the aftershock of the breakup of his marriage, his distress about the triangle with Frank, a loss of desire resulting from Rand's early and increasing demands for emotional intimacy, posited on morality—all were partly responsible for his retreat. Age was another barrier, though not the crucial one. He had felt genuinely baffled by his growing love for Patrecia, worried about Rand, and was ashamed of the pain he was causing everyone. He had struggled to find a way to make her happy. But he had not been impotent.

"Get him down here," Rand said quietly and menacingly.

Blumenthal tried to intervene. Nathaniel couldn't handle a confrontation right now, he told her, and was already filled with horror and remorse.

"*Get that bastard down here or I'll drag him here myself!*" she hissed.

Branden had been waiting in his apartment. He rode the elevator to six. Rand met him at the front door and pointed to a straight chair in the foyer. "Sit there," she told him. She did not want him to enter the living room. He slouched in the chair, appearing numb and exhausted. She launched into a tirade of indignation and abuse that was almost unintelligible at times, so thick and rasping did her Russian accent suddenly become. She seemed not always to know that it was 1968 and that "it was Nathaniel she was denouncing," Barbara recalled in 1986. "She was in Russia, she was a girl again, and she was damning [all] those who had inflicted upon her a lifetime of rejection." "You have rejected *me*?" she shouted. "You have dared to reject *me*? *Me*, your highest value, you said, the woman you couldn't live without, the woman you had dreamed of but never hoped to find!" Did he even begin to grasp what he had thrown away? Did he understand the magnitude of the prize that she had offered him—*her* love and *her* name, which she had wrested out of the opposition of a jealous world? Did he realize that he had abandoned the universe of *Atlas Shrugged*? And for what? For a social metaphysician's backstairs romance, sealed by a winking familiarity with each other's weaknesses and flaws! If Nathaniel were the man he pretended to be, he would have been blind to all other women on earth and would feel sexual desire for her "even if I were eighty years old and in a wheelchair!" she railed at him, in grief and rage, according to both Brandens.

As she spoke, her eyes were glaring. Her mouth was loose and wide. She didn't speak about Patrecia. With her gift for translating twists of plot and character into a tapestry of ideas, she chose not to address the blunt fact of sex between her protégé and her beautiful young rival. Patrecia physically resembled Dominique and Dagny and possessed the kind of Nordic glamour Rand had always celebrated and could never have. But *she* was the one who controlled her fictional fair-haired heroines; *she* maneuvered them into position with her mind and awarded them their dashing lovers based on their allegiance to her values. She had even managed to steer the courtship and marriage of Barbara and Nathaniel. Somehow, Patrecia had escaped from the world of symbols and abstractions, of "Patrecia or some equivalent," and now taunted the novelist from beyond the covers of her books. Her loss was immense. Branden had been her "reward for everything—my life, my work" and the only man who had ever really made "visible" and touched the hot-blooded woman in Ayn Rand. His lying and apparent intellectual looting enraged her. Again, she did not admit to sexual jealousy. Yet when she cried that he had hurt her more effectively than her enemies ever could, she was speaking for that wounded stranger, pain, who was absorbing a mortal blow.

She had created Branden and she would destroy him, she thundered. When she got through with him he wouldn't have a career or money or prestige. "You'll have nothing!" she shouted. She would stop the publication of his book, *The Psychology of Self-Esteem*. She would remove his name from the dedication page of future editions of *Atlas Shrugged*. She would denounce and pauperize him.

Suddenly, she paused. She moved ominously closer to his chair. Had he told Patrecia about his relationship with her? she asked.

Yes. He'd had to, he answered.

Enraged by this final betrayal, she raised her hand and brought it down, once, twice, three times across his face. "God damn you!" she spat as red marks appeared on his cheek. "Now get out of here." He rose to go, murmuring, "I'm sorry," but she had one more thing to say. "If you have an ounce of morality left in you, an ounce of psychological health," she said, "you'll be impotent for the next twenty years." And if by some chance he were not impotent, she added, any sexual pleasure he found would be a further sign of immorality.

Before leaving, Branden looked at Frank. The older man's eyes were open but vacant as he sat half swallowed by his armchair. Gazing at Ayn one last time, Branden was struck by an insight all pervasive in *Atlas Shrugged.* If she was hoping to injure him with her recriminations, he reflected, she must still believe he was a moral man; otherwise, she would know that he couldn't be hurt by her malice. Ironically, it was *she* who was now depending on the sanction of the victim (himself), he thought, and closed the door behind him.

Much has been made by Rand aficionados of her parting curse against her lover, first described in Barbara Branden's *The Passion of Ayn Rand.* Such harsh invective proves that she was behaving as a woman scorned, said some. The incident didn't happen, or it was the outcome of her love of justice, insisted others. In fact, it was fully consistent with her evolving appraisal of Branden's character over the preceding months. One day after he handed her his "age" paper, when she still assumed that he was impotent, she wrote in her journal, "I believe that he has been attempting to cure himself by the primitive, concrete-bound notion of watching his emotions and waiting for some woman to arouse his sexual response somehow. . . . And if, by some accident of random factors and evasion, he succeeds in desiring some woman and in sleeping with her—it will not and cannot last; he will lose his sex power again, only with a stronger feeling of hopelessness and despair." This had always been her credo: "To say 'I love you' one must know first how to say the 'I.'" Branden desired "Patrecia or the equivalent" out of weakness, inadequacy to reach his utmost values, including her, and an erosion of self-esteem, Rand suggested in her journal, stating, "*The horrible truth is that he ha[s] no self to assert.*" If her final malediction against Branden was rage dressed as philosophy, or delusion refusing to pay homage to reality, it was also a reflection of half a century of reasoning and concentrated imaginative power. It was Rand's world, her creation, and it was closing down.

The deterioration of her lover from a young Howard Roark into a self-destructive Leo Kovalensky, Kira's gifted young lover who becomes a gigolo in *We the Living*, was complete. It was almost as though Rand had created Branden and then clung to what he might have been, just as Kira did with Leo. This time there would be no second chances. Ayn Rand never saw her protégé of nineteen years again.

There are many who remember the period that followed. During the dog days of that explosive summer of 1968—pivotal for the protest- and riot-torn nation as well as for Rand—she notified key contacts that she had severed her relationship with Branden; she told them only that she had discovered immoral actions on his part. She gave no hint of her sexual history with him, then or ever. Not until after her death did Leonard Peikoff, her final heir and lone remaining full-time follower, uncover evidence of the fourteen-year affair. When, on August 24, she met with her attorney and "legal bodyguard," Hank Holzer, she told him curtly, "I have broken with Nathan," and explained that he had lied to her. Holzer and his wife, Erika, were as shocked "as if she had said that the sun wasn't coming up tomorrow morning," but they asked no probing questions. She told them that she had also become suspicious of Branden's business conduct, and Holzer agreed to review the books of *The Objectivist*. It wasn't long before he found the $25,000 loan made by *The Objectivist* to the diminished accounts of NBI. In the nine months since then, there had been no payments on the loan, except for a series of monthly rental credits to the magazine, whose offices were now also in the Empire State Building as a subtenant of NBI.

Later that day, Rand met with Barbara and, in effect, forgave her for protecting Branden. Where there were divided loyalties, she said, it was understandable that a man-worshipping woman would stand by the man she had married. She embraced the younger woman as her heir apparent and offered her a salary to assume Branden's former position as co-editor of *The Objectivist*. She also either encouraged Barbara to draft a plan to continue operations at NBI or reluctantly agreed to let her do so. She sent Barbara to inform her disgraced heir of certain nonnegotiable demands: that he cede his half interest in *The Objectivist* to Rand, without compensation; that he transfer ownership of NBI to Barbara; that he inform the staff and all associates that he was relinquishing par-

ticipation in Rand-related enterprises; and that he limit himself to saying only that he was guilty of immoral behavior of such severity that
Rand had broken with him. If he did not comply with these demands,
Rand would create a public scandal. If he did comply, she would write a
short paragraph for *The Objectivist* explaining that, because of certain
improprieties, he no longer spoke for Objectivism or for her.

The designated guilty party agreed to give up *The Objectivist*, but
only if Rand conveyed copyrights to him on dozens of essays he had
published over the years. The essays formed the spine of his partly finished book. She agreed but refused to commit her promise to writing.

On August 28, Branden held an NBI staff meeting and formally resigned from both the magazine and the institute. According to his
nephew, Jonathan Hirschfeld, who attended the meeting with Branden's
sister Florence, his presentation was brief and anguished. He had done
something "unforgivable" and had "betrayed the principles of Objectivism," he announced, and Ayn had therefore required him to withdraw
from NBI. Since he didn't explain what he had done, he "left everybody
completely mystified," recalled Hirschfeld. "But you could see that he
was [a] broken [man], and that he was confessing to something real."
The volunteers and secretaries were shocked and frightened, both for
their mission and their jobs. Then, beginning the next day, hundreds of
followers began to phone or arrive at the office, crying and begging to be
told what had come between their two icons. Said Branden later, "We
were like mother and father figures" to thousands of young members of
the movement. Rumors "spread like wildfire," he wrote in 1989: he was
a drug addict, a drinker, a thief, and a child molester. In his years of lecturing, prescribing, and sometimes posturing or bullying from his position of authority, he had made few friends, and some associates were
not unhappy to see him go.

The issue of NBI became moot. Barbara and Wilfred Schwartz, the
business manager, drafted a plan for a scaled-down but potentially still-
profitable lecture organization. By the time they and Hank Holzer, who
had approved the plan, presented it to Rand, she had decided against
continuing NBI. She was weary of the risks and obligations she bore as
the figurehead of a crusade that was often in the news. NBI had been
central in adding "philosopher" to her designation as a novelist, a development she had appreciated and enjoyed—and then adding "cult leader"
to her reputation as a thinker. "I am not a teacher by professional and

personal inclination," she wrote some weeks later. "My way of spreading ideas is by the written, not the spoken word." To Barbara, she said, "I won't hand my endorsement and reputation to *anyone,* for *any* reason! I can't run a business and I can't let anyone else run it when it carries my name!" She spoke with such vehemence that Barbara didn't argue; indeed, Barbara remembered, it was with a sense of liberation that she agreed to close the doors of NBI. But she was angered by Rand's escalating accusations and threats against Nathaniel, which the older woman shouted out in bursts of anger mixed with grief and fear. She swore that she would not merely write a paragraph in *The Objectivist*—she would expose him to the world. She would deny his book a chance at publication and create a public scandal that would deprive him of a license to practice psychology, which he had recently applied for in New Jersey.

Ironically, Rand made her decision to close NBI on September 2, exactly twenty-two years to the day after she had written, "Who is John Galt?" at the head of a blank sheet of paper. No doubt, she was relieved to be rid of a set of duties she did not enjoy. "I never wanted and do not now want to be the leader of a 'movement,' " she wrote in *The Objectivist*. A philosophical and cultural movement had been Branden's idea and his accomplishment. Now that her brilliant star, as she once called him, had faded in the light of day, his business ventures and the organized following he had built held little interest for her.

Barbara, too, was quickly pulled into the gravitational field of Rand's anger. On September 3, she confided to two close friends that she was concerned about the woman's deteriorating mental condition and increasingly "reckless" behavior. Predictably, one of them told Rand, and that evening Rand summoned Barbara to a meeting to explain her comments in front of Rand and the group. Barbara knew the script and refused to go. In absentia, her friends found her guilty of making false and immoral statements; and after nineteen years of almost daily contact with the writer and visionary she had loved, she was summarily dismissed. Without much evidence, the great woman and generations of her disciples linked Barbara's apparent "sudden switch" of attitude toward Rand to the loss of NBI, casting her along with Nathaniel as the successfully wily looter of an aging naïf. In this, Rand's supporters draw an erroneously unflattering picture of their idol. Rand was not unobservant, and was not easily surprised. She was worn out with anger. She and Barbara would see each other only once again, shortly before the older woman's death.

It didn't end there. Rand made good on her threat to damage Branden, or protect herself, or both. She contacted her agent Perry Knowlton at Curtis Brown, Ltd., and her editors at NAL and asked them to block publication of Branden's book. The literary agency declined to participate, but when Branden missed his deadline, NAL's affiliate World Publishing canceled his contract. She also refused to return his copyrights to him—that is, unless he and Barbara agreed in writing never to discuss the nature of Nathaniel's relationship with her or answer any public accusations she might make against them. "I knew that this was plain, undiluted evil," Branden wrote somewhat hyperbolically in 1989. "What happened to property rights?" he scornfully asked Holzer, and refused to sign. A year later, Ed Nash, a savvy marketer, launched a small company to publish *The Psychology of Self-Esteem*—without copyrights, and without any trouble from Rand. This was followed by *Breaking Free* in 1970, *The Disowned Self* in 1971, and many other books on aspects of self-esteem. Thus did Branden become known as the father of the self-esteem movement in the 1970s and 1980s. Rand also rescinded her letters of support for Branden's licensing application, but in spite of this he was certified by New Jersey in 1969.

Now the Brandens went on the defensive. "You've got to understand," Branden recalled Barbara telling him. "Ayn wants you dead!" The novelist's allies began to hear reports that the Brandens had been screaming hysterical insults and threats against Rand in front of staffers who were being laid off and were packing to go. "The substance of [the Brandens'] accusations was that I had been unjust to them," she mildly wrote in the October issue of *The Objectivist;* by then she had ordered the magazine moved into a new office, on East Thirty-fourth Street. In fact, as she knew, they had gone further in their comments in an effort to safeguard themselves against the damage they were aware was being done to them.

One afternoon, Holzer recalled, Branden's sister and longtime office manager, Elayne Kalberman, called and asked him to come to NBI. According to Holzer's recollection, he entered the half-emptied office to find staffers milling about, while Elayne, her husband, Harry, Barbara, and Nathaniel stood conferring in low voices. "Tell him. Tell him," he recalled Nathaniel urging Barbara when he joined them. Barbara took Holzer into her private office, closed the door, and nervously informed him that Ayn and Nathaniel had been having an affair. Holzer didn't believe it. "Nathan had so much to lose—he had built this whole empire," Holzer said in an interview in 2006. "I thought he would say anything [including making up an affair] to keep it going." Agitated himself, the attorney hurried home to his apartment (located across the street from Rand's) and phoned his star client, whom he perceived to be an innocent victim of Branden's lies. Rand listened as he repeated what he had been told, then asked calmly, "What do *you* think?" He answered, "It's unthinkable," and added a comment to the effect that the very possibility was too disgusting to consider. She said mildly, "Oh, yes, I see." But "from then on, I think my days were numbered," Holzer recalled. Eighteen months later, in early 1970, she gave him and his wife their walking papers, on the pretext that they had repeated an item of gossip that wasn't true. "I carried through everything to do with the breakup," he remarked, "and then she [found] a reason to get rid of me." It wasn't until many years later that he was persuaded of the truth of the affair, and then he understood that his expression of disgust had deeply angered and offended her.

Memories fade over the course of forty years, perhaps especially in matters of sequence and timing. In a statement Barbara circulated a few weeks after the incident, she described it differently. According to her, she did not divulge Rand's secret. She conveyed a threat, telling Holzer she "was worried that [Ayn's] attacks would compel [Nathaniel], in self-defense, to reveal information which would be painful and embarrassing to Miss Rand. I did not say what this information consisted of." In addition, she stated, under duress Nathaniel had shouted loudly, in a tone of moral outrage, in front of Holzer and the staff, "How long is she [Miss Rand] going to count on me to remain silent?" In any event, Rand did not heed the Brandens' indirect warnings. But, with very few exceptions, they kept their vow to remain silent about the affair until after she had died.

Among the exceptions were Branden's sisters, Florence, Elayne, and Reva. All three believed their brother's account, but their sense of unity ended there. Elayne and Reva sided with Rand. Florence flew from Toronto to New York to support her little brother. She asked for a meeting with Rand, which was granted and lasted for five hours. In the presence of Frank and a watchful Holzer, she asked outright whether there had been a romantic relationship between the older woman and Nathaniel. Rand dismissed the question as preposterous, as she would later dismiss the questions of less intimate acquaintances. Yet she spoke heatedly about Nathaniel's moral degeneracy in choosing Patrecia over her. He was evil, depraved, a gigolo, Rand told Florence. At last, she asked, in a convulsion of loneliness and frustration, "Florence, am I *real* to you?" Yes, Florence answered in a letter written a few months later, she was real, both in the magnitude of her genius and in the fraudulence and cruelty of her pretence of being an innocent victim in a fourteen-year affair with a younger man.

Florence recalled that Rand became more and more inflamed as she discussed Nathaniel and his outrages against her. "The thing that really got to me was that she was leaning against a desk, with her legs spreading farther and farther apart as she talked about him," Florence recalled. She interpreted the gesture as a graphic indication that there *had* been a sexual relationship between them. Finally, Rand shouted that if Nathaniel had been half the man he pretended to be, he would have been in love with her rather than with Patrecia. When the meeting ended, Holzer followed Florence out into the hallway and warned that if one word were said to any third party about what had just transpired, he would deny it. During both of these encounters, Frank sat by silently.

As a last direct strike, Rand and her attorney set to work on a blistering condemnation of the Brandens. When the statement appeared as a letter in the October issue of *The Objectivist*, entitled, "To Whom It May Concern," it ran to fifty-three paragraphs, each contributing to a controlled, chronological though ultimately vague impeachment of Branden and, to a lesser extent, Barbara. The writing was elegant, without a trace of shriek or sprawl, but it seemed to protest in too much detail. It began:

> This is to inform my readers and all those interested in Objectivism that Nathaniel Branden and Barbara Branden are no longer associated with this magazine, with me or with my philosophy.
>
> I have permanently broken all personal, professional and business associations with them, and have withdrawn from them the permission to use my name in connection with their commercial, professional, intellectual or other activities.
>
> I hereby withdraw my endorsement of them and of their future works and activities. I repudiate both of them, totally and permanently, as spokesmen for me or for Objectivism.

There it might have ended, but she went on. Her reasons, she explained, began with Mr. Branden's three-year drift away from the principles of Objectivism and toward frivolous pursuits. Her personal relationship with him had also deteriorated, turning into "a series of his constant demands on my time, constant pleas for advice, for help with his writing, for long discussions of his personal, philosophical and psychological problems." After she had warned him that she would not tolerate this treatment forever, he began to reveal certain unacceptable traits. "This year . . . I was shocked to discover that he was consistently failing to apply to his own personal life and conduct, not only the fundamental philosophical principles of Objectivism, but also the psychological principles he himself had enunciated and had written and lectured about." The example she gave: He had told her that he sometimes acted "on the basis of unidentified feelings," a charge that only Randian true believers could find surprising. She added, "He did not practice what he preached."

The problems had multiplied, she wrote. In the previous two months he had presented her with a paper "so irrational and offensive to me that I had to break my personal association with him." Next, she had learned from Mrs. Branden that he had long been concealing "ugly actions and irrational behavior in his private life" that had involved the deliberate deception of a number of persons, including herself, and amounted to a conscious breach of morality. She implied, but did not state, that he had committed financial malfeasance in the matter of the $25,000 loan. That he "was exploiting me [not only] intellectually and professionally [but also] financially . . . was grotesquely sickening," she wrote. Thus she had ended their professional association, too.

All this time, she continued, Mrs. Branden had pretended to be her ally. Yet almost as soon as she had refused Mrs. Branden's proposed business plan for NBI, the younger woman was heard to utter "veiled threats" against her. Mr. Branden joined his ex-wife in engaging in "unbelievably hysterical" behavior in the presence of her attorney and the NBI staff. "Since this change in their attitude occurred when they realized that . . . the gold mine involved in the use of my name was shut down, draw your own conclusions about the cause and motive of their behavior."

Finally, with an apology to subscribers and others who had trusted the Brandens on her recommendation, she held herself blameless for the rupture and the blow it might represent to thousands of her admirers. "No one stays here by faking reality in any manner whatsoever," John Galt tells Dagny when she crash-lands in utopia. "I do not fake reality and never have," she declared in her published statement. Even so, she did not celebrate the tragic downfall of "an unusually intelligent man who had the potential to become a great man." The lesson was that her philosophy made no allowances for personal contradictions or hypocrisy. It "will stifle the mind" that attempts to adopt it in part or play games with it. "Objectivism, like reality," she wrote, "is its own avenger."

And so it was.

Within a week or two, the Brandens answered her letter with one of their own. In a tone of barely controlled outrage, Nathaniel pointed out that he had repaid the $25,000 loan within ten days of Miss Rand's belated objections to it. "So much for my alleged financial exploitation of Miss Rand," he wrote. In fact, she had exploited *him,* he continued. She had coerced him into giving up his share of *The Objectivist* while refusing to keep her promise to return his copyrights, an infringement of their original partnership agreement. She had taken more of *his* time for *her* personal problems than he had taken of hers. And in the realm of their personal dealings, he announced, she had pressed for a relationship that he could not agree to. The paper that she had found so "irrational and offensive," he declared in a concluding sentence that fueled decades of speculation, had really been "a tortured, awkward, excruciatingly embarrassed attempt to make clear to her why I felt that an age distance between us of twenty-five years constituted an insuperable barrier, for me, to a romantic relationship."

Years later, in an interview in a small libertarian magazine, long after the scandal had harmed the reputations of everyone involved, Hank Holzer admitted that Nathaniel was innocent of all financial charges. He "did not steal any money from Ayn Rand. If that is the charge, I can tell you in my very considered, researched judgment that that did not occur. It is an unfair charge." At the time, however, he was silent.

In her own rebuttal, Barbara stated that her friendship with Rand had never been motivated by financial considerations. "It was precisely my horror of accepting the financial gain about to be showered upon me that caused me to tell her" about Nathaniel's unspecified "ugly acts," she wrote. She then predicted that anyone who expressed sympathy for the evil Brandens or tried to remain neutral in the break would be pronounced immoral themselves and ostracized. As the bright, clear days of autumn reached their zenith, she and Nathaniel mailed their letter, entitled "In Answer to Ayn Rand," to 21,000 subscribers of *The Objectivist.* Then Barbara and, separately, Nathaniel and Patrecia, left New York to begin new lives in Los Angeles.

The reaction to Rand's charges against the Brandens exceeded Barbara's prediction. Alan Greenspan, Leonard Peikoff, and others signed a terse coda to Rand's "To Whom It May Concern" in which they renounced all future contact with the Brandens. Lest Branden disclose more information about a romantic relationship with Rand, he was discredited as a confessed liar and thief whose word on any subject could not be trusted. No questions needed to be asked or answered. If the author of the greatest book ever written declared that the Brandens "had lied to preserve their money pot and association with Ayn," as one contemporary described the prevailing wisdom, well, then, who could doubt it? Not Allan Blumenthal—not after his philosophical torchbearer had explained that *Nathaniel* had been the sexual aggressor at every stage of their affair and had exploited her financially for years. Not Peikoff or Holzer. They disseminated and enforced the party line— "You're either for Miss Rand or you're against her"—setting in motion a wave of Soviet-style loyalty oaths and excommunications that would eventually slow Rand's movement to a trickle. A witch-hunt atmosphere took hold. As attorney Holzer recalled, "Ayn wanted to know on whom she could rely." The lawyer phoned NBI tape-transcription reps, seeking evidence of any suspicious behavior on the part of Branden, while Peikoff notified the representatives and others that the Brandens were now official "enemies" and that any who objected to the phone calls or forced taking of sides would be blackballed. When Peikoff, now thirty-four years old, launched his own series of non-NBI lectures in the spring of 1969, students had to sign a waiver promising not to contact either of the pair or buy Nathaniel's forthcoming book or subsequent books. In New York, therapists dismissed patients who asked for explanations with an air of disapproval that baffled some for years and haunts a few to this day. Holzer reportedly refused to represent some clients in midcase. Recalled Joan Kennedy Taylor, "He was supposedly handling the estate of my father [Deems Taylor]. Before 'To Whom It May Concern' came out, he called me and said, 'There's been a break. Don't feel I'm singling you out, but I'm asking all my clients: Which side are you on? If you give me the wrong answer I can no longer represent you.' I told him I didn't know what he meant by the wrong answer . . . to which his answer was, 'Then you must understand that I can no longer represent you.' And he didn't." Taylor and a number of other of Rand's more grown-up, independent-minded followers and friends, including Florence Hirschfeld and Al Ramrus, continued to admire her thought and work but never again attempted to see her.

By the beginning of 1970, with the Holzers gone and others disillusioned or scattered, Rand's full-time following dwindled to a few newcomers and five or six inner-circle members competing for her favor in the absence of the Brandens. They were, they had to be, prepared to act as unquestioning loyalists and, in some cases, willing avengers in her cause. And the greatest of these was Leonard Peikoff.

SIXTEEN

IN THE NAME OF THE
BEST WITHIN US

1969–1982

❦

*When people look back at their childhood or youth, their wistfulness
comes from the memory, not of what their lives had been in those years,
but of what life had then promised to be. The expectation of some
indefinable splendor, of the unusual, the exciting, the great, is an attribute of youth—and the process of aging is the process of that expectation's gradual extinction.*

*One does not have to let it happen. But that fire dies for lack of
fuel, under the gray weight of disappointments.*

—Introduction to Victor Hugo's *Ninety-Three,* 1962

The 1970s found Ayn Rand's ideas gliding quietly—almost anony-
mously—into the conservative mainstream, including the *National
Review* and two Republican administrations. (Gerald Ford told a
convention of small businessmen that Washington was "an instrument of philanthropic collectivism," for example.) But her ideas
roared and shouted within a new group of young right-wing libertarians
who were disgusted with the economic policies of the Republican Party
and determined to found a party of their own, which they called the Libertarian Party. In its "Statement of Principles" it rejected "the cult of the

omnipotent state" and called for the restoration of each individual's right to "exercise sole dominion over his own life." It recommended a speedy return to the gold standard and, when seeking its first presidential candidate in 1972, it chose Rand's erstwhile friend John Hospers. Its founders and members, many of whom were self-declared Objectivists, almost universally revered Rand as the guiding light and most courageous exponent of limited government and free markets.

Rand rejected the libertarian cause, alleging that its promoters had stolen her ideas while failing even to try to master her complete philosophy. The presence of Murray Rothbard and John Hospers among the movement's leadership didn't improve her opinion. In fact, after the departure of Branden she wasn't much interested in praise from the idealistic young. The world was small and personal.

She removed Branden's name from the dedication page of all future editions of *Atlas Shrugged* and made a new will, bequeathing her estate jointly, at first, to Leonard Peikoff and Allan Blumenthal. Keeping to her practice of revising her history with former friends and allies, she diminished the importance of the Brandens and denied the originality of Nathaniel's work. But she did not expunge his essays from future printings of *The Virtue of Selfishness* or *Capitalism: The Unknown Ideal*. And for two long years, she brooded over the questions of Branden's character and motives. Had he always been corrupt, or had he gradually become so? When had the evil in his soul begun to dominate? Was he a con man? A common crook? Had he ever loved her? She and her remaining loyalists insisted that he had stolen and exploited her ideas, and they tried unsuccessfully to quash an early attempt he made to market his NBI lecture tapes under his own name. Only Frank and the Blumenthals were aware of the sexual component of Rand and Branden's relationship, and with them she agonized over various explanations of his sexual psychology. On the one hand, she needed to understand his betrayal of her in order to restore the rule of reason in her life. Lacking the ability or willingness to be honest with herself about his conduct or to scrutinize her own, however, she could not find an adequate explanation. Gradually she stopped speaking about him, or even referring to him, with anyone other than members of her household: Frank, her housekeeper, her personal secretary Barbara Weiss, and perhaps Leonard Peikoff. As the 1970s wore on—a politically dreary sequence of years beginning with Nixon's wage and price controls and final abandonment of the gold standard and ending with the fourteen-month-long Iran hostage crisis—she largely retreated from the public eye.

Like a younger son stepping out of his elder brother's shadow, Peikoff took charge of Rand's physical and emotional well-being. Now in his middle thirties, he was still young for his age, with a high-pitched voice, thick glasses, and a tendency toward excitability. He deeply revered Rand; he believed, and regularly said, that hers was the greatest mind in the universe. When asked to compare what he had learned from her with what he had learned in school, he once answered, "How would you compare . . . going to the Metropolitan [Opera House] and watching a ballet versus living in Auschwitz?" By way of explanation, he said, "If you took the total of my mind, whatever rational knowledge I have is ninety-eight percent from her, and one or two percent of simply historical data from fourteen years of universities." She called him by the Russian pet name "Leonush" but still sometimes flew into a rage at his mistakes or oversights. Her verbal abuse seemed only to intensify his love. Said a member of Rand's 1970s inner circle, "Sometimes she would wipe the floor with him. You'd think he had threatened to kill her. I finally said, 'How can you let her do that?' He said, 'I would let her step on my face if she wanted.' "

If he heard rumors about sex between Rand and Branden, as he almost surely did, he dismissed them as slanders against Rand. He regarded her as a spiritual mother figure and could not imagine even the villainous Branden breaking the constraints of a universal taboo—let alone with the willing participation of his idol. He did his best to replace the vaunted genius Branden as her interpreter, buffer, publicist, and enforcer. In January 1969, he launched his own private lecture series, beginning with an "Introduction to Logic," followed by a twelve-part series, "The Philosophy of Objectivism." During his first lecture in the logic course, he answered a question about Branden's forthcoming book, *The Psychology of Self-Esteem,* with a stern warning that no one was to buy or read it. "Either you deal with him or you deal with Ayn Rand and myself," he reportedly declared. *"Either/or.* If you have dealings with him, I don't want you in this course." One student walked out of the auditorium and withdrew from the class. Her money was refunded but her name was stricken from *The Objectivist* subscriber rolls and she was barred from all future lectures and events. As letters of inquiry or protest arrived about the demands that students take sides, hundreds of others were report-edly added to a blacklist. Yet so tied to Rand or to the group were some of these defectors that they adopted pseudonyms to enroll secretly in lec-tures and subscribe to the magazine. In turn, loyalists later spoke of using false names on mailing lists, as means of ensuring that Rand's new enemies weren't communicating with subscribers by using the approved list. After one of his lectures, Rand herself was asked whether she and Branden had had a sexual relationship, as the bold questioner thought was implied by parts of Branden's "In Answer to Ayn Rand." "If you could ask such a question you would not be able to believe the answer," she replied, sophistically, to her supporters' admiration. Presumably the fifth columnist was removed from the room.

She bound Peikoff to her tightly, partly through a scholarly book he had been working on since the early 1960s. Called *The Ominous Paral-lels: The End of Freedom in America,* its purpose was to amplify Rand's controversial argument in "The Fascist New Frontier" that America was marching toward Fascism, by comparing postwar American ideology with German philosophical ideas he argued had given rise to the Third Reich. He became preoccupied with Nazi atrocities against thinkers and Jews, tracing them to Kant and Hegel. The book was scheduled to appear in 1969, by arrangement with Weybright and Talley, a publish-ing firm founded by Victor Weybright, Rand's friend at NAL. But Rand demanded more revisions, and more revisions after that. For the next thirteen years, Peikoff produced draft after unsatisfactory draft of the manuscript. "She was making him rewrite the book, rewrite the book," one of Rand's employees recalled. "He was trying to prove to himself [the depth of] his devotion." Phillip Smith, a member of the reconfigured inner circle in the late 1960s and early 1970s, said, "We were *always* hear-ing [that] Leonard had finished a chapter and was going to [consult] with Ayn, and then he would come back and say, 'It has to be all rewritten.' " In the end, she rewarded him with an introduction like the one Branden had been waiting for and never got. But the tribute she wrote was muted. She praised *The Ominous Parallels* as "the first book by an Objectivist philosopher other than myself" and as a philosophical bulwark against the collectivist ideas that were still helping to destroy the lives of people around the world. Paraphrasing Dr. Robert Stadler in *Atlas Shrugged,* she ended the introduction by exclaiming, "It's so wonderful to see a great, new, crucial achievement which is not mine." The statement was overtly grandiose, but it was also subtly deflating. Dr. Stadler, speaking to Dagny after examining Galt's newly recovered electric motor, says, "It's so wonderful to see a great, new, crucial *idea* which is not mine!" Rand was signaling that the ideas in *The Ominous Parallels* were not new and were fundamentally hers rather than Peikoff's. The book was finally published, complete with introduction, three months after her death in 1982.

She kept him off balance by favoring him as her "number-one man" without designating him her official philosophical successor or "intellectual heir." After Branden, it is unlikely that she would again invest a follower with so much trust and power. Yet he must have wanted the validation that came with the title "intellectual heir," for he claimed it after her death, even posting it on his Web site, implying to others that she had bestowed it on him in her will (there is no such reference). While she lived, he tried not to repeat the mistakes that had caused her to punish him in the middle 1960s; overcompensating, perhaps, he relentlessly proselytized for her in social and academic settings. He paid a price. The open, witty boy who had felt "total awe" on meeting her in 1951 gradually became humorless and dutiful. He was known as a gifted teacher. Employed as a junior philosophy professor at colleges including Hunter, New York University, and the Polytechnic Institute of Brooklyn, however, he couldn't resist trying to "convert" his students to Rand's ideas, in spite of warnings. As a result, he lost his teaching posts and damaged his future prospects. By the middle 1970s his university teaching career was over, although he continued to seek jobs throughout the 1980s. In 1987, when he was fifty-four years old and living in California, his second wife, Cynthia Pastor, wrote a poignant letter to Sidney Hook, her husband's former academic adviser at NYU, pleading for help in finding her husband a post in which to exercise "his talent and passion for teaching." Peikoff had applied to three hundred colleges and universities, she wrote. He had been granted three interviews and had been "explicitly rejected because of his views." Hook replied, not unkindly, that before recommending his former student for another teaching job, he would have to be satisfied that Peikoff would not inject, where inappropriate, Randian dogma into classroom instruction. "I made that a condition before giving him a couple of classes to teach at NYU many years ago," Hook wrote. "He didn't live up to the condition . . . I still recommended him in hopes he would mature and try to follow the pedagogic model to which he had been exposed in my classes. . . . I do not believe, concerned as he is with teaching *the* message, he is interested in students as individual human beings and helping them develop their own independent personalities." The eminent professor also cited longstanding reports of Peikoff's "spiteful fury" against associates who differed with him, manifested in boycott campaigns against colleagues' books and in nuisance lawsuits, in the intensity of which he exceeded even Rand.

She also named him an editor of *The Objectivist* and of its scaled-down successor publication, *The Ayn Rand Letter,* until late 1974, when the *Letter* was discontinued. "I am tired of saying 'I told you so,' " she wrote. The essays she contributed to almost every issue were not the sweeping policy statements of the 1960s; they were sometimes illuminating, more often bitter assessments of current events. She published position papers against the war on poverty, "selfless" hippies, affirmative action, government funding of the arts, international relief aid, the Watergate Committee—as well as in opposition to the Vietnam War and a wave of 1970s anti-obscenity legislation. She crafted a brilliant and farsighted critique of B. F. Skinner's 1971 behaviorist manifesto, *Beyond Freedom and Dignity,* in which she aptly quoted Victor Hugo: "And he [the student Marius in *Les Misérables*] blesses God for having given him these two riches which many of the rich are lacking: work, which gives him freedom, and thought, which gives him dignity." More often, she quoted from her own work in rebuttal to the prevailing wisdom of the decade's altruists and shallow thinkers.

In 1969, she led a course in nonfiction writing, with the announced purpose of training a new brigade of contributors to *The Objectivist.* The class met on Saturday evenings in her apartment, where she offered detailed if conventional advice about content and composition. Edited, these lessons appeared posthumously as *The Art of Nonfiction.* Also in 1969, she published *The Romantic Manifesto,* a collection of essays reflecting on the philosophical meaning of art as "sense of life" and as "a selective re-creation of reality according to an artist's metaphysical value judgments," which was Rand's definition of the romantic strain in which she wrote. She continued to present her popular annual lectures at the Ford Hall Forum in Boston but accepted few other public engagements.

There were memorable exceptions. In July 1969, Alan Greenspan, then a member of President Nixon's Gates Commission on the draft, arranged for her to be present for NASA's launch of Apollo 11 at Cape Kennedy, Florida, an event that for the first time placed men on the surface of the moon. She was thrilled by the sight of the powerful rocket lifting into the sky. "What we had seen, in naked essentials, was the concentrated abstraction of man's greatness," she wrote in *The Objectivist.* When the spacecraft landed on the Moon, she praised Neil Armstrong's broadcast comment, which might have come from *Atlas Shrugged:* "That's one small step for a man, one giant leap for mankind." Although she didn't approve of government funding for scientific projects except in military matters, she restated what she had written about the atomic bomb: "It is not coercion, not the physical force or threat of a gun that created Apollo 11. The scientists, the technologists, the engineers, the astronauts were free men acting of their own choice." The family with whom she and O'Connor stayed in Titusville, NASA's pleasant bedroom town for Kennedy Space Center employees, remembered that she was wearing a new diamond-and-ruby ring. The ring had forty rubies, one for each year she had been married to Frank, and she told the family that he had given it to her for their wedding anniversary in April. On Rand's return to New York, Barbara Weiss reflected that she had never seen the great woman in a better frame of mind. And yet there was unremitting anger. "Those who suggest we substitute a war on poverty for the space program should ask themselves whether the premises and values that form the character of an astronaut would be satisfied by a lifetime of carrying bedpans and teaching the alphabet to the mentally retarded," she wrote in *The Objectivist.* This, like her praise, was a scrap of old rhetoric, and was unseemly.

Another high point was an address she gave in March 1974 to members of the senior class of the United States Military Academy at West Point. She spoke at the invitation of Colonel Herman Ivey, a philosophy instructor who had completed two tours of duty as a pilot in Vietnam and was an admirer of *Atlas Shrugged.* The Vietnam War was officially over. But the eleventh-hour airlift of American support personnel out of Saigon was still a year away, and the bitter criticism of the military for its conduct of the war charged the atmosphere at West Point. Rand made it clear to Colonel Ivey that she admired the cadets' and officers' voluntary service as exemplary of the strength, competence, restraint, and honor that characterized American military tradition, and this made him more eager to present her to his students.

The speech she gave, later published as "Philosophy: Who Needs It" in a book of the same name, proved an emotional epiphany for everyone

present and was an example of Rand at her most stirring. It opened with
a parable. A spaceship crashes on an unknown planet. The astronaut re-
gains consciousness amid a strange landscape, under a foreboding sky.
He knows that he should ask himself certain questions, which Rand
identified as the basic questions of philosophy: Where am I? How can I
discover where I am? and, Once I know where I am, what should I do?
The astronaut, however, is filled with fear. If he pursues these questions,
he may discover that he is in dangerous territory or too far from Earth to
manage a return. He spots some odd-looking creatures approaching his
spaceship from a distance and decides to wait and see if *they* have answers. He is never heard from again.

The three questions, Rand explained, are the province of three
branches of philosophy: metaphysics, epistemology, and ethics. Conventional wisdom would answer them this way: (1) The astronaut is in an incomprehensible world, whether he is in space or on Earth; (2) his mind
is powerless to discover anything for certain; and (3) there is nothing he
can do. Therefore he is helpless in the face of his destroyers. The habit of
rationality would answer differently: (1) He is in a universe governed by
natural laws; (2) he can acquire knowledge of those laws through observation and reason; and (3) he must act, and act on his own behalf. "You
have no choice about the necessity to integrate your observations, your
experiences, your knowledge into abstract ideas, i.e., into principles," she
told the cadets in a famous defense of philosophical reflection. "Your
only choice is whether these principles are true or false, whether they
represent your conscious rational convictions—or a grab bag of notions
snatched at random, whose sources, validity, context and consequences
you do not know, notions which, more often than not, you would drop
like a hot potato if you knew." She extolled Aristotle and warned against
"the Kantian-Hegelian-collectivist establishment," which, she declared,
had sown confusion for two centuries among practical leaders such as
themselves. In effect, said Colonel Ivey, she told the nation's aspiring
young officers that they not only had the ability to understand the differences between right and wrong but also the responsibility to act on their
convictions. Whereas other guest speakers had maintained a diplomatic
silence on the subject of the cadets' military mission, she praised them
for preserving "qualities of character which were typical at the time
of America's birth, but are virtually non-existent today: earnestness—
dedication—a sense of honor. Honor," she added, "is self-esteem made

visible in action." At the end of the speech, the cadets and officers stood and cheered.

Afterward, Rand, accompanied by Frank, Allan and Joan Blumenthal, Rand's secretary Barbara Weiss, Nathaniel's sister Elayne Kalberman (who had temporarily sided with Rand against her brother), Elayne's husband Harry Kalberman, Leonard Peikoff and his new (first) wife, a broadcast technician named Sue Ludel—Rand's diminished inner circle—walked to the West Point officers' club to answer questions and sign autographs. "Men were standing on other men's shoulders to hear her," said Barbara Weiss. "There was a wall of men. They didn't want to miss a word." Yet even within the shared context of the military academy, there were those who were displeased by her ideas. "My impression was that the cadets and the faculty were very much taken with [her speech]," said Brigadier General Jack Capps, then deputy head of the English department. "But when they had time to sit down and think it over, some of the things Miss Rand had advocated were things that they had gone to war against." He mentioned her answer to a cadet's question about the moral legitimacy of federal raids on the Sioux reservation at Wounded Knee, South Dakota, and, in general, the history of U.S. aggression against American Indians (as they were then called). When cultures clash, she answered coolly, the superior technological culture will always prevail against the inferior, less developed one. Moreover, she said, the tribes that had occupied the land for five thousand years had done nothing with it and should stand aside for those who would. She didn't know that the cadet who had asked the question was a native American, but the other cadets and officers knew and were embarrassed, said Brigadier General Capps. Before she returned to New York, Colonel Ivey asked permission to publish her speech as an introduction to a new West Point philosophy textbook, and Rand proudly agreed. For the most part, "it was a dream trip" for the sixty-nine-year-old writer, recalled Barbara Weiss.

One complication of the visit was her labored breathing. For months she had experienced increasing shortness of breath and fatigue, but at the academy she realized that she couldn't walk more than a few yards without stopping to rest. Back in Manhattan, she paid a visit to Murray Dworetzky, her GP since the early 1960s. As usual, the doctor chided her about her smoking. His headstrong patient, inhaling smoke through her long cigarette holder while sitting in his office, answered, as usual, "Give me a rational reason why I should not smoke." Just then his assistant knocked, entered, and handed him a set of X-rays. The doctor placed her chest X-ray onto a viewing box and, stunned, replied, "Here is a good reason." There was a lesion on one of her lungs. She had lung cancer. She stubbed out her cigarette. The doctor began searching through his Rolodex for surgeons.

She took the news calmly—more calmly than she took any indication of physical ill health in Frank. She entered New York Hospital and had one lung removed. In accord with the practice of the time, she remained in the hospital for nearly a month. She was an obstreperous patient, even though she was medicated heavily for pain. One day, she pointed to her ninth-floor hospital-room window and said to Joan Blumenthal, "Isn't it funny, Joan? I wonder how that tree can be nine stories tall." Blumenthal glanced at the window and realized that Rand was seeing not a tree but the reflection of her IV pole, and told her so. As with her UFO sighting years earlier in California, Rand believed the evidence of her senses, and she flew into a rage. Blumenthal, who visited her every day, mentioned the incident to her husband, Allan, and Allan mentioned it to Peikoff, who was staying in Rand's apartment, caring for Frank. Peikoff dutifully reported the Blumenthals' concerns to Rand, who remained furious for months. Home again, she would phone Joan and scold the younger woman for having tried to undermine her rationality. Meanwhile, the thinker who insisted that a heroic sense of life grants no importance to mental suffering proved to have little tolerance for physical pain. Finding movement difficult, she would not sit or walk. Her medical attendants, like her mother long ago, exhorted her to *move*— even to wiggle her toes—to prevent blood clots, but she would not cooperate. She changed position without protest only when she was arguing with someone, Blumenthal recalled wryly; then, she waved her arms.

She often reverted to childlike demeanor during the period of her recovery. Peikoff remembered bringing her home from the hospital, an event he later described as the most cheerful moment in his life with her. "She was finding it difficult to walk," he recalled, "and she sort of stumbled into the apartment." At her request, he put on her "tiddlywink" music. Buoyed by the gay spirit of the melodies of her youth, "she got [her] little baton and started to march around the room, tossing her head, grinning at us, conducting the music. That was very happy." Yet she refused to take walks around the neighborhood or exercise—that is, until doctors also ordered Frank to walk. Then they would go out together. Mostly, she preferred to stay in bed, watching TV game shows during the daytime and prime-time dramas in the evening and reading mysteries. She worked with her secretary to answer accumulated fan mail and sometimes played solitaire.

She gave up smoking but refused the Blumenthals' requests to make her decision public, even though, as they reminded her, she had indirectly or directly encouraged her fans to smoke. She still denied that there was any conclusive, nonstatistical evidence to prove that smoking caused cancer. The Blumenthals understood that she was all but unable to admit to imperfections or mistakes. And they knew that she was trying to absorb a number of profound and painful psychic blows, including the loss of her protégé and a mutiny by her body. But she was testing their patience and, to some degree, their admiration.

Perhaps the most stunning blow had come a year before her cancer diagnosis. In 1972, half a world away in Leningrad, her youngest sister, Nora, now also in her sixties, stumbled on a copy of a Russian-language magazine published and distributed by the U.S. Information Agency in Washington, D.C. The magazine contained an article about the range of political opinion in America and included a thumbnail sketch of Rand. Nora was familiar with her older sister's pen name but had heard nothing about her since 1937, when the first-time novelist had, perforce, stopped writing to her family. The decades-long Soviet barricade against Western influences had insulated Nora and her husband, a retired factory engineer named Fedor Andreyevich Drobyshev, from all knowledge of Rand's best-selling novels and her fame as a polemicist. In March 1973, Nora contacted the U.S. embassy in Moscow and, with its help, sent a letter of inquiry about Rand to the USIA magazine. A translation of the letter crossed the desk of an assistant editor named Lilyan Courtois, who phoned Rand. "Do you have a sister in Russia?" Courtois asked. "I don't think I do anymore," Rand answered. Told that her beloved sister Nora had been trying to contact her, she burst into tears. "She's alive!" she exclaimed, again and again. "She's alive! All these years, I thought she was dead!" Courtois wept, too. "It was unbearably moving," Courtois later said.

In 1973, Rand was already experiencing early symptoms of lung disease. Energized by relief and affection, however, she began a campaign to bring Nora to the United States. This was an old and treasured dream; at least until Nora's marriage in 1931, she had wanted to show *this* most

compatible sister the splendors of America. Lest even now direct communication from her endanger Nora with the Soviet authorities, she turned
to the U.S. State Department for advice. A plan was hatched: The USIA
magazine dispatched a brief reply to Nora, signaling between the lines
that Rand had received her sister's letter. Soon afterward, the women
were able to write to each other, the more easily because of Nora's flu-
ency in English. Then phone calls flew back and forth, and, to everyone's
surprise, when Nora and her husband applied for foreign travel papers
the Soviet government granted a permit with relatively little fuss. (Later,
it came to light that the government was all too willing to rid itself permanently of retired residents such as Nora and Fedor, who were collecting government pensions.) Rand rented a furnished apartment in her
building and had it cleaned and fitted out with telephones and a television set. She stocked the refrigerator with Western treats unavailable in
the Soviet Union and placed long-treasured objects Rand had carried
from St. Petersburg in the rooms to make Nora feel at home, including
one of her sister's early Art Deco–style drawings. She considered buying
the couple a little house in a Russian-American community in New Jersey, if they agreed to defect and resettle, as she hoped they would. In letters, she rejoiced in her and her sister's similarities. When Nora wrote
about her love for her husband, Rand replied, "Everything you wrote
about Fedya, I can say (and often *have* said) about Frank, even using the
same words. . . . Our friends say we have an ideal marriage." In another
letter, she told her darling Norochka that "I have not changed at all, except to age," and she imagined that Nora hadn't, either.

At Kennedy Airport, Rand spotted her sister and brother-in-law sitting on a bench in the waiting room, looking lost, foreign, shabbily
clothed, and anxious. Nora's large, dark eyes set among thick features
gave her face a striking resemblance to Rand's, but she was taller and
heavier. The women clung to each other and wept in greeting. Frank
and Fedor shook hands. But even before the two couples reached home
in the chauffeured limousine Rand had hired for the occasion, there
came a first discordant note. Nora, having lived all but a few years of her
life under a Communist system in which neighbors and shopkeepers
might be government agents, whispered to Rand that their driver was an
informant planted by the U.S. government to monitor their movements
and conversations. Rand explained that spying on visitors wasn't a feature of American life, but Nora and Fedor were insistent. Once at home,

they were pleased with their apartment but showed no response to Rand's girlhood mementos or the sight of Nora's drawing; this upset Rand, because she considered the drawing emblematic of the best part of Nora. During a welcoming dinner in Rand's apartment that evening, Nora and Fedor were afraid that Eloise Huggins, Rand's cook and housekeeper, was also an informant. And they were so sourly suspicious of Leonard Peikoff, who joined the group after dinner, that they answered his polite questions in monosyllables. Their hostess, who possessed her own streak of paranoia that had deepened with age, began to take it amiss that they couldn't or wouldn't recognize that America was a *free* country. For their part, the Drobyshevs were disappointed in Rand's standard of living. They had expected a "rich, noble lady" in a three-story house, Nora later said.

If Rand hadn't fundamentally changed, Nora had. Rand remembered her as a spirited girl of sixteen who admired Western fashions, loved to draw, and worshipped her older sister. Now she appeared to be an average, aging Russian woman, satisfied to be cared for by the state. She and Fedor were childless, and they lived in a one-room apartment that was regarded as luxurious in a period when many Russian families had to double or triple up. After teaching for a few years, Nora had made a career in display design. Fedor had invented a piece of factory equipment that earned him a larger than ordinary pension. Although they were not Communists, they thought of themselves as loyal Soviet citizens, attended shul, and were proud of their relatively comfortable position. When Rand or one of her circle argued against Soviet totalitarianism and in favor of individual liberties, Nora responded, "What good is political freedom to me? I'm not an activist." She quarreled with her sister over the benefits of capitalism and the evils of altruism, about which she later said, "It was the altruism of our entire family that enabled Alyssa to get out to the United States in the first place." Of course, Nora misunderstood Rand's definition of "altruism," as many others also have.

Worse, perhaps, Nora didn't approve of America. She disliked American conveniences, which left her with nothing to do all day; she preferred her old routine of waiting in food lines and gossiping with her friends, she told Elayne Kalberman. When Kalberman asked what she and her friends talked about, she said that they discussed freedom and what it would be like to do and say anything they wanted, adding, however, that they really didn't mind the Soviet way of life. One day, she went into a store to buy a tube of toothpaste and found herself over-

whelmed by the number of brands and sizes and became angry when a
clerk wasn't willing to help her choose. Why were there so many kinds
of everything? How did New Yorkers stand the crowds of strangers?
Why was Central Park so dirty? The one thing she wanted to do was to
visit Hollywood, and Rand disappointed her in this; the writer had a
deadline to meet for *The Ayn Rand Letter* and, besides, she lacked the
physical stamina to travel or act as a tour guide. "But you are a rich and
famous person!" Nora objected. "You can do whatever you want!" Naturally, Rand was indignant. How dare this opinionated woman criticize
America and make demands? What had happened to the little sister
who had shared her love of Western values?

Worst of all, Nora did not admire Rand's novels. On the Drobyshevs'
first evening in New York, Rand had proudly presented Nora with copies
of all four: taken together, they were the heart of Rand's life's achievement, which until now no one in her family had ever seen or read. Rand
had fulfilled her youthful promise, in every sense. But she gained no
recognition from Nora. With the exception of part of *We the Living,* Nora
did not read any of the books; of *We the Living* she later said that the little she had read was offensive and contrived. "[My sister] had just artificially constructed everything," Nora told an interviewer in 1997. "She
had made up all of our lives." Setting aside *Anthem, The Fountainhead,*
and *Atlas Shrugged,* Nora borrowed or bought a volume by Aleksandr
Solzhenitsyn, whose more subversive works were unavailable in Russia
and who in 1974 would be charged with treason and forced to emigrate,
eventually settling in Vermont. Rand hated Solzhenitsyn for his outspoken anti-Western views and his religiosity, and when she discovered that
Nora preferred his writing to her own, she demanded that Nora return
her books. Nora complied. All told, the little sister pronounced her older
sister's writing to be "fake" and "lacking in talent," and she paid no more
attention to it.

In the second or third week, Fedor, who had a history of heart disease, collapsed with a sudden heart attack. By then, Rand had stopped
speaking to her sister. Nora managed to dial 911, and an ambulance
took Fedor to Bellevue Hospital, where he underwent successful surgery. Nora called Rand, but Rand did not come, either that day or during
the two weeks of her brother-in-law's hospitalization. After he had been
discharged and taken a few days to recuperate, Rand suggested that the
pair return to Russia. She did not see them off. She did contact her

lawyer, Eugene Winick, to assure herself that Nora would not automatically inherit any of her money when she died. Nora would not, he told her. Nor, as it turned out, did Nora wish to; the younger sister resembled the older in her stubbornness and her propensity to mix anger with contempt. When Nora and Fedor were gone, Rand's friends discovered that their vacated apartment was "filthy, with rotten food in the refrigerator," said one. "It was a disgrace."

Ever after Nora's return to Russia, Rand avoided speaking of her sister. Yet she must have sorely felt the loss—if not of the living Nora, then of a long-cherished illusion that, once upon a time, she had possessed a girlhood soul mate. "She had hoped that the idea of freedom was still burning in her sister," recalled Elayne Kalberman. But the lure of freedom may never have been as powerful for Nora as it was for Rand. Although childhood had been the time "when I liked everything about [my sister]," Nora recalled in 1997, "I was [merely] her shadow and yes-man. . . . She always wanted adoring fans." Nora died in St. Petersburg in 1999, at the age of eighty-eight, without ever again speaking to Rand.

Rand never fully recovered from her lung surgery. But by the autumn of 1974 she was well enough to travel to Washington, D.C., for another uplifting occasion, the swearing in of her most famous protégé, Alan Greenspan, as the chairman of President Gerald Ford's Council of Economic Advisers. An Oval Office photograph of the occasion shows Rand, looking proud but frail, standing beside Greenspan as the president embraces the new chairman's diminutive mother, Rose. Three weeks later, *Time* noted that during one of Greenspan's first official meetings, convened to discuss a soaring inflation rate, John Kenneth Galbraith joked that the only known remedies for inflation applied alike to "Bolsheviks and devoted supporters of Ayn Rand, if there are any present," whereupon Greenspan called out, "There's at least one." Rand was immensely pleased by the public recognition of her Sleeping Giant. By all accounts she did not pester him to advocate for her antigovernment agenda. "I am a philosopher, not an economist," she told *Time.* "Alan doesn't seek my advice on these matters." But they clashed over his leadership of a committee whose purpose was to bolster Social Security (a benefit she deplored as socialistic but, unlike Isabel Paterson, accepted, because she had paid into the fund). And during one of their semimonthly dinners at the sedate University Club when he visited New York, she scolded him so vehemently that other diners turned and stared. They remained loyal friends. He met his second wife, Andrea Mitchell, a journalist, a year after Rand's death, and, unable to enact the Objectivist custom of taking prospective spouses to meet the famous author, he showed Mitchell a copy of an anti-antitrust article he had contributed to *The Objectivist Newsletter* in 1963, and they discussed it—on their first date. In *The Age of Turbulence,* the former Federal Reserve chairman paid further tribute to his philosophical mentor. She had drawn him from a world of empiricism and statistics into a deeper engagement with human beings, "their values, how they work, what they do and why they do it, and how they think and why they think. This broadened my horizons far beyond the models of economics I had learned," he wrote. "I'm grateful for the influence she had on my life."

There were other friends with whom she clashed—and parted. In 1970, she bid farewell to the Holzers. In 1973, she banished two long-time followers named Phillip and Kay Nolte Smith, who combined careers in the theater with Rand-inspired writing and art. The *casus belli* was a mistake Kay Smith made during an Off-Broadway production of *The Night of January 16th,* Rand's 1930s courtroom drama, which the Smiths had mounted at the McAlpin Rooftop Theater on West Thirty-fourth Street. Like Barbara Branden before them, they appear to have been motivated by a wish to please their friend and honor her work. They restored the play's original title, *Penthouse Legend,* and used its original script, minus Al Woods's props and innovations—giving Rand and the public their first experience of the play as she had written it. The revival stirred unusual interest, and for the first time in many years Rand gave extensive interviews to newspaper reporters. On opening night, jubilant fans filled the theater. But the play was not favorably reviewed. (In *The New York Times,* Clive Barnes wrote mockingly, if irrelevantly, "[*Penthouse Legend*] is the kind of play that makes you wish Perry Mason had become a Supreme Court judge.") It closed after thirty performances. During one of the last of these, Kay Smith altered or cut a line, or a few lines (how many is not clear), of Rand's dialogue, either because the lines were generating unwanted laughter from the audience or because the actor playing the role requested a change, or both. Outraged that a so-called student of Objectivism had tampered with her lines, Rand dismissed both Smiths and banned them from her inner circle and her world. "One mistake was all it took to be drummed out for life," said Kay Smith bitterly in 1992. "She was"—or became—"a cruel woman."

Although some professional connections and incidental acquaintances still described Rand as modest, unaffected, and charming, those who were closest to her witnessed increasing pathology. From the Blumenthals and Leonard Peikoff, she demanded a foot soldier's forfeiture of privacy. "She was relentless in pursuit of psychological errors," Allan recalled, and she seemed abnormally preoccupied with uprooting all deviations from her convictions and aesthetic tastes. Throughout the 1970s, she needled Allan about his penchant for playing Beethoven and other pre- or post-Romantic composers privately, on his own piano, and ridiculed Joan for her appreciation of painters including Rembrandt, whose "visual distortions" Rand so disliked that she had positioned one of Rembrandt's etchings above the writing desk of the abominable Ellsworth Toohey in *The Fountainhead*. After an evening's bickering about the immorality of the Blumenthals' "sense of life," she would phone the next day to find out whether they had reconsidered their opinions; if not, she renewed the argument the following evening, and the evening after that. She questioned their choices of entertainment, travel, and friends and accused them of being secretive when they withheld information from her. "By then, there was something almost reckless in Ayn's attitude toward us," Joan Blumenthal recalled. "Along with Leonard, she considered us her closest friends, but, often, she would seem to deliberately insult and antagonize us. . . . She seemed almost to invite a break." In 1978, these friends of twenty-five years' standing phoned to tell her they would no longer see her. She talked about "denouncing" them but was persuaded that another public falling-out might further undermine her reputation. They were quietly designated enemies and Allan was written out of her will.

Elayne and Harry Kalberman also drifted away. Although Branden had recited to his sister the full story of his affair with Rand in 1968, Elayne and her husband had remained in Rand's camp for a decade. By the late 1970s, however, Frank's health had sharply declined. Rand's response was to badger him with demands that he try harder and get better. Her behavior with him shocked and upset the Kalbermans, and they were further offended by her harsh invective against the Blumenthals, who, they pointed out, had nursed her and O'Connor through adversity and illness. The Kalbermans eventually reconciled with Branden.

Rand also had a final rift with Robert Hessen, her tireless advocate and helper. In his spare time, Hessen, a research fellow at the Hoover

Institution at Stanford University, managed an independent West Coast book service based on the defunct NBI model, selling books that championed or complemented Objectivism. In 1981, he decided to list *The Watcher,* the first novel of "enemy" theatrical producer Kay Nolte Smith, and refused to back down when Rand threatened to withdraw her own books from the service. She viewed his rebellion as "siding with her enemy," he recalled in 2004, and never spoke to him again. On the advice of her secretary, Barbara Weiss, who reminded her of the income she received from Hessen's sales of her books, she rescinded her threat and once again refrained from a public rupture.

Barbara Weiss resigned. Over the course of fifteen years, Weiss had looked on as dozens of hapless followers had endured interrogation and humiliation. At first, she had attributed her employer's anger to a blind, passionate, highly charged moral temperament. Later, "I saw how repressed she was, and I knew [her anger] had to come from fear," Weiss said, echoing an observation made two decades earlier by Random House copy editor Bertha Krantz. "I decided she was possibly the most fearful person I had ever met." After the Blumenthals' departure, Weiss decided that Rand was not, after all, unconscious of the turbulence and pain she had caused in the lives of people who had cared for her, including Frank. "She just robbed him of everything," the secretary said. "I [came to] look on her as a killer of people."

Thus Peikoff became the sole heir to her copyrights, manuscripts, and savings and, except for Eloise Huggins, often her sole companion. He had grown anxiously possessive of her, a wound-up version of an attentive son. Her enemies were his, of course, and as she became more isolated he supplemented his own visits with visits from his friends, including his first wife, Susan Ludel, and his second wife, Cynthia Pastor, both of whom served, successively, as Rand's secretaries. Two decades after her death, married for the third time, he was still pursuing her vendettas, mounting acrimonious attacks on heretics, and prosecuting legal threats against outsiders. While she lived, he was the only acolyte who remained close to her, and—whether she knew it or not—he had to further stifle his spirit. "Leonard was destroyed," said an acquaintance. "He was a robot at the end."

Amid illnesses and a diminished social life, Rand pursued two major preoccupations in the years before her death. One was to see *Atlas Shrugged* brought to a wider audience by means of a movie or television production. Because she believed that she had been betrayed by the makers of *The Fountainhead*, she was determined to exert control over every aspect of any adaptation of her masterpiece, including approval of the cast. For years, no producer would agree to her requirements. Then, in May 1972, her agent introduced her to Albert Ruddy, an independent Paramount producer who had just released *The Godfather* and who accepted all her terms. They held a press conference at the "21" Club. But when Rand demanded veto rights over film editing, the deal dissolved.

It was during the Ruddy negotiations that Daryn Kent, the actress whom Branden had berated as an Ellsworth Toohey in the 1950s, was acutely disillusioned. She asked Rand to allow her to audition for the part of Dagny. Rand, whom Kent had heard say, "You should aim high and have a *right* to aim high," answered, pragmatically, "Don't aim too high, Daryn." Three decades later, Kent could recall the intensity of her surprise and distress. But she never lost her love and admiration for the author who she felt had identified monumentally important principles "for man to live by. I still want that world" that Ayn Rand envisioned half a century ago, she said in 2008.

In 1976 or 1977, producers Henry Jaffe and his son, Michael, approached Rand with a proposal to turn *Atlas Shrugged* into an eight-hour miniseries for NBC. With support from network executives, they reached an agreement giving her broad decision-making power. They hired Stirling Silliphant, who had won an Academy Award for his screenplay for *In the Heat of the Night*, to adapt the novel for television. Rand and the writer worked together well, and she enjoyed the Jaffes' attention and solicitude. For years, she had made a game of casting the characters of *Atlas Shrugged*; now she decided that she wanted Raquel Welch or Farrah Fawcett-Majors as Dagny, Clint Eastwood as Rearden, and (at the Jaffes' suggestion) the French actor Alain Delon as Francisco d'Anconia. "She never had [an actor to play] Galt," Susan Ludel recalled.

Silliphant finished an outline sometime in 1978. He and Rand had begun working on revisions when NBC installed a new chief executive, Fred Silverman, who scuttled the project. The Jaffes took the idea to other television studios, but the outline was long, the staging next to impossible, and the terms Rand demanded unusual and onerous. With prospects fading, Silliphant arranged to have a final meeting with Rand in New York and then fly out to meet another author and possible collabora-

tor on a new project at her home in the San Juan Islands, off the coast of
Washington State: Ruth Beebe Hill, Rand's sharp-witted former friend
from California, who had written her own soon-to-be best-selling novel
called *Hanta Yo* and was considering the possibility of turning *it* into a
miniseries. Without being aware beforehand that Hill knew Rand, Silliphant told her a harrowing story. He had made an appointment to meet
Rand in the lobby of her building, where they often conducted business.
He waited but she didn't appear, so he took the elevator up to her apartment and knocked on the door. She opened it an inch or two, recognized
him, said, "Just a minute!" and closed it again. He heard movement and
some muffled conversation, and had the impression that she had pushed
O'Connor into another room. She reopened the door a crack. "With a yell
he'd never heard before, or a cry, or an expression of being frantic," Hill recalled Silliphant telling her, Rand rushed into the bathroom and closed
and latched the bathroom door, leaving the apartment door ajar. He pulled
it closed and left. Hill was frightened by Silliphant's description of the terrible scene, not least because she didn't know until later that Frank was
suffering from arteriosclerosis, let alone that he was by now in the throes
of full dementia. Silliphant surmised that Rand had been trying to hide
her husband, although he didn't know why.

Frank was Rand's other preoccupation, and by far the deeper and
more painful one. After the loss of Nathaniel, she had turned back to
him—to the warm, patient, often witty man who, if he had never satisfied her yearning for an idea-driven, sexually dominating partner, had
never been disloyal to her. But she was too late. Even then, he was failing. One evening in the early 1970s, he collapsed and was taken to the
hospital. Doctors believed that he had suffered a mild heart attack; if so,
they said, the cause was probably arteriosclerosis. Those who met him
afterward assumed that he was inebriated or had had a stroke, since he
found it hard to speak and seemed to be aphasic. He grew increasingly
fragile, vacant, hard to reach. Rand was terrified of losing him, and for
the rest of his life she—anxiously, even intrusively—monitored his exercise and eating.

But she did not acknowledge his mental deterioration, just as she had
never really acknowledged the fact of his separate mental life. When
conversation was still within his power, he had sometimes told Eloise,
the housekeeper, or one of Rand's secretaries how much he missed the
open spaces and greenery of the San Fernando Valley. "But he *hated* Cal-

ifornia," Rand would say. "He loves New York." She nagged at him continually, to onlookers' distress. "Don't humor him," she told Barbara Weiss, before the woman resigned. "Make him try to remember." She insisted that his mental lapses were "psycho-epistemological," and she gave him long, grueling lessons in how to think and remember. She assigned him papers on aspects of his mental functioning, which he was entirely unable to write. At one point she asked his niece Mimi Sutton, now widowed and living in Chicago, to come to New York to help care for him, but Mimi sensed that her uncle and aunt were in a state of conflict and said no. For months and years Rand went on goading him, out of fear, horror, or, perhaps, a cultivated prejudice that what is not rational is not quite human. "He never got kindness from her," said Weiss.

Perhaps it's not surprising that he drank heavily whenever he could. He reportedly ordered beer or hard liquor from neighborhood stores and took delivery in his studio, where he still spent many afternoons, or when she was out of the apartment. "If Ayn happened to open the door, she'd send it back," said a regular visitor during those years. "Once he asked her about it. 'Are you trying to take this away from me, too?' " he said. He drank at night, so that morning callers smelled liquor on his breath. Eloise Huggins later disclosed to a confidante that every week she removed empty bottles from the studio. After the death of both O'Connors, Peikoff took stock of the neglected studio, found old liquor bottles, and told friends that Frank had used them for mixing paints, although he hadn't been able to paint in many years.

And yet Rand valued him above all others. Even in the period of her greatest frustration with him, just before Nathaniel Branden entered her life, the possibility of her leaving him was very small. She loved to look at him. Until the end of her life, "she [always] talk[ed] about how he looked, how good-looking he was," said Huggins. She never tired of his company or his touch. She genuinely prized his early, vital contributions to her work—his American optimism, his fund of idiomatic language, his active interest in her writing, his wit. (In *The Fountainhead*, for example, Roark's response to Ellsworth Toohey's second-handed inquiry, "Why don't you tell me what you think of me?" was borrowed from Frank: "But I don't think of you," as Frank had once told a troublemaker.) He understood her origins and frame of reference better than anyone ever had; he understood her. And whatever it might have cost him, he deferred to her natural gifts and superior sense of purpose. Something she had written to Gerald Loeb in 1944 remained always true. "I [have] had Frank, which is the greatest mercy God has ever granted me (and I say that without being religious)."

Her impossible expectations of him arose partly from her need. With this exceptionally handsome, affable, and apparently doting man by her side, she was not an aberration or an idol but a woman who belonged on earth. One year, when Frank wasn't strong enough to accompany her to Boston for her annual Ford Hall Forum speech, she shook with anxiety during the four-hour drive in a hired car. She was frightened but she didn't call it that. "She said, 'I am very nervous. I am worried about him,'" said an employee who escorted her to Boston. "But she wasn't worried about him. She [gave her speech and] got an ovation, and her worry about Frank disappeared." Having known Rand and O'Connor for many years, this acquaintance said, "I knew she didn't love him. But he was something in her life that was really crucial. She needed him by her side to make her a person, a woman, something. She said she'd never travel without him again."

In the spring of 1979, New American Library published her *Introduction to Objectivist Epistemology,* a theoretical treatise on the nature of human reason first published in several installments in *The Objectivist.* Surprisingly, perhaps, she made an appearance on *The Phil Donahue Show* to promote the book. She also posed for a *Look* magazine photograph, a majestic portrait showing her, with arms flung wide, standing above the main concourse of Grand Central Terminal, a Beaux Arts monument to the American industrial era she loved.

In the late 1970s, Frank's condition worsened. He became housebound and didn't always recognize familiar faces. In an attempt to anchor his mind to the present, she gave him household chores to do, such as feeding the cats, and became agitated when he forgot to do them. He refused to eat, and she tried to force him, in spite of the fact that he appeared to be "frightened, terribly frightened," Peikoff's first wife, Susan Ludel, recalled. "Don't eat the food," he whispered to Barbara Weiss. "She's trying to poison me. She might try to poison you." Sometimes she was cruel. When he became incontinent, she referred to his diapers in the presence of a friend. One day, she confided to the same friend that he had tried to hit her. ("I was sorry he missed," said the friend.) Yet he still rose to his feet when a woman entered the room. Out of loneliness, devotion, depression, or the fear that she was running out of time with the man she had most deeply loved and deeply betrayed, she slept beside him on rubber sheets. Eventually, friends persuaded her to buy a hospital bed. During his final days and nights, she sat by his side, held his hands, and wept.

Frank O'Connor died on November 7, 1979. Rand asked Evva Pryor, an attentive young associate at her lawyers' office, to help arrange a memorial service in the city and choose a gravesite in the countryside. At the service, held in the Frank E. Campbell Funeral Chapel on the Upper East Side of Manhattan, she sat silently, apparently exercising steely self-control, while dozens of old acquaintances and former students filed past, offering condolences. Later, she, Leonard, and a small group of Leonard's friends drove to the nonsectarian Kensico Cemetery in Valhalla, New York. David Kelley, a student of Leonard's (later a philosophy professor at Vassar, whom Leonard excommunicated), read "When Earth's Last Picture Is Painted" by Rudyard Kipling, a writer from the heroic age of Ayn's and Frank's childhoods. Then she watched as her husband was lowered into the ground, beside an empty plot she had purchased for herself. She had heard that long-married couples often die within months of each other. "I won't have to suffer long," she told one of Leonard's friends. Her fellow exile and favorite composer, Sergei Rachmaninoff, lay in a grave nearby.

Although the last three years of Ayn Rand's life were scored with private sadness and ill health, they were not entirely lacking in contentment. Perhaps her happiest moments took place when she was able to reminisce about Frank with Peikoff or Huggins, who was her closest companion after her husband's death. She spoke often with Frank's niece Mimi Sutton and begged Mimi to call collect and tell her family stories about his boyhood and young manhood. " 'Mimi, talk to me about Frank,' she would say. 'Tell me everything you can remember.' I feared she would commit suicide," Mimi reflected. "Every time I called, she was alone." At first, her days were blank with bewilderment and loss. Slowly, she revived. She began to take antidepressant medication. Leonard introduced her to his student Cynthia Pastor. Together, the two women tackled the stacks of letters, bills, and invitations that had gone unattended, and Rand began to receive visitors again. Evva Pryor came to play Scrabble once a week. Alan Greenspan stopped in to see her when he was in New York. She occasionally spoke to George Reisman, Murray Rothbard's onetime crony, who was teaching Austrian-school economics at Pepperdine University in Los Angeles, and she grew close to Reisman's romantic partner, Edith Packer, a psychologist and Objectivist stalwart who lived in New York.

With encouragement from Eloise, she began to take short walks, sometimes in street clothes and sometimes in a housedress and slippers. A neighborhood rental agent who knew her encountered the women walking and had to look twice at Rand, who was almost unrecognizable in a shabby dress and a babushka. "She looked like a poor old Russian woman," said the agent, Roberta Satro.

She watched reruns of a 1960s television series called *The Rat Patrol* and developed a crush on a German-American actor named Hans Gudegast. Straight and slender, with European manners and an aristocratic bearing, Gudegast, also known as Eric Braeden, struck her as a living representation of Francisco d'Anconia. He "look[ed] like Cyrus," observed an acquaintance of the time who later saw reproductions of the original 1914 drawings of Cyrus and his rescuers. With the actor as her inspiration, she began to compose her own script for a miniseries of *Atlas Shrugged*.

An ex-NBI student named Kathryn Eickhoff, a vice-president of Greenspan's former Wall Street consulting firm, Townsend-Greenspan, paid regular visits to counsel her about her finances. Eickhoff tried to disguise her dismay when Rand revealed that all her money was in a savings bank across the street from the apartment; the champion of capitalism had no time to research stocks and disapproved of government savings bonds, she told Eickhoff, who eventually persuaded her to invest her savings in money-market funds. When Eickhoff learned that Rand was drafting a new teleplay of *Atlas Shrugged,* she asked if she and her husband, a jazz club owner, could help finance the project. So did Ed Snider, a Rand fan and the founder of a sports conglomerate. Thus buoyed, Rand wrote steadily, and during evening Scrabble games with Pryor or one of Peikoff's friends, she returned to the pastime of casting *Atlas Shrugged*. About a third of the script was completed when she died.

In 1980, Harry Binswanger, a philosophy professor and a longtime believer in Objectivism, founded a sixteen-page bimonthly magazine called *The Objectivist Forum*. Rand gave her consent to the endeavor and donated her old *Objectivist* mailing lists. But she did not endorse the publication, as she pointed out in an odd and astringent letter to readers in the first issue. She could not guarantee that the editors would accurately convey the tenets of Objectivism, she wrote. In case readers didn't understand why she was so protective of the term "Objectivism," "my reason is that 'Objectivism' is the name I have given to *my* philosophy—therefore, anyone using that name for some hodgepodge of his own, without my knowledge or consent, is guilty of the fraudulent presumption of trying to put thoughts into *my* brain." She and her philosophical system had become a unit. Other matters also gave rise to bouts of solipsism and paranoia. Despite her sister's safe return to Russia, for example, she warned acquaintances that the Soviet authorities were plotting to capture her. She told Al Ruddy that she could not fly on a commercial plane to the West Coast, explaining, "Darling, if the Russians find out I'm flying on an airliner, they'll hijack it." She also warned him that the Russians might try to buy Paramount to block a film of *Atlas Shrugged*.

Phil Donahue had treated her cordially during her 1979 appearance on *The Phil Donahue Show*. In the spring of 1980, she agreed to return as part of a Great Minds of America series, which also included Milton Friedman. On screen, she looked old and frail, even in a bright blue dress and with her hair colored a coppery red. As Donahue fired philosophical questions at her, she grew more energetic, however, and when the audience laughed appreciatively at their bantering and applauded, she seemed surprised but greatly pleased. Then an audience member broke the spell by challenging her views on the merits of selfishness and the "Me Society." Speaking above Donahue's attempts to mediate, she angrily repeated the point she had made in *The Objectivist Forum*. "I want to hold only *my* ideas," she said, almost pleading. "I don't approve of those who preach the opposite." At the age of seventy-five, she could no longer bear to listen to anyone who differed with her. Turning to Donahue, she said quaveringly, "I would love to see an honorable adversary, but I've stopped hoping for it." Toward the end of the hour, he asked about the recent loss of her husband. Had it in any way changed her philosophy? "No," she answered. "It has only altered my position in regard to the world. I lost my top value. I'm not too interested in anything else." Wasn't she tempted to believe in a heaven where she and her husband might be reunited? "I've asked myself just that," she answered soberly. "And if I really believed that for five minutes, I'd commit suicide immediately to get to him. . . . I've [also] asked myself how I'd feel if I thought that he was now on trial before God or Saint Peter," she continued. "My first desire would be to run and help him, to say how good he was."

Her final Ford Hall Forum address, in April 1981, titled "The Age of Mediocrity," was a prophetic polemic against "family values," creationism, and other religious pieties of the Reagan-era Right. When she returned home from Boston, she received a visit from Barbara Branden. It had been thirteen years since she had seen her lover's wife, who had been moved to phone her after watching her speak about Frank to Donahue. Seated in the living room where they had spent hundreds of hours together, the women reconciled. They spoke about the past, but there were no recriminations. Rand, unconsciously perhaps, had forgiven Barbara long ago. Like herself, she seemed to say, Barbara was a hero-worshiper, and whatever mistakes the younger woman had made were a consequence of loyalty to her husband. Rand did *not* and never would forgive Nathaniel, and so they talked not of failures or betrayals but of politics, philosophy, former friends—and Frank. An afternoon had passed and the sun was setting when Barbara stood at the apartment door, saying good-bye, and Ayn Rand blew her a kiss. "It was not 1981, it was 1950," Barbara wrote, "we were young and the world was young, and the glow of ideas outshone the sun." Yet when Barbara wrote to her a few months later, announcing that she planned to write a book about Rand's life, the aged lioness retreated into silence.

She made her last public appearance—before three thousand of the hundreds of thousands, perhaps millions, of men and women whose minds and lives her work had changed—at an economic conference in New Orleans on Saturday, November 18, 1981. James Blanchard, a goldbug and founder of the sponsoring organization, the National Committee for Monetary Reform, enticed her with regal transportation in a private railway car, complete with a butler, a gourmet cook, and a formal dining room. It was the same kind of railway car that had carried Dagny Taggart across the country as the heroine tried to save both her own company and the last best hope of Earth. Rand had never traveled in one. She took a small entourage with her: Peikoff, Cynthia Pastor, Harry Binswanger, Binswanger's girlfriend Molly Hays, and her housekeeper Eloise. After a two-and-a-half-day journey, limousines collected them at New Orleans's Union Station, designed by Louis Sullivan and Frank Lloyd Wright in 1892. The cars took them to an oversized suite of rooms at the Hilton

Hotel—"the size of three houses," said Molly Hays—and on to a round of elaborate lunches, dinners, and parties. At 3:00 a.m. on the night before her speech, she sat alone at a table, still writing it, as crowds of admirers and well-wishers milled in and out of the rooms. The speech was called "The Sanction of the Victims," Rand and Francisco's phrase for the unwitting cooperation great men and women often grant, in the name of charity, to their adversaries and destroyers. She walked across the stage to ebullient applause by the economists, businessmen, and financiers who filled the hall. She was animated but obviously in poor health, and she occasionally gasped for breath. She began to speak and then interrupted herself to ask that people stop taking pictures of her. "Please, gentlemen, don't photograph me," she said, sounding vexed and sad. "I am much too *old* for that. Just leave me as I am." She ended her speech with a quotation from John Galt, filled with the unattainable absolutes that she had come to trust. "But to win requires your total dedication and a total break with the world of your past," she read. "Fight for the value of your person. Fight for the virtue of your pride. Fight for the essence of that which is man: for his sovereign rational mind. Fight with the radiant certainty and absolute rectitude of knowing that yours is the Morality of Life and that yours is the battle for *any* achievement, *any* value, *any* grandeur, *any* goodness, *any* joy that has ever existed on this earth. Thank you." She was visibly affected by the reading and by the emotion of the audience, and she tried not to weep as men and women jumped to their feet and cheered as though they wished never to stop.

She fell ill on the train ride back. Home again, she was nursed by Eloise and shifts of professional nurses, but she gradually grew weaker. On New Year's Day 1982, she rose and wrote the first page of the second part of her script for *Atlas Shrugged,* observing, as she always had, the Russian tradition of welcoming the new year by doing what you hope to do for the following twelve months. But she was losing heart. She had encountered facts about the politics and character of Hans Gudegast that did not mesh with her fantasies of him. Prospects for additional private financing of a miniseries had fallen through. She was hospitalized for the month of February but was released to die at home. "She had no will to live, so it was a simple thing," said Eloise in 1997.

Peikoff spent many days and evenings by her side. He guarded others' access to her. One evening, Mimi Sutton phoned to wish her aunt a belated happy birthday; there had been no answer when she called on

February 2. Mimi was shocked to learn from Peikoff that her aunt was gravely ill. "Miss Rand cannot possibly come to the phone," he said. Mimi would not take a near stranger's haughty dismissal as final. She found the doctor in charge of Rand's case and secured his permission to speak to her aunt. Peikoff was absent on the evening when she called again, and Eloise gave the phone to Rand. "I'm probably the last person she talked to who she knew who she was talking to," Mimi told an interviewer in 1983. "I told her, 'It's Mimi. I love you,' and we cried."

Ayn Rand died on that night, March 6, 1982. The cause of death was congestive heart failure, or, as the nineteenth-century Romantic novelists and poets she had loved in her youth might have hinted, a broken heart. Newspapers around the world announced her death, and most were respectful of her accomplishments. Only a few, such as *The New York Times* and *National Review,* took the occasion to be cool or carping. Eight hundred friends and followers crowded into the Frank E. Campbell Funeral Chapel for the memorial service, where guards were posted, needlessly, to repulse the Brandens should they try to enter. One hundred gathered at the gravesite, in the snow, where David Kelley read another poem by Rudyard Kipling, the stoical "If." She was buried next to the man she had loved as thoroughly as her lonely, driven, and revolutionary nature permitted her to love, in Valhalla, New York.

"It is not I who will die, it is the world that will end," she liked to say. Of course, the world went on. But her extraordinary achievement extended far beyond the collapse, later in the decade, of the Communist tyranny she so abhorred, and still informs our thoughts about the competing values of liberty and safety, individual rights and the social contract, ownership and equity, and the sometimes flickering light of freedom.

AFTERWORD

Some of the central figures in Ayn Rand's circle of the 1950s and 1960s are still at large.

NATHANIEL BRANDEN lives with his fourth wife, Leigh Horton, in a high-rise apartment in Brentwood. He maintains a therapeutic practice in his home office and by phone. In the 1960s, 1970s, and 1980s, he published a dozen books of popular psychology, some of which were best-sellers, and as a result earned the appellation "father of the self-esteem movement." In his writing and practice, he has remained faithful to Rand's major tenets but has departed from her strict emphasis on rationality by restating the importance of emotions. Turning Rand's maxim "Emotions are not tools of cognition" on its head, Branden advised a college audience to "feel clearly to think clearly" shortly after Rand's death in 1982. Over the years, he has expressed regret for his harsh manner with former followers, saying in 1971, for example, "I feel I owe an apology to . . . every student of Objectivism who ever heard me lecture at NBI—not only for perpetuating the Ayn Rand mystique but also for contributing to that dreadful atmosphere of intellectual repressiveness that pervades the Objectivist movement." In and out of his workshops and lectures, he makes it a special point to counsel Objectivists on emotional health. Yet in many ways, Rand remains Branden's lodestar. In 2009, he was preparing to publish for the first time the twenty original lectures of the NBI series "The Basic Principles of Objectivism," which he developed under Rand's guidance, along with commentary reflecting his current views.

B A R B A R A   B R A N D E N lives a few miles from Nathaniel, in West Hollywood. She and her former husband attend many of the same Objectivist and libertarian conferences and parties. Barbara serves as a guide to what Rand-inspired Web sites call "neo-Objectivist" thought and practice, meaning Rand's philosophy tempered by a suitable sense of human limitations and the occasional need for kindness. In 1986, she published the only previous biography of Rand, *The Passion of Ayn Rand;* there, for the first time, she made public Rand and her former husband's sexual affair, igniting yet another firestorm of moral outrage and debate among the five to ten thousand dedicated Randians remaining. Leonard Peikoff claims never to have read his cousin Barbara's book, and the two have not seen or spoken to each other since the fall of 1968.

At eighty and seventy-nine, respectively, Barbara and Nathaniel remain the objects of fitful but intense vituperation by a second and third generation of zealous Randians. These younger men and women, most of whom didn't know Rand, have adopted her famous injunction to "judge, and be prepared to be judged." Hard as it is to believe, twenty-five years after her death they, too, seem to be vying for her approval.

P A T R E C I A   B R A N D E N (née Gullison) married Nathaniel in 1969 in a civil ceremony in Las Vegas. She died in a drowning accident in 1977.

Rand's sole legal heir, L E O N A R D   P E I K O F F, at seventy-six remains her most faithful adherent. In his 1982 book, *The Ominous Parallels,* he traced the causes of the Holocaust to collectivism and altruism, his mentor's bêtes noires. In 1985, he co-founded the Ayn Rand Institute (ARI) with Philadelphia Eagles owner Ed Snider. ARI promotes Rand's books and ideas and provides support to approved Rand study groups around the world. It also acts as a repository for the author's papers, which, according to Rand's stated wishes in the 1960s and 1970s, the Library of Congress in Washington, D.C., had expected to receive upon her death. In 1991, Peikoff did make a donation of the original manuscripts and galley proofs of her four novels—from his hospital bed, after a heart attack. When he recovered his health, he accepted a million-dollar tax deduction for his donation but delayed making further gifts of her papers. In 1998, in an interview with the *Los Angeles Times*, he revealed that when he had donated the manuscripts he "stole," or kept back, both the first and last pages of the handwritten first draft of *The Fountainhead*, and the Library of Congress, backed by the Department of Justice, threatened to sue. The dispute smoldered for a few years, but Peikoff eventually agreed to relinquish the manuscript pages, and in 2002 the library sent a conservator to Peikoff's Los Angeles home to remove the framed pages from the wall. The next day, hundreds of angry e-mails sent by Objectivists arrived in the mailboxes of library staff members and assorted others, including employees of the congressional committee that oversees the library's operations. The Peikoff supporters were furious at what they regarded as government theft of private property. The librarians were "thugs with guns," the e-mails claimed, using one of Rand's favorite designations for government officials. This is one of many peculiar incidents I heard about that indicate the Ayn Rand cult endures into the twenty-first century.

Peikoff was recently divorced from his third wife, Amy Peikoff, and lives in Riverside, California. He keeps a Web site at peikoff.com. His daughter, Kira Peikoff, is a 2007 graduate of New York University with a major in journalism and, according to her university Web site, an aspiration to write a novel.

ACKNOWLEDGMENTS

Special thanks to Elena Tsvetkova of Blitz research services in St. Petersburg, Russia, who provided information and documents concerning Ayn Rand's Russian childhood, youth, and family. Also: John Allen; Thaddeus Ashby; Iris Bell; Susan Belter; Indira Berndtson, The Frank Lloyd Wright Foundation and Archives; Michael Berliner; Kathy Berlowe; Robert Bidinotto; Kai Bird; Alice Lotvin Birney, Literary Manuscript Historian, Library of Congress; Jude Blanchette; Joan and Allan Blumenthal; Nell Boeschenstein (research); Leonard Bogat; Jeff Britting, archivist, Ayn Rand Institute; Fern Brown; William F. Buckley, Jr. (deceased); Roger J. Callahan; Becky Cape, the Literary Guild; Stephanie Cassidy, archivist, Art Students League; Margaret Cheney, The Lorain, Ohio, Genealogy Society; John Christensen, librarian, Harold B. Lee Library, Brigham Young University Library; Simon Elliott, Charles E. Young Research Library, Department of Special Collections, Manuscripts Division; Mary Marshall Clark, director, Columbia University Oral History Project; Lee Clifford; Frederick H. Cookinham; Richard Cornuelle; Lilyan Courtois; Stephen D. Cox; Aura Davies (research); Wendy de Weese; Frederick Dews, National Archives and Records Administration; Mary Beth Dunhouse, Ford Hall Forum Archives; Murray Dworetsky, M.D.; Jenny Eiger; Katie Eiger; Albert Ellis; Marsha Enright; John Enright; Walter Flamenbaum, M.D.; Joel Frank; Bettina Bien Greaves; Liesha Gullison; Avner Hacohen; Barbara Hall, oral historian, the Margaret Herrick Library of the Academy of Motion Picture Arts and Sciences; Muriel Welles Hall (deceased); Don Hauptman; Molly Hays;

Margaret Smith Heller; Hertog Fellowships at Columbia University School of the Arts, Writing Division, and Susan and Roger Hertog; Robert Hessen; Dalma Heyn; Ruth Beebe Hill; Florence Hirschfeld; Leonard Hirschfeld; Jonathan Hirschfeld; Tony Hiss; Beth Hoffman, archivist, Foundation for Economic Education; John Hospers; Gerry Howard; Spencer Howard, Herbert Hoover Presidential Library; Edward Hudgins; Elayne Kalberman; David Kelley; Michael Stuart Kelly; Daryn Kent-Duncan; George Kline; June Kurisu; Jenny Lee, Columbia Rare Book and Manuscript Library, Columbia University; Winnie Lee (photo research); Justin Martin; Scott McConnell; Ed Nash; Patricia Neal; Ruth Ohman; Kerry O'Quinn; Suze Orman; Connie Papurt; Jack Portnoy; Al Ramrus; Justin Raimondo; Shelly Reuben; Llewellyn H. Rockwell, Jr., Ludwig von Mises Institute; Bernice Glatzer Rosenthal; Allan Ryskind; Roger Salamon; Roberta Satro; Wilfred Schwartz; Marc Schwalb; Chris Matthew Sciabarra; Duncan Scott, director, the Objectivist History Project; Marian L. Smith, historian, History Office and Library, U.S. Citizenship and Immigration Services, Department of Homeland Security; Betsy Speicher; Ellen Stuttle; Joan Kennedy Taylor (deceased); William Thomas, director of programs at the Atlas Society; John Thornton; Henry Teitel; Alvin Toffler; James S. Valliant; Don Ventura; Jeffrey Walker; Mike Wallace; Greg Walsh, archivist, the Margaret Herrick Library of the Academy of Motion Picture Arts and Sciences; Eugene Winick; Marna Wolf.

Special thanks to Barbara Branden, who gave generously of her time, knowledge, and resources; to Nathaniel Branden, who spoke with me at length, on multiple occasions; and to Patricia O'Toole, without whose encouragement this book would not have been written.

And thanks, always, to my parents, Neil and Miriam Smith Heller.

ABBREVIATION KEY

KEY TO NAMES, PLACES, THINGS

ARI	Ayn Rand Institute
JMB	Joan Mitchell Blumenthal
BB	Barbara Branden
NB	Nathaniel Branden
JB	Jeff Britting
FB	Fern Brown
WFB	William F. Buckley, Jr.
BC	Bennett Cerf
RBH	Ruth Beebe Hill
JH	John Hospers
EK	Elayne Kalberman
MSC	Marc Schwalb Collection
LVM	Ludwig von Mises
NBI	Nathaniel Branden Institute
OHP	Objectivist History Project
FO	Frank O'Connor
IP	Isabel Paterson
LP	Leonard Peikoff
AR	Ayn Rand
NR	Nora (Eleanora) Rosenbaum
MR	Murray Rothbard
MS	Mimi Sutton
JKT	Joan Kennedy Taylor
JW	Jeff Walker
MW	Marna Wolf
FLW	Frank Lloyd Wright

KEY TO FREQUENTLY USED SOURCES

100 Voices	*100 Voices: An Oral History of Ayn Rand* (Scott McConnell, ed.)
AS	*Atlas Shrugged* (Ayn Rand)
AR	*Ayn Rand* (Jeff Britting)
AR: SOL	*Ayn Rand: A Sense of Life,* book (Michael Paxton)
AR: SOL DVD	*Ayn Rand: A Sense of Life,* DVD (Michael Paxton)
BBTBI	Barbara Branden taped biographical interviews, 1960–61
EOA	*Essays on Ayn Rand's "Anthem"* (Robert Mayhew, ed.)
EOTF	*Essays on Ayn Rand's "The Fountainhead"* (Robert Mayhew, ed.)
EOWTL	*Essays on Ayn Rand's "We the Living"* (Robert Mayhew, ed.)
FTNI	*For the New Intellectual* (Ayn Rand)
JD	*Judgment Day* (Nathaniel Branden)
JOAR	*Journals of Ayn Rand* (David Harriman, ed.)
LOAR	*The Letters of Ayn Rand* (Michael S. Berliner, ed.)
LOC	Library of Congress
MYWAR	*My Years with Ayn Rand* (Nathaniel Branden)
NYP	*New York Post*
NYT	*New York Times*
RPJ	Rand's private journals from 1967 to 1968, as quoted in *The Passion of Ayn Rand's Critics* (James Valliant)
TEAR	*The Early Ayn Rand: A Selection from Her Unpublished Fiction* (Leonard Peikoff, ed.)
TF	*The Fountainhead* (Ayn Rand)
TON	*The Objectivist Newsletter*
TPOAR	*The Passion of Ayn Rand* (Barbara Branden)
TPOARC	*The Passion of Ayn Rand's Critics* (James Valliant)
TVOS	*The Virtue of Selfishness: A New Concept of Egoism* (Ayn Rand)
VOR	*The Voice of Reason: Essays in Objectivist Thought* (Ayn Rand)
WIAR	*Who Is Ayn Rand?* (Barbara and Nathaniel Branden)
WTL	*We the Living* (Ayn Rand)

NOTES

ONE: BEFORE THE
REVOLUTION: 1905–1917

1 **If a life can have a theme song:**
From a four-page biographical sketch
that AR wrote at age thirty-one in
1936 to promote the British edition
of *WTL* (Michael Paxton, *Ayn Rand:
A Sense of Life* [Layton, Utah: Gibbs
Smith, 1998], pp. 17–18).

1 **"My philosophy, in essence":**
"About the Author," in Ayn Rand,
Atlas Shrugged (New York: Plume,
1999), p. 1070.

2 **the brief but bloody uprising:**
Bruce W. Lincoln, *In War's Dark
Shadow: The Russians Before the
Great War* (New York: Dial Press,
1983), p. 290.

2 **The slaughter gave rise to days
of rioting:** Orlando Figes, *A People's
Tragedy: The Russian Revolution,
1891–1924* (New York: Penguin
Books, 1996), pp. 173–80.

2 **Rand's parents, who:** Anna and
Zinovy Rosenbaum were married on
April 20 (May 3, new calendar),
1904, in the St. Petersburg Choral
Synagogue; synagogue register of
marriages of merchants, Central

State Historic Archive of St. Petersburg, file 386, fond 422, inventory 3.

2 **"The Russian Revolution has
begun":** *A People's Tragedy,* p. 179.

3 **Jews were ready-made scapegoats:** *A People's Tragedy,* pp. 80–81.

3 **this period brought the worst
anti-Semitic violence:** Paul Johnson, *A History of the Jews* (New York:
Harper Perennial, 1987, 1988), pp.
364–65.

3 **The czar's police:** *A People's Tragedy,*
p. 197.

3 **By 1914, the statutes circumscribing Jewish activities:** *History
of the Jews,* pp. 359–60.

3 **made up no more than 2 percent of the city's population:** In
1910, 35,000 registered Jews lived
in St. Petersburg (Solomon Volkov,
St. Petersburg: A Cultural History
[New York: The Free Press, 1995],
p. 183).

3 **subject to police searches at
all times:** Mikhail Beizer, *The Jews
of St. Petersburg* (Philadelphia: The
Jewish Publication Society, 1989),
pp. 6–8; Stacy Schiff, *Vera: Mrs.
Vladimir Nabokov* (New York: Random House, 1999), pp. 20–21.

3 **one of the professions:** *Jews of St. Petersburg,* p. 61.

4 **her sister Natasha:** Natasha was also known as Natalia, which is the way she is listed in the archives of the Crimean school both she and AR attended from 1918–21.

4 **faced Znamenskaya Square:** This is now called Vosstaniya Square (Jeff Britting, *Ayn Rand* [New York: The Overlook Press, 2004], p. 3).

4 **named Isaac Guzarchik:** Scott McConnell, "Recollections of Ayn Rand I," speech delivered at the Oslo Objectivist Conference, Oslo, October 18, 2003; Scott McConnell, *100 Voices: An Oral History of Ayn Rand* (Irvine, Calif.: ARI Press), interviews with AR's sister NR in 1997 and 1998 (NR died in 1999), pp. 13–14.

4 **There the family lived:** McConnell, "Recollections of Ayn Rand I," based on interviews with AR's sister NR.

4 **unreasonably treated in such matters:** Michael S. Berliner, "Ayn Rand in Russia," lecture at the Lyceum International, Brussels, Belgium, 1997.

4 **"a tyrant":** *100 Voices,* NR, p. 11.

5 **Why won't they let me have what I want?:** Harry Binswanger, "AR's Life: Highlights and Sidelights," taped speech delivered at the Thomas Jefferson School, San Francisco, 1993; Barbara Branden, "Holding Court," rebirthofreason .com, July 2005.

5 **thought that she had been three:** Binswanger reports this incident as having occurred when AR was three, but according to the *All St. Petersburg Directory,* 1907–11, the Rosenbaums moved from Zalbalkanskii Prospekt to Nevsky Prospekt in the fall of 1909 or the winter of 1910, when AR would have been ap-

proaching her fifth birthday (Binswanger, "Ayn Rand's Life").

5 **recalled sitting at a window:** AR seems to have believed that she was two and a half at the time of this incident, but, again, she appears to have been older. The streetcar line opened on Nevsky Prospekt in September 1907, and the Rosenbaums moved to Nevsky only in late 1909 or early 1910, when AR was close to age five, according to the *All St. Petersburg Directory.* AR may have been remembering a visit she and her father paid to friends or relatives on Nevsky Prospekt ("Ayn Rand's Life"; "Holding Court").

5 **explaining the way the streetcars worked:** "Ayn Rand's Life."

5 **became the co-owner of Klinge's pharmacy:** *The Directory of the St. Petersburg Merchant Administration,* 1906–11, 1916, St. Petersburg.

5 **bought the deed:** *AR,* p. 3.

5 **Anna hired a cook:** Barbara Branden, *The Passion of Ayn Rand* (New York: Doubleday, 1986), p. 4.

6 **took music and drawing lessons:** *AR,* p. 4.

6 **whom . . . she called by the Russian variant:** "Ayn Rand in Russia."

6 **capricious, nagging:** "Ayn Rand's Life"; Dina Schein, "Ayn Rand's Home Atmosphere: Her Family in Russia," a lecture based on letters to AR from the Rosenbaums, 1926–35, July 9, 2005, ARI Centennial Conference, Santa Barbara, California.

6 **considered her eldest daughter to be "difficult":** "Holding Court."

6 **"Make motions, Alice, make motions!":** Author interview with NB, May 5, 2004.

6 **exasperated by her penchant for becoming violently enthusiastic:** "Ayn Rand's Life."

6 **"Every man is an architect of**

his own fortune": "Ayn Rand in Russia."

6 **named the family cats after American states and cities:** One cat was named Los Angeles, possibly by AR, and another was called Missouri ("Home Atmosphere").

6 **Anna came from a more privileged background:** I was unable to find a full record of Anna's birth, in 1880, but Anna's older brother Josel (also known as Jakov) was born in St. Petersburg in 1877, three years before Anna's birth, and attended the tenth St. Petersburg Secondary School (*All St. Petersburg Directory,* 1900–04). He went on to Kharkov University, in the Ukraine, to study medicine, and returned to St. Petersburg in about 1900, where he opened a business selling ready-made dresses. His birth in St. Petersburg suggests that Anna was also born there.

6 **owned a factory:** Information about AR's maternal grandfather has been taken from the archives of the *All St. Petersburg Directory* for the years 1902–6. FB, AR's second cousin, and other relatives of AR's mother living in Chicago at the time she arrived there believed that Berko Kaplan was a boot maker, as reported in Barbara Branden, *The Passion of Ayn Rand* (New York: Doubleday, 1986).

7 **extended family also lived nearby:** *All St. Petersburg Directory,* 1900, 1904. Interestingly, one of Anna's brothers, Josel Kaplan, lived at number 17 Zagorodnyi Prospekt, the street on which Osip Mandelstam, the great Russian Jewish poet, grew up at number 70. Mandelstam was fourteen years older than AR, but the two could easily have known each other, especially since AR's father also lived on Zagorodnyi

Prospekt—at number 12—in 1904, before he and Anna were married. As it happened, the oldest and most active Russian Jewish educational organization of the time, called the Society for the Spread of Enlightenment among the Jews of Russia, occupied number 23 Zagorodnyi Prospekt during the period under discussion (*Jews of St. Petersburg,* pp. 126, 128–9).

7 **at least a few of Zinovy's eight brothers and sisters:** *AR,* p. 3.

7 **read and spoke English, French, and German:** Robert Mayhew, ed., *Essays on Ayn Rand's "We the Living"* (Lanham, Md.: Lexington Books, 2004), p. 58.

7 **taught Rand and Natasha to read and write in French:** "Ayn Rand's Life."

7 **an aspiring member of the St. Petersburg intelligentsia:** *EOWTL,* p. 58.

7 **Rand read and was strongly influenced by:** *TPOAR,* p. 11.

7 **focused on her refusal to play with other children:** "Ayn Rand's Life."

7 **never wanted children:** "Ayn Rand's Life."

7 **broke the leg of a doll that Rand was fond of:** "Ayn Rand's Life."

8 **had given everything to an orphanage:** "Ayn Rand's Life."

8 **developed a keen sense that anything she liked had to be *hers*:** "Ayn Rand's Life."

8 **the perverse and complicated character of Dominique:** Some of AR's memories of her childhood thoughts and attitudes may have been colored by her later reading of Friedrich Nietzsche's *Thus Spoke Zarathustra* and *Beyond Good and Evil.* Passages she underlined as a young adult in her copies of these

books, now owned by the ARI, echo both her characterization of Dominique Francon and her recollections of her childhood. For example, from *Beyond Good and Evil* (Modern Library edition, 1917, pp. 47–48), she marked the following: " 'Good' is no longer good when one's neighbor takes it into his mouth" (Robert Mayhew, ed., *Essays on Ayn Rand's "The Fountainhead"* [Lanham, Md., Lexington Books, 2007], p. 25).

8 **construct a universe of moral principles:** According to JMB, an artist, "Fitting in became something Ayn *didn't* do, because she couldn't." Dr. Blumenthal, a psychiatrist, added, "So she became a superior human being. . . . If you can't do small talk, you create a philosophical system which makes small talk stupid, or immoral." This theme is explored in later chapters. Author interview with Joan and Dr. Allan Blumenthal, who knew AR intimately from 1951 until 1978, March 23, 2004.

8 **a certain kind of turn-of-the-century music:** Yaron Brook, "Ayn Rand's Musical Biography," a speech given at the AR Centenary Conference, New York, April 23, 2005.

8 **one of the first in St. Petersburg:** "Ayn Rand in Russia."

8 **She would pick out songs:** "Ayn Rand in Russia."

9 **buying Rand a chest of drawers:** Jeff Britting, "An Illustrated Life," speech given at the Ayn Rand Centenary Conference, New York, April 23, 2005.

9 **known to the family as Z.Z.:** "Ayn Rand in Russia."

9 **"thick hair, powerful body":** Ayn Rand, *We the Living* (New York: Signet, 1995), p. 34.

9 **for the most part, silent:** "Ayn Rand in Russia."

9 **proud of his accomplishments as a self-made businessman:** "Ayn Rand in Russia."

9 **An avid reader of Russian literature:** *EOWTL*, p. 56.

9 **wanted to be a writer, too:** "Ayn Rand's Home Atmosphere."

9 **from the University of Warsaw in 1899:** Directories of the universities of Derpt (Yuriev), Vilno, and Warsaw, for the academic years 1887–99.

9 **popular with the Jewish residents:** Author correspondence with Blitz research service.

9 **an opening in that department for a Jew:** *TPOAR*, p. 4.

9 **begin his course of study until age twenty-seven:** Or age twenty-nine, depending on whether you go by the record of his marriage (St. Petersburg Choral Synagogue, synagogue register of marriages of merchants, Central State Historic Archive of St. Petersburg, file 386, fond 422, inventory 3) or the ARI's records.

9 **helped all but one of his eight brothers and sisters:** *TPOAR*, p. 4.

9 **how his parents earned their living:** I could not discover the birthplace or professions of Zinovy Rosenbaum's parents, but these may be known to the archivists at the ARI, which controls access to AR's papers and declined to make them available to me. Information about Zinovy's uncle and cousins comes from the Russian Medical List and the St. Petersburg Merchant Administration Directory for the years 1905–1916.

10 **later a strict atheist:** "Ayn Rand's Life."

10 **believed in God:** "Ayn Rand's Life."

10 **experimenting with the idea of**

God: "Ayn Rand's Life"; "An Illustrated Life."

11 **her parents tried to protect her:** Forbidding her to read newspapers, for example (*TPOAR*, p. 16).

11 **an impassioned defense of gifted, productive Jews:** Jeffrey Walker, *Go Ask Alyssa*, an unpublished book-length study of AR, Judaism, and Nietzsche, courtesy of author.

11 **she must have been *frighteningly* intelligent:** Author interview with Robert Bidinotto, Vancouver, July 9, 2004.

11 **little interest to anyone:** "Ayn Rand's Life."

11 **family "shrugged impatiently":** *WTL*, p. 47.

11 **the same was true of her classmates:** *TPOAR*, p. 17.

11 **sure that such social awkwardness:** "Ayn Rand's Life."

11 **thought Nora was *like* her:** *TPOAR*, p. 31.

12 **"shadow and yes-man":** *100 Voices*, NR, p. 13.

12 **It presented Catherine:** This is the account AR gave fifty years later. AR had an unusually good memory, so her version may have been the way the story was written for the children of the time, but if so, it was historically inaccurate. In reality, Catherine was a German princess who came to St. Petersburg to marry Peter III, the grandson of Peter the Great. After his death, she ruled Russia for thirty-four years, bringing Western ideas and methods to a still largely Asiatic empire. In the 1790s, she also created the infamous Pale of Settlement through usurpation and partitioning of lands that had belonged to Poland.

12 **"something between a misfit and an ugly duckling":** "Ayn Rand's Life."

12 **meant for an exceptional fate:** "Ayn Rand's Life."

13 **according to Bill Bucko's translation:** *The Mysterious Valley* has been translated from French and republished in the United States in book form as *The Mysterious Valley*, Bill Bucko, trans., introduction by Harry Binswanger (Lafayette, Co.: The Atlantean Press, 1994).

13 **"my present kind of hero":** Introduction to *The Mysterious Valley*, p. xiii.

13 **All things British:** Brian Boyd, *Vladimir Nabokov: The Russian Years* (Princeton: Princeton University Press, 1990), p. 76.

13 **never forgot this girl, whose name was Daisy:** This was Daisy Gerhardie, sister of British novelist William Gerhardie. Interestingly, when speaking about Daisy and another equally tall, slender, blue-eyed girl she had glimpsed the year before, she called them "symbols. I admired them from afar as though with a movie-star infatuation." What's interesting here is that her infatuation was *theatrical;* since she couldn't hope to emulate or become these long-legged girls, she could only fantasize about them. She went on to say, "Those were the first value steps in my development"; in both cases, they were steps away from being Russian and Jewish ("Ayn Rand's Life").

14 **"ideal country":** "Ayn Rand's Life."

14 **describe reason:** Ayn Rand, *The Virtue of Selfishness: A New Concept of Egoism* (New York: Signet, 1964), p. 28.

14 **He was her "exclusive love":** *The Mysterious Valley*, p. xiii.

14 **something that none of them could see or share:** *The Mysterious Valley*, p. xiii.

14 **her feeling for Cyrus was of "unbearable intensity":** *The Mysterious Valley*, p. xiii.

15 **conducting official business before he headed off to Sarajevo:** Frederic Morton, *Thunder at Twilight: Vienna 1913/1914* (New York: Charles Scribner's Sons, 1989).

16 **moved on to Switzerland and Paris:** *TPOAR*, p. 14.

16 **Rand found a rare playmate:** *TPOAR*, p. 14.

16 **what she had always thought existence would be like:** "Ayn Rand's Life."

16 **she decided to become a writer:** "Ayn Rand's Life."

17 **sailed on a packed ship:** *AR*, p. 9.

17 **"The war marked the end of the world":** *TPOAR*, p. 14.

17 **mistakenly believing that St. Petersburg was a Germanic name:** Arthur L. and Elena George, *St. Petersburg: Russia's Window to the Future* (Oxford, UK: Taylor Trade Publishing, 2003), p. 409.

17 **began a classical course of study:** AR is listed as one of thirty-nine second-year students at Stoiunin in the Central Historic Archive of St. Petersburg. Individual students' records were not preserved, but a list of students, their teachers, and the courses they taught were. (Fond 148, file 420, inventory 1, pp. 1–2.)

17 **Founded in 1889:** Dostoevsky File, fond 100, Manuscript Department of the Institute of Russian Literature (Pushkin House), St. Petersburg.

17 **The school had an extraordinary faculty:** Chris Matthew Sciabarra, *The Russian Radical* (University Park: Pennsylvania State University Press, 1995), pp. 41–42.

18 **sidestepped official quotas on Jewish students:** Jews were limited to at most 10 percent of places in Russian grammar schools, even in towns made up mostly of Jews. In general, education involved "ceaseless chicanery, deception, and humiliation" for the Jewish population of Russia (Chaim Weitzman, quoted in *A History of the Jews*, pp. 424–25).

18 **Almost a third of Rand's second-year class:** *Vladimir Nabokov: The Russian Years*, p. 101. AR, the Nabokov family, and the Stoiunins and Losskys cross paths in many different ways, as I describe later in this chapter.

18 **student there from 1914 until 1918:** Until recently, AR's attendance at Stoiunin was unproved; Sciabarra found incontrovertible evidence of it, and so did my researchers at Blitz research services. Blitz obtained and searched the school archives, which revealed all the facts contained here. A collection of documents from the Stoiunin school exists in St. Petersburg's Central Historic Archive, fond 148, including class lists and lists of teachers from the 1880s on. (Chris Matthew Sciabarra, "The Ayn Rand Transcript," *The Journal of Ayn Rand Studies*, Fall 1999 [vol. 1, no. 1], pp. 1–26.)

18 **studied French and German:** Unfortunately, the academic files of AR and other students have not been preserved.

18 **Jewish girls had to attend:** the Central Historic Archive of St. Petersburg (fond 148) and the Manuscript Department of the Russian National Library.

18 **"revoltingly dark":** "Ayn Rand's Life."

18 **Russian Orthodox prayer:** The late George Walsh, a former professor of philosophy at Salisbury State University, related this personal an-

ecdote to Dr. Sciabarra. (Author interview with Chris Matthew Sciabarra, November 13, 2003.)

18 **"Any man [who has] a serious central ambition"**: Ayn Rand, *The Art of Fiction* (New York: Plume Books, 2000), p. 61.

18 **"a tremendous sense of intellectual power"**: "Ayn Rand's Life."

19 **The teacher asked the class**: "An Illustrated Life."

19 **to play boring games and read silly books**: Later, AR would also decry both Descartes and Pascal ("An Illustrated Life").

19 **known as "the brain"**: *TPOAR,* p. 32.

20 **a ridiculous thing to say**: Nathaniel Branden and Barbara Branden, *Who Is Ayn Rand?* (New York: Random House, 1962), p. 160.

20 **"the first most important event"**: *TPOAR,* p. 26.

20 **writing novels at home and in school**: "Ayn Rand's Life."

20 **Russian military losses**: *St. Petersburg: Russia's Window,* p. 411.

21 **"stood alone against everyone"**: NB speculates that AR learned of Joan of Arc through reading Friedrich Schiller's play *The Maid of Orleans* (author interview with NB, August 10, 2004). It is the part of Joan in this play that Vesta Dunning is rehearsing when Howard Roark first meets her in an excised section of *TF* (Ayn Rand, *The Early Ayn Rand: A Selection of Her Unpublished Fiction,* Leonard Peikoff, ed. [New York: Signet, 2005], p. 441). According to another former friend, the philosophy professor and 1972 Libertarian Party presidential candidate JH, Schiller was AR's favorite playwright (John Hospers, "Conversations with Ayn Rand," *Liberty,* July 1990, p. 25).

21 **didn't expect to publish anything**: "Ayn Rand's Life."

21 **"You [always] planned to be greater than Columbus"**: "Ayn Rand in Russia."

21 **hated the stocky shape of her developing body**: *AR,* p. 11.

21 **was again desperately lonely**: "Ayn Rand's Life."

TWO: LOOTERS: 1917–1925

22 **"There is a fundamental conviction"**: Ayn Rand, "Inexplicable Personal Alchemy," *The Objectivist,* January 1969, bound volume, p. 579.

22 **"faithful to the truth"**: Meryle Secrest, *Frank Lloyd Wright* (Chicago: The University of Chicago Press, 1992), p. 375.

22 **"On the shore of empty waves"**: These are the opening lines of Alexander Pushkin's poem "The Bronze Horseman," which takes its name from the Etienne Falconet statue of Peter the Great in St. Petersburg's Senate Square. In the poem, "he" is the czar Peter (1672–1725), and the empty waves represent the desolate spot on which he chose to build St. Petersburg (*St. Petersburg,* pp. 3–7).

23 **a "city of stone"**: *WTL,* pp. 238–39.

23 **"to astonish Russia and the civilized world"**: *St. Petersburg,* p. 9.

23 **"St. Petersburg was … a vast, almost utopian, project"**: Orlando Figes, *Natasha's Dance: A Cultural History of Russia* (New York: Metropolitan Books, 2002), p. 10.

24 **broad squares of St. Petersburg**: Bruce W. Lincoln, *Red Victory: A History of the Russian Civil War 1918–1921* (New York: Simon & Schuster, 1989), p. 34.

24 **Temperatures stood at twenty or thirty degrees below zero:** *A People's Tragedy*, p. 307.

24 **Six million Russians:** *Red Victory*, pp. 38–39.

24 **shortages of food:** *Red Victory*, p. 32.

24 **railway system had long since broken down:** *A People's Tragedy*, pp. 282–83.

24 **Crime was rampant:** *St. Petersburg*, p. 197.

24 **Czarist "Black Hundreds":** *A People's Tragedy*, p. 277.

24 **retreated from the advancing Germans:** *A History of the Jews*, pp. 423–24; Salo W. Baron, *The Russian Jew under the Tsars and Soviets* (New York: Macmillan, 1964), pp. 188–95. Under pressure from Russia's war allies and bankers, the czar's ministers had abolished the Pale of Settlement in August 1915 (Bruce W. Lincoln, *Passage Through Armageddon: The Russians in War and Revolution* [New York: Simon & Schuster, 1986], p. 143), but I refer to it here for the sake of convenience.

24 **welcomed temporary German occupation:** *A History of the Jews*, pp. 423–24; *Russian Jew*, pp. 188–95.

25 **as were most Russian Jews:** *A History of the Jews*, p. 452.

25 **Short for her age:** "Ayn Rand's Life."

25 **She assigned herself a new task:** "Ayn Rand's Life."

25 **The job of the adolescent:** Ayn Rand, *The Romantic Manifesto* (New York: Signet, 1971), p. 28.

26 **her first close friend:** Olga was born on January 5, 1903. She is listed as a member of AR's 1915–16 Stoiunin class (fond 148, inventory 1, file 420, pp. 1–2 in the Central Historic Archive of St. Petersburg). She

also attended the school during the 1916–17 academic year, according to research by Chris Sciabarra ("The Ayn Rand Transcript," p. 6).

26 **a cultured heiress:** *Vladimir Nabokov: The Russian Years*, quoting I. V. Hessen, p. 33. I am indebted to Boyd's book and to *Vera*, by Stacy Schiff, for much of the information about Olga's family.

26 **advocacy of political rights for Jews:** The adult AR promoted a view of herself in which she was indifferent to her Jewish background. This is unlikely, as I try to show later. Yet it's doubtful whether she could have befriended a Russian Orthodox girl whose family wasn't pro-Semitic; Russian anti-Semitism was too pervasive and too deep. Olga's father, like her grandfather, was an active champion of Russia's Jews; according to biographer Boyd (*Vladimir Nabokov: The Russian Years*, p. 27), V. D. Nabokov was "the most outspoken defender of Jewish rights among all Russian gentiles trained in the law." Olga's famous brother Vladimir married a Jewish St. Petersburg girl three years older than AR, whom he met in exile in Berlin (*Vera*, pp. 9–11, 13–14).

26 **Olga's father, V. D. Nabokov:** Lionel Kochan, ed., *The Jews in Soviet Russia since 1917* (London: Oxford University Press, 1970), p. 17.

26 **a member of Rand's class since 1915:** Central Historic Archive of St. Petersburg, fond 148.

26 **looked after by footmen:** *Vladimir Nabokov: The Russian Years*, pp. 48–90.

26 **paid many visits to the family home in 1917:** The quoted material is based on Dr. Sciabarra's personal correspondence with Helene

Sikorski in 1996, in which Mme. Sikorski recalled her sister's "dear" friendship with AR in 1917 ("The Ayn Rand Transcript," p. 6).

26 **"vast":** WTL, p. 45.

26 **"stately granite mansion":** WTL, p. 21.

26 **"a maid in black":** WTL, p. 45. In AR's handwritten first draft of WTL, when Kira Argounova pretends to ask a militiaman for directions home, she asks for Morskaia [sic] Street, where the Nabokovs lived; noticing her slip, perhaps, AR crossed out "Morskaia" and wrote in "Mioka," the street on which the fictional Argounovas have an apartment (Ayn Rand Papers, LOC, Washington, D.C., box 26, folder 4, p. 152/22). In her first draft, she also wrote that the Argounovas left St. Petersburg for the Crimea in the fall of 1917, as Rand believed the Nabokovs did. The Rosenbaums left in 1918 (Ayn Rand Papers, LOC, box 26, folder 1, p. 7).

26 **frustration with her daughter's gracelessness:** "Ayn Rand's Life."

27 **She and Olga "conversed endlessly":** "The AR Transcript," p. 6, citing Helene Sikorski's correspondence.

27 **Rand wanted a republic:** "Ayn Rand's Life."

27 **Rand's tendency to argue:** "Ayn Rand's Life."

27 **International Women's Day march:** Details of events from February 23 to March 3, 1917, are based on A People's Tragedy, pp. 307–45; Red Victory, pp. 38–39; Passage Through Armageddon, pp. 320–45.

27 **one hundred thousand hungry, war-weary workers:** A People's Tragedy, p. 308.

27 **recklessly shouting, "Down with the czar!":** Red Victory, p. 33.

27 **stood on their apartment balcony:** TPOAR, p. 18; and AR, p. 14, based on material in the Ayn Rand Papers. (In AR:SOL, p. 38, Paxton writes, "She saw red flags rise up on the streets. Armed Cossacks appeared and one man descended from a horse. He walked into the crowd, raised his sword, and brought it down.")

28 **ceded his right of succession:** Nabokov wrote Mikhail's abdication letter with the help of another lawyer, Baron Boris Nolde (A People's Tragedy, p. 345; Vladimir Nabokov: The Russian Years, p. 129).

28 **Russia cheered the fall of the czar:** A People's Tragedy, p. 346. Alexander Blok, the man who AR would later tell friends was her favorite poet, wrote to his mother, "A miracle has happened!" (A People's Tragedy, p. 351).

28 **a period of unparalleled excitement:** "Ayn Rand's Life."

28 **"synchronized with history":** Stephen Cox, Dictionary of Literary Biography, "Ayn Rand," Gale Literary Databases, volume 279, "American Philosophers, 1950–2000," Philip B. Dematteis and Leemon B. McHenry, eds. (California State University, Northridge: Gale Group, 2003), pp. 255–72.

28 **"flare up and fume":** Red Victory, p. 43.

28 **stockpiling cash:** AR, p. 16.

28 **one of the happiest summers of Rand's childhood:** AR, p. 14.

28 **was reading Ivanhoe:** Chronology, Michael S. Berliner, The Letters of Ayn Rand (New York: Dutton, 1995), p. xix.

29 **"need, not achievement, is the source of rights":** "Check Your Premises: Is Atlas Shrugging?" The Objectivist Newsletter, August 1964 (vol. 3, no. 8), p. 29.

29 **confer equal rights on Jews:** *Jews in Soviet Russia,* p. 5.

29 **granted basic freedoms:** *Vladimir Nabokov: The Russian Years,* p. 126.

29 **began to ration bread:** *A People's Tragedy,* p. 358.

29 **running on a promise to end the war:** *A People's Tragedy,* pp. 457–58.

29 **sure his troops could defeat the radicals:** *Vladimir Nabokov: The Russian Years,* p. 132, citing V. D. Nabokov.

30 **Then, to worldwide dismay:** *A People's Tragedy,* pp. 483–94.

30 **spent the rest of his life:** In 1918, Kerensky fled to Paris and then, in 1940, to the United States. For many years he divided his time between Paris, New York City, and northern California, where he was a fellow at the Hoover Institution on War, Revolution and Peace at Stanford University. Though AR lionized him in 1917, she later viewed his performance as prime minister as having been weak and unprincipled (Ayn Rand, "Cashing In: The Student 'Rebellion,'" in *For the New Intellectual* [New York: Signet, 1963], p. 25). He would be Russia's last prime minister for seventy-four years, until the election of Boris Yeltsin in 1991.

30 **Rand kept a diary:** "Ayn Rand's Life."

30 **God was obviously an invention:** "Ayn Rand's Life."

30 **she burned it:** In "Ayn Rand's Life"; AR is quoted as saying that she kept her diary for a year, then burned it. JB quotes AR as recalling that she kept the diary through mid-1921 and burned it as she and her family were returning from the Crimea to St. Petersburg (*AR,* p. 18).

30 **People have a right to live for themselves:** "Ayn Rand's Life."

30 **"Whoever tells you to exist for the state is, or wants to be, the state":** *The Phil Donahue Show,* broadcast from Madison Square Garden, May 1979.

31 **she began making notes for** *We the Living***:** She began making notes in 1929 (*EOWTL,* p. 3).

31 **As scholars have noted:** *A People's Tragedy,* p. 129.

31 **referred to her own novels as anti-Communist propaganda:** Letter to Gerald Loeb, August 4, 1944 (*LOAR,* p. 157).

31 **viewed national politics as a morality play:** In *Politics and the Novel,* Irving Howe writes, "In 19th-century Russia, the usual categories of discourse tend to break down. Politics, religion, literature, philosophy—these do not fall into neat departments of the mind. Pressed together by the Tsarist censorship, ideas acquire an extraordinary concentration; the novel, which in the West is generally regarded as a means of portraying human behavior, acquires the tone and manner of prophetic passion. . . . Where ideas cannot be modulated through practice, they keep their original purity." Howe quotes Nikolai Chernyshevsky as saying, "Literature in Russia constitutes almost the sum-total of our intellectual life" (Irving Howe, "Dostoevsky: The Politics of Salvation," *Politics and the Novel* [New York: Columbia University Press, 1957], p. 51).

31 **no copies and few accounts of these exist:** *AR:SOL,* p. 38.

31 **immigrated via Constantinople:** *Vladimir Nabokov: The Russian Years,* pp. 133–40.

31 **Rand never saw any of them again:** Author interview with AR's

friend, the author JKT, May 21, 2004. It was in 1962, when JKT was soliciting AR's advice about whether to interview Vladimir Nabokov for a New York City radio program she hosted, that AR first mentioned her friendship with Olga. Chris Sciabarra unearthed many details of that friendship in 1998 ("The Ayn Rand Transcript," p. 6).

31 **consciously initiated the Red Terror:** *A People's Tragedy*, p. 525. Figes also observes that at the beginning of the Red Terror, Jews were strongly identified with the targeted middle class and that "the words 'burzhooi' [Russian for "bourgeois"], 'speculator,' 'German' and 'Jew' were virtually synonymous" (p. 523).

31 **Rand was in the store:** *TPOAR*, p. 21.

32 **began to read the novels of Victor Hugo:** "I discovered Hugo when I was thirteen, in the stifling, sordid ugliness of Soviet Russia," she wrote in an introduction to the Lowell Bair translation of Victor Hugo's *Ninety-Three* (New York: Bantam Books, 1962); her introduction is reprinted in Ayn Rand, *The Romantic Manifesto* (New York: Signet, 1971), p. 160.

32 **only novelist she ever acknowledged:** Ayn Rand, lecture on "The Art of Fiction," January–June 1958, New York, private notes courtesy of John Allen.

32 **Anna would read aloud:** Ayn Rand, "Victor Hugo Allows a Peek at Grandeur," *Los Angeles Times*, September 16, 1962, p. 12.

32 **The first one of his novels she read:** *WIAR*, p. 158.

33 **she retained traces of the plotting techniques:** For an excellent discussion of Hugo's influence on AR, see Shoshana Milgram's "We the Living* and Victor Hugo" in *EOWTL*, pp. 223–56.

33 **"greatest novelist in world literature":** Ayn Rand, introduction to *Ninety-Three, The Romantic Manifesto*, p. 154.

33 **spent in search of rationed millet, peas, and cooking oil:** *100 Voices*, NR, p. 14; *WTL*, p. xv.

33 **forced to walk all the way from Leningrad:** JH, "Conversations with Ayn Rand," p. 32; details provided in a telephone interview with author, December 13, 2004.

33 **she told another friend:** *TPOAR*, p. 30.

33 **robbed by a gang of bandits:** *EOWTL*, p. 61.

33 **Zinovy managed to safeguard his savings:** *TPOAR*, p. 30.

34 **"not of Russia nor the horrors":** *EOWTL*, p. 243; *TPOAR*, p. 30.

34 **where a number of Zinovy's cousins practiced medicine:** Issues of the *Russian Medical List*, 1905–08, 1910, 1916, and *The Directory of the St. Petersburg Merchant Administration*, 1901, 1906–11, 1915. These cousins included Iosif Wolfovitch Rosenbaum, a pharmacist in Rostov; Feiga Aronovna Rosenbaum, a dentist in Poltava; and Leia Jankelevna Rosenbaum, a dentist in Odessa.

34 **she believed that Olga and her family had left the country in 1917:** BB reports on p. 27 of *TPOAR* that the Nabokovs left Russia in 1917, presumably based on AR's belief that this was so.

34 **found a small, damp, unheated house in which to live:** *TPOAR*, p. 30.

34 **opened a pharmacy:** *AR*, p. 17.

34 **looted and shut down:** *Red Victory*, p. 477; *A People's Tragedy*, p. 717.

34 **Rand remembered the terror of the Red Army:** Ayn Rand, "The Lessons of Vietnam," in Leonard Peikoff, ed., *The Voice of Reason: Essays in Objectivist Thought* (New York: New American Library, 1989), pp. 138–39.

34 **The family lived "on a battlefield":** "Ayn Rand," *Dictionary of Literary Biography,* pp. 255–72.

35 **attended a private girls' school:** From the Crimea Department of the State Archive of the Ukraine, Simferopol, fond 72, inventory 1, file 15, pp. 3–7, and fond 72, inventory 1, file 160, pp. 159, 160, 170.

35 **free of the Communist curriculum:** *The Russian Radical,* p. 72.

35 **expected to "be against" Aristotle:** BBTBI.

35 **She also studied political economy:** Chris Matthew Sciabarra, "The AR Transcript, Revisited," *Journal of Ayn Rand Studies,* Fall 2005, pp. 4–14, based on research provided by the author.

35 **introduction to the Declaration of Independence:** Robert Mayhew, *Ayn Rand and "Song of Russia": Communism and Anti-Communism in 1940s Hollywood* (Lanham, Md.: Scarecrow Press, 2005), p. 72.

35 **America's constitutional guarantee:** *AR,* p. 18.

35 **"I cried my eyes out":** *TPOAR,* p. 36.

35 **learned the play by heart:** Shoshana Milgram, "Three Inspirations for the Ideal Man," *EOTF,* p. 189.

35 **caused her mother to complain:** "Ayn Rand's Life."

35 **This was in the late spring of 1921:** AR graduated from secondary school on June 30, 1921 (Petrograd State University Archives, fond 7240, inventory 5, file 3576; personal file of the student A. Z. Rosenbaum.

36 **loaded everybody into French and British ships:** *Red Victory,* pp. 448–49.

36 **set sail from the docks at Yevpatoria:** *Red Victory,* pp. 448–49.

36 **he promised, they would reclaim their business:** *TPOAR,* p. 38.

36 **mock trials, burnings, and hangings:** *TPOAR,* p. 37.

36 **one classmate's father was summarily and publicly shot:** *TPOAR,* p. 37.

36 **five billion of these rubles:** To the Bolsheviks, the disappearance of money was a sign that the social order was nearing full Communism (Steve H. Hanke, Lars Jonung, and Kurt Schuler, *Russian Currency and Finance* [New York: Routledge, 1993]).

36 **"first adult novel":** "An Illustrated Life."

36 **Rand admired feudalism:** "An Illustrated Life."

36 **By age thirty:** "An Illustrated Life."

36 **gifted at teaching:** *TPOAR,* p. 38.

37 **they had lost their gamble:** AR's grandmother, Rozalia Pavlovna Kaplan, may have died at about this time, since AR's grandfather Berko Itskovitch Kaplan was the only grandparent listed in official documents as a member of the Rosenbaum household after their return to St. Petersburg. What happened to the Rosenbaum and Kaplan uncles, aunts, and cousins who remained in Brest-Litovsk is unknown, but, as Germany temporarily acquired most of the Russian Pale by virtue of the 1918 Treaty of Brest-Litovsk, they may have become German citizens and perished in the Holocaust.

37 **There's no better description:** In 1960–61, AR told BB, "And then we started back for Petrograd, and the way we traveled was exactly de-

scribed in *We the Living.* . . . I mean the conditions and the trains and the bundles" (*EOWTL*, p. 50).

37 **The audience for her plays and stories would be immense:** Shoshana Milgram, "Ayn Rand as a Public Speaker: A Philosopher Who Lived on Earth," Objectivist Conference, Boston, July 7, 2006.

37 **smaller by two-thirds:** Ida Mett, *The Kronstadt Commune,* ch. 2, and *A History of the Russian Civil War,* pp. 466, 493–94.

37 **inhabited by a sign painter:** *AR,* p. 20; *EOWTL,* p. 49.

38 **Zinovy obtained a position in a cooperative pharmacy:** *AR,* p. 20.

38 **"wouldn't do anything":** *EOWTL,* p. 57.

38 **She began to refer to her husband:** *TPOAR,* p. 135.

38 **traveled the city by tram:** It appears that Anna Rosenbaum had to prove to Petrograd State University administrators that she was capable of supporting her daughter before AR could be admitted (the Central Historic Archive of St. Petersburg, fond 7240, inventory 5, file 3576).

38 **earning much-needed money:** *EOWTL,* p. 76; "AR in Russia."

38 **Anna marveled at her daughter's ability to choose:** *EOWTL,* p. 76.

38 **"You and I have our love of work in common":** "AR in Russia."

38 **Zinovy was placed in charge of keeping house:** McConnell, "Recollections of AR I."

38 **This division combined the old disciplines:** *The Russian Radical,* pp. 75–76, and "The Ayn Rand Transcript," pp. 3–19.

38 **She declared a major in history:** Petrograd State University Archives, fond 7240, inventory 5, file 3576; personal file of the student A. Z. Rosenbaum.

39 **She took ancient, medieval, Western, and Russian history:** "The Ayn Rand Transcript," pp. 10–19.

39 **She read Hegel and Marx:** Nathaniel Branden, *Judgment Day* (Boston: Houghton Mifflin, 1989), p. 88.

39 **He "gives me the feeling":** Ayn Rand, *The Romantic Manifesto,* p. 43.

39 **a decree was issued:** "Novelist Tells of Russia in Lavery's Suit," *Los Angeles Times,* August 8, 1951, p. 18.

39 **If a young man, he said:** "Ayn Rand as a Public Speaker," July 7, 2006.

39 **the freedom to think:** *FTNI,* p. 127.

40 **she felt real love for him:** "Ayn Rand's Life."

40 **disapproved of his wife's working for the Communists:** *TPOAR,* p. 44.

40 **Anna was a little "pink":** *100 Voices,* NR, p. 11.

40 **"You must see clearly":** "Ayn Rand in Russia."

40 **"She spoke about him with more respect":** author interview with JMB and Dr. Allan Blumenthal, March 23, 2004.

40 **the crucial role that work and money play:** *A People's Tragedy,* p. 772.

40 **Natasha studied piano:** "Home Atmosphere."

40 **fellow students Igor Stravinsky, Sergei Prokofiev, and Dmitri Shostakovich:** *St. Petersburg,* pp. 336, 340–57.

40 **Anna approved of Natasha's choice:** "Ayn Rand's Life."

41 **became a teacher like her mother:** "Ayn Rand in Russia"; *100 Voices,* NR, p. 4.

41 **"to have a factual knowledge of man's past":** "About the Author," *AS,* p. 1070.

41   **make a living as a writer:**
TPOAR, p. 41–42.

41   **N. O. Lossky:** *The Russian Radical,*
pp. 83–89.

41   **surveyed the pre-Socratic philosophers:** "The Ayn Rand Transcript," pp. 3–4.

41   **she learned from Lossky:** Dr.
Sciabarra was the first scholar to
point out this important element in
AR's training and its effect on her
thinking (introduction to *The Russian Radical,* p. 11).

41   **people often didn't want to talk
to her:** "Ayn Rand's Life."

41   **no known friends:** McConnell,
"Recollections of Ayn Rand I."

42   **"beat me to all my ideas":** *AR,*
p. 22.

42   **Nietzsche's work was popular
among intellectuals:** Bernice
Glatzer Rosenthal, *New Myth, New
World: From Nietzsche to Stalinism*
(University Park: Pennsylvania State
University Press, 2002), pp. 1–25.

42   **"that it doesn't have to be collective":** *EOTF,* p. 37.

42   **It wasn't until she was writing
The Fountainhead:** As an adult, AR
once said that she would never commit suicide as long as she had a copy
of *Thus Spoke Zarathustra* (Shosana
Milgram, "The Road to Roark,"
speech presented at an ARI Conference in Industry Hills, California, July 2003, based on material
in the ARI Archives). For a fascinating discussion of AR and Nietzsche,
see Ronald Merrill, *The Ideas of Ayn
Rand* (Chicago: Open Court Press,
1991).

42   **leader of a group:** *EOWTL,* p. 52;
100 Voices, NR, p. 14.

42   **His name was Lev Bekkerman:**
All information about AR and Lev
Bekkerman is based on *EOWTL,*
pp. 52–56, and *AR,* p. 22.

42   **An engineering student at St.
Petersburg Technical Institute:**
Like Leo Kovalensky, Kira Ar-
gounova bore a resemblance to Lev
Bekkerman, in that she was an engi-
neering student at St. Petersburg
Technical Institute.

43   **"The first time I saw him":** *EOTF,*
p. 52.

43   **bought cheap seats:** Ayn Rand,
"No," *TEAR,* p. 232; McConnell,
"Recollections of AR I."

43   **lifelong favorite, Emmerich Kálmán's *Die Bajadere*:** "Ayn Rand in
Russia."

43   **sat "solemn, erect":** *WTL,* p. 208.

43   **"I knew he didn't like it":**
EOWTL, p. 53.

43   **he pointedly ignored her:** *TPOAR,*
p. 48.

43   **"The whole issue [of Lev]":**
EOWTL, p. 54.

44   **he had been accused of plotting:**
EOWTL, pp. 55–56.

44   **she would almost certainly have
remained in Russia:** *EOWTL,* pp.
55–56.

44   **"I would have stayed":** *TPOAR,*
p. 49.

44   **By the time she spoke about it:**
That is, on tape to BB in 1960–61.

44   **"yelling in despair":** *AR,* p. 27.

44   **favorite piece for the year 1924:**
"Ayn Rand's Musical Biography."

44   **Rand developed a passion:** Operettas "really saved my life," AR
once said. In the years during which
Stalin was rising to power, "my sense
of life was kept going on that" (*AR:
SOL,* p. 5).

44   **that . . . the Bolshevik government made available:** "Ayn Rand
in Russia."

44   **"I was there every Saturday":**
EOWTL, p. 120.

44   **attending Russian-made movies:**
"An Illustrated Life."

45 **sophisticated American and European films:** "Ayn Rand in Russia."

45 **seeing more than one hundred movies:** Ayn Rand, *Russian Writings on Hollywood,* Michael S. Berliner, ed., Dina Garmong, trans. (Los Angeles: ARI Press, 1999), pp. 173–89.

45 **"It was almost as if I had a private avenue":** "Ayn Rand in Russia."

45 **Her favorite film:** "Ayn Rand in Russia."

45 **Veidt, a German Jew:** *A History of the Jews,* p. 479.

45 **She had chosen him:** "Ayn Rand in Russia."

45 **"a heart like a pavement, trampled by many feet":** *WTL,* p. 43.

45 **first glimpse of the New York skyline:** One of the films she may have seen was *The Lights of New York,* a 1922 Fox Film Corporation production. The brother of her second cousin Burt Stone's first wife, Sarah Stone, was a cellist in the Fox Studio Orchestra in Hollywood. According to Susan Belter, the great-granddaughter of Burt and Sarah Stone, AR knew of this cellist and saw him onscreen, sitting in the orchestra pit, in at least one movie she viewed in Russia (*Russian Writings on Hollywood,* p. 9; author interview with Susan Belter, October 24, 2006).

45 **nonsense, or "applesauce":** "Woman Novelist Reveals Soviet Tyranny's Horror," *New York American,* June 15, 1936.

45 **Her enthusiasm for America:** *Russian Writings on Hollywood,* p. 9.

46 **"Atlantis": the ideal existence:** "Ayn Rand in Russia."

46 **Lenin had been preoccupied:** *Passage Through Armageddon,* p. 465.

46 **Diseases of dirt and poverty:** *A People's Tragedy,* pp. 784–85.

46 **becoming an informant against fellow students:** "Woman Novelist Reveals Soviet Tyranny's Horror."

46 **Candid speech was dangerous:** *St. Petersburg,* p. 335–39.

46 **Leonid Konheim joined them:** St. Petersburg address rolls, Central Archive.

46 **cakes made of potato peelings:** *EOWTL,* p. 72.

46 **carrot greens, coffee grounds, and acorns:** "Russian Girl Jeers at Depression Complaint," *Oakland Tribune,* October 7, 1932, p. 9.

46 **her one party dress:** *EOWTL,* p. 74.

46 **her eminent professor N. O. Lossky:** Archive of the St. Petersburg FSB Office, archival file 14493, concerning criminal case 1625. See also Leslie Chamberlain, *The Philosophy Steamer: Lenin and the Exile of the Intelligentsia* (London: Atlantic Books, 2006).

47 **On Mme. Stoiunina's arrest:** Archive of the St. Petersburg FSB Office, archival file 14493, concerning criminal case 1625.

47 **the university announced the largest purge:** *The Russian Radical,* p. 92.

47 **She was one of four thousand students expelled:** *EOWTL,* pp. 62–63.

47 **"young girls and boys I knew":** *Current Biography Yearbook 1982,* (New York: H. W. Wilson), p. 332.

47 **"not fulfilling academic requirements":** Petrograd State University Archive, personal file of A. Z. Rosenbaum, list N 1361 from November 28, 1923.

47 **"all kinds of anti-Soviet remarks":** *EOWTL,* p. 50.

47 **When a group of visiting Western scientists:** *EOWTL,* p. 51.

47 **Her university records show:** Petrograd State University Archive, per-

sonal file of A. Z. Rosenbaum, list N 1361 from November 28, 1923.

47 **"with highest honors":** *TPOAR,* p. 42. AR told BB that she (AR) had also been awarded a perfect score in a course on the history of ancient philosophy with N. O. Lossky, whom she described as famous for his tough grading and contempt for women. Dr. Sciabarra has cast doubt on these assertions, including AR's description of Professor Lossky as "an international authority on Plato" (*TPOAR,* p. 42), whom AR considered a philosophical malefactor. According to Dr. Sciabarra, Professor Lossky published nearly three hundred works on philosophy, "and not one of them even mentions Plato in the title" (*The Russian Radical,* p. 86). Lossky was a specialist in dialectics and in Kant, among other thinkers ("The Ayn Rand Transcript," pp. 5–9).

47 **Rand joined local writers' clubs:** "Woman Novelist Reveals Soviet Tyranny's Horror."

47 **The text of the novella seems to be lost:** "Ayn Rand's Life." Presumably, if the ARI or the estate owned the manuscript, Binswanger would have stated that he had read it. As it is, he quotes from AR's recollection of it.

48 **The explanation may lie:** *Natasha's Dance,* pp. 447–50; *St. Petersburg,* pp. 359, 369–92.

48 ***Anthem* clearly reflects their influence:** On the other hand, AR may have gotten the idea for her story from seeing airplanes in silent movies. According to Greg Walsh, a librarian at the Margaret Herrick Library of the Academy of Motion Picture Arts and Sciences, Beverly Hills, California, aircraft first ap-

peared on screen circa 1913; in the following ten years, at least forty films featured airplanes or aviators as an integral plot component.

48 **too fearful to fly in a plane:** Her first plane ride was in 1963, to Portland, Oregon, to accept an honorary degree (*TPOAR,* p. 318).

48 **Dagny Taggart and John Galt both fly solo:** *AS,* pp. 634–640.

48 **In a 1969 essay:** Ayn Rand, "Apollo 11," *The Objectivist,* September 1969, pp. 708–10.

49 **The heiress's assistant in the novel:** "An Illustrated Life."

49 **In October 1924:** *Art Life* and *Laborer and Theatre,* back issues for the years 1923–25; *St. Petersburg Academy of Theatre Art, Pages of History.*

49 **Rand probably would not have been admitted:** Petrograd State University Archives, fond 7240, inventory 5, file 3576, personal file of A. Z. Rosenbaum.

49 **She and her mother both foresaw:** Scott McConnell, "Ayn Rand's Family and Friends, 1926–1951," a lecture presented at ICON 2004, London, England, September 25, 2004.

49 **In the late 1890s:** Ellis Island documents provided by FB.

49 **one of Anna's aunts, Eva Kaplan, had immigrated:** Two of Eva's children were born in the United States; taped interview with Minna Goldberg, FB, and MS, conducted by BB, February 20, 1983, courtesy of MSC.

50 **Sarah Lipton:** Anna Rosenbaum's cousin Sarah Lipton was married four times. In publications by the Estate of Ayn Rand, she is also referred to as Sarah Lipsky, Sarah Collier, or Sarah Satrin. Rand knew her best when she was Sarah Lipton.

50   **sponsor her for a visit to America:**
     Author interview with AR's second
     cousin, Eva Kaplan's granddaughter
     FB, June 21, 2004.

50   **The Chicago cousins had
     brought over other Russian Jews:**
     Author interview with FB, June 21,
     2004.

50   **Sarah Lipton owned and oper-
     ated a Chicago movie theater:**
     author correspondence with FB, De-
     cember 16, 2004; *AR*, p. 29.

50   **declared intention of visiting the
     United States:** *AR*, p. 29.

50   **almost every other window of
     escape would slam shut:** By
     1927, AR recalled, the Soviet gov-
     ernment required a payment of five
     hundred dollars in gold or foreign
     currency to apply for a passport—
     kinds and amounts of wealth that
     Russians could be put to death for
     possessing. So the only way to get
     out of Russia was to be ransomed
     by a wealthy foreigner ("Woman
     Novelist Reveals Soviet Tyranny's
     Horror").

50   **In the essay, which was dis-
     covered:** "Editor's Note on 'Pola
     Negri,'" *Russian Writings on Holly-
     wood*, p. 15.

50   **"ready to crush the man who
     dared to stand in her way":**
     Russian Writings on Hollywood, pp.
     31–33.

50   **She was granted a passport:** *AR*,
     p. 30; *AR:SOL*, DVD.

50   **She and her mother sent away
     for French passenger ships' bro-
     chures:** *TPOAR*, p. 59.

51   **Harry Portnoy, Eva Kaplan's
     widowered husband:** National Ar-
     chives and Records Administration,
     De Grasse Manifest of Alien Passen-
     gers for the United States, Feb-
     ruary 10, 1926, column 19.

51   **At Anna Rosenbaum's sugges-
     tion:** Author correspondence with
     Michael Berliner, June 2, 2005.

51   **She would have to travel three
     hundred miles:** Latvia was still an
     independent nation. The United
     States had no embassy or consulate
     in Russia.

51   **acquaintances . . . looked for-
     ward to seeing her back home
     again:** Letter to Lev Bekkerman,
     August 28, 1926 (*LOAR*, p. 2).

51   **sold the last of the family jew-
     elry:** *AR*, p. 30.

51   **"the freest country on earth":**
     "America's Persecuted Minority: Big
     Business," *Capitalism, The Unknown
     Ideal* (New York: Signet, 1967), p. 48.

51   **packed her few clothes and her
     typewriter:** *TPOAR*, p. 60.

51   **slipped on her mother's old Per-
     sian lamb jacket:** BBTBI.

51   **She had asked Lev Bekkerman
     to be there:** Author interview with
     BB, September 15, 2005.

51   **the first and last time he kissed
     her hand:** *TPOAR*, p. 60

51   **"Just you wait!":** *AR*, p. 30.

THREE: FREEDOM TO THINK: 1926–1934

52   **"When I am questioned about
     myself":** Ayn Rand, "To the Readers
     of *The Fountainhead*," 1945 (*LOAR*,
     p. 669).

52   **she met her cousin Vera:** *AR*, p.
     31. Vera later moved from Berlin to
     Paris to work at the Pasteur Institute.
     She married a Frenchman and relo-
     cated to Lyon, where she lived under
     the Nazi occupation. She and AR
     were briefly reunited in New York in
     the early 1960s (*100 Voices*, Lisette
     Hassanil, pp. 257–59).

52   **The two young women were pho-tographed together:** *AR*, p. 31.

52   **they saw *Der Wilderer*:** *Illustri-erter Film Kurier*, 7. Jahrgang, 1925. Thanks to Joan McDonald of the Carl de Vogt Society and to Peter Doll for the translation.

52   **Carl de Vogt ... whom Rand adored:** Michael Paxton, from the documentary film *AR: SOL*, DVD. In 1933, de Vogt joined the Nazi Party and became a brownshirt (thanks to Joan McDonald for this informa-tion).

52   **sailed for America aboard the French liner S.S. *De Grasse*:** *De Grasse* Ship Manifest, February 19, 1926; vol. 8626, p. 2, line 13, Na-tional Archives Microfilm Publica-tion T715, roll 3800, "Passenger and Crew Lists of Vessels Arriving at New York, N.Y., 1897–1957," National Archives and Records Administration Northeast Region, New York, N.Y.

52   **She had a first-class cabin:** *AR:SOL*, DVD.

52   **the five-foot-two, dark-eyed Rus-sian girl:** Her Russian passport stated her height as five foot four, ac-cording to ARI (*100 Voices*, p. 539), but she said she was five foot two, and acquaintances recalled her as closer to that height.

53   **a light snow had begun to fall:** *TPOAR*, p. 63.

53   **This was the dollar decade:** James Warren Prothro, *The Dollar Decade* (Baton Rouge: Louisiana State University Press, 1954), p. 39.

53   **"the will of man made visible":** Ayn Rand, *The Fountainhead* (New York: Plume, 1994), p. 463; also, "finger of God" (Nora Ephron, "A Strange Kind of Simplicity," *NYT Book Review*, May 5, 1968, p. 8).

53   **The ship's manifest noted that she had promised to return:** National Archives and Records Administration, *De Grasse* Mani-fest of Alien Passengers for the United States, February 10, 1926, column 19.

53   **that she was engaged to marry a Russian man:** Quoted in a syndi-cated interview with AR, "New York Notes," appearing in the *Marion [Ohio] Star*, June 9, 1936.

53   **re-enter the United States:** *TPOAR*, p. 68.

54   **"One must never attempt to fake reality in any manner":** "The Ob-jectivist Ethics," *TVOS*, p. 28.

54   **an obligation to be truthful ends:** *TPOAR*, p. 354.

54   **She stayed in New York for four days:** Author interview with Susan Belton, great-granddaughter of Man-del and Anna Stone, October 24, 2006.

54   **the guest of relatives of Mandel Stone:** Author correspondence with FB, April 10 and 17, 2005.

54   **lived in a new, stately enclave:** Author interview with Susan Belton, October 24, 2006.

54   **she had only fifty dollars of her travel money left:** *TPOAR*, p. 63.

54   **"all mispronounced":** Jack Stin-nett, "A New Yorker at Large," syn-dicated column appearing in the *Florence [S.C.] Morning News*, May 22, 1936, p. 4.

54   **"I'll never forget it":** *TPOAR*, p. 68.

54   **movies, which then cost thirty-five or fifty cents:** *1927 Film Year Book*, cited in a note to author by Greg Walsh, librarian, the Margaret Herrick Library.

55   **She kept a journal:** *Russian Writ-ings on Hollywood*, pp. 173–214.

55   **By the time she boarded a New York Central train:** AR's present-day followers at ARI have stated that she chose her two-part pseudonym

while still in Russia and cite as evidence an unpublished letter written to AR by her mother, mentioning the name "Ayn Rand" while the *De Grasse* was still at sea.

55   **knew she would need a professional name:** *AR:SOL,* p. 59.

55   **"Ayn" was a Finnish female name:** Letter to a fan, January 30, 1937 (*LOAR,* p. 40).

55   **borrowed it from a Finnish writer:** *TPOAR,* p. 63. There has been some speculation that AR was referring to Finnish novelist Aino Kallas (1878–1956).

55   **once claiming that she made it up herself:** Author correspondence with JMB, March 21, 2005.

55   **Remington Rand typewriter:** "I can swear that I remember giving her her last name—from her typewriter, the Remington Rand," FB told me in 2004. "Sitting in my mother's dining room, where we were sleeping, was an old-fashioned round table. She had her typewriter. We were looking—[I] said, 'Should it be Remington?' She said no, she liked a small name. And I said, 'What about "Ayn Rand"?' and we took the name right off the Remington Rand" (author interview with FB, March 18, 2004).

55   **Rand repeated this story:** AR told the typewriter story to BB, who repeated it in her book *TPOAR.* BB later told me in an interview that AR must have lied to her about this, though she wasn't able to explain why.

55   **the Remington Rand was not yet on the market in 1926:** The Remington Rand Company was formed in 1927.

55   **her family seems to have been aware of her new surname before she wrote to them:** James S.

Valliant, *The Passion of Ayn Rand's Critics: The Case against the Brandens* (Dallas: Durban House, 2005), p. 13. Valliant, a former San Diego prosecuting attorney, makes this claim in a passionate book-length condemnation of two of AR's early followers. In writing the book, he had access to many of AR's personal papers stored at the Ayn Rand Papers, which are closed to independent scholars; therefore, this assertion may be based on Rosenbaum family letters.

55   **an abbreviation of her Russian surname:** The ARI Newsletter, *Impact,* June 2000; John Kobler, "The Curious Cult of Ayn Rand," *The Saturday Evening Post,* November 11, 1961, p. 100.

55   **a number of followers believed:** *Impact,* May 1997.

56   **the self-made soul:** *AS,* p. 937.

56   **a habitué of lectures:** The acquaintance was Betsy Speicher, a writer who was a student at Objectivist lectures in the 1960s. She told AR that her father had called her "Ayin—two syllables," meaning " 'bright eyes' in Jewish," Speicher informed me. "I asked [AR] if her father ever called her that, and she smiled and nodded. I took that to be a yes." Author correspondence with Betsy Speicher, August 17, 2004.

56   **a letter from Anna Rosenbaum:** "Ayn Rand in Russia." "Notchka" is a Russian diminutive signaling affection.

56   **a perfect ... endearment for a little girl with bright, bold, hypnotizing eyes:** As referenced in a 1934 letter to AR from Anna Rosenbaum; "Ayn Rand in Russia."

56   **derivation of the surname "Rand":** Some aficionados speculate that Rand is a reference to the gold-

mining district of South Africa or to the Rand McNally railroad timetables used in Russia and around the world.

56 **she did not reveal her birth name to American acquaintances:** The exceptions were her husband, FO, his brother Nick Carter, and possibly another brother, Joe O'Connor.

56 **"She didn't want anyone to know":** Taped interview with MS, conducted by BB, January 20, 1983. Millicent Patton, a friend of the O'Connors' in the 1930s, independently recalled in 1982, "I never heard Mimi's last name" (taped interview, conducted by BB, December 5, 1982).

56 **"They all changed their names":** Author interview with Susan Belton, October 24, 2006.

57 **knew her real name when she died:** TPOAR, p. 72.

57 **first book she purchased in America:** Jeff Walker, taped unpublished interview with John Ridpath, an associate professor at York University in Toronto and a member of the board of ARI, 1991. Ridpath claims to own this book. AR also purchased English translations of *Beyond Good and Evil* and *The Anti-Christ*, all in 1917 Modern Library editions (*EOTF*, p. 24).

57 **Russian-Jewish "greenhorns":** Author interview with FB, March 18, 2004. "We brought over anybody who wanted to come. She wasn't the only one."

57 **rating of four out of five in her journal:** *Russian Writings on Hollywood*, p. 190.

57 **She had been invited to stay:** Author interview with Susan Belton, October 24, 2006.

57 **after some difficulty about the**

family schedule: Author interview with FB, March 18, 2004; taped interview with Minna Goldberg, FB, and MS, conducted by BB, February 20, 1983.

57 **parents slept in the front bedroom:** "Ayn Rand's Family and Friends."

57 **Harry Portnoy:** Eva Portnoy, née Kaplan, seems to have been the sister of Anna Rosenbaum's father, Berko Kaplan.

57 **occupied a back alcove:** Taped interview with Minna Goldberg, JB, and MS, conducted by BB, February 20, 1983.

57 **referred to as "conquering Hollywood":** Author interview with FB, March 18, 2004.

57 **She wrote these in Russian:** *AR*, p. 32. However, in 1983 Minna Goldberg told BB that AR wrote in halting *English* and that a cousin put her writing in "better English" (taped interview with Minna Goldberg, FB, and MS, conducted by BB, Chicago, February 20, 1983). As to who translated or polished these early scenarios, Sarah Lipton's grandson, Roger Salamon, recalled that his mother, Beatrice Collier, did (*100 Voices*, Roger Salamon, p. 260).

57 **she let the hot water run:** *100 Voices*, Harvey Portnoy, p. 28. Typhoid and cholera were common illnesses in St. Petersburg after the revolution. AR would be "phobic" about germs (as Minna Goldberg put it in a taped interview with BB in 1983) until she died.

58 **"I'm Sitting on Top of the World":** Author interview with FB, June 21, 2004. Fern sang the song for me as AR had sung it.

58 **substituted "z's" for American "th's":** Harry Binswanger, "Recol-

lections of AR," talk presented to the NYU Objectivist Club, November 20, 2007.

58 **where she was able to eat as much as she wanted:** Author interview with FB, June 21, 2004; *TPOAR*, p. 76.

58 **"as though the subject didn't interest her":** Author interview with FB, March 18, 2004; *TPOAR*, p. 71.

58 **"Yessir, That's My Baby":** McConnell, "Recollections of AR I."

58 **American proletarian novels:** *100 Voices*, NR, p. 9.

58 **"all she talked about was what *she* was going to be and going to do":** *TPOAR*, p. 71.

58 **"being of self-made soul":** *AS*, p. 934.

58 **"I felt I was not yet in an American city":** *TPOAR*, p. 69.

59 **She spent her time in movie theaters:** Author correspondence with FB, December 16, 2004; "Ayn Rand's Family and Friends."

59 **138 movies between late February and August 1926:** *Russian Writings on Hollywood*, pp. 190–202.

59 **her then-favorite film director:** *TPOAR*, p. 77.

59 **read and even think in her new language:** Letter to Lev Bekkerman, August 28, 1926 (*LOAR*, p. 1). The letter was written in Russian and is the only surviving letter from AR's early years in America, according to *LOAR* editor Berliner.

59 **picked up period words and phrases:** *The Skyscraper*, July–September 1927 (*JOAR*, p. 8).

59 **a letter, written in Russian:** Letter to Lev Bekkerman, August 28, 1926 (*LOAR*, p. 1).

59 **Sarah Lipton inveigled a film distributor:** Author interview with

Roger Salamon, Sarah Lipton's grandson, July 2004.

60 **By late August 1926, she was ready to go:** Author interview with FB, June 21, 2004.

60 **four completed scenarios:** *AR:SOL*, DVD.

60 **"a noble crook":** Quoted in *TPOAR*, p. 73.

60 **"heavy, hopeless stupidity":** circa February 1928 (*JOAR*, pp. 24–25).

60 **they believed she would be famous:** Author interview with FB, June 21, 2004.

60 **tart stories were still being told:** Author interview with FB, June 21, 2004. Fern's mother, Minna Goldberg, "had some very strong feelings about her," Fern told me. "She couldn't wait to get rid of Ayn."

61 **"Rolls-Royce and a mink coat":** "I didn't get five cents," said Minna Goldberg in a 1983 taped interview with BB. Said Roger Salamon, Fern's cousin, "The family was annoyed because when Ayn got into the upper brackets she forgot where she came from and how she got there. There was a feeling of—shall I say disappointment? I'm being kind." Author interview with Roger Salamon, October 30, 2006; also, author interview with FB, April 13, 2004.

61 **On return visits—one in 1949:** Letter to Pincus Berner, September 10, 1949 (*LOAR*, p. 456).

61 **and one or two in the 1960s:** Author correspondence with FB, April 25, 2005.

61 **acolytes told newspapers that she had no family in America:** Author interview with FB, March 18, 2004.

61 **"She never talked about her family":** Taped interview with Minna Goldberg, FB, and MS, conducted by BB, February 20, 1983.

61 **"The [extended] family had enough money"**: Author interview with Susan Belton, October 24, 2006.

61 **she made up her mind to marry:** The basics of this version of the story are told by JB in "An Illustrated Life" and by Michael Paxton in his film and companion book, *AR:SOL*. Both JB and Paxton had access to the Ayn Rand Papers.

61 **the nerve to ask his name:** AR told this version to a reporter in 1932 ("Russian Girl Finds End of the Rainbow in Hollywood," *Chicago Times,* September 26, 1932).

61 **she saw him before he saw her:** *TPOAR,* pp. 76–77.

62 **"She never left a thing to chance":** Author interview with FB, March 18, 2004; said Roger Salamon, "There were no coincidences in Ayn's life. What Ayn wanted to do, she did."

62 **proper and delightful Hollywood Studio Club:** *TPOAR,* p. 75; *AR,* p. 33.

62 **created specifically to shelter aspiring actresses:** At various times, the Studio Club housed Maureen O'Sullivan, Donna Reed, Marilyn Monroe, Kim Novak, and other stars of screen and stage.

62 **brand-new quarters on Lodi Place:** "Studio Club Opens Tomorrow," *Los Angeles Times,* May 6, 1926, p. A7.

62 **residents had use of a well-stocked library:** Grace Kingsley, "Film Club is Joy Haven," *Los Angeles Times,* September 5, 1921, p. II, 9.

62 **typically a waiting list:** "Studio Club Opens Tomorrow," p. A7.

62 **Mrs. Cecil B. DeMille:** "Studio Club Bids Called," *Los Angeles Times,* May 8, 1925, p. A1.

62 **as he later claimed he did:** *TPOAR,* p. 77.

62 **told them her new first name:** *AR: SOL,* p. 70. AR and her family wrote hundreds of letters to each other from 1926 to 1936, but only the family's letters to AR survive; hers were lost during the Nazi blockade of Leningrad in World War II (McConnell, "Recollections of Ayn Rand I," based on interviews with AR's sister NR). As to how AR and her parents and sisters overcame the problem of Soviet censors, BB recalled AR telling her that they wrote to each other through a third-party contact in Finland (interview with BB, September 15, 2005). Chances are, their mail would have been opened and read in any case.

62 **"the embodiment of the world's glory and glamour":** "Home Atmosphere."

62 **In 1926, the Hollywood film studios:** Cecil B. DeMille, *The Autobiography of Cecil B. DeMille,* David Hayne, ed. (New York: Grandland Publishing, 1989; originally Englewood Cliffs, N.J.: Prentice Hall, 1959).

63 **During her first day on the set:** *TPOAR,* p. 77.

63 **she complained:** *TPOAR,* p. 78.

63 **a woman named E. K. Adams:** Payroll files, Cecil B. DeMille Collection, L. Tom Perry Special Collections, Harold B. Lee Library, Brigham Young University, Provo, Utah, box 778, folder 1.

63 **"like last year's newspaper":** *The Art of Fiction,* pp. 75–76.

63 **"I still hate [that woman] to this day":** *TPOAR,* p. 78.

63 **spoke of her early days in Hollywood as "grim":** Zeanette Moore, "Studio Club Bolsters Film Novices' Courage," *Los Angeles Times,* June 24, 1945, p. B1.

63 **dislike the movie capital of America and its "barbarians":** Ayn

Rand, book review of *Lillian Gish: The Movies, Mr. Griffith, and Me* (by Lillian Gish with Ann Pinchot), *The Objectivist,* November 1969, p. 751.

63 **"an intruder with all the world laughing at [her]":** Letter to Marjorie Williams, June 18, 1936 (*LOAR,* p. 32). In the same letter, AR first states a theme that will become a motif in *TF* and *AS.* In thanking Williams for the Studio Club's help to gifted women, she writes: "Who is more worthy of help—the subnormal or the above-normal? Which of the two suffers more acutely: the misfit, who doesn't know what he is missing, or the talented one who knows it only too well?"

64 **$7.50 a day:** *AR,* p. 36; *The Autobiography of Cecil B. DeMille,* p. 281.

64 **enough to pay her room and board:** *TPOAR,* p. 78.

64 **she was able to borrow:** BBTBI.

64 **first professional effort in English:** A manuscript of *His Dog* is on file in the Cecil B. DeMille Collection, L. Tom Perry Special Collections, Harold B. Lee Library, Brigham Young University, box 1017, folder 6, with the following comment written in DeMille's hand: "Do not return, as this was written only as a test and for her instruction."

64 **competent set piece:** The same story was adapted very differently by another writer and released in 1927, starring Joseph Schildkraut. AR saw the movie in August and rated it a "four-minus" on a scale of one to five (*Russian Writings on Hollywood,* p. 207).

64 **earning twenty-five dollars a week:** "Summary of Charges to Future Productions," May through September 1927, from the Cecil B. DeMille Collection, box 783, folder 20.

64 ***The Angel of Broadway*:** "Completed Productions" for the week ending April 14, 1927, from the Cecil B. DeMille Archives Collection, box 784, folder 1. The script was rewritten and released in the fall of 1927. It starred Leatrice Joy and Ivan Lebedeff, with the writing credit given to Lenore J. Coffee. *American Film Index Catalog,* taken from *NYT,* November 6, 1927.

64 **In *Craig's Wife*:** *Craig's Wife,* adapted by the original playwright and another writer, was released in 1928. AR's versions of *Angel of Broadway* and *Craig's Wife* can be found in the Cecil B. DeMille Collection box 1017, folders 6, 15, and 24.

65 **frustrated by the secondhandedness of the work:** *TPOAR,* p. 83.

65 **Rand's fingerprints are especially evident:** Notes for *The Skyscraper,* July–September 1927 (*JOAR,* pp. 6–15).

65 ***The Skyscraper* ends with a triumphant architect:** The final film version of *The Skyscraper,* featuring William Boyd and Alan Hale, was released in its original form, more or less—as the story of two steelworkers—in April 1928. The adaptation credit went to Elliot Clawson and Tay Garnett. *American Film Index Catalog,* taken from *Film Daily,* April 15, 1928.

65 **"Achievement is the aim of life":** July–September 1927 (*JOAR,* p. 8).

65 **Born Charles Francis O'Connor . . . in 1897:** "Mrs. O'Connor Dies Today," *Lorain [Ohio] Times Herald,* July 19, 1911, p. 1. Also, author interview with FO's niece MW, June 21, 2004.

65 **a hard-drinking Catholic steelworker:** "Pioneer Lorain Steelman Dies," obituary of Dennis O'Connor, FO's father, *Lorain [Ohio] Journal,* December 22, 1938, p. 15.

65 **Mary Agnes O'Connor became ill with breast cancer:** "Mrs. O'Connor Dies Today," *Lorain [Ohio] Times Herald,* July 19, 1911, p. 1.

66 **dropped out of his Catholic high school:** O'Connor dropped out of school in the summer of 1911.

66 **"even more of an atheist than I am":** *The Phil Donahue Show,* April 29, 1980.

66 **spelled phonetically:** According to RBH and her husband, Dr. Burroughs Hill, friends of AR's and FO's during the 1940s, FO could hardly spell. In 1951, the Hills received a thirteen-page letter from FO, the only example of his writing they had ever seen. The letter shocked RBH. "It wasn't the case of a poor speller," she said. "He didn't know how to spell words." Not wanting anyone to say that FO "wasn't intelligent," she destroyed the letter. (Author interview with RBH, May 26, 2005).

66 **a rubber worker in the tire mills at Akron:** *Fourteenth Census of the United States: 1920—Population,"* State of Ohio, County of Summit, Department of Commerce, Bureau of the Census, National Archives, Washington, D.C.

66 **a film extra for D. W. Griffith:** *AR:SOL,* DVD.

66 **"Frank had some feminine tendencies":** Taped interview with Millicent Patton, a friend of AR and the O'Connor brothers from 1929 through the 1930s, in California and New York, conducted by BB, December 5, 1982.

66 **was his first part in Hollywood:** *AR:SOL,* DVD.

66 **later told the tale of their meeting and courtship:** *TPOAR,* pp. 78–94.

66 **"What I couldn't forget [was] the profile":** *AR,* p. 35.

66 **"it was an absolute that this was the man I wanted":** *TPOAR,* p. 81.

67 **he couldn't understand a word she said:** *TPOAR,* p. 81.

67 **where eighty-odd young women:** "Studio Club Bids Called: Promoters Will Meet at Home of Mrs. DeMille Next Week," *Los Angeles Times,* May 8, 1925, p. A1.

67 **Joe, also an aspiring actor:** Author interview with MW, FO's niece, June 21, 2004.

67 **"grim and remote":** *TPOAR,* p. 92.

67 **bought black silk lingerie:** *TPOAR,* p. 92.

67 **the studio had stopped providing her with full-time work:** From January until April, DeMille paid AR only fifty dollars, the equivalent of two weeks' work and the smallest sum paid to any of the studio's dozen writers ("Administration Expenses," January 1, 1928 to April 14, 1928 [Cecil B. DeMille Collection, Harold B. Lee Library, box 784, folder 1]).

67 **DeMille closed his studio:** *The Autobiography of Cecil B. DeMille,* p. 290.

68 **didn't take Rand with him:** DeMille took a dozen or so of his former staff members with him to MGM, including scriptwriter Jeannie Macpherson (note dated July 2, 1928 [Cecil B. DeMille Collection, Harold B. Lee Library, mss. 1400, box 778, folder 1]).

68 **she was left without a job:** She, in turn, lost some of her reverence for DeMille in 1928. She came to see him as a "box-office chaser" (BBTBI).

68 **worked as a waitress:** "New Yorker at Large," p. 4.

68 **famous within a year of reaching Hollywood:** BBTBI.

68 **borrow small sums from her Chicago relatives:** Author interview with FB, June 21, 2004.

68 **twenty-five-dollar monthly subsidy from them:** Author correspondence with Michael Berliner, September 27, 2005, who consulted unpublished Rosenbaum family letters on my behalf. In a 1997 interview conducted by ARI oral historians for *100 Voices,* AR's youngest sister recalled that AR had sent the family photographs of herself from Hollywood and that Anna and Natasha had taken them to the state bank and received permission to send AR money every month.

68 **the custom in the movie industry:** Author interview with Marian L. Smith, historian, History Office and Library, U.S. Citizenship and Immigration Services, Department of Homeland Security, May 19, 2005, who said, "I don't think they would be extending [a visa] for a waitress, but if she had a patron like DeMille—when the movie people wanted [a visa] extended, then it would be extended."

68 **Anna actually urged her to come back:** "Ayn Rand in Russia."

68 **working in a restaurant alongside Nick and Joe:** *TPOAR,* p. 91

68 **to see the woman in Ayn Rand:** The phrase comes from notes AR made on Kira Argounova's feelings for Leo Kovalensky and Andrei, circa 1930 (*JOAR,* p. 50).

68 **romance should never be mixed with suffering or pity:** *AS,* p. 348.

68 **a woman should avoid cooking or cleaning:** "The Husband I Bought," *TEAR,* p. 13.

68 **"an answering voice, an answering hymn, an echo":** *Ideal,* an unproduced play written in 1934, *TEAR,* p. 287.

69 **practiced her new language:** These letters have been lost, according to the ARI.

69 **"put so much weight on success and so little on failure":** "Ayn Rand in Russia."

69 **signed two unpublished stories from that period "O. O. Lyons":** Editor's preface to "Escort," *TEAR,* p. 103. Rand admirer Fred Cookinham points out that "O. O." probably referred to Oscar and Oswald, stuffed lions given as a gift to Rand by O'Connor.

69 **absorbing the civil-libertarian iconoclasm:** AR would have known of Garrett's work, but whether or not she actually read it is a subject of dispute. Journalist Justin Raimondo accuses her of pirating narrative devices from Garrett's *The Driver* (1922) when writing *AS* (Justin Raimondo, *Reclaiming the American Right: The Lost Legacy of the Conservative Movement* [Burlingame, Calif.: Center for Libertarian Studies, 1993], pp. 196–205).

69 ***Calumet "K":*** Letter to Barbara Brandt, December 11, 1945 (*LOAR,* p. 252).

69 **books she didn't like:** *TPOAR,* p. 101.

69 **"The Husband I Bought" (circa 1926):** As the story appears in *TEAR,* it seems too nuanced and sophisticated to have been written in 1926 and gives the impression of having been edited (*TEAR,* pp. 3–39).

70 **exercise in grieving for Lev Bekkerman:** My thanks to LP for making this point in his introduction to "The Husband I Bought," *TEAR,* p. 4.

70 **"human herds":** July–September 1927 (*JOAR,* p. 35).

70 **strangle and dismember an eight-year-old Los Angeles girl:** "Marion Parker's Murder Confessed by Hickman," *Los Angeles Times,* December 27, 1927.

70   **"A strong man can eventually trample society"**: July–September 1927 (*JOAR*, p. 38).

70   **"All the crimes in history have always been perpetrated by the mob"**: Letter to John Temple Graves, August 12, 1936 (*LOAR*, p. 34).

71   **"She hated being afraid"**: Author interview with Joan and Dr. Allan Blumenthal, March 24, 2004.

71   **"From now on, [you will permit] no thought about yourself"**: July–September 1927 (*JOAR*, p. 48).

71   **Ayn Rand and Frank O'Connor were married:** In his book *AR:SOL,* Paxton states that AR's temporary visa was set to expire permanently in April 1929. Yet based on handwritten notes recording her visa extensions on the official ship manifest of the S.S. *De Grasse,* her final extension was granted in July 1928, suggesting that her visa had already expired by the time of her marriage (*De Grasse* Ship Manifest, February 19, 1926; vol. 8626, p. 2, line 13, National Archives Microfilm Publication T715, roll 3800, "Passenger and Crew Lists of Vessels Arriving at New York, N.Y., 1897–1957," National Archives and Records Administration Northeast Region, New York, N.Y.).

71   **she and her husband took a borrowed car:** The car belonged to one of the friends who acted as official witnesses: Dorotha Bensinger and Harrison James Carter ("Application for Immigration Visa," C-file number C-3447608, U.S. Citizenship and Immigration Services, Department of Homeland Security, Washington, D.C.). One of her procedural witnesses was her boss in the RKO wardrobe department, costume designer Walter Plunkett ("Petition for Citizenship No. 32336," National Archives, N.Y.).

71   **She recrossed the border:** Henceforth she seems to have reported her original immigration date as 1929 instead of 1926 (Bureau of the Census, *Fiftieth Census of the United States: 1930,* Los Angeles, Assembly District 55, April 10, 1930).

71   **a rapid evaluation to become a permanent resident:** Author interview with Marian L. Smith, historian, Department of Homeland Security, May 19, 2005.

71   **proved that she wasn't wanted for crimes in Soviet Russia:** Alice O'Connor's petition for citizenship, courtesy of Marian L. Smith, historian, Department of Homeland Security.

71   **"a shotgun wedding"**: *TPOAR,* p. 93.

71   **which of them would marry her and rescue her from deportation:** *TPOAR,* p. 93.

72   **Months earlier she had moved out:** AR shared her first apartment with a Studio Club friend named Nell McKenzie. O'Connor family lore had it that Nell had to leave when FO visited (taped interview with MS, conducted by BB, February 18, 1983).

72   **"He loved Ayn better"**: Taped interview with MS, conducted by BB, February 18, 1983.

72   **a small apartment at 823 North Gower Street:** 1930 U.S. Census, City of Los Angeles, sheet 11A, lines 8–9.

72   **"Just after the wedding, Ayn said"**: Taped interview with Millicent Patton, conducted by BB, December 5, 1982.

72   **July 1929:** Noted in AR's "Application for a Certificate of Arrival and Preliminary Form for Petition of Citizenship," October 15, 1930 (C-File number C-3447608, U.S.

Citizenship and Immigration Services, Washington, D.C.).

72 **Ivan Lebedeff:** *AR*, p. 36.

72 **version of *The Angel of Broadway*:** Ivan Lebedeff also played Rosengoltz in the 1943 film *Mission to Moscow*, the subject of AR's voluntary testimony before the House Un-American Activities Committee in October 1947.

72 **helped Rand to get a full-time clerical job:** *AR*, p. 36; McConnell, "Paramount Studio Tour," speech given on the Paramount Studio lot at the ARI premiere of the movie *Ayn Rand: A Sense of Life*, November 2, 1996.

72 **eventually became the department boss:** Millicent Patton told an interviewer in 1982 about AR's career in the RKO wardrobe department: "Anybody who got in her way she just brushed aside and stepped ahead. Anybody who was over her she naturally just—she'd see to it that that person got out of her way and would rise up over that one and get to the next one. She had such drive. Maybe she just learned a few little things about somebody who wasn't doing what they should be doing and just let it be known." This, of course, is a tactic Peter Keating perfects in *TF* (taped interview with Millicent Patton, conducted by BB, December 15, 1982).

72 **started at a salary of twenty dollars:** *TPOAR*, p. 94.

72 **began to send money:** Author correspondence with Michael Berliner, September 27 and 28, 2005, based on unpublished Rosenbaum family letters.

72 **Soviet government was desperate for foreign currency:** Thanks to Bernice Glatzer Rosenthal, professor of Russian and European intellectual

history at Fordham University in New York, who provided this information and also cited Eugene Lyons's *Assignment in Utopia* (New York: Harcourt Brace, 1937).

72 **"I loathed [that job]":** *TPOAR*, pp. 93–94.

73 **"to cook, and wash dishes, and such":** Unpublished letter to Sarah Lipton, November 27, 1932, courtesy of FB.

73 **He decorated their new apartment:** BBTBI.

73 **"I came to America to write":** Unpublished letter to Sarah Lipton, November 27, 1932, courtesy of FB.

73 **film scenario, called *Red Pawn*:** AR apparently composed two film scenarios in 1930–31, *Red Pawn* and another called *Treason*, which has been lost ("Ayn Rand's Family and Friends").

73 **The story begins:** In a thirteen-page synopsis of *Red Pawn* later written by AR, the American character Joan becomes a Russian character called Tania Sokolova. Tania seduces the prison commandant by teaching him the basic joy of living rather than the specific sensual superiority of Western values. Paramount owned *Red Pawn*, and AR showed the new version to both Hal Wallis and Barbara Stanwyck (letter to Barbara Stanwyck, September 7, 1946 [*LOAR*, pp. 317–18]; copy of the synopsis courtesy of Al Ramrus, to whom AR gave it in the 1960s).

73 **displaying too much "ability":** *Red Pawn, TEAR*, pp. 154–227.

73 **"a right to the joy of living":** Letter to Hollywood producer Kenneth MacGowan, May 18, 1934 (*LOAR*, p. 6).

73 **"building a story in tiers":** Letter to Kenneth MacGowan, May 18, 1934 (*LOAR*, p. 6).

74 **the kind of romantic triad that Rand was now elaborating:** *AR:SOL*, p. 3.

74 **powerful Myron Selznick agency:** "Ayn Rand's Family and Friends"; *EOWTL*, p. 259.

74 **The agent, coincidentally named Nick Carter:** Paramount appears to have rejected *Red Pawn* in 1932 but then changed its mind and acquired the script from Universal in 1934 with Dietrich in mind ("Paramount Gets *Red Pawn*, Maybe for Dietrich," *The Hollywood Reporter*, June 20, 1934, p. 1).

74 **According to the author:** "Russian Girl Finds End of Rainbow in Hollywood."

74 **Gouverneur Morris:** Lee Shippey, "The Lee Side o' L.A.," *Los Angeles Times*, March 11, 1936, p. A4. Morris happened to be the great-grandson and namesake of a signer of the U.S. Declaration of Independence. His grandfather was a vice president of the New York and Harlem Railroad.

74 **"[Red Pawn] was the first script sent me":** "Russian Girl Finds End of Rainbow in Hollywood"; unpublished letter to Sarah Lipton, November 27, 1932; letter to Jean Wick, August 29, 1934 (*LOAR*, p. 14).

74 **"From that point on, you couldn't stop her":** *100 Voices*, Marcella Rabwin, p. 41.

74 **studios "were interested in Russian stories":** Unpublished letter to Sarah Lipton, November 27, 1932.

75 **"The high-priced executive in Russia":** "Russian Girl Jeers at Depression Complaint," p. 9.

75 **Universal hired her to rewrite an unrelated project:** Unpublished letter to Sarah Lipton, November 27, 1932. AR was assigned the job rewriting others' attempts at a screenplay called *Black Pearls*, which does

not appear to have been released by Universal.

75 **Red Pawn was never produced:** Two years later, in June 1934, Paramount acquired *Red Pawn* by trading a twenty-thousand-dollar property it owned, called *The Great Impersonation,* for the script. Paramount wanted Josef von Sternberg to direct it, with Marlene Dietrich in the starring role. AR spent four weeks at Paramount, earning one hundred dollars a week, waiting for orders to revise the script. For a second time, von Sternberg decided against the project (*EOWTL*, pp. 259–60).

75 **He was landing small parts:** My thanks to David Hayes for compiling FO's movie titles. The list appears at http://movies.davidhayes.net.

75 **earning enough to buy his young wife:** *AR:SOL*, DVD.

75 **"Ayn; adorable":** Bonhams & Butterfields, *The Library of Ayn Rand,* auction catalog, Los Angeles, June 28, 2005, p. 40.

75 **"a real big novel . . . about Russia":** Unpublished letter to Sarah Lipton, November 27, 1932.

75 **Rand originally called it Penthouse Legend:** The play has been edited and re-edited many times. The "authorized" edition appears in *Three Plays.*

75 **"sense-of-life" play:** *Three Plays,* p. 3.

75 **Swedish Match King and con man Ivar Kreuger:** *Three Plays,* p. 5.

76 **her growing preoccupation with the envy:** Echoing Nietzsche, she describes Bjorn Faulkner as "young, tall, with an arrogant smile, with kingdoms and nations in the palm of one hand—and a whip in the other" (*Three Plays,* p. 21).

76 **She later renounced her roman-**

tic fascination with criminals: *TPOAR*, p. 110.

76 audience juries overwhelmingly found in favor of Karen Andre: "Jury in Drama Usually Votes for Acquittal," *Los Angeles Times*, November 13, 1934, p. 12.

76 She wrote *The Night of January 16th* in a few months' time: *TPOAR*, p. 110.

76 opened as *Woman on Trial*: Lee Shippey, "The Lee Side o' L.A.," *Los Angeles Times*, October 22, 1934, p. A4.

76 Critics and a star-studded first-night audience: Advertisement, *The Hollywood Citizen*, October 19, 1934; "That Certain Party," *Los Angeles Times*, October 28, 1934, p. A1; "Window to Civilization," quoted in *AR:SOL*, DVD.

77 at a party Lebedeff threw: "That Certain Party," p. A1.

77 she had felt uncomfortable at the party: *TPOAR*, p. 110.

77 "superlatives or nothing": *TPOAR*, p. 111.

77 for Loretta Young: Thanks to archivist Jenny Romero of the Margaret Herrick Library.

77 wasn't able to write comedy to order: *TPOAR*, p. 111.

78 She had come to despise: BBTBI.

78 a box-office chaser: BBTBI.

78 advantageous to her as a writer: Letter to Jean Wick, July 19, 1934 (*LOAR*, p. 12).

78 he wasn't earning much money: O'Connor earned about seven dollars a day as a film extra (*100 Voices*, Marcella Rabwin, p. 41).

78 Rand began to chafe under the impression: BBTBI.

78 described as heartbreaking: BBTBI.

78 very good in the parts he got: BBTBI.

78 he didn't publicly express it: At least one friend at the time believed that AR preferred O'Connor *not* to be successful. "If Ayn had *wanted* him out there [in front of movie audiences], she would have pushed. But I think she wanted him right there, by her side," said Millicent Patton (taped interview with Millicent Patton, conducted by BB on December 15, 1982).

78 closed in late November 1934: " 'The Night of January 16th' Unique Courtroom Drama," *Los Angeles Times*, March 2, 1936, p. 17.

78 "killed his ambition to work as an actor": AR:SOL, DVD.

78 "enormous contempt" for the whole movie business: *TPOAR*, p. 135.

79 "His downfall was his enormous respect for her": Taped interview with MS, conducted by BB, January 20, 1983.

79 "the greatest monument to the potency of man's mind": *FTNI*, p. 49.

79 translated it into Russian: "Ayn Rand in Russia."

79 compared the beauty and economy of her language: "Home Atmosphere."

79 a sketch of a theater marquee: *AR:SOL*, p. 71.

79 "A is A": "Ayn Rand in Russia."

80 determined belief in her abilities: "Ayn Rand in Russia."

FOUR: WE ARE NOT LIKE OUR BROTHERS: 1934–1938

81 "Men have been taught": *TF*, p. 713.

81 left Los Angeles in their second-hand Nash: Letter to Jean Wick, November 24, 1934 (*LOAR*, p. 20).

81 **in Virginia the car hit a pothole:** *TPOAR*, p. 119.

81 **She had already begun to make mental notes:** According to *JOAR*, p. 77, AR made her first actual notes for *TF* on December 4, 1935. Shoshana Milgram, who has access to the ARI Archives, claims that AR was already working on an outline when she traveled from California to New York (Shoshana Milgram, "The Hero in the Soul Manifested in the World," a lecture presented at the ARI's Centenary Conference, New York, April 23, 2005).

82 **The car was wrecked:** "The Hero in the Soul, Manifested in the World."

82 **She also got on well:** Letter to Mary Inloes, December 10, 1934 (*LOAR*, pp. 20–21).

82 **one-room furnished apartment:** Harry Binswanger, dinner lecture, ARI Centenary Conference, April 24, 2005; thanks to Fred Cookinham for his notes. In *TPOAR*, p. 120, BB mistakes the address as being on East Sixty-fifth Street.

82 **Woods informed her that the play would not open:** *TPOAR*, p. 120.

82 **she needed money:** Letter to Mary Inloes, March 16, 1935 (*LOAR*, pp. 21–22).

82 **cash advance against the play's New York box office:** "Contract with A. H. Woods, Ltd.," November 14, 1934 (A. Watkins Collection, Columbia University Rare Book and Manuscript Library, New York, New York, box 80).

82 **complained in a letter to Mary Inloes:** Letter to Mary Inloes, March 16, 1935 (*LOAR*, pp. 21–22).

83 **"It was just a matter of what she had to do":** Taped interview with Millicent Patton, conducted by BB, December 5, 1982.

83 **literary agent, a woman named Jean Wick:** Letter to Jean Wick, July 19, 1934 (*LOAR*, p. 12).

83 **"the *Uncle Tom's Cabin* of Soviet Russia":** Letter to Jean Wick, October 27, 1934 (*LOAR*, p. 19).

83 **warned that its anti-Communist message might hurt it:** Letter to Jean Wick, June 19, 1934 (*LOAR*, p. 10). "The literary set also turned against H. L. Mencken . . . because of his opposition to the New Deal" (from Llewellyn H. Rockwell, Jr., "Biography of Henry Hazlitt," http://www.mises.org).

83 **disbelief and indignation:** BBTBI; JMB, a friend of AR's from the early 1950s until the 1970s, told Jeff Walker, a Canadian Broadcasting Corporation reporter, "She had such a glamorous view of America as a child and as a young person in Russia that she was genuinely horrified that there were such things as liberals and socialists; she couldn't believe that it was true of this country at first, and then of course she came to believe that there was little else" (from taped, unpublished interviews by journalist JW in preparation for a CBC special report on the tenth anniversary of AR's death, titled *Ideas: The Legacy of Ayn Rand*, 1992).

83 **couldn't be more than a handful of Communists:** BBTBI.

83 **Americans would "scream with horror":** Letter to Jean Wick, October 27, 1934 (*LOAR*, p. 18).

84 **first vote as a U.S. citizen:** *TPOAR*, p. 158.

84 **she had been intimate with relatively few people:** BBTBI.

84 **"pink" penetration in America:** *Ayn Rand and the Song of Russia*, p. 75.

84 **Matthew Josephson:** Josephson's book *The Robber Barons* (New York: Harcourt Brace, 1962) set the tone

for much 1930s writing about ruthless, greedy industrialists. Cited in John Chamberlain, *A Life with the Printed Word* (Chicago: Regnery Gateway, 1982), p. 47. It was a point of view that AR would attempt to refute in *AS*.

84 **"Red Dawn":** Page Smith, *Redeeming the Time* (New York: McGraw Hill, 1987), p. 532. It's not impossible that AR had heard this phrase in Hollywood and had named her screenplay *Red Pawn* as an ironic commentary on it.

84 **the extent of the pro-Communist bias:** BBTBI; by mid-1936, she was writing to Gouverneur Morris, "New York is full of people sold bodies and souls to the Soviets. The extent of it almost frightens me" (letter to Gouverneur Morris, April 14, 1936 [*LOAR*, p. 28]).

84 **vowed to confront the messengers of collectivism:** Letter to H. L. Mencken, July 28, 1934 (*LOAR*, p. 13).

84 **began a program of extensive reading:** *The Library of Ayn Rand*, pp. 34–51; "The Hero in the Soul Manifested in the World."

85 **the most persuasive:** AR's youngest sister, NR, who turned against AR in old age, didn't think the novel was persuasive. In a 1997 interview, NR said, "I can't admire this falsehood. Go ahead, judge me! She had just artificially constructed the whole thing while living in America, that's all. She had made up all of our lives, do you understand?" (*100 Voices*, NR, p. 4).

85 **"Russia is a huge cemetery":** *TPOAR*, p. 60.

85 **"we are dying here":** Isabel Paterson, "Turns with a Bookworm," *New York Herald Tribune*, June 29, 1941. In 1925, many Russians still believed that if Western countries only understood their plight, they would be rescued.

85 **St. Petersburg, or Petrograd, in 1922 and 1923:** The Argounovas' fictional return to St. Petersburg takes place a year later than the Rosenbaums' actual return in 1921. Kira Argounova is depicted as being a little more than a year older than AR at the time of the events of the novel; specifically, Kira is said to have been born on April 11, 1904, a few days before Anna and Zinovy Rosenbaum's wedding on April 20, 1904. In the first typed draft of *We the Living* on file at the Library of Congress, AR originally made Kira her own age. " 'Born in 1905, eh?' said the Soviet official" is crossed out, and "1904" is penciled in, presumably to avoid giving the impression that the novel was purely autobiographical. (Ayn Rand Papers, LOC, box 26, reel 17, p. 108, begun on April 18, 1933.)

85 **she enrolls in the city's free State Technical Institute:** Lev Bekkerman was an engineering student at Petrograd Technical Institute from 1918 until 1925 (*EOWTL*, p. 54). In the novel, Leo Kovalensky is said to be a student of history and philosophy at Petrograd State University, otherwise known as St. Petersburg University, just as AR was.

85 **son of a slain aristocrat:** *WTL*, p. 62. Leo Kovalensky's father, Admiral Leo Kovalensky, who AR suggests served heroically in World War I and was executed without a trial (*WTL*, p. 48), may be based on the husband of the woman who tutored AR in English in 1925, one Marie von Strachow. Her deceased husband had been an admiral; author correspondence with Michael Berliner, June 2, 2005.

85 **just as Rand was during the same years:** AR was a student of history and philosophy from 1921 until 1924. In an earlier draft of *WTL*, Kira Argounova was also a student of history.

85 **campus GPU leader:** The GPU, Russia's secret police force, was the forerunner of the KGB.

86 **"the rule of brute force":** Preface to *WTL* (written in 1958 and reprinted in the Signet edition, 1995), p. xv.

86 **"The individual against the masses":** Letter to Jean Wick, October 27, 1934 (*LOAR*, pp. 17–19).

86 **"too strong to compromise":** This description also characterizes AR's father after 1921 (*EOWTL*, p. 23).

86 **a mouth "like that of an ancient chieftain":** *WTL*, p. 61.

86 **spiritual self-destruction:** *EOWTL*, p. 54; BBTBI.

86 **upholding values, even in the airtight atmosphere:** AR's circa 1930 working title for *WTL* was *Airtight: A Story of Red Russia* (*JOAR*, pp. 56–57).

87 **"the state," "the public," or "the common good":** Quoted phrases from Ayn Rand, *Capitalism: The Unknown Ideal* (New York: New American Library, 1966), pp. 11–34.

87 **cannot be broken:** circa 1930 (*JOAR*, p. 59).

87 **would have chanced death:** *TPOAR*, p. 60. In about 1930, AR told Millicent Patton that she *had* risked death by walking across the Russian border, working her way west from St. Petersburg and finally "creeping through barbed wire in the snow." If Patton was remembering correctly, AR seemed to be trying Kira Argounova's story on for size (taped interview with Millicent Patton, conducted by BB, December 5, 1982).

87 **she re-edited it:** Revised for publication in 1959 (*EOWTL*, p. 185).

87 **"I loathe your ideals":** *WTL*, pp. 41, 92–3.

88 **St. Petersburg section was her favorite:** BBTBI.

88 **was writing for newspapers:** Taped interview with MS, conducted by BB, February 18, 1983, courtesy of MSC.

88 **Ivan Lebedeff was in and out of town:** *TPOAR*, p. 121.

88 **friend of Sinclair Lewis:** Hiram Haydn, *Words & Faces* (New York: Harcourt Brace Jovanovich, 1954, 1974), p. 93.

88 **"All achievement and progress":** Unpublished correspondence with Ethel Boileau; cited in "The Hero in the Soul Manifested in the World."

88 **aspiring playwright named Albert Mannheimer:** *TPOAR*, p. 121.

88 **graduate student at the Yale School of Drama:** Mannheimer attended but did not graduate, according to the archives of the Yale School of Drama; phone interview, December 5, 2005.

88 **tall, fair, and curly haired:** Interview with Frances Schloss, who dated Mannheimer in 1950–51, December 8, 2005.

88 **screenwriter Budd Schulberg:** BBTBI. Schulberg is best remembered for his best-selling 1947 novel *What Makes Sammy Run?* Interestingly, the narrator is named Al Manheim, and Manheim's lover, a woman "who likes sex," is called Billie Rand.

88 **Ring Lardner, Jr.:** "Ayn Rand's Family and Friends."

88 **a mutual theatrical acquaintance introduced them:** BBTBI.

88 **it was she who would convert him:** BBTBI.

89 **a vehement advocate of capital-**

ism: AR, quoted in "Ayn Rand's Family and Friends."

89 **recently staged a play by John Howard Lawson:** Lawson's *Gentlewoman* had been staged at the Cort Theater in the spring of 1934. On Lawson as a Communist, see Kenneth Lloyd Billingsley's *Hollywood Party* (Rocklin, Calif.: Forum, 1998), pp. 47–48.

89 **would . . . share the spotlight:** AR and Hellman were the first screenwriters hired by Wallis when he started his own production company after storming off a Warner Bros. set (Paramount Contracts Collection, Margaret Herrick Library, file 3, box 95).

90 **kept promising that casting and rehearsals would begin any day:** Letter to Mary Inloes, March 16, 1935 (*LOAR*, p. 21).

90 **her "highfalutin" courtroom speeches:** *TPOAR*, p. 122.

90 **reportedly Shubert's mistress:** *TPOAR*, p. 122.

90 **tirades about how ponderous ideas had no place:** What AR could not have known was that ex-millionaire Woods was broke at the time of the production and was under pressure to turn *The Night of January 16th* into a commercial hit. Royalties from the play were one of his few discovered sources of income when he declared bankruptcy in February 1936. By then, he was a mere employee of the Shubert Organization, working for $150 a week ("Ex-millionaire Reported Broke," *Los Angeles Times,* February 8, 1936, p. 2).

90 **removing elements of the motivation of her characters:** Unpublished letter cited in Shoshana Milgram's "Ayn Rand's Unique and Enduring Contributions to Literature," lecture, ARI Centenary Conference, July 7, 2005, San Diego. According to Milgram, AR wrote about what was taken out of her play and the fact that she found the first "tier" unsatisfactory as a result.

90 **she reportedly told him:** "The Hero in the Soul Manifested in the World."

90 **Hayes and Weitzenkorn:** "Second Arbitration on Play Royalties," *NYT,* January 17, 1936, p. 15.

90 **to siphon off one-tenth of her royalties:** "Agency Agreement with Ann Watkins," October 30, 1935 (A. Watkins Collection, Columbia University Rare Book and Manuscript Library, box 80).

90 **the support of Mrs. Vincent Astor:** "News of the Stage," *NYT,* January 27, 1936, p. 20.

90 **"miserably painful":** "The Hero in the Soul Manifested in the World."

91 **"Don't read that! I'm going to destroy it":** Author interview with RBH, June 8, 2005.

91 **Wick didn't always pass their comments along to Rand:** BBTBI.

91 **wasn't merely about postrevolutionary Russia:** Letter to Jean Wick, July 19, 1934 (*LOAR*, p. 12).

91 **the first novel on the subject written in English by a Russian writer:** Based on a survey of fictional representations of Stalin in Russia by Rosalind Marsh, a professor of Russian studies at the University of Bath in England, AR's claim appears to be true (Rosalind Marsh, *Images of Dictatorship: Portraits of Stalin in Literature* [Oxford: Routledge, 1989]).

91 **as Wick took to arguing it did:** BBTBI.

91 **This was a theme the American public . . . needed to hear:** Ayn Rand, "The Only Path to Tomorrow," *Reader's Digest,* January 1944, p. 88.

91 **"the greatest problem of our century":** Letter to Jean Wick, October 27, 1934 (*LOAR*, pp. 17–19).

91 ***"We the Living* is not a story about Soviet Russia in 1925":** Foreword to *WTL*, p. xiii.

91 **all this sounded much too intellectual:** BBTBI.

92 **On September 8, Rand, O'Connor, and Nick Carter headed for Philadelphia:** "Play Uses Audience in Jury Box on Stage," *NYT,* September 10, 1935, p. 26.

92 **summoned to make yet another round of last-minute changes:** *TPOAR*, p. 123.

92 **felt as if she were about to go under the knife:** *TPOAR*, p. 123.

92 **frustrated tears:** "The Hero in the Soul Manifested in the World."

92 **the most wonderful thing:** Letter to Gouverneur Morris, November 29, 1935 (*LOAR*, p. 23).

92 ***The Night of January 16th* premiered:** The play opened on Monday, September 16. The weather was reported in *NYT,* September 17, 1935, p. 25.

92 **The theater was packed:** Brooks Atkinson, "The Play," *NYT,* September 17, 1935, p. 26.

92 **The celebrity jury:** "The Play," p. 26.

92 ***The Wall Street Journal*:** "Audience Does Jury Duty," *Wall Street Journal,* September 19, 1935, p. 11.

92 **sat in the back row of the theater on opening night:** *TPOAR*, p. 124.

92 **this was no longer Ayn Rand's work:** The 1935 production version of *The Night of January 16th* was first published by Longmans Green & Co. in 1936 (RKO contract), and a separate, "cleaned-up" version for amateur theatricals appeared in print slightly later (Ayn Rand, introduction to *The Night of January 16th, Three Plays,*

p. 3). In 1968, New American Library issued an authorized version of the play, with an introduction by AR.

93 **publisher did not ask for cutting:** Letter to Gouverneur Morris, November 29, 1935 (*LOAR*, p. 23).

93 **recounted the story in the early 1960s:** *TPOAR*, pp. 124–25.

93 **Hicks had recently joined the U.S. Communist Party:** Leah Levinson and Jerry Natterstad, *Granville Hicks: The Intellectual in Mass Society* (Philadelphia: Temple University Press, 1993), pp. 53–56, 85, and 195–99.

93 **an admiring biography of the American Communist John Reed:** Granville Hicks, *John Reed: The Making of a Revolutionary* (New York: Macmillan, 1936). Ironically, Hicks's book appeared on the same Macmillan list as did *WTL*.

93 **published *We the Living* on April 7, 1936:** "Books Published Today," *NYT,* April 7, 1936.

93 **"my American father":** "Ayn Rand's Family and Friends."

93 **Rand told a *New York Times* reporter:** "Books and Authors," *NYT,* April 26, 1936, p. BR14.

94 **"wild cry for the right[s] of the individual":** Ida Zeitlin, "A Passionate and Powerful Novel of Conflicts in the Red Land," *New York Herald Tribune Books,* April 19, 1936, sec. VII, p. 4. Zeitlin was married to Russian refugee artist Theodore Nadejen. Russian émigrés gave the novel some of its best reviews.

94 **"would cause Boccaccio":** J. C. Rogers, "Reds and Whites: Ayn Rand's *We the Living* Portrays Aristocrats Amid Russian Revolution," *Washington Post,* April 26, 1936, p. B8.

94 **her work compared with that of Joseph Conrad:** AR may never have

read Conrad. At least, she was unaware that he called himself a romantic realist (a designation she took as her own) according to longtime acquaintance JKT (author interview with JKT, May 21, 2004).

94 **"inherent sentimentality":** "New Yorker at Large," p. 1.

94 **"slavishly warped to the dictates of propaganda":** Harold Strauss, "Soviet Triangle," *NYT Book Review,* April 19, 1936, p. 7.

94 **"out to puncture a bubble—with a bludgeon":** Ben Belitt, "The Red and the White," *The Nation,* April 22, 1936, p. 523.

94 **ended Ayn Rand's expectations of receiving literary "justice":** BBTBI.

95 **average American incomes were well under $1,500 a year:** Based on data from the "Statistics of Income" report, IRS archives.

95 **royalties of between $200 and $1,200 a week:** Royalty statements, various dates (A. Watkins Collection, Columbia University Rare Book and Manuscript Library, box 178).

95 **closed on April 4, 1936:** "Agreement with RKO Radio Pictures," July 13, 1938 (A. Watkins Collection, Columbia University Rare Book and Manuscript Library, box 152).

95 **theatrical rights had been sold:** "Agreement with RKO Radio Pictures," July 13, 1938 (A. Watkins Collection, Columbia University Rare Book and Manuscript Library, box 152); Lee Shippey, "The Lee Side o' L.A.," *Los Angeles Times,* March 31, 1936, p. A4.

95 **filling seats in the El Capitan Theatre:** Lee Shippey, "The Lee Side o' L.A.," *Los Angeles Times,* March 31, 1936, p. A4; "The Night of January 16 Unique Courtroom Drama," *Los Angeles Times,* March 2, 1936, p. 17.

95 **road show was about to open in Chicago:** Introduction to *The Night of January 16th, Three Plays,* p. 3.

95 **royalties of ten dollars:** "Royalty Statements," various dates (A. Watkins Collection, Columbia University Rare Book and Manuscript Library, box 178).

95 **certain that she was being ostracized:** TPOAR, p. 127.

95 **"She talks too much about Soviet Russia":** Shoshana Milgram, "AR as a Public Speaker."

96 **"This [blacklisting] lasted until *The Fountainhead*":** Ayn Rand and Song of Russia, p. 77.

96 **called herself shy:** "The Hero in the Soul Manifested in the World."

96 **lectured at the then-famous New York Town Hall Club:** "Book Notes," *NYT,* May 14, 1936, p. 23; "Ayn Rand to Speak Tuesday," *NYT,* May 22, 1936.

96 **"two million snow-white [Stalinist] angels":** "Ayn Rand as a Public Speaker," quoting the *New York Journal American* from May 1936.

96 **In one New York newspaper interview:** "Only High Ransom for Passports Opens Border, Says Miss Ayn Rand," *New York American,* June 15, 1936.

97 **to get an affidavit of support:** AR, p. 52; Binswanger, dinner lecture, April 24, 2005. A question arises here, for AR's Chicago relatives possessed more than enough money to sponsor the whole Rosenbaum family and pay their passage, had AR asked them for help. In fact, some of them never forgave AR for not alerting them to the dire conditions her family faced in St. Petersburg (taped interview with Minna Goldberg, FB, and MS, conducted by BB, Chicago, February 20, 1983).

97 **Soviet agents might be watching**

her: As far as I was able to discover, neither AR nor the Rosenbaums has a GPU or KGB file.

97 **notorious for their ruthlessness and skill:** Author interview with Bernice Rosenthal, Ph.D., July 5, 2005.

97 **was more compelling:** Later, AR would occasionally recommend filial love above truth-telling, as in an aside at a 1960s lecture.

97 **"She lied":** Interview with BB, July 5, 2006.

97 **fallen in love with an engineer named Fedor Drobyshev:** AR, p. 45; NR was married in 1931 (100 Voices, NR, p. 7).

97 **married and teaching in a Soviet school:** AR, p. 52; Binswanger, dinner lecture, April 24, 2005.

97 **willing to make the journey:** TPOAR, p. 125.

98 **One of the reasons:** Unpublished letter to Sarah Lipton, June 4, 1936.

98 **letters between Rand and the Rosenbaums ceased:** In 1997 or 1998, AR's youngest sister, NR, told an interviewer, "Actually, she [AR] was the one who stopped writing to us. Probably because she did not have any use for us any longer" (100 Voices, NR, p. 18). Why NR would have assumed, bitterly, in the 1930s that her émigré sister had lost interest in the family is not clear. In 1974, when the sisters were briefly reunited in New York, AR was "extremely excited," said a friend of the time, but the reunion was a disaster. See Chapter 16.

98 **left Sixty-sixth Street:** Binswanger, dinner lecture, April 24, 2005.

98 **where the newspaper photograph was taken:** Binswanger, dinner lecture, April 24, 2005; "A New Yorker at Large," p. 4. Sixty-six Park Avenue is now the Kitano New York hotel.

98 **bought a set of blond Art Deco**

bedroom furniture: Photographs, Binswanger, dinner lecture, April 24, 2005.

98 **became her trademark in the 1940s:** TPOAR, p. 137.

98 **musing about its theme since her late teens:** BBTBI.

98 **made her first extensive notes about it in December 1935:** December 4, 1935 (JOAR, p. 82).

98 **life on earth:** BBTBI.

98 **now she was ready:** BBTBI.

99 **earned the right:** BBTBI.

99 **the first notes of marital discord:** Based on taped interview with MS, conducted by BB, January 20, 1983.

99 **far from sexually dominant, or even highly sexed:** Author interviews with Thaddeus Ashby, RBH, and BB. Thaddeus Ashby, interviewed on June 19, 2005, called O'Connor "undersexed."

99 **didn't fit her romantic image of him:** BBTBI.

99 **decorated their apartments inexpensively:** Taped interview with MS, conducted by BB, January 20, 1983.

99 **take over many household chores:** TPOAR, pp. 94, 137.

99 **"Mr. Ayn Rand":** TPOAR, p. 136.

99 **"there would not have been so much hurt pride":** Taped interview with MS, conducted by BB, January 20, 1983.

99 **did not complain:** TPOAR, p. 148. On the other hand, in an interview with Mike Wallace in 1959, she seemed embarrassed to admit that she supported him.

99 **withdrew from conversation:** TPOAR, p. 135.

99 **brimming with new ideas:** March 13, 1936 to August 15, 1938 (JOAR, pp. 117–64).

100 **dinner almost every night:** TPOAR, p. 121.

100 **charming, funny, well read, intel-**

ligent: Interview with MW, June 21, 2004.

100 **collected disability payments:** Letter to Nick Carter, October 5, 1944 (*LOAR*, p. 164). "Nick wanted to [write] but didn't have the drive to succeed," Millicent Patton recalled in 1982. "He was trying to write books but ended up writing a few articles" (taped interview with Millicent Patton, conducted by BB, December 5, 1982).

100 **"He was Noel Coward":** Taped interview with MS, conducted by BB, February 18, 1983.

100 **"peasant" face and figure:** Taped interview with Millicent Patton, conducted by BB, December 5, 1982.

100 **"My father was appalled":** Taped interview with MS, conducted by BB, February 18, 1983.

100 **"a small white Dutch hat":** *TPOAR*, p. 137.

100 **He was a homosexual:** Author interview with MW, June 21, 2004.

100 **"She would have been the last person on earth":** Author interview with JMB and Dr. Allan Blumenthal, June 21, 2004, quoting BB.

101 **whom Rand had met at the Studio Club:** Marjorie Booth Hiss was married to Philip Hiss, Alger's cousin (author interview with Alger's son Tony Hiss, February 21, 2008); AR met her in the Studio Club (BB interview with MS).

101 **called him Cubbyhole:** Letters to FO ("Cubby"), August 19 and August 21, 1936. In a taped interview from 1983, MS recalled having been told by Ayn that the nickname Cubbyhole came from a joke Nick told, which included the line, "Papa bear couldn't find the cubbyhole" (*LOAR*, pp. 36–38).

101 **called her Fluff:** *TPOAR*, p. 185.

101 **poring over architectural texts:** *EOTF*, p. 38.

101 **turn *We the Living* into a stage play:** Letters to FO, August 19, 1936, and to Hollywood friend Gladys Unger, July 6, 1937 (*LOAR*, pp. 36, 41); retitled *The Unconquered*, the play version of *WTL* ran for five nights and closed on February 17, 1940 (IBDB.com).

101 **At Ann Watkins's urging:** *TPOAR*, p. 148.

101 **rewrote a novella she had completed:** *Three Plays*, p. 193. In his preface, LP seems to have misstated the date of composition of AR's final play, *Think Twice*. AR's correspondence suggests she wrote it in 1941, not 1939.

101 **Called *Ideal*:** Published in play form in 1983 and again in 2005 by Signet.

101 **Greta Garbo–like movie star:** Kay Gonda says to her ideal fan, the drifter Johnnie Dawes, "There was a great man once who said, 'I love those who know not how to live today' " (*Three Plays*, p. 178). The quote from *Thus Spoke Zarathustra* is: "I love those that know not how to live, except by going under, for they are those who cross over. I love the great despisers, because they are the great reverers and arrows of longing for the other shore" (Friedrich Nietzsche, *Thus Spoke Zarathustra*, Walter Kaufmann, trans. [New York: Penguin, 1978]).

101 **"a string trembling to a note of ecstasy no man had ever heard":** *Three Plays*, p. 170.

101 **first glimpse of Howard Roark:** An observation neatly made by Merrill in *The Ideas of Ayn Rand*, p. 44.

102 **negotiations broke down:** "Ayn Rand's Family and Friends."

102 **"truly heroic man":** Unpublished letter to Ann Watkins, cited in "The Hero in the Soul Manifested in the World."

102 **In July 1937:** Letter to Gladys Unger, July 6, 1937 (*LOAR,* p. 41).

102 **told friends, she was soon doing her best work:** Letter to Gladys Unger, July 6, 1937 (*LOAR,* p. 41).

102 **"It will be very good experience for him":** Letter to Gladys Unger, July 6, 1937 (*LOAR,* p. 41).

102 **walked on the beach with visitors:** See photo, *AR,* p. 65.

102 **"I was going crazy":** BBTBI.

102 **composed the short, futuristic novel:** BBTBI.

102 **"We are nothing":** Ayn Rand, *Anthem* (New York: Signet, 1995), p. 21.

103 **"either condemned or exalted it":** Bernice Glatzer Rosenthal, "The Russian Subtext of *Atlas Shrugged* and *The Fountainhead,*" *Journal of Ayn Rand Studies,* Fall 2004 (vol. 6, no. 1).

103 **conceived *Anthem* as a four-act play:** Leonard Peikoff, introduction to *Anthem,* p. viii.

103 **during her university years:** "An Illustrated Life."

103 **short story that tracks a primitive future man:** Stephen Vincent Benét, "The Place of the Gods," *The Saturday Evening Post,* July 31, 1937, p. 10.

103 **start to finish in three weeks:** Leonard Peikoff, introduction to *Anthem,* p. ix; Robert Mayhew, ed., *Essays on Ayn Rand's "Anthem"* (Lanham, Md.: Lexington Books, 2005), p. 163.

103 **admirers point out another, related difference:** *WIAR,* p. 113.

104 **couldn't place *Anthem*:** *EOA,* p. 24.

104 **"does not understand socialism":** *EOA,* p. 24.

104 **illustrated magazine version appeared in 1953:** In June 1953 *Famous Fantastic Mysteries* devoted an entire issue to an illustrated *Anthem.*

104 **three and a half million copies have been sold:** *EOA,* p. 27.

104 **"more precious to me than anything I have ever considered writing":** Unpublished letter to Norman Flowers, January 2, 1938; cited in *EOA,* p. 27.

104 **fond of Watkins:** Unpublished letter to Ann Watkins, circa 1940, cited in "The Hero in the Soul Manifested in the World."

104 **in the fall of 1937:** BBTBI.

105 **this calamity was compounded:** Royalty statements, A. Watkins Collection, Columbia University Rare Book and Manuscript Library, box 178.

105 **Rand walked away:** BBTBI.

105 **taking the copyright to *We the Living* with her:** "Copywright Reassignment for *We the Living,*" A. Watkins Collection, Columbia University Rare Book and Manuscript Library, box 178.

105 **settled on the Upper East Side of Manhattan:** AR lived at 173 East Seventy-fourth Street from October 1937 to September 1938, and at 160 East Eighty-ninth Street from October 1938 to September 1940 (Binswanger, dinner lecture, April 24, 2005). At that time, New Yorkers traditionally changed apartments on October 1.

105 **throw a party in Town Hall:** "The Hero in the Soul Manifested in the World," based on a newspaper account.

105 **pronounced the FBI director "charming":** Hope Ridings Miller, "Lady Boileau, Here, Finds G-Men Most Interesting," *Washington Post,* February 23, 1938, p. X14.

105 **would try, and fail, to see him:** AR was denied permission to see J. Edgar Hoover twice, once in October 1947,

when she made a trip to Washington, D.C., to serve as a friendly witness before the House Un-American Activities Committee, and once in January 1966; FBI archives, U.S. Department of Justice, FOIA memo to author from U.S. Department of Justice, December 11, 2003.

105 **offer of ten thousand dollars:** Contract between AR, A. H. Woods, Ltd., and RKO Radio Pictures, July 13, 1938 (A. Watkins Collection, Columbia University Rare Book and Manuscript Library, box 152); see also *The Saturday Evening Post,* November 11, 1961, p. 100.

105 **intended to cast Claudette Colbert:** News clippings about RKO stars and American Film Institute archive notes; thanks to Jenny Romero of the Margaret Herrick Library.

106 **came to think of as "a phony":** BBTBI.

106 **signed a contract with Knopf:** Contract with Alfred A. Knopf, June 27, 1938 (A. Watkins Collection, Columbia University Rare Book and Manuscript Library, box 152).

FIVE: *THE FOUNTAINHEAD:* 1936–1941

107 **"I do not recognize anyone's right to one minute of my life":** *TF,* p. 685.

107 **how a moral man can live in a corrupt society:** BBTBI.

108 **just as Rand remembered Cyrus laughing:** BBTBI. In a lecture entitled "The Road to Roark," Milgram points out that AR remembered incorrectly. Nowhere in *The Mysterious Valley* does Cyrus laugh (ARI Conference in Industry Hills, California,

July 2003). Nietzsche's Zarathustra *does* laugh, however, and he avers that "not by wrath does one kill, but by laughter" (*Thus Spoke Zarathustra,* p. 315).

108 **as supple as a cat:** AR often described FO this way.

108 **Like Zarathustra, he welcomes difficulties:** *Thus Spoke Zarathustra,* pp. 25–27.

108 **"walk over corpses":** *TF,* p. 89.

108 **"a soul that has reverence for itself":** December 26, 1935 (*JOAR,* p. 88). AR is quoting Nietzsche's *Beyond Good and Evil.* The passage reads: "What is noble? What does the word 'noble' still mean to us today? How do noble people reveal who they are, how can they be recognized under this heavy, overcast sky of incipient mob rule that makes everything leaden and opaque? There are no actions that prove who they are, actions are always ambiguous, always unfathomable; and there are no 'works' either. Among artists and scholars these days, you will find plenty of people whose work reveals them to be driven by a deep desire for nobility. But this very need *for* nobility is fundamentally different from the needs *of* the noble soul itself, and almost serves as an eloquent and dangerous testimony to the absence of such needs. It is not works, it is *faith* that is decisive here, faith that establishes rank order (this old, religious formula now acquires a new and deeper meaning): some fundamental certainty that a noble soul has about itself, something that cannot be looked for, cannot be found, and perhaps cannot be lost either. *The noble soul has reverence for itself.*" (Judith Norman trans. [Cambridge: Cambridge University Press,

2002], p. 172.) From her earliest notes, AR used this passage as an inscription to *TF*, but just before publication in 1943, she removed it. By then, she disapproved of Nietzsche's discussion of faith.

108 **archetype of the creator:** BBTBI.

108 **the first germ of the idea:** BBTBI.

109 **In 1931 or 1932:** The dates are based on the fact that Selznick came to RKO in 1931 and that AR left RKO in 1932 (*AR*, p. 50; *TPOAR*, p. 132; BBTBI).

109 **fascinated by her next-door neighbor, Marcella Bannert:** BBTBI.

109 **helped her to place *Red Pawn* at Universal Pictures:** "Ayn Rand's Family and Friends."

109 **If some people had an automobile:** BBTBI.

109 **would want people to know:** In 1996, when Scott McConnell of ARI found and interviewed Marcella Bannert (by then married and named Rabwin), the woman had no recollection of this exchange with AR. As for her attitude toward AR in the 1930s, she was as unimpressed with AR as AR was contemptuous of her. Bannert said, "She [AR] was rough. She was masculine. . . . She was the worst-dressed woman I have ever known in my life. She had a terrible figure in the first place. She went around with no makeup on" (*100 Voices*, Marcella [Bannert] Rabwin, pp. 42–43).

110 **a genius surrounded by mediocrities:** "Ayn Rand in Russia."

110 **"the collectivist motivation":** BBTBI.

110 **they love what is average:** February 22, 1937 (*JOAR*, p. 107).

110 **"He was great":** *TF*, p. 188.

110 **a seeming change of personality in her sister:** AR remembered NR

as an independent, nonconforming child, with tastes and attitudes like her own; NR remembered herself as Ayn's "shadow and yes-man." AR's evidently mistaken perception of her favorite sister as a soul mate rather than a follower foreshadows her relationship with her young acolyte and lover, NB, in the 1950s (quote from NR comes from *100 Voices*, p. 13).

111 **seemed to live to make others jealous:** The letter was written in 1933 ("Ayn Rand in Russia"). This was not an entirely new development in NR; sixteen when AR left Russia, NR had been known to imitate her successful older sister's handwriting and prose style and to hoard the letters and stories AR sent home.

111 **Roark chuckles:** *TF*, p. 634.

111 **based on Louis Sullivan:** The mentoring relationship between Cameron and Roark resembles the early apprenticeship of FLW with Louis Sullivan, as described in Wright's autobiography. Frank Lloyd Wright. *An Autobiography* (London: Longmans Green, 1932; rev. ed. Petaluma, Calif.: Pomegranate Communications, 1943).

112 **a flame he holds on a leash:** *TF*, p. 85.

112 **thrusts and shoots through the earth's crust:** *TF*, p. 726.

112 **"convulsion of anger, of protest, of resistance":** *TF*, p. 207.

113 **"a first cause":** *TF*, p. 711.

113 **"The act of a master":** *TF*, p. 220.

113 **finally made and met someone who does:** That AR is not advocating rape in an ordinary sense is made clear in a letter she wrote to a fan in 1946: "You write as if you thought that the lesson to be derived from [the relationship of Howard Roark and Dominique Francon] is that a man should force himself on a

woman. But the fact is that Howard Roark did not actually rape Dominique; she had asked for it and he knew she wanted it. A man who would force himself on a woman against her wishes would be committing a dreadful crime. What Dominique liked about Roark was the fact that he took responsibility for the romance and his own actions. Most men nowadays, like Peter Keating, expect to seduce a woman, or rather they let her seduce them and they shift the responsibility to her"; letter to Waldo Coleman, June 6, 1946 (*LOAR*, p. 282). In the 1960s, some of AR's male followers would make the mistake the letter writer made and try to force themselves on girls whom they considered "Dominiques."

113 **a contorted form of hero worship:** *TF*, p. 245.

113 **"myself in a bad mood":** *TPOAR*, p. 134.

114 **find ecstasy in their struggle:** *TF*, p. 221.

114 **opens in 1922:** March 8, 1938 (*JOAR*, p. 166).

114 **materials on architectural history:** BBTBI; in an essay by Shoshana Milgram entitled *"The Fountainhead* from Notebook to Novel," in *EOTF*, a footnote states that on March 18, 1936, Jennie M. Flexner, readers' advisor at the New York Public Library, prepared an annotated list of recommended architectural texts for AR.

114 **studying the masters:** BBTBI.

114 **she had barely heard of Wright:** BBTBI.

115 **"temple to man":** Wright, *An Autobiography,* p. 154.

115 **echoes the young Wright's argument:** Wright, *An Autobiography,* pp. 125–28.

115 **substitutes the name of H. L.**

Mencken: April 25, 1938 (*JOAR*, p. 182).

115 **"Dear Mr. Rand":** Letter from Eugene Masselink, December 31, 1937, Frank Lloyd Wright Archives, Frank Lloyd Wright Foundation, Taliesin West, Scottsdale, Arizona, R022D05.

115 **Taliesin West:** *Frank Lloyd Wright,* p. 495.

115 **arranged to be introduced:** According to Secrest, the intermediaries were Blanche Knopf and Ely Jacques Kahn; *Frank Lloyd Wright,* p. 496.

115 **"I felt this would be an unrepeatable occasion":** *TPOAR*, p. 189.

115 **felt no immediate rapport:** *Frank Lloyd Wright,* p. 496.

115 **imploring him to see her:** Letters to FLW dated December 12, 1937, and November 7, 1938 (*LOAR*, pp. 108–111); thanks to the Frank Lloyd Wright Foundation, Taliesin West, Scottsdale, Ariz., for authentication of Wright's letters to AR.

116 **compared their attitudes to those of Wright:** February 23, 1937 to November 28, 1937 (*JOAR*, pp. 122–44).

116 **Lewis Mumford:** Mumford was the author of an architectural survey called *Sticks and Stones.* Toohey's fictional history of architecture was called *Sermons in Stone.*

116 **"You could sense the bared teeth behind [his] smile":** BBTBI.

116 **Toohey in the flesh:** BBTBI.

116 **in 1935:** December 26, 1935 (*JOAR*, p. 89).

117 **"You held a leash":** *TF*, p. 691.

117 **"rules the mob":** *JOAR*, p. 89.

117 **"individualism versus collectivism":** In BB's biographical interviews from 1960–61, AR stated that she had understood her theme in 1935. The quoted description is from 1942 (undated entry, *JOAR*, p. 223).

118 **the rights of the creative individual:** BBTBI.

118 **vindication of modern architecture:** BBTBI.

118 **brought her along to professional seminars:** December 6, 1937 (*JOAR*, p. 152).

118 **helped to engineer her introduction to Frank Lloyd Wright:** *Frank Lloyd Wright*, p. 496.

119 **"valorizes [that group's] cacophony":** Author interview with Bernice Glatzer Rosenthal, July 5, 2005.

119 **based on the department store magnate Marshall Field III:** Note from Bobbs-Merrill editor Archibald Ogden to company president D. L. Chambers, March 6, 1943; Bobbs-Merrill Collection, courtesy of the Manuscripts Department, Lilly Library, Indiana University, Bloomington, Indiana.

119 **completing a dream:** Richard Siklos, "Hearst's New Home: Xanadu in Manhattan," *NYT*, June 5, 2006, p. C6.

120 **"in its real meaning":** "The first purpose of this book is a defense of egoism in its real meaning" were the first words AR wrote in her notes on *TF* (December 4, 1935 [*JOAR*, p. 77]).

120 **"All that which proceeds":** February 22, 1937 (*JOAR*, p. 105).

120 **either they are "economic man":** Albert Jay Nock, *Our Enemy, the State* (Tampa, Fla.: Hallberg Publishing Corp., 1983), cited in Raimondo's *Reclaiming the American Right*, p. 116. Nock, also the author of *Memoirs of a Superfluous Man* (Lanham, Md.: University Press of America, 2002), was an outspoken and articulate opponent of both a government-managed economy and the Left's faith in the "wisdom of the common man." AR met Nock in late

1940 or early 1941. See chapter 6, note 51, and chapter 10, note 20.

120 **"The creator's concern":** *TF*, p. 712

120 **a nineteenth-century Eastern European Jew:** Thanks to JW and his unpublished book, *Go Ask Alyssa: The Jewish/Nietzschean Worldview of Ayn Rand,* courtesy of author.

121 **"Enjoyment is not my destiny":** *TF*, p. 664.

121 **Compromise is said to be an insult in Russia:** "The Russian Subtext of *Atlas Shrugged* and *The Fountainhead*."

121 **envied him his simple pleasure:** JW's taped, unpublished interviews with Philip and Kay Nolte Smith in preparation for a CBC special report on the tenth anniversary of AR's death, titled *Ideas: The Legacy of Ayn Rand* (1992).

122 **wrote and rewrote:** *TPOAR*, p. 147.

122 **"makes John Barrymore look like an office boy":** *100 Voices*, Al Ramrus, p. 162.

122 **about a third of the novel in first draft:** Ayn Rand Papers, LOC, box 18, folder 11.

122 **couldn't say with certainty:** BBTBI.

122 **contract with the publisher was canceled:** The contract was officially nullified in October 1940 (unpublished letter from Blanche H. Knopf to Ann Watkins, October 25, 1940 [A. Watkins Collection, Columbia University Rare Book and Manuscript Library, box 80]).

SIX: THE SOUL OF AN INDIVIDUALIST: 1939–1942

123 **"Renunciation":** Introduction to *The Romantic Manifesto* (New York: World Publishing, 1969).

123 **"My research material"**: Quoted in Milgram, "The Road to Roark."

123 **four and a half years**: The first page of the first handwritten draft of *TF* is dated June 26, 1938 (Ayn Rand Papers, LOC, box 18, folder 1).

123 **"Frank was the fuel"**: Introduction to the twenty-fifth-anniversary edition of *TF* (New York: Bobbs-Merrill, 1968), p. viii.

124 **conflated him with her heroes**: *TPOAR*, p. 136.

124 **"He's on strike"**: *TPOAR*, p. 135.

124 **father died in late December 1938**: Dennis O'Connor died on December 21, 1938, State of Ohio death certificate for Dennis O'Connor, Archives of the Lorain, Ohio, City Health Department.

124 **curious to see Lorain, Ohio**: *TPOAR*, p. 152, based on an interview with MS.

124 **the rest of the O'Connor family**: AR and FO also traveled to Cleveland during the 1938 trip to Ohio, and that's where AR first met the Papurt family (author interview with MW, December 16, 2006).

124 **Roman Catholic funeral ceremony**: Death notices, *Lorain [Ohio] Journal*, December 23, 1938, p. 18.

124 **small talk remained something she didn't do well**: Author interview with JMB and Dr. Allan Blumenthal, March 3, 2004.

124 **"drab and homely"**: Author interview with MW, June 21, 2004.

125 **During one dinner**: This took place in 1947, at the Essex House in New York (author interview with MW, December 16, 2006).

125 **Rand did increase the distance**: *TPOAR*, p. 153; taped interview with MS, conducted by BB, January 20, 1983.

125 **modern red-brick apartment building**: At 160 East Eighty-ninth Street.

125 **served a Russian dinner**: FB, from a taped interview by BB with FB, Minna Goldberg, and MS in Chicago, February 20, 1983.

125 **"The man cooking"**: FB, from a taped interview by BB with FB, Minna Goldberg, and MS in Chicago, February 20, 1983.

125 **twenty young-adult biographies and novels**: Author correspondence with FB, February 18, 2006.

126 **"architecture by committee"**: Wright, *An Autobiography*, p. 152.

126 **Mimi, also twenty**: Facts about MS thanks to MW, December 11, 2005.

126 **first met**: Note from BB, June 21, 2006, based on her interview with MS in the early 1980s.

126 **offered to produce the play**: *TPOAR*, p. 150.

126 **one-hundred-dollar-a-month stipend**: "Contract with George Abbott" dated May 9, 1939 (A. Watkins Collection, Columbia University Rare Book and Manuscript Library, box 178).

127 **her mind rebelled against reshaping it**: BBTBI.

127 **"the folks next door"**: *TPOAR*, p. 150.

127 **might hurt her nascent Hollywood career**: Taped interview with MS, conducted by BB, February 18, 1983. Gregory Ratoff would later direct the movie *Song of Russia*, which was AR's primary example of the glamorization of Russia by Hollywood in her 1947 testimony to the House Un-American Activities Committee.

127 **never saw or spoke to Leontovich again**: Taped interview with MS, conducted by BB, February 18, 1983.

128 **"Almost everybody"**: Taped interview with MS, conducted by BB, February 18, 1983.

128 **most often drawn to Ayn Rand's brains**: *TPOAR*, p. 154.

128 **"You're absolutely right"**: Taped interview with MS, conducted by BB, February 18, 1983; *TPOAR*, p. 154.

128 **appeared less guarded**: *TPOAR*, p. 153.

128 **"it wouldn't fit with Ayn"**: Taped interview with MS, conducted by BB, February 18, 1983.

128 **decision to have an abortion**: Agnes Papurt told her daughter MW that she, MW, had been a toddler when this event took place, which would set it in the early 1930s (author interviews with MW, June 21, 2004, and December 21, 2005).

129 **Based on material in her journals**: Author correspondence with James S. Valliant, author of *The Passion of Ayn Rand's Critics: The Case against the Brandens*, May 24, 2007.

129 **"Where have you *been*?"**: Taped interview with MS, conducted by BB, January 20, 1983.

129 **February 13, 1940**: "News of the Stage," *NYT*, January 4, 1940, p. 18.

129 **theatrical and film-world celebrities**: *TPOAR*, p. 154.

129 **"one of the season's mishaps"**: Richard Watts, Jr., "Red Terror," *New York Herald Tribune*, February 14, 1940, p. 14.

129 **"there would be a play"**: "The Play," *NYT*, February 14, 1940, p. 28.

129 **days in bed, despondent**: Taped interview with MS, conducted by BB, February 18, 1983.

129 **safeguarding the individual**: Letter to Tom Girdler, July 12, 1943 (*LOAR*, p. 81).

130 **left off again in May**: February 18,

1940, to April 22, 1940 (*JOAR*, pp. 205–15).

130 **One night in early June**: Thanks to Shoshana Milgram for her analysis of the timing of this incident in "The Road to Roark."

130 **"Frank talked to me"**: "The Road to Roark." This statement appears, in a slightly different form, in AR's twenty-fifth-anniversary introduction to *TF*, pp. viii–ix.

130 **Rand had written a letter**: Letter to Aleksandr Kerensky, undated (*LOAR*, p. 42).

131 **government-backed manufacturing cartels**: *Redeeming the Time*, pp. 454–55.

131 **from Stalinism to syphilis**: *Redeeming the Time*, p. 612.

131 **there might never be another federal election**: Stephen Cox, *The Woman and the Dynamo: Isabel Paterson and the Idea of America* (Piscataway, N.J.: Transaction Publishers, 2004), p. 219.

131 **"against the worst madman"**: "The Hero in the Soul Manifested in the World."

132 **preferred to let Hitler march**: Reported by LP in a 1982 philosophy course, according to a student's detailed notes.

132 **"the old reliance"**: 1933 radio speech by Franklin Delano Roosevelt (cited in *Redeeming the Time*, p. 449).

132 **"only the strong can be free"**: Quoted in Ellsworth Bernard, *Wendell Willkie: Fighter for Freedom* (Marquette, Mich.: Northern Michigan University Press, 1966), p. 207.

132 **"to strike a balance"**: Foundation Day address by Wendell Willkie, May 4, 1938, at Indiana University; quoted in *Wendell Wilkie*, p. 145.

132 **working out an agreement**: Unpublished letter from Blanche Knopf to Ann Watkins, October 25, 1940

(A. Watkins Collection, Columbia University Rare Book and Manuscript Library, box 80).

132 **National Willkie Clubs headquarters:** Letter to Gerald Loeb, August 5, 1944 (*LOAR*, p. 154).

132 **"pure selfishness":** *TPOAR*, p. 160.

132 **spoke out against the New Deal:** *AR:SOL*, DVD.

132 **"I was a marvelous propagandist":** "Ayn Rand as a Public Speaker."

132 **she mesmerized her audiences:** "Of all the guest speakers who came to talk there and share the podium with me," Swanson wrote, "the most notable by far was AR, who had a fascinating mind and held audiences hypnotized" (Gloria Swanson, *Swanson on Swanson* [New York: Random House, 1980], p. 462). In April 1943, AR sent Swanson a copy of *TF*, inscribed, "To Gloria Swanson, from your fellow fighter of Fourteenth Street" (Gloria Swanson Collection, Library Books, Harry Ransom Humanities Research Center, University of Texas at Austin).

132 **especially good when challenged:** Letter to DeWitt Emery, August 14, 1941 (*LOAR*, p. 57).

132 **"I chose to be an American":** *TPOAR*, p. 161.

133 **a larger number of interesting men and women:** Letter to Gerald Loeb, August 15, 1944 (*LOAR*, p. 154).

133 **Channing Pollock:** "The Hero in the Soul Manifested in the World."

133 **several of the key ideas:** From Nock, AR learned to distinguish between political man and economic man, i.e., between those who live by imposing taxes on what other people produce and those who do the producing. This concept appears explicitly in AR's "The Individualist Manifesto," written in the spring of 1941; its psychological correlative permeates *TF*.

133 **"America's Joan of Arc":** "The Hero in the Soul Manifested in the World."

133 **"barbarism and poverty to affluence and culture":** Jennifer Burns, "Godless Capitalism: Ayn Rand and the Conservative Movement," *Modern Intellectual History*, 2004 (vol. 1, no. 3), p. 367.

133 **"violent" indignation:** *TPOAR*, p. 162.

133 **perceived him as having knuckled under:** Until January 1940, Willkie had been a lifelong Democrat, so the fact that he shared FDR's opinions on some issues should not have come as a surprise to his supporters.

133 **"Willkie was the guiltiest man":** *TPOAR*, p. 161.

134 **men and women of strong convictions:** Letter to Gerald Loeb, August 5, 1944 (*LOAR*, p. 155).

134 **wrote broadsides and letters:** One of these appeared in the *St. Louis Post-Dispatch* (*Wendell Willkie*, pp. 384–85 and p. 577, note 18; see also "Ex-Willkie Aids Assail Him for G.O.P. 'Betrayal,'" *Chicago Daily Tribune*, December 6, 1942, p. 22).

134 **organization of conservative intellectuals:** Letter to Channing Pollock, May 27, 1941 (*LOAR*, p. 47).

134 **apartment on East Thirty-fifth Street:** From October 1940 through September 1941, the O'Connors lived at 349 East Forty-ninth Street; from October 1941 until December 1943, they lived in apartment 1N of the Bromley apartment house at 139 East Thirty-fifth Street (Binswanger, dinner lecture, April 24, 2005).

134 **down to less than nine hundred dollars:** BBTBI; in *TPOAR*, p. 160, BB mistakenly quotes the figure as seven hundred dollars.

134 **quirkily Christian fifty-four-year-old:** IP was born on January 22, 1886, on Manitoulin Island in northern Ontario.

134 **the older woman didn't remember the encounter:** *The Woman and the Dynamo,* p. 219.

134 **hardships could be instructive:** *The Woman and the Dynamo,* p. 219; Isabel Paterson, "Turns with a Bookworm," *New York Herald Tribune,* May 31, 1935, p. 15.

134 **most outspoken critic:** Stephen Cox, "*Atlas* and the Bible: Ayn Rand's Debt to Isabel Paterson," in Edward W. Younkins, ed., *Ayn Rand's "Atlas Shrugged": A Philosophical and Literary Companion* (Aldershot: Ashgate, 2007), pp. 351–60.

135 **had been asking for Rand's phone number:** BBTBI.

135 **liked her "enormously":** BBTBI.

135 **gathered to proofread:** Author interview with Muriel Hall, IP's friend and executor, July 7, 2004.

135 **a conservative Round Table:** *A Life with the Printed Word,* p. 55.

135 **remarking later:** BBTBI.

135 **Paterson had a theory about capitalism:** *The Woman and the Dynamo,* pp. 254–55.

136 **a "marvelous mind":** BBTBI.

136 **was a genius:** *TPOAR,* p. 165, based on an interview with Muriel Hall.

136 **"sat at the master's feet":** Samuel Gardner Welles, Jr., was IP's literary executor and Muriel Hall's older brother; quoted by Muriel Hall; see also *The Woman and the Dynamo,* p. 220, quoting Welles.

136 **"guru and teacher":** *TPOAR,* p. 166.

136 **her opinion of a riddle:** BBTBI; *The Woman and the Dynamo,* pp. 310–11 and p. 401, note 46. Cox speculates that AR had not read Boswell and misremembered the

ethical dilemma IP presented. In Boswell's *Life of Johnson,* the biographer asks the man of letters what he would do if he were shut up with a child in a castle. Dr. Johnson imagines that he wouldn't much enjoy the company but would probably feed and bathe the child; this appears under the date Thursday, October 26, 1769, on p. 420 of the Oxford University Press edition. Perhaps IP misconstrued the passage from Boswell. Thanks to Stephen Cox, author correspondence, March 9, 2006.

137 **preponderance of evidence is on her side:** In *The Woman and the Dynamo,* Cox argues this persuasively, pp. 310–14.

137 **"an ungulfable bridge":** Isabel Paterson, "Turns with a Bookworm," *New York Herald Tribune,* August 25, 1946; undated note by IP, cited in *The Woman and the Dynamo,* p. 391, note 58.

137 **"Will you write my autobiography?":** *TPOAR,* p. 165, based on an interview with Muriel Hall.

137 **"She is afraid of traffic":** Isabel Paterson, "Turns with a Bookworm," *New York Herald Tribune,* September 23, 1945.

137 **"To All Innocent Fifth Columnists":** "Fifth columnist" was coined during the Spanish civil war to mean a turncoat or traitor within the ranks.

137 **"Of such as you is the Kingdom of Hitler and Stalin":** Ayn Rand, "To All Innocent Fifth Columnists," circa 1940 (*JOAR,* p. 345).

137 **wanted to do for free-market capitalism:** Letter to Channing Pollock, April 28, 1941 (*LOAR,* p. 45).

138 ***Think Twice:*** *Three Plays,* pp. 196–291. The play seems never to have been professionally produced.

138 **written in three weeks:** Author cor-

respondence with Michael Berliner, December 20, 2005.

138 **the month of January 1941:** Unpublished letter from AR to H. N. Swanson, a film-industry agent, October 10, 1948 (H. N. Swanson Collection, Margaret Herrick Library, box 56).

138 **"I had not heard or dreamed of the atom bomb":** Unpublished letter to H. H. Swanson (H. N. Swanson Collection, Margaret Herrick Library, box 56).

138 **Two months later, in April:** Unless otherwise stated, all quotations and other information about the unpublished essay "The Individualist Manifesto" come from Jeff Britting, "*Anthem* and 'The Individualist Manifesto,' " in *EOA*, pp. 70–80. For date of composition, see p. 79, note 2; for essay length, see p. 72.

139 **citizens owe the government nothing:** "Government Financing in a Free Society," *TVOS*, pp. 135–40.

140 **"mud to be ground underfoot":** 1936 edition; original *WTL* manuscript, Ayn Rand Papers, LOC, box 18, quoted in *EOWTL*, p. 211.

140 **"Man, each *single, solitary, individual* man":** "To All Innocent Fifth Columnists," circa 1940 (*JOAR*, p. 350).

140 **sent the author's outline:** BBTBI.

141 **"bad" disappointment:** Perhaps it is no coincidence that she named the malevolent milquetoast of a U.S. president in *AS* Mr. Thompson.

141 **found this episode funny:** *TPOAR*, p. 156.

141 **book might sell:** BBTBI.

141 **ran out of money:** BBTBI.

141 **criticizing her to others:** BBTBI.

142 **making it impossible to sell:** BBTBI.

142 **resigned in protest:** "You did not want to handle *TF* further because

you told me that I made it impossible to sell it," AR reportedly wrote; "The Hero in the Soul Manifested in the World."

142 **or because Rand abruptly broke off with her:** *TPOAR*, p. 156.

142 **"Even instincts have reasons":** "The Hero in the Soul Manifested in the World."

142 **lost a champion:** "The Hero in the Soul Manifested in the World." Of course, Ann Watkins lived to regret her loss of confidence in *TF*, just as Macmillan and Knopf may have regretted not investing $1,200 and $1,000, respectively.

142 **She was a slow reader:** Author interview with Robert Hessen, October 17, 2007.

142 **took her under their wing:** *TPOAR*, pp. 168–69.

143 **placid definitions:** "The Only Path to Tomorrow," pp. 88–90; the essay was condensed from "The Moral Basis of Individualism," written in 1943 but not published (August 18, 1943 to March 22, 1946 [*JOAR*, pp. 243–310]), which in turn was based on "The Individualist Manifesto." AR's definitions of individualism and collectivism did not change from the 1930s on.

143 **proved surprisingly controversial:** Letters to Channing Pollock, March–August 1941 (*LOAR*, pp. 44–56).

143 **struck her as anti-intellectual and smug:** *TPOAR*, p. 163.

143 **Nazis occupied Kiev:** Martin Gilbert, *The Holocaust: A History of the Jews of Europe During the Second World War* (New York: Holt, Rinehart and Winston, 1985), p. 202.

143 **"If I were a defender of Communism":** Letter to DeWitt Emery (executive of the Small Businessmen's Association), September 10, 1941 (*LOAR*, p. 58).

143 **Mostly, she yearned for the resources:** *TPOAR,* p. 168.

143 **gathering dust on her desktop:** BBTBI.

144 **Park Avenue and Thirty-first Street:** In the early 1940s, Bobbs-Merrill's New York offices were located at 468 Fourth Avenue; thanks to Becky Cape at the Lilly Library at the University of Indiana.

144 **reminded her of Peter Keating:** BBTBI.

144 **"Pat had contacts there":** Author interview with Muriel Hall, July 7, 2004. Hall provided the same account to Stephen Cox, IP's biographer, who wrote, "I don't doubt Muriel's account" (author correspondence with Cox, May 17, 2006).

144 **"Far be it from me to dampen such enthusiasm":** *TPOAR,* p. 171.

145 **second congratulatory phone call:** BBTBI.

145 **famously frugal boss:** *Words & Faces,* p. 33.

145 **"Marionettes at Midnight":** According to ARI, AR said that Kurt Noack's "Marionetten um Mitternacht" was her favorite piece of music in the early 1940s ("Ayn Rand's Musical Biography").

145 **whenever she was happy:** Author interview with JMB and Dr. Allan Blumenthal, March 23, 2004.

145 **Oscar and Oswald:** *TPOAR,* p. 185.

145 **promised to deliver *The Fountainhead*:** *EOTF,* p. 6.

145 **now began the happiest year:** "The Hero in the Soul Manifested in the World."

145 **excuse for backing out:** BBTBI.

146 **easily available in pill form:** *TPOAR,* p. 173; interviews with the Blumenthals, the Brandens, Roger Callahan; unpublished correspondence with IP (Isabel Paterson Papers, Herbert Hoover Presidential Library, box 23).

146 **"clean and respectable":** Letter to Archibald Ogden, February 19, 1942 (*LOAR,* p. 62).

146 **worked for thirty hours straight:** "The Hero in the Soul Manifested in the World."

146 **type her new pages:** Author interviews with June Kurisu (May 19, 2004) and Daryn Kent-Duncan (April 25, 2005).

146 **"You are really writing about collectivism":** *The Art of Fiction,* p. 163.

146 **Nick claimed that he had even written:** Taped interview with Millicent Patton, conducted by BB on December 15, 1982.

147 **on file at the U.S. Library of Congress:** Ayn Rand Papers, LOC, boxes 18–20.

147 **averaged a chapter a week:** Hand-dated manuscript chapters, first draft (Ayn Rand Papers, LOC, boxes 18–19).

147 **On July 4, 1942:** Ayn Rand Papers, LOC, box 19, folder 10.

147 **"The year at Monadnock Valley":** *TF,* p. 532.

148 **see who could finish first:** *TPOAR,* p. 171.

148 **won by a week or two:** Author correspondence with Stephen Cox, who writes: "[Pat] worked on [*The God of the Machine*] during 1942. . . . During January and early February 1943, her correspondence shows her fixing some details. Page proofs were sent by [the publisher] to Pat's friend Col. Robert Henry on March 17, 1943." AR finished correcting the page proofs of her book on or about March 30, 1943, as she noted in a letter on that date to D. L. Chambers (*LOAR,* p. 66).

148 **"Whoever is fortunate enough":** Isabel Paterson, *The God of the*

Machine (Palo Alto, Calif.: Palo Alto Book Service reissue, 1983), p. 306.

148 **"breaks through the clay":** *TF,* pp. 726–27.

SEVEN: MONEY: 1943

149 **"Many words have been granted Me":** *Anthem,* p. 95.

149 **delivered to bookstores on May 7, 1943:** "Books Published Today," *NYT,* May 7, 1943, p. 17.

149 **copies remained unsold:** BBTBI. In 1960–61, AR told BB that there was no second printing of *TF* until late summer 1943, but in a letter written to Archibald Ogden on July 29, 1943, she seems to make reference to a recent *third* printing of the book (*LOAR,* p. 86). Sales figures come from secondary sources. The Bobbs-Merrill Archives at the Lilly Library at Indiana University in Bloomington, Indiana, contain no contracts or sales reports, and ARI denied the author access to the Curtis Brown literary agency archives at Columbia University, where copies of AR's contracts and royalty statements can presumably be found.

150 **new and better novels about architecture:** Orville Prescott, "Books of the Times," *NYT,* May 12, 1943, p. 23.

150 **prepublication buzz:** BBTBI.

150 **endorsed the novel:** Kenneth Horan, "Three Unusual Novels with Widely Different Settings," *Chicago Daily Tribune,* May 30, 1943, p. E10.

150 **Irita Van Doren assigned the book:** Albert Guerard, "Novel on Architectural Genius," *New York Herald Tribune Weekly Book Review,* May 30, 1943, p. 2.

150 **as she colorfully put it:** BBTBI.

150 **"Anyone who is taken in":** Diana Trilling, "Fiction in Review," *The Nation,* June 12, 1943, p. 843.

150 **If the book contract had been delayed:** BBTBI.

151 **To save paper:** The deleted section of the novel can be read as a reconstructed narrative in *TEAR* (pp. 440–76) or in its original context in AR's first-draft manuscript on file at the LOC.

151 **Rand always thought:** BBTBI.

151 ***The Fountainhead* was *her* book:** BBTBI.

151 **hinted that she might sue:** Letter to Ralph E. Lewis, of Prescott & Files, March 22, 1944 (*LOAR,* p. 128); also, Bobbs-Merrill Collection, Lilly Library.

151 **The single most perceptive review:** Lorine Pruette, "Battle Against Evil: *The Fountainhead,*" *NYT,* May 16, 1943, BR7.

151 **she would be happy to hear this:** *TPOAR,* p. 179.

152 **"my kind of readers":** BBTBI.

152 **at best to commit a social gaffe:** BBTBI.

152 **chronicles of the period bear her out:** An especially interesting view is provided by Kai Bird and Martin J. Sherwin in *American Prometheus: The Triumph and Tragedy of J. Robert Oppenheimer* (New York: Random House, 2005).

152 **"practically in every line":** Letter to DeWitt Emery, May 17, 1943 (*LOAR,* pp. 72–77).

152 **other publications gradually took it up:** For example, *Mansfield [Ohio] News-Journal,* July 8, 1943, p. 8.

152 **"individualism" would re-enter the language:** BBTBI.

153 **Ogden lacked the power:** BBTBI.

153 **The public mood "is going our way":** Letter to DeWitt Emery,

May 17, 1943 (*LOAR*, pp. 72–77); letter to Lorine Pruette, May 18, 1943 (*LOAR*, p. 75).

154 **wait to collect any royalties:** BBTBI.

154 **she estimated the ten thousand dollars she needed:** Letter to Monroe Shakespeare, November 16, 1943 (*LOAR*, p. 100).

154 **approach to the du Pont family:** BBTBI. The intermediary may have been Rose Wilder Lane, a libertarian and the author of another individualist book in 1943, *The Discovery of Freedom*. She apparently knew the du Ponts (*The Woman and the Dynamo*, p. 287).

154 **only prospective donor:** Letter to Monroe Shakespeare, October 10, 1943 (*LOAR*, p. 94).

154 **minimum wage of thirty cents an hour:** U.S. Department of Labor, "History of Federal Minimum Wage Rates Under the Fair Labor Standards Act, 1938–1996."

154 **another job selling shoes:** BBTBI.

154 **who asked him to stay on as a manager:** BBTBI.

154 **"a gray desert":** Introduction to the twenty-fifth-anniversary edition of *TF*.

154 **the author of eight moderately successful novels:** *The Woman and the Dynamo*, p. 326.

154 **she considered *The Fountainhead* to be so good:** BBTBI.

155 **those two weeks were the only formal vacation:** BBTBI.

155 **reached the right minds in the country:** BBTBI.

155 **Albert Jay Nock's famous concept:** "Isaiah's Job," *The Atlantic Monthly,* June 1936, p. 641. Nock explained that it is Isaiah's job, like John Galt's, to preach to and encourage the conservative Remnant to hang on until Judgment Day. In real life, AR and others accepted this

task as their own. She never acknowledged her intellectual debt to Nock, and it has never before been pointed out, as far as I know. In biographical interviews, she referred to Nock as cynical and weary.

155 **One hundred thousand copies:** BBTBI.

155 **designated each other "sisters":** Unpublished letter from IP to AR, October 7, 1943 (Isabel Paterson Papers, Herbert Hoover Presidential Library, box 4); AR's reply to IP, October 10, 1943 (*LOAR*, p. 174).

155 **"Really, those women":** Author interview with Muriel Welles Hall, July 7, 2004.

155 **"little sister [from] St. Petersburg":** Author interview with Muriel Welles Hall, July 7, 2004.

155 **Council on Books in Wartime:** Council on Books in Wartime Archives, 1942–47, Princeton University Library Department of Rare Books and Special Collections, Princeton, N.J.

156 **"It takes a book to save or destroy the world":** Letter to Earle H. Balch, November 28, 1943 (*LOAR*, p. 101).

156 **as her own publisher was beginning to be inclined:** In interoffice correspondence contained in the Bobbs-Merrill Archive, AR is often spoken of as unpredictable and volatile after Ogden's departure.

156 **By Thanksgiving:** BBTBI. Again, this is what AR told BB in 1960–61. In a letter written on November 28, 1943, to one of IP's editors at G. P. Putnam's Sons, she estimated sales of *TF* at 25,000. Either she was underestimating her early sales to BB or she exaggerated them to the editor at Putnam, perhaps to support the argument that more money should be invested in promoting IP's *The God of the Machine*.

156 **he proposed a deal:** BBTBI.

156 **bold new full-page ads:** Letter to IP, October 10, 1943 (*LOAR*, p. 174).

157 **$25,000 for *The Glass Key*:** Figures courtesy of Greg Walsh at the Margaret Herrick Library.

157 **made a hefty profit:** In 1934, Universal Studios, which paid AR $700 for *Red Pawn*, traded it to Paramount Pictures in exchange for an E. Phillips Oppenheimer story that had cost Paramount $20,000 (*TPOAR*, p. 106). In 1938 or 1939, MGM sold *The Night of January 16th* to RKO for $10,000, significantly more than it had paid AR in 1934. A year later, MGM resold the rights to Paramount for $35,000 (Paramount Production Records); Paramount released a film under that name in 1941 (American Film Institute archives).

157 **made the hoped-for offer:** Contracts negotiated on AR's behalf by Alan Collins of Curtis Brown, Ltd., are on file in the Curtis Brown Archives at Columbia University's Rare Book and Manuscript Library. I was denied access to those files by the ARI. This account was relayed by AR to BB in 1960–61.

158 **They stayed awake all night:** BBTBI.

158 **moment would not have been as sweet:** BBTBI.

158 **she jested to her friend:** Letter to Ruth Alexander, October 22, 1943 (*LOAR*, p. 99).

158 **"Money is the root of all good":** *AS*, pp. 380–85.

159 **considered both ponderous and ludicrously mystical:** *TPOAR*, p. 101.

159 **send a signed copy of *The Fountainhead*:** Author interview with FB, March 18, 2004.

159 **an oversight that was not forgotten:** Author interview with FB, June 21, 2004.

159 **Now I can pay:** BBTBI.

160 **That notion quickly gave way:** BBTBI.

160 **"You can choose any kind of coat":** *TPOAR*, p. 184.

160 **modeled the coat:** *The Woman and the Dynamo*, p. 289, based on Cox's interview with IP's assistant Gertrude Vogt.

160 **"I couldn't find any purpose":** *AS*, pp. 346–47.

EIGHT: FAME: 1943–1946

161 **"I decided to become a writer":** "To the Readers of *The Fountainhead*," 1945 (*LOAR*, 669).

161 **Warner Bros. had sent them to Chicago:** Letter to Archibald Ogden, December 18, 1943 (*LOAR*, p. 105).

161 **"The only advantage of poverty":** *TPOAR*, p. 184.

162 **Tartalia, Russian for "Turtle Cat":** Interview with Thaddeus Ashby, June 20, 2005.

162 **not far from Hollywood Boulevard:** Howard Koch, *As Time Goes By* (New York: Harcourt Brace, 1979), p. 90.

162 **"Only my wife":** BBTBI.

162 **"mink-coat" conditions:** Letter to Archibald Ogden, December 18, 1943 (*LOAR*, p. 105).

162 **"I didn't know you were this way":** *As Time Goes By*, p. 90.

162 **her new boss, Henry Blanke:** BBTBI.

163 **"It's *magnificent*":** *TPOAR*, p. 184.

163 **By early February, she had completed:** United Artists Collection, Series 1.2, Warner Bros. Scripts, the Wisconsin Historical Society, box 138, folder 4. JB, on p. 68 of *AR*, mistakenly reports that the first script was 283 pages long; that was the length of the second script, dated

February 25, 1947, according to studio records. In taped biographical interviews from 1961, AR recalled that the first screenplay had been 380-some-odd pages long (BBTBI).

163 **preserved all the novel's major characters:** BBTBI.

163 **her impassioned love scenes and her styled dialogue:** Letter to Archibald Ogden, December 18, 1943 (*LOAR*, p. 105).

163 **put *The Fountainhead* on hold:** Letter to Nick Carter, October 5, 1944 (*LOAR*, p. 166).

163 **keep the dark-eyed beauty's dialogue:** BBTBI.

164 **co-invented and patented:** Joseph Carr, *The Technician's Radio Receiver Handbook* (Oxford, UK: Butterworth-Heinemann, 2001), p. 233.

164 **hated Hollywood as both shabby and vicious:** Letter from IP quoting a letter from AR, December 15, 1943, Isabel Paterson Papers, Herbert Hoover Memorial Presidential Library, box 4.

164 **"Frank says what I love is not the real city":** Letter to Archibald Ogden, December 18, 1943 (*LOAR*, p. 105). On her assumed return to New York, AR intended to go back to work on weekends for Richard Meland at Paramount, in spite of her new wealth (letter from IP, March 21, 1944, Isabel Paterson Papers, Herbert Hoover Presidential Library, box 4).

164 **invited Rand to join him as his first employee:** BBTBI.

164 **second was Lillian Hellman:** Letter to Archibald Ogden, July 19, 1944 (*LOAR*, p. 148).

164 **"lost no opportunity to run down":** Patricia Neal, quoted in Stephen Michael Shearer, *Patricia Neal: An Unquiet Life* (Lexington: University of Kentucky Press, 2006),

p. 66. Neal knew both AR and Hellman. In 1946, she played Regina Hubbard in Hellman's *Another Part of the Forest* and in 1949 starred in the movie *TF*.

164 **caricatured her as an anti-Communist puppet:** Lillian Hellman, *Scoundrel Time* (Boston: Little, Brown and Co., 1976), pp. 3–5.

164 **scheduled to begin in July:** Unpublished letter from agent Bert Allenberg to Hal Wallis, dated April 8, 1944, and "Multiple Picture Contract with Ayn Rand," dated July 5, 1944, both from the Hal Wallis Collection, Margaret Herrick Library, box 95.

164 **"pictures [I write] would be done *my* way":** Letter to IP, July 26, 1945 (*LOAR*, p. 178).

165 **"the mind on strike":** TPOAR, p. 218.

165 **bought a 1936 Packard car:** Unpublished letter to Richard Meland, February 20, 1944, courtesy of JB.

165 **wavering between 5 and 7 percent:** "Historical CPI [Consumer Price Index]," 1943–44, Bureau of Labor Statistics.

165 **arranged to buy an astoundingly Roarkian house:** TPOAR, pp. 186–87.

166 **fantastic sum of $24,000:** TPOAR, p. 186.

166 **asked Frank's brother:** BBTBI.

166 **"chronically and permanently happy":** Letter to Nick Carter, October 5, 1944 (*LOAR*, p. 164).

166 **she confided to a few friends:** Interviews with RBH and with June Kurisu, May 19 and December 31, 2004.

166 **spell of active tuberculosis:** Letter to Nick Carter, October 5, 1944 (*LOAR*, p. 164).

166 **was buried on Long Island:** Gravesite locator, the U.S. Department of Veterans Affairs.

166 **Tuberculosis had weakened his heart:** Taped interview with Millicent Patton, conducted by BB, December 5, 1982.

166 **sent him a long, affectionate letter:** Letter to Nick Carter, October 5, 1944 (*LOAR,* pp. 164–68).

166 **By Christmas 1944:** Harry Hanson, "*The Fountainhead* Enjoys a Fresh Wave of Popularity," December 24, 1944, p. 19.

166 **Every two or three weeks:** In the 1940s, *The New York Times* published regional lists, showing which novels and nonfiction books were bestsellers in Detroit, Cleveland, New Orleans, Los Angeles, New York, etc.

166 **This occurred twenty-six times:** "A Strange Kind of Simplicity," p. 8.

166 **Fan mail was pouring in to Bobbs-Merrill:** The Bobbs-Merrill Collection, courtesy of the Lilly Library.

167 **a way of bolstering morale:** NB, "The Benefits and Hazards of the Philosophy of Ayn Rand," lecture given at the University of California, San Diego, May 25, 1982.

167 **"great and exceptional" stand:** Kevin Bazzana, *Lost Genius: the Curious and Tragic Story of an Extraordinary Musical Prodigy* (New York: Carroll and Graf, 2007), pp. 200–201.

167 **"compliment" of being addressed as "Mr. Rand":** Letter to Sylvia Bailey, July 5, 1943 (*LOAR,* p. 79).

167 **the number of logical contradictions:** BBTBI.

167 **invited her to speak:** BBTBI. In 1943 she spoke before the New York chapter of the American Institute of Architects ("Books—Authors," *NYT,* June 23, 1943, p. 19); in 1945 she spoke before the Southern California chapter of the same group ("Ayn Rand as a Public Speaker").

167 **told the group of architects:** From her speech to the New York chapter of the American Institute of Architects, June 1943; "Ayn Rand as a Public Speaker."

167 **Joan Crawford gave a dinner party:** BBTBI.

168 **preferred Garbo:** Letter to Gerald Loeb, April 23, 1944 (*LOAR,* p. 132).

168 **MGM reportedly responded:** Erskine Johnson, "This is Hollywood," syndicated in the *Zanesville [Ohio] Times Recorder,* March 21, 1957, p. 4.

168 **"the big man in Hollywood":** Letter to Archibald Ogden, July 19, 1944 (*LOAR,* p. 148).

168 **Hedda Hopper and *The New York Times:*** Hedda Hopper, "Looking at Hollywood," *Los Angeles Times,* July 21, 1944, p. A7; "Screen News," *NYT,* June 26, 1944, p. 21.

168 **tried to pry her away from Wallis:** Unpublished letter from IP, November 1944 (Isabel Paterson Papers, Herbert Hoover Presidential Library, box 4); "Paramount Studio Tour."

168 **suffered over his 1938 letter to her:** *TPOAR,* pp. 189–90.

168 **"Your thesis is the great one":** Letter from FLW, April 23, 1944 (*LOAR,* p. 112); thanks to the Frank Lloyd Wright Foundation for authentication.

168 **should have had a mane of white hair:** *TPOAR,* p. 190.

168 **Loeb demurred:** Letter to Gerald Loeb (and footnote), August 5, 1944 (*LOAR,* p. 162).

169 **his houses were an expression:** Letter to FLW (*LOAR,* p. 113).

169 **"I think I am made of asbestos":** Letter to FLW (*LOAR,* p. 113).

169 **eager to get Wright to design:** Secrest, *Frank Lloyd Wright,* p. 497.

169 **demand for prior approval:** BBTBI.

169 **reminiscent of his 1935 master-piece, Fallingwater:** Roderick Grant, "Wright and Rand," *Journal of the Taliesin Fellows,* Spring 1997 (iss. 27), pp. 19–24.

169 **he told her the price, $35,000:** Secrest, *Frank Lloyd Wright,* p. 497.

169 **"My dear lady":** *TPOAR,* p. 191.

169 **compared them to medieval serfs:** *TPOAR,* p. 190.

170 **the charge that she required hero worship:** In "Born Eccentric" in *Newsweek* of March 27, 1961, and "The Curious Cult of Ayn Rand" in *The Saturday Evening Post* of November 11, 1961.

170 **was disappointed by the visit:** Oral history of William Wesley Peters, recorded on September 24, 1989, courtesy of the Frank Lloyd Wright Archives.

170 **need for admiration, strong tendency to moralize:** Secrest, *Frank Lloyd Wright,* p. 497.

170 **reportedly grabbed her cigarette:** Ada Louise Huxtable, *Frank Lloyd Wright* (New York: Penguin, 2004), p. 227. Secrest tells this story somewhat differently, reporting that Wright walked out rather than expelling AR, p. 497.

170 **"I deny the paternity":** Huxtable, *Frank Lloyd Wright,* p. 226.

170 **nicknamed "Boss":** Unpublished letter to Hal Wallis, June 18, 1945 (Hal Wallis Collection, Margaret Herrick Library, box 95).

170 **a critical failure:** See, for example, Bosley Crowther, "The Screen," *NYT,* August 27, 1945, p. 22.

170 **"wet nurse":** Thanks to David Hayes in "Ayn Rand vs. Hollywood Censorship, Part 3," footnote 3, *Axiomatic,* December 2005, for making this observation.

170 **four distinctly different endings:** Dates courtesy of project-specific file cards archived in the Hal Wallis Collection, box 95, and the Paramount Script Collection, box 57, housed at the Margaret Herrick Library.

171 **which she had read on the recommendation:** Letter to Pincus Berner, February 3, 1945 (*LOAR,* p. 220).

171 **tried unsuccessfully to interest Wallis:** Letter to Barbara Stanwyck, September 7, 1946 (*LOAR,* p. 318). AR tried to interest Paramount in *Red Pawn* one more time, in 1963, when she asked screenwriter Al Ramrus to write a new screenplay and enlisted Robert Stack to play Commandant Kareyev. Paramount expressed no interest, and the film was never made (*100 Voices,* Al Ramrus, pp. 160–61).

171 **flirted mildly:** About a photograph of himself Hal Wallis gave her, she wrote, "That's the way I like to see you look—hard and ruthless (except in relation to *my* scripts)"; letter to Hal Wallis, June 18, 1945 (*LOAR,* p. 227).

171 **to buy the collected works of Aristotle:** Richard McKeon's *Basic Works of Aristotle,* containing selections from the complete works (*100 Voices,* Allan Gotthelf, p. 345).

171 **three new outfits by Adrian:** *TPOAR,* p. 192.

171 **the nature of human existence:** Letter to IP, July 26, 1945 (*LOAR,* p. 179).

171 **the faculty of "rational consciousness":** July 30, 1945 (*JOAR,* p. 300).

171 **Keating and Toohey are examples:** September 18 and 30, 1943 (*JOAR,* p. 259).

172 **"You have been the one encounter in my life":** *TF,* p. 684.

172 **echoed Roark's mixed sympathies:** Thanks to Stephen Cox for pointing this out in *The Woman and the Dynamo,* p. 304.

172 **thought that the Christian moral-ity would one day:** *The Woman and the Dynamo,* p. 306.

172 **"The best possible kindergarten of communism":** December 4, 1935 (*JOAR,* p. 80).

172 **"an omniscient being":** Letter to IP, August 4, 1945 (*LOAR,* p. 184).

172 **Rand trusted deductive reasoning too much:** Unpublished letter from IP to AR, July 30, 1945 (Isabel Paterson Papers, Herbert Hoover Presidential Library, box 4). Thanks to Stephen Cox for his patient explanations of the nature of IP's intellectual differences with AR.

173 **"the fiat of revelation":** Letter to IP, August 4, 1945 (*LOAR,* p. 184).

173 **reminding Paterson:** Letter to IP, July 26, 1945 (*LOAR,* pp. 179–80).

174 **"sometimes I [think]":** Unpublished letter from IP to AR, July 30, 1945 (Isabel Paterson Papers, Herbert Hoover Presidential Library, box 4).

174 **"Stop taking that benzedrine":** Unpublished letter from IP to AR, January 19, 1944 (Isabel Paterson Papers, Herbert Hoover Presidential Library, box 4).

174 **Rand's reply is missing:** This letter, if it exists, was excluded from the published *LOAR,* and a copy was not provided by ARI to the Isabel Paterson Papers at the Herbert Hoover Presidential Library, although copies of other letters appear to be on file there.

174 **"I am seriously vexed":** Unpublished letter from IP, November 1944 (Isabel Paterson Papers, Herbert Hoover Presidential Library, box 4).

174 **"If you take any more of that benzedrine":** Unpublished letter from IP, June 7, 1944 (Isabel Paterson Papers, Herbert Hoover Presidential Library, box 4).

174 **She looked forward to seeing Pa-terson:** Letter to IP, August 28, 1945 (*LOAR,* pp. 186–87).

174 **but the two women must have argued:** There are no surviving letters between AR and IP from August 28, 1945, to February 7, 1948, following another trip by AR from California to New York.

175 **He was a mere zero:** BBTBI.

175 **"You can knock the world for a loop now":** Unpublished letters from IP, February 17, 1944, and July 30, 1945 (Isabel Paterson Papers, Herbert Hoover Presidential Library, box 4).

175 **"I admired her":** Author interview with Ruth Ohman and Allan Ryskind, August 24, 2006. Ryskind, Ohman's brother and the owner and editor of *Human Events,* recalled AR more acerbically. "There were a couple of times when she was talking about anti-Communism when she was not so much attractive as a tractor. She would be making a lot of sense, and then go way over the edge," he said.

175 **"furiously nervous":** Letter to Gerald Loeb, April 23, 1944 (*LOAR,* p. 135).

175 **"I am becoming more antisocial":** Letter to IP, July 26, 1945 (*LOAR,* p. 179).

175 **came to live on the ranch in the spring of 1945:** Account is based on two interviews with Thaddeus Ashby, conducted for the author by Wendy de Weese in Hawaii, June 19 and July 17, 2005.

176 **invited him to lunch:** BBTBI.

176 **remained for between five months and a year:** In an unpublished interview conducted by BB in 1960–61, AR set his visit at five or six months; BBTBI.

176 **spending long weekends at the ranch:** "Ayn Rand's Family and Friends."

176 **part-time secretary during those years:** June Kurisu worked as AR's secretary from June 1947 until November 1949 (*100 Voices,* June Kurisu, pp. 86, 89).

176 **intensive planning of *Atlas Shrugged*:** April 6, 1946, to August 31, 1946 (*JOAR,* pp. 399–548).

176 **"They spent an awful lot of time in there":** Author interview with June Kurisu, December 31, 2004. In an interview with ARI oral historian Scott McConnell, Kurisu said of FO, "He always seemed like the strong one that could stand on his own and be the guard to the castle" (*100 Voices,* June Kurisu, p. 106).

177 **another young man named Walter Abbott:** BBTBI.

177 **couldn't raise the additional capital:** BBTBI.

177 **at $150 a week:** Project-specific file cards archived in the Hal Wallis Collection, Margaret Herrick Library, box 95. In an example of AR's willingness to help others who she believed deserved help, she also offered to assist June Kurisu in getting a secretarial position at Paramount (McConnell, "Recollections of Ayn Rand I," based on his interview with Kurisu).

177 **Bernstein . . . tried out for the composer's role:** Thomas Pryor, "Young Conductor May Star in Film," *NYT,* August 21, 1945, p. 17.

177 **Monogram announced plans for its own Tchaikovsky movie:** "Two Studios to Film Tchaikovsky's Life," *NYT,* October 3, 1946, p. 38. According to this report, Abbott started writing the script in 1945.

177 **saw a lot of Jack Bungay:** Unpublished letter from Bert Allenberg to Hal Wallis, April 12, 1944 (Hal Wallis Collection, Margaret Herrick Library, box 95).

177 **joined the male trio:** Unpublished letter from Albert Mannheimer to IP, April 26, 1947 (Isabel Paterson Papers, Herbert Hoover Presidential Library, box 23).

177 **"She was a very sensual woman":** *100 Voices,* Jack Bungay, pp. 59–63.

178 **were her only regular visitors:** BBTBI.

178 **"He looked like Frank":** Author interview with RBH, June 8, 2005.

178 **"a lot of sex in her face":** *100 Voices,* Jack Bungay, p. 59.

178 **"I don't know what would have happened":** *TPOAR,* p. 250.

179 **developed a paranoid fixation:** Interview with Thaddeus Ashby, July 17, 2005. The fact that von Strachow knew Rand's American name is evidence that Rand's parents and their friends also knew it.

179 **Marie von Strachow:** Author correspondence with Michael Berliner, June 2, 2005.

179 **fled Russia for Western Europe:** Letter to John C. Gall, AR's attorney, January 29, 1947 (*LOAR,* p. 360) and author correspondence with Michael Berliner. AR told Gall that Strachow left Russia in 1918, but she must have left later, in the middle or late 1920s.

179 **the elder Rosenbaums' deaths:** Letter to Marie von Strachow, August 8, 1946 (*LOAR,* p. 301).

179 **perished from cancer:** Archive of the Kuibyshev district of Leningrad, card 1696.

179 **Rand later learned:** *EOWTL,* p. 78; *100 Voices,* NR, p. 7.

179 **sent . . . packages of food and clothing:** *100 Voices,* Lisette Hassani, p. 257.

179 **Rand's lively and much-beloved youngest sister, Nora:** Author correspondence with BB, Feb-

ruary 4, 2008 ("Ayn never told us about her parents' deaths, nor about bringing this woman over, although the woman must have left not long before we met Ayn. I'm thinking of the also odd fact that she never said a word about experiencing anti-Semitism in Russia. And another odd fact: I would never, from what Ayn told me, have expected NR to refuse to speak to me about Ayn's childhood because 'we don't speak ill of the dead'—which suggests childhood problems between the sisters and perhaps more widely than that and which Ayn never so much as hinted at. There's a mystery here and some sort of deliberate rewriting of history that I can't figure out").

180 **working on a difficult and important section:** This was the wedding-anniversary party scene in the Reardens' house in Pennsylvania, where almost all the major characters come together for the first time (*JOAR*, pp. 583–85).

180 **to live elsewhere in California:** Author interview with June Kurisu, December 31, 2004.

180 **Two of Rand's Chicago cousins stopped by:** Probably in the summer of 1946.

180 **Jack noticed that she had a needle:** Author interview with Jack Portnoy, August 17, 2004.

180 **Joe O'Connor, now an itinerant actor:** Author interview with MW, June 21, 2004.

180 **The four were talking about a newspaper article:** *100 Voices,* Rosalie Wilson, pp. 29–36.

181 **On hearing this story:** Author correspondence with Barbara Branden, September 17, 2008.

181 **A few years later she would tell a friend:** Author interview with

Nathaniel Branden, December 11, 2008.

181 **Marna, had quit high school:** Letter to Mimi Sutton, April 30, 1946 (*LOAR,* p. 275).

181 **She and Frank agreed to pay:** Letter to Mimi Sutton, March 24, 1946 (*LOAR,* pp. 265–66).

181 **a strain developed:** Author interview with MW, June 21, 2004.

182 **she did not see it as a moral duty:** Alvin Toffler, "The *Playboy* Interview: Ayn Rand," *Playboy,* March 1964, p. 40.

182 **the old and the lame, she complained:** Letter to Marjorie Williams, June 18, 1936 (*LOAR,* p. 32).

182 **"I considered it an investment":** Author interview with MW, June 21, 2004.

182 **Similarly, when discussing Thaddeus Ashby's long residence:** BBTBI.

182 **"She had a certain tone of voice":** Interview with Thaddeus Ashby, July 17, 2005.

183 **plot of a story she had read at the studio:** I was unable to identify this story.

183 **worked for tiny libertarian magazines:** Brian Doherty, *Radicals for Capitalism: A Freewheeling History of the Modern Libertarian Movement* (Washington, D.C.: Public Affairs, 2007), pp. 278–79.

183 **sent her a long letter:** BBTBI.

183 **Rand had written lovingly:** Letter to IP, August 4, 1954 (*LOAR,* p. 185).

183 **becoming impatient with each other:** *TPOAR,* p. 210.

183 **her way of ceding control:** *JD,* pp. 65–66.

184 **heard him snap:** *TPOAR,* p. 210, based on interview with RBH.

184 **Frank, visibly angry:** Interview with Thaddeus Ashby, July 17, 2005.

184 **"Sometimes I think I am the throne,":** *100 Voices,* RBH, p. 126.

184 **Another acquaintance:** *TPOAR,* p. 210.

184 **"To the Readers of *The Fountainhead*":** *LOAR,* pp. 669–73.

184 **"or as near to it as anyone I know":** Letter to Gerald James, August 18, 1945 (*LOAR,* p. 228), on which "To the Readers of *The Fountainhead*" was partly based.

NINE: THE TOP AND THE BOTTOM: 1946–1949

185 **"The average man":** April 29, 1946 (*JOAR,* p. 474).

185 **"I had in my mind":** "To the Readers of *The Fountainhead*" (*LOAR,* pp. 669–73).

186 **questions concerning her background:** Letter to Ross Baker, November 21, 1945 (*LOAR,* p. 233).

186 **scores of characters:** She created almost two hundred characters in her four novels (Mimi Reisel Gladstein, *The Ayn Rand Companion* [Westport, Conn.: Greenwood Press, 1984], pp. 41–69).

186 **"I am interested in men only":** "To the Readers of *The Fountainhead*" (*LOAR,* pp. 669–73).

186 **"An abstract theory":** *WIAR,* pp. 107–8.

187 **"Do not underestimate":** Letter to Henry Blanke, December 6, 1945 (*LOAR,* p. 247).

187 **Literary Guild issued its own edition:** Letters to Ross Baker of Bobbs-Merrill, December 18, 1943, and December 11, 1945 (*LOAR,* pp. 107, 249); author correspondence with Becky Cape, archivist for the Literary Guild, August 10, 2006.

187 **without a guarantee:** Letter to Walter Hurley, January 23, 1944 (*LOAR,* p. 121).

187 **the hand-drawn . . . illustrations:** The illustrations were created by a well-known commercial artist named F. O. Godwin.

187 **"The artist has done a wonderful job":** Letter to MS, December 2, 1945 (*LOAR,* p. 240).

187 **Dominique is a passable replica of Rand:** See *The Illustrated "Fountainhead"* (Irvine, Calif.: ARI, 1998), p. 18.

188 **loved the luminous rationality:** *AS,* p. 54.

188 **assigned her to a silly gangster movie:** Project-specific file cards listing scripts AR worked on and start and completion dates (Hal Wallis Collection, Margaret Herrick Library, box 95).

188 **stood for man's greatness:** January 2, 1946 (*JOAR,* pp. 312–26).

189 **"The responsibility of making [this] picture:** *JOAR,* p. 312.

189 **"If there is such a thing as an average man":** Letter to M. Curtiss, November 30, 1945 (*LOAR,* p. 237).

189 **who had returned to his teaching post:** *American Prometheus,* p. 351.

189 **endorsed her interpretation of Germany's failure:** *TPOAR,* p. 193.

189 **and told her, thrillingly:** January 19, 1946 (*JOAR,* p. 342).

189 **found Oppenheimer enormously intelligent:** January 15, 1946 (*JOAR,* p. 329).

189 **model for the character of Dr. Robert Stadler:** BBTBI.

189 **borrowed the details of his office:** *TPOAR,* p. 193.

190 **"Man can harness the universe":** January 19, 1946 (*JOAR,* p. 344).

190 **she had completed her outline:** Editor's note (*JOAR,* p. 311).

190 **on the verge of filming its own movie:** According to David Harriman, editor of *JOAR,* Wallis knew about the MGM project from the beginning (*JOAR,* p. 311). The MGM film, *The Beginning or the End,* was released in 1947 and criticized for its muddled history and sentimental subplots.

190 **She was furious:** TPOAR, p. 193.

190 **she figured out:** "Paramount Studio Tour."

190 **She wrote a second memo:** Letter to Hal Wallis, March 19, 1946 (*LOAR,* p. 263).

190 **left the studio a week later:** Dates courtesy of project-specific file cards and "Multiple Picture Contract with Ayn Rand," dated July 5, 1944, both from Hal Wallis Collection, Margaret Herrick Library, box 95.

190 **drafted its first chapter:** Ayn Rand Papers, LOC, box 6, folder 1.

190 **a prolonged tantrum:** Beverly Fields, "Ayn Rand Rants for 1,168 Pages."

192 **"Whatever pride of person I hold":** AS, pp. 235–36.

193 **"I'll give you a hint":** AS, p. 188.

193 **"a raw commodity":** *A People's Tragedy,* p. 73.

193 **The novel is full of detailed parallels:** Author interview with Bernice Glatzer Rosenthal, July 5, 2005.

195 **"This [Galt's face] was the world":** AS, p. 643.

196 **a railroad map above her desk:** Lewis Nichols, "Talk with Ayn Rand," *NYT,* October 13, 1957, p. 272.

196 **Rand wrote hundreds of pages:** Editor's note, *JOAR,* p. 390.

196 **She was setting out, she wrote, to show:** January 1, 1945 (*JOAR,* p. 394).

196 **John Galt, like Howard Roark:** BBTBI.

196 **was basing Dagny Taggart:** BBTBI.

196 **"hunger for her own kind":** April 14, 1946 (*JOAR,* p. 417).

196 **based on this view of O'Connor:** January 1, 1945 (*JOAR,* p. 398).

196 **"the sensitive, poetic kind of writer":** April 13, 1946 (*JOAR,* p. 411).

197 **"she cannot reach her enemies":** April 11, 1946, to April 17, 1946 (*JOAR,* pp. 410–18).

197 **"I think I represent":** May 4, 1946 (*JOAR,* p. 480).

197 **had given a dinner party in her honor:** BBTBI.

197 **"I have written such a book":** Leonard Read, foreword to the Caxton Press edition of *Anthem,* originally published in July 1953 (Caldwell, Idaho: Caxton, 2004), p. 8.

198 **had already issued:** John Blundell, "Liberty at Its Nadir: Interview with Leonard Liggio," *Liberty,* July 2004 (vol. 18, no. 7).

198 **ninety-eight-page booklet:** James Howard, "Nightshirt Fringe Applauds Ayn Rand's Ten-Year-Old Book," *PM,* October 22, 1947.

198 **appeared in July 1946:** "Author's Foreword" to Pamphleteer's edition of *Anthem,* written in April 1946 (copy of the first printing of *Anthem,* Bennett A. Cerf Collection, Columbia University Rare Book and Manuscript Library, New York, box 436; letter to Walt Disney, September 5, 1946 [*LOAR,* p. 317]).

198 **sold for a dollar a copy:** Unpublished letter from Leonard Read to Ann Watkins, April 10, 1946/7 [two dates on letter, one a typo] (A. Watkins Collection, Columbia University Rare Book and Manuscript Library, box 152).

198 **U.S. purveyor of *The Protocols***

of the Elders of Zion: "Nightshirt Fringe." The reporter, and *PM,* unfairly used the connection to discredit AR and *Anthem.*

198 **"What can be loved":** *Thus Spoke Zarathustra,* pp. 14–15.

198 **"Ayn Rand is a phenomenon":** Quoted in *EOA,* p. 58.

199 **the parent of *The Fountainhead:*** Letter to Henry Blanke, September 5, 1946 (*LOAR,* p. 315).

199 **Stanwyck wasn't interested:** Letter to Barbara Stanwyck, September 7, 1946 (*LOAR,* pp. 317–18).

199 **Wallis turned it down:** "Paramount Studio Tour."

199 **With the rumored silent backing:** Robert Mayhew, *Ayn Rand and "Song of Russia"* (Lanham, Md.: Scarecrow Press, 2005), p. 78.

199 **"the rising tide" of Communism:** Motion Picture Alliance "Statement of Principles," AMPTP Collection, Margaret Herrick Library, box 11, MPA folder. The MPA was organized in February 1944; Rand joined in the summer of 1944, as soon as it was clear that she was going to remain in Hollywood.

199 **Members met weekly at MGM:** *An Oral History with Robert M. W. Vogel,* interviewed by Barbara Hall, Beverly Hills, Calif.: Academy of Motion Pictures Arts and Sciences, Oral History Program, 1991.

199 **Rand sat on the MPA executive board:** Motion Picture Alliance records, Hedda Hopper Collection, Margaret Herrick Library.

199 **The Vigil:** "Textbook of Americanism," 1946; Motion Picture Alliance Records.

200 **"Fascist anti-Semites!":** After the end of the Nazi-Soviet Pact, American opponents of the Soviet Union were accused of being pro-Hitler, i.e., pro-Fascist and anti-Semitic ("Emergency Committee of Hollywood Guilds and Unions Announcement," *Hollywood Reporter,* June 23, 1944; "To the Membership of the Motion Picture Alliance," *Hollywood Reporter,* June 27, 1944; James Kevin McGuinness, "Double Cross in Hollywood," *The New Leader,* July 15, 1944, p. 119; Morrie Ryskind, "A Reply to Elmer Rice about the MPAPAI," *The New Leader,* December 23, 1944.)

200 **suspected her own treasured literary agent:** Unpublished letters to Benjamin Stolberg, September 26, 1946, and October 9, 1946 (Benjamin Stolberg Collection, Columbia University Rare Book and Manuscript Library).

200 **remained her New York agents:** Alan Collins died in 1968. Perry Knowlton, who later replaced Collins as president of Curtis Brown, Ltd., in the United States, acted as her primary agent from 1957 until 1982 (*100 Voices,* Perry Knowlton, p. 307).

200 **"we were all seeing ghosts":** *An Oral History with Robert M. W. Vogel,* interviewed by Barbara Hall, Beverly Hills, Calif.: Academy of Motion Pictures Arts and Sciences, Oral History Program, 1991.

200 **monopoly over the nation's literary output:** "Writers Form Group to Combat Control by Unit Assailed as Red," *NYT,* September 13, 1946, p. 1.

200 **formed the American Writers Association:** "Cain Plan Scored by Writers' Group," *NYT,* May 8, 1947, p. 14; "22 Authors on Board," *NYT,* October 16, 1947, p. 34.

200 **joined the board:** Letter to Benjamin Stolberg, September 27, 1947 (*LOAR,* p. 380).

200 **"chop his head off":** "Paramount Studio Tour."

201 **met as often as three times a week:** *Song of Russia*, p. 79, based on AR's desk calendars.

201 **composed the "Screen Guide for Americans":** "Screen Guide for Americans" was published in the November 1947 issue of *Plain Talk*.

201 **wrote the first sentence:** Ayn Rand Papers, LOC, first draft of *AS*, reel 2, chapter 1.

201 **worked on a movie called *House of Mist:*** Dates courtesy of project-specific file cards (Hal Wallis Collection, Margaret Herrick Library, box 95).

201 **"I don't believe in unhappiness":** "First Temporary Yellow" screenplay of *House of Mist*, dated December 30, 1946, Hal Wallis Collection, Margaret Herrick Library, box 95.

202 **shelved in October 1947:** Dates courtesy of project-specific file cards (Hal Wallis Collection, Margaret Herrick Library, box 95).

202 **never to return:** Her contract was cancelled in November 1948 ("Termination of Employment Agreement," November 29, 1948, Hal Wallis Collection, Margaret Herrick Library, box 95).

202 **steering Dagny and Hank Rearden:** First draft of *AS*, Ayn Rand Papers, LOC, reel 3, chapter 6, "The Noncommercial."

202 **predicted that she would finish it:** Letter to Alan Collins, June 24, 1946 (*LOAR*, p. 284).

202 **But when she began to consider:** BBTBI.

202 **"Why is the mind important?":** October 6, 1949 (*JOAR*, p. 610).

202 **boarded a train for the nation's capital:** *Song of Russia*, p. 79.

202 **hottest show in town:** Willard Edwards, "List 18 as Leaders in Red Film Invasion," *Chicago Tribune*, October 21, 1947, p. 1.

202 **supplied most of the twenty-four friendly witnesses:** *Hollywood Party*, p. 178.

202 **"Are you now, or have you ever been":** Victor Navasky, *Naming Names* (New York: Viking, 1980), p. viii.

203 **"a lot of fools":** "Ayn Rand's HUAC Testimony," appendix 1, in *Song of Russia*, pp. 179–90.

203 **later identified themselves as members:** Patrick McGilligan and Paul Buhle, *Tender Comrades: A Backstory of the Hollywood Blacklist* (New York: St. Martin's Press, 1997); see McGilligan's interview with Paul Jarrico, pp. 326–50. During HUAC testimony in 1951, Richard Collins stated that he had been a Communist Party member and also named his *Song of Russia* co-script writer, Jarrico.

203 **naming sixteen:** Samuel A. Tower, "Film Men Admit Activity by Reds, Sam Wood Lists Writers by Name," *NYT*, October 21, 1947, p. 1.

204 **not be able to secure work for the next seven years:** *Naming Names*, pp. 104–06.

204 **a "little black book":** Neal Gabler, *An Empire of Their Own: How the Jews Invented Hollywood* (New York: Anchor Books, 1989), p. 363.

204 **accused seven screenwriters:** "Film Men Admit Activity by Reds, Sam Wood Lists Writers by Name."

204 **had been promised an opportunity to make a full statement:** *Song of Russia*, p. 96.

204 **Not listed in the schedule:** "From the FBI Files: Schedule for the October 1947 HUAC Hearings," FBI FOIA file no. 100-138754, appendix 3; *Song of Russia*, pp. 195–99.

204 **she remembered having a "violent scene":** *Song of Russia*, p. 97.

205 **"Still handling the chicken shit, I see":** *Tender Comrades,* p. 414.

205 **press coverage had turned negative:** "Hearing Halt Laid to Move by Reds," *Washington Post,* November 1, 1937, p. 3.

205 **flacks hailed the curtailment of the hearings:** Joseph Loftus, "Expert Balked It," *NYT,* October 31, 1947, p. 1.

205 **"nothing but disappointments":** *Song of Russia,* p. 97.

205 **"nightshirt fringe":** "Nightshirt Fringe Applauds Ayn Rand's Ten-Year-Old Book," *PM,* October 22, 1947.

205 **fair game in the political as well as the literary press:** Thanks to Robert Mayhew's research on the public reaction to AR's testimony in *Song of Russia,* pp. 159–69; *Naming Names,* p. 80.

205 **annoyed Louis B. Mayer:** *Song of Russia,* p. 173, based on AR's notes in preparation for her HUAC testimony.

205 **"a disgusting spectacle":** *TPOAR,* p. 201.

206 *was* **a crime:** "Suggestions Regarding the Congressional Investigation of Communism," 1947 (*JOAR,* pp. 381–86).

206 **Hoover, who turned her down:** Memorandum from A. B. Hood of the Los Angeles Bureau of the FBI to J. Edgar Hoover, October 17, 1947, FOIA. AR asked to see Hoover again in 1957 and was again turned down (FOIA memo to author from U.S. Department of Justice, December 11, 2003).

206 **real-life equivalent:** This job was held by a man named A. H. Wright (letter to William Duce, AR's tax attorney, October 1, 1949 [*LOAR,* p. 457]).

206 **showed Archibald Ogden:** Letter to William Duce, AR's tax attorney, October 1, 1949 (*LOAR,* p. 457).

206 **finally met Rose Wilder Lane:** Letter to Rose Wilder Lane, December 13, 1947 (*LOAR,* p. 383).

206 **In their hotel room after dinner:** Author interview with MW, December 16, 2006.

206 **"You are the ultimate in human beings":** Quoted in "AR's Family and Friends."

207 **"She was afraid that she would lose him":** Taped interview with MS, conducted by BB, January 20, 1983.

207 **"The 'Screen Guide for Americans' did it":** *Song of Russia,* p. 176.

207 *Plain Talk,* **whose editor:** Letter to William Duce, October 1, 1949 (*LOAR,* p. 457).

207 **The Sunday** *New York Times* **picked up the story:** Thomas F. Brady, "Hollywood Don'ts," *NYT,* November 16, 1947, p. X5.

207 **"all the points I made":** *Song of Russia,* p. 176.

207 **preferred to sell screen rights outright:** Thomas F. Brady, "Hollywood's Uneasy Labor Truce," *NYT,* November 2, 1947, p. X5.

207 **finally able to get hold of a print of the film:** She first saw the film in May 1947 (letter to John C. Gall, May 28, 1947 [*LOAR,* p. 368]). She also sat for a viewing in New York (letter to William B. Duce, October 1, 1949 [*LOAR,* p. 458]).

207 **From Valli:** R. W. Bradford, "The Search for *We the Living,*" *Liberty,* November 1988, p. 24, citing AR's friend Erika Holzer.

207 **opened to packed theaters:** The 1942 movie apparently also "had a big box office" in Nazi Germany and Vichy France (unpublished letter from Donald Downes to Armitage Watkins, May 16, 1946; A. Watkins Collection, Columbia University Rare Book and Manuscript Library, box 80).

207 **ordered the film to be withdrawn:**
Letter to John C. Gall, July 12, 1947,
LOAR, p. 370.

207 **and prints and negatives destroyed:** "The Search for *We the Living,"* p. 22, quoting Massimo Ferrara, legal counsel to Scalera Films in 1942. Based on additional interviews with experts and historians, Bradford goes on to argue that the film *wasn't* banned and that (1) the actors Alida Valli and possibly Rossano Brazzi lied to Rand, or (2) that Rand made the story up herself for publicity purposes, or (3) Rand and the actors misunderstood each other based on difficulties with English.

207 **on the grounds that it was anti-Fascist:** Ironically, according to documents in the A. Watkins Collection, AR had been just about to sell Italian film rights to a production company headed by Mussolini's second son, Vittorio Mussolini, in March 1940. The war intervened; otherwise it might have been Vittorio's production that his father's troops would allegedly have seized.

207 **This proved the kinship:** Letter to John C. Gall, July 12, 1947 (*LOAR,* p. 370).

207 **Rossano Brazzi:** In R. W. Bradford's chronicle of the film in *Liberty,* Brazzi is quoted as saying that he and Rand became "very good friends." Brazzi went on: "She was a funny woman, very strong. Difficult woman. She was bisexual. She loved women. But . . . what a mind!"

208 **Rand contacted Jack Warner:** Letter to Jack Warner, February 14, 1948 (*LOAR,* p. 385).

208 **paid her $35,000:** "The Search for *We the Living,"* p. 24.

208 **buy a new mink coat:** *TPOAR,* p. 317.

208 **It was not until 1972:** Rand re-portedly obtained her own print of the film but lost it sometime in the 1950s. In 1968, Henry and Erika Holzer, both attorneys, set out to find a copy. Unable to obtain one from Brazzi or Valli, in August 1968 they located the original negative and a print through a vintage film dealer in Rome, purchased it, and, with film producer Duncan Scott, re-edited it and added subtitles. Since then, Scott has offered occasional screenings of the film ("The Search for *We the Living,"* pp. 25–26).

208 **item in a Hollywood gossip column:** Hedda Hopper, "Looking at Hollywood," *Los Angeles Times,* January 29, 1948, p. 18, and February 16, 1948, p. 14.

208 **Cooper was welcome news:** Gary Cooper was AR's favorite film actor. But according to AR's second cousin FB, AR wrote the family a letter saying she expected FO to get the part of Howard Roark and "was livid" when Gary Cooper got it; taped interview with FB, Minna Goldberg, and MS, conducted by BB, February 20, 1983.

208 **she fired her Hollywood agent:** Unpublished telegram from Alan Collins to H. N. Swanson, March 10, 1948, and unpublished letter from H. N. Swanson to Alan Collins, March 30, 1948 (H. N. Swanson Collection, Margaret Herrick Library, box 27).

208 **She "went through hell":** BBTBI.

208 **back in a Warner Bros. office:** Letter to John B. Williams, March 27, 1948 (*LOAR,* p. 393).

208 **hinted that Lauren Bacall had accepted the part:** Hedda Hopper, "Looking at Hollywood," *Los Angeles Times,* February 16, 1948, p. 14.

208 **Margaret Sullavan said she wanted it:** Hedda Hopper, "Looking

at Hollywood," *Los Angeles Times,*
May 7, 1948, p. 19.

208 **his eye on Jennifer Jones:** BBTBI.

208 **In early June:** *Patricia Neal,* p. 58.

208 **a twenty-two-year-old ingenue:**
Hedda Hopper, "Looking at Hollywood," *Los Angeles Times,* June 21,
1948, p. 16.

209 **she was horrified:** BBTBI.

209 **"After dinner we never saw the
two of them again":** Stuart M.
Kaminsky, *Coop: The Life and Legend of Gary Cooper* (New York: St.
Martin's Press, 1980), p. 154.

209 **completed the screenplay in late
June:** Letter to John L. B. Williams,
June 26, 1948 (*LOAR,* p. 398).

209 **a quarry near Fresno:** Letter to
Archibald Ogden, July 10, 1948
(*LOAR,* p. 402).

209 **remained on the lot:** TPOAR, p.
209.

209 **turned in her script in a blaze of
glory:** Letter to Archibald Ogden,
June 26, 1948 (*LOAR,* p. 398).

209 **promised not to make any
changes:** Letter to Henry Blanke,
June 26, 1948 (*LOAR,* p. 397).

209 **was an excellent director:** Letter
to Archibald Ogden, June 26, 1948
(*LOAR,* p. 398).

209 **ended with her plot and theme
intact:** She saw a rough cut the week
of October 2 (letter to Ross Baker,
October 2, 1948 [*LOAR,* p. 407]).

209 **"For the first time in Hollywood
history":** Letter to John Chamberlain, November 27, 1948, *LOAR,*
p. 415.

209 **were in an uproar of excitement:**
Letter to Alan Collins, January 8,
1949 (*LOAR,* p. 419).

209 **"The whole thing was an enormously miserable experience":**
TPOAR, p. 210.

209 **constantly caved in to pressure:**
BBTBI.

209 **on time and under budget:** BBTBI.

210 **no more changes made to the
script:** AR:SOL, DVD.

210 **she defied them all:** TPOAR, p.
211.

210 **one line *had* been cut in final
editing:** BBTBI.

211 **wrote a second article:** Bosely
Crowther, "The Screen in Review"
and "In a Glass House," *NYT,* July 9
and July 17, 1949, pp. 8 and XI, respectively. AR wrote and the *Times*
published a long rebuttal, in which
she said, confusingly, "My script was
shot verbatim; this, to my knowledge, was the first and only instance
of its kind in Hollywood" ("Ayn Rand
Replies to Criticism of Her Film,"
NYT, July 24, 1949, p. X4).

211 **"Cooper in Race for Longest-
Speech Oscar":** Harold Heffernan,
The Bell Syndicate, 1949.

211 **"In all the years I knew her":** Barbara Branden, "It's a Dirty Job,
But . . . ," unpublished essay, 2007,
courtesy of the author.

211 **It was the trip of a lifetime:** Letters to IP, February 7 and February 14, 1948 (*LOAR,* pp. 188–96).

211 **contacted her good pal:** *The
Woman and the Dynamo,* p. 304.

212 **didn't mention her former mentor's help:** Author interview with BB,
December 16, 2005.

212 **"I have seldom enjoyed anything":** Letter to IP, February 7
(*LOAR,* p. 188).

212 **"It was the security of being
first":** AS, p. 225; italics the author's.

212 **the greatness of man:** Letter to IP,
April 24, 1948 (*LOAR,* p. 212).

213 **she reminded Paterson:** Letter to
IP, May 8, 1948 (*LOAR,* p. 211).

213 **Altruism was like sawdust:** Letter
from IP to AR, May 13, 1948 (*LOAR,*
p. 214).

213 **She conceded to having:** Letter

to IP, May 17, 1948 (*LOAR*, pp. 215–17).

213 **raise money for a new magazine:** BBTBI.

213 **in honor of Albert Jay Nock's 1920s libertarian weekly:** *A Life with the Printed Word*, pp. 136–37.

213 **She wrote to the older woman:** Letter to IP, May 17, 1948 (*LOAR*, p. 216).

213 **She had not enjoyed the flight:** *The Woman and the Dynamo*, p. 312.

214 **would never really work again:** *The Woman and the Dynamo*, p. 322.

214 **The first hint of trouble:** Summary of Paterson's 1948 visit based on BBTBI.

214 **After Ryskind left:** *TPOAR*, p. 203.

214 **The next incident took place:** BBTBI.

214 **"[That woman] ought to be kept out of sight":** *The Woman and the Dynamo*, p. 313.

215 **Rand suspected:** "I suspect that [Paterson] really hated *The Fountainhead*," Rand once told Barbara Branden, "that she liked certain aspects of it dutifully, or rather that she talked herself into liking it" (BBTBI).

215 **According to Rand's later account:** BBTBI.

215 **She didn't like the sex:** Author interview with NB, May 5, 2004.

215 **was "gone" . . . was "no good":** BBTBI.

215 **in February 1959:** Author interview with Muriel Hall, July 4, 2004.

216 **she also hoped:** *The Woman and the Dynamo*, p. 381.

216 **admitted that she had reservations:** *The Woman and the Dynamo*, p. 382.

216 **He couldn't imagine:** Author interview with NB, May 5, 2004.

216 **Close friends had no idea:** It was BB who discovered the friendship between Rand and Paterson while researching *TPOAR*.

216 **"No one helped me":** AR expanded on this heroic version of herself on *The Les Crane Show* in the fall of 1964. Asked to give her view of taxation, she erupted, "I had the longest period of struggle [before *TF* was purchased as a movie]. I was not paid by any big business interests. I had a dreadful period of struggle to reach the day when I could make money. I had to write part time while holding odd jobs and making a living. No one helped me in that period, nor did I at any time or any moment believe that anybody should. I never expected the government or other people to help me with my struggle. I earned what I made. I felt that [taxes on my income were] a monstrous moral injustice with which I had to put up"; *Selfishness as a Virtue*, audio CD of AR's appearance on *The Les Crane Show*.

216 **had as little reality for her:** In a famous exchange in *TF*, Toohey says to Roark, "We're alone here. Why don't you tell me what you think of me?" and Roark replies, "But I don't think of you" (*TF*, p. 389). Roark's line came from FO, AR tells us in her introduction to the twenty-fifth-anniversary edition.

216 **"If she didn't love it":** Author interview with BB, December 16, 2005.

216 **"She was not interested in process":** Author interview with NB, May 5, 2004.

TEN: THE MEANS AND THE END: 1950–1953

218 **"I have nothing to sell":** *WTL*, first handwritten draft, dated April 18, 1933 (Ayn Rand Papers, LOC, box

26, folder 2, p. 35). Quoted in *EOWTL*, pp. 26–27.

218 **opened in July 1949, to moderate box-office success:** *TF* press book, Warner Bros. Press Books, Series 1.4, United Artists Collection, courtesy of the Wisconsin Center for Film and Theater Research.

218 **"Monumental Best-Seller!":** *TF* press book, Warner Bros. Press Books, Series 1.4, United Artists Collection, courtesy of the Wisconsin Center for Film and Theater Research.

219 **ample books waiting in local bookstores:** Internal note dated June 16, 1949, Bobbs-Merrill Collection, courtesy of the Lilly Library.

219 **In three weeks, fifty thousand copies were sold:** BBTBI.

219 **"It was the greatest word-of-mouth book":** "A Strange Kind of Simplicity," p. 8.

219 **By the mid-2000s:** Courtesy of the ARI, May 2007.

219 **"metaphysics, morality, politics, economics and sex":** BBTBI. ARI archivist JB notes that AR first described her work this way during an interview with a reporter from the *Los Angeles Herald Examiner* in mid-1948, during the filming of *TF*; correspondence with the author, May 14, 2007.

219 **only one had personal meaning:** BBTBI.

219 **He was trying to write a novel:** Author correspondence with BB, June 24, 2008.

219 **he could summarize:** "The Benefits and Hazards," p. 40.

219 **would like to know more:** *JD*, p. 39; letter to NB, December 2, 1949 (*LOAR*, p. 461).

220 **he sent another letter:** *TPOAR*, p. 232; *JD*, p. 40.

220 **ended her letter with a short reading list:** She recommended IP's *The God of the Machine* and Henry Hazlitt's *Economics in One Lesson* (*LOAR*, p. 465).

220 **just starting a difficult chapter:** When AR received NB's second letter, in January 1950, she had just begun the chapter called "The Sanction of the Victim" (part 2, chapter 4), in which Francisco d'Anconia speaks at length to Hank Rearden about the purpose and meaning of sex (Ayn Rand Papers, LOC, box 7, folder 6).

220 **asked for his telephone number:** Letter to NB, January 13, 1950 (*LOAR*, pp. 462–65).

220 **phoned the Hollywood apartment:** Author interview with EK, December 13, 2008.

220 **interpreted his lack of fear:** *JD*, pp. 40–43.

221 **sensed that she had made a discovery:** BBTBI.

221 **His . . . parents had never fully assimilated:** *JD*, p. 16.

221 **"Oh, foolish child":** *JD*, p. 44. NB's other favorite book in his teen years was Romain Rolland's ten-volume novel *Jean-Christophe*. AR argued him out of his attachment to the book by calling attention to the author's sympathy with socialism and by asking, characteristically, "Tell, me, would you want to meet Jean-Christophe in real life?" "No," NB answered, "but I *would* want to meet Howard Roark." Thus in their first meeting NB gave his full allegiance to AR (Ayn Rand, "The Goal of My Writing," *The Objectivist Newsletter*, October 1963, p. 37).

221 **things as they might be and ought to be:** Again, AR may have picked up Aristotle's dictum about the difference between history and literature from Albert Jay Nock, who quoted it, both in English and in

Greek, in *Memoirs of a Superfluous Man. Memoirs* appeared in 1943, alongside *TF*; AR owned a copy of the book and annotated it with margin notes (*The Library of Ayn Rand,* p. 39). Her first published reference to things as they "might be and ought to be" appeared in 1945, in "To the Readers of *The Fountainhead*," *LOAR,* p. 670.

222 **she was the only Jewish child:** Karen Reedstrom, "An Interview with Barbara Branden," *Full Context,* October 1992, p. 1.

222 **She liked him and admired him:** Author interview with BB, December 16, 2005.

222 **continued to want more:** *JD,* pp. 30–39.

222 **"Ayn Rand is fascinating":** *TPOAR,* p. 233.

222 **feel appreciated, understood:** *JD,* p. 46.

222 **Rand had given every appearance of liking him, too:** *JD,* p. 45.

223 **phoned on Sunday evening:** *WIAR,* p. 221.

223 **"seemed to be staring right down to the bottom of your soul":** BB to Ron Grossman, "Passions: A Disciple Confronts Ayn Rand's Power," *Chicago Tribune,* September 9, 1986, p. 1.

223 **"It's a wonderful fiction event!":** *TPOAR,* p. 235.

223 **"ideas *matter*":** *TPOAR,* p. 236.

223 **astounded by her energy:** BB, radio interview with Don Swaim, WOUB (Ohio University) online, June 27, 1986.

223 **conversation could go on for hours:** "The Curious Cult of Ayn Rand," p. 101; "The Benefits and Hazards."

223 **"You will":** *JD,* p. 60.

223 **worked for days and sometimes weeks:** BBTBI.

224 **looking after the alfalfa:** *100 Voices,* RBH, p. 126.

224 **"Not the sort of thing Howard Roark would do!":** Author interview with RBH, June 2, 2005.

224 **Rand never met Aretha:** Interview with RBH, June 8, 2005.

224 **her "kind of face":** BBTBI.

224 **possessed the best mind:** *JD,* p. 62.

224 **"and I really mean *genius*":** BBTBI.

224 **finally found one:** BBTBI, reprinted on Objectivistliving.com.

225 **as "the children":** Lewis Nichols, "In and Out of Books: Class of '43," *NYT,* December 22, 1957, p. 136.

225 **didn't mean anything parental by it:** *JD,* p. 57.

225 **"relatives through choice, not blood":** Author interview with RBH, June 2, 2005.

225 **"Certainly not":** *JD,* p. 64.

225 **shared her view of families:** *JD,* p. 55.

225 **like one of his mother's cousins:** *JD,* p. 82.

225 **warning "the children":** *TPOAR,* p. 241.

225 **"One could not encounter a human being":** *TPOAR,* p. 235.

225 **"She had a Sherlock Holmes ability":** Author interview with NB, December 11, 2008.

226 **"everything is something":** *AS,* p. 136.

226 **defined as "the faculty that identifies and integrates":** "The Objectivist Ethics," *VOS,* p. 20.

226 **both lacked respect for the human will:** Letter to Stanley Greben, October 15, 1950 (*LOAR,* p. 482).

226 **"Emotions are not tools of cognition":** *FTNI,* p. 17.

227 **"the head has its reasons":** AR was reformulating JH's reformulation

of Pascal, who wrote in *Les Pensées*, "The heart has its reasons that reason does not understand" (letter to JH, January 3, 1961 [*LOAR*, p. 526]).

227 **claimed that she could account rationally:** *TPOAR*, p. 194.

227 **Branden talked of more personal matters:** *JD*, p. 70.

227 **bet he wouldn't even notice:** Author interview with NB, December 11, 2008.

227 **If she could make his life's path any easier:** Nathaniel Branden, *My Years with Ayn Rand* (Hoboken, N.J.: Jossey-Bass, 1990), p. 67.

227 **could see that Barbara was very intelligent:** BBTBI.

227 **some kind of mind-body split:** *MYWAR*, p. 29. Years later, in a private journal, AR suggested that it was NB who had the mind-body split. " 'I felt, give me the intellect and sex,' " AR quoted NB as having said to her, " 'and to hell with emotions, leave them to others!' Through all the years this seems to have been his attitude, which never changed," AR wrote. "Yet emotions are the form in which one experiences one's values" (*TPOARC*, RPJ, July 4, 1968, p. 320).

227 **sorting them helped her organize:** Author correspondence with RBH, August 21, 2005.

228 **a girl as bright as Barbara:** *MYWAR*, p. 59.

228 **wasn't madly, passionately, sexually in love:** *TPOAR*, p. 238.

228 **"Love is our response":** *AS*, p. 454.

228 **Rand's doctrine of man worship:** Author correspondence with BB, June 23, 2008.

229 **summer of 1950:** *JD*, p. 78.

229 **gave them eighteen completed chapters:** Author interview with NB, May 5, 2004; letter to NB, September 1, 1950 (*LOAR*, p. 479).

229 **who had already heard each new section:** Letter to Archibald Ogden, April 23, 1949 (*LOAR*, p. 437).

229 **"We were hearing":** *TPOAR*, p. 245.

229 **"I can't fully communicate the exhilaration":** "Interview with Barbara Branden," p. 12.

229 **"plot, theme, characterization, style":** *TPOAR*, p. 242.

229 **selected some of Barbara's favorite passages:** *The Art of Fiction*, p. 10, from contemporaneous recordings of private lectures. Interestingly, AR is quoted as saying that Thomas Wolfe's "appeal is usually to people under twenty. Wolfe presents an empty mold to be filled by any reader, the general intention being aspiration, undefined idealism, the desire to escape from the commonplace and to find 'something better in Life' " (p. 111). Except for the reference to "an empty mold," AR could be describing her own appeal.

230 **"into a destructive vise":** *TPOAR*, p. 243.

230 **She wore short skirts:** *JD*, p. 65; *TPOAR*, p. 240.

230 **snapped at her about such carelessness:** *TPOAR*, p. 210.

230 **"top value":** *The Phil Donahue Show*, April 29, 1980.

230 **"Frank is my rock":** *TPOAR*, p. 248.

230 **"too disgusted with people":** *JD*, p. 66.

230 **she didn't divorce Frank:** "Interview with Nathaniel Branden," Karen Reedstrom, *Full Context*, September 1996, p. 7.

230 **held his hand as they strolled:** *TPOAR*, p. 247.

231 **such as Zorro and the Scarlet Pimpernel:** *JD*, p. 84.

231 **raised by a doting mother and grandmother:** Author interview

with Florence Hirschfeld, Jonathan Hirschfeld, and EK, August 25, 2006.

231 **Lavery ... alleged that Mrs. Rogers had defamed him:** "Debate Suits Ask $2,000,000," *Los Angeles Times,* September 11, 1947, p. A1, and "Unproduced Play's Value Question in Lavery Suit," *Los Angeles Times,* August 4, 1951, p. B18.

231 **settled for thirty thousand dollars:** "Lavery Awarded $30,000," *Los Angeles Times,* August 14, 1951, p. 2.

231 **flirted pleasantly with Barbara:** Author interview with BB, June 9, 2006.

231 **lasted for only twenty-eight performances:** In 1948, *The Bees and the Flowers* was released as the MGM movie *Three Daring Daughters* with Jeanette MacDonald.

231 **When a girlfriend committed suicide:** *TPOAR,* p. 193.

232 **affected his rationality:** *JD,* p. 63.

232 **"I think we replaced him":** Author interview with BB, June 9, 2006.

232 **"the only two ... which I consider serious":** BBTBI.

232 **"She was very, very close":** Author interview with BB, June 9, 2006.

232 **"That's the Dominique premise":** *JD,* p. 64.

232 **Ruth Beebe Hill and her husband:** Dr. Borroughs Hill was a cancer research physician at UCLA Medical Center. RBH later wrote and published a prize-winning novel, called *Hanta Yo,* about the Teton Sioux Indians (New York: Doubleday, 1979).

233 **"Plato? The father of Communism?":** Author interview with RBH, May 25, 2005.

233 **"I saw it":** Author interview with RBH, June 8, 2005.

234 **had become lovers again:** *TPOAR,* p. 249.

234 **not anticipated the emptiness she felt:** BBTBI.

234 **"It's the kids!":** Author interview with RBH, May 26, 2005.

234 **wasn't aware that he was behaving seductively:** *JD,* p. 105.

235 **"I was so cautious":** *JD,* p. 62.

235 **"If Ayn had designs on Nathaniel":** Author correspondence with BB, November 8, 2006.

235 **the third and final part of the novel:** At the time, "Atlantis" was the beginning of part 2; the novel was originally planned in two parts (Ayn Rand Papers, LOC, box 9, folder 1).

235 **expected to see it at sixteen:** *AS,* p. 643.

235 **"He says ... I can't live without you!":** *JD,* p. 107.

235 **long drive in Frank's new Cadillac convertible:** Author interview with NB, April 3, 2008.

235 **whose surroundings contributed to the topography:** In a letter to philosopher JH written in August 1960, AR noted that she had marked Ouray on a map of Colorado as the right place for Galt's Gulch "long before I saw it." She added, "It is the most beautifully dramatic spot in the whole state," although "Galt's Valley would be somewhat larger" (*LOAR,* p. 509).

235 **provided a model for the revolutionary new motor:** AR's proofreader, the ex-marine Evan Wright, who was also an electrical engineer, remembered that AR was still looking for a new source of power for Galt's invention in 1951 and that in discussions they eliminated lightning as too difficult to capture (*100 Voices,* Evan Wright, p. 142).

235 **Dr. Stadler's terrifying weapon:** "Death Ray for Planes," *NYT,* September 22, 1940, p. D7.

236 **"He uncuffed it for dinner":** Au-

thor interview with Connie Papurt, September 21, 2004.

236 **On October 24, they took occupancy:** Letter to Pincus Berner, October 12, 1951 (*LOAR*, p. 494).

236 **who were to live at the ranch while they were away:** The Hills moved into the Chatsworth house in summer 1952 (*100 Voices*, RBH, p. 127).

236 **gave their convertible car to Branden:** Author interview with NB, April 3, 2008.

236 **aware of having reservations:** Author interview with BB, November 2, 2006.

236 **enrolled at NYU:** *TPOAR*, p. 249.

236 **"I wanted it desperately":** Author interview with BB, November 2, 2006.

236 **"The Fountain Pen, by Frank O'Connor":** Author interview with RBH, May 26, 2005.

237 **insisted on paying rent:** Undated note from RBH to BB, courtesy of MSC.

237 **In 1962:** *100 Voices*, RBH, p. 129.

237 **for a price of $175,000:** *TPOAR*, p. 186.

237 **"That property was his business and his world":** Author interview with RBH, June 8, 2005.

237 **"She said it too insistently":** *TPOAR*, p. 251.

238 **"Francisco, the Lobbyist":** Mary Ann and Charles Sures, *Facets of Ayn Rand* (Irvine, Calif.: ARI Press, 2001), p. 117.

238 **began to paint—figures, cityscapes:** *Facets of Ayn Rand*, p. 118.

238 **heaped from countertops:** Author correspondence with RBH, August 2005.

238 **apart from whatever they may have taken:** Ruth Beebe Hill, "Shared Moments with a Famous Author," *The Journal of the San Juan Islands*, July 23, 1986, p. 1.

238 **cats sharpened their claws:** *Facets of Ayn Rand*, pp. 40–41.

238 **bill collectors sometimes showed up:** Author interview with Roberta Satro, July 20, 2006.

238 **job to pay the bills:** *TPOAR*, p. 252.

238 **natural and charming:** Author interview with Iris Bell, March 8, 2004; *Facets of Ayn Rand*, p. 46.

238 **foyer doubled as the dining room:** Mary Ann Sures, "Portrait of an Artist," *Impact*, September 1997, p. 1.

239 **see the Empire State Building:** *Facets of Ayn Rand*, pp. 32–33; *TPOAR*, p. 251.

239 **launched into a spirited discussion of John Galt:** *JD*, pp. 109–10.

239 **"One does not approach a god too closely":** *JD*, p. 109.

240 **Rand had written back:** Author interview with BB, December 16, 2005.

240 **"a pain that . . . was excruciating":** *JD*, pp. 110–13.

240 **Barbara remembered Rand's manner:** Note from BB to author, November 7, 2006.

240 **become her "moral mentor":** "The *Liberty* Interview: Barbara Branden," *Liberty*, January 1990, p. 55.

240 **refrain from seeking *his* mentor's advice again:** Author interview with BB, November 2, 2006.

240 **should have ended their relationship that night:** *JD*, p. 111.

240 **"He was going to help me":** "The *Liberty* Interview: Barbara Branden," p. 55. Interview quote was altered slightly for grammatical correctness, at the request of the subject.

240 **"expand our circle":** *MYWAR*, p. 108.

241 **German and Polish Jew:** Justin

Martin, *Greenspan: The Man Behind the Money* (Cambridge, Mass.: Perseus, 2000), p. 3.

241 **"Alan had his own relationship with her":** From taped, unpublished interviews by journalist JW in preparation for a CBC special report on the tenth anniversary of AR's death, titled *Ideas: The Legacy of Ayn Rand* (1992).

241 **they dressed with care:** Author correspondence with Al Ramrus, March 1, 2007.

242 **"Is Roark idealistic":** *MYWAR,* p. 60.

242 **"total awe, as though I were on a different planet":** *Ideas and Action,* videotaped interview with LP by James Valliant, WJM Productions, August 5, 1995.

242 **her deepening interest in Nathaniel Branden:** In an author interview with two of NB's sisters and Jonathan Hirschfeld, a nephew, in Toronto in August 2006, Hirschfeld, who knew the group members well, said, "I think that, for her, the main draw was NB. I suspect that the rest of it happened and she participated and she cared, but she didn't need [a following]."

242 **"I've always seen [the Collective]:** BBTBI.

242 **at a pivotal point:** Rand was writing part III, chapter 2, "The Utopia of Greed" (Ayn Rand Papers, LOC, box 9, folder 4; begun November 6, 1951).

243 **the strain could cost her two or three days' work:** *TPOAR,* p. 255.

243 **"When I'm writing":** *JD,* p. 120.

243 **"What? What is it?":** Author interview with BB, November 2, 2006.

243 **politely raised their hands:** In and Out of Books, "Class of '43," p. 136.

243 **"It was the world of *Atlas Shrugged*":** Author interview with NB, August 10, 2004.

243 **returned to their new studio apartment:** *TPOAR,* p. 253–54.

243 **some of Nathaniel's relatives noticed:** Author interview with NB's sisters Florence Hirschfeld and EK, August 25, 2006. In a December 2005 interview, BB told the author that both NB's and LP's mothers were jealous of AR. "They knew that if [their sons] had to choose, they would probably choose Ayn."

244 **"he liked Ayn better than he liked her":** Author interview with Florence Hirschfeld, Jonathan Hirschfeld, and EK, August 25, 2006.

244 **165 East Thirty-fifth Street:** *MYWAR,* p. 100.

ELEVEN: THE IMMOVABLE MOVER: 1953–1957

245 **"Only the man who extols":** *AS,* p. 454.

245 **it hadn't yet splintered:** "Godless Capitalism," pp. 359–85.

245 **penthouse apartment of J. B. Matthews:** Author interview with William F. Buckley, Jr., June 12, 2006.

245 **reformed Communist fellow-traveler:** "J. B. Matthews, R.I.P.," *National Review,* August 9, 1966. Matthews is credited with having coined the phrase "fellow-traveler" (Margit von Mises, *My Years with Ludwig von Mises* [Bel Air, Calif.: Arlington House, 1984], p. 157).

246 **often stopped in at Matthews's:** "J. B. Matthews, R.I.P."

246 **first met McCarthy:** Author correspondence with BB, who was present, September 17, 2008.

246 **"Tell me your premises"**: *MYWAR,* p. 185.

246 **"singular"**: Author interview with WFB, June 13, 2006.

246 **"Mr. Buckley, you arrrr too intelligent"**: WFB, "Recollection of Ayn Rand," syndicated in the *Chicago Sun-Times,* March 13, 1982.

246 **"That certainly is an icebreaker"**: WFB, "Ayn Rand, R.I.P." *National Review,* April 2, 1982, p. 380.

246 **"I had just written a book about him"**: The book was *McCarthy and His Enemies: The Record and Its Meaning* (Washington, D.C.: Regnery Publishing, 1954).

246 **"an instantly communicable charm"**: Author interview with WFB, June 12, 2006.

246 **written in liturgical Latin, as a joke:** "Ayn Rand, R.I.P." p. 380.

246 **payback for earlier leftist allegations:** Discussed in Ralph Raico's taped speech, "Murray Rothbard, Ludwig von Mises, and Ayn Rand," Ludwig von Mises Institute lecture.

247 **"Oh, I see. The Big Lie"**: Author interview with JKT, May 21, 2004.

247 **told a young friend:** *100 Voices,* Susan Ludel, p. 412.

247 **"From an author who voted for him"**: *100 Voices,* Richard L. Phillips, p. 137.

247 **reportedly didn't vote:** According to a student's notes, LP told a class of philosophy students that Rand hadn't voted in either election; notes courtesy of MSC.

247 **Branden recalled her indignation:** *MYWAR,* pp. 117–18.

247 **"I was hard put to it when [Zhukor] insisted:** Quoted in "No Invitations, Please," *Time,* July 29, 1957.

247 **"the noblest, freest country"**: *MYWAR,* p. 118.

248 **newly appointed editor of *The Freeman:*** Beginning in 1950, AR's and IP's mutual friend Leonard Read financed *The Freeman* through the Foundation for Economic Education, a libertarian think tank he founded, based in Irvington, New York. By the early 1950s, AR had broken with him, too, over a "pernicious" pamphlet he published called *Roofs or Ceilings?* by Milton Friedman and George Stigler. Friedman, at that time a self-declared Keynesian, would become famous as an advocate of free markets, but he and AR continued to be at odds (Murray Rothbard, "Milton Friedman Unraveled," 1971, reprinted in *Journal of Libertarian Studies,* Fall 2002). At the height of Friedman's fame in 1979, they would appear on the same *Phil Donahue* show in May 1980.

248 **Frank Meyer and Willie Schlamm:** Interview with Bettina Bien Greaves, January 6, 2007.

248 **Mises, as he was known:** Though LVM would ordinarily be referred to as *von* Mises, his American admirers called him Mises.

248 **didn't see eye to eye:** George Reisman, "Reisman on Murray Rothbard, Ludwig von Mises, and Ayn Rand," speech presented to the Ludwig von Mises Institute.

248 **dinner party he and Frances gave in 1941 or 1942:** Unpublished letter from Henry Hazlitt to WFB, March 13, 1982, courtesy of Bettina Bien Greaves. Hazlitt, correcting Buckley's errors in the *National Review* obituary of AR, tells the story and sets the date as approximately 1942. Over the years, Hazlitt recalled different dates for the famous argument, ranging from the early 1940s to 1950 (unpublished inter-

views with Hazlitt by Mrs. Greaves, courtesy of Mrs. Greaves), but in all other details the narrative remained the same.

248 **assuming that they were arguing about the doctrine of natural rights:** Author interview with Bettina Bien Greaves, December 22, 2006; also "Books," *TON,* September 1963, p. 34.

249 **peace was restored:** Unpublished letter from Henry Hazlitt to WFB, March 13, 1982, courtesy of Bettina Bien Greaves.

249 **during one of Hazlitt's trips to Los Angeles:** Author correspondence with BB, June 24, 2008.

249 **"Did he really say *man*?":** Unpublished letter from Henry Hazlitt to WFB, March 13, 1982, courtesy of Bettina Bien Greaves.

249 **irritated by Mises's rejection of a moral . . . argument:** *MYWAR,* p. 116.

249 **"allowed normal human considerations":** *MYWAR,* p. 116.

249 **with the Brandens in attendance:** Author correspondence with BB, June 24, 2006.

249 **He liked to stop by her apartment:** Author interview with Richard Cornuelle, August 5, 2006.

249 **and helped him to promote his books:** Through the NBI Book Service.

249 **Cornuelle was half relieved:** Author interview with Richard Cornuelle, August 5, 2006.

250 **added embellishment that she wept:** That AR wept was a detail added by Frances Hazlitt, who was present at the dinner party, according to Bettina Bien Greaves, January 6, 2007.

250 **requesting a written denial:** NB wrote to LVM in response to a re-port that the conservative theorist Russell Kirk had told the story of "the silly little Jewish girl" during a lecture he gave at the University of Wisconsin in 1962. Unpublished letters from Winfred Blevins to NB, May 16, 1962, and from NB to LVM, June 20, 1962, both courtesy of Edward Hudgins.

250 **Mises, then in his eighties, complied:** Unpublished letter from LVM to Russell Kirk, July 5, 1962, courtesy of Edward Hudgins.

250 **immediately after Rand's death he wrote:** Unpublished letter from Henry Hazlitt to WFB, March 13, 1982, courtesy of Bettina Bien Greaves. In *The Passion of Ayn Rand's Critics,* James S. Valliant cites a 1950s letter from Hazlitt to Russell Kirk denying that the "Jewish girl" incident took place. The letter is in the ARI Archives, Valliant writes, and so I haven't seen it. I *have* seen the 1982 affirmative letter from Hazlitt to Buckley.

250 **"She felt no pity":** *AS,* p. 560.

251 **"all the years of ugliness":** *AS,* p. 702.

251 **Rothbard found the experience of paying court to her:** Letter from MR to Richard Cornuelle, August 11, 1954, quoted in Justin Raimondo, *An Enemy of the State* (Amherst, Mass.: Prometheus, 2000), p. 110.

251 **called themselves the Circle Bastiat:** The group was named after Claude Frédéric Bastiat, a nineteenth-century French political economist.

251 **The date was set for a Saturday evening:** The meetings took place on July 10 and July 17, 1954, according to George Reisman ("Reisman on Murray Rothbard, Ludwig von Mises, and Ayn Rand").

251 **arrayed on the sofa:** "Reisman on Murray Rothbard, Ludwig von Mises, and Ayn Rand."

252 **"the voice of Judgment":** "Reisman on Murray Rothbard, Ludwig von Mises, and Ayn Rand."

253 **"While I agreed":** Letter from MR to Richard Corneulle, August 11, 1954, quoted in *An Enemy of the State*, p. 110.

253 **"an enhanced sense of male power":** *JD*, p. 140.

253 **Heretofore apprehensive in his relationships:** Author interview with BB, July 1, 2008.

254 **would claim that he and Rand were still unaware:** Broadcast interview with NB by Ken Wilber, *Integral Naked* online, 2005.

254 **advised him, and also Barbara:** *JD*, p. 126.

254 **a capacity for sexual passion:** *JD*, p. 140.

254 **on Father's Day of 1951:** *JD*, p. 100.

254 **which is a perfect anagram:** Nora Ephron first pointed out the "ben Rand" connection in "A Strange Kind of Simplicity." NB and BB have frequently and strenuously denied that their chosen surname has anything to do with the last name of their mentor. BB has stated that she and NB chose the name from a New York City telephone book.

255 **jointly fielding questions:** Author correspondence with BB, June 24, 2008.

255 **They felt a degree of spiritual unity:** *MYWAR*, p. 121.

255 **he had never really contemplated:** Author interview with NB, August 10, 2004.

256 **"I am in love with you":** *JD*, pp. 142–47.

256 **Rand suggested that the affair:** *JD*, p. 153.

256 **"It was not named but it was felt":** *JD*, p. 154.

256 **Not so Barbara:** *MYWAR*, p. 133.

256 **"There is nothing in our feeling":** *TPOAR*, pp. 258–59.

256 **turned pale and looked downcast:** *JD*, p. 156; *TPOAR*, p. 259.

256 **We don't hold our values":** *JD*, p. 155.

257 **"No! I won't be part of this":** *TPOAR*, p. 259.

257 **only wanted to spend a little time together:** *JD*, p. 157.

257 **"With Ayn's mind":** "Passions: A Disciple Confronts Ayn Rand's Power," p. 1.

257 **series of conversations with their spouses:** *TPOAR*, p. 259.

257 **"You both know how little I've had":** *JD*, p. 159.

257 **"What we're asking for is temporary":** *JD*, p. 160.

257 **"the epitome and standard of the human potential":** "Passions: A Disciple Confronts Ayn Rand's Power," p. 1.

258 **approved of the affair:** *TPOARC*, pp. 135–41.

258 **"arouses his sexual desire":** August 28, 1949 (*JOAR*, p. 605).

258 **"On the right philosophical premise about sex":** October 6, 1949 (*JOAR*, p. 609; italics added).

258 **swore everyone to silence:** *TPOAR*, p. 272.

258 **"involve all four of us in a life of deception":** "It's a Dirty Job, But . . ."

258 **"an old woman pursuing a younger man":** *TPOAR*, p. 260.

259 **"If the four of us were of lesser stature":** *JD*, p. 160.

259 **"I'm amused that you condemned":** "Home Atmosphere."

259 **"Ayn frightened most people":** *JD*, pp. 158–61.

260 **drafted the first line of the**

speech: The opening page of "This Is John Galt Speaking" is dated July 4, 1953 (Ayn Rand Papers, LOC, box 11, folder 3).

260 **allotted roughly three months to its completion:** *TPOAR*, p. 266.

260 **"I swear by my life":** *AS*, pp. 670, 979.

260 **"a dramatized summation of the Objectivist ethics":** "The *Playboy* Interview: Ayn Rand," p. 38.

260 **"Just as there are no contradictions":** *AS*, pp. 939–40.

261 **It was while working on this famous section:** Author interview with BB, July 1, 2008.

261 **"drops-of-water-in-a-desert kind of torture":** *TPOAR*, p. 267.

261 **her favorite nightgown:** *Facets of Ayn Rand*, p. 34.

261 **for thirty-three days:** *WIAR*, p. 226.

261 **seeing no one but her husband:** *JD*, p. 177.

261 **nagged at O'Connor:** *MYWAR*, pp. 169, 189.

261 **pushed her to the limits of her endurance:** *TPOAR*, p. 267.

261 **tendencies became more marked:** *TPOAR*, pp. 267–70.

261 **"You are my reward for everything":** Author interview with NB, December 11, 2008.

261 **"A mind":** *JD*, p. 163.

261 **both Barbara and Frank:** *MYWAR*, pp. 168–69.

262 **felt both too large and too small:** *JD*, p. 218.

262 **"Do you think only of yourself?":** *TPOAR*, p. 277.

262 **"Why should *I* be victimized?":** JD, pp. 167–168.

262 **What's the matter with you?:** "It's a Dirty Job, But . . ."

262 **"Repression":** Ayn Rand, *The New Left: The Anti-Industrial Revolution* (New York: Signet, 1971), p. 62.

262 **"She became more than a stranger":** *MYWAR*, p. 169.

262 **She often phoned him:** "It's a Dirty Job, But . . ."

263 **"emotionalist":** *TPOAR*, p. 272.

263 **"You cannot imagine what a nightmare":** R. W. Bradford, "Ayn Rand and Her Movement: An Interview with Barbara Branden," *Liberty*, January 1990, pp. 7–8.

263 **anxiety as a crisis of self-esteem:** NB, *The Psychology of Self-Esteem* (Los Angeles, Nash Publishing, 1969), pp. 160–65.

263 **considered turning the theory into a book:** *MYWAR*, p. 147.

263 **began to offer therapy:** NB recalled that he charged five dollars an hour, beginning in the spring of 1955 (*JD*, p. 169).

263 **assertion that has been bitterly disputed:** *TPOAR*, p. 272, and *JD*, p. 166; *TPOARC*, p. 142. Because of its implications for the cruel effect of the affair on FO, the extent of his drinking has been a subject of controversy. The Brandens present evidence that FO drank alcoholically. AR's executor, LP, and other acquaintances dispute this. My research suggests that, at least toward the end of his life, FO drank heavily and secretly.

264 **"I confused loneliness":** Speech by NB, New York City, June 22, 1989; courtesy of Liberty Audio and Film Service, 2214 Hey Road, Richmond, VA 23224.

264 **"This affair is sexual":** *JD*, p. 217.

264 **"Where have you gone to?":** *MYWAR*, p. 142.

264 **he told himself:** *JD*, p. 163.

264 **"I never did, until things started showing at the seams":** Author interview with JMB and Allan Blumenthal, March 23, 2004.

264 **"Ayn wasn't very clean":** Taped in-

terview with Barbara Weiss, AR's secretary from the early 1960s until the late 1970s, conducted by BB, September 25, 1983.

264 **"In a world that was hurtling toward collectivism":** Author interview with Al Ramrus, March 5, 2007.

264 **"as though I were entering Atlantis":** Leonard Peikoff, "My Thirty Years with Ayn Rand," *The Voice of Reason,* p. 353.

265 **"She wanted us to discuss":** Author interview with EK, July 21, 2006.

265 **"like an old tank":** *Facets of Ayn Rand,* pp. 33, 39.

265 **aware of the author standing half hidden:** Author interview with Daryn Kent-Duncan, April 25, 2005.

265 **gave them the going wage:** *Facets of Ayn Rand,* p. 38; interview with Daryn Kent-Duncan, April 25, 2005.

265 **rent check slipped their minds:** Videotaped interview with Hank and Erica Holzer, AR's personal attorneys, 1965–70, by Duncan Scott, the Objectivist History Project, February 9, 2006.

265 **packets of fan letters arrived from Bobbs-Merrill:** Author interview with BB, October 14, 2007.

265 **"very good—to be answered":** Videotaped interview with Robert Hessen by Duncan Scott, OHP, November 10, 2004.

266 **Nickerson began to attend:** *100 Voices,* Kathleen and Richard Nickerson, p. 180.

266 **"spiritual bodyguard":** Author interview with NB, December 11, 2008.

266 **"desperately":** Author interview with Daryn Kent-Duncan, April 25, 2005.

266 **paid little attention to girls:** Author interviews with BB (October 14, 2007) and others.

267 **"devastating":** Author interview

with Daryn Kent-Duncan, April 25, 2005.

267 **"who neither agrees or disagrees":** *AS,* p. 971.

267 **"kangaroo courts":** Ayn Rand and Her Movement," p. 8.

267 **Peikoff was a particular target:** *MYWAR,* p. 158.

268 **"When she laid out her argument":** Author interview with BB, December 16, 2005.

268 **"The six months I had spent":** Author interview with Daryn Kent-Duncan, April 25, 2005.

268 **"he regards reason and emotion as antagonists":** *MYWAR,* p. 165.

268 **he who "pulled the trigger":** *MYWAR,* p. 172.

269 **that is, Albert Jay Nock's Remnant:** AR's returning strikers mirror Nock's Remnant of conservative true believers who will one day redeem the world, a tribute she may be slyly acknowledging when she writes, in John Galt's speech, "Whoever you are, you who are hearing me now, I am speaking to whatever living remnant is left uncorrupted within you, to the remnant of the human, your mind" (*AS,* p. 932).

TWELVE: *ATLAS SHRUGGED: 1957*

270 **"If anyone should ask me":** "The Goal of My Writing," *The Romantic Manifesto,* p. 172.

270 **"Those who are anti-business are anti-life":** Letter to John Chamberlain, November 27, 1948 (*LOAR,* p. 413).

271 **decided not to show the text:** *JD,* p. 201.

271 **"To the glory of mankind":** *AS,* p. 385.

271 **"the book is unsaleable and unpublishable":** *TPOAR,* p. 284.

271 **tripped over itself to court her:** TPOAR, p. 285.

271 **dozen companies phoned or wrote:** Reported by BC in a 1971 oral history interview from which his memoir At Random (1977) was taken; recorded by Robin Hawkins, 1968, for the Columbia University Oral History Project, Columbia University Rare Book and Manuscript Library, New York, used by permission of Christopher Cerf; number 719, p. 945.

272 **Bennett Cerf and Donald Klopfer, were Communists:** Words & Faces, p. 260. In his oral history interview, BC said that AR had explained to Hiram Haydn that, in Cerf's words, "her sycophants had told her that we were way over on the left" (p. 944). In TPOAR, BB writes that the novelist had long considered Random House to be a leftwing publisher (p. 285).

272 **"the exact replica":** Words & Faces, p. 257.

272 **she tolerated him [Hayden]:** Although "he would not have known it," BB recalled, "she didn't like him." In fact, "with a few exceptions, I can't remember her ever saying that she liked someone without adding a list of qualifications" (author correspondence with BB, June 26, 2008).

273 **lunch took place in the Trianon Room:** Words & Faces, p. 260.

273 **"an infinite number" of questions:** Bennett Cerf, At Random: The Reminiscences of Bennett Cerf (New York: Random House, 1977).

273 **was delighted with his answer:** Words & Faces, p. 261.

273 **"nobody is going to try to censor you":** At Random. BC later claimed that he meant he would publish anything she wrote as fiction.

273 **posthumously published memoir:**

At Random was edited by Christopher Cerf and published posthumously, based on BC's oral history interview on file at Columbia University's Oral History Project, number 719.

273 **"They spoke as I would want":** TPOAR, p. 286.

274 **To all of these terms the men agreed:** Internal memo, Bennett Cerf Collection, Columbia University Rare Book and Manuscript Library, box 57.

274 **should not exceed 600,000 words:** Letter to AR from BC (Bennett Cerf Collection, Columbia Rare Book and Manuscript Library, box 57).

274 **"This is life as it should be":** JD, p. 202.

274 **"They didn't pretend to be converted":** TPOAR, p. 288.

274 **"What I loved to do":** BC's oral history interview, p. 943.

275 **"she peers right through you":** BC's oral history interview, p. 944.

275 **"a remarkable woman":** Donald Klopfer, in an oral history interview on file at the Columbia University Oral History Project archives, number 1091, p. 79.

275 **a spell of bright optimism:** TPOAR, p. 290.

275 **"I am challenging the cultural tradition":** TPOAR, p. 294.

275 **"Whether or not the world":** Unpublished letter to AR from BB, August 29, 1951, courtesy of MSC.

275 **foresaw a renaissance of political liberty:** TPOAR, p. 294; author interview with NB, May 5, 2004.

275 **Alan Greenspan:** MYWAR, p. 167.

275 **He often said that Ayn Rand put the moral basis:** Author interview with JMB, March 23, 2004. "I was limited until I met her," Greenspan wrote in his 2007 memoir, The Age of Turbulence (New York: Penguin

Press). "Rand persuaded me to look at human beings, their values, how they work, what they do, and why they do it. . . . She introduced me to a vast realm from which I'd shut myself off" (p. 53).

276 **Until 2008:** *NYT,* October 23, 2008; *TON,* August 1963, p. 31.

276 **early months of 1957:** First draft of *AS* (Ayn Rand Papers, LOC, box 11, folders 10–12).

276 **he would slip away to paint:** *TPOAR,* p. 281; "Portrait of An Artist," p. 1.

276 **what she called his "exalted sense of life":** *Facets of Ayn Rand,* p. 119.

276 **"There were no historical influences at all in his work":** *WIAR,* p. 230. Since this book was written under AR's supervision and with her guidance, this view of FO's originality was almost surely hers.

276 **he enrolled in the Art Students League:** Author correspondence with Stephanie Cassidy, archivist, Art Students League; *Facets of Ayn Rand,* pp. 118–19.

276 **Robert Brackman and Robert Beverly Hale:** Author interview with Don Ventura, March 19, 2004.

276 **popular among the students:** McConnell, "Recollections of Ayn Rand I."

276 **women, particularly, admired his good looks:** *TPOAR,* p. 282.

276 **"I did not yet know about his drinking":** *MYWAR,* p. 162.

277 **Rand had honored her lover:** About becoming AR's "intellectual heir," NB said in 2004, "[Now] I don't know what it means, but I thought I did then. I guess it meant 'the anointed one to carry on the tradition,' 'the keeper of the flame' " (author interview with NB, May 5, 2004).

277 **"The idea of the greatest literary masterpiece":** *MYWAR,* p. 194.

277 **didn't occur to him until later:** *MYWAR,* pp. 176–77.

277 **limit his freedom:** Author interview with NB, April 6, 2008.

277 **"my manifesto, my profession of faith":** Unpublished letter to Newman Flower, January 2, 1938 (quoted in *EOA,* p. 71).

278 **had best-seller stamped all over it:** *Words & Faces,* p. 261.

278 **"contextual absolutism" and "contextualism":** Rand also used the word *opsolitism* to describe her philosophy in a 1961 speech at the University of Michigan.

278 **"showed us how to live without truth":** Norman Podhoretz, "Intellectuals and Writers, Then and Now," *Partisan Review,* Fall 2002 (vol. 69, no. 4), pp. 507–40.

279 **"One word leads to another!":** "Ayn Rand and *Atlas Shrugged,*" recorded speech by BB, Cato Institute, Washington, D.C., October 6, 2007.

279 **the last recorded concerto of Richard Halley:** Halley's Fifth Concerto was inspired by love songs from Boris Godunov, according to follower Howard Odzer (*100 Voices,* Howard Odzer, p. 191–92).

279 **"drab" prose style and core ideas:** *Words & Faces,* p. 262.

279 **"Nobody's going to read that [speech]":** BC's oral history interview on file at the Columbia University Oral History Project archives (number 719, p. 950.)

279 **to pay for the additional paper:** Unpublished letter to AR from BC, May 9, 1957, Bennett Cerf Collection, Columbia Rare Book and Manuscript Library, box 57.

279 **"an obsession with her":** *Words & Faces,* p. 261.

280 **"They were putting a great deal [of money]":** Unpublished taped

interview with Bertha Krantz, conducted by BB, September 20, 1983.

281 **"a slave to the image she built"**: Unpublished taped interview with Bertha Krantz, conducted by BB, September 20, 1983.

281 **A few months before *Atlas Shrugged*:** BC's oral history interview, p. 948.

282 **"Metaphysics: objective reality"**: *TPOAR*, p. 294.

282 **presented packages to Rand:** *TPOAR*, p. 295.

282 **"This is John Galt"**: *TPOAR*, p. 296.

282 **"That's us!"**: *TPOAR*, p. 294.

282 **old nemesis from the 1930s, Granville Hicks:** By 1957, Hicks had left the Communist Party. In the *Times,* he was identified as a literary consultant to *The New Leader,* a biweekly magazine published by the American Labor Conference on International Affairs.

282 **"howl" by a harpy:** Granville Hicks, "A Parable of Buried Talents," *NYT,* October 13, 1957, p. 266.

282 **"where it's equally easy to hate both sides"**: Earl P. Brown, "From the U.S.A.," *Washington Post,* October 13, 1957, p. E6.

283 **compared her ideas on mysticism to those of Hitler:** Earl Wagenknecht, "As Thriller or Parable, Novel Is Absorbing," *Chicago Daily Tribune,* October 13, 1957, p. B1.

283 **"Is it a novel? Is it a nightmare?"**: "The Solid-Gold Dollar Sign," *Time,* October 14, 1957.

283 **"display of grotesque eccentricity"**: Robert R. Kirsch, "The Book Report," *Los Angeles Times,* October 15, 1957, p. B5.

283 **"the globe's two billion or so incompetents"**: Donald Malcolm, "The New Rand Atlas," *The New Yorker,* October 26, 1957, pp. 194–96.

283 **"crackbrained ratiocination"**: "Come the Revolution," *Atlantic Monthly,* November 1957, pp. 249–50.

283 **ambition and intellectual intensity:** John Chamberlain, "Ayn Rand's Political Parable and Thundering Melodrama," *New York Herald Tribune,* October 15, 1957, section 6, p. 1.

283 **"Ayn Rand is destined to rank in history"**: *TPOAR,* p. 298.

283 **"I am now able to say it"**: Unpublished letter to AR from William C. Mullendore, William C. Mullendore Papers, Herbert Hoover Presidential Library, Subject Series, box 23, folder "Ayn Rand."

283 **"a cogent analysis of the evils"**: Unpublished letter from LVM, January 23, 1958, courtesy of Bettina Bien Greaves.

283 **"No one writes about the bureaucrats the way Ayn Rand does"**: Author interview with Bettina Bien Greaves, December 22, 2006.

284 **"we thought that we were going to be hooked"**: BC's oral history interview, p. 945.

284 **partly in an attempt:** "Godless Capitalism," pp. 359–85.

284 **"To a gas chamber—go!"**: Whittaker Chambers, "Big Sister Is Watching You," *National Review,* December 28, 1957, p. 120.

285 **"is not, and by its essential nature cannot conceivably be"**: Whittaker Chambers, *Odyssey of a Friend: Whittaker Chambers' Letters to William F. Buckley, Jr.,* 1969, pp. 227–28, cited in "Godless Capitalism," p. 375.

285 **She had expected attacks:** AR claimed never to have read the Whittaker Chambers review of *AS* (*LOAR,* p. 572) but to have been told about it by others.

285 **Anguished, she asked Barbara:** *TPOAR,* p. 304.

285 **"even earlier than I imagined":** *MYWAR,* p. 203.

285 **Paterson sent an indignant letter:** *The Woman and the Dynamo,* p. 351.

285 **if so, she refused to go:** Author interview with WFB, June 12, 2006.

285 **lampooned her:** William F. Buckley, Jr., *Getting It Right* (Washington, D.C.: Regnery Publishing, 2003).

286 **"I believe she died under the impression":** Author interview with WFB, June 12, 2006.

286 **thought that he had been drinking:** *MYWAR,* p. 201.

286 **"She was a valiant human being":** Author interview with WFB, June 12, 2006.

286 **confused its author's increasingly authoritarian personality:** *TPOAR,* p. 302.

286 **"To hear a woman":** "Ayn Rand and *Atlas Shrugged."*

286 **"Her personal bitterness was at odds with her philosophy":** "An Interview with Barbara Branden," p. 8.

286 **ascended to number five:** "Best Seller List," *NYT Book Review,* October 27, 1957, p. 4.

286 **Five years after its first printing:** TON, December 1962 (vol. 1, no. 12), p. 47.

287 **150,000 copies a year:** Author correspondence with Richard Ralston, publishing manager of ARI, March 3, 2004.

287 **the intelligent common man:** Author interview with JKT, May 21, 2004.

287 **"the largely abandoned class":** Claudia Roth Pierpont, "Twilight of the Goddess," *The New Yorker,* July 24, 1995, p. 76.

288 **Other notes identify:** JOAR, pp. 706–716.

288 **She would resume musing:** "Two Possible Books," November 30, 1957, and February 10, 1959 (*JOAR,* pp. 706–11).

288 **organized a letter-writing campaign:** "In and Out of Books: Class of '43," p. 136.

288 **"We were all strongly encouraged":** Author interview with EK, NB's sister, on July 21, 2006.

288 **wrote to *The New York Times*:** "Letters to the Editor," *NYT,* November 3, 1957, p. 283.

288 **lacked compassion and "proceeds from hate":** Patricia Donegan, "A Point of View," *Commonweal,* November 8, 1957, p. 156.

288 **he pointed out:** "Communications," *Commonweal,* December 20, 1957, p. 313.

288 **Leonard Peikoff, Daryn Kent, and . . . John Chamberlain:** "Letters to the Editor," *National Review,* January 18, 1958, p. 71.

288 **canceling subscriptions to *Time*:** *100 Voices,* Kathleen Nickerson, p. 181.

288 **Her life's mission to create:** December 15, 1960 (*JOAR,* p. 704).

288 **"She had left Galt's Gulch":** "Ayn Rand and Her Movement," p. 7.

289 **"Ayn had disappeared into [the] alternate reality":** *MYWAR,* p. 195.

289 **"Something was gone":** "Interview with Nathaniel Branden," p. 6.

289 **"What kind of world is this?":** *MYWAR,* p. 205.

289 **"I felt like my job was to protect her":** Author interview with NB, May 5, 2004.

289 **"one part of my destiny":** *MYWAR,* p. 194.

289 **"With my lecture course":** Author interview with NB, May 5, 2004.

289 **she didn't want to give her enemies an opportunity:** Author interview with Robert Hessen, October 17, 2007.

289 **Bennett Cerf and Hiram Haydn pled a shortage of time:** Unpublished taped interview of Bertha Krantz by BB, dated September 20, 1983.

289 **mentioned the author's name in the first line of copy:** Circular advertising NB's first lecture series, Hiram Haydn correspondence, Bennett Cerf Collection, Columbia University Rare Book and Manuscript Library, box 436.

290 **"she-messiah":** "Born Eccentric," *Newsweek*, March 27, 1961.

290 **"We [are] like Siamese twins":** *MYWAR*, pp. 121–22.

THIRTEEN: THE PUBLIC PHILOSOPHER: 1958–1963

291 **"My personal life is a postscript to my novels":** "About the Author," *AS*, p. 107.

291 **"hangers-on," "brown-nosers":** From BC's oral history interview on file at the Columbia University Oral History Project archives, number 719, conducted by Mary R. Hawkins, 1971, pp. 903–952.

291 **"the very whining, toadying quality":** *Words & Faces*, p. 258.

292 **"If anyone can pick a single rational flaw":** Mike Wallace, "Should the Strong Inherit the Earth?" *NYP*, December 9, 1957, ghosted by Edith Efron.

292 **Barbara and Nathaniel persuaded her:** Author correspondence with BB, June 27, 2008.

292 **gave a lecture called "Faith and Force":** "Ayn Rand as a Public Speaker."

292 **At Brooklyn College:** In April 1958; "Ayn Rand as a Public Speaker."

292 **"I was awed by the power":** *100 Voices*, Fred Feingersh, p. 176.

293 **"Why Human Beings Repress and Drive Underground":** NBI flyer, September 1964, courtesy of Lee Clifford.

293 **"Lectures on Objectivism":** Advertisement, *NYT*, October 7, 1962, p. X4.

293 **attendance rose steadily:** *MYWAR*, p. 206.

293 **During the question periods:** *TPOAR*, p. 329.

293 **"every word, every sentence was magic":** "Interview with Henry Mark Holzer," p. 6.

293 **enlisted Alan Greenspan:** *TPOAR*, p. 307.

294 **By popular demand:** *100 Voices*, Kathleen Nickerson, p. 181. AR's lectures on plot, theme, characterization, and style were recorded, transcribed, edited, and, in 2000, published as *The Art of Fiction*.

294 **began in early 1958:** *100 Voices*, Larry Abrams, p. 194.

294 **For six months:** *100 Voices*, Larry Abrams, footnote, p. 194.

294 **if self-referential:** In another example of her tendency toward self-reference, during an NBI question-and-answer period she mentioned that her favorite painting was Salvador Dali's *Crucifixion*. Students, who all knew that she was an atheist, were confused. She explained that the Christ in the painting reminded her of Galt on the torture device at the end of *AS* (*100 Voices*, Allan Gotthelf, p. 330).

294 **critique the very passages:** *TPOAR*, p. 278; *100 Voices*, Kathleen Nickerson, p. 183.

294 **"Good Copy":** "Good Copy" appears in *TEAR*, p. 56.

294 **"she began to shout in outrage":** *TPOAR*, p. 278.

295 **"a philosophy for living on earth"**: "Philosophy: Who Needs It," *The Ayn Rand Letter,* January 14, 1974 (vol. 3, no. 8), p. 284.

295 **while researching a New York newspaper interview:** This was the *NYP* interview in which AR suggested that she was the world's most creative philosopher. At that time, Wallace had not yet met or talked to her.

295 **"spouting these strange ideas":** Author interview with Al Ramrus, March 1, 2007.

295 **Two days later, along came:** Author correspondence with Al Ramrus, March 19, 2007.

295 **"was hugely impressed":** Author interview with Al Ramrus, March 1, 2007.

295 **"was inspiring and, by example, empowering":** Author correspondence with Al Ramrus, March 14, 2007.

295 **joined the circle surrounding Rand:** Author interview with Al Ramrus, March 1, 2007.

295 **obtained early copies of *Atlas Shrugged*:** OHP interview with Robert Hessen, November 10, 2004.

296 **"since [Ayn's followers] all have":** Unpublished letter from MR to Richard Cornuelle, August 11, 1954, quoted in *Radicals for Capitalism,* p. 261.

296 **"the greatest novel ever written":** Unpublished letter from MR to AR, October 3, 1957, copy courtesy of Justin Raimondo.

297 **He also entered into a course of psychotherapy with Branden:** "Ayn Rand and Her Movement," pp. 3, 8.

297 **On the basis of such assurances:** Unpublished letter from MR to NB, July 15, 1958, courtesy of Justin Raimondo.

297 **considered him to be an established genius:** *MYWAR,* p. 97.

298 **"Nathan was everybody's therapist":** "Ayn Rand and Her Movement," pp. 7, 8.

298 **would get one in 1973:** In 1973, NB received his Ph.D. in psychology from the unaccredited California Graduate Institute. In an interview, NB explained that, once settled in California, he opted to obtain a California license to practice marriage and family counseling rather than apply for the "super, super, super tough" license to practice psychotherapy. As a result, he said, he cannot refer to himself in print as a psychologist; "The *Liberty* Interview: Nathaniel Branden Speaks," *Liberty,* September 1999 (vol. 13, no. 9), pp. 41–42.

298 **He had applied for:** Jeff Walker, *The Ayn Rand Cult* (Chicago: Open Court, 1999), p. 156.

298 **obtain certification in New Jersey:** Unpublished letter from MR to Kenneth Templeton, September 3, 1958, courtesy of Justin Raimondo; *The Ayn Rand Cult,* pp. 156–58; "The *Liberty* Interview: Nathaniel Branden Speaks," p. 41.

298 **pressure on Rothbard intensified:** Murray Rothbard, "My Break with Nathaniel Branden and the Rand Cult," *Liberty,* September 1989, p. 30; *An Enemy of the State,* pp. 125–26.

298 **Educational events were augmented:** "My Break with Nathaniel Branden and the Rand Cult," p. 27; *100 Voices,* Howard Odzer, p. 191.

298 **"Why is it you don't see us more often?":** "My Break with Nathaniel Branden and the Rand Cult," p. 29.

299 **"Those parties were very hierarchical":** Author interview with Ed Nash, January 6, 2005.

299 **"They were absolutely a nightmare"**: Author interview with BB, December 16, 2005.

299 **Once, Rand bought a new dining room table**: *100 Voices,* Shelly Reuben, p. 373.

299 **tragic, "malevolent" Beethoven**: Author interview with JMB and Dr. Allan Blumenthal, March 23, 2004.

299 **she described Brahms as "worthless"**: Author correspondence with BB, June 26, 2008.

299 **rushed to give away his collection**: He gave them to EK (author interview with EK, July 21, 2006).

299 **When not in his studio painting**: *100 Voices,* Al Ramrus, p. 163.

299 **Rothbard gave Branden a copy**: Unpublished letter from MR to Helmut Schoeck, August 30, 1958, courtesy of Justin Raimondo.

299 **Helmut Schoeck, a well-known scholar**: Schoeck is best remembered for his 1969 book *Envy: A Theory of Social Behaviour.* In it, he examined one of AR's lifelong preoccupations, envy, and defined it as "a drive which lies at the core of man's life as a social being." AR made marginal notes in her copy of the book, to the effect that envy is the characteristic of a second-hander, not a universal force that governs the social order (Helmut Schoeck, *Envy: A Theory of Social Behaviour* [Indianapolis, Ind.: Liberty Fund, 1987]; Robert Mayhew, ed., *Ayn Rand's Marginalia* [Irvine, Calif.: Second Renaissance, 1995]), p. 98.

300 **one from Rand's attorney Pincus Berner**: Mentioned in an unpublished letter from Helmut Schoeck to James Wiggins, August 13, 1958, courtesy of Justin Raimondo.

300 **The paper, titled**: Rothbard, "The Mantle of Science," unpublished paper prepared for the symposium Scientism and the Study of Man, 1958, courtesy of Justin Raimondo.

300 **based on Rand's fallacy of the stolen concept**: An example of "the stolen concept" frequently cited by Rand is the attempt to negate reason by means of reason (*Introduction to Objectivist Ethics* [New York: New American Library, 1989], p. 81).

301 **"Prior to our break with him"**: *MYWAR,* p. 231.

301 **Rand's habit of self-promotion**: Unpublished letter from Helmut Schoeck to James Wiggins, August 13, 1958; letter from LVM to MR, July 22, 1958. Both courtesy of Justin Raimondo.

301 **discovered what it felt like to be someone**: Unpublished letter from George Reisman to Ralph Raico, July 25, 1958, courtesy of Justin Raimondo.

301 **He remained loyal to organized Objectivism**: MR later wrote extensively about the rise and fall of the AR movement. A few years before he died, he published "My Break with Nathaniel Branden and the Rand Cult," which gives a blow-by-blow account of his version of events. Earlier, in an essay called "The Sociology of the Ayn Rand Cult" (1972; reprinted by the Center for Libertarian Studies, 1990), he analyzed AR's appeal.

301 **later described his single therapeutic session**: *The Ayn Rand Cult,* pp. 145–46; author interview with Robert Hessen, October 17, 2007.

301 **watched Branden pace the room like a panther**: "I'd rather have gone into therapy with Stalin," Hessen told Duncan Scott of the OHP; author interview with Robert Hessen, November 2, 2007.

301 **went to work as Rand's part-time personal secretary:** "The Genesis of a Great Gift," Robert Hessen's introduction to the auction catalog "The Papers of Ayn Rand," Bonhams and Butterfield, November 18, 1998.

301 **She purged him, too:** OHP, Robert Hessen, November 10, 2004.

301 **she established the atmosphere:** Author interview with Shelly Reuben, November 19, 2007.

302 **"She was very controversial":** OHP, Robert Hessen, November 10, 2004.

302 **to declare their agreement:** John Lobler, "The Curious Cult of Ayn Rand," p. 101. A 1964 NBI brochure stated that the lectures are addressed exclusively to those who have read *TF, AS,* and *FTNI,* are in agreement with the essentials of the philosophy presented in these books, and seek an amplification (NBI brochure, 1964).

302 **"I went to a [lecture] once":** Unpublished taped interview with Bertha Krantz, conducted by BB, September 30, 1983.

302 **gave up her job as a junior editor:** Earlier, Barbara had worked for Archibald Ogden at RKO in New York.

302 **"If one considers that Ayn was God":** "Ayn Rand and Her Movement," p. 8.

302 **"the most beautiful woman in the world":** Author interview with Don Ventura, March 19, 2004.

302 **"I learned repression":** TPOAR, pp. 243, 304–305.

302 **"the greatest human being":** MYWAR, p. 226.

303 **struck her as well meaning:** BBTBI.

303 **"I saw her change":** Author interview with JKT, May 21, 2004.

303 **"I thought that my fans disappointed and depressed me":** http://www.solopassion.com/node/1257.

303 **At first, no one noticed:** MYWAR, p. 209.

303 **arrived by the hundreds every week:** About two hundred; OHP, Robert Hessen, November 10, 2004.

304 **stopped giving lectures on college campuses:** AR seems to have made no college appearances between mid-1958 and 1960; "Ayn Rand as a Public Speaker."

304 **"I cannot fight lice":** MYWAR, p. 211.

304 **spent hours playing solitaire:** "The *Liberty* Interview: Barbara Branden," p. 51.

304 **"John Galt wouldn't feel this":** "An Interview with Barbara Branden," p. 8.

304 **"I would hate for him to see me like this":** MYWAR, p. 213. In private notes from 1968, excerpted in Valliant's TPOARC, AR writes that during this period she experienced "self-protective withdrawal—and I realized that this is a state without any use for one's mind or rational faculty."

305 **carrying a jar of Dexedrine:** Dr. Allan Blumenthal recalled that AR took Dexedrine, an amphetamine, in the 1950s and 1960s. BB has mentioned that she took Dexamyl (TPOAR, p. 173), a combination of Dexedrine and amobarbital, a barbiturate.

305 **"Oh, these are for Ayn":** Author interview with Roger J. Callahan, November 4, 2003. There were other rumors over the years. For example, in February 1969, a person close to AR and the Brandens wrote a concerned letter to Barbara about rumors that the novelist's doctor was upping her dose.

305 **"she'd take another two":** Jeff Walker, "Ayn Rand, Objectivism and

All That," an interview with Roy A. Childs, Jr., *Liberty*, April 1993, p. 33.·

305 **"She *was* wired up":** Author interview with Robert Hessen, October 17, 2007.

305 **"as well as Swiss chocolates":** Author correspondence with BB, June 26, 2008.

305 **Joan Blumenthal recalled that Rand:** Author interview with JMB and Dr. Allan Blumenthal, March 23, 2004.

305 **"always had a very elevated pulse rate":** Author interview with JMB and Dr. Allan Blumenthal, September 2, 2004.

305 **the telltale symptoms of suspicion:** Everett H. Ellinwood, George King, and Tong H. Lee, "Chronic Amphetamine Use and Abuse," in Floyd Bloom and Donald Kupfer, eds., *Psychopharmacology: The Fourth Generation of Progress* (Nashville, Tenn.: American College of Neuropsychopharmacology, 2000).

305 **"The atmosphere was like that of a hospital":** Author interview with NB, May 5, 2004.

305 **withdrew into his painting:** *MYWAR*, p. 212.

305 **some of which she sometimes conceded:** BBTBI.

305 **"You are my lifeline":** *MYWAR*, p. 210.

305 **"disappearing professor" act:** *TPOARC*, RPJ, July 4, 1968, p. 323.

305 **"he had always been arrogant":** *TPOAR*, p. 304.

306 **"If all of you who look at me":** "Ideal," *Three Plays*, p. 177.

306 **She was paralyzed by disgust:** *TPOAR*, pp. 302–3.

306 **"Thinking is all I do":** *JD*, p. 240.

306 **able to renew their intimacy:** *TPOAR*, p. 304; *MYWAR*, p. 219.

307 **She was never fastidious:** According to RBH, AR's friend from Chatsworth, California, NB approached BB and "asked her to ask AR to 'clean up her act,' though it wasn't her act he wanted cleaned up." RBH claimed to have heard this from BB, with whom she became friendly in the 1980s and 1990s. According to RBH, BB confided that "NB found her physically—unclean, not clean"; author interview with RBH, June 8, 2005. When asked if this story was true, Barbara replied, "No comment."

307 **"I needed all of my resources":** *MYWAR*, p. 219.

307 **"How is it possible that we can be accused":** *MYWAR*, p. 209.

307 **"it was more and more true":** Author interview with NB, August 10, 2004.

308 **"the founder of a new and unusual philosophy":** *The Mike Wallace Interview*, February 25, 1959.

308 **told the same story to both Brandens:** The untruth that AR told to Wallace and the Brandens "is puzzling," said BB in 2007 (author correspondence with BB, 2007).

309 **Mr. Branden had received six hundred letters:** *The Mike Wallace Interview*, February 25, 1959.

309 **dumbfounded that Wallace had devoted half an hour:** Author interview with Al Ramrus, March 1, 2007.

309 **"Most of the media":** Author interview with Al Ramrus, March 1, 2007.

309 **enjoyed the interview and admired her courage:** Author interview with Mike Wallace, February 15, 2007.

309 **"I remember with amusement her haircut":** *100 Voices*, Mike Wallace, p. 156.

309 **he and she dined together:** Author interview with Mike Wallace, February 15, 2007.

309 **"creature who sat on her shoul-**

der": Author interview with Mike Wallace, February 15, 2007.

309 **"slavish followers":** Author interview with Mike Wallace, February 15, 2007.

310 **received an advance copy of the novel:** Also, like MR, JKT initially had an adverse reaction to NB. "When I first met Nathan at Ayn's, my immediate reaction to him was that he might be a wife-swapper in some sense. But then I said, ah, no" (Karen Reedstrom, "Interview with Joan Kennedy Taylor," *Full Context,* October 1993, p. 4).

310 **"when the whole world wanted her attention":** Author interview with JKT, May 21, 2004.

310 **"I think she was kinder to people":** "Interview with Joan Kennedy Taylor," p. 3.

310 **"she respected creative people":** Author interview with JKT, May 21, 2004.

310 **didn't want to compose atonal music:** "Interview with Joan Kennedy Taylor," p. 3.

310 **pulled up chairs and listened to their conversation:** *100 Voices,* Mickey Spillane, p. 232.

311 **loved the fact that Spillane's potboiling plots:** BBTBI.

311 **"Grays don't interest me":** "The Curious Cult of Ayn Rand," p. 100.

311 **the *Los Angeles Times* and in other forums:** In her private lectures on the art of writing, she often mentioned him as a favorable example of descriptive writing and use of slang. In her short-lived weekly column of commentary in the *Los Angeles Times,* she devoted a column to his writing, beginning with the sentence, "Mickey Spillane is one of the best writers of our time" ("The Ayn Rand Column," *Los Angeles Times,* September 2, 1962).

311 **following their joint appearance:** The broadcast aired on October 11, 1961; no videotape seems to have survived.

311 **threw back her head and laughed:** Author interview with Al Ramrus, February 7, 2007.

311 **They formed a mutual admiration society:** Spillane also met Rand's followers. "I was never at her place when they weren't there," he told an interviewer. "Every time one of us would talk, all [their] heads would follow that person" (*100 Voices,* Mickey Spillane, pp. 235–38).

311 **"Ayn Rand and I, we don't have to shrug":** *100 Voices,* Mickey Spillane, pp. 235–38.

311 **"vicious injustice on the part of the 'intellectuals' ":** "The Ayn Rand Column," *Los Angeles Times,* September 2, 1962.

311 **"moral cannibals":** *AS,* p. 928.

311 **Rand paid for her hotel:** Letter to Vera Glarner, née Guzarchik, March 2, 1962 (*LOAR,* p. 595).

312 **deeply impressed by their American cousin's fame:** *100 Voices,* Lisette Hassanil, pp. 257–59.

312 **Rand wrote that she missed her:** Letter to Vera Glarner, August 4, 1962 (*LOAR,* p. 599).

312 **hosted a radio program:** "Interview with Joan Kennedy Taylor," p. 3. The station was WEVD, New York.

312 **didn't comment on Nabokov's lurid subject:** In a March 1964 *Playboy* interview, AR told Alvin Toffler that she regarded Nabokov as a brilliant stylist but that his subjects and "sense of life" were evil; "The *Playboy* Interview: Ayn Rand," p. 40.

312 **"Oh, Nabokov!":** Author interview with JKT, May 21, 2004.

312 **never contacted his sister Olga:** Brian Boyd, *Vladimir Nabokov: The*

American Years (Princeton, N.J.: Princeton University Press, 1991), p. 388. Interestingly, Boyd describes a speech Nabokov gave at Cornell in 1958 in which he reenacted a love scene from Fyodor Gladkov's 1930s Russian industrial novel *Energiya*, about the building of a Russian dam, in which the hero confesses love to the heroine while operating a pneumatic drill. "Social Realism's ideal love scene—boy and girl with pneumatic drill," Boyd quotes Nabokov as saying gleefully (p. 360).

312 **"She was very, um, cautious":** Author interview with JKT, May 21, 2004.

312 **Mannheimer turned up in New York:** Author interview with BB, June 9, 2006. NB didn't remember seeing Mannheimer as a client but thought that sending the screenwriter to him "sounded like something Ayn would do"; author interview with NB, April 3, 2008.

312 **appearing anxious, stiff, and visibly frightened:** Author interview with BB, June 9, 2006.

312 **having seen almost nothing of Rand:** Author interview with BB, June 9, 2006.

312 **fatally shot himself:** Obituaries, *Variety*, March 15, 1972.

313 **"Too bad":** Author interview with Joan Blumenthal, October 10, 2007.

313 **saw little of Frances and Henry:** Karen Reedstrom, "Interview with Erika Holzer," *Full Context*, February 1996, p. 3.

313 **struck her as a betrayal:** Author interview with BB, October 12, 2007.

313 **never had a good word to say:** Author interview with BB, December 16, 2005.

313 **the sensation she created:** Author interview with Bettina Bien Greaves, December 22, 2006.

313 **Mises's eightieth-birthday party:** William Henry Chamberlain, "Ludwig von Mises at 80," *Wall Street Journal*, October 20, 1961, p. 10; *My Years with Ludwig von Mises*, p. 163. The party was held at the University Club of New York.

313 **"LSD steps up our voltage":** Quoted in *Radicals for Capitalism*, p. 280.

313 **editing a quasi-religious libertarian magazine:** *Radicals for Capitalism*, p. 276.

313 **"Whenever I wrote anything":** Interview with Thaddeus Ashby, conducted by Wendy de Weese, June 20, 2005.

314 **she attended the awards ceremony and enjoyed herself:** Author interview with JKT, May 21, 2004.

314 **three million copies in print:** *EOWTL*, p. 143. Oddly, in spite of the fact that the cold war was at its height and that two years earlier Khrushchev had disclosed the mass killings committed by Stalin at about the time *WTL* had first been published, the reissued novel attracted little attention. The hardback edition seems to have been reviewed only in the *Miami Herald* and the *Detroit Jewish News* (*EOWTL*, p. 151).

314 **advertising reply card for NBI:** The reply card was the brainstorm of Robert Hessen, at that time a graduate student at Columbia University and part-time employee of NBI. Hessen recalls one evening in 1961 or 1962 when AR and NB assembled the Collective and a few other Objectivists to bawl them out for not contributing enough to the advancement of AR's philosophy. They named Hessen as an example to the contrary, praising his ideas for the reply card, the book service, and the soon-to-be-launched tape tran-

scription service; "I was mortified." Author interview with Robert Hessen, October 17, 2007.

314 **most expensive paperback ever sold:** TPOAR, p. 299.

314 **NAL republished Anthem:** The NAL edition of Anthem was published in September 1961. By late 1963, there were five hundred thousand copies of Anthem in print ("Objectivist Calendar," TON, January 1962 and November 1963, pp. 1, 41).

314 **Participants arrived once a week:** Author interview with Florence Hirschfeld, Jonathan Hirschfeld, and EK, August 25, 2006.

314 **each paying half the New York rate:** NBI flyer, September 1964, courtesy of Lee Clifford.

314 **gave readings of Rand's plays:** "Objectivist Calendar," TON, October 1963 and May 1965, p. 22.

314 **wrote proudly of having aided Rand's transformation:** MYWAR, p. 237.

315 **it was the buzz and growing influence:** http://www.solopassion.com/node/1257.

315 **"infinitely more rational":** BBTBI.

315 **"whole enormous response to Nathan":** http://www.solopassion.com/node/1257.

315 **"I hate bitterness":** MYWAR, p. 251.

315 **"I'm inclined to think, in the end, no":** Author interview with NB, May 5, 2004.

FOURTEEN: ACCOUNT
OVERDRAWN: 1962–1967

317 **"It does not matter that only a few in each generation":** Introduction to TF, p. xii.

317 **Yale Law School's prestigious**

Challenge series: The lecture took place on February 17, 1960.

317 **In a car on the way to New Haven:** TPOAR, p. 315.

317 **the New Haven Symphony Orchestra:** "Down with Altruism," Time, February 29, 1960.

317 **thought of Yale as a breeding ground for liberals:** Author interview with Robert Hessen, October 17, 2007; TPOAR, p. 315.

318 **the overflow was so great:** From an unpublished 1984 tribute to AR by Larry Scott, who was a Yale student at the time of AR's speech; courtesy of MSC.

318 **"Young man: the janitors!":** TPOAR, p. 316.

318 **several times interrupted by applause:** Ed Barthelmes, "First mailed copy" for Time article ("Personal newspaper clippings 1916–1960," Isabel Paterson Papers, Herbert Hoover Presidential Library, box 6).

318 **"Do not confuse altruism":** "Faith and Force: Destroyers of the Modern World," reprinted in Philosophy: Who Needs It (New York: Bobbs-Merrill, 1982).

318 **a revealing anecdote:** Ed Barthelmes, "First mailed copy" for Time article.

318 **she said that she hated speaking:** Author correspondence with BB, June 17, 2008.

318 **"As an advocate of reason, freedom":** The speech, delivered at the Ford Hall Forum on March 26, 1961, was titled "The Intellectual Bankruptcy of Our Age"; a version appears in The Voice of Reason, Leonard Peikoff, ed. (New York: New American Library, 1989); quote is from AR, p. 94.

319 **"radical for capitalism":** "Conservatism: An Obituary" was delivered at Princeton University on Decem-

ber 7, 1960, and was reprinted in *Capitalism, the Unknown Ideal.*

319 **nearly twice as many students:** "Ayn Rand as a Public Speaker."

319 **addressed an overflow audience in Ferris Booth Hall:** The speech was "Faith and Force: Destroyers of the Modern World," delivered at Columbia University, May 5, 1960. ·

319 **"That's when I was struck":** Unpublished taped interview of Bertha Krantz by BB, dated September 20, 1983.

319 **at the University of Michigan:** On May, 15, 1961, the University of Michigan filmed a postlecture interview with AR on the subject of "The New Intellectual." "The man who defines the basic, fundamental ideas of a culture is the man who determines history," she told the interviewer, a professor of philosophy.

319 **Boston University, Brown, Purdue:** "Ayn Rand as a Public Speaker."

319 **she gave a lecture entitled "The Objectivist Ethics":** AR gave this lecture at the University of Wisconsin on February 9, 1961. (Quotes are from *TVOS*, pp. 13–39.)

320 **from as far away as Africa:** *100 Voices,* Frances Smith, president of the Ford Hall Forum, p. 222.

320 **even the night before:** Author correspondence with BB, June 27, 2008.

320 **exchange ideas, news, and gossip:** Author interview with Molly Hays, February 29, 2004.

320 **on WBAI-FM:** Together and separately, AR and NB taped radio programs for WBAI from 1961 to 1965. From 1965 to 1969, AR had a regular biweekly program of her own.

320 **turned young adversaries into grudging admirers:** "I've seen audiences start booing and end up cheering," said LP; *AR:SOL,* DVD.

320 **"Abortion is a moral right":** AR,

"Of Living Death," speech given at the Ford Hall Forum, December 8, 1968, reprinted in *The Objectivist,* September–November 1968, p. 534.

321 **although Branden later denied it:** Nathaniel Branden, "In Answer to Ayn Rand," *The Objectivist,* October 1968.

321 **primarily because its purpose:** May 4, 1946 (*JOAR,* p. 479).

321 **She wasn't convinced:** *MYWAR,* p. 211.

321 **composing essays was child's play:** Harry Binswanger, "Recollections of Ayn Rand."

321 **clarity and logic:** *MYWAR,* p. 297.

322 **warns against defining national emergencies too broadly:** Ayn Rand, "The Ethics of Emergencies," *TON,* February 1963; reprinted in *TVOS,* p. 49.

322 **"for the gold standard's inherent price stability":** *The Age of Turbulence,* p. 481.

322 **she endorsed Goldwater:** *TON,* October 1963 and March, July, September, and October 1964.

323 **helped to found the club and magazine:** Author interview with JKT, May 21, 2004.

323 **famous Goldwater rally:** This took place on May 12, 1964.

323 **"It made his points in his voice":** Unpublished taped interview with Barbara Weiss, conducted by BB, September 25, 1983.

323 **took the document to Goldwater's temporary office:** Author interview with BB, October 14, 2007.

323 **didn't receive the speech in time:** I haven't been able to find a copy of this speech in the Goldwater archives or among the papers of his senior staff.

323 **imprecision of his language:** Ayn Rand, "Check Your Premises: The

Argument from Intimidation," *TON,* July 1964, p. 26.

323 **"Daisy" television ad:** The ad, broadcast by the Democrats in September 1964, showed a little girl sitting in a green field counting the petals of a daisy. A male voice also begins to count—a countdown to a nuclear explosion. The implication was that Barry Goldwater's stance against a nuclear test-ban treaty with Russia would end in a nuclear war.

323 **"In former campaigns":** Ayn Rand, "Check Your Premises: It Is Earlier Than You Think," *TON,* December 1964, p. 49.

324 **March 1964 *Playboy* interview:** "The *Playboy* Interview: Ayn Rand," pp. 38–43, 64.

324 **Alvin Toffler:** Toffler visited AR's apartment to conduct the interview. At first, she struck him as "a nice Russian-Jewish grandma." When he admitted that he had not read *AS,* she ordered him out and told him not to return until he had read it. After a subsequent, more successful interview, he recalled that his transcriptionist couldn't decipher her words through her thick Russian accent. Finally, on receiving proofs, she edited not only her answers to his questions but also the questions and his introduction. Toffler wasn't impressed by her philosophy. "It was like Marxism turned upside down," he said. But he liked her and invited her to dinner with his wife and guests (author interview with Alvin Toffler, May 27, 2007).

324 **reached two and a half million people:** Don Hauptman, "The 'Lost' Parts of Ayn Rand's *Playboy* Interview," *Navigator,* March 2004, p. 9.

324 **attributed the suffering of mankind:** NB named these archetypes (*JD,* p. 281).

325 **"chief destroyer of the modern world":** Ayn Rand, "Brief Summary," *The Objectivist,* September 1971, p. 1091. Interestingly, Nietzsche also hated Kant. In *The Anti-Christ,* he wrote that Kant and others like him regarded "beautiful feelings" as arguments, "the heaving breast as the bellows of divine inspiration," and conviction as the criterion of truth. "German *decadence* as a philosophy—that is *Kant!*" he wrote in 1895 (trans., H. L. Mencken, 1920).

325 **a "New Intellectual":** "New man" was a popular concept in the Russia of AR's youth, appearing, for example, in Lenin's favorite novel, Nikolai Chernyshevsky's *What Is to Be Done?* and in *Thus Spoke Zarathustra.* Chernyshevsky's new man is, however, a mythic revolutionary struggling to create a collective social order (see *New Myth, New World: From Nietzsche to Stalinism,* pp. 189–202).

325 **One hundred or so "new intellectuals":** "Born Eccentric," *Newsweek,* March 27, 1961. A day or two after the piece appeared, NB distributed an open letter to NBI students urging them to cancel their *Newsweek* subscriptions ("An Open Letter from NB to Our Readers," March 22, 1961).

325 **"a glare [that] would wilt a cactus":** "Born Eccentric."

326 **"the free enterprise system's Joan of Arc":** "The Curious Cult of Ayn Rand," pp. 99–102.

326 **by now she made it a point never to read:** Author interview with Robert Hessen, October 17, 2007.

326 **"nearly perfect in its immorality":** Gore Vidal, "Comment," *Esquire,* July 1961, pp. 24–28.

326 **sitting around "in booths":** "The Book Shelf," *Wall Street Journal,* March 24, 1961, p. 10.

326 **did read Sidney Hook's review:** Sidney Hook, "Each Man for Himself," *NYT Book Review,* April 9, 1961, p. 3.

326 **the children would have starved to death:** Nathaniel Branden, "Concerning Ayn Rand's *For the New Intellectual*" display ad, *NYT,* May 28, 1961, p. B14.

327 **had been Barbara Branden's master's-thesis advisor:** *TPOAR,* p. 321.

327 **exempted them from challenging him:** Author interview with BB, October 14, 2007.

327 **he constructed a point-by-point:** "Concerning Ayn Rand's *For the New Intellectual,*" p. B14.

327 **"It was almost worth Hook's review":** *MYWAR,* p. 248.

327 **proud of his ability:** *JD,* p. 282.

327 **his "failure":** Author interview with NB, May 5, 2004.

328 ***Who Is Ayn Rand?*:** The book was based on a series of talks NB presented on WBAI-FM in New York in 1961.

328 **the Brandens later disavowed it:** Michael Etchison, "Break Free!" interview with NB, *Reason,* reprint, October 1971, p. 1.

328 **"She could hardly complain":** *MYWAR,* p. 249.

328 **"enormous enthusiasm was expected":** "Objectivism Past and Future."

328 **"Right and wrong, rational and irrational":** Author interview with JMB and Dr. Allan Blumenthal, March 23, 2004.

328 **"Judge, and be prepared to be judged":** *TVOS,* p. 83.

328 **"Moral judgments were required":** Unpublished taped interview with Barbara Weiss, conducted by BB, September 25, 1983.

328 **new emphasis on "sense of life":** Author interview with Jonathan Hirschfeld, NB's nephew, who spent summers working at NBI and attended social functions. "Every thought implies a value judgment," AR wrote (January 9, 1954 [*JOAR,* p. 659]).

328 **"Most people were walking on eggshells":** "Interview with Henry Mark Holzer," p. 6. In 2006, Holzer told another interviewer, "Sometimes it was like walking on eggshells, and sometimes it was like walking on air" (OHP, Hank and Erika Holzer, February 9, 2006).

329 **"Her idea of encouraging a person":** "Break Free! interview with Nathaniel Branden," p. 9.

329 **"She was the Evel Knievel of leaping to conclusions":** Author interview with Robert Hessen, November 2, 2007.

329 **"There was very little psychological privacy":** "The *Liberty* Interview: Nathaniel Branden Speaks," pp. 38–39.

329 **"his denunciation was much more damaging":** "Ayn Rand and Her Movement," pp. 7, 8. In 1999, NB disputed this assessment, telling an interviewer, "Ayn took, uh, denunciation, judgmentalism, to a . . . an intensity that nobody [chuckles] could approach!" (ellipsis and interjection in the original); "The *Liberty* Interview: Nathaniel Branden Speaks," p. 39.

329 **a rising academic thinker:** JH went on to serve as chair of the philosophy department of the University of Southern California.

330 **"bowled over":** John Hospers, "Memories of Ayn Rand," *Full Context,* May 1998, p. 3.

330 **which Hospers praised in depth:** Karen Minto, "Interview with John Hospers," *Full Context,* May 1998, p. 8.

330 **didn't remember her answer:** "Conversations with Ayn Rand," p. 23.

330 **"which could warm you and freeze you by turns":** "Memories of Ayn Rand," p. 3.

330 **"She read almost no philosophy at all":** "Conversations with Ayn Rand," p. 47.

330 **her ideas "had come full-blown from her head":** JH, from taped, unpublished interviews by journalist JW in preparation for a CBC special report on the tenth anniversary of AR's death, titled *Ideas: The Legacy of Ayn Rand* (1992).

331 **"relegated to the scrap-heap":** "Conversations with Ayn Rand," p. 24.

331 **"shivering, scared children":** John Hospers, "Remembrance of Things Past," *Liberty,* August 2006, pp. 19–22.

331 **" 'Undigested agreement' does not interest or concern me":** Letter to JH, January 3, 1961 (*LOAR,* p. 531).

331 **If she didn't find it:** Author correspondence with BB, June 27, 2008.

331 **she saw the realm of ideas:** John Hospers, "Conversations with Ayn Rand II," *Liberty,* September 1990, page 51.

331 **"Any hint of thinking as one formerly had":** "Conversations with Ayn Rand II," p. 52.

331 **"to the stratosphere in anger":** "Conversations with Ayn Rand II," p. 42.

332 **She had frequently complained to him:** JH from taped, unpublished interviews by journalist JW in preparation for a CBC special report on the tenth anniversary of AR's death, titled *Ideas: The Legacy of Ayn Rand* (1992).

332 **She gave a formal, twenty-minute paper:** Or "Art *and* Sense of Life," a version of which appears under that title in *The Romantic Manifesto.*

332 **According to Barbara:** Author correspondence with BB, June 27, 2008.

332 **brought him close to tears:** "Memories of Ayn Rand," pp. 5, 7.

332 **spoke to twenty-five hundred fans:** "Ayn Rand Rips Trust Laws," *Chicago Tribune,* September 30, 1963, p. 22.

332 **traveled hundreds of miles to hear her:** Author interview with Ed Nash, former Chicago NBI representative, January 6, 2005.

332 **On Rand's mother's side:** Letter to Esther Stone, August 17, 1963 (*LOAR,* p. 611).

333 **Luckily, it was a hoax:** *100 Voices,* Iris Bell, p. 228.

333 **Rand's black dress:** Author interview with Susan Belter, December 18, 2006.

333 **"It was polite but formal":** Unpublished, taped interview with MS, conducted by BB, February 20, 1983.

333 **"She was like a queen on a throne":** *100 Voices,* FB, p. 27.

333 **specifically the 1890 Sherman Antitrust Act:** "Ayn Rand Rips Trust Laws," p. 22.

333 **didn't come to the funeral:** AR's second cousin Roger Salamon (Sarah Lipton's grandson) recalls that AR attended Burt Stone's funeral, but FB and Burt Stone's granddaughter Susan Belter remember her absence. All agree that relations with AR cooled over time and the family lost touch with her in the middle 1960s.

333 **"He was very rude":** Interview with MS, conducted by BB, February 20, 1983.

333 **left Chicago by plane for Portland, Oregon:** The Brandens, who accompanied AR, couldn't remember whether they also flew from New York to Chicago on the first leg of the trip.

Either way, once in the plane she lost her fear of flying. "The unknown frightened her," Barbara observed, "a fact of reality did not" (*TPOAR*, p. 318). She flew again in the 1970s.

333 **Rand was joining him for a question-and-answer session:** "Objectivist Calendar," *TON*, September 1963, p. 36.

333 **so crammed that a janitor called the fire department:** *100 Voices*, Jan Schulman, p. 248.

334 **heard Frank's voice through an open window:** Author interview with RBH, May 19, 2005.

334 **for years had been displeased:** *MYWAR*, p. 203.

334 **"a chicken and unloyal":** *100 Voices*, Perry Knowlton, p. 307.

334 **suggested publishing a second collection:** *TPOAR*, pp. 321–22.

335 **"The Fascist New Frontier":** This essay was based on a speech by the same name given at the Ford Hall Forum on December 16, 1962.

335 **would have to remove the essay and change the title:** Second draft of an unpublished letter from BC to AR, October 18, 1963 (Bennett Cerf Collection, Columbia University Rare Book and Manuscript Library, box 57).

335 **"He made the decision not to publish":** *TPOAR*, p. 322.

335 **One day in mid-October:** They met on October 16, 1963; second draft of an unpublished letter from BC to AR, October 18, 1963.

335 **her whole point:** Manuscript letter to BC, October 30, 1963 (Bennett Cerf Collection, Columbia University Rare Book and Manuscript Library, box 57).

335 **"Get yourself another publisher":** BC's oral history interview on file at the Columbia University Oral History Project archives, number 719,

p. 951; letter to BC, October 30, 1963 (*LOAR*, pp. 617–21).

336 **had contracted to pay:** *100 Voices*, Perry Knowlton, p. 307.

336 **new "unrequited love story":** *JOAR*, p. 709.

336 **paid many of the bills at NAL:** *100 Voices*, Patrick McConnell (one of AR's editors at New American Library), p. 451.

336 **had to nag and coax the editors:** *100 Voices*, Perry Knowlton, p. 312.

336 **"delegated to Ayn Rand duty":** Author interview with former New American Library editor Gerry Howard, March 2, 2004.

336 **"She asked me at lunch":** Author interview with former New American Library editor John Thornton, who was assigned to AR from 1975–79; March 4, 2004.

336 **"That's not funny":** *100 Voices*, Patrick McConnell, p. 451.

337 **"no conflicts of interest among rational men":** *TVOS*, p. 57.

337 **The *Virtue of Selfishness* did not include:** NBI published "The Fascist New Frontier" as a pamphlet in 1963.

337 **"I hope you will agree":** Manuscript letter from BC to AR, November 26, 1963 (Bennett Cerf Collection, Columbia University Rare Book and Manuscript Library, box 57).

337 **"She said the assassination":** BC, Columbia University Oral History Project interview, p. 952.

337 **"I think you are one of the most wonderful people":** Unpublished letter from BC to AR, March 29, 1965 (Bennett Cerf Collection, Columbia University Rare Book and Manuscript Library, box 57).

337 **She also wished him well:** Letter to BC, April 3, 1965 (*LOAR*, pp. 634–35).

337 **Cerf blamed her followers:** Cerf, Columbia University Oral History Project interview, p. 952.

337 **"She was a revolutionary":** JH, from taped, unpublished interviews by journalist JW in preparation for a CBC special report on the tenth anniversary of AR's death, titled *Ideas: The Legacy of Ayn Rand* (1992).

337 **"She could be immensely empathetic":** Author interview with BB, October 12, 2007.

338 **"This is exactly how I feel about myself":** *100 Voices,* Ilona Royce Smithkin, p. 214.

338 **At least twice a year:** "Objectivist Calendar," *TON.*

338 **also tape-recorded answers:** Author interview with Shelly Reuben, November 19, 2007.

338 **without accepting any remuneration:** *MYWAR,* p. 206.

338 **NBI "was certainly profitable":** "The *Liberty* Interview: Barbara Branden, p. 54.

338 **She let it be known that he, and only he:** "Conversations with Ayn Rand," p. 35.

338 **traded their set of rooms:** The Brandens had earlier moved from their single room into a one-bedroom apartment at 165 East Thirty-fifth Street before moving into 120 East Thirty-fourth.

339 **Elayne Kalberman managed the newsletter staff:** Author interview with EK, July 21, 2006.

339 **transferred his paints:** Author interview with Don Ventura, March 19, 2004.

339 **An intercom joined the O'Connors' apartment with the Brandens':** BB, in a taped interview with MS, February 18, 1983.

339 **she tended to have fixed ideas about drawing:** "Art and Cognition," *The Romantic Manifesto,* p. 49.

339 **She might point out that his colors:** *Facets of Ayn Rand,* pp. 120–21.

339 **she phoned her favorite painter:** Author interview with JMB and Dr. Allan Blumenthal, March 23, 2004.

339 **she asked knowledgable friends:** *Facets of Ayn Rand,* p. 121.

339 **"He is a tiger at the easel":** *Facets of Ayn Rand,* p. 121.

339 **"It was the only time":** Author interview with Don Ventura, March 19, 2004.

340 **"That's what she was concerned about":** Author interview with JMB and Dr. Allan Blumenthal, September 2, 2004.

340 **she forbade him to sell his paintings:** Author interview with Don Ventura, March 19, 2004; author correspondence with BB, September 17, 2008.

340 **she was discovered:** Author interview with Roberta Satro, July 20, 2006. Satro was the on-site rental agent for 120 East Thirty-fourth Street and several other Murray Hill apartment buildings in the 1970s; in 1979 or 1980, she came upon Rand putting the painting in a trash can and asked if she could take it home. Rand agreed.

340 **"I'm coming back to life":** *JD,* p. 314.

341 **was the most important person in the world to him:** *TPOAR,* p. 335.

341 **offered to counsel the unhappy couple:** *JD,* p. 314.

341 **a therapeutic technique that she categorically rejected:** "The Benefits and Hazards."

341 **resented what he later characterized as:** "The Benefits and Hazards."

341 **"kill one's capacity to be certain of anything":** Nathaniel Branden, "Mental Health versus Mysticism and Self-Sacrifice," *TON,* March 1963, p. 9.

341 **"Ayn sometimes seemed like a pussycat in comparison"**: "The *Liberty* Interview: Barbara Branden," p. 52, amended by BB in a note to the author, September 17, 2008.

341 **displaying a seductive mixture**: Roy Childs, from taped, unpublished interviews by journalist JW in preparation for a CBC special report on the tenth anniversary of AR's death, titled *Ideas: The Legacy of Ayn Rand* (1992).

341 **"so strong on purity"**: Sinclair Lewis, *Elmer Gantry* (New York: Signet, 1970), p. 297.

341 **"Omnisciate and inflamminate"**: Author correspondence with Robert Hessen, December 8, 2007.

341 **"he would go off on shopping sprees"**: Author interview with Robert Hessen, October 17, 2007.

341 **"Nathan had a theory about 'men as tools' "**: Unpublished, taped interview with Barbara Weiss by BB, September 25, 1983.

342 **typists found her exceptionally fair**: Everyone who worked for AR professionally, from June Kurisu in the 1940s to Shelly Reuben in the 1960s, remembered her as scrupulously courteous and careful.

342 **"She didn't know how he'd been treating us"**: Unpublished, taped interview with Barbara Weiss by BB, September 25, 1983.

342 **"broke out into the most beautiful smile"**: *100 Voices*, Shelly Reuben, p. 373.

342 **"I did it myself!"**: *TPOAR*, p. 329.

342 **spent hours a week**: "Interview with Henry Mark Holzer," p. 5.

342 **"Miss Rand, would it be an infringement of your rights"**: Unpublished, taped interview with Betty Scourby, conducted by Fred Cookinham, March 3, 2003.

342 **"She had a huge number of young people"**: Interview with JKT, from taped, unpublished interviews by journalist JW in preparation for a CBC special report on the tenth anniversary of AR's death, titled *Ideas: The Legacy of Ayn Rand* (1992).

343 **"The expression on her face"**: Author interview with Don Ventura, April 28, 2004.

343 **"frightening, really frightening"**: Unpublished, taped interview with Betty Scourby, conducted by Fred Cookinham, March 3, 2003.

343 **"In those days, people worshipped the ground he walked on"**: Author interview with Don Ventura, March 19, 2004.

343 **he won disciples**: Author interview with Roger J. Callahan, November 4, 2003.

343 **"except for a few blemishes"**: *TPOARC*, p. 221.

343 **He made it clear**: "The *Liberty* Interview: Barbara Branden," p. 57.

343 **"He was the one who made a crusade"**: "The *Liberty* Interview: Barbara Branden," p. 57.

343 **"This was before anyone knew"**: The call took place on September 13, 1965 (author interview with Lee Clifford, November 5, 2007; letter from Clifford to BB, August 26, 1965, courtesy of Lee Clifford).

343 **only moral giants could possibly pull it off**: Karen Reedstrom, "Interview with Nathaniel Branden, Part 2," *Full Context*, October 1996, p. 4; Al Ramrus (author correspondence, March 5, 2007). Bill Bucko, an NBI student and the translator of *The Mysterious Valley* into English, reports two occasions on which NB answered this question. The first time, early in the 1960s, he said, no, it is not possible to be in love with two women at the same time. "Such a man [would be] unclear

about his values." The second time, he answered yes. "How?" asked the questioner. "Get a bigger bed," reportedly said NB, then added, "It would take a giant of introspection to do so"; reprinted from http://forums.4aynrandfans.com/index, which seems to have been removed from the Web.

343 **"It sounded like bullshit at the time":** Author interview with Ed Nash, January 6, 2005.

343 **sometimes said much the same thing:** MYWAR, p. 304. JMB recalled that NB and AR "were [both] going around playing dangerous games. One night a bunch of us were eating in a restaurant and they started a conversation about how [truly] superior people would be able to do exactly what they were doing, which I didn't buy for a second. But I thought, I can see why they are saying this" (author interview, March 23, 2004).

344 **"No, but you can be half in love":** Reported by Betsy Speicher on http://forums.4aynrandfans.com/index, which seems to have been removed from the Web.

344 **good-looking advertising account executive:** Author interview with Iris Bell, March 8, 2004.

344 **encouraged one of his male students:** Author interview with Robert Hessen, whom NB urged to date Patrecia, November 2, 2007.

344 **offered her and Larry Scott free marriage counseling:** "Ayn Rand and Her Movement," p. 8; notes on a November 12, 1968, conversation with Larry Scott by Al Ramrus, courtesy of Ramrus. Since conducting marriage counseling while flirting with or sleeping with one spouse would be unethical, both NB and

BB point out that the therapy was unofficial and unpaid.

344 **"as if she were entering a temple":** MYWAR, p. 281.

344 **She hadn't gone to college:** JD, p. 290.

344 **Unconditional female admiration:** Author interview with Florence Hirschfeld, Jonathan Hirschfeld, and EK, August 25, 2006.

344 **"what Nathan had never had in his life":** Author interview with BB, December 15, 2005.

345 **"You would see an explosion":** MYWAR, p. 288.

345 **he described her as an "Eddie Willers":** Author correspondence with BB, June 27, 2008.

345 **good premises but no special gifts:** TPOARC, RPJ, July 4, 1968, p. 326.

345 **His body "will not obey him":** AS, p. 454.

345 **The thought of being without her was intolerable:** "It's a Dirty Job, But . . ."

345 **his attraction to Patrecia would pass:** MYWAR, p. 288.

345 **turned down modeling jobs:** MYWAR, p. 290.

345 **"to lie expertly":** JD, p. 328.

345 **Branden "really cared for me":** Author correspondence with BB, June 27, 2008.

346 **took him at his word:** "The Liberty Interview: Barbara Branden," p. 56.

346 **Branden gradually lost discretion:** Author interviews with Iris Bell, March 8, 2004, and Peter Crosby, June 13, 2007.

346 **"the truth was evident":** TPOAR, p. 334.

346 **He moved out:** MYWAR, p. 309.

346 **penthouse apartment on the twentieth floor:** Author interview with BB, June 2, 2008.

346 **a marriage he half hoped:** Author correspondence with BB, June 27, 2008.

346 **"operated as a shield":** *JD*, p. 339.

346 **Rand spent many hours:** *TPOARC*, RPJ, July 4, 1968, p. 207.

346 **treated them with a kindness:** *TPOAR*, p. 333.

346 **attended the sessions under protest:** Author correspondence with BB, June 27, 2008.

347 **informed their unofficial therapist:** *TPOARC*, RPJ, November 27, 1967, p. 237.

347 **"Now, darling":** *MYWAR*, p. 309.

347 **"a sense of [emotional] deadness":** *JD*, pp. 364–65.

347 **her allegiance to Frank was difficult for him:** *JD*, p. 367.

347 **"if the ability to think of people":** *TPOARC*, RPJ, July 4, 1968, p. 319.

347 **"You will always be a sexual being":** *JD*, p. 352.

347 **"You have no equals at any age":** *JD*, p. 371.

347 **"happiness of a kind I had never known before":** *JD*, p. 358.

348 **recover her reason:** *MYWAR*, p. 299.

348 **"She's very American looking":** *MYWAR*, p. 291.

348 **"What is magnificent":** *MYWAR*, p. 316.

348 **volunteered as artist's models:** Author interviews with JMB, March 23, 2004, and Don Ventura, March 19, 2004.

348 **assuming that she was supposed to keep her legs crossed:** *100 Voices*, Don Ventura, apparently referring to the *Tonight Show Starring Johnny Carson* broadcast on August 11, 1967, p. 244.

348 **"When you're with Patrecia":** *JD*, p. 302.

348 **"I hated the calculations":** *MYWAR*, p. 315.

348 **"I cannot stand people with 'acts' ":** *TPOARC*, RPJ, January 30, 1968, p. 283.

348 **She was disturbed by their friendship:** *TPOARC*, RPJ, February 14, 1968, p. 287.

349 **"man-worship":** *TPOARC*, RPJ, July 4, 1968, p. 326.

349 **"When, if not now?":** *MYWAR*, p. 299.

349 **"We don't want people to think":** *MYWAR*, p. 313. In 1966, Larry Scott left New York for California. Almost three years passed before he learned of his wife's affair with NB. According to Iris Bell, who became friendly with Scott in Los Angeles, until then he ruminated about his broken marriage. He told Bell that "he would go off on his business trips. Then he would come back [to New York] and not understand what was going on in his marriage." After one such trip, "he brought back a necklace for Patrecia and made a sexual overture. She was very cold. He talked to NB about that. NB said, 'Well that's how women are. You have to give her time to get back into the same mood with you,' " Bell recalled. "Larry was telling me about how much he loved Patrecia and how he had no understanding of why his marriage had fallen apart. It wasn't until much later that I realized that while NB was talking to Larry this way, he was having an affair with Patrecia. Larry said that NB was never able to help him understand why his marriage fell apart." At least until 1967, Scott displayed separate framed photographs of his ex-wife and of NB in the bedroom of his Los Angeles apartment. He

learned about the affair between NB and Patrecia in the fall of 1968. He died in the 1990s (author interview with Iris Bell, March 8, 2004, and author correspondence with Al Ramrus, March 4, 2007).

349 **"We're just incompatible":** *MYWAR,* p. 313.

350 **he could barely tolerate the strain:** *JD,* p. 359.

350 **Once separated and living apart:** Author correspondence with BB, June 27, 2008.

350 **when he begged for time:** *TPOAR,* p. 336.

350 *The Psychology of Self-Esteem:* This would be published, sans introduction, in 1969, after AR had broken with him, under the auspices of a publishing company founded for this purpose by Objectivist Ed Nash. The book has never been out of print.

350 **a work of genius:** *JD,* p. 370.

350 **"Just wait until [Ayn] writes the introduction":** "The *Liberty* Interview: Barbara Branden," p. 57. In 1996, NB told an interviewer about the introduction, which was never written: "I believe that was owed me, after all the work I had done fighting for her work and all the compliments she had paid my book" ("Interview with Nathaniel Branden," p. 7).

350 **four hundred thousand dollars:** Ayn Rand, "To Whom It May Concern," *The Objectivist,* May 1968 issue (published October 1968), p. 450.

350 **affordable on paper:** A year later the NBI business manager Wilfred Schwartz was able to sell the lease to a new tenant for a premium of $55,000 (author correspondence with BB, June 27, 2008).

350 **always paid back in the fall:** Author correspondence with BB, June 27, 2008.

350 **Rand had told Nathaniel not to bother her:** Author correspondence with BB, September 17, 2008.

350 **was only mildly put out:** "To Whom It May Concern," p. 452.

351 **"I felt we were really in trouble":** Unpublished taped interview with Barbara Weiss, conducted by BB, September 25, 1983.

351 **"Patrecia's involvement":** *JD,* p. 370.

351 **expected it to open:** *TPOAR,* p. 342.

351 **considered Patrecia:** Files from 1967–68 on NBI Theater, Inc., and on production budgets, schedules, etc., for the aborted production of BB's adaptation of *TF,* courtesy of MSC; author correspondence with BB, June 27, 2008.

FIFTEEN: EITHER/OR (THE BREAK): 1967–1968

352 **"Pity for the guilty":** Rand, *The Romantic Manifesto,* p. 131.

352 **a book-length essay:** Ayn Rand, *Introduction to Objectivist Epistemology, The Objectivist,* July 1966 to February 1967; republished as a paperback original by the Objectivist Press in June 1967. An expanded paperback edition is available from Plume.

352 **Never among her popular works:** As of mid-2008, the paperback edition had sold about 146,000 copies, according to ARI.

352n. **In Ayn Rand's view:** "Introduction to Objectivist Epistemology," part 1, *The Objectivist,* July 1966, p. 103.

352 **and a fiery, farsighted speech:** "The Wreckage of the Consensus," April and May 1967, reprinted in *The Objectivist,* April 1967, pp. 241–45, 257–64.

352 **Marital counseling having ended:** *TPOARC*, RPJ, July 4, 1968, p. 327. In notes to herself, AR recalled that it was NB who asked for the "psychotherapy" she provided; *TPOARC*, RPJ, July 4, 1968, p. 327. BB recalled that the sessions were an example of AR's increasingly compulsive tendency to "psychologize"; "It's a Dirty Job, But . . ."

352 **placed their active relationship on hold:** *TPOARC*, RPJ, July 4, 1968, p. 327.

353 **He rationalized, improvised:** *TPOAR*, p. 338.

353 **he knew "years ago":** *TPOARC*, RPJ, November 27, 1967, p. 243.

353 **"I feel real *fear*":** *TPOARC*, RPJ, November 27, 1967, p. 241.

353 **Also, although he said he wanted:** *TPOARC*, RPJ, February 14, 1968, p. 287.

353 **"business, theatrical business":** *TPOARC*, RPJ, November 27, 1967, p. 242.

353 **"in a man of Branden's rationality":** *TPOARC*, RPJ, November 27, 1967, p. 241.

353 **she had been unable to "project":** *TPOARC*, RPJ, November 27, 1967, p. 243.

354 **"or, rather, admired":** *TPOARC*, RPJ, November 27, 1967, p. 240; "I do not fully believe that hypothesis," she wrote regarding NB's possible narcissism.

354 **"Here is a man who":** *TPOARC*, RPJ, November 27, 1967, p. 244.

354 **"on the same level as Kant and Hegel":** *The Ayn Rand Cult*, p. 151.

354 **"vanity, flattery-seeking":** *TPOARC*, RPJ, January 25, 1968, p. 256.

354 **To "break with him entirely":** *TPOARC*, RPJ, November 27, 1967, p. 244.

355 **By the late 1960s, her media ap-** pearances: OHP, Hank and Erika Holzer, February 9, 2006.

355 **"You won't attack me?":** The network tapes of AR's appearances on *The Tonight Show* (August 11, October 26, and December 13, 1967) were reportedly destroyed in a fire. I watched a homemade videotape, courtesy of Kerry O'Quinn, an acquaintance of AR in the 1960s and 1970s.

355 **all but twelve of them positive:** *TPOAR*, p. 325.

355 **"more openly, romantically expressive":** *TPOARC*, RPJ, July 4, 1968, pp. 330–31.

355 **His eyes were lifeless:** *TPOARC*, RPJ, July 4, 1968, p. 331.

355 **danced too often with Patrecia:** *MYWAR*, pp. 324–25.

355 **"sex problem":** *TPOARC*, RPJ, July 4, 1968, p. 331.

356 **a "subconscious, *total renunciation*":** *TPOARC*, RPJ, January 30, 1968, p. 278.

356 **might help to thaw:** *TPOARC*, RPJ, July 4, 1968, p. 335.

356 **very secret, very private, and very spiritual romance:** *TPOARC*, RPJ, July 4, 1968, p. 335.

356 **she seems briefly to have considered:** *TPOARC*, RPJ, February 14, 1968, p. 335.

356 **"I would be the only remnant":** *TPOARC*, RPJ, March 30, 1968, p. 297.

356 **"You have no right to casual friendships":** *MYWAR*, p. 331.

357 **"I will not be Cyrano":** *TPOARC*, RPJ, February 14, 1968, p. 291.

357 **He had surgery:** *TPOAR*, p. 334.

357 **returned to his classes:** Author correspondence with Stephanie Cassidy, archivist of the Art Students League, April 22, 2007.

357 **"I wish you hadn't said it":** Author interview with JMB and Dr. Allan Blumenthal, March 23, 2004.

357 **a young sculptor named Don Ventura:** This section is based on author interviews with Ventura, March 19, 2004, and April 28, 2004.

358 **he thought her accent was cute:** AR never liked her Russian accent. When JMB once asked her why she didn't try to correct it, Rand replied that it wasn't in her to imitate anyone, as people who came to New York with accents had to do; this shows a certain self-consciousness and pride that AR had not exhibited when learning English in the 1920s (author interview with JMB and Dr. Allan Blumenthal, March 23, 2004).

359 **surviving witnesses couldn't explain:** For example, the Brandens and Al Ramrus.

359 **the magazine published a notice:** *The Objectivist,* June 1967, p. 288.

359 **Afterward, in a familiar pattern, Rand spoke disparagingly:** "An Interview with Nathaniel Branden," p. 12.

359 **the woman's eighteen-year-old son, Leonard:** Author interview with Leonard Bogat, January 22, 2007.

359 **"a horrible woman":** Author interview with Leonard Bogat, February 1, 2007.

360 **"had been seeking an identity":** Author interviews with Don Ventura, March 19, 2004, and April 28, 2004.

360 **O'Connor ceased painting:** "Portrait of an Artist," p. 1.

360 **O'Connor stopped taking classes:** This occurred in May 1966, according to Stephanie Cassidy (author interview, 2007).

360 **"she insisted that Frank be present":** Author interview with BB, September 15, 2005.

360 **"That man [Nathaniel] is no damn good!":** *TPOAR,* pp. 338–39.

360 **He flew into violent rages:** *MYWAR,* p. 329.

361 **"I want to leave her":** Author interview with BB, September 15, 2005.

361 **expanded his popular . . . lecture:** "The Objectivist Calendar," *The Objectivist,* March 1967, p. 239.

361 **he was rehearsing the role:** "The *Liberty* Interview: Nathaniel Branden Speaks," p. 56.

361 **visited psychedelic nightclubs:** Author interview with Iris Bell, March 8, 2004.

361 **"Branden was off in a corner":** Author interview with Al Ramrus, February 22, 2007.

361 **"He was having a slow-motion":** Author interview with Iris Bell, March 8, 2004.

361 **Yet he did not cut back:** *TPOARC, RPJ,* March 20, 1968, p. 296.

361 **lurched between impossible choices:** *TPOAR,* p. 338.

361 **"[I used to race] from my office":** *TPOAR,* p. 338.

362 **"not [Nathaniel] the person":** BB during unpublished taped interview with Barbara Weiss, September 25, 1983.

362 **Again, she urged him to confess:** *TPOAR,* p. 336.

362 **built small followings:** Of one of these disciples, NB's nephew, Jonathan Hirschfeld, recalled, "[This person] presided over her little universe in the same way that NB presided over his and AR presided over hers, which meant that [she] was handing out points and making people feel uncertain of themselves and insecure. It wasn't comfortable. It wasn't adventuresome. It wasn't curious. It was filled with an assumption about the negativity of the world, about the decadence of the world, about the corruption of the world" (author interview with Jonathan Hirschfeld, August 25, 2006).

362 **Prescription drugs, including**

tranquilizers: Author interviews with Roger J. Callahan, November 4, 2003, and Don Ventura, April 28, 2004.

362 **"disgusting":** AR said this in a question-and-answer period after a speech called "The Moratorium on Brains," at Ford Hall Forum on November 14, 1971. As a matter of policy, she opposed state intervention in sexual matters and favored the repeal of sodomy laws then on the books in most states (Chris M. Scia-barra, *Ayn Rand, Homosexuality, and Human Liberation* [Stow, Ohio: Leap Publishing, 2003], p. 8). She was also personally naïve. Once, JMB remarked to LP that Rudolf Nureyev, whom she had just seen perform, was gay. LP told AR, and AR came to see JMB. " 'Did you say this?' she said. 'Certainly,' I said. 'He is a known homosexual and I can see it every time I watch him.' Her whole demeanor changed, because it was a subject she didn't know anything about, and she said to me, 'I can hardly believe it! He's so well en-dowed' " (author interview with JMB and Dr. Allan Blumenthal, September 2, 2004).

362 **"It was a wild time":** Author interview with Kerry O'Quinn, May 20, 2004.

362 **Some entered into therapy:** During a public debate in May 1967, for example, NB answered a question about how he measured psychotherapeutic success this way: "If a homosexual comes in—if he goes out heterosexual and stays heterosexual, that's a success" (NB and Albert Ellis debate, May 26, 1967, unpublished tape courtesy of MSC).

363 **relied on a small group of thera-pists:** Author interview with Roger J. Callahan, November 4, 2003.

363 **an investor:** Partnership agreement, courtesy of MSC.

363 **surrendered his license:** Ellen Plasil, *Therapist* (New York: St. Mar-tin's, 1985), p. 221.

363 **"There were those who were ex-tremely hypocritical":** Author interview with Don Ventura, March 19, 2004.

363 **"unreal" and "utterly impossible":** Albert Ellis, *Is Objectivism a Religion?* (New York: Institute for Rational Living Press, 1968), p. 288.

363 **"Am *I* unreal?":** *MYWAR,* p. 317.

364 **later described Rand:** Author interview with Albert Ellis, September 12, 2003.

364 **he published a short book:** The book was *Is Objectivism a Religion?*

364 **"the excess of a virtue":** BB to Bar-bara Weiss; taped, unpublished interview with Weiss conducted by BB, September 25, 1983.

364 **"One of the most astonishing phenomena":** "A Strange Kind of Simplicity," p. 8.

364 *Man Also Rises:* AR, p. 101.

364 **"He gave me, in the hours of my own days":** Introduction to the twenty-fifth-anniversary edition of *TF,* p. viii.

365 **"physical alienation":** *TPOARC,* RPJ, July 4, 1968, p. 324.

365 **The letter itself appears:** Author interview with NB, April 3, 2008.

365 **thought it was as diplomatic:** *TPOAR,* p. 340.

365 **"You *bastard*!":** *TPOAR,* p. 340.

365 **"Face twisted in hatred":** *MYWAR,* p. 334.

365 **"Everyone else profits from my ideas":** *TPOAR,* p. 341.

365 **His paper was the worst:** *TPOARC,* RPJ, November 27, 1967, p. 244.

365 **rebuffed the offer as offensive:** *TPOARC,* RPJ, July 4, 1968, p. 317.

365 **accused him of immorality:** *TPOAR*, p. 341.

366 **"I can't predict":** *TPOAR*, p. 341.

366 **"pretentious, presumptuous":** *TPOARC*, RPJ, January 30, 1968, p. 283.

366 **"girl next door":** *TPOARC*, RPJ, July 12, 1968, p. 369.

366 **"Appalled by Ayn's terms":** *TPOAR*, p. 342.

366 **Rand expressed hope:** *TPOAR*, p. 342.

366 **But if he didn't, she would ruin him:** *MYWAR*, p. 334.

366 **"NB's mind worked excellently":** *TPOARC*, RPJ, July 12, 1968, p. 367.

367 **gave Barbara the assignment:** *TPOARC*, RPJ, July 13, 1968, p. 378.

367 **"I do believe":** *TPOARC*, RPJ, July 4, 1967, pp. 324–25.

367 **"filthy soul":** *TPOARC*, RPJ, July 8, 1968, p. 351.

367 **At times, she wept in grief:** *MYWAR*, p. 337.

367 **a fascinating conjecture:** *TPOARC*, RPJ, July 4, 1968, p. 337.

367 **"ought" to do:** *TPOARC*, RPJ, July 4, 1968, p. 341.

367 **"at least to the extent":** *TPOARC*, RPJ, July 4, 1968, p. 322.

368 **She was *too much* for Nathaniel Branden:** *TPOARC*, RPJ, July 4, 1968, p. 323.

368 **Since she was also the mirror:** *TPOARC*, RPJ, July 8, 1968, p. 361.

368 **"a real Objectivist hero and creative genius":** TPOARC, RPJ, July 4, 1968, p. 324.

368 **"But I am too much for the role-playing imitation":** *TPOARC*, RPJ, July 4, 1968, p. 323.

368 **The first was the publication:** *TPOARC*, RPJ, March 20, 1968, p. 295.

368 **"our relationship became":** *TPOARC*, RPJ, July 4, 1968, p. 323.

368 **The second turning point:** *TPOARC*, RPJ, July 4, 1968, p. 325.

368 **"wheeling-dealing" . . . "intangible pleasure":** *TPOARC*, RPJ, July 4, 1968, pp. 312, 339.

368 **general rubric of role-playing:** *TPOARC*, RPJ, March 20, 1968, p. 295.

369 **Inexplicably, she didn't question:** *TPOARC*, RPJ, January 30, 1968, pp. 280–81.

369 **"notary public" soul:** TPOARC, RPJ, July 4, 1968, p. 328.

369 **"a sexual urge":** *TPOARC*, RPJ, July 8, 1968, p. 351.

369 **In mid-July:** *MYWAR*, p. 339; *TPOAR*, p. 342.

369 **"I know what this must mean to you":** *TPOAR*, p. 342.

369 **So did all communication with Nathaniel:** *MYWAR*, p. 341.

369 **cut Branden out of her will:** "Affidavit of Services," Probate Proceedings, Will of Alice O'Connor, a.k.a. Ayn Rand, New York County Surrogates Court, November 16, 1983, p. 2.

369 **"I intend *you* to be my heir":** *TPOAR*, p. 343.

369 **"afraid to say it":** Author interview with JMB and Dr. Allan Blumenthal, March 3, 2004.

369 **"How could [Ayn] have failed":** *TPOAR*, p. 344.

370 **"Get him down here":** *TPOAR*, pp. 345–46.

370 **backstairs romance:** *TPOARC*, RPJ, July 4, 1968, p. 344.

371 **"even if I were eighty years old":** Author interview with NB, August 10, 2004. That AR was sexually without age appears originally to have been *his* idea, as when he told her, "You will always be a sexual being" and "You have no equals at any age"; *TPOAR*, p. 346.

371 **As she spoke, her eyes were glaring:** *TPOAR*, p. 346.

371 **more effectively than her enemies:** *MYWAR*, p. 343.

372 **"If you have an ounce of morality":** *MYWAR*, p. 345; *TPOAR*, p. 347; also, cited in an unpublished letter from Florence Hirschfeld to AR, early 1969, courtesy of Florence Hirschfeld.

372 **"I believe that he has been attempting to cure himself":** *TPOARC*, RPJ, July 4, 1968, pp. 347–48.

372 **"To say 'I love you' ":** *TF*, p. 388.

372 **out of weakness:** *TPOARC*, RPJ, July 4, 1968, p. 320.

373 **the period that followed:** The final confrontation with NB took place three days before the opening of the 1968 Democratic National Convention in Chicago and as Soviet Russia began to crush the Prague Spring movement for individual liberty in Czechoslovakia.

373 **She gave no hint of her sexual history:** *TPOAR*, p. 349.

373 **"I have broken with Nathan":** OHP, Hank and Erika Holzer, February 9, 2006.

373 **as her heir apparent:** "To Whom It May Concern," p. 453.

373 **She also either encouraged:** Nathaniel Branden and Barbara Branden, "In Answer to Ayn Rand," October 1968, independently published and distributed; "To Whom It May Concern," p. 348.

373 **that he cede his half interest:** "In Answer to Ayn Rand"; "To Whom It May Concern," p. 453.

374 **On August 28, Branden held an NBI staff meeting:** *MYWAR*, p. 350.

374 **According to his nephew, Jonathan Hirschfeld:** Author interview with Jonathan Hirschfeld, August 26, 2006.

374 **beginning the next day:** Author interview with NB, May 5, 2004.

374 **"We were like mother and father figures":** Author interview with NB, May 5, 2004.

374 **Rumors "spread like wildfire":** *MYWAR*, p. 351.

374 **Barbara and Wilfred Schwartz:** *TPOAR*, p. 350.

374 **"I am not a teacher":** "To Whom It May Concern," p. 454.

375 **To Barbara, she said, "I won't":** *TPOAR*, p. 350.

375 **a sense of liberation:** Author interview with BB, June 2, 2008.

375 **She swore that she would not merely write:** *TPOAR*, p. 351.

375 **"I never wanted":** "To Whom It May Concern," p. 454.

375 **On September 3:** *TPOAR*, p. 351.

376 **The literary agency declined to participate:** *MYWAR*, p. 355.

376 **"What happened to property rights?":** *MYWAR*, p. 357.

376 **A year later, Ed Nash:** *TPOAR*, p. 349.

376 **Rand also kept her threat:** *TPOARC*, p. 122, based on copies of AR's unpublished letters in the Rand archive at ARI.

376 **According to Holzer's recollection:** OHP interview with Hank and Erika Holzer, February 9, 2006.

377 **described it differently:** "In Answer to Ayn Rand."

377 **as she would later dismiss the questions:** Robert Hessen remembered: "Sometime later that fall [1968], when Leonard began to give lectures, Ayn agreed to participate in the question periods. Nathan had by now published his 'Answer,' with its elliptical last line about its being impossible to carry on a romantic

relationship given the age difference. And someone said, 'Is it true, as Nathan said it was, that you and he had a sexual relationship and that your break was over the end of that?' And she said, 'If you could ask me a question like that, what reason would you have to trust my answer?' It was an ingenious and manipulative answer," recalled Hessen. "And I thought, Either it's a rehearsed answer, because it's very brilliant, it throws the questioner off, or it's a spontaneous answer, which is even more brilliant. I remained friends with her for the next twelve years, and we never talked about Nathan"; author interview with Robert Hessen, October 17, 2007.

378 **Yes, Florence answered:** Unmailed, unpublished letter from Florence Hirschfeld to AR, reviewing the points made during their fall 1968 meeting; undated, early 1969, courtesy of Florence Hirschfeld.

378 **"The thing that really got to me":** Author interview with Florence Hirschfeld, Jonathan Hirschfeld, and EK, August 25, 2006.

378 **in the October issue:** It was labeled May 1968 but was published in October.

380 **Within a week or two:** "In Answer to Ayn Rand."

380 **He "did not steal any money from Ayn Rand":** "Interview with Henry Mark Holzer," p. 6.

381 **a terse coda:** "For the Record," *The Objectivist,* May 1968, p. 457.

381 **he was discredited:** *MYWAR,* p. 368.

381 **If the author of the greatest book:** Author interview with Leonard Hirschfeld, December 15, 2006.

381 **"Ayn wanted to know":** OHP, Hank and Erika Holzer, February 9, 2006.

381 **The lawyer phoned NBI tape-transcription reps:** JW, citing Keith Edwards, NBI Detroit business rep, *The Ayn Rand Cult,* p. 45.

381 **Peikoff notified the representatives:** *MYWAR,* p. 358.

381 **students had to sign a waiver:** *TPOAR,* p. 357.

381 **In New York, therapists dismissed patients:** Author interview with John Allen, January 3, 2005.

381 **"He was supposedly handling":** JKT, from taped, unpublished interviews by journalist JW in preparation for a CBC special report on the tenth anniversary of AR's death, titled *Ideas: The Legacy of AR* (1992).

SIXTEEN: IN THE NAME OF THE BEST WITHIN US: 1969–1982

383 **"When people look back at their childhood":** Ayn Rand, "Introduction to *Ninety-Three* [by Victor Hugo]," *TON,* October 1962.

383 **"an instrument of philanthropic collectivism":** Quoted in "TRB from Washington," *The New Republic,* July 19, 1975.

384 **She removed Branden's name:** Author interview with JMB and Dr. Allan Blumenthal, October 7, 2007.

384 **tried unsuccessfully to quash:** Henry Mark Holzer, "Legal Notice," *The Objectivist,* May 1969.

385 **"How would you compare":** "Ideas in Action," videotaped interview of Leonard Peikoff by James Valliant, WJM Productions, August 5, 1995.

385 **"Sometimes she would wipe the floor with him":** Author interviews with EK, July 21 and August 25, 2006.

385 **"Either you deal with him":** Taped interview with Betty Scourby,

conducted by Fred Cookinham, March 30, 2003.

386 **In turn, loyalists later spoke:** *100 Voices,* Daniel Sutton, p. 263.

386 **"If you could ask such a question":** Author interview with Robert Hessen, October 17, 2007.

386 **scheduled to appear in 1969:** "Objectivist Calendar," *The Objectivist,* August 1968, p. 496.

386 **"She was making him rewrite":** Unpublished taped interview with Barbara Weiss, conducted by BB, September 25, 1983.

386 **"We were *always* hearing":** Phillip Smith, from taped, unpublished interviews by journalist JW in preparation for a CBC special report on the tenth anniversary of AR's death, titled "Ideas: The Legacy of AR" (1992).

386 **"the first book by an Objectivist philosopher":** Ayn Rand, introduction, in Leonard Peikoff, *The Ominous Parallels* (New York: Stein and Day, 1982).

387 **"It's so wonderful to see a great, new, crucial *idea*":** AS, p. 333.

387 **"number-one man":** Author interview with Molly Hays, February 29, 2004.

387 **on his Web site:** http://www.peikoff .com/op/ home.htm.

387 **at colleges including Hunter, New York University:** Unpublished letter from AR to Sidney Hook, undated, 1957. Sidney Hook Papers, Hoover Institution Library and Archives, box 24, folder 27, Stanford University, Palo Alto, California.

387 **In 1987, when he was fifty-four years old:** Unpublished letter from Cynthia Peikoff to Sidney Hook, April 16, 1987, and unpublished reply from Sidney Hook to Cynthia Peikoff, April 21, 1987; Sidney Hook Papers, Hoover Institution Library and Archives, box 23, folder 43.

388 **She also named him an editor of *The Objectivist:*** "Objectivist Calendar," *The Objectivist,* September 1968, p. 528.

388 **in which she aptly quoted Victor Hugo:** *The Ayn Rand Letter,* January 31, 1972, p. 42.

388 **appeared posthumously:** Ayn Rand, *The Art of Nonfiction: A Guide for Writers and Readers,* Robert Mayhew, ed. (New York: Plume, 2001).

388 **Also in 1969:** *The Romantic Manifesto* (New York: World Publishing, 1969), p. 45.

388 **Alan Greenspan arranged:** Karen Minot and David Oyerly, "Interview with Henry Mark Holzer," *Full Context,* July/August 2001, p. 5.

389 **"It is not coercion, not the physical force":** In her introduction to the 1958 edition of *We the Living,* Rand compared the Russian successful launch of Sputnik I and II in 1957, which shocked Americans, to Project X in *Atlas Shrugged.* "But how can we explain the 'Sputnik'?" she wrote. "Read the story of 'Project X' in *Atlas Shrugged.*"

389 **a new diamond-and-ruby ring:** *100 Voices,* the Vaught family, pp. 414–21.

389 **On Rand's return to New York:** Taped, unpublished interview with Barbara Weiss, conducted by BB, September 23, 1983.

389 **"Those who suggest we substitute":** "Apollo 11," p. 717.

389 **She spoke at the invitation of Colonel Herman Ivey:** *100 Voices,* Brigadier General Jack Capps, p. 496.

389 **The speech she gave:** *Philosophy: Who Needs It* (New York: Bobbs-Merrill, 1982).

390 **In effect, said Colonel Ivey:** *100 Voices,* Colonel Herman Ivey, p. 493.

391 **Afterward, Rand, accompanied**

by Frank: Author interview with EK, July 21, 2006.

391 **"Men were standing on other men's shoulders":** Taped, unpublished interview with Barbara Weiss, conducted by BB, September 23, 1983.

391 **"My impression was":** *100 Voices,* Brigadier General Jack Capps, pp. 497–98.

391 **For the most part, "it was a dream trip":** Taped, unpublished interview with Barbara Weiss, conducted by BB, September 25, 1983.

391 **couldn't walk more than a few yards:** *100 Voices,* Colonel Herman Ivey, pp. 488–89.

391 **one lung removed:** MS, unpublished, taped interview with FB, Minna Goldberg, and MS, conducted by BB, February 20, 1983.

391 **One day, she pointed:** Author interview with JMB and Dr. Allan Blumenthal, March 23, 2004.

392 **"She was finding it difficult to walk":** Peikoff, from taped, unpublished interviews by journalist JW in preparation for a CBC special report on the tenth anniversary of AR's death, titled "Ideas: The Legacy of AR" (1992).

392 **Yet she refused to take walks:** *TPOAR,* p. 383.

393 **But she was testing their patience:** Author interview with JMB and Dr. Allan Blumenthal, March 23, 2004.

393 **A translation of the letter:** Author interview with Lilyan Courtois, September 5, 2006.

393 **She had wanted to show:** *100 Voices,* FB, p. 23.

394 **When Nora wrote about her love:** Letter to Nora Drobyshev, May 5, 1973 (*LOAR,* p. 657).

394 **At Kennedy Airport:** *TPOAR,* p. 374.

394 **striking resemblance:** Author interview with EK, August 25, 2006.

394 **whispered to Rand:** *TPOAR,* p. 374.

395 **They had expected a "rich, noble lady":** *100 Voices,* Eleanora Drobysheva, p. 10.

395 **"What good is political freedom to me?":** Author interview with EK, August 25, 2006.

395 **"It was the altruism of our entire family":** *100 Voices,* Eleanora Drobysheva, p. 9.

396 **"But you are a rich and famous person!":** Author interview with EK, August 25, 2006.

396 **"[My sister] had just artificially constructed":** *100 Voices,* Eleanora Drobysheva, p. 4.

396 **"fake" and "lacking in talent":** *100 Voices,* Eleanora Drobysheva, p. 5.

396 **Nora called Rand:** *100 Voices,* Eleanora Drobysheva, p. 9.

396 **She did contact her lawyer:** *100 Voices,* Evva Pryor of Ernst, Cane, Gitlin & Winick, p. 526.

397 **Nor, as it turned out, did Nora wish to:** Probate Proceedings, "Report of Guardian *Ad Litem,*" November 16, 1983, p. 6.

397 **When Nora and Fedor were gone:** Author interview with EK, August 25, 2006.

397 **"when I liked everything about [my sister]":** *100 Voices,* Eleanora Drobysheva, pp. 10–13.

397 **Time noted:** "The Chairman's Favorite Author," *Time,* September 30, 1974.

397 **during one of their semimonthly dinners:** Author interview with JMB and Dr. Allan Blumenthal, October 7, 2007.

398 **he showed Mitchell a copy of an anti-trust article:** *The Age of Turbulence,* p. 97; "The Assault on Integrity," *TON,* August 1963, pp. 31–32.

398 **She had drawn him from a world of empiricism:** *The Age of Turbulence*, pp. 52–53.

398 **The revival stirred unusual interest:** Allen McCauley, "Ayn Rand, a Radical for True Capitalism," *Bergen County Record*, February 22, 1973.

398 **"[Penthouse Legend] is the kind of play":** Clive Barnes, "Stage: 'Penthouse Legend,' a Courtroom Drama," *NYT*, February 23, 1973, p. 20.

398 **It closed after thirty performances:** "Closing the Record Book on 1972–1973," *NYT*, Arts & Leisure, July 1, 1973, p. 3.

398 **a line, or a few lines:** The issue in dispute is whether AR's anger about the changes in her dialogue was justified, or even reasonable.

398 **"One mistake was all it took":** Taped, unpublished interview with Phillip and Kay Nolte Smith by journalist JW in preparation for a CBC special report on the tenth anniversary of AR's death, entitled "Ideas: The Legacy of AR" (1992).

399 **"She was relentless in pursuit":** *TPOAR*, p. 387.

399 **"visual distortions":** "Art and Sense of Life," *The Objectivist*, March 1966, p. 38.

399 **"By then, there was something almost reckless":** *TPOAR*, p. 387.

399 **She talked about "denouncing" them:** Taped, unpublished interview with Barbara Weiss, conducted by BB, September 23, 1983.

399 **Her behavior with him shocked and upset the Kalbermans:** Author interview with EK, July 21, 2006.

400 **She viewed his rebellion:** OHP, Robert Hessen, November 10, 2004.

400 **On the advice of her secretary:** Taped, unpublished interview with Barbara Weiss, conducted by BB, September 25, 1983.

400 **"Leonard was destroyed":** Taped, unpublished interview with Barbara Weiss, conducted by BB, September 25, 1983.

401 **For years, no producer:** *100 Voices*, Perry Knowlton, p. 315.

401 **They held a press conference:** "On His Own, Al Ruddy Readying Ayn Rand's 1957 *Atlas Shrugged*," *Variety*, May 17, 1972, p. 32.

401 **It was during the Ruddy negotiations:** Author interview with Daryn Kent-Duncan, April 25, 2005.

401 **now she decided that she wanted Raquel Welch:** *100 Voices*, Michael Jaffe, p. 516.

401 **the French actor Alain Delon:** *100 Voices*, Albert S. Ruddy, p. 510.

401 **"She never had [an actor to play] Galt":** *100 Voices*, Susan Ludel, p. 401.

401 **He and Rand had begun working:** Author interview with RBH, June 8, 2005.

402 **her own soon-to-be best-selling novel:** *Hanta Yo: An American Saga* (New York: Doubleday, 1979) became a 1984 ABC miniseries entitled *The Mystic Warrior*, adapted by Jeb Rosebrook.

402 **Silliphant told her a harrowing story:** Author interview with RBH, June 8, 2005.

402 **One evening in the early 1970s:** *TPOAR*, p. 366.

402 **Those who met him afterward:** Author interview with Martha and John Enright, July 6, 2006.

402 **"But he *hated* California":** *TPOAR*, p. 384.

403 **"Don't humor him":** Taped, unpublished interview with Barbara Weiss, conducted by BB, September 25, 1983.

403 **She assigned him papers:** *TPOAR*, p. 365.

403 **At one point she asked:** Taped,

unpublished interview with MS, conducted by BB, February 20, 1983.

403 **"He never got kindness from her":** Taped, unpublished interview with Barbara Weiss, conducted by BB, September 25, 1983.

403 **He apparently ordered beer:** *100 Voices,* Eloise Huggins, p. 440.

403 **"If Ayn happened to open the door":** Author interview with Florence Hirschfeld, Jonathan Hirschfeld, and EK, August 25, 2006.

403 **Eloise Huggins later disclosed to a confidante:** Taped, unpublished interview with Barbara Weiss, conducted by BB, September 25, 1983.

403 **"she [always] talk[ed] about":** *100 Voices,* Eloise Huggins, p. 439.

404 **"I [have] had Frank":** Letter to Gerald Loeb, August 5, 1944 (*LOAR,* p. 154).

404 **One year, when Frank wasn't strong enough:** Taped, unpublished interview with Barbara Weiss, conducted by BB, September 25, 1983.

404 **In the spring of 1979:** Ayn Rand, *Introduction to Objectivist Epistemology* (New York: New American Library, 1979).

404 **Surprisingly, perhaps, she made an appearance:** *The Phil Donahue Show,* broadcast from Madison Square Garden, May 1979.

404 **She also posed for a *Look* magazine photograph:** "Ayn Rand Returns," *Look,* May 14, 1979, pp. 72–73.

404 **"frightened, terribly frightened":** *100 Voices,* Susan Ludel, p. 530.

404 **"Don't eat the food":** Taped, unpublished interview with Barbara Weiss, conducted by BB, September 25, 1983.

405 **she slept beside him on rubber sheets:** Taped, unpublished interview with Barbara Weiss, conducted by BB, September 25, 1983.

405 **Frank O'Connor died on November 7, 1979:** "Charles Francis O'Connor, Artist, Husband of the Writer Ayn Rand," *NYT,* November 12, 1979, p. D11.

405 **Rand asked Evva Pryor:** *100 Voices,* Evva Pryor, p. 526.

405 **At the service, held in the Frank E. Campbell Funeral Chapel:** Taped, unpublished interview with Barbara Weiss, conducted by BB, September 25, 1983.

405 **David Kelley, a student of Leonard's:** David Kelley's journal notes from November 12, 1979, courtesy of Kelley.

405 **"I won't have to suffer long":** Binswanger, "Recollections of Ayn Rand."

405 **"'Mimi, talk to me about Frank'":** Taped, unpublished interview with MS, January 20, 1983, courtesy of MSC.

405 **She began to take antidepressant medication:** *100 Voices,* Harry Binswanger, p. 601.

405 **Alan Greenspan stopped in to see her:** Taped, unpublished interview with Barbara Weiss, conducted by BB, September 25, 1983.

406 **A neighborhood rental agent:** Author interview with Roberta Satro, July 20, 2006.

406 **He "look[ed] like Cyrus":** "Recollections of Ayn Rand."

406 **Eickhoff tried to disguise her dismay:** *100 Voices,* Kathryn Eickhoff, p. 276.

406 **So did Ed Snider:** Taped, unpublished interview with Barbara Weiss, conducted by BB, September 25, 1983.

406 **Rand gave her consent:** "Recollections of Ayn Rand."

407 **"my reason is that 'Objectivism'":** Ayn Rand, *The Objectivist Forum,* February 1980, p. 1.

407 **"Darling, if the Russians find**

out": *100 Voices,* Albert Ruddy, p. 50.

407 **Speaking above Donahue's attempts to mediate:** *The Phil Donahue Show,* April 29, 1980.

408 **"It was not 1981, it was 1950":** *TPOAR,* p. 399; Harry Binswanger, in an interview published in *100 Voices,* says that AR gave him a differing account of the meeting but doesn't specify the differences.

408 **She made her last public appearance:** Author interview with Molly Hays, February 29, 2004.

409 **"Please, gentlemen, don't photograph me":** Videotape of "The Sanc-

tion of the Victims," November 18, 1981.

409 **"But to win":** "The Sanction of the Victims," *The Objectivist Forum,* April 1982, p. 9.

409 **On New Year's Day 1982:** "Recollections of Ayn Rand."

409 **Mimi Sutton phoned:** Taped, unpublished interview with MS, January 20, 1983, courtesy of MSC.

410 **guards were posted:** Author interview with David Kelley, January 25, 2005.

410 **"It is not I who will die, it is the world that will end":** *TPOAR,* p. 403.

SELECTED BIBLIOGRAPHY

BY AYN RAND

Anthem (England: Cassell, 1938; 50th anniversary edition, New York: Signet, 1995).

The Art of Fiction, Tore Boeckmann, ed. (New York: Plume, 2000).

The Art of Nonfiction, Robert Mayhew, ed. (New York: Plume, 2001).

Atlas Shrugged (New York: Random House, 1957; New York: New American Library, 1957; Plume, 1999).

Ayn Rand Answers, Robert Mayhew, ed. (New York: New American Library, 2005).

Ayn Rand's Marginalia, Robert Mayhew, ed. (Irvine, Calif.: Second Renaissance Books, 1995).

Capitalism: The Unknown Ideal (New York: New American Library, 1966; New York: Signet, 1967).

The Early Ayn Rand: A Selection from Her Unpublished Fiction, Leonard Peikoff, ed. (New York: New American Library, 1984; New York: Signet, 1986).

For the New Intellectual (New York: Random House, 1961; New York: Signet, 1963).

The Fountainhead (New York: Bobbs-Merrill, 1943; 25th anniversary edition, New York: New American Library, 1971; New York: Plume, 1994).

The Illustrated Fountainhead (Irvine, Calif.: Ayn Rand Institute, 1998).

Introduction to Objectivist Epistemology (New York: New American Library, 1979; New York: Meridian, 1990).

Journals of Ayn Rand, David Harriman, ed., Dina Garmong, trans. (New York: Dutton, 1997; New York: Plume, 1999).

Letters of Ayn Rand, Michael S. Berliner, ed., Dina Garmong, trans. (New York: Dutton, 1995; New York: Plume, 1999).

Philosophy: Who Needs It (New York: Bobbs-Merrill, 1982).

The New Left: The Anti-Industrial Revolution (New York: Signet, 1971).

The Romantic Manifesto (New York: World Publishing Company, 1969; New York: Signet, 1971).

Russian Writings on Hollywood, Michael S. Berliner, ed., Dina Garmong, trans. (Los Angeles: Ayn Rand Institute Press, 1999).

The Voice of Reason: Essays in Objectivist Thought, Leonard Peikoff, ed. (New York: New American Library, 1989; New York: Meridian, 1990).

Three Plays (New York: Signet, 2005).

The Virtue of Selfishness: A New Concept of Egoism (New York: Signet, 1963; New York: New American Library, 1964).

We the Living (New York: Macmillan, 1936; New York: Signet, 1995).

OBJECTIVIST (AND ASSOCIATED) PUBLICATIONS

The Ayn Rand Letter, 1971–75, Harry Binswanger, ed. (New York: The Ayn Rand Letter, Inc.; New Milford, Conn.: Second Renaissance Books, 1990).

Barbara Branden and Nathaniel Branden, *Who Is Ayn Rand?* (New York: Random House, 1962).

Robert Mayhew, ed., *Essays on Ayn Rand's "We the Living"* (United Kingdom: Lexington Books, 2004).

———, *Essays on Ayn Rand's "Anthem"* (United Kingdom: Lexington Books, 2005).

———, *Essays on Ayn Rand's "The Fountainhead"* (United Kingdom: Lexington Books, 2007).

Scott McConnell, *100 Voices: An Oral History of Ayn Rand* (Irvine, Calif.: Ayn Rand Institute Press, to be published).

Ronald E. Merrill, *The Ideas of Ayn Rand* (Chicago: Open Court Press, 1991).

The Objectivist Newsletter, 1962–65 (New York: The Objectivist, Inc.; New Milford, Conn.: Second Renaissance Books, 1991).

The Objectivist, 1966–71 (New York: The Objectivist, Inc.; New Milford, Conn.: Second Renaissance Books, 1990).

Edward W. Younkins, ed., *Ayn Rand's "Atlas Shrugged": A Philosophical and Literary Companion* (Aldershot, UK: Ashgate, 2007).

MANUSCRIPT COLLECTIONS

Alliance of Motion Picture and Television Producers Collection, Margaret Herrick Library of the Academy of Motion Picture Arts and Sciences, Beverly Hills, Calif.

AMPTP Collection, Margaret Herrick Library of the Academy of Motion Picture Arts and Sciences, Beverly Hills, Calif.

Bennett Cerf Collection, Columbia Rare Book and Manuscript Library, Columbia University, New York.

Bobbs-Merrill Collection, Lilly Library, Indiana University, Bloomington.

Cecil B. DeMille Collection, L. Tom Perry Special Collections, Harold B. Lee Library, Brigham Young University, Provo, Utah.

Hedda Hopper Collection, Margaret Herrick Library of the Academy of Motion Picture Arts and Sciences, Beverly Hills, Calif.

National Archives and Records Administration, Northeast Region, New York and Washington, D.C.

Paramount Contracts Collection, Margaret Herrick Library of the Academy of Motion Picture Arts and Sciences, Beverly Hills, Calif.

Isabel Paterson Papers, Herbert Hoover Presidential Library, West Branch, Iowa.

Ayn Rand Papers, Library of Congress, Washington, D.C.

Random House Collection, Columbia Rare Book and Manuscript Library, Columbia University, New York.

Benjamin Stohlberg Collection, Columbia Rare Book and Manuscript Library, Columbia University, New York.

H. N. Swanson Collection, Margaret Herrick Library of the Academy of Motion Picture Arts and Sciences, Beverly Hills, Calif.

United Artists Collection, Wisconsin Center for Film and Theater Research, Wisconsin Historical Society, Madison.

U.S. Department of Justice, Federal Bureau of Investigation, Records Management Division, Washington, D.C.

Hal Wallis Collection, Margaret Herrick Library of the Academy of Motion Picture Arts and Sciences, Beverly Hills, Calif.

A. Watkins Collection, Columbia University Rare Book and Manuscript Library, Columbia University, New York.

Frank Lloyd Wright Archives, Frank Lloyd Wright Foundation, Taliesin West, Scottsdale, Ariz.

BOOKS

Salo W. Baron, *The Russian Jew under the Tsars and Soviets* (New York: Macmillan, 1964).

Kevin Bazzana, *Lost Genius: the Curious and Tragic Story of an Extraordinary Musical Prodigy* (New York: Carroll and Graf, 2007).

Mikhail Beizer, *The Jews of St. Petersburg* (Philadelphia: The Jewish Publication Society, 1989).

Ellsworth Bernard, *Wendell Willkie: Fighter for Freedom* (Marquette: Northern Michigan University Press, 1966).

Kenneth Lloyd Billingsley, *Hollywood Party: How Communism Seduced the American Film Industry in the 1930s and 1940s* (Rocklin, Calif.: Forum, 1998).

Harry Binswanger, *The Ayn Rand Lexicon: Objectivism from A to Z* (New York: New American Library, 1986).

Kai Bird and Martin J. Sherwin, *American Prometheus: The Triumph and Tragedy of J. Robert Oppenheimer* (New York: Random House, 2005).

Brian Boyd, *Vladimir Nabokov: The Russian Years* (Princeton, N.J.: Princeton University Press, 1990).

———, *Vladimir Nabokov: The American Years* (Princeton, N.J.: Princeton University Press, 1991).

Barbara Branden, *The Passion of Ayn Rand* (New York: Doubleday, 1986).

———, Barbara Branden and Nathaniel Branden, *Who Is Ayn Rand?* (New York: Random House, 1962).

Nathaniel Branden, *Judgment Day* (Boston: Houghton Mifflin, 1989).

———, *My Years with Ayn Rand* (Hoboken, N.J.: Jossey-Bass, 1999).

Jeff Britting, *Ayn Rand* (New York: The Overlook Press, 2004).

William F. Buckley, Jr., *McCarthy and His Enemies: The Record and Its Meaning* (Washington, D.C.: Regnery Publishing, 1954).

———, *Getting It Right* (Washington, D.C.: Regnery Publishing, 2003).

———, *Odyssey of a Friend: Whittaker Chambers' Letters to William F. Buckley, Jr., 1954–61* (Washington, D.C.: Regnery Publishing, 1970).

Joseph Carr, *The Technician's Radio Receiver Handbook* (Oxford, UK: Butterworth-Heinemann, 2001).

Bennett Cerf, *At Random: The Reminiscences of Bennett Cerf* (New York: Random House, 1977).

John Chamberlain, *A Life with the Printed Word* (Chicago: Regnery Gateway, 1982).

Leslie Chamberlain, *The Philosophy Steamer: Lenin and the Exile of the Intelligentsia* (London: Atlantic Books, 2006).

Whittaker Chambers, *Witness* (New York: Random House, 1952).

Maurice Champagne, *The Mysterious Valley,* Bill Bucko, trans., intro. by Harry Binswanger (Lafayette, Colo.: The Atlantean Press, 1994).

Stephen Cox, *The Woman and the Dynamo: Isabel Paterson and the Idea of America* (Piscataway, N.J.: Transaction Publishers, 2004).

Cecil B. DeMille, *The Autobiography of Cecil B. DeMille,* David Hayne, ed. (Englewood Cliffs, N.J.: Prentice Hall, 1959; New York: Garland Publishing, 1989).

Brian Doherty, *Radicals for Capitalism: A Freewheeling History of the Modern Libertarian Movement* (New York: Public Affairs, 2007).

Albert Ellis, *Is Objectivism a Religion?* (New York: Institute for Rational Living Press, 1968).

Orlando Figes, *Natasha's Dance: A Cultural History of Russia* (New York: Metropolitan Books, 2002).

———, *A People's Tragedy: The Russian Revolution, 1891–1924* (New York: Penguin Books, 1996).

Neal Gabler, *An Empire of Their Own: How the Jews Invented Hollywood* (New York: Anchor Books, 1989).

Arthur L. George and Elena George, *St. Petersburg: Russia's Window to the Future* (Oxford, UK: Taylor Trade Publishing, 2003).

Martin Gilbert, *The Holocaust: A History of the Jews of Europe During the Second World War* (New York: Holt, Rinehart and Winston, 1985).

Mimi Reisel Gladstein, *The Ayn Rand Companion* (Westport, Conn.: Greenwood Press, 1984).

Alan Greenspan, *The Age of Turbulence: Adventures in a New World* (New York: Penguin, 2007).

Virginia L. L. Hamel, *In Defense of Ayn Rand* (Brookline, Mass.: New Beacon Publications, 1990).

Steve H. Hanke, with Lars Jonung and Kurt Schuler, *Russian Currency and Finance* (New York: Routledge, 1993).

Hiram Haydn, *Words & Faces* (New York: Harcourt Brace, 1974).

Lillian Hellman, *Scoundrel Time* (Boston: Little, Brown, 1976).

Granville Hicks, *John Reed: The Making of a Revolutionary* (New York: Macmillan, 1936).

Victor Hugo, *Ninety-Three,* trans. Lowell Bair (New York: Bantam Books, 1962).

Ada Louise Huxtable, *Frank Lloyd Wright* (New York: Penguin, 2004).

Paul Johnson, *A History of the Jews* (New York: Harper Perennial, 1987, 1988).

Matthew Josephson, *The Robber Barons* (New York: Harcourt Brace, 1962).

Stuart M. Kaminsky, *Coop: The Life and Legend of Gary Cooper* (New York: St. Martin's Press, 1980).

Howard Koch, *As Time Goes By* (New York: Harcourt Brace Jovanovich, 1979).

Lionel Kochan, ed., *The Jews in Soviet Russia since 1917* (London: Oxford University Press, 1970).

Leah Levinson and Jerry Natterstad, *Granville Hicks: The Intellectual in Mass Society* (Philadelphia: Temple University Press, 1993).

Sinclair Lewis, *Elmer Gantry* (New York: Harcourt Brace, 1927; New York: Signet, 1970).

W. Bruce Lincoln, *In War's Dark Shadow: The Russians Before the Great War* (New York: Dial Press, 1983).

———, *Passage Through Armageddon: The Russians in War and Revolution* (New York: Simon & Schuster, 1986).

———, *Red Victory: A History of the Russian Civil War 1918–1921* (New York: Simon & Schuster, 1989).

Eugene Lyons, *Assignment in Utopia* (New York: Harcourt Brace, 1937).

Justin Martin, *Greenspan: The Man Behind the Money* (Cambridge, Mass.: Perseus, 2000).

Robert Mayhew, *Ayn Rand and "Song of Russia": Communism and Anti-Communism in 1940s Hollywood* (Lanham, Md.: Scarecrow Press, 2005).

Patrick McGilligan and Paul Buhle, *Tender Comrades: A Backstory of the Hollywood Blacklist* (New York: St. Martin's Press, 1997).

Frederic Morton, *Thunder at Twilight: Vienna 1913/1914* (New York: Charles Scribner's Sons, 1989).

Victor Navasky, *Naming Names* (New York: Viking, 1980).

Friedrich Nietzsche, *Thus Spoke Zarathustra,* Walter Kaufmann, trans. (New York: Penguin, 1978).

———, *Beyond Good and Evil,* Judith Norman, trans. (Cambridge: Cambridge University Press, 2002).

Albert Jay Nock, *Our Enemy, the State* (Tampa, Fla.: Hallberg Publishing Corp., 1983).

———, *The Memoirs of a Superfluous Man* (Lanham, Md.: University Press of America, 2002).

Isabel Paterson, *The God of the Machine* (Palo Alto, Calif.: Palo Alto Book Service reissue, 1983).

Michael Paxton, *Ayn Rand: A Sense of Life* (Layton, Utah: Gibbs Smith, 1998).

Ellen Plasil, *Therapist* (New York: St. Martin's Press, 1985).

James Warren Prothro, *The Dollar Decade* (Baton Rouge: Louisiana State University Press, 1954).

Justin Raimondo, *Reclaiming the Right: The Lost Legacy of the Conservative Movement* (Burlingame, Calif.: Center for Libertarian Studies, 1993).

———, *An Enemy of the State* (Amherst, N.Y.: Prometheus Books, 2000).

Bernice Rosenthal, *New Myth, New World: From Nietzsche to Stalinism* (University Park: Pennsylvania State University Press, 2002).

Stacy Schiff, *Vera: Mrs. Vladimir Nabokov* (New York: Random House, 1999).

Helmut Schoeck, *Envy: A Theory of Social Behaviour* (Indianapolis, Ind.: Liberty Fund, 1987).

Chris Matthew Sciabarra, *Ayn Rand: The Russian Radical* (University Park: Pennsylvania State University Press, 1995).

————, *Ayn Rand, Homosexuality, and Human Liberation* (Cape Town, South Africa: Leap Publishing, 2003).

Meryle Secrest, *Frank Lloyd Wright* (Chicago: The University of Chicago Press, 1992).

Stephen Michael Shearer, *Patricia Neal: An Unquiet Life* (Lexington: University Press of Kentucky, 2006).

Page Smith, *Redeeming the Time* (New York: McGraw-Hill, 1987).

Mary Ann Sures and Charles Sures, *Facets of Ayn Rand* (Irvine, Calif.: Ayn Rand Institute Press, 2001).

Gloria Swanson, *Swanson on Swanson* (New York: Random House, 1980).

James S. Valliant, *The Passion of Ayn Rand's Critics: The Case Against the Brandens* (Dallas, Tex.: Durban House, 2005).

Solomon Volkov, *St. Petersburg: A Cultural History,* Antonina W. Bouis, trans. (New York: The Free Press, 1995).

Margit von Mises, *My Life with Ludwig von Mises* (Bel Air, Calif.: Arlington House, 1984).

Frank Lloyd Wright, *An Autobiography* (London: Longmans, Green and Co., 1932; the revised 1943 edition was reissued by Pomegranate Communications, Petaluma, Calif., 2005).

ARTICLES AND PRINT INTERVIEWS

Brooks Atkinson, "The Play," *New York Times,* September 17, 1935.

"Ayn Rand," *Current Biography Yearbook,* 1982.

Frederick Babcock, "Book Award Winners," *New York Times,* March 6, 1958.

Ben Belitt, "The Red and the White," *The Nation,* April 22, 1936.

John Blundell, "Liberty at Its Nadir: Interview with Leonard Liggio," *Liberty,* July 2004, vol. 18, no. 7, pp. 36–42.

R. W. Bradford, "The Search for *We the Living,*" *Liberty,* November 1988, vol. 2, no. 2, pp. 17–29.

————, "Ayn Rand and Her Movement: An Interview with Barbara Branden," reprinted from *Liberty* by Liberty Publishing, 1991; erratum between pp. 7 and 8.

Thomas F. Brady, "Hollywood Don'ts," *New York Times,* November 16, 1947, p. X5.

Nathaniel Branden, "Mental Health versus Mysticism and Self-Sacrifice," *TON,* March 1963, p. 9.

———, "Concerning Ayn Rand's *For the New Intellectual,*" display ad, *New York Times,* May 28, 1961, p. B14.

"Disturber of the Peace," *Mademoiselle,* May 1962, pp. 172–96.

Kimberly Brown, "Ayn Rand No Longer Has Script Approval," *New York Times,* January 14, 2007.

William F. Buckley, Jr., "Recollection of Ayn Rand," syndicated in the *Chicago Sun-Times,* March 13, 1982.

———, "Ayn Rand, RIP," *National Review,* April 2, 1982, p. 380.

Jennifer Burns, "Godless Capitalism: Ayn Rand and the Conservative Movement," *Modern Intellectual History,* 2004, vol. 1, no. 3, pp. 359–85.

William Henry Chamberlain, "Von Mises at 80," *Wall Street Journal,* October 20, 1961, p. 10.

Stephen Cox, "The Craft of Ayn Rand," *Liberty,* January 2006, vol. 20, no. 1, pp. 31–33.

———, "The Evolution of Ayn Rand," *Liberty,* July 1998, vol. 11, no. 6, pp. 49–57.

———, "The Films of Ayn Rand," *Liberty,* August 1987, vol. 1, no. 1, pp. 5–10.

Patricia Donegan, "A Point of View," *Commonweal,* November 8, 1957, pp. 155–56.

"Down with Altruism," *Time,* February 29, 1960, pp. 94–95.

Willard Edwards, "List 18 as Leaders in Red Film Invasion," *Chicago Tribune,* October 21, 1947, p. 1.

Everett H. Ellinwood, George King, and Tong H. Lee, "Chronic Amphetamine Use and Abuse," in Floyd Bloom and Donald Kupfer, eds. *Psychopharmacology: The Fourth Generation of Progress* (Nashville, Tenn.: American College of Neuropsychopharmacology, 2000).

Nora Ephron, "A Strange Kind of Simplicity," *New York Times,* May 5, 1968.

Roderick Grant, "Wright and Rand," *Journal of the Taliesin Fellows,* Spring 1997, issue 21, pp. 5–24.

Ron Grossman, "Passions: A Disciple Confronts Ayn Rand's Power," *Chicago Tribune,* September 9, 1986, p. 1.

Albert Guerard, "Novel on Architectural Genius," *New York Herald Tribune Weekly Book Review,* May 30, 1943, p. 2.

Dora Jane Hamblin, "The Cult of Angry Ayn Rand," *Life,* April 7, 1967, pp. 44–50.

Leslie Hanscom, "Born Eccentric," *Newsweek,* March 27, 1961, pp. 104–105.

Harry Hanson, "*The Fountainhead* Enjoys Fresh Wave of Popularity," *Chicago Daily Tribune,* December 24, 1944, p. 19.

Don Hauptman, "The 'Lost' Parts of Ayn Rand's *Playboy* Interview," *Navigator,* March 2004, pp. 9–11.

Granville Hicks, "A Parable of Buried Talents," *New York Times,* October 13, 1957, p. 266.

Ruth Beebe Hill, "Shared Moments with a Famous Author," *The Journal of the San Juan Islands,* July 23, 1986, p. 1.

Sidney Hook, "Each Man for Himself," *New York Times,* April 9, 1961, p. BR3.

Hedda Hopper, "Looking at Hollywood," *Los Angeles Times,* July 21, 1944, January 29, 1948, February 16, 1948, May 7, 1948, and June 21, 1948, p. A7.

Kenneth Horan, "Three Unusual Novels with Widely Different Settings," *Chicago Daily Tribune,* May 30, 1943, p. E10.

John Hospers, "Conversations with Ayn Rand," *Liberty,* July 1990.

———, "Conversations with Ayn Rand II," *Liberty,* September 1990.

———, "Memories of Ayn Rand," *Full Context,* May 1998.

———, "Remembrance of Things Past," *Liberty,* August 2006.

James Howard, "Nightshirt Fringe Applauds Ayn Rand's Ten-Year-Old Book," *PM,* October 22, 1947.

Lester Hunt, "Thus Spoke Howard Roark: The Transformation of Nietzschean Ideas in *The Fountainhead,*" *Philosophy and Literature,* 2006, vol. 30, no. 1.

Erskine Johnson, "This Is Hollywood," syndicated in the *Zanesville [Ohio] Times Recorder,* March 21, 1957.

John Kobler, "The Curious Cult of Ayn Rand," *The Saturday Evening Post,* November 11, 1961, vol. 234, no. 45, pp. 98–101.

Joseph Loftus, "Expert Balked It," *New York Times,* October 31, 1947, p. 1.

James Kevin McGuinness, "Double Cross in Hollywood," *The New Leader,* July 15, 1944.

Hope Ridings Miller, "Lady Boileau, Here, Finds G-Men Most Interesting," *Washington Post,* February 23, 1938, p. X14.

Karen Minto, "Interview with John Hospers," *Full Context,* May 1998.

Karen Minto and David Oyerly, "Interview with Henry Mark Holzer, Part II, *Full Context,* September/October 2001.

Lewis Nichols, "Talk with Ayn Rand," *New York Times,* October 13, 1957, p. 272.

———, "In and Out of Books: Class of '43," *New York Times,* December 22, 1957, p. 136.

Albert Jay Nock, "Isaiah's Job," *The Atlantic Monthly,* June 1936.

Claudia Pierpont, "Twilight of the Goddess," *The New Yorker,* July 24, 1996, pp. 70–81.

Norman Podhoretz, "Intellectuals and Writers, Then and Now," *Partisan Review,* Fall 2002, vol. 69, no. 4, pp. 507–40.

Orville Prescott, "Books of the Times," *New York Times,* May 12, 1943, p. 23.

Thomas Pryor, "Young Conductor May Star in Film," *New York Times,* August 21, 1945, p. 17.

Rex Reed, "Controversial Eye in a New Hurricane of Excitement," syndicated in *Chicago Tribune,* February 25, 1973, pp. D7, D11.

Karen Reedstrom, "Interview with Barbara Branden," *Full Context,* October 1992.

———, "Interview with Joan Kennedy Taylor," *Full Context,* October 1993.

———, "Interview with Erika Holzer," *Full Context,* February 1996.

———, "Interview with Nathaniel Branden," *Full Context,* September 1996.

J. C. Rogers, "Reds and Whites: Ayn Rand's *We the Living* Portrays Aristocrats Amid Russian Revolution," *Washington Post,* April 26, 1936, p. B8.

Bernice Glatzer Rosenthal, "The Russian Subtext of *Atlas Shrugged* and *The Fountainhead,*" *The Journal of Ayn Rand Studies,* Fall 2004, vol. 6, no. 1.

Murray Rothbard, "My Break with Branden and the Rand Cult," *Liberty,* September 1989, pp. 27–32.

———, "The Sociology of the Ayn Rand Cult," monograph, Liberty Publishing, 1987.

"Russian Girl Finds End of Rainbow in Hollywood," *Chicago Daily Times,* September 26, 1932.

Morrie Ryskind, "A Reply to Elmer Rice about the MPAPAI," *The New Leader,* December 23, 1944.

Nora Sayre, "The Cult of Ayn Rand," *New Statesman,* March 11, 1966, p. 332.

Chris Matthew Sciabarra, "The Rand Transcript," *The Journal of Ayn Rand Studies,* Fall 1999, vol. 1, no. 1, pp. 1–26.

———, "The Rand Transcript, Revisited," *The Journal of Ayn Rand Studies,* Fall 2005, vol. 7, no. 1, pp. 1–17.

Lee Shippley, "The Lee Side o' L.A.," *Los Angeles Times,* October 22, 1934, March 11, 1936, March 31, 1936.

Richard Siklos, "Hearst's New Home: Xanadu in Manhattan," *New York Times,* June 5, 2006, p. C6.

Jack Stinnett, "A New Yorker at Large," syndicated column appearing in the *Florence [S.C.] Morning News,* May 22, 1936.

Harold Strauss, "Soviet Triangle," *New York Times Book Review,* April 19, 1936, p. 7.

Alvin Toffler, "The *Playboy* Interview: Ayn Rand," *Playboy,* March 1964, p. 38–43, 64.

Samuel A. Tower, "Film Men Admit Activity by Reds, Sam Wood Lists Writers by Name," *New York Times,* October 21, 1947.

Diana Trilling, "Fiction in Review," *The Nation,* June 12, 1943, p. 843.

"Novelist Tells of Russia in Lavery's Suit," *Los Angeles Times,* August 8, 1951.

"Russian Girl Jeers at U.S. for Depression Complaint," syndicated in the *Oakland Tribune,* October 7, 1932, p. 9.

Gore Vidal, "Comment," *Esquire,* November 1961.

Jeffrey Walker, "Ayn Rand, Objectivism and All That," an interview with Roy A. Childs, Jr., *Liberty,* April 1993.

Mike Wallace, "Mike Wallace Asks," *New York Post,* December 9, 1957, ghosted by Edith Efron.

Richard Watts, Jr., "Red Terror," *New York Herald Tribune,* February 14, 1940.

"Woman Novelist Reveals Soviet Tyranny's Horror," *New York American,* June 15, 1936.

Ida Zeitlin, "A Passionate and Powerful Novel of Conflicts in the Red Land," *New York Herald Tribune Books,* April 19, 1936, section VII, p. 4.

SPEECHES AND LECTURES

Michael S. Berliner, "Ayn Rand in Russia," a lecture presented in three parts (Letters/Music/Movies) at the Lyceum International, Brussels, Belgium, 1997.

Harry Binswanger, "Ayn Rand's Life: Highlights and Sidelights," taped speech delivered at the Thomas Jefferson School, San Francisco, 1993.

————, dinner lecture, ARI Centenary Conference, April 24, 2005.

————, "Recollections of Ayn Rand," talk presented to the NYU Objectivist Club, November 20, 2007.

Nathaniel Branden, "The Benefits and Hazards of the Philosophy of Ayn Rand," lecture given at the University of California at San Diego, May 25, 1982.

————, "Objectivism Past and Future," speech delivered at California Institute for Applied Objectivism, November 1996, Laissez Faire Books.

Jeff Britting, "An Illustrated Life," speech given at the Ayn Rand Centenary Conference, New York, April 23, 2005.

Yaron Brook, "Rand's Musical Biography," speech given at the Ayn Rand Centenary Conference, New York, April 23, 2005.

Scott McConnell, "Paramount Studio Tour," speech given on the Paramount Studio lot at the Ayn Rand Institute premiere of *Ayn Rand: A Sense of Life,* November 2, 1996.

————, "Recollections of Ayn Rand I," speech delivered at the Oslo Objectivist Conference, Oslo, Norway, October 18, 2003.

————, "Ayn Rand's Family and Friends, 1926–1951," a lecture presented at ICON 2004, London, England, September 25, 2004, based on Ayn Rand Institute Oral History Project interviews and material in the Ayn Rand Institute Archives.

Shoshana Milgram, "The Road to Roark," speech presented at an ARI Conference in Industry Hills, California, July 2003, based on material in the Ayn Rand Institute Archives.

———, "The Hero in the Soul Manifested in the World," a lecture presented at the Ayn Rand Institute's Centenary Conference, New York, April 23, 2005.

———, "Ayn Rand's Unique and Enduring Contributions to Literature," lecture, ARI Centenary Conference, July 7, 2005, San Diego.

———, "Ayn Rand as a Public Speaker: A Philosopher Who Lived on Earth," lecture given at the Objectivist Conference, Boston, July 7, 2006.

George Reisman, "Memories of Mises, Rothbard and Rand," taped speech presented to the Mises Institute, 2005.

Dina Schein, "Ayn Rand's Home Atmosphere: Her Family in Russia," a lecture on letters to Rand from the Rosenbaums, 1926–35, July 9, 2005, Ayn Rand Institute Centennial Conference, Santa Barbara, California.

MISCELLANEOUS SOURCES

Ayn Rand: A Sense of Life, a film produced, directed, and written by Michael Paxton; associate produced and music composed by Jeff Britting, 35 mm, 2 hr. 24 min. (Santa Monica, Calif.: Strand Releasing, 1998).

Bonhams and Butterfields, *The Library of Ayn Rand,* auction catalog, Los Angeles, June 28, 2005.

Barbara Branden, "It's a Dirty Job, But . . . ," an unpublished essay written in 2007, courtesy of the author.

Jeffrey Walker, *Go Ask Alyssa,* an unpublished book-length study of Rand, Judaism, and Nietzsche, courtesy of author.

Nathaniel Branden and Barbara Branden, "In Answer to AR," independently published and distributed mailer, October 1968.

PERMISSIONS ACKNOWLEDGMENTS

TEXT CREDITS

Grateful acknowledgment is made to the following for permission to reprint previously published and unpublished material:

Academy of Motion Picture Arts and Sciences: Excerpts from *An Oral History with Robert M.W. Vogel,* interviewed by Barbara Hall (Beverly Hills, CA: Academy of Motion Picture Arts and Sciences, Oral History Program, 1991). Reprinted by permission of Barbara Hall, on behalf of Academy of Motion Picture Arts and Sciences.

The Ayn Rand Institute: Excerpts from *100 Voices: An Oral History of Ayn Rand* by Scott McConnell, an unpublished project of the Ayn Rand Archives (Irvine, CA: Ayn Rand Institute Press, forthcoming). The Ayn Rand Archives at The Ayn Rand Institute is a reference source. Use of its materials by this author does not constitute endorsement or recommendation of this work by The Ayn Rand Institute. Reprinted by permission of The Ayn Rand Institute.

Michael Berliner: Excerpts form "Ayn Rand in Russia," a lecture presented at the Lyceum International, Brussels, in 1997. Reprinted by permission of Michael Berliner.

Nathaniel Branden: Excerpts from *Judgment Day* by Nathaniel Branden (Boston: Houghton Mifflin, 1989). Reprinted by permission of Nathaniel Branden.

Doubleday and Barbara Branden: Excerpts from *The Passion of Ayn Rand* by Barbara Branden, copyright © 1986 by Barbara Branden. Reprinted by permission of Doubleday, a division of Random House, Inc., and Barbara Branden.

John Wiley & Sons, Inc., and Nathaniel Branden: Excerpts from *My Years with Ayn Rand* by Nathaniel Branden, copyright © 1999 by Nathaniel Branden. Reprinted by permission of John Wiley & Sons, Inc., and Nathaniel Branden.

James Valliant: Excerpts from *The Passion of Ayn Rand's Critics: The Case Against the Brandens* by James Valliant, copyright © 2005 by James S. Valliant. Reprinted by permission of James Valliant.

ILLUSTRATION CREDITS

First Insert

PAGE 1   Top: Courtesy of Barbara Branden. Bottom: Courtesy of The Ayn Rand Institute.

PAGE 2   Top: © The New York Times/Redux.

PAGE 3   Top: Courtesy of Barbara Branden. Middle: Courtesy of Barbara Branden. Bottom: David E. Scherman/Time & Life Pictures/Getty Images.

PAGE 4   Top: © J. Paul Getty Trust. Used with permission. Julius Schulman Photography Archive. Research Library at the Getty Research Institute. Bottom: Courtesy of University of Southern California, on behalf of the USC Libraries Special Collections.

PAGE 5   © J. Paul Getty Trust. Used with permission. Julius Schulman Photography Archive. Research Library at the Getty Research Institute.

PAGE 6   Top: Leonard McCombe/Time & Life Pictures/Getty Images.

PAGE 7   Top: Leonard McCombe/Time & Life Pictures/Getty Images. Middle: Courtesy of Calumet Regional Archives, Indiana University Northwest. Bottom: © J. Paul Getty Trust. Used with permission. Julius Schulman Photography Archive. Research Library at the Getty Research Institute.

PAGE 8   Top: THE FOUNTAINHEAD © Turner Entertainment Co. A Warner Bros. Entertainment Company. All Rights Reserved. Bottom: Courtesy of University of Southern California, on behalf of the USC Libraries Special Collections.

Second Insert

PAGE 1   Top: Courtesy of Nathaniel Branden. Middle: Courtesy of Nathaniel Branden. Bottom: Courtesy of Nathaniel Branden.

PAGE 2   Top: Courtesy of Nathaniel Branden. Bottom, left: Courtesy of Nathaniel Branden. Bottom, right: Courtesy of Nathaniel Branden.

PAGE 3   Top: Courtesy of Christopher and Jonathan Cerf. Bottom: Alfred Eisenstaedt/Time & Life Pictures/Getty Images.

PAGE 4   Top: Courtesy of Barbara Branden. Bottom: Courtesy of Barbara Branden.

PAGE 5   Courtesy of The Everett Collection. Photograph by Lester Kraus.

PAGE 6   Top: Courtesy Gerald R. Ford Library. Middle: © Edward Sorel. Bottom: Courtesy of The Ayn Rand Institute.

PAGE 7   Courtesy of Theo Westenberger Photography.

PAGE 8   Painting courtesy of Roberta Satro. Photograph by Jill LeVine.

INDEX

Abbott, George, 126, 127
Abbott, Walter, 177, 196–97, 225
Abortion issue, 320–21
Adams, E. K., 63
Addio, Kira! (film), 207–8
Adelphi University, 335
Adrian (designer), 63, 171, 175, 214, 231, 233, 243
Agee, James, 313
Age of Turbulence, The (Greenspan), 322, 398
Alexander, Ruth, 133, 158, 283
Alfred A. Knopf, Inc., 106, 122, 126, 130, 131, 141, 186, 272, 310, 465*n*
Alger, Horatio, 116
Allenberg, Bert, 164, 207, 208
Altruism, 8, 213, 326–27
American Authors Authority, 200
American Society for Aesthetics, 332
American Writers Association, 200
Amphetamines, 146, 147, 174, 261, 304, 502*n*
Anderson, Martin, 322, 323
Anderson, Sherwood, 70
Anthem (aka *Ego*), 33, 48, 127, 133, 138, 149, 178, 232, 247, 271, 277–78, 334, 396

American publication, in 1946, 197–99
critical reaction, 198–99
cultural status, 287
literary influences, 103
1984 and, 103–4
proposed operatic adaptation, 310
publication history, 104, 456*n*
republication in 1961, 314
revisions, 198
sales, 104
story line, 102–3
writing of, 102, 103
Anti-Communist movement in America, 199–201, 202–6, 207, 245–47
Anti-Semitism, 3, 11, 24, 32, 34, 250–51
Apollo 11 space flight, 48, 388–89
Architecture, Rand's research, 114–16, 118
Aristotle, 35, 41, 171, 221, 226, 278, 284, 300, 308, 315, 326, 327, 390, 472*n*
Armstrong, Neil, 389
Arrowsmith (Lewis), 18
Art Students League, 276, 338, 357, 358, 360

Ashby, Thaddeus, 175–76, 177, 179,
    219, 221, 225, 230, 313
    Rand's relationship with, 182–83
"Assault on Integrity, The"
    (Greenspan), 276n
Associated Ex-Willkie Workers
    Against Willkie, 134
Astor, Mrs. Vincent, 90
Atheism, 10–11, 30, 66, 172–73
Atkinson, Brooks, 92, 119
Atlantic Monthly, The, 283
Atlantis (myth of), 46, 263, 264, 310,
    433n
Atlas Shrugged, xi, 5, 13, 40, 48, 49,
    104, 117, 131, 140, 164, 176,
    180, 182, 212, 217, 245, 246,
    247, 252, 257, 270, 292, 293,
    295, 300, 302, 306, 320, 324,
    330, 368, 372
    "About the Author" section, 291
    anti-Semitism and, 250–51
    "Atlantis" (chapter), 235, 240, 251
    Nathaniel Branden's affair with
        Gullison and, 345
    Brandens' discussions with Rand
        about, 225–26, 229, 239
    capitalism, theme of, 270–71
    characters in
        Francisco d'Anconia, xi, 16, 158,
            159n, 191–95, 226, 228, 230,
            258, 269, 271, 280, 300, 345,
            401, 406, 409
        Ragnar Danneskjöld, 29, 269
        Balph Eubank, 225, 228, 327
        John Galt, xi, 14, 41, 48, 49, 178,
            191, 195–96, 226, 235, 239, 254,
            258, 259–60, 268–69, 283, 304,
            309, 326, 328, 336, 342, 343,
            352, 361, 364, 380, 387, 409
        Richard Halley, 279, 310
        Simon Pritchett, 225, 228, 327
        Hank Rearden, 160, 191–95,
            201, 228, 258, 274, 345
        Dr. Robert Stadler, 189, 386–87

Cherryl Taggart (suicide of), 262
Dagny Taggart, 16, 20, 48, 49,
    160, 191–95, 196, 197, 202,
    206, 211, 228, 235, 239,
    242–43, 250–51, 255, 258,
    269, 274, 279, 318, 348, 367,
    371, 380, 387, 401, 408
James Taggart, 191, 226, 271
"Wet Nurse," 170, 190
Eddie Willers, 49, 345, 348
Collective and, 242–43
critical reaction, 282–86, 287,
    288
cultural status, xii, 287
dedication, 277, 384
editing, 279–80
ending, 48
film and TV miniseries adaptation
    projects, 336, 400–401, 406,
    409
fur coat scene, 160
"Galt's Gulch," 195, 235, 239, 242,
    250, 253, 260, 288, 310, 487n
Galt's speech, 195, 196, 259–61,
    263, 264, 266, 267, 268, 271,
    279, 292, 293, 299, 302, 319,
    357, 361, 494n
manuscript, safeguarding of, 236
marketing, 281–82
"money speech," xi–xii, 158–59,
    159n, 271
National Book Awards and,
    313–14
Nock's influence, 155
original title, 38
paperback edition, 310, 314
Paterson and, 136, 197, 216, 285
publisher for, 271–74
Rand-Branden sexual relationship
    and, 258
Randian subculture and, 242–43,
    264–65, 266, 275–76, 288
Rand's acquaintances as models for
    characters, 196–97

Rand's railroad research, 206,
211–12
readers' reactions, 287
Rothbard's assessment, 296
sales, xii, 286–87, 314
sex based on rational self-interest,
theory of, 228
story line, 190–96, 268–69
"strike" theme, 165, 190, 196, 197
Tesla's influence on, 235–36
Think Twice and, 138
timeless atmosphere, 146
uniformity of "Galt's Gulch" in, 253
Wayne-Falkland Hotel, 89
working title (*The Strike*), 38, 164
writing of, 190, 196, 201, 202, 235,
237, 259–61, 268–69, 275,
278–79
Atomic bomb, 187–89, 389
At Random (Bennett Cerf), 273
Autobiography, An (Frank Lloyd
Wright), 114–15
Axelrod, George, 274–75
Ayn Rand clubs, 292, 320
Ayn Rand cult. *See* Randian
subculture
Ayn Rand Institute (ARI), xii, xiv,
412–13
Ayn Rand Letter, The, 388, 396

Bacall, Lauren, 208
Bajadere, Die (Kálmán), 43
Baker, Ross, 271
Balch, Earle, 156
Ball, Lucille, 105
Bannert, Marcella, 74, 109, 216
Barnes, Clive, 398
Barrymore, John, 122
Bedford, Barbara, 76
Behrman, S. N., 127
Bekkerman, Lev, 42–44, 51, 59, 66,
70, 86
Bell, Iris, 361

Bellow, Saul, 245
Benét, Stephen Vincent, 103
"Benevolent universe" premise, 221,
280
Benzedrine. *See* Amphetamines
Berner, Pincus, 88, 116, 119, 171,
235, 236, 238, 300, 369
Bernstein, Leonard, 177
Bertini, Francesca, 50
Bessie, Alvah, 202
Beyond Freedom and Dignity
(Skinner), 388
Biberman, Herbert, 202
Bidinotto, Robert, 11
Binswanger, Harry, 406, 408
Birell, Tala, 74
Blanchard, James, 408
Blanke, Henry, 162–63, 164, 167,
169, 187, 199, 208, 209, 210
Blumenthal, Allan, 71, 241, 264, 298,
301, 305, 343, 349, 358, 359,
366, 369–70, 381, 384, 391,
392, 393, 399
Blumenthal, Dinah, 243–44
Blumenthal, Elayne. *See* Kalberman,
Elayne Blumenthal
Blumenthal, Florence. *See* Hirschfeld,
Florence Blumenthal
Blumenthal, Joan Mitchell, 241, 264,
276, 278–79, 305, 313, 328,
340, 348, 357, 358, 359, 369,
391, 392, 393, 399
Blumenthal, Reva, 241, 377
Bobbs-Merrill Company, 144–45,
150–51, 153, 155, 156, 163,
166, 171, 185–87, 219, 260,
265, 271, 272, 364
Bogart, Humphrey, 168
Boileau, Ethel (Lady), 88, 105, 131
Bombal, Maria Luisa, 201
Born Yesterday (play), 231
Boston University, 319
Brackman, Robert, 276
Brahms, Johannes, 299

Branden, Barbara Weidman, xiv, 97,
225, 261, 266, 267, 268, 273,
274, 275, 276, 277, 282, 285,
288, 292, 293, 297, 298–99,
305, 309, 314, 318, 322, 323,
328, 329, 332, 333, 335, 338,
339, 341, 343, 356, 360, 361
Atlas Shrugged and, 225–26, 229,
239, 286
banishment from Randian
subculture, 375
Nathaniel Branden
affair with Gullison and, 344,
345–46, 349–50
divorce from, 346–47, 349
psychotherapeutic work with, 263
relationship with, 222, 227–28,
229, 234, 239–40, 243–44, 254
California, conversations with Rand
in, 220–23
Collective and, 241
extramarital affair, 345
Hook and, 327
man worship, attitude toward, 228
mock trials of Rand's followers and,
329
New York, move to, 234, 236
panic attacks and night terrors of,
262
Passion of Ayn Rand, 286, 372, 412
physical appearance, 222
post-Rand life, 412
Rand-Branden relationship and,
235, 255, 256–57, 258–59, 262,
361–62, 365, 367, 369, 370,
376–77, 380
Randian subculture, status in, 301,
302
Rand's break with, 375, 378–81
Rand's last meeting with, 408
Rand's relationship with, 229–30,
294, 373
Branden, Nathaniel (born Nathan
Blumenthal), xiv, 247, 249, 250,
282, 285, 292, 334, 399
arrogance, 305–6, 341–42
Atlas Shrugged, discussions with
Rand about, 225–26, 229, 239
Atlas Shrugged's dedication to, 277,
384
Atlas Shrugged's negative reviews,
response to, 288
background, 221
banishment from Randian
subculture, 373–75, 381
belated adolescence in 1960s, 361
Barbara Branden
divorce from, 346–47, 349
relationship with, 222, 227–28,
229, 234, 239–40, 243–44, 254
Cerf's attitude toward, 291
Collective and, 240–41, 243
conformity program for Rand's
followers, 302–3
discussion gatherings for Rand's
followers, 298–99
fame, enjoyment of, 343
Fountainhead, reaction to, 219, 221
Gullison, affair with, 344–46,
347–50, 353, 356–57, 366,
368–69, 370, 371, 381
Hook, attacks on, 327
leadership role in Randian
subculture, 266, 301
lecture series on Objectivism,
289–90, 293–94, 309, 333, 361
mock trials of Rand's followers,
266–67
name change, 219, 254
Nathaniel Branden Institute (NBI),
289, 314–15, 325, 337–39,
350–51, 373
New York, move to, 234, 236
"Objectivism" name for Rand's
philosophy, coining of, 278
Objectivist publications, 320, 321,
373
Peikoff-Kent relationship and, 266
plagiarism charge against Rothbard,
299–300

post-Rand life, 411–12
Psychology of Self-Esteem, 350, 371,
    376, 385
psychotherapeutic career, 227, 263,
    267, 297–98, 300, 301, 312,
    322, 329, 341, 343, 376
on Rand's need for loyalty from her
    followers, 328, 329
Rand's relationship with. *See*
    Branden, Nathaniel, Rand's
    relationship with
on Rand's self-pity, 315–16
recruitment of new followers for
    Rand, 297, 298
satirical barbs targeting Rand,
    intolerance of, 299
self-esteem, theory of, 227
speaking technique, 341
Wallace's attitude toward, 309
Who Is Ayn Rand?, 328
Branden, Nathaniel, Rand's
    relationship with
apartments rented in same
    building, 338–39
Branden's affair with Gullison and,
    344–45, 347–50, 353, 356–57,
    366, 368–69, 370, 371
Branden's designation as
    intellectual heir, 277–78
Branden's essays published in
    Rand's books, 336, 338
Branden's mother and, 243–44
Branden's "paper" to Rand, 365,
    367, 369, 379, 380
Branden's possessiveness, 232
Branden's public defense of Rand,
    327–28
Branden's "repression" of feelings,
    262
Branden's "sexual freeze," 355–56
Barbara Branden and, 235, 255,
    256–57, 258–59, 262, 361–62,
    365, 367, 369, 370, 376–77,
    380
Brandens' divorce and, 346–47

Brandens' post-break comments on,
    376–77, 380
Brandens' relationship and,
    227–28, 254
break in relations, 287–88, 354–55,
    364–66, 369–73
California conversations, 220–23
Collective and, 242
first contacts, 219–20
flirtations, 230–31, 234–35
O'Connor and, 220, 221, 222, 234,
    256–59, 261–62, 263, 276–77,
    360–61
parent-child aspect, 225, 254
Peikoff's attitude toward, 385
Randian subculture and, 264, 363
Rand's angry outbursts and, 363–64
Rand's depression and, 305
Rand's fear of intellectual betrayal,
    366
Rand's interview comments on, 309
Rand's loneliness and, 223–24
Rand's move to New York and, 237
Rand's post-break actions against
    Branden, 375, 376
Rand's post-break comments on,
    373, 377–80, 386
Rand's post-break rationalizing of,
    384
Rand's psychological analysis of,
    352–54, 366–69, 372
Rand's ranking of Branden as
    genius, 224–25
sexual relationship, 253–59,
    261–62, 263–64, 268, 306–7,
    337, 340–41, 343–44, 346, 347
Sutton's assessment, 333
Branden, Patrecia Gullison, 344–46,
    347–50, 351, 353, 355, 356–57,
    362, 366, 368–69, 370, 371,
    381, 412
Brazzi, Rossano, 207–8
Breaking Free (Branden), 376
Brest-Litovsk, Russian Pale of
    Settlement, 9–10, 24

Brooklyn College, 292
Broun, Heywood, 84, 116
Brown, Fern, 55, 57, 58, 60, 62, 125,
    159, 332
Brown University, 319
Bryant, Leland, 75
Buckley, William F., Jr., 247, 250,
    284, 313
  Rand's relationship with, 246,
    285–86
Bucko, Bill, 13
Bungay, Jack, 177–78, 223
Bunshaft, Gordon, 119

Cain, James M., 200
California Graduate Institute, 500*n*
Callahan, Roger, 339, 363
Calumet "K" (novel), 69, 338
Cane, Melville, 88, 90
Capitalism, 139–40, 221–22,
    270–71, 326
Capitalism the Creator (Snyder), 133
Capps, Brig. Gen. Jack, 391
Capra, Frank, 77
Capuletti, José Manuel, 329, 339
Carson, Johnny, 355
Carter, Nick (agent), 74
Carter, Nick (O'Connor's brother),
    67, 68, 71, 79, 88, 92, 99, 102,
    125, 126, 129, 229
  death, 166
  Fountainhead's writing and, 146–47
  homosexuality of, 100
  O'Connor-Rand relationship and,
    72, 100
  Rand's relationship with, 100
Cassell & Company, 95, 104
Catherine the Great, 12, 15, 23
Caxton Press, 479*n*
Cerf, Bennett, 281, 287, 289, 324,
    328
  Atlas Shrugged's publication and,
    272, 273–74, 279, 282, 284
  Randian subculture and, 291

Rand's break with, 334–35, 337
Rand's relationship with, 274–75
Cerf, Phyllis, 274
Chamberlain, John, 135, 209, 213,
    270, 283, 288
Chambers, D. L., 144, 156
Chambers, Whittaker, 272–73,
    284–85, 286
Champagne, Maurice, 12
Charity, 181–82
Chase, Gordon, 214
Cheever, John, 313, 314
Chernyshevsky, Nikolai, 31
Chevalier, Haakon, 205
Chicago Daily Tribune, 150, 283
Childs, Roy, 305
Chodorov, Frank, 133
Circle Bastiat, 251–53, 295–96, 301
Civil rights movement, 320
Clifford, Lee, 343
Clive, E. E., 76
Cognitive psychology, 227
Cohn, Roy, 251–52
Colbert, Claudette, 105
Cold War, 187
Cole, Lester, 202, 204–5
Collective, the, 240–43, 244
Collectivism, 13, 84, 88, 91
    (definition of), 99, 110, 117,
    120, 131, 143, 146, 152, 191,
    221, 264, 318, 383, 412
Collier, Beatrice and Harry, 97
Collins, Alan, 156, 157, 168, 200,
    209, 260, 271–72, 274, 282
Collins, Richard, 203
Columbia Missourian, 198
Columbia University, 319, 320
Commonweal magazine, 288
Communism in United States, 83–84
  anti-Communist movement,
    199–201, 202–6, 207, 245–47
Communist Manifesto, The, 137
Concept formation, theory of, 352
Conference of Studio Unions, 199
Conrad, Joseph, 94

Cooper, Gary, 45, 168, 208, 209
Cornuelle, Herbert, 231, 250, 251
Cornuelle, Richard, 231, 249–50, 251, 296
Cotten, Joseph, 170
Council of Economic Advisers, 322, 397
Council on Books in Wartime, 155
Courtois, Lilyan, 393
Cowley, Malcolm, 84
Cox, Christopher, xii
Cox, Stephen, 134, 213, 214
Craig, Helen, 127
Crawford, Joan, 167
Crimea, 3, 33–37, 39, 46, 85, 86
Crowther, Bosley, 211
Culture clashes, 391
Curtis Brown, Ltd., 172, 376
Cyrano de Bergerac (Rostand), 35, 170, 357
Cyrus (Rand's childhood fictional hero), 12–14, 61, 63, 108, 112, 187, 232, 269, 361, 406

Dawson, David, 323
De Grasse, S.S., 52
Delon, Alain, 401
DeMille, Cecil B., 44, 59, 60, 61–64, 67, 68, 69, 78, 93, 142, 168, 199
  Rand's hiring by, 61–62
Dempsey, Jack, 92
Descartes, René, 19
Determinism, 39, 300, 330
Dewey, John, 267, 278, 327
Dexamyl. See Amphetamines
Dexedrine. See Amphetamines
Dickens, Charles, xiii
Dietrich, Marlene, 74, 77, 166
Disney, Walt, 199, 202
Disowned Self, The (Branden), 376
Dmytryk, Edward, 202
Donahue, Phil, 404, 407
Dos Passos, John, 84, 200
Dostoyevsky, Fyodor, 31, 39, 70

Doubleday publishing company, 140–41
Dreiser, Theodore, 84, 153
Dreyfus, Alfred, 251–52
Drobyshev, Fedor, 97, 393, 394–95, 396
Dworetzky, Murray, 391

Eastwood, Clint, 401
Economic Council Review of Books, 198
Economics in One Lesson (Hazlitt), 248
Efron, Edith, 295, 297, 309, 354, 359–60, 361
Efron, Leonard, 359–60
Efron, Robert, 360
Eickhoff, Kathryn, 406
Einstein, Albert, 188
Eisenhower, Dwight D., 247
Eliot, George, 15
Elliott, Jean, 232
Ellis, Albert, 363–64
Emery, DeWitt, 153
Emory, John, 126
Emory University, 297
Emotionalism, 263, 347
Empire State Building, 89, 239, 350, 373
Engels, Wera, 101
Enjolras (character in Les Misérables), 33, 34, 43, 108
Ephron, Nora, 364
Esquire magazine, 326
Evil, 39, 116, 117, 118, 120, 141, 165, 194, 211, 224, 307, 311, 330, 358, 363, 376, 378, 380, 384

Fadiman, Clifton, 116, 274
Farrell, James T., 200
Faulkner, William, 331
Fawcett-Majors, Farrah, 401

Fermi, Enrico, 188

Field, Marshall, III, 119

Figes, Orlando, 193

Finneran, William, 219

Fisher, Aretha, 224, 236

Fitzgerald, Rosalie, 180–81

Forbes magazine, xii–xiii

Ford, Gerald, 322, 383, 397

Ford, John, 199

Ford Hall Forum, 320, 321, 352, 362, 388, 404, 408

Fortune magazine, xii–xiii

Foundations of Morality, The (Hazlitt), 313

Fountainhead, The (novel), xi, 8, 60, 81, 107, 128, 140, 182, 196, 202, 232, 245, 260, 265, 270, 271, 274, 399, 413

  ad campaign for, 153–54, 156

  as allegory of good and evil, 141

  Nathaniel Branden's reaction to, 219, 221, 222, 223, 241, 242

  characters in

    Henry Cameron, 59, 111, 114, 118

    Vesta Dunning (cut), 151

    Dominique Francon, 8, 20, 66, 81–82, 112–14, 115, 116, 148, 150, 151, 187, 215, 232, 264, 271

    Guy Francon, 112, 118

    Peter Keating, 74, 108–11, 118, 119, 121, 126, 171, 191

    Howard Roark, 14, 22, 23, 41, 52, 58, 60, 65, 71, 81, 82, 98, 99, 102, 107–8, 110–14, 115–19, 120–21, 122, 123, 126, 130, 141, 147, 148, 150, 151, 152, 153, 163, 167, 184, 185, 186, 187, 196, 197, 211, 216, 224, 228, 231, 239, 269, 296, 307, 309, 347, 373, 403

    Ellsworth M. Toohey, 19, 65, 107, 114, 116, 117, 118, 119, 121, 138, 152, 168, 171, 216, 274, 367, 399

    Gail Wynand, 116–18, 119, 121, 151, 172, 342

  condensations and serializations, 187

  cover illustration featuring O'Connor's *Man Also Rises,* 364

  critical reaction, 149–50, 151–52

  cultural status, xii, 287

  Dana Building, 118–19

  dedication to O'Connor, 130

  deleted portions, 151

  Dominique's country mansion, 81–82

  ending, 148

  Ideal and, 101

  individualism theme, 117–18, 152–53

  Introduction to the twenty-fifth-anniversary edition, 317

  March of the Centuries exposition in, 126

  Nock's influence, 120

  O'Connor's influence, 403

  original title, 109

  paper shortage concerns and, 150–51

  parodic aspects, 118–19

  Paterson and, 136, 144, 146, 215

  Peter the Great and, 22–23

  publisher for, 105–6, 122, 132, 140–41, 143–45

  quarry scene, 102

  Rand's explanatory writings on, 171–72, 185–86

  Rand's need for success with, 154–55

  Rand's study of architecture for, 114–16, 118

  readers' reactions, 166–67, 265

  Roark's speech, 120, 152

  Roark's tribute to Wynand, 172

  Russian influences, 121

sales, xii, 149, 156, 166, 173,
218–19, 364
sex scenes, 112–13, 121, 178
Skyscraper screenplay and, 65
stage adaptation project, 351, 366
Johnny Stokes flashback, 19
story line, 107–8, 111–14, 116–17,
119–20
Think Twice and, 138
timeless atmosphere, 146
twenty-fifth-anniversary edition,
317, 364
Watkins's reservations about,
141–42
Wright and, 22, 114–16, 119,
168–69, 170
writing of, 98–99, 102, 121–22,
123, 129–30, 145–48
Fountainhead, The (film)
actors' interest in appearing in, 163,
167–68
Blanke's interest in producing,
162–63
box-office success, 218–19
casting, 208–9
critical reaction, 211
editing, 210
"on hold" status of production, 163,
208
Rand's unhappiness with, 209–11
rights for film version, 156–58,
168
screenplay, 157, 163, 208, 209
shooting, 209–10
Wright's participation in, 169
Franz Ferdinand, Archduke, 15–16
Freeman magazine, 213–14, 248
Free Speech Movement, 321
Free will, 39, 226
Friedman, Milton, 407

Gable, Clark, 168, 202
Gabler, Neal, 204

Galbraith, John Kenneth, 397
Gall, John C., 133
Gapon, Father, 2
Garbo, Greta, 168, 208
Garrett, Garet, 69
Gaynor, Janet, 63, 214, 231
Gerhardie, Daisy, 423*n*
Getting It Right (Buckley), 286
Giffey, René, 12
Gilbert, Cass, 119
Gippius, V. V., 18
Glarner, Lisette, 311–12
God and Man at Yale (Buckley), 246
God of the Machine, The (Paterson),
148, 154, 156, 173, 174, 213,
217, 248
Goldberg, Minna, 50, 57, 58, 60–61,
159, 332, 333
Goldberg, Sam, 57, 332
Golden Rule, 281–82
Gold standard, 322
Goldwater, Barry, 322–23
Gone with the Wind (novel), 93, 95
Gorky, Maxim, 2, 28, 31
Grand Central Terminal, 54, 206,
212, 404
Greenspan, Alan, xii, 159*n,* 251, 252,
264, 275–76, 276*n,* 288, 293,
322, 338, 355, 381, 388,
405–6
government service, 322, 397
Rand's relationship with, 241, 242,
397–98
Greenspan, Rose, 397
Griffith, D. W., 44, 66
Groves, Gen. Leslie, 189
Gudegast, Hans, 406, 409
Guerard, Albert, 150
Guervin, Helen, 178–79
Gullison, Liesha, 346, 348, 355, 357,
362
Gullison, Patrecia. *See* Branden,
Patrecia Gullison
Guzarchik, Isaac, 4

Guzarchik, Nina, 41, 42, 43, 179
Guzarchik, Vera, 41–42, 52, 179, 311–12

Hale, Robert Beverly, 276, 358
Hall, Muriel Welles, 136, 144, 155, 285
Hammett, Dashiell, 157
Hamowy, Ron, 299
Hanta Yo (Hill), 402, 487*n*
Harvard University, 320
Haydn, Hiram, 260, 272–74, 278, 279, 280, 289, 291
Hays, Molly, 408, 409
Hazlitt, Frances, 142, 145, 154, 248, 313
Hazlitt, Henry, 142, 213, 248–49, 250–51, 313
Heard, Gerald, 313
Hearst, William Randolph, 116, 119, 283
Hegel, G. W. F., 39, 278, 354, 386
Heinlein, Robert, 183
Hellman, Lillian, 89, 164, 205
Hemingway, Ernest, 69, 157
Henreid, Paul, 163
Henry, O., 69
Henry, Col. Robert S., 211
Hessen, Robert, 297, 301–2, 305, 322, 323, 329, 341, 399–400
Hickman, William, 70
Hicks, Granville, 84, 93, 104, 282
Hill, Borroughs ("Buzzy"), 178, 232, 233, 234, 236–37, 238, 334
Hill, Ruth Beebe, 178, 179, 232–34, 236–38, 333, 334, 402
Hillel, Rabbi, 281–82
Hirschfeld, Florence Blumenthal, 241, 314, 374, 377–78, 382
Hirschfeld, Jonathan, 374
Hirschfeld, Leonard, 522*n*
Hiss, Alger, 273
Hiss, Marjorie, 101
Hitchcock, Alfred, 329

Hitler, Adolf, 131, 132
Hollywood Studio Club, 62, 63, 65, 71, 182
Hollywood Ten, 202–3
Holmes, Oliver Wendell, 278
Holzer, Erika, 241, 300, 323, 373, 398
Holzer, Henry, 300, 323, 328–29, 342, 355, 373, 374, 376, 378, 380, 381–82, 398
Homosexuality, 100, 362–63
Hook, Sidney, 326–27, 331, 387–88
Hoover, J. Edgar, 105, 206
Hoover Institution, 297
Hopper, Hedda, 168, 208
Horton, Leigh, 411
Hospers, John, xii, 329–32, 337, 384
Houchin, Katharine, 237
House Committee on Un-American Activities (HUAC), 200–206, 211, 246
Huggins, Eloise, 395, 400, 402, 403, 405, 406, 408, 409, 410
Hughes, Langston, 84
Hugo, Victor, 32–33, 36, 87–88, 338, 388
Human Action (Mises), 249
Humphrey, Hubert, 323
Hunter College, 387
Huxley, Aldous, 103

Ideal, 101–2, 104, 133, 306, 316, 364
  Kay Gonda (character in), 110, 113, 342, 455*n*
"In Answer to Ayn Rand" (Brandens), 380–81, 386
Indian Tomb, The (film), 45
Individualism, 30, 117–18, 137, 138–40, 143, 152–53, 171, 253
Inloes, Mary, 82
"Isaiah's Job" (Nock), 155
Is Objectivism a Religion? (Ellis), 364, 535*n*

Ivanhoe (Scott), 28–29
Ivey, Col. Herman, 389, 390, 391

Jaffe, Henry and Michael, 401
Jagger, Dean, 126, 128, 129
Jarrico, Paul, 203
Joan of Arc, 21, 133
Johnson, Lyndon B., 323
Jones, Jennifer, 170, 208
Josephson, Matthew, 84
Judgment Day (*My Years with Ayn
Rand,* Branden), 240

Kahn, Ely Jacques, 118, 119, 167
Kalberman, Elayne Blumenthal, 220,
241, 254, 255, 265, 339, 376,
377, 391, 395, 397, 399
Kalberman, Harry, 242, 376–77, 391,
399
Kálmán, Emmerich, 43
Kanin, Garson, 231
Kant, Immanuel, 278, 324–25, 354,
386
Kaplan, Berko Itskovitch, 6, 46, 49
Kaplan, Dobrulia, 4, 10
Kaplan, Rozalia Pavlovna, 6–7, 8, 9
Kelley, David, 405, 410
Kelly, George, 64
Kennedy, John F., 307, 335, 337
Kensico Cemetery, 405, 410
Kent, Daryn, 265–67, 268, 288,
401
Kerensky, Aleksandr, 28, 29, 30, 39,
130
Rand's meeting with, 174–75
King Features, 187
King of Kings (film), 61, 63, 65, 66
Kipling, Rudyard, 13, 405, 410
Kirk, Russell, 246, 250
Kirsch, Robert, 283
Klinge, Aleksandr, 4, 5
Klopfer, Donald, 272, 273–74, 275
Knopf, Blanche, 106, 122, 132

Knowlton, Perry, 200, 334, 335, 336,
376
Kobler, John, 326
Koch, Howard, 162, 204
Konheim, Iezekiil, 4, 10
Konheim, Leonid, 46
Krantz, Bertha, 279–81, 302, 319,
400
Kreuger, Ivar, 75
Kurisu, June, 176–77, 179–80

Ladd, Alan, 168
Lake, Veronica, 167–68
Lamarr, Hedy, 163–64
Lane, Rose Wilder, 198, 206
Lang, Fritz, 44, 162
Lardner, Ring, Jr., 88, 203, 204–5
Laski, Harold, 116
Lasky, Jesse, 77
Lavery, Emmet, 231
Lawson, John Howard, 89, 203
Lebedeff, Ivan, 72, 77, 83, 88, 93,
128
Lenin, Vladimir, 15, 28, 30, 31, 32,
39, 46, 49
Leonard, Lonnie, 363
Leontovich, Eugenie, 126, 127, 128
Lewis, Sinclair, 18, 69, 70, 341
Lewis and Clark College, 333
Libertarian movement, 290, 383–84
Library of Congress. *See* U.S. Library
of Congress
Lipton, Sarah, 50, 59, 73, 74, 93,
97, 98
Literary Guild, 187
Little, Brown and Company, 144
Lodge, John Davis, 126
Loeb, Gerald, 168, 404
Logic, 172
Lolita (Nabokov), 26
London, England, Rand in, 16
Look magazine, 404
Los Angeles Times, 283, 311
Lossky, N. O., 18, 41, 46

Lubitsch, Ernst, 162
Ludel, Susan, 391, 400, 401, 404
Lugosi, Bela, 177
Lyons, Eugene, 144, 171, 174, 246

MacArthur, Gen. Douglas, 247
Macmillan publishing company, 92,
    93, 94, 104–5, 186
Magic Mountain, The (Mann), 69,
    159
Malcolm, Donald, 283
"Malevolent universe" premise, 25,
    221, 340
Maltz, Albert, 203
Man Also Rises (O'Connor), 364
Mannheimer, Albert, 100, 101, 102,
    148, 183, 200, 223, 232, 277
    death, 312–13
    psychotherapy with Nathaniel
      Branden, 312
    Rand's relationship with, 88–89,
      176–77, 206, 231–32
    writing career, 231, 312
Marx, Karl, 284
Massie, Christopher, 170
Matthews, Chris, xii
Matthews, J. B., 245–46, 313
May, Joe, 45
Mayer, Jerome, 95, 101, 102, 126
Mayer, Louis B., 199, 203, 204,
    205
McAlpin Rooftop Theater, 398
McCarthy, Joseph R., 245, 246–47,
    251
McCarthy, Mary, 275
McGraw-Hill publishing company,
    272
McGuinness, James, 199
Mealand, Richard, 142, 143–44, 145,
    154
Mencken, H. L., 69, 83, 84, 88, 115,
    133
Menjou, Adolphe, 202

Metaphysics, 226, 260, 282, 390
Meyer, Frank, 248
MGM, 77, 78, 79, 89, 105, 157, 168,
    190, 199, 203, 204, 205
Mike Wallace Interview, The (TV
    show), 307–9
Military draft, 249, 323–24
Mind, theory of, 226–27
Mind-body split, 227–28, 257
Mises, Ludwig von, 198, 301, 313
    Atlas Shrugged, assessment of,
      283–84
    Rand's relationship with, 248–49,
      250
Mission to Moscow (film), 162
MIT, 319, 320
Mitchell, Andrea, 398
Money, defense of, xi, 135–36,
    158–59, 270, 271
Mont Pelerin Society, 313
Moore, Stephen, xii
Moral judgment, 267, 328
Morris, Gouverneur, 69, 74, 83, 92,
    93, 99
Motion Picture Alliance for the
    Preservation of American Ideals
    (MPA), 199–200, 201, 202, 207,
    214
Mozart, Wolfgang Amadeus, 299
Mullendore, William, 197, 214–15,
    231, 248, 283, 313
Mumford, Lewis, 116
Murphy, Dudley, 65
Mussolini, Benito, 131, 207
Mysterious Valley, The (Champagne
    and Giffey), 12–14, 15, 45, 187,
    193, 195, 439*n*

Nabokov, Olga, 26–27, 31, 312
Nabokov, V. D., 26, 28, 29, 31
Nabokov, Vladimir, 18, 26, 312,
    313
Nash, Ed, 332, 333, 376

Nathaniel Branden Institute (NBI),
    289, 293–94, 314–15, 325,
    337–39, 350–51, 373–75
National Committee for Monetary
    Reform, 408
National Review, 246, 250, 284, 285,
    286, 288, 313, 383, 410
Nation magazine, 94, 150
Native Americans, 391
Nazi Germany, 91, 130, 131, 143,
    146, 162, 179, 181, 188, 203,
    246, 386
NBC, 401
Neal, Patricia, 208–9
Negri, Pola, 50, 76–77
Neutra, Richard, 166
New American Library (NAL), 310,
    314, 335–36, 376, 404
New Economic Policy (NEP) in
    Russia, 38, 45, 46
New School for Social Research,
    116
Newsweek magazine, 213, 290, 308,
    325, 327
New York Central Railroad, 55, 206
    Twentieth Century Limited, 161,
    212
New York Daily Mirror, 283
New Yorker, The, 283
New York Herald Tribune, 94, 129,
    134, 135, 150, 155, 214, 215,
    283, 285
New York Hospital, 392
New York Post, 292
New York Public Library, 114, 132,
    325
New York Times, 92, 94, 129, 149,
    151, 168, 207, 211, 282, 286,
    293, 326, 327, 364, 398, 410
New York University (NYU), 234,
    241, 249, 251, 263, 292, 387,
    413
New York World's Fair of 1939,
    125–26

New York Young Republican Club,
    323
Nicholas II, Czar, 3, 5, 17, 24, 27, 28
Nickerson, Kathleen, 266
Nietzsche, Friedrich, 41–42, 60, 63,
    65, 70, 101, 102, 108, 117, 150,
    198, 212, 284, 300, 314, 324
Night of January 16th, The (aka
    *Penthouse Legend; Woman on
    Trial*), 60, 101, 142, 259
    "audience as jury" innovation, 76
    Broadway production, 78, 79, 82,
    90–91, 92, 95
    critical reaction, 77, 92, 398
    film rights, 77–78, 105, 157
    Hollywood production, 76–77, 78
    Off-Broadway production, 398
    Rosenbaums' reaction, 79
    royalties from, 95
    script alterations, 90–91, 92
    story line, 75–76
    WPA-supported productions, 95
1984 (Orwell), 103–4
Nixon, Richard M., 200, 322, 323,
    324
Nock, Albert Jay, 69, 120, 133, 139,
    155, 213, 269, 469*n*
Noi Viva (film), 207–8
Nyiregyházi, Erwin, 167

"Objectivism," name for Rand's
    philosophy
    "Basic Principles of Objectivism,
    The" (Branden), 289–90
    coining of name, 278
    as "cult," 298, 300–301, 359, 265,
    385–86, 398, 400, 406–7, 411
Objectivist Forum magazine, 406–7
Objectivist movement. *See* Randian
    subculture
Objectivist Newsletter, The (aka *The
    Objectivist*), 321–22, 338–39,
    350, 373–74, 376, 388

O'Connor, Dennis, 93, 124
O'Connor, Frank (Rand's husband),
    xiv, 14, 38, 88, 92, 96, 122, 127,
    132, 146, 147, 158, 160, 162,
    164, 165, 169, 176, 177, 180,
    181, 196, 202, 206, 212, 213,
    215, 223, 229, 233, 236–37,
    251, 254, 261, 266, 279, 299,
    332, 333, 334, 348, 355, 372,
    377, 378, 391, 394, 400
  absentmindedness in practical
    affairs, 238, 265
  acting career, 66, 75, 78–79, 101,
    102, 126
  atheism, 66
  Atlas Shrugged
    dedication to, 277
    manuscript, safeguarding of, 236
    marketing and, 282
  background, 65–66
  death, 405, 407–8
  drinking habit, 263, 360, 403
  Fisher and, 224
  flower business, 224
  Fountainhead, dedication to, 130
  Fountainhead, influence on, 403
  health problems, 357, 360, 399,
    402–3, 404
  marriage to Rand; *see* O'Connor-
    Rand relationship
  painting career, 121, 238, 276–77,
    281, 339–40, 357, 358, 359,
    360, 364
  personal qualities, 99
  physical appearance, 65
  Rand-Branden relationship and,
    220, 221, 222, 234, 256–59,
    261–62, 263, 276–77, 360–61
  sales work and, 154
  Ventura and, 357–59, 360
O'Connor, Harry. *See* Carter, Nick.
O'Connor, Joe, 67, 68, 100, 125, 175,
    180
O'Connor, Mary Agnes, 65
O'Connor family, 124–25

O'Connor-Rand relationship
  Brandens' wedding and, 243
  Nick Carter and, 72, 100
  children and, 128
  diamond-and-ruby ring for Rand,
    389
  divorce, Rand's consideration of,
    184, 230
  late life, tenor of, 402–5
  love letters, 101
  married life, 72–73, 75, 99, 125,
    183–84, 206–7, 230
  meeting and courtship, 66–67,
    68–69
  New York move in 1934, 78–79,
    81–82
  New York move in 1951, 235–36,
    237–38
  O'Connor's death, Rand's
    reflections on, 407–8
  O'Connor's nostalgia for early days,
    358
  O'Connor's painting career and,
    339–40
  ranch purchase in California,
    165–66
  ranch sale, 237
  Rand's depression and, 305
  Rand's feelings for O'Connor,
    123–24, 125, 184, 308–9, 403–4
  Rand's public thanks to O'Connor,
    364
  Rand's role as breadwinner, 99,
    308–9
  sexual relationship, 128–29, 182,
    230
  Thirty-sixth Street apartment (New
    York), 236, 238–39
  wedding, 71–72
Odets, Clifford, 89
Ogden, Archibald, 144–45, 150, 151,
    153, 155, 162, 163, 164, 165,
    168, 206, 209, 272
Ohman, Ruth, 175
Old Right, 133, 245–46

Ominous Parallels, The (Peikoff), 386–87, 412
Omnibook magazine, 187
Oppenheimer, J. Robert, 188, 189, 199, 205
O'Quinn, Kerry, 362
Orman, Suze, xi
Ornitz, Samuel, 203
Orsini, Frank, 128
Orwell, George, 103–4
Ouray, Colorado, 235, 487*n*

Packer, Edith, 406
Pamphleteers, Inc., 198
Papurt, Agnes O'Connor, 125, 236
Papurt, A. M., 128, 181
Papurt, Connie, 236
Papurt, Marna. *See* Wolf, Marna Papurt
Papurt, Mimi. *See* Sutton, Mimi Papurt
Paramount Building, 120
Paramount Pictures, 74, 78, 89, 142, 143–44, 145, 154, 164, 168, 170, 171, 176, 184, 187, 201, 401, 407
Pascal, Blaise, 19
Passion of Ayn Rand, The (Barbara Branden), 286, 372, 412
Pastor, Cynthia, 387, 400, 405, 408, 412
Paterson, Isabel, 139, 150, 154, 160, 164, 165, 171, 175, 183, 206, 224, 248, 326, 397, 410
  alleged appropriation of Rand's ideas, 173
  Atlas Shrugged and, 136, 197, 216, 285
  Fountainhead and, 136, 144, 146, 215
  God of the Machine and, 148, 156, 173, 174, 217
  Monday-night get-togethers with, 135
  Rand's falling out with, 211–15
  Rand's final meeting with, 215–16
  Rand's relationship with, 134–37, 140, 146, 155–56, 172–74, 232
Patton, Millicent, 72, 82–83, 100, 146–47
Paul, Ron, xii
Pegler, Westbrook, 246
Peikoff, Amy, 413
Peikoff, Kira, 413
Peikoff, Leonard, 241, 251, 264, 275, 278–79, 288, 293, 299, 307, 313, 322, 323, 339, 362, 373, 381, 382, 384, 391, 392, 395, 399, 403, 405, 408, 409, 410
  Hook and, 327
  Kent and, 266
  leadership role of in Randian subculture, 385, 386–87, 388
  Ominous Parallels and, 386–87, 412
  post-Rand life, 412–13
  Rand-Branden relationship and, 385
  Rand's relationship with, 242, 385, 386–87, 388, 400
  as target of mock trials, 267
  teaching career, 387–88
Penthouse Legend. See Night of January 16th, The
Pepperdine University, 252, 406
Persuasion magazine, 323
Plain Talk magazine, 207
Peter the Great, 4, 22–23
Petrograd Conservatory, 40, 177
Petrograd State University, 38–39, 41, 47
Phil Donahue Show, The (TV show), 404, 407
Picasso, Pablo, 331
Pickford, Mary, 50, 77
Pidgeon, Walter, 90
Pierpont, Claudia, 287
"Place of the Gods, The" (Benét), 103
Plato, 35, 41, 232–33

Playboy magazine, interview in, 260, 324

Pnin (Nabokov), 313

Podhoretz, Norman, 278

Pollock, Channing, 133, 134, 137, 142, 147

Polytechnic Institute of Brooklyn, 387

Portnoy, Eva Kaplan, 49

Portnoy, Harry, 49, 51, 57

Portnoy, Harvey, 57

Portnoy, Jack, 180

Prescott, Orville, 149–50

Princeton University, 319

Pro-American Information Bureau, 198

Protocols of the Elders of Zion, The, 198

Pruette, Lorine, 151–52, 159, 199

Pryor, Evva, 405, 406

Psychology of Self-Esteem, The (Branden), 350, 371, 376, 385

Purdue University, 319

Pushkin, Aleksandr, 22, 425*n*

Putnam, James, 105

Queens College, 292, 297

Rachmaninoff, Sergei, 299, 405

Raico, Ralph, 251, 299, 301

Ramrus, Al, 295, 297, 307, 309, 349, 361, 382

Rand, Ayn (born Alissa Rosenbaum)
  abortion, 128, 181
  adolescent years, 25–27, 28–29, 30–51
  air travel, fascination with, 48
  amphetamine habit, 146, 174, 261, 304–5
  arrival in America, 52–57
  belittling of former friends, 216–17
  birth, 1–2
  British culture, attraction to, 13–14
  charitable activities, 181–82

  in Chicago, following arrival in United States, 57–61
  childhood years, 3–6, 7–9, 10–21
  childishness, 145, 233, 392
  clothing preferences, 98, 100, 233, 236, 261, 272
  collecting hobby, 8–9
  color preferences, 220
  Crimea stay (1918–1921), 33–37, 39
  death, xi, 409–10
  defamation lawsuit against, 231
  depressed period, 303–6, 307, 315
  dishonesty by, 308
  drawing and painting, ideas about, 339
  education, 11, 17–20, 26, 32, 35, 36, 38–39, 41, 47, 49, 50
  English language and, 51, 59
  European tour in 1914, 15–17
  exceptionality of herself, belief in, 12
  fearfulness, 280, 400, 404
  financial situation, 82–83, 95, 105, 122, 134, 142, 153–54, 158, 160
  first memory, 5
  friendship terminations, 127–28, 133–34, 249, 313, 332–35, 337, 377, 398–400
  germ phobia, 125, 280
  glamorous lifestyle, 175
  handwriting, 147
  impressiveness, 295
  intellectual possessiveness, 45
  intelligence, 11
  Jewish background, obscuring of, 56–57, 180–81, 280
  joy in the present moment, inability to experience, 212
  last three years of life, 405–10
  lung cancer, 391–93
  malapropisms, 137
  marriage of; *see* O'Connor-Rand relationship
  menial jobs in Hollywood, 68

mink coat purchases, 159–60, 208
mistakes, inability to admit to, 211, 393
money management, 406
money's meaning for, 158–59
musical taste, 8, 44, 145, 279, 299
name change, 55–57
New York, first experience of, 53, 54
papers at Ayn Rand Institute, 412–13
pathological behavior in later years, 399
physical appearance, 6, 25, 35, 54, 220, 223, 272, 406
physical exertion, disinterest in, 145–46, 392–93
political activities, 84, 130–33, 322–23, 324
portraits, 338, 340
refugees, assistance for, 179–80
romances and love affairs of, 14, 42–44, 128, 178; see also Branden, Nathaniel, Rand's relationship with
Russian culture, attitude toward, 2, 16
secretarial training, 64
self-made woman, self-concept as, 58, 216, 308
self-pity, 315–16
sexuality, 178, 182–83, 259
skyscrapers, enthusiasm for, 53, 89
smoking, attitude toward, 391–92, 393
social difficulties, 11, 19–20, 21, 26–27, 41, 109–11, 175, 312
solipsism and paranoia of later years, 407
Soviet surveillance, concerns about, 312
space program, support for, 388–89
teaching work, 36–37
"tiddlywink" music, 233, 279, 288

UFO sighting, 233–34, 392
United States
  citizenship, 71, 97
  early enthusiasm for, 35, 45–46
  immigration to, 49–51, 52–53
untidiness, 230, 238, 264, 280–81, 307
will (legal), 384, 387, 399
See also Rand, Ayn, literary/philosophical career of; Rand, Ayn, motion picture career of; Randian subculture; specific persons
Rand, Ayn, literary/philosophical career of
  "Age of Mediocrity," 408
  altruism and, 8, 213, 326–27
  American writers, study of, 69
  "America's Persecuted Minority: Big Business," 332–33
  anti-Communist activism, 96, 199–201, 202–6, 207
  anti-Semitism and, 11, 250–51
  arguing, method of, 252, 272
  Aristotle's influence, 35, 41, 221, 226, 308
  "Art as Sense of Life," 332
  Art of Fiction, 229
  Art of Nonfiction, 388
  atheism and, 10–11, 30, 172–73
  atomic bomb and, 188–89
  "Autobiographical Sketch," 1
  Capitalism: The Unknown Ideal, 338, 355, 384
  capitalism and, 139–40, 221–22, 270–71, 326
  cardinal values and virtues of her philosophy, 319–20
  charity and, 181–82
  childhood, denunciation of, 19
  childhood experiences and, 5, 7–8, 10–11, 21
  childhood literary influences, 12–14, 28–29, 35

Rand, Ayn, literary/philosophical
    career of (*cont.*)
  childhood writings, 16, 19,
    20–21, 31
  childrearing and, 128
  collectivism and, 110
  concept formation, theory of, 352
  "Conservatism: An Obituary," 319
  culture clashes and, 391
  decision on writing career, 16
  education in philosophy, 39, 41
  emotions and, 268
  "Ethics of Emergencies," 322
  "exceptional individual against the
    mob" theme, 70–71
  expository writing, shift to, 321–22
  "Faith and Force: Destroyers of the
    Modern World," 292, 317–18
  "fascistic" charge against her
    philosophy, 42
  "Fascist New Frontier," 335, 337
  fiction as means for advancing
    philosophical ideas, 31
  fiction-writing workshops, 294,
    298
  films' impact on writings, 59
  first adult novel, 36
  "For the New Intellectual," 319
  *For the New Intellectual: The
    Philosophy of Ayn Rand,* 324–25,
    326–27
  free will and, 39, 226
  "Goal of My Writing," 270
  "Good Copy," 294
  government's role, views on, 139,
    199
  honesty and, 53–54
  Hook's criticism of her philosophy,
    326–27
  Hugo's influence, 32–33, 36
  "Husband I Bought," 69–70
  Ideal, 101–2, 133, 306, 316, 364
  individualism and, 30, 117–18,
    137, 138–40, 143, 152–53, 171,
    253

"Individualist Manifesto," 137,
    138–40, 143
"Inexplicable Personal Alchemy," 22
interviews with the media, 260,
    292, 307–9, 324, 348, 355, 404,
    407
introduction to Hugo's *Ninety-
    Three,* 383
*Introduction to Objectivist
    Epistemology,* 352, 404
Introduction to Peikoff's *The
    Ominous Parallels,* 386–87
journals and diaries, 30, 55, 85–86,
    185, 321, 349, 353, 354, 355,
    356–57, 367–69, 372
larger-than-life fictional characters,
    34, 60
libertarian movement and, 383–84
Little Street, 60, 70–71, 239, 347
logic and, 172
male point of view, writing from,
    14–15
"malevolent universe" premise and,
    340
"Man's Rights," 322
"man worship" theme, 44, 69–70,
    87, 228
metaphysics and, 226
mind, theory of, 226–27
money, perspective on, xi
Moral Basis of Individualism,
    171–72
moral judgment and, 267
mother's influence, 6
"Nature of Government," 322
Nietzsche's influence, 41–42
Objectivism
  coining of name, 278
  protectiveness toward name, 407
Objectivist essays of 1970s, 388
"Objectivist Ethics," 319–20,
    336–37
one-party nature of Rand's
    philosophical system, 253
"Only Path to Tomorrow," 171

Paterson's criticism of Rand, 172–73

Paterson's influence, 135–37, 140

philosopher, self-identification as, 261, 292

"Philosophy Ship," 47

"Philosophy: Who Needs It," 48, 389–91

plagiarism concerns, 299–300, 342

"pre-philosophy" of adolescence, 25

psychology and, 297

public appearances, 96, 132, 167, 178–79, 292–93, 317–20, 325, 332–33, 342–43, 388–91, 408–9

radio talk-show programs, hosting of, 320

reason-versus-mysticism theme, 221–22

the Right and, 245–50, 319, 383

Romantic Manifesto, 123, 352, 388

"romantic realism" of writings, 221

"Roots of War," 322

"Sanction of the Victims," 409

"Screen Guide for Americans"; *see* Rand, Ayn, motion picture career of

screenplays; *see* Rand, Ayn, motion picture career of

selfishness and, 110, 136–37, 139

selflessness and, 109

sex based on rational self-interest, theory of, 228, 257

"sexual triangles" theme, 74

social issues of 1960s and, 320–21

sponsors for books and plays, alleged difficulties in finding, 93–94

summations of her philosophy, 1, 281–82

syndicated column, 311

Think Twice, 137, 138

"To All Innocent Fifth Columnists," 137, 140

To Lorne Dieterling, 287–88, 306, 336, 368

"To the Readers of *The Fountainhead*," 52, 161, 184, 185–86

university-period writings, 47–49

Virtue of Selfishness, 5, 336–37, 338, 384

"What Is the Basic Issue in the World Today?," 199

"What Is the Proper Function of Government?," 199

whim-worship and, 13

"Whitewashed Russia," 96

"Zero Worship," 292

See also Anthem; Atlas Shrugged; Fountainhead, The; Night of January 16th, The; Randian subculture; We the Living

Rand, Ayn, motion picture career of

Angel of Broadway screenplay, 64

anti-Communist activism, 199–201, 202–6, 207

blacklisting due to anti-Communist views, 95–96

clerical job at RKO, 72

Conspirators screenplay, 163

Craig's Wife screenplay, 64–65

Crying Sisters screenplay, 171

DeMille, hiring by, 61–62

end of screenwriting, 210

extra work, 63, 64

His Dog screenplay, 64

Hollywood, dislike of, 63–64, 78, 164

House of Mist screenplay, 201–2

I Walk Alone screenplay, 188

Love Letters screenplay, 170

moviegoing in Russia, 44–46

moviegoing in United States, 54–55, 57, 59

Night of January 16th screenplay, 77

Pola Negri essay, 50

Rand, Ayn, motion picture career
      of (cont.)
   ranking of films seen, 55
   Red Pawn screenplay, 73–75, 83,
      157, 171, 199
   "Screen Guide for Americans," 201,
      204, 207
   screenwriting, 57, 64–65, 67–68,
      163, 170–71, 188–90, 201–2
   screenwriting education, 49
   Skyscraper screenplay
      adaptation, 65
      original, 60
   studio accommodations in 1943,
      162
   Tchaikovsky screenplay, 177
   Top Secret screenplay, 188–90
   Wallis, hiring by, 164–65
   work as script reader, 82, 142
   You Came Along screenplay,
      170–71
   See also Fountainhead, The (film)
Randian subculture
   apartments for followers in
      proximity to one another, 339
   Art Reproduction service, 338
   Atlas Shrugged and, 242–43,
      264–65, 266, 275–76, 288
   attraction of Rand's philosophy
      for susceptible persons, 300
   Ayn Rand clubs, 292, 320
   banishment of disfavored
      followers, 299–301, 329,
      331–32, 358–60, 373–75,
      377, 381–82, 398
   beginning of Rand's public legend,
      185–87
   Barbara Branden's status in, 301,
      302
   Nathaniel Branden's leadership
      role in and status as Rand's
      intellectual heir, 266, 277–78,
      301
   Brandens' banishment from,
      373–75, 381

Brandens' divorce and, 349
Cerf's attitude toward, 291
Circle Bastiat and, 251–53
closing down of business ventures,
   373–75
Collective, 240–43, 244
conformity, program of, 302–3
"cult" designation, Rand's rejection
   of, 187
discussion gatherings, 298–99
Ellis's attitude toward, 364
film series, 338
financial problems of business
   ventures, 350–51, 373
homosexuality, intolerance of,
   362–63
Hook, attacks on, 327
lecture series on Objectivism,
   289–90, 293–94, 309, 314,
   333–34, 361, 385
Mannheimer as first follower,
   88–89
media coverage, 325–26
military draft, opposition to,
   323–24
mock trials ("kangaroo courts"),
   266–68, 329
Nathaniel Branden Institute, 289,
   314–15, 325, 337–39, 350–51,
   373–75
Objectivist publications, 321–22,
   338–39, 350, 373–74, 376,
   388
Peikoff's rise following Nathaniel
   Branden's banishment, 385,
   386–87, 388
persecution, sense of, 307
psychotherapy for followers, 263,
   297–98, 300, 301, 343
publishing venture, 337–38
Rand-Branden relationship and,
   264, 363
"Rand or Branden" ultimatum
   made to followers, 381–82,
   385–86

Rand's need for loyalty and adulation, 288–89, 328–29, 331–32

Rand's relationship with followers, 291–92, 298–99, 303, 318

recruitment of new followers, 265–66, 295–97, 298

rules of admission, 301–2

satirical barbs, intolerance of, 299

staffers, Nathaniel Branden's treatment of, 341–42

Stalinist tyranny, potential for, 296, 300–301, 329

tape-transcription service, 314

theatrical venture, 351

Wallace's attitude toward, 309

witch-hunt atmosphere following Rand-Branden break, 381–82

young men of Hollywood, 175–78

Random House publishing company, 272–74, 282–83, 284, 314, 335–337

Rankin, John, 200

Rational emotive behavioral therapy, 363

Ratoff, Gregory, 127

Read, Leonard, 197, 198, 248, 313

Reader's Digest, 171

Reagan, Ronald, 322

Red Decade: The Stalinist Penetration of America (Lyons), 144, 171

Red Pawn, 73–75, 83, 85, 89, 109, 157, 171, 199, 445*n*

Reed, John, 93

Reisman, George, 251–52, 253, 297, 299, 301, 322, 406

Rembrandt, 399

Reuben, Shelly, 299, 342

RKO, 72, 78, 82, 109, 274

Robin Hood, 29, 269

Rockefeller, Nelson A., 322

Rogers, Ginger, 202, 274

Rogers, Lela, 199, 231, 274

Roosevelt, Franklin D., 84, 95, 125, 130–31, 132, 133, 138, 162, 187

Rosenbaum, Anna Kaplan (Rand's mother), 2, 4, 5, 17, 21, 25, 26, 32, 35, 36, 40–41, 44, 49, 51, 56, 58, 62, 68, 69, 72, 79–80, 110–11

background, 6–7

death, 179

marriage, 10

as mother, 4–5, 7–8

Rand's efforts to bring to United States, 96–98

Rand's relationship with, 6, 7–8

teaching career, 36, 38

Rosenbaum, Aron (Rand's great-uncle), 9

Rosenbaum, Natasha (Rand's sister), 4, 7–8, 17, 35, 40–41, 58, 97, 177, 179

Rosenbaum, Nora (Rand's sister), 4, 17, 35, 40, 41, 58, 62, 79, 97, 110–11, 179, 308, 312

Rand's relationship with, 11–12

visit with Rand in 1970s, 393–97

Rosenbaum, Zinovy (Rand's father), 2, 5, 28, 31–32, 33, 34, 36, 49, 51, 69, 72, 79, 259

background, 9–10

death, 179

marriage, 10

pharmacy business, 3, 4, 5, 9

Rand's efforts to bring to United States, 96–98

Rand's relationship with, 9, 11, 38, 39–40, 41

unemployment in Communist period, 38

Rosenthal, Bernice, 103, 119

Rostand, Edmond, 35, 170, 357

Rothbard, Joey, 298

Rothbard, Murray, 251, 252, 253, 288, 295–97, 298, 299–301, 384

Royce-Smithkin, Ilona, 338

Ruddy, Albert, 401, 407

Russell, Bertrand, 267

Russia/Soviet Union
  anti-Semitism, 3, 11, 24, 32, 34
  Cold War, 187
  Crimea's conquest by Red Army,
    35–36
  Red Terror, 31–32
  repression of Soviet period, 46–47
  Revolution of 1905, 2
  Revolution of 1917, 2, 17, 24–25,
    27–28, 29–30, 49
  St. Petersburg, 3, 17, 22–24, 37,
    143
  World War I, 24
  World War II, 143, 152
Ryskind, Morrie, 175, 199, 214,
    231

Salamon, Roger, 97
"Sanction of the victim," 195, 372,
    409
Sarah Lawrence College, 319
Saroyan, William, 119
Sartre, Jean-Paul, 278
Satenstein, Sidney, 82, 90, 92
Satro, Roberta, 406
Saturday Evening Post, 55, 69, 103,
    104, 302, 325–26
Schiller, Friedrich von, 39, 425n
Schlamm, Willie, 248
Schoeck, Helmut, 299, 301
Schulberg, Budd, 88, 450n
Schwalb, Marc, xiv
Schwartz, Wilfred, 339, 374
Scott, Adrian, 203
Scott, Larry, 344, 345, 349
Scott, Sir Walter, 28–29
Scoundrel Time (Hellman), 164,
    205
Screen Writers Guild, 89, 199, 200,
    231
Secrest, Meryle, 170
Seeley, Mabel, 171
Self-esteem movement, 227, 376
Selfishness, 110, 136–37, 139

Selflessness, 109
"Sense of life," 25, 30, 41, 65, 71,
    75, 76, 77, 90, 92, 109, 123,
    225, 226, 230, 263, 276, 305,
    328–29, 364, 399
Sex based on rational self-interest,
    theory of, 228, 257
Shakespeare, Monroe, 154
Shakespeare, William, 39, 79
Shaw, George Bernard, 281–82
Shayne, Robert and Elizabeth,
    127–28
Sheed, Wilfrid, 246
Shubert, Lee, 90
Shulman, Lee, 363, 364
Sikorski, Helene Nabokov, 26, 27
Silliphant, Stirling, 401–2
Silverman, Fred, 401
Simon & Schuster publishing
    company, 140, 141
"Simple Aveu" (Thomé), 44
Sinatra, Frank, 358
Skinner, B. F., 388
Smith, Adam, 300
Smith, Kay Nolte, 398, 400
Smith, Phillip, 358, 386, 398
Smith, Robert, 170
Snider, Ed, 406, 412
Snyder, Carl, 133
Social Security, 131, 397
Sokolsky, George, 133
Solitaire (game), 304, 306, 393
Solzhenitsyn, Aleksandr, 396
Song of Russia (film), 203, 204, 205
Southern California Edison, 197
Soviet Union. *See* Russia/Soviet
    Union
Space program, 388–89
Spillane, Mickey, 309, 310–11
Stalin, Joseph, 46, 162
Stanford University, 150, 400
Stanwyck, Barbara, 163, 167, 199,
    208
State Technicum for Screen Arts, 49
Stein, Gertrude, 119

Sternberg, Josef von, 74, 166
St. Martin's Press, 302
St. Petersburg, 3, 17, 22–24, 37, 143
St. Petersburg Technical Institute, 43, 85
Stoiunin, M. N. and V. J., 17, 46–47
Stoiunin school, 17–20, 26, 32, 47
Stolberg, Benjamin, 200
Stone, Anna, 50, 51, 57, 60
Stone, Burt, 180, 332, 333
Stone, Mandel, 54, 57
Strachow, Marie von, 179–80, 308
Sullavan, Margaret, 208
Sullivan, Louis, 58–59, 111, 114, 118, 408
Sures, Mary Ann Rukavina, 241, 264, 265, 276, 278–79, 293
Sutton, Mimi Papurt, 56, 72, 79, 99, 100, 124, 125, 126, 127, 128, 129, 136, 181, 187, 206–7, 332, 333, 403, 405, 409–10
Swanson, Gloria, 50, 77, 132, 133
Switzerland, Rand in, 16, 27
Syracuse University, 319

Taft, Robert, 247
Taliesin East, Taliesin West. See Wright, Frank Lloyd
Taylor, Deems, 310, 381
Taylor, Joan Kennedy, 247, 287, 289, 303, 310, 312, 314, 323, 342, 381–82
Taylor, Robert, 202, 203
Tchaikovsky, Pyotr, 40, 177, 190, 201
Tesla, Nikola, 235–36
Thomas, J. Parnell, 200, 204–5
Thomé, Francis, 44
Thompson, Dorothy, 200
Thus Spoke Zarathustra (Nietzsche), 42, 57, 198, 284
Time magazine, 188, 283, 318
Toffler, Alvin, 324

Tonight Show, The (TV show), 355
"To Whom It May Concern" (Rand's condemnation of Brandens), 378–80, 381
Traviata, La, 8
Town Hall Club, 96, 105, 129
Town Hall Meeting of the Air, 231
Trial of Mary Dugan, The (Veiller), 75, 76, 77
Trilling, Diana, 150
Trilling, Lionel, 275
Trotsky, Leon, 15, 141
Truman, Harry, 187
Trumbo, Dalton, 203
Turgenev, Ivan, 31

Uncle Tom's Cabin (We the Living compared to Stowe's novel), 83
Unconquered, The, 95, 101, 102, 126–27, 129, 133
Universal Pictures, 74, 75, 109, 157
University of California at Los Angeles (UCLA), 222, 225, 242, 254
University of Denver, 267
University of Michigan, 319
University of Warsaw, 9
University of Wisconsin, 319
U.S. Information Agency, 393
U.S. Library of Congress, 147, 412

Valli, Alida, 207
Van Doren, Irita, 134–35, 150, 214
Veidt, Conrad, 45
Ventura, Don, 357–59, 360, 363
Vidal, Gore, 326
Vidor, King, 59, 199, 208, 209–10
Vienna, Austria (Rosenbaums' 1914 visit to), 15–16
Vietnam War, 320, 352, 389
Viking Press, 272
Vogel, Robert, 199, 200
Vogt, Carl de, 52

Vogt, Gertrude, 285
von Mises, Ludwig. *See* Mises,
    Ludwig von

Walker, Jeff, xiv
Wallace, Mike, 295, 307–9
Wallis, Hal, 89, 163, 164, 168, 170,
    171, 177, 188, 189, 190, 199,
    201
Wall Street Journal, 92, 326
Warner, Jack, 164, 203–4, 205, 208,
    210
Warner Bros., 156–58, 162, 168
Washington Post, 94, 282–83
Watkins, Ann, 91, 92, 95, 101, 104,
    105, 122, 132, 133, 135, 140,
    141–42
We (Zamiatin), 103
Weiss, Barbara, 384, 389, 391, 400,
    403, 404
Welch, Raquel, 401
Welles, Sam, 135, 136
Wells, H. G., 103
Westinghouse, 5, 311
West Point Military Academy, 389–91
We the Living, 7, 9, 11, 13, 23, 30,
    31, 33, 37, 38, 40, 47, 67, 75,
    98, 128, 130, 133, 140, 142,
    218, 220, 235, 270, 373
  anti-Communist message, 83
  characters in
    Kira Argounova, 7, 11, 14, 26, 40,
      42, 44, 47, 67, 85–87, 117, 140,
      218, 228, 324, 373
    Irina Dunaeva, 43, 86
    Leo Kovalensky, 33, 42, 43–44,
      85, 86, 87, 108, 113, 218, 235,
      373
    Andrei Taganov, 33, 67, 85, 87,
      88, 94, 108, 324
    Uncle Vasili (Dunaev), 9, 38, 86
  critical reaction, 94
  cultural status, 287
  foreword, 91
  Hugo's influence, 33, 87–88
  Italian film version, 207–8
  man worship in, 87
  Mencken's assessment, 83
  Nabokov family and, 26
  paperback edition, 314
  as political novel, 85–86
  postpublication mishandling,
    104–5
  publisher for, 83, 91, 92, 93
  Random House edition in 1958,
    314
  Rand's efforts on behalf of her
    parents and, 97
  Rand's explanations about, 91
  revisions, 87
  Nora Rosenbaum's assessment, 396
  sales, 94–95
  stage adaptation (*The
    Unconquered*), 95, 101, 102,
    126–27, 129, 133
  story line, 85
  tragic ending, 87
  U.K. edition, 95
  writing of, 74, 84–85
Weybright, Victor, 335–36, 386
Whim-worship, 13
Who Is Ayn Rand? (Brandens), 328
Wick, Jean, 83, 86, 88, 91, 141
Willkie, Wendell, 134, 135
  presidential campaign, 130,
    132–33
Wilson, Edmund, 84, 275
Wilson, Woodrow, 324
Winick, Eugene, 369, 397
Witness (Chambers), 273
Wolf, Marna Papurt, 124–25, 181,
    182, 206, 332, 333
Wolfe, Thomas, 229–30, 294
*Woman on Trial. See The Night of
    January 16th*
Women's movement, 320
Wood, Sam, 199, 203, 204
Woods, A. H., 78, 79, 82, 88, 90, 92,
    105

Words & Faces (Haydn), 272
Works Progress Administration
    (WPA), 95
World Publishing, 350, 376
World War I, 15, 17, 24
World War II, 131–32, 143, 145, 152,
    187
Wright, Evan, 178
Wright, Frank Lloyd, 58, 118, 119,
    126, 166, 168, 265, 295, 408
    Atlas Shrugged and, 197
    Fountainhead and, 22, 114–16,
        119, 168–69, 170
    Fountainhead film and, 169
    Frank Lloyd Wright Foundation,
        169
    house design for Rand, 169
    Rand's meetings with, 115–16,
        168, 169–70
    Taliesin East studio/residence,
        169–70
    Taliesin West studio/residence, 115

Yale University, 317–18, 319
Young, Loretta, 77
Young, Stanley, 93

Zamiatin, Yevgeny, 103
Zhukov, Marshal Georgy, 247
Zola, Emile, 251–52